ECDL Advanced

Word Processing

Paula Kelly

Blackrock Education Centre

2002

© Blackrock Education Centre

ISBN   0 9540287 0 8

Published by
Blackrock Education Centre
Kill Avenue, Dún Laoghaire
Co. Dublin, Ireland.

Tel. (+353 1) 2 365 000   Fax. (+3531) 2 365 050
E-mail. bec@blackrock-edu.ie   Web. www.blackrock-edu.ie

First published   2002

Blackrock Education Centre

Director/Stiurthóir: Séamus Cannon / Séamus Ó Canainn
Walter Cullinane (Chairperson), Deirdre Keyes (Vice Chairperson), Betty Behan,
John Brennan, Phil Caulfield, Dóirín Creamer, Patrick Fox, Kieran Griffin,
Jean Hughes, Thérèse McPhillips, Matt Reville, Donal Ryan, Cora Uí Chuinn.

Blackrock Learning

This manual is produced by the Blackrock Learning division of
Blackrock Education Centre. Executive Director: Siobhán Cluskey.
Project Manager for this production was John Brennan.

Credits

Design and Layout
Paula Kelly

Editorial Consultants
Tom Mc Mahon

Frank Kirk

Cover Design
Vermillion

Acknowledgements

The assistance of the following staff members is also acknowledged:

Aileen Benson, Geraldine Byrne, Emer Bradley, Val Collins, Monica Dowdall
Adela Fernandez, Phil Halpin, Evelyn Logan, Lil Lynch, Jenny Masterson,
Helen McGoey, Chris Murphy, Tomás Ó Briain, Róisín Phillips, Mary Sorohan, Heather Friel.

Blackrock Education Centre is an accredited ECDL Test Centre

Contents

About This Book

The Manual

'ECDL Advanced Word Processing' offers a practical, step-by-step guide for any person who wishes to increase their knowledge and competence in using Microsoft Word. It has been designed as a study aid for the advanced word processing module of the European Computer Driving Licence (the International Computer Driving Licence – ICDL – outside Europe). However, as is characteristic of Blackrock Education Centre training materials, the content of this manual offers far more by way of additional support information through explanations, demonstrations and practical exercises as well as a support website, **www.ecdlmanual.org**. Particular attention has been given to providing students with additional information on syllabus items to assist their understanding.

Design

Every use has been made of the expertise we have gained from working closely with ECDL over the last several years. Additionally, the knowledge and skills of our substantial pool of trainers hugely influenced the content and layout of the material.

We use plain English, not computer jargon. We take you point by point through detailed explanations and action sequences. We pay particular attention to relating what you see on the pages of the manual to what you see on the computer screen.

You will also find that the A4 size of the manual, the side-by-side layout of graphics and text, and the spiral binding all combine to make it an ideal *desk-top-friendly* training manual.

Exercises

At the end of each section, there are two kinds of exercises. There are self-check questions designed to jog your memory of important details. There are also practical exercises that have been designed to revise some of the more important skills associated with using Microsoft Word.

In successfully completing a set of exercises, you can be confident of your progress in learning the skills associated with each section of the syllabus.

Web Support

Support material is available on the Internet at **www.ecdlmanual.org** – a sister site of Blackrock Education Centre (**www.blackrock-edu.ie**). Should there be any minor amendments to the ECDL syllabus in the future, updates and/or additional material will be posted there.

This manual was produced – text, design and layout – using only the Microsoft Office suite of programs and the skills described in the manual. The screen shots were captured using a small utility program and most were inserted directly onto the page.

Foreword

Blackrock Education Centre provides support services to teachers and to partners in education under the auspices of the Department of Education and Science in Ireland. It is one of a network of thirty Centres dispersed throughout the country. For many years the Education Centre has provided training for teachers in the use of Information and Communications Technology. While introductory courses were always popular, we frequently experienced difficulties in progressing beyond the basics. There was a large gap between the introductory course and what was being offered at university, with little in between that was both comprehensive and practical. There was a need for a training programme that measured progressive development of competency across a range of skills.

The European Computer Driving Licence – ECDL (ICDL outside Europe) – provides a very good framework for such a training programme. Blackrock Education Centre put a programme in place on a pilot basis in 1997 and subsequently opened it up to larger numbers. The initial response was very encouraging and demand has grown dramatically over the years. More recently, a clear need emerged for advanced manuals which would expand and develop teacher knowledge in particular modules. This advanced manual is the first in what we hope will be a series.

The key attractions of ECDL/ICDL are the focus on practical competency and the flexible syllabus, independent of platform or software. These enabled us to tailor our training while maintaining standards that are recognised internationally. It is the experience of Blackrock Education Centre that completing the ECDL/ICDL programme gives the user confidence in using the computer, a significant level of practical skill and an excellent preparation for further study.

In the Information Age, all of us are required to engage in continuous lifelong learning. We have been aware that many of the schools we work with want to offer a programme to parents and to other members of the community. Increased access to learning opportunities, through libraries and other community institutions, is more and more the norm. Our training programme has encouraged this development and many schools have themselves become accredited ECDL/ICDL test centres offering local training. In addition, *Training for ECDL*, our first manual, has come to be used extensively in the commercial and corporate training sectors, both in Ireland and abroad.

We are pleased to note how many users of our training manuals comment on their continued usefulness as reference materials after they have completed their courses. We believe this reflects well on all who work on our development projects who deserve great credit in maintaining high standards. Particular thanks are due to Director Séamus Ó Canainn, to John Brennan, Project Manager, to Paula Kelly the author, Tom Mac Mahon and Frank Kirk who gave valuable assistance and to Siobhán Cluskey, the Executive Director of Blackrock Learning. These training materials are a testament to the thoroughness with which they have addressed the requirements of lifelong learning in the Information Age.

Walter Cullinane
Chairperson

Blackrock Education Centre
August 2002

E C D L

The European Computer Driving Licence
(ICDL outside Europe)

The European Computer Driving Licence is a means of indicating that you have acquired the basic skills to use a computer in a wide variety of applications, just as your standard Driving Licence indicates that you have acquired the skills necessary to drive a car on public roads.

As with learning to drive a car, a variety of skills has to be learnt before the licence is issued. Also, it is important that these skills be acquired by actually using the computer: one does not expect to have a vehicle Driving Licence issued just by reading all about it and answering questions in a written examination.

The ECDL concept originated in Finland in 1988 and has spread all over Europe since then, with headquarters now established in Dublin. In each country, ECDL operates under the auspices of and in association with the national computer society. In Ireland, this is the Computer Society of Ireland.

The success of ECDL throughout Europe has been due to the well thought out and structured modular approach which allows training establishments to provide flexible training in basic computer skills with varying degrees of emphasis according to the candidates' needs, while at the same time maintaining uniformly high standards.

ECDL has now spread beyond European borders and attracted the attention of trainers and training establishments in many parts of the world. It is now known internationally as ICDL – the International Computer Driving Licence.

On enrolling for an Advanced ECDL/ICDL course, candidates are issued with an Automated Test Unit number (ATU) which is used to register their successful completion of the course examination. The test for Module AM3, Word Processing – Advanced Level, is of one hour's duration. It is a practical hands-on test at the computer. On successful completion of the test, the result is returned to the national ECDL/ICDL office which then issues the appropriate Advanced ECDL certificate.

The issue of the Advanced certificate is administered in Ireland by ECDL Ireland, which controls accreditation and provides tester training on a national level. It also monitors very closely the standards under which ECDL/ICDL training and testing are carried out at the hundreds of accredited training centres throughout the country.

Training and training materials for the ECDL/ICDL are the responsibility of the individual training establishment. Blackrock Education Centre has over twenty years' experience in Information Technology training and has been closely associated with ECDL Ireland from the beginning, organising and administering one of the first ECDL/ICDL pilot projects in this country.

Chapter 1

Editing

Syllabus

Module AM3

Word Processing – Advanced Level

Word Processing – Advanced Level, requires the candidate to use the word processing application to produce what are deemed to be advanced word processing documents outputs.
The candidate shall be able to operate effectively at more than a basic level of competence and be able to produce advanced word processing outputs, illustrating sophisticated typographical, formatting and layout presentations, including tables, forms or graphics.
The candidate shall be able to use tools such as macros and to carry out more advanced mail merge operations within the word processing application.

Chapter One: AM 3.1 – Editing

Editing

Editing is the process of making changes to an existing file or document. The file may exist on a storage medium, such as a hard disk, a zip drive and so on, or it may simply be held within the temporary storage, RAM, awaiting action. Such changes are characterised by amendments to the text, paragraph formats, document templates, page layout and so on.

It is important to understand that when changes are made to a document as they appear on the computer screen, these are only temporary and it is not until the file has been saved under its original name or new name that the amendments are added. Editing programs distinguish between the stored document and the document of the same name that is copied into the working memory to be edited. Should the edited document be assigned a new name when it is saved, as far as the computer is concerned, this will be a completely new and unrelated document to the one that was opened initially.

Editing programs normally supply a small safeguard routine to protect against overwriting a file or including unintended or inadvertent amendments. Typically, as is the case with Word, confirmation is required before a document can be saved using an existing file name other than its own i.e., another file's name. It is important to understand that the original file will cease to exist when the new file is saved over it.

However, if you are not renaming your document any editing you save as your work will overwrite the original document. The only alert available in this instance occurs if you choose to close down your document when it contains unsaved edits. Word will ask you if you wish to save the changes you made.

Section 1   Formatting Text (3.1.1.1) + (3.1.1.2)

1.1   Standard Text Formatting

One of the more obvious forms of editing is that which applies to a document's text. Text can be edited, formatted or changed in many ways. Typical formatting options in Word provide a whole range of text or character enhancing features from applying bold and underlining to special animation effects. The full list of character features available is accessed through the **Font** option on the **Format** menu. However, most of the regularly used character formatting options are readily available through the Formatting Toolbar.

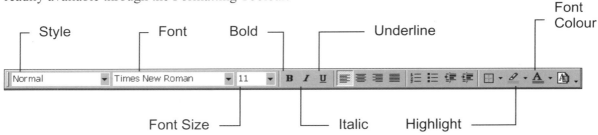

Toggle buttons on the Formatting Toolbar provide various formatting options. Click the button once to apply the format option and then click it again to cancel it.

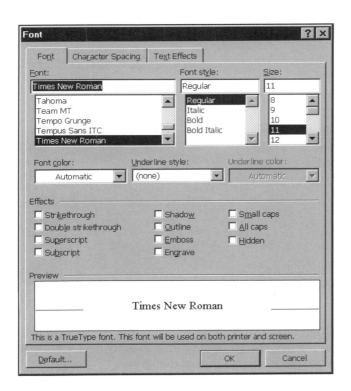

To access the Font window choose **Font** from the **Format** menu. You can apply a number of different formatting changes within the Font window all of which will be applied to the selected text when you click the **OK** button.

The Preview panel at the bottom of the window will show a sample of your text and how the formatting you choose will affect it. This helps you to decide whether or not a particular formatting option should be used.

NOTE

Formatting applies to any text that has been selected. Otherwise, the formatting choices you make apply to any new text that you type from that point onwards.

CHAPTER 1
Editing

1.2 Changing Font Properties

Each time you start a new document, Word provides the "*Normal*" style font ready for you to start typing. The Normal style is set by default to the Times New Roman font at 12 points. However, you can select from a wide range of other font styles as well as various font sizes, colours and positions. Additionally, words and phrases can be highlighted using different colours to emphasis parts of your document as well as the colour of the font itself being changed.

1.2.1 Choosing a Font

You can select a new font for your entire document or only selected parts of the document. It is advised, however, that you keep the number of fonts used in a document to a minimum. Usually, the rule of thumb is not to use more than three font types in one file. It is actually better in most cases to use only one or two font types and simply increase or decrease the size of the font to emphasise parts of your document, such as headings, titles, etc.

- Click on the arrow on the **Font** box on the Formatting Toolbar to display a list of available fonts.

- Use the scroll bar to view the range of fonts.

- Click the font of your choice to apply the font to previously selected text or to set the font type for new text you are about to type.

1.2.2 Changing the Font Size

One way to emphasise or distinguish specific text is by changing the font size. The font size can either be increased or decreased to suit your requirements.

- Click the arrow on the **Font Size** box on the Formatting Toolbar.

- Use the scroll bar to view the range of sizes.

- Click the font size of your choice.

NOTE

In addition to the standard font sizes shown in the Font Size box, you can also create a font size of your own, such as 13 points, 15 points, etc. Simply click on the arrow in the **Font Size** box and then highlight the font size that is displayed. Type your own font size over the top of the existing one and then press **ENTER**.

1.2.3 Using the Highlighter

There may be occasions when you wish to emphasise portions of text by highlighting with a specific highlighting colour.

- Click the arrow on the **Highlight** button on the Formatting Toolbar.

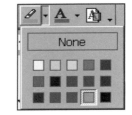

- Select the highlight colour you wish to use from the available colour palette. The cursor changes into the I-beam pointer with the highlighting marker attached.

- Select the text that you wish to highlight by dragging the mouse across the individual portions of text. The highlighter remains active until you have finished highlighting.

- Click the **Highlight** button again to turn the highlighter off.

NOTE

If you have already selected text before you click on the Highlight button on the Formatting Toolbar, only this portion of text will be highlighted with the colour of your choice. Therefore, if you wish to highlight a number of different sections of your document, ensure that you do not select any text before you click the Highlight button.

1.2.4 Changing the Font Colour

Whether you are typing a simple document or designing a poster, Word has a huge range of colour options available for you to use. To apply a colour to selected text:

- Click on the arrow on the **Font Colour** button on the Formatting Toolbar.

- Select the colour of your choice from the available palette of colours. Should you require a further choice of colours, click on the **More Colours** button. You can then select from a more extensive range of Standard colours or create your own Custom colour.

NOTE

If you wish to remove a font colour from existing text, select the text and then click the **Font Colour** button. Click on the **Automatic** option at the top of the colour palette to return to the default font colour for your document.

NOTE

All of the above changes to the font properties can also be made using the Font window.

Exercise 1A

1   Open the document named "**Sydney - Formatting**".

2   Select the heading "**Hotel Isis Darling Harbour**". Using the Formatting Toolbar, apply the following formatting changes to this text:

> **Bold**
> **Font = Comic Sans MS**
> **Size = 12pt**
> **Highlight Colour = Grey-25%**
> **Font Colour = Red**

3   Now apply the same formatting to the remaining headings:

> **Newton Hotel Darling Harbour**
> **Hyde Park Place**

4   Save the document but do not close it.

1.3   Changing Font Effects

Using the Font window, you can set a range of different formatting effects, such as strikethrough, shadow, small caps, etc. These formatting options are not usually accessible from the Toolbar buttons.

- Select the text you wish to format.

- Choose **Font** in the **Format** menu. The Font window will be displayed.

- Make any necessary formatting selections. The Preview box will show you how each option will apply to your selected text.

- Click **OK** to apply the formatting changes and return to your document.

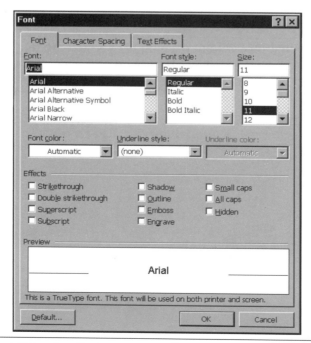

1.3.1 Text Effects (3.1.1.1)

There are a number of "non-animated" formatting effects that can be set on the Font tab of the Font window. A sample of each of choices is displayed below.

Strikethrough	~~Holidays~~
Double Strikethrough	~~Holidays~~
Superscript	Holi^{days}
Subscript	Holi_{days}
Shadow	Holidays
Outline	Holidays
Emboss	Holidays
Engrave	Holidays
Small Caps	Holidays
All Caps	HOLIDAYS
Hidden	

1.3.2 Animated Text Effects (3.1.1.2)

Animated effects are useful for enhancing and emphasising portions of text for on-screen display rather than for printed results. Only one animation effect may be applied at one time.

- Select the appropriate text to be formatted.

- Choose **Font** in the **Format** menu. The Font window will be displayed.

- Click on the **Text Effects** tab.

- Select an effect from the available list of **Animations**. The Preview box will display a sample of the effect you have chosen.

- Click **OK** to apply the animation formatting.

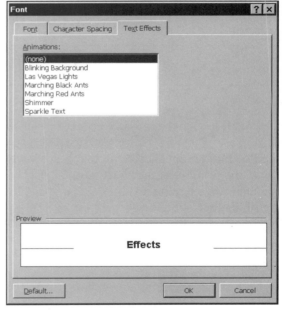

TIP

Try not to use too many animated effects in one document as this can become very annoying to your readers when they are viewing them online.

1.3.3 Character Spacing

On occasions you may need to be very precise with the spacing and scaling between letters and words. This precision can be achieved using the **Character Spacing** tab in the Font window.

- Select the text you wish to format.

- Choose **Font** in the **Format** menu. The Font window will be displayed.

- Click on the **Character Spacing** tab.

- Select the spacing settings you require. The Preview box will display the formatting effects you have selected.

- Click **OK** to apply the formatting.

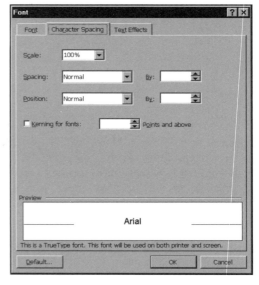

Scaling

Scaling allows you to adjust the size of selected text as a percentage of its normal size, with normal being 100%.

Spacing

Spacing provides a condensed and expanded option to determine the space between characters. Whichever option you choose, Word will enter suggestions in the **By** box which you may either accept or amend. The effects are demonstrated below.

Normal	JL	Once upon a time
Expanded by 2.5 pts	JL	Once upon a time
Condensed by 6 pts	L	

Position

The **Position** option allows you to raise or lower the placement of text on a line. In the sample below, the position of the word "normal" has been raised 30 pts to centre it on to the bigger "JL" characters on the same text line. Raising and lowering text in this manner does not change the size of the font.

Normal	JL

Kerning

Kerning allows Word to "tighten" the spacing between individual characters. To activate kerning you need to check the **Kerning for Points option** and then set a measurement, in points, in the **Points and Above** box that controls when kerning should be applied. For example, if you set the **Points And Above** box to **36pts** only characters that are 36 points and above will be kerned.

NOTE

The effect of kerning and the need for kerning will depend on the actual font you have used to format the text.

Venezuela Vacations

In the example above, the two words "Venezuela Vacations" have been formatted to Times New Roman, 48 points, no kerning.

Venezuela Vacations

In the example above, the two words "Venezuela Vacations" have been formatted to Times New Roman, 48 points, with the Kerning set to **48 Points and Above**, so that the individual spacing between the initial capital letters and the first lowercase letters is tightened.

Exercise 1B

1   Ensure you are working in the "**Sydney - Formatting**" document at the top of page 1.

2   Select the heading "**All about Sydney**" and using the **Font** window, apply the following formatting to this text:

> **Font style = bold**
> **Size = 24 pts**
> **Effects = shadow, small caps**

3   View the changes to the heading in your document.

4   Select the "**All about Sydney**" heading and again choose **Font** in the **Format** menu to access the Font window. Click on the **Text Effects** tab and move the cursor down through the list of available effects to see what each one does. Select the **Sparkle Text** option and then click **OK** to return to the document.

5   Select the "**All about Sydney**" heading and again choose **Font** in the **Format** menu to access the Font window. Set the **Animation** effect to **(none)**. Click on the **Character Spacing** tab and set the **Spacing** to **Expanded** by **1.3 pts**. Click **OK** to return to the document.

6   Go to the end of the document.   The three hotel headings use the font **Comic Sans MS**. Notice that some of the characters in these headings appear very close together. Using the Font window, expand the spacing for all of these headings by **1pt** only.

7   Return to page 1. Save the document but do not close it.

12

1.4   Creating a Drop Capital

The use of an initial "dropped" capital letter is a text feature found in a whole range of writing materials, from articles in magazines to literary works. The sample text below shows one of the two possible drop capital options available in Word.

V enezuela Vacations are now offering special travel packages for trips between May and October. Please contact you local travel agent for further details.

To create a drop cap:

- Ensure you are working in the Print Layout view.

- Click anywhere within the paragraph you wish to format with an in initial drop cap. Word will identify the first character of the paragraph to be formatted.

- Choose **Drop Cap** in the **Format** menu.

- Select an appropriate choice from the **Position** box. Change any of the **Options** if appropriate, such as changing the font for the drop capital or increasing the number of lines of the drop.

- Click **OK** to apply the formatting.

NOTE

When a drop capital is created, a special text frame is placed around the drop capital letter at the start of the paragraph. A sample of the frame is shown in the example below.

V enezuela Vacations are now offering special travel packages for trips between May and October. Please contact you local travel agent for further details.

1.5   Changing the Case of Typed Text

If you have already typed a portion of text and then decide you would prefer it to be in another *case*, you can quickly and easily change it without having to retype the information again. For example, you may have accidentally had the caps lock on and typed an entire paragraph in capitals. Using the Change Case window you can format the paragraph into sentence case rather than retyping the text again.

- Select the text you wish to format.

- Choose **Change Case** in the **Format** menu.   The Change Case window appears.

- Select the appropriate case option and then click **O K**. Please see below for an example of the different case options.

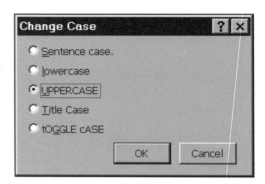

Sentence Case
Capitalises the first letter of the first word in the selected sentences. All other text is formatted to lowercase.

Lowercase
Formats all selected text into lowercase letters.

Uppercase
Formats all selected text into uppercase letters.

Title Case
Capitalises the first letter of each word in the selected text. All other letters in each word are formatted to lowercase.

Toggle Case
Formats all lowercase letters to uppercase and vice versa.

TIP

You can also use a speed key combination to change the case of a selected piece of text. Simply highlight the text and then press **SHIFT+F3** until the text appears in the case you require.

Exercise 1C

1   Ensure you are working in the "**Sydney - Formatting**" document.

2   Click in the heading "**Arriving in Sydney**". Using the **Format** menu, create a drop capital for this heading. Set the drop cap. to the **In margin** position with **4** lines to drop.

3   Now change the drop cap. position for the same heading to **Dropped**. View the changes in your document.

4   Select the heading "**Public Transport**" and then choose **Change Case** in the **Format** menu. Select **Uppercase** and then click **OK**. Now apply the same formatting to the remaining headings:

> **Banking Hours**
> **Climate**
> **Visitors Information Centres**
> **Accommodation**

5   Save the document, closing it on completion.

CHAPTER 1
Editing

Section 2   Automated Text Procedures

2.1   Automatic Text Correction (3.1.1.3)

AutoCorrect is a proofing tool within Word that identifies and corrects words and phrases that are commonly misspelt. For example, common typographical errors, such as "**adn**" for "**and**" and "**teh**" for "**the**" can be corrected, as well as punctuation errors and grammar mistakes. Capital letters automatically replace lowercase letters at the start of a new sentence and so on according to the preset rules of the AutoCorrect feature. It is important to note that AutoCorrect is active by default and needs to be turned off, if you do not wish to work with the feature.

To access the AutoCorrect window:

- Choose **AutoCorrect** in the **Tools** menu. The AutoCorrect window will be displayed.

If you don't want to use AutoCorrect within your document, uncheck the **Replace text as you type** box.

The two main columns show the error in the left-hand column and the replacement in the right-hand one.

Check this box if you want Word to automatically make suggestions based on the spelling checker if no other replacement is available.

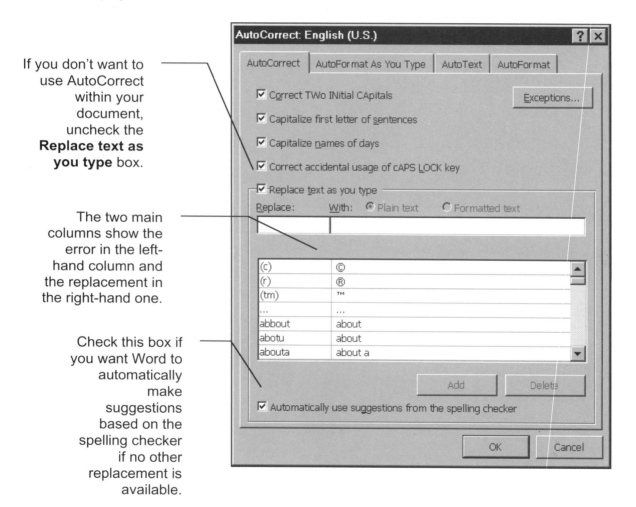

Correct Two Initial Capitals

If this option is checked, then if you type two capital letters together, the second one is automatically converted into a lowercase letter. For example:

"**THis one…**" becomes "**This one…**"

Capitalise First Letter of Sentences

If this option is checked, then the first letter after a full stop is automatic changed to uppercase if it is typed as lowercase.

"**this one…**" becomes "**This one…**"

Capitalise Names of Days

If this option is checked, then days of the week are automatically given an initial capital if a lowercase letter is used instead.

"**This monday …**" becomes "**This Monday…**"

Correct Accidental Usage of Caps Lock Key

If you accidental type when the Caps Lock key is on, then Word will convert the errors for you.

"**tHIS ONE …**" becomes "**This one…**"

2.1.1 Adding AutoCorrect Entries

The AutoCorrect window contains some initial settings which you can change or add to.

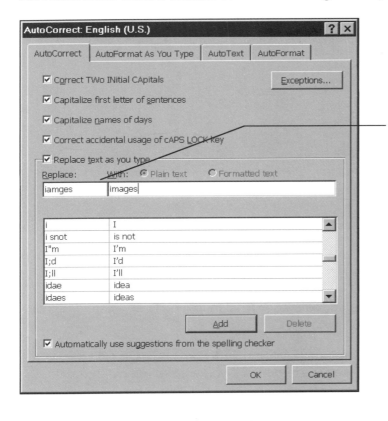

Enter the error in the **Replace** box and your correction in the **With** box. Then click the **Add** button at the bottom of the window to complete the process. Add as many other entries as you would like.

2.1.2 Adding Shortcuts to AutoCorrect

AutoCorrect also facilitates the use of useful shortcuts. For example, some predefined shortcuts are available, such as if you type (c) Word converts it to © or if you type (r) Word converts it to ®. You can create your own shortcuts within AutoCorrect at anytime, simply by using the **Replace** and **With** boxes. For example, you may wish to create a shortcut for the company **Happy Holidays International**, using **hhi** as the **Replace** text.

NOTE

Watch out for using abbreviations that have other meanings. For example, imagine if you used **ltd** as an abbreviation with the replacement entry of "**local travel destinations**". Problems would occur when you try to use **Ltd** within a company name as Word will automatically replace it with your AutoCorrect example.

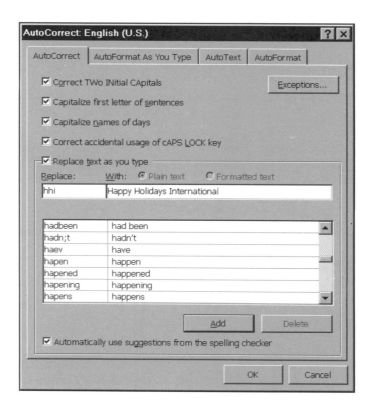

2.1.3 Amending AutoCorrect Entries

You can modify any of the AutoCorrect entries at any time or you can delete those that are no longer appropriate.

- Access the AutoCorrect window.

- Scroll down until you have located the entry you wish to modify or delete and then click on this entry.

- Change either the text in the **Replace** or **With** boxes and then click **Add** to update it. Alternatively, click th4e **Delete** button if you wish to remove the entry altogether.

- Click **OK** to return to your document.

2.1.4 Exceptions

For every rule there are exceptions and you can use the AutoCorrect **Exceptions** button to identify any that are appropriate to you. For example, you may regularly use the abbreviation "eg.". If you type a fullstop after the abbreviation, Word will automatically capitalise the first letter of the next word you type. However, using the **First Letter** tab in the **AutoCorrect Exceptions** box, you could specify that you don't wish to capitalise after "**eg.**" Has been typed.

- Choose **AutoCorrect** in the **Tools** menu. The AutoCorrect window will be displayed.

- Click on the **Exceptions** button. The AutoCorrect Exceptions dialolgue box will be displayed.

Use the available tabs to specify your exceptions. Use the **Add** and **Delete** buttons to add new exceptions or to remove existing ones.

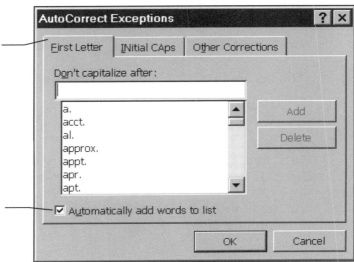

If this box is checked, Word will automatically create an exception for you, if you have used the **BACKSPACE** key to undo an AutoCorrect suggestion.

NOTE

If AutoCorrect changes something in your typing automatically and for that instance you do not want it to, you can use the Undo feature to revert the typing back to how you inserted it. Either click the Undo button on the Standard Toolbar or press **CTRL+Z**. One example is if you are temporarily typing something in Irish and you don't want an "**i**" on it's own to become a capital "**I**". Rather than deleting this replacement from the AutoCorrect entries permanently, you could use the Undo feature in this instance when you wish an "i" on it's own to remain as lowercase.

Exercise 2A

1   Ensure you are working in a new blank document.

2   Access the AutoCorrect window by choosing **AutoCorrect** in the **Tools** menu.

3   Scroll through the various mistakes and their corrections in the lower half of the window. What are some of your favourite mistakes - are they listed or would you need to add them yourself?

4   Click **Cancel** to exit the window without making any changes.

5   Type the following sentence (sometimes it's hard to type incorrectly on purpose!!).

     "Teh libary might of been closed on taht occassion."

     AutoCorrect should automatically change the sentence to read:

     "The library might have been closed on that occasion."

6   On a blank line, type (c) and then press the **SPACEBAR**. AutoCorrect should insert the © symbol for you.

7   On a blank line, type the following text. When Word capitalizes the word "travel", use undo to revert back to a lowercase letter.

     "All personnel, eg. travel consultants, tour co-ordinators, etc, will need to arrive before 8am."

8   Access the AutoCorrect window by choosing **AutoCorrect** in the **Tools** menu. In the **Replace** box type *hhi* and in the **With** box type *Happy Holidays International*. Click the **Add** button and then click **OK**. Test out your new replacement by typing *hhi* and then pressing the **SPACEBAR**.

9   Access the AutoCorrect window and delete the rule that you have just created. Return to the document on completion.

10   Close the document without saving the changes.

Section 3   Automatically Formatting Text (3.1.1.4)

Consistent formatting in your documents not only saves you time but all provides a specific "look and feel" to your work.   Word makes it easy for us to format our documents in a standard way, using the AutoFormat tool. You can either let AutoFormat work with you as you type or leave it until the document is complete and then have AutoFormat do the checking and correcting for you.

3.1   Using AutoFormat as you Type

Word will automatically format your text as you type as the AutoFormat is active by default. You may, however, wish to change some of the AutoFormat As You Type options to ensure that what Word is doing suits your own formatting requirements.

To change the AutoFormat options:

- Choose **AutoFormat** in the **Format** menu. The AutoFormat window will be displayed.

- Click the **Options** button to display the AutoCorrect window. Then click on the **AutoFormat As You Type** tab.

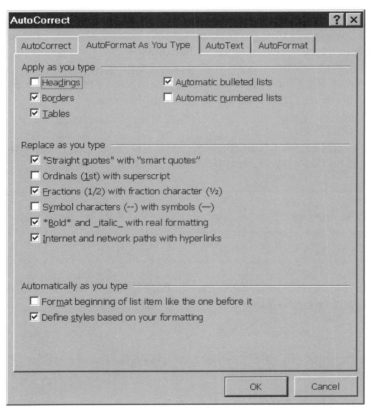

- Make any necessary changes and then click **O K** to return to your document. Please see the following page for more details on the AutoFormat As You Type options.

3.1.1 Apply As You Type Options

Headings

If this option is checked, then headings styles are automatically applied to your text, depending on certain circumstances, such as in the example outlined below.

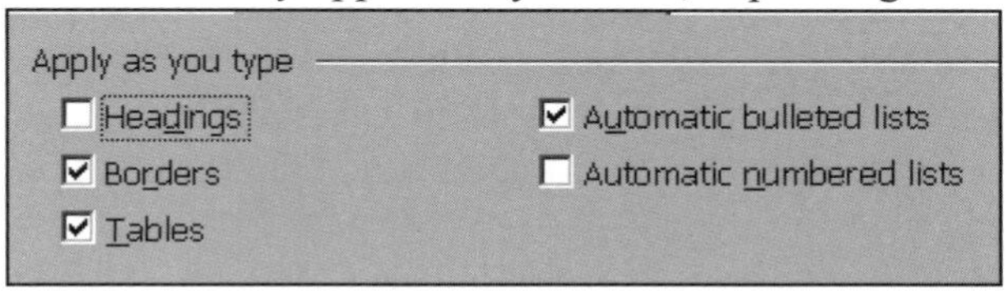

```
Apply as you type
  □ Headings              ☑ Automatic bulleted lists
  ☑ Borders               □ Automatic numbered lists
  ☑ Tables
```

If you :	Type a line of text Do not include a full stop Enter a blank line Press the **ENTER** key twice

The text is formatted using the **Heading 1** style

If you :	Start with a blank line Type a line of text Do not include a full stop Press the **TAB** key once

The text is formatted using the **Heading 2** style

Each time you include an extra tab space the heading style is taken to the next level, such as Heading 3, Heading 4, all the way up to Heading 9

Borders

If you check the **Borders** option in the Apply as you type section, borders can be added above or below a paragraph by typing three or more of the special characters listed below.

If you:	Type three or more hyphens (-) or underscores (_)and then press **ENTER**, a single line border will be inserted by the AutoFormat feature.

_____

If you:	Type three or more equal signs (=) and then press **ENTER**, a double line border will be inserted by the AutoFormat feature.

═══

If you:	Type three or more asterisks (*) and then press **ENTER**, a dotted line border will be inserted by the AutoFormat feature.

••

If you:	Type three or more tildes (~) and then press **ENTER**, the AutoFormat feature will insert a wavy line border.

∼∼

If you:	Type three or more hashes (#) and then press **ENTER**, the AutoFormat feature will insert a decorative line border.

═══

Tables

If you check the Table option in the Apply as you type section, you can create tables by using the plus sign (+) to indicate a column border and hyphens (-) or underscores (_) to indicate the column width. Then press **ENTER** to create the table.

+_____+_____+_____+_____+

Automatic Bulleted Lists

If you check the **Automatic bulleted lists** option in the Apply as you type section, Word will automatically format a list for you with the bullet symbol you use for the first line of the list. Each time you press the **ENTER** key, Word provides you with another bullet symbol for the next item. When you press **ENTER** twice, Word considers that you have finished the list.

Automatic Numbered Lists

If you check the **Automatic numbered lists** option in the Apply as you type section, Word will automatically format a list for you with a numbering system based on the number or letter you use for the first line of the list. Each time you press the **ENTER** key, Word provides you with another number/letter in the sequence for the next item. When you press **ENTER** twice, Word considers that you have finished the list.

Exercise 3A

1   Ensure you are working in a new blank document.

2   Choose **AutoFormat** in the **Format** menu and then select **Options**. Click on the **AutoFormat As Your Type** tab. Set the **Apply As You Type** options as shown in the example below:

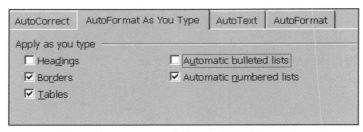

3   Click **OK** to accept the changes and then click **Close** to return to the document.

4   Type three tildes (~~~) on a blank line and then press **ENTER**. A wavy line should appear. Now type three asterisks (***) on a blank line and press **ENTER**. A dotted line should appear.

5   On a blank line, type the following example and then press **ENTER**.

+-----------------------------+------------+--------+---------+

6   On a blank line type the sequence **a)** then press the **TAB** key. Type **Cats** and then press **ENTER**. On the next line type **Dogs** and press **ENTER**. On the last line type **Ponies** and this time press **ENTER** twice to end the numbered list.

7   Close the document without saving it.

3.1.2   Replace As You Type Options

The **Replace as you type** options can be used to control the automatic replacement of specific text. This is activated by pressing the **SPACEBAR** after the text has been typed.

```
Replace as you type
  ☑ "Straight quotes" with "smart quotes"
  ☐ Ordinals (1st) with superscript
  ☑ Fractions (1/2) with fraction character (½)
  ☐ Symbol characters (--) with symbols (—)
  ☑ *Bold* and _italic_ with real formatting
  ☑ Internet and network paths with hyperlinks
```

Straight Quotes with Smart Quotes
If checked, standard quotation marks ("text") are replaced with smart quotes ("text").

Ordinals (1st) with Superscript
If checked, ordinals (st, nd, rd, th, etc) are enhanced with superscript formatting. For example, 1st, 2nd, 3rd, 4th, etc become 1st, 2nd, 3rd, 4th, etc.

Fractions (1/2) with Fraction Character (_)
If checked, fractions separated by the slash symbol (/) are automatically formatted as fraction characters. For example, 1/2 becomes _, 1/4 becomes _ and so on.

Symbol Characters (--) with Symbols
If checked, you can type a special shortcut of characters and when you press the **SPACEBAR**, AutoFormat automatically inserts the symbol the shortcut represents. For example:

(r) changes to ®, (TM) changes to ™, (c) changes to © and -- changes to —

Bold and _Italic_ With Real Formatting
If checked, when you type a word or phrase that starts and finishes with an asterisk (*) the text between the two asterisks will be changed to bold. If you use the underscore character (_) then the text between the two underscores changes to italics.

Internet and Network Paths with Hyperlinks
If this option is checked, if you enter a web address, such as **www.blackrock.edu.ie**, then AutoFormat will automatically convert the address into a hyperlink, such as www.blackrock.edu.ie. This means that if someone clicks on the link, their internet browser is opened and the address is searched for on the web.

Exercise 3B

1   Ensure you are working in a new blank document.

2   Access the **AutoFormat as You Type** tab in the **AutoFormat** window.

3   Set the **Apply as You Type** options as shown in the example below.

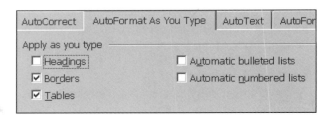

4   Ensure that the **Replace as You Type** options are also set as shown in the example below.

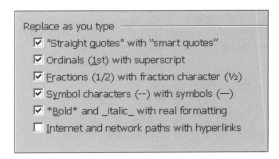

5   Click **OK** and then choose **Close** to return to your document.

6   Type the following lines of text:

"I think, therefore I am".

If not on the 1ˢᵗ June then perhaps the 2nd?

You will need 1/2 a kilo of flour and 1/4 of a kilo of sugar.

Microsoft Outlook (r) is Microsoft (TM) product.

***This is bold* and _this is italics_.**

7   Within the **AutoFormat As You Type** tab of the AutoFormat window, turn on the **Internet and network paths with hyperlinks** option. Upon returning to the document, type the following web address: **www.blackrock.edu.ie**. Once this text has been converted into a hyperlink click on it to access the website via your browser if this facility is available to you.

8   Close the document on completion, without saving it.

3.1.3 Automatically As You Type Options

> Automatically as you type ————
> ☐ For<u>m</u>at beginning of list item like the one before it
> ☑ Define <u>s</u>tyles based on your formatting

Format Beginning of List Item Like the One Before It

If this option is checked, Word automatically repeats the character formatting that you apply to the beginning of a list item. For example, if the first word or phrase of a list is in italics, Word automatically applies italic formatting to the first word or phrase of the next list item.

Define Styles Based on Your Formatting

If this option is checked, Word automatically creates new paragraph styles based on the manual formatting you apply to your document. You can apply these styles to other locations in your document.

For example, imagine that you turn on bold, italics and change the font colour to red and then type an entire paragraph, after which you turn the formatting options off. Word would automatically create a "**body text**" style containing the formatting choices you have used. This style could then be applied to other paragraphs in your document.   If you then use other formatting for another paragraph, Word will create a "**body text 2**" style and so on.

Exercise 3C

1   Ensure you are working in a new blank document.

2   Access the **AutoFormat as You Type** tab in the **AutoFormat** window.

3   Set the **Automatically as You Type** options as shown in the example below.

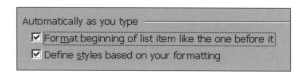

4   Click **OK** to accept your changes and then click **Close** to return to your document.

5   On a new blank line type the first line of text shown below. Ensure that only the word **Monday** is bold. Then press **ENTER** and type the next line in the list. You will not need to turn bold on or off for this line as AutoFormat will do it automatically for you. Press **ENTER** again and type the last line of text and then press **ENTER** twice to end the list.

- **Monday** – agency meeting with all travel personnel
- **Tuesday** – visit exhibition centre
- **Wednesday** – transportation of all exhibition materials

6   On a blank line, insert the file named "**This is section two.doc**".

7   Select the first paragraph of the newly inserted information and press **CTRL+M** to indent the entire paragraph by one tab stop. Click away from the paragraph and then click back into it. Notice in the **Style** box on the Formatting Toolbar that this paragraph is now using a **Body Text** style. Select the third paragraph of the document and, using the **Style** box on the Formatting Toolbar, change the paragraph style to the same **Body Text** style used for the first paragraph.

8   Close the document on completion without saving the changes.

CHAPTER 1
Editing

3.2   AutoFormatting a Finished Document

Instead of autoformatting as you type, you can leave it until you're finished the document or part of it, e.g. a paragraph or section. . Using AutoFormat Word is able to apply all of the autoformatting settings in "one pass". Having completed the AutoFormat routine, Word will allow you to review all of the changes it has made so that you can decide whether to accept or reject them.

3.2.1   Setting the AutoFormat Options

Just as you can set AutoFormat options for as you are typing (please see 3.1 for more details). You can also set AutoFormat options for use when you are checking a completed document. The options are very much the same, with only a few differences.

To set the AutoFormat options:

- Choose **AutoFormat** in the **Format** menu.

- Click the **Options** button.

- Select the **AutoFormat** tab and then make any appropriate changes. Most of the options are the same as for AutoFormat As You Type but the differences are identified below.

- Click **OK** to accept your changes.

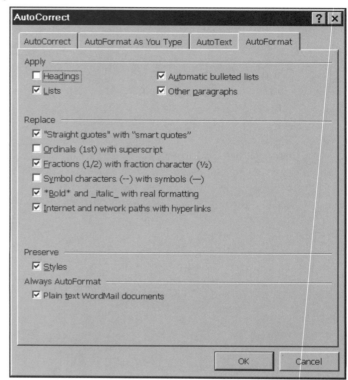

Headings
Formats the headings in your document using the styles Heading 1 to Heading 9.

Lists
Lists, including numbered lists, are identified and assigned a list style.

Automatic Bulleted Lists
Depending on the differing levels of indentation, Word assigns different bullet styles to the lists. Additionally, bullets created using asterisks or hyphens are automatically formatted with bullet symbols instead.

Other Paragraphs
The main body of text, that is text excluding the headings, lists, bulleted lists, etc, are assigned an appropriate paragraph style.

Preserve Styles

This option keeps any styles you create yourself and does not replace them with standard Word styles.

Always AutoFormat Plain Text Email Documents

If you are using Word as your "email editor", then email messages that are in plain text are automatically autoformatted when they are opened.

3.2.2 Running AutoFormat

Once you have set your AutoFormat options you are ready to run the AutoFormat process.

- Click anywhere in the document to AutoFormat the entire file or highlight the portion of the document you wish to check.

- Choose **AutoFormat** in the **Format** menu. The AutoFormat window will be displayed.

- If you wish to run the process through the document without reviewing any recommended changes, select **AutoFormat Now**. Alternatively, select **AutoFormat and review each change** so that you can decide whether or accept or reject the suggestions made by the AutoFormat routine.

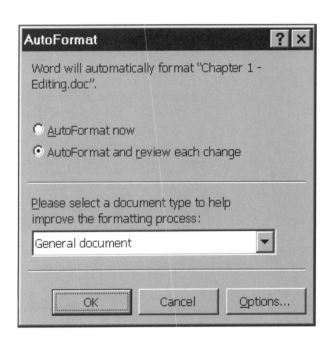

- Select what type of document you are going to AutoFormat from the available list box. The choices are **General document**, **Letter** or **Email**.

- Click **OK** to begin the AutoFormat process.

- If you have selected to AutoFormat and review the changes before the document is reformatted, the document will appear in an updated format and the following window will be displayed.

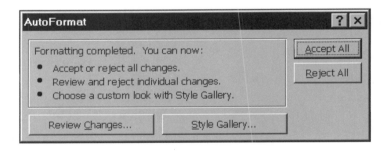

- If you wish, you can **Accept All** of the changes to the document or **Reject All** of the changes to leave the document as it was originally. You can, however, use the **Review Changes** button to control which changes are kept and which are to be rejected.

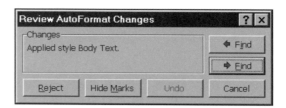

3.2.2.2 The Review AutoFormat Changes Window

If you have decided to review each of the changes before you decide whether each one is accepted or rejected, the Review AutoFormat Changes window will be displayed and the first change in the document will be highlighted.

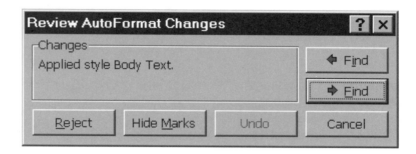

- If you want to reject a formatting change, click the **Reject** button.

- To move between the next or previous changes, click the Find buttons.

- Editing marks will be displayed in the document to help you distinguish where formatting changes have been made. If you do not wish to see these marks, click the **Hide Marks** button. Editing marks are only for the purpose of on-screen display and will not appear on the page when it is printed.

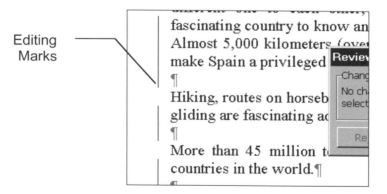

Editing Marks

- If you have rejected a formatting suggestion and then change your mind, you can click the **Undo** button to reverse the last change you have made.

- When you have reviewed all of the suggested changes, you will be returned to the AutoFormat window. Alternatively, if you do not want to go through each change, you can click **Cancel** at any time to return to the AutoFormat window.

You can then choose to **Accept All** or **Reject All** as before. If you choose **Accept All** then it will be assumed that you accept any suggested formatting that you have not already rejected.

- You can now click **Accept All** to accept all the formatting suggestions that have not been rejected or cancel all of them by clicking the **Reject All** button.

3.2.2.3 Style Gallery

When you AutoFormat a document, Word bases the formatting changes on the settings you made in the AutoFormat window as well as the standard "styles" available in the template upon which your document is based. You can, however, choose the styles from another template and this is achieved by clicking the **Style Gallery** button. This should be done, however, before you review the changes or accept those that have been proposed.

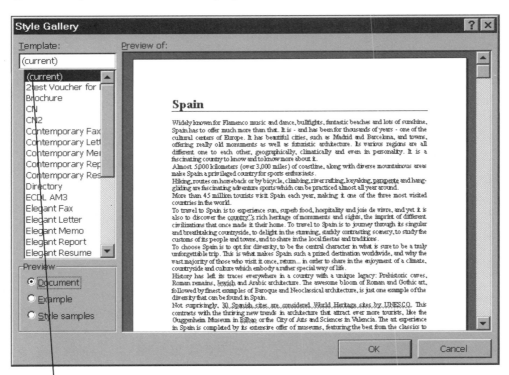

Select a template from the available list. The contents of your document will change in the **Preview of** window to display how the newly selected styles will update your document. Click **OK** once you have made the appropriate selection to return to the **AutoFormat** window.

Exercise 3D

1   Open the document named **AutoFormat Report**. This document contains some *generic* type text. No styles have been used in the document and only some basic formatting for each heading level has been applied.

2   Choose **AutoFormat** from the **Format** menu. Select **AutoFormat and review each change**. Click the **Options** button and ensure the **AutoFormat** tab is selected. Check all boxes in the **Apply** section and then click **OK**. Click **OK** again for the AutoFormat process to take place. Notice that some changes occur in your document. You can click outside of the **AutoFormat** window if you want to see what heading styles or other styles have been applied in your document. Click back inside the window again to continue.

3   Click the **Review Changes** button to see the editing marks within your document. Click **Cancel** to return to the **AutoFormat** window.

4   Click the **Style Gallery** button. Click on the **Professional Report** style and notice the changes in your document. Click **OK** to accept this format. Click the **Accept All** button to update your document.

5   Save the document, closing it on completion.

Section 4   Automatic Text Entry (3.1.1.5)

Most of the text in a document is typed used the keyboard. However, using AutoText, Word can help you to insert regularly used words or phrases quickly and easily at any time.   AutoText works with the *AutoComplete* feature to anticipate the words you are preparing to enter and to insert them for you. By spending the time to teach Word about the words, terms and phrases you often use in your documents, you can save text entry time and also ensure accuracy.

4.1   Inserting Predefined AutoText Entries

Word includes a number of standard, predefined AutoText entries that can you can insert automatically into your documents.

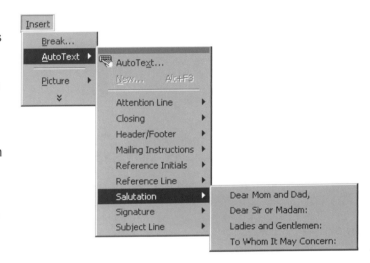

- Place the insertion point where the AutoText entry is to appear.

- Choose **AutoText** from the **Insert** menu.

- From the sub-menu, select an AutoText category (such as Attention Line, Closing, etc).

- Click on the AutoText entry to insert it.

4.2   Creating Your Own AutoText Entries

There will be many words, phrases or sentences that you use on a day-to-day basis that could be added as an AutoText entry to save you time in typing them each time they need to be used.

- In the usual way, type the text that you wish to include as an AutoText entry. Include any formatting that may be appropriate.

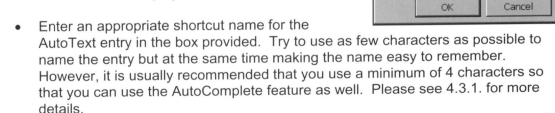

- Highlight the text and then choose **AutoText** in the **Insert** menu and then select **New**. Alternatively, press the shortcut keyboard combination **ALT+F3**. The **Create AutoText** window will be displayed.

- Enter an appropriate shortcut name for the AutoText entry in the box provided. Try to use as few characters as possible to name the entry but at the same time making the name easy to remember. However, it is usually recommended that you use a minimum of 4 characters so that you can use the AutoComplete feature as well. Please see 4.3.1. for more details.

- Click **OK** to return to the document.

Exercise 4A

1   Ensure you are working in a new blank document.

2   Type the following text:

Happy Holidays International

For further details please contact your local Happy Holidays Travel office.

All passengers have a free allowance of 20kgs.

Fitzroy House
77 Gloucester Road
LONDON SW7

3   Highlight the company name. Choose **AutoText** from the **Insert** menu and then
           select **New**. Name the entry **Happy** and then click **OK**.

4   Highlight the second line "For further details…". Press **ALT+F3** to access the
           Create AutoText window. The suggested named should be **For further**. Click
           OK to accept this name.

5   Highlight the third line "All passengers have…". Create an AutoText entry for this
           sentence, naming it **baggage**.

6   Highlight the remaining address and create an AutoText entry called **address**.

7   Close the document without saving it.

4.3   Inserting AutoText Entries

Using the same process you did for predefined AutoText entries, you can also insert your own AutoText entries.

- Choose **AutoText** from the **Insert** menu.

- Select one of your AutoText entries from the available menu list.

Alternatively, you can use a shortcut method.

- Type the name of your AutoText entry into your document and immediately after press the **F3** key to insert the entry.

4.3.1   Using AutoComplete to Insert an AutoText Entry

AutoComplete is an inbuilt tool within Word to help you to insert dates and/or AutoText entries. Simply start by typing the name of the AutoText entry and notice how Word proposes a ScreenTip above the word or phrase. If this is the correct entry that you wish to use, simply press **ENTER** to insert it. If not, continue typing and the ScreenTip will disappear.

NOTE

You need to use at least four characters of the AutoText shortcut entry for the ScreenTip to appear.

If you wish to use the AutoComplete tool, you need to activate on the AutoText options page.

- Choose **AutoText** in the **Insert** menu. Select **AutoText** and then click on the **AutoText** tab if it is not already selected.

- Ensure the **Show AutoComplete tip for AutoText and dates** box is checked.

- Click **OK** to return to your document.

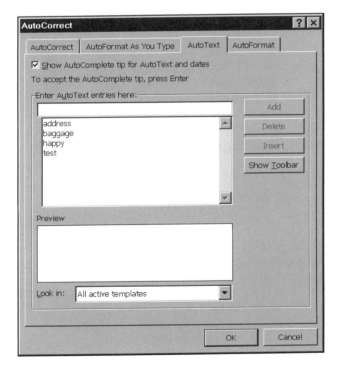

Exercise 4B

1   Ensure you are working in a new blank document. Choose **AutoText** from the **Insert** menu and then select **AutoText** again. Click on the **AutoText** tab and ensure the **Show AutoComplete tip for AutoText and dates** box is checked. Click **OK** to return to your document.

2   Type **address** and then press **F3** to insert the AutoText entry.

3   Type **Happy** and then press **F3** to insert the company name.

4   On a blank line, type **For fur** and notice the ScreenTip that appears. Press **ENTER** to insert the AutoText entry.

5   On another blank line, type **bagg** and then press **ENTER** when the ScreenTip appears.

4.4   Managing AutoText Entries

Over a period of time you may wish to add more and more AutoText entries and then find that some of them become redundant.   Those entries that are no longer needed should be deleted so that they are not accidentally used, particularly with the AutoComplete feature.

- Choose **AutoText** from the **Insert** menu. Select **AutoText** and then **AutoCorrect** window appears. Ensure you are working on the **AutoText** tab.

- Select the entry you wish to remove and then click the **Delete** button.

- Click **OK** once you have deleted all appropriate AutoText entries.

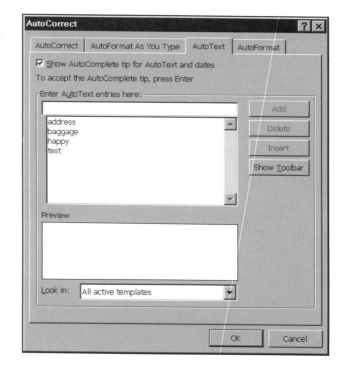

4.4.1   The AutoText Toolbar

The AutoText toolbar can be used to help you add, insert or manage your AutoText entries.   The toolbar can be displayed in the usual way; that is by right mouse clicking on any currently displayed toolbar or from the AutoCorrect window.

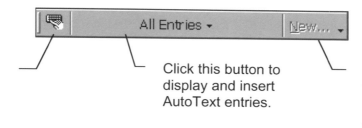

Click this button to access the AutoText in the AutoCorrect window.

Click this button to display and insert AutoText entries.

Click the **New** button when you are creating a new AutoText entry.

4.4.2 Editing an AutoText Entry

The contents or formatting of an AutoText entry may need to change from time to time. Using the AutoText feature you can quickly and easily edit an existing entry.

- Using the AutoText feature, insert the entry you wish to modify into a document.

- Make any necessary changes.

- Highlight the entry and choose **AutoText** from the **Insert** menu. Choose **AutoText** again.

- When the AutoCorrect window appears, ensure you are working on the **AutoText** tab. Click on the AutoText name for the entry you have just modified. Click the **Add** button. A question box will appear.

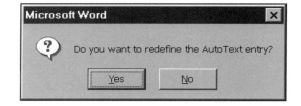

- Click **Yes** to update the AutoText entry.

Exercise 4C

1   Insert the **address** AutoText entry into your document.

2   Change the street address to "**97 Gloucester Road**". Highlight the entire address again. Choose **AutoText** from the **Insert** menu and then **AutoText** again. Click on the **address** name and then click **Add**. Choose **Yes** to update the entry. Insert the entry to ensure that it has been successfully modified.

3   Access the AutoText tab in the AutoComplete window. Click the **Show Toolbar**. Using the **All Entries** button, practice inserting some AutoText entries.

4   Access the AutoText tab again in the AutoComplete window. Delete the four entries that you have created: **address**, **baggage**, **happy** and **For further**. Return to your document on completion.

5   Close the current document, without saving.

Section 5   Text Wrapping (3.1.1.6)

In Word, when a graphic is placed on a page, it is placed "in line" within the line of text that is active. This means that until it is formatted, it cannot be moved or dragged freely within the document. It is treated in the same way as any other single character (except that it may be a bit bigger!) and therefore is confined to normal text movements. However, in most instances, it is important to be able to place the graphic more appropriately on the page and to be able to manage effectively the text around it.

5.1   Basic Text Wrapping Options

The most regularly used text wrapping options are available within the Format Picture window on the **Layout** tab. The graphical representation of each of the options helps to demonstrate to you their effect on the text surrounding the graphic you have selected.

To change the text wrapping options for a graphic:

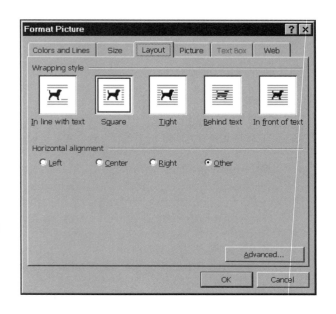

- Right mouse click on the graphic for which you wish to change the text wrapping options.

- Select **Format Picture** from the shortcut menu.

- Click on the **Layout** tab.

- Make an appropriate selection from the **Wrapping style** options and also the **Horizontal alignment** settings.

- Click **OK** to return to your document.

5.1.1 Wrapping Styles

In Line with Text
This style places the object at the insertion point in a line of text. The object remains on the same layer as the text.

Square
This style wraps text around all sides of the square object box for the selected object.

Tight
This style wraps text tightly around the edges of the actual image rather than the object's box.

Behind Text
This style removes text wrapping and places the object behind the text.

In Front of Text
This style removes text wrapping and places the object in front of the text in the document.

Exercise 5A

1   Open the document named **Sports and Locations in Spain**.

2   Notice the graphic that has been inserted on the page 1. Try dragging it to a new location on the page. It is confined to normal text movements as its wrapping style is "In line with text". Click **Undo** to return the graphic to its original position.

3   Click once on the picture to select it, then right mouse click and choose **Format Picture**. Click on the **Layout** tab. Select the **Square** wrapping style and then **Right** horizontal alignment. Click **OK** to return to the document. If you wish, you can drag the image with the mouse to slightly adjust its position on the right side of the page.

4   Now change the layout for your graphic so that it is using the **Behind text** wrapping style on the **Left** for the horizontal alignment. View the changes on the page.

5   Return to the **Format Picture** window and change the layout for the image so that it uses the **Square** wrapping style in the **Centre** for the horizontal alignment.

6   Now change the layout for the image so that it is still in the centre but this time the wrapping style is **Tight**.

7   Move the graphic to another location on the page and observe what happens to the wrapping style when the graphic is repositioned.

8   Go to page 2 and select the graphic under the heading "**About Spain and its Locations**".   Right mouse click and choose **Format Picture**. Set the layout so that the graphic is using the **Square** wrapping style in the **Centre** horizontal position. Click **OK** to return to the document. Notice the position of the graphic on the page and within the paragraph with which it is associated.

9   Save the document but do not close it.

5.2   Advanced Text Wrapping Options

The advanced text wrapping options provide additional styles with more specific options that allow you greater flexibility to control the text around your graphics.

To change the advanced text wrapping options:

- Right mouse click on the graphic for which you wish to change the text wrapping options.

- Click on the **Layout** tab. Select a **Wrapping style** and **Horizontal alignment** setting now, if you haven't already done so.

- Click the **Advanced** button. The **Advanced Layout** window will be displayed.

- Click on the **Text Wrapping** tab.

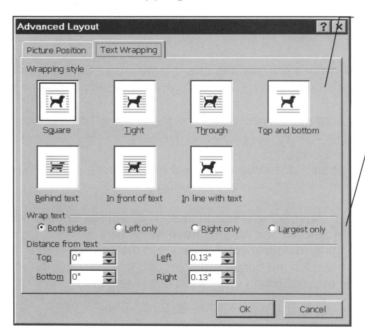

Two additional wrapping styles are available: Through and Top and bottom. See 5.2.1 below for further details.

Wraps text on either the left or right depending on which is wider. This can only be achieved when using Through, Tight or Square for the wrapping style.

- Make a selection in the **Wrapping style** section, if appropriate.

- Choose an appropriate option in the **Wrap text** section to control whether the text wraps on both the left and right sides of the graphic or on one side only.

- Use the **Distance from text** options to control the space between the graphic and the text which wraps around it.

- Click **OK** to return to the Format Picture window and then click **OK** again to return to your document.

5.2.1   Through and Top and Bottom Wrapping Styles

 Through, this wrapping style will wrap text tight up against the graphic and will also fill any available empty spaces within the graphic.

 Top and bottom: this wrapping style will wrap text above and below the graphic. The left and right sides will not contain any text.

5.3   Changing Wrapping Points

Each picture has what is known as *wrapping points* around it which control where the text will flow around if you select any of the wrapping styles, except **In line with text** or **Top and bottom**. The wrapping points around a picture may be altered to further control where text flows around it.

- Select the graphic you wish to change the wrapping points for. Ensure you have specified an appropriate wrapping style for this graphic on the **Layout** tab of the Format Picture window.

- Ensure the **Picture** Toolbar is displayed (this should appear automatically whenever you click on a graphic). Click the **Text Wrapping** button and choose **Edit Wrap Points**. Wrapping points will appear around the graphic that can be dragged and dropped as required.

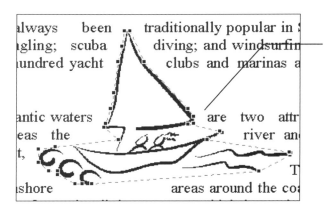

Wrapping points surround the graphic. They can be dragged and dropped to alter the wrapping points for the image.

- When you have finished setting the wrapping points, click the **Text Wrapping** button again on the Picture Toolbar and choose **Edit Wrap Points** to turn the feature off.

CHAPTER 1
Editing

Exercise 5B

1   Ensure you are working in the document named **Sports and Locations in Spain**.

2   Access the **Format Picture** window again for the selected graphic. Click on the **Layout** tab and then click the **Advanced** button. Click on the **Text Wrapping** tab. In the **Distance from text** section, set the **Left** setting to **.05** and the same for the **Right** setting. Click on the **Picture Position** tab and in the **Vertical** section, set the **Absolute position** to **.3"** below the **Paragraph**. Click **OK** twice to return to the document.

3   Return to page 1 of the document and select the graphic on this page. Ensure that the **Picture Toolbar** is displayed and then click on the **Text Wrapping** button. Select the **Edit Wrap Points** option. *Wrap points* will appear around the "boat" image. Using the mouse, drag the wrap points in and out to alter how the text wraps around the image. When you have finished, click on the **Text Wrapping** button again on the **Picture Toolbar**. Select **Edit Wrap Points** to turn the option off.

4   Save the document, closing it on completion.

Section 6   Text Orientation (3.1.1.7)

The standard orientation of text is *horizontal* - that is the text flows from the left side of the page to the right side of the page horizontally. There may be occasions however when you wish to change the orientation of text so that it flows vertical, either up or down the page. Word provides a *Text Direction* facility which allows for the vertical positioning of text. However, the Text Direction feature will only work on text that is typed within a table or a text box. See Chapter 4 for information on text boxes.

To change the direction of text:

- Select the text to be modified within a table or a text box.

- Choose **Text Direction** from the **Format** menu. The **Text Direction** window will be displayed.

- Select a direction of your choice from the **Orientation** box. A sample of how your text will appear displays in the **Preview** box.

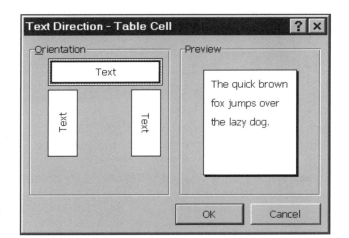

- Click **OK** to return to your document.

Exercise 6A

1   Open the document named **Weather around the World**.

2   Click in the cell of the table containing the word "**January**". Choose **Text Direction** from the **Format** menu. Select the second vertical orientation (that is the one on the right side of the **Orientation** box). Click **OK** to return to your document.

3   Select the remaining months, from **February** to **December**, and format them in the same text direction as the "**January**" heading.

4   Select all of the monthly headings and change the text direction so that they are using the first vertical orientation (that is the one on the left side of the **Orientation** box). You may need to increase the depth of the first row cells so that each month is fully displayed in its individual cell.

5   Select the text in the text box next to the photograph of the storm.   Change the text direction to a vertical setting of your choice. You may need to alter the width of the box on completion.

6   Save the document and then close it.

Section 7   Text Galleries (3.1.1.8)

WordArt is a graphical text feature available within Word. It provides a gallery of different "text styles" which can be used to enhance elements of your document, such as headings, banners, information notes, etc.

Once you have inserted a WordArt "object" it can be manipulated in many different ways. The management of text produced using WordArt is more closely related to the management of graphic items than normal text. A WordArt object can be resized, moved, reshaped, coloured, rotated as well as having various effects added to further enhance it. When it is inserted into a document, a WordArt object is a floating graphic so that it can be freely moved around the page as soon as it is inserted and then formatted to appear behind, in front of, or beside normal text and other graphics.

7.1   Inserting a WordArt Object

There are over thirty different WordArt styles to choose from when you insert a WordArt object. You can insert WordArt either using the Insert menu option or using the Drawing Toolbar.

- Click where you want the WordArt object to initially appear.

- Choose **Picture** from the **Insert** menu and then select **WordArt** or click the **WordArt** 🔲 button on the Drawing Toolbar. The **WordArt Gallery** window will appear.

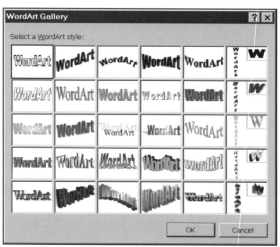

- Select a style of your choice and then click **OK**.

- The Edit WordArt Text window will appear. Over-type the "Your Text Here" caption with the text you wish to use. The text will wrap within the box provided but this does not affect the appearance of the text when it is inserted into your document.

- You can change the **Font** and **Size** if you wish. You can also use **Bold** and **Italics** for your text.

- Click **OK** to insert your WordArt object onto the page.

7.1.1 The WordArt Object

When you click on a WordArt object to select it, several things happen. Sizing handles appear around the outside of the object, a *skew handle* appears which can be used to change the object's tilt or slant and the **WordArt** Toolbar appears.

Sizing
Handles

Skew Handle

WordArt
Toolbar

Exercise 7A

1   Ensure you are working in a new blank document.

2   Click on the WordArt button on the **Drawing Toolbar** to open the WordArt Gallery window.

3   Select the WordArt style in the second row, first box across. Click **OK** to continue. When the **Edit WordArt Text** box appears, change the **Size** to **24** and then type the following text: **Happy Holidays** (do not press ENTER at the end of the last word). Click **OK** to continue. The WordArt image should be placed on the page with the WordArt Toolbar displayed. Click away from the WordArt image and the WordArt Toolbar disappears.

4   Save the document as "**Happy Holidays Logo**" but do not close it.

7.2   Editing a WordArt Object

Once you have inserted a WordArt object into a document, you may wish to change its text and or the font and its font attributes.

To edit an existing WordArt object:

- Double click the WordArt object or select it and click on the **Edit Text** button on the WordArt Toolbar. The Edit WordArt Text window will appear.

- Make any necessary changes, such as the font type or size, and then click **OK** to return to your document.

7.3   Changing the Style for a WordArt Object

When you create a WordArt object you initially select a *style* from the WordArt Gallery. You can, however, change this style once the object has been inserted into the document.

- Click on the WordArt object to select it.

- Click the **WordArt Gallery** button on the WordArt Toolbar. The WordArt Gallery window will be displayed. Make a selection of your choice and then click **OK** to return to your document.

Exercise 7B

1   Ensure you are working in the **Happy Holidays Logo** document.

2   Select the WordArt object and then click on the **WordArt Gallery** button. Change the style for the object so that it is using the style in the second row but the **third** box across from the left. Click **OK** to return to your document.

3   Double click the WordArt object to access the **Edit WordArt Text** window. Change the text so that it reads **Happy Holidays International**. Change the font size to **28** points. Return to the document. You may need to *drag* the WordArt object over to the left so that the logo sits more centrally on the page.

4   Save the document, but do not close it.

7.4   WordArt Colour and Line Formats

You can further enhance your WordArt object by changing its colour and line formats.

- Click on the WordArt object to select it.

- Click the **Format WordArt** button on the WordArt Toolbar. The Format WordArt window will be displayed.

- Click on the **Colours and Lines** tab.

- Choose the options appropriate to your object using the drop-down arrows to change the settings in the **Fill** and **Line** sections. **Colour** applies to the body of the character and **Line** refers to the bordering on each character.

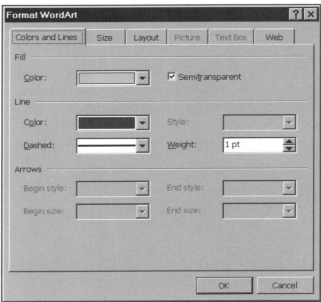

CHAPTER 1
Editing

7.5   Sizing and Rotating a WordArt Object

The size of any piece of WordArt text can be easily changed by grabbing and dragging the resize handles. However, more advanced size editing is available when using the **Size** tab in the **Format WordArt** window. You can have much greater control over the formatting of height, width and rotation settings. There is also a scaling choice as well as an *aspect ratio*, which maintains the original relationship between the height and width of the object.

- Click the WordArt object to select it.

- Click the **Format WordArt** button on the WordArt Toolbar. The Format WordArt window will be displayed.

- Click on the **Size** tab.

- Make any necessary changes such as altering the WordArt's height or width. Click **OK** to return to your document.

You can rotate the WordArt object in degrees using the Size tab on the Format WordArt window. However, you may wish to have more flexibility over the rotation of the object and this can be achieved using the Rotate button on the WordArt Toolbar. See 7.7 for more details.

Exercise 7C

1   Ensure you are working in the **Happy Holidays Logo** document.

2   Click on the WordArt object to select it and to display the WordArt Toolbar.

3   Click on the **Format WordArt** button on the WordArt Toolbar. Select the **Colours and Lines** tab.   Click in the **Fill Colour** and select the **Light Yellow** shade. For the **Line Colour** select **Grey, 50%**. Click **OK** to return to the document and view the changes to the WordArt object.

4   Access the **Format WordArt** window again and this time click on the **Size** tab. Set the **Height** for the **Size and Rotate** box to **0.67**" and then click **OK**. View the changes to the WordArt object.

5   Save the document but do not close it.

7.6   Reshaping a WordArt Object

In addition to the style that is used for a WordArt object, you can also change the *shape* of the object to further enhance its appearance.

- Click the WordArt object to select it.

- Click the **WordArt Shape** button on the WordArt Toolbar. A palette of shapes will appear. Click on the shape you wish to use.

NOTE

Some shapes can cause the text of a WordArt object to become a little unreadable. If this happens, you can either select another shape, or use the **Skew Handle** on the object to manipulate the text slightly to make it more readable.

7.7   Adjusting the Rotation of a WordArt Object

You can change the rotation of a WordArt object so that it does not sit purely in a horizontal position. For example, you may wish to rotate a WordArt object so that it slants down the page.

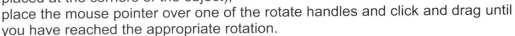
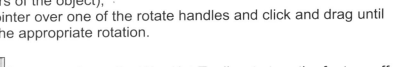
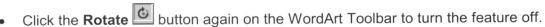

- Click the WordArt object to select it.

- Click on the **Rotate** button on the WordArt Toolbar. When the rotate handles appear (green circles usually placed at the corners of the object), place the mouse pointer over one of the rotate handles and click and drag until you have reached the appropriate rotation.

- Click the **Rotate** button again on the WordArt Toolbar to turn the feature off.

NOTE

You can also change the rotation of a WordArt object within the Format WordArt window. See **7.5 Sizing and Rotating a WordArt Object** for more information.

Exercise 7D

1   Ensure you are working in the **Happy Holidays Logo** document.

2   Ensure the WordArt object is selected and the WordArt Toolbar displayed.

3   Click on the **WordArt Shape** button on the WordArt Toolbar and from the available menu select the **Slant Up** style. Notice the changes to your WordArt object.

4   Now change the shape of your WordArt object so that it is using the **Wave 1** style.

5   With your WordArt object selected, click on the **Free Rotate** button on the WordArt Toolbar. Using one of the rotation handles, slightly adjust the rotation of the object until it appears to your satisfaction. Click the **Free Rotate** button again to turn off this feature.

6   Save the document, but do not close it.

7.8   WordArt Text Wrapping

If you wish to have 'normal' text surrounding a WordArt object, you can also control the text wrapping as you would for any other object, such as a picture. Please see Section 5 page 38 for more information on **Text Wrapping**.

- Click the WordArt object to select it.

- Click the **Text Wrapping**  button on the WordArt Toolbar.   Make an appropriate selection from the drop-down list that is displayed.

NOTE

You can also make changes to the wrapping style of a WordArt object using the **Format WordArt** window. Click on the object and then click the **Format WordArt** button on the WordArt Toolbar. Click on the **Layout** tab and make any necessary selections.

7.9   WordArt Character Arrangements

The last four buttons on the WordArt Toolbar facilitate the adjustment and arrangement of the characters within a piece of WordArt text.

7.9.1 Same Letter Height

Click the **WordArt Same Letter Heights** button to set the letters of the object at the same height regardless of whether they are uppercase or lowercase letters. By clicking the button again, you can return to the original letter height for the WordArt object.

7.9.2 Vertical Text

Using the **WordArt Vertical Text** button, you can switch the WordArt object to a vertical position and then back to the horizontal position, depending on your requirements.

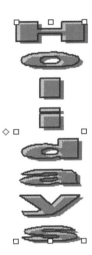

Exercise 7E

1   Ensure you are working in the **Happy Holidays Logo** document.

2   Ensure the WordArt object is selected and the WordArt Toolbar displayed.

3   Click on the **WordArt Same Letter Heights** button on the WordArt Toolbar. Notice the change to your WordArt object. Click the **WordArt Same Letter Heights** button again to turn this feature off.

4   Click on the **WordArt Character Spacing** button and select **Loose**. Now change the choice to **Very Tight** and then finally **Tight**.

5   Save the document, but do not close it.

7.9.3 Text Alignment

The **WordArt Alignment** button aligns text within the WordArt object, which is a *frame* within which the text appears. It is difficult to see the alignment options if you only have a single line of text within the WordArt object. Multiple lines of text (that is text ended with an ENTER) demonstrates the settings more clearly.

Left Align WordArt Alignment

Centre Align WordArt Alignment

Right Align WordArt Alignment

Word Justify WordArt Alignment

Letter Justify WordArt Alignment

Stretch Justify WordArt Alignment

Exercise 7F

1   Ensure you are working in the **Happy Holidays Logo** document.

2   Ensure the WordArt object is selected and the WordArt Toolbar displayed.

3   Click on the **WordArt Same Letter Heights** button on the WordArt Toolbar.
             Notice the change to your WordArt object. Click the **WordArt Same Letter
             Heights** button again to turn this feature off.

4   Click on the **WordArt Character Spacing** button and select **Loose**. Now change
             the choice to **Very Tight** and then finally **Tight**.

5   Save the document, but do not close it.

7.10 Additional Formatting Features

In addition to the formatting enhancements that can be made to a WordArt object using the
WordArt Toolbar, you can also make use of some additional features on the Drawing Toolbar,
namely the Shadow effect and the 3D effect.

7.10.1 WordArt Shadow Effects

Shadow effects can add further emphasis to your WordArt object.

- Click on the WordArt object to select it.

- Click on the **Shadow** ⬛ button on the Drawing Toolbar. The Shadow palette will
  be displayed.

- Select a shadow style of your choice to update your WordArt object.

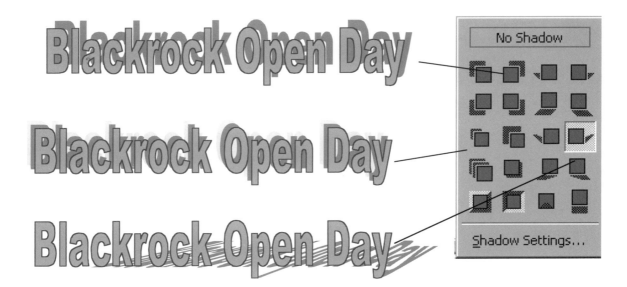

The Shadow Settings option allows you to edit the shadow options settings as illustrated in the graphic below.

Turn the
shadow
on or off

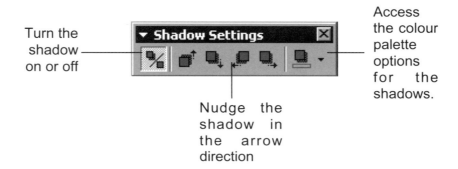

Access
the colour
palette
options
for the
shadows.

Nudge the
shadow in
the arrow
direction

7.10.2 WordArt 3D Effects

3D effects can emphasise a WordArt object but cannot be used with all of the styles that are available for a WordArt image as sometimes it can distort the text and make it unreadable.

- Click on the WordArt object to select it.

- Click on the **3D** [▣] button on the Drawing Toolbar. The 3D palette will be displayed.

- Select a 3D style of your choice to update your WordArt object.

54

The 3D option allows you to edit the shadow options settings as described in the graphic below.

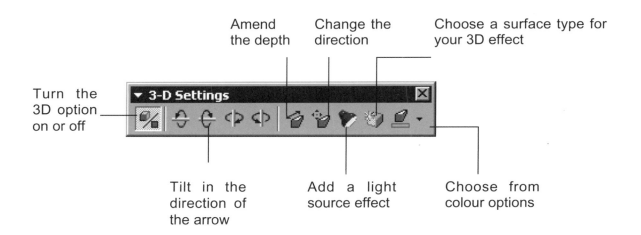

Exercise 7G

1   Ensure you are working in the **Happy Holidays Logo** document.

2   Ensure the WordArt object is selected and the WordArt Toolbar displayed.

3   Using the **Drawing Toolbar**, click on the **Shadow** button. Practice applying
         different shadow styles until you find one that you like the most.

4   Using the **3D** button on the **Drawing Toolbar**, practice applying some 3D effects.
         As 3D effects will dramatically change your WordArt object because of its current
         formatting, we don't really wish to use a 3D effect. Use **Undo** after each 3D
         selection to return it to its previous format.

5   If you wish, you may now like to change any of the formatting characteristics of
         your WordArt object, until the logo is to your satisfaction. On completion,
         however, save the document and then close it.

CHAPTER 1
Editing

Section 8   Working with Paragraphs

A paragraph is any text that is ended with a hard return where the ENTER key has been pressed to end the line or paragraph.

Paragraphs can be formatted to change their alignment, indentation, line spacing, shading as well as other more advanced formatting features.

8.1   Paragraph Shading (3.1.2.1)

You can shade paragraphs within a document to give them extra emphasis and attention.

To shade a paragraph:

- Click anywhere in the paragraph you wish to shade or select a range of paragraphs.

- Choose **Borders and Shading** in the **Format** menu.

- Click the **Shading** tab when the Borders and Shading window appears.

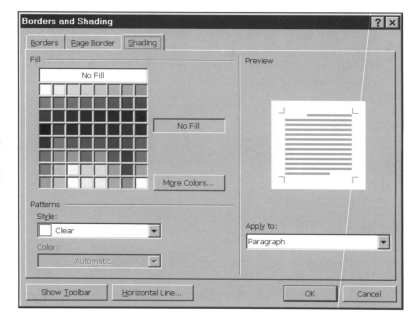

- In the **Fill** section, choose a colour option or choose the **More Colours** button to select from a wider range.

- From the **Patterns** section, choose a style from the available drop-down list.

- Click **OK** to return to your document.

8.2   Paragraph Borders (3.1.2.2)

Using the **Borders** function within Word, you can add borders to an entire paragraph or to only selected sides of the paragraph.   Borders can be applied in conjunction with shading options (please see above for more information). You can apply borders and shading to headings, titles, paragraphs, even entire pages.

To apply a border to a paragraph:

- Click anywhere in the paragraph you wish to shade or select a range of paragraphs.

- Choose **Borders and Shading** in the **Format** menu.

- Click the **Borders** tab when the Borders and Shading window appears.

- Use the **Setting** section to select a border style.

- In the **Style** section, choose a line style, a colour and a width for the line that is to make up the border.

- The **Preview** pane shows an example of how your paragraph will be formatted, based on the choices you have made. You can also use the **Border lines** to turn specific borders on or off.

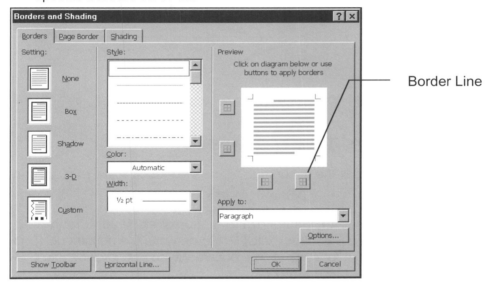

Border Line

- If you wish to control the distances between each border and the text of the paragraph, use the **Options** button.

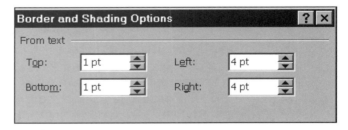

- Click **OK** to return to your document.

NOTE

Using the Borders button on the Formatting Toolbar you can also apply a limited number of border formats to selected areas of a document.

8.2.1 Altering Border Dimensions

When you add a full border to a paragraph, Word determines the border lines from the paragraph indents (displayed in the Ruler Line at the top of the page). A paragraph that does not have a substantial amount of text, such as a heading or title, may not appear correctly in a border that stretches from the left margin to the right margin.

Happy Holidays International

To change the width of a bordered area:

Select the bordered area you wish to modify.

- Drag the indent markers on the left and right of the Ruler until the appropriate dimensions have been reached.

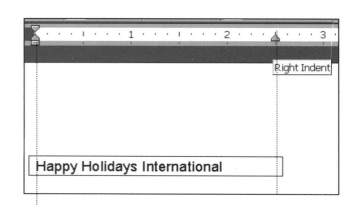

Exercise 8A

1   Open the document named "**Getaway to Tunisia**".

2   Select the first paragraph of the document "*Tunisia is a short three to four hour flight…*".

3   Choose **Borders and Shading** in the **Format** menu. Click on the **Shading** tab. Select the shade **Grey, 50%** and then click **OK** to return to the document. This shade appears to be a little too dark for our document, so now change it to **Grey, 25%** using the **Borders and Shading** window.

4   Ensure the first paragraph is still selected. Choose **Borders and Shading** in the **Format** menu. Click on the **Borders** tab. Select the **Shadow** setting and change the **Width** to **1 _ pt**. Click **OK** to return to the document.

5   With the first paragraph still selected, return to the **Borders and Shading** window. On the **Borders** tab select the **Box** setting and change the width to **2 _ pt**. From the **Style** list, scroll down until you find the line style that has a thick top line and a thin lower line (this one should be just below the *triple* line style). As we only want the lines to appear on the top and bottom borders of the paragraph, click on the left border in the Preview panel to turn this border off. Do the same to the right border and then click **OK** to return to your document. Notice the changes that have occurred.

6   To make our first paragraph stand out even further, we will indent it slightly from the other paragraphs. Select the first paragraph and then, using the markers on the Ruler, drag the left and right markers in approximately one inch each. Click away from the paragraph on completion.

Holidays in Tunisia

Tunisia is a short three to four hour flight from London. The beaches are fine, sunbleached and stretch for miles. Endless blue skies and sunfilled days - all year round. Excellent golf, tennis, watersports - everything for a fun-filled holiday.

---

7   Save the document, but do not close it.

8.3 Widows and Orphans (3.1.2.3)

Paragraphs can sometimes split at the bottom of a page leaving a line or two separated from the rest of the paragraph either at the bottom of the page or the start of the next page. This is what is known as *widows and orphans*. By default, Word has the **Widow/Orphan Control** feature turned on so that it will automatically rectify the situation, should it arise. It does this by keeping the first and last lines of a paragraph with the remainder of the paragraph.

To turn the Widow/Orphan control on and off:

- Choose **Paragraph** in the **Format** menu.

- Click on the **Line and Page Breaks** tab when the **Paragraph** window appears.

- Ensure that the **Widow/Orphan control** box is checked if you want Word to automatically correct widows and orphans within your document.

- Click **OK** to return to the document.

8.4 Styles

In Word, the term *style* refers to a collection of formatting options that are grouped together and given a name. To apply a style, you simply select the text to which the style is to apply and then select the appropriate style name from the **Style** box on the Formatting Toolbar.

Style box on the
Formatting Toolbar

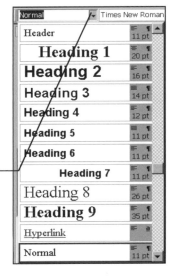

In Word, there are two main types of style: a character style and a paragraph style.

A **paragraph** style affects all the properties associated with a paragraph's appearance, such as its alignment, line spacing, tab stop positions, borders, shading, etc. Paragraph styles can also include *character* formatting.

A **character** style affects selected text (a word, sentence, line, paragraph, page, etc) with such character formatting effects as bold, underline, italics, font size, font type, etc.

Word provides a number of inbuilt styles when you first start your document. These styles reside in a *template* upon which your document is based. The default template for a new blank document is the **Normal.dot** template.

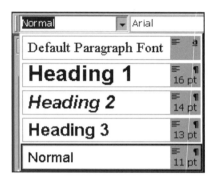

The example to the right shows the default styles available in the **Style** box when a new document is started. These defaults may differ from one Word installation to the next, depending on the settings of the **Normal.dot** template.

8.4.1 Paragraph Styles

As we have already discussed, a paragraph style is a collection of formatting that affects the entire appearance of a paragraph. The default paragraph style is known as **Normal**. It has the following default settings.

<u>**Normal Style**</u>
Font: Times New Roman
Font Colour : Black
Font Size : 12 points
Line Spacing: Single
Alignment: Left

8.4.1.1 Applying a Paragraph Style

- Click within the paragraph you wish to format or select a range of paragraphs.

- Click on the arrow on the **Style** box on the Formatting Toolbar.

- Select a paragraph style from the available list.

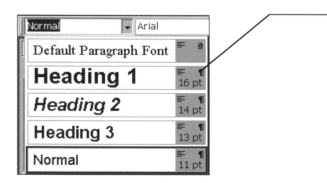

The paragraph mark (¶) next to a style name indicates that it is a paragraph style and not a character style.

8.5.1   Character Styles

Character styles apply a group of formatting features to individual characters, words, phrases, etc. They have a more limited range of formatting features than a paragraph style.

It is important to understand that character styles may include formatting features in common with the surrounding text that has been formatted with a paragraph style. Emboldening a word for example, distinguishes it from the surrounding text, but the word still shares the common formation imposed by the paragraph style.

8.5.1.1 Applying a Character Style

- Select the text you wish to format.

- Click on the arrow on the **Style** box on the Formatting Toolbar.

- Select a character style from the available list.

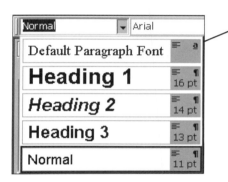

The character mark (**a**) next to a style name indicates that it is a character style and not a paragraph style.

8.5.2   Applying Styles Using the Style Window

In addition to using the **Style** box on the Formatting Toolbar, you can also apply a style from the **Style** window.

- Select the text you wish to format with the selected style.

- Choose **Style** from the **Format** menu.

- Select a style from the **Styles** box. The formatting for the style appears in the **Description** box.

- Click **Apply** to return to your document.

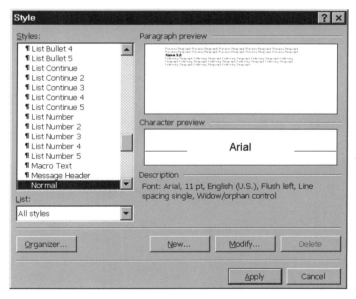

Exercise 8B

1   Ensure you are working in the "**Getaway to Tunisia**" document.

2   Select the heading at the top of the document "*Holidays in Tunisia*". Using the **Style** box on the **Formatting Toolbar**, change the style for this heading to **Heading 1**.

3   Select the subheading "*Hammamet Yasmine*" and choose **Style** from the **Format** menu. Select the **Heading 2** style from the list and then click **Apply**. Apply the same style to the next subheading "*Hammamet*".

4   Select the text "*Tunisia's major new resort development*" under the first heading "Hammamet Yasmine". Now, apply the character style named "**Strong**". If you need help:

         Select the text and then choose **Style** in the **Format** menu. Locate the character style named **Strong**. Click on it and then click **Apply**.

5   Select the first paragraph in the document "*Tunisia is a short three to four hour flight…*". Using the **Style** window, apply the character style named **Emphasis**.

6   Save the document, but do not close it.

8.6   Creating Your Own Styles (3.1.2.4)

Whilst the standard styles that are available within a template, such as the **Normal.dot** template, are useful, you may wish to create your own styles to format specific elements of your document.

To create your own style:

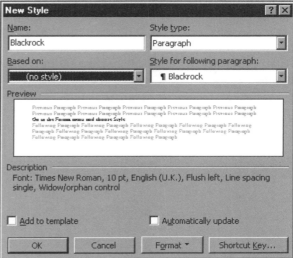

- Select Style in the **Format** menu.

- When the **Style** window appears, click the **New** button. The **New Style** window will be displayed.

- Type the name of your style in the **Name** box.

- In the **Style type** box select either **Paragraph** or **Character** depending on which type of style you are creating.

- Go to the **Based on** box and choose **No Style**. Alternatively, you may use the formatting of a previously defined style for the basis of your new style.

- In the **Style for the following paragraph** box choose a style you want to use for paragraphs that follow the one using the style you are creating. This option is only available when creating a **Paragraph** style.

- Click the **Format** button at the bottom of the **New Style** window to display the **Format** menu. Each menu item gives you access to the dedicated formatting window for each of the style items. Make sure to exit the windows appropriately to apply the properties, i.e., use the **OK** key.

- Having defined the formatting properties, click **OK** to return to the **Style** window.

- Click **OK** to save the style and apply it to your document.

CHAPTER 1
Editing

The table below outlines information on some of the options available within the **New Style** window

Style Window Optional Feature Detail

Add to template

If you wish to automatically add the new style to the template upon which your document is based, click the **Add to template** check box. If you don't, the style will only be available in the current document.

Automatically update

This option is only applicable when you are using **Paragraph** styles.

When you create a paragraph style, you can ask Word to update the style automatically whenever you apply manual formatting to text formatted with the selected style. For example, imagine that you have created a paragraph style called "**question**" and have applied it within your document. The formatting characteristics of this style are: Normal font, italics, single spaced, indented 2cm on the left and contained within a single border. However, whilst you are working in your document, you decide that text using the "**question**" style should also be centre aligned. If you select one of the paragraphs using the "**question**" style and then centre it, the style will also update to include this formatting feature so all previous paragraphs using the "**question**" style and all subsequent ones will have the updated format. This only occurs if you have checked the **Automatically update** option in the **New Style** window when you were creating it.

NOTE

When a paragraph style is configured to update automatically, you can still perform character formatting tasks within the paragraph without affecting the style or other paragraphs formatted with that style. Automatic updates only occur when you select the **ENTIRE** paragraph (that is the text and the paragraph mark at the end of it) and then apply a formatting change. To show paragraph marks in a document, click on the Show/Hide button on the Standard Toolbar.

Based on

Choosing the **No style** option from the menu list is the recommended option. Amending a style that is already available provides you with a ready-made list of formatting features, font, size, spacing, indents and so on, however, all styles related to this *base* style will have the new feature incorporated into their formatting features.

Style for the following paragraph

By default, Word applies the style created to the next paragraph your document. To apply a different style to the following paragraph, choose one from the menu list in the **Style for following paragraph** box.
This does not apply to character style formatting.

Exercise 8C

1   Ensure you are working in the "**Getaway to Tunisia**" document.

2   Go to the last page of the document. Format the heading "*Testimonials*" so that is using the **Heading 2** style.

3   Select the first paragraph under the heading "*We had such an amazing holiday…*" so that we can use this paragraph as our sample whilst we create a paragraph style of our own.

4   Choose **Style** in the **Format** menu. Click on the **New** button. In the **Name** box type *Testimonial* for the name of your new style. Ensure the **Style type** is set to **Paragraph**. Change the **Based on** box to **(no style)** and the **Style for following paragraph** to **Normal**.

5   Click the **Format** button and then choose **Font**.   Change the Size to **14 pts**, the Font style to **Bold Italic** and the Font Colour to **Grey, 50%**. Click **OK** to confirm the changes.

6   Click the **Format** button and this time choose **Paragraph**. Change the Alignment to **Centred** and the Line Spacing to **At Least** and the At box to **18 pt**. Click on the **Line and Page Breaks** tab and check that the **Widow/Orphan Control** option is checked (it should be as this is the default). Click **OK** to confirm the changes to the Paragraph settings. Click **OK** again to complete the formatting for the new style and then click **Apply**. Notice the changes to the paragraph you originally selected. Now apply the same style to the remaining two sentences.

7   Save the document, but do not close it.

8.7   Modifying Styles (3.1.2.5)

Just as it is quick and easy to create a new style, it is also a simple process to make changes to an existing style. However, it is important to understand that when you modify a style in a document, all the text that has been formatted using the modified style will be amended to incorporate the new formatting features.

WARNING

Should you *mistakenly* modify the **Normal** style, all styles based on it will be automatically modified. This means that all text using styles that were based on the Normal style will be changed – and quite a lot of styles are based on it.

8.7.1 Modifying a Style Using the Style Window

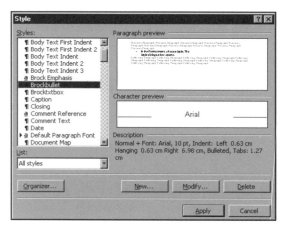

- Choose **Style** in the F**ormat** menu. The Style window will be displayed.

- Select the style you want to modify from the **Styles** box and click the **Modify** button. The Modify Style window appears.

- To rename the style, simply overtype the content in the **Name** box. (The names of styles are case and style, sensitive.)

- If you have used a base style, you can change it by selecting a new one from the **Based on** box.

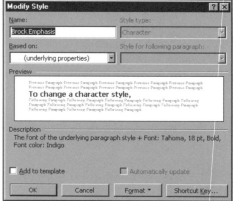

- Click the **Format** button to display the formatting items available to you. Make any necessary changes using these options.

- As you make adjustments you will notice them being applied in the **Description** section of the window.

- Click the **Format** button to obtain set the options as required.

- You will also notice the Description section of the box being amended as you change the formatting. The Preview box will also display a sample of how the formatting will appear in your document.

- Having completed amending the formatting options, click the **OK** button to store your changes and to return to the **Style** window.

- In the **Style** window, click the **Apply** button to apply the modifications to the text in your document. Alternatively, if you are not highlighting text that is to use the updated style, click the **Close** button.

8.7.2 Modifying a Style from within the Document

Whilst you can easily use the **Style** window to make changes to any of your previously created styles, you can also quickly update a style from within the document itself.

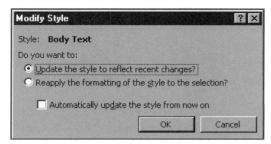

- Select the paragraph or text whose style you want to format. The **Style** box in the Formatting Toolbar will display the currently applied style name.

- Format the selected text or character as required.

- Select the style name in the **Style** box on the Formatting Toolbar and then press the **ENTER** key and the **Modify Style** box will appear.

- To update the style with the new changes ensure the **Update the style to reflect recent changes?** option is selected. The alternative option removes the formatting you have directly applied and leaves the style as originally defined.

- If you click the **Automatically update the style from now on** box, any changes you make to the style will automatically update all text using that style. The Modify Style window will not be displayed to ask you whether or not you wish to confirm the update.

- Click the **OK** button to update your style.

Exercise 8D

1   Ensure you are working in the "**Getaway to Tunisia**" document.

2   Return to the top of the document.

3   Select the first heading "*Holidays in Tunisia*". Change the font size to **20 pt** and the font colour to **Red**. With the heading still select, click on the style name **Heading 1** in the **Style** box on the Formatting Toolbar. When the Modify Style box appears, click **Update the style to reflect recent changes** and then click **OK**. The style will now have updated. To check that it has, select the second heading "*Hammamet Yasmine*" and apply **Heading 1** to it. Once you have verified that the style has been updated, apply **Heading 2** to the second heading.

4   Select the second heading "*Hammamet Yasmine*" and then choose **Style** in the **Format** menu. Click the **Modify** button and then choose **Format** and **Font**. Change the font style to **Bold** and the size to **16 pt**. Click **OK**. Choose **Format** and then **Border**. Change the border width to **1 ½ pt** and then click the bottom border ONLY in the Preview panel. Click **OK** to confirm your changes. Now click **OK** and **Apply** to return to your document. Scroll through the text to ensure that all headings that use the **Heading 2** style now appear with the updated format.

5   Save the document, closing it on completion.

Section 9   Templates

Every document that you create in Word is based on a ***template***. A template is a special file that contains the structure and layout for a specific type of document, such as a report, fax, memo, letter, and so on.

Templates can contain settings for fonts, styles, page layouts, AutoText entries, special formatting and much, much more. By default, Word bases all new blank documents on a template known as **Normal.dot** which contains its own page layout, basic styles, and default font.

The main purpose of a template is to make formatting and the inserting of information as efficient and convenient as possible. They also provide a way of creating documents of a similar type, to have a consistent look and feel to them as they provide a standard structure into which your text is entered.

9.1   Using a Standard Word Template

In addition to the **Normal** template that is used for new blank documents, Word also provides a number of other predefined templates.

To use a Word template:

- Choose **New** from the **File** menu.

- Select **More Word Templates** and the **New** window will be displayed. If you are using an earlier version than Word 2000, you will not have the **More Word Templates** option. Selecting **File**, **New** will simply take you to the New window.

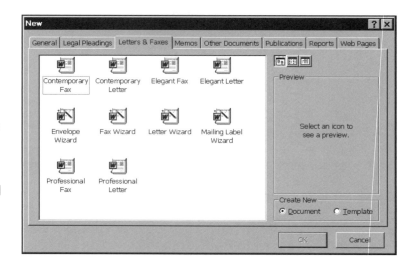

- Click on any of the tabs to display the available templates for that category.

- Click on the template you wish to use and then click **OK**.

NOTE

Some of the predefined Word templates contain standard text as well as formatting. You can replace the suggested text with your own information before saving to an ordinary file in the usual way.

Exercise 9A

1   Practice creating new documents based on some of the available templates in the **New** window. Close each new document after you have looked at its structure and the contents of the **Style** box on the Formatting Toolbar.

9.1.1   Creating a New Template (3.1.3.2)

Creating a template is much the same as creating a document. It is, however, in the saving of the document that the major difference occurs.

- Choose **New** in the **File** menu. The **New** window will appear.

- Select the **Template** option in the **Create New** section of the window.

- Select a template that is closest to your needs, e.g., the **Contemporary Report**, **Professional Fax**, etc. If you want to create your own template that does not correspond to any of the standard templates available to you, you can base your template on the **Blank Document** template. This template is the same as **Normal.dot** - it does not contain any standard text only some standard formatting in the Styles box.

- Click **OK** to create the template.

- Make any changes to the template such as adding/deleting styles or text, changing the page layout, etc.

- Choose **Save As** in the **File** menu. The **Save As** window will be displayed.

- Name your template in the **File name** box.

- The **Save as type** box will automatically be set to **Document Template (*.dot)**.

- Click **Save** to save the template.

NOTE

When you save a template, as opposed to a document, the template is stored in the default *template folder*. The location of this folder is specified in the **Options** window under the **File Locations** tab. To access this window select **Options** from the **Tools** menu.

CHAPTER 1
Editing

Location
for user-
defined
templates

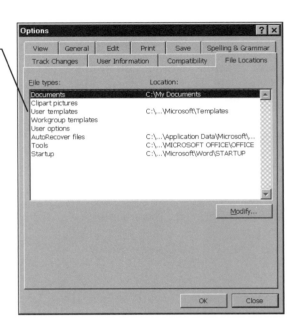

9.1.2 Modifying a Template

Once you have created a template, you can use it for the basis of a new document, over and over again. You may, however, at some stage wish to modify the template to update it with such things as formatting enhancements, additional standard text, etc.

To edit an existing template:

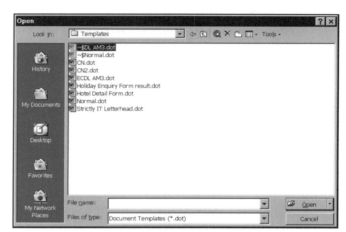

- Choose **Open** from the **File** menu. The **Open** window will be displayed.

- Change the **Files of type** box to **Document Templates (*.dot)**.

- Select the appropriate template name from the available list and then click **Open**.

- Make any necessary changes to the template.

- Save and close the template on completion.

9.1.2.1 Changing the Page Layout for a Template (3.1.3.1)

In addition to all of the other changes you can make whilst you are modifying your template, you can also alter the page setup, should you wish.

To change the page layout for the template:

- Open the **Page Setup** window in the **File** menu.

- Choose the appropriate tab to access the formatting features you wish to amend and enter the appropriate changes.

- Click **OK** to accept your changes.

- Choose **Save** on the **File** menu to update your template file.

Exercise 9B

1   In this exercise we are going to create a *hotel overview* template that provides a standard document structure for each of the hotels that we recommend.   Every time we wish to include a new hotel, we would use the template as the basis for the document and then add in the particulars of the specific hotel.

2   Choose **New** from the **File** menu. Select **More Word Templates** and click on the **General** tab when the **New** window appears (remember you do not need to use this step if you are working in a pre-Word 2000 version). Click on the **Template** option in the **Create New** section and then click on the **Blank Document** template.   Click **OK** to create the template. Our new template will now be based on the **Normal** template. It is essential before you make any changes, that you save the template under a new name.   Choose **Save As** in the **File** menu. In the **File name** box type **Hotel Detail Form**. Notice that the **Save as type** option is set to **Document template (*.dot)**. Click **Save** to continue.

3   Enter the following headings one below another, placing THREE blank lines between each.

> **Hotel Name**
> **Overview**
> **Amenities and Sports**
> **Entertainment**
> **For Children**
> **Meals**
> **Air Conditioning**
> **Prices**
> **Official Rating**

4   Format the first heading "*Hotel Name*" so that it uses the **Heading 1** style.

5   Format all of the remaining headings so that they use the **Heading 2** style. (Make sure you do each heading separately otherwise the lines in between will also be formatted with the Heading 2 style.

6   Highlight the "*Hotel Name*" heading and change its font size to **24 pt**, the font colour to **Red** and place a bottom border on the text using a width of **1 ½ pt**. Now select the entire heading and click the **Heading 1** style in the **Style** box on the Formatting Toolbar. When the Modify Style window appears, choose **Update the style to reflect recent changes** and then click **OK**.

7   Select the "*Overview*" heading.   Change its font size to **20 pt**, the font colour to **Grey, 50%** and underline the text. Now select the entire heading and click the **Heading 2** style in the **Style** box on the Formatting Toolbar. When the Modify Style window appears, choose **Update the style to reflect recent changes** and then click **OK**. All of the other headings should now update as well.

8   Click below the heading "*Prices*" and insert a file named "*Hotel Prices Table*".   If you need help:

Choose **File** in the **Insert** menu. Select the "*Hotel Prices Table*" file and then click **Insert**.

9   For now we have completed our template so you can save it once more (remember that it has been named as a template and not a document) and then you may close it on completion.

10   Now create a new document based on the "*Hotel Detail Form*" template. If you need help:

Choose **New** in the **File** menu. Select **More Word Templates** to display the New window. Select the "*Hotel Detail Form*" and then click **OK**.

11   Select the *Hotel Name* heading and type "**Hotel Assis**". Whilst the rest of the form is ready for us to complete, for now we will simply save it and leave it for someone else to finish!! Save the document as **Hotel Assis**, closing it on completion.

Section 10   Document Content Management

10.1 Outline View

Outline View allows you to manage and manipulate your document text without the distraction of formatting features, page layout, graphics and so on. The Outline View presents your document as a series of headings, sub-headings and associated text. Essentially, this tool allows you to view your document content, browse through headings at various levels, rearrange headings and their levels, reorganise blocks of text and so on. When you view your document in Outline View, the text is presented in hierarchical levels as demonstrated in the screenshot below.

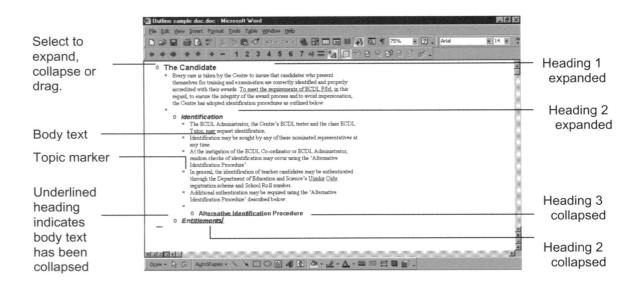

The **Outlining Toolbar** appears at the top of the document every time you activate the Outline View.

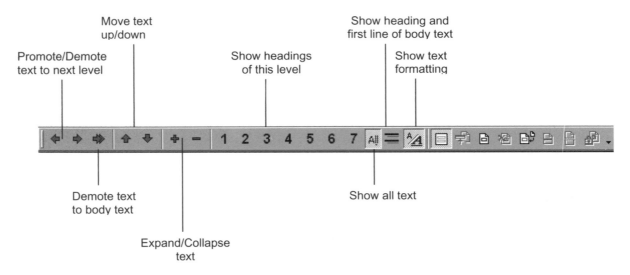

These buttons are explained in the following sections.

10.2 Document Navigation

Before considering the various procedures available within the Outline View, it is worth reviewing the two document navigation tools Word makes available, i.e. the vertical scroll bar and Document Map. They are particularly useful when you are handling large documents.

By simply dragging the slider on the vertical scroll bar, Word displays a screen tip on the page that displays the page number and text from the previous heading it has located as you scroll. To ensure this feature is activated, do the following.

- Choose **Options** in the **Tools** menu.

- Click on the View tab.

- In the **Show** section, select **Screen Tips**.

- Click **OK** to return to your document.

> Page: 45
>
> 10.1 Document Navigation

Additionally, **Document Map** provides a very useful and efficient navigation option to quickly find and locate parts of your document, especially if it is a long document. To access Document Map, use the button on the Standard Toolbar or select **Document Map** from the **View** menu. The Document Map presents itself as a separate pane on the left side of the screen with the main pane on the right containing the document itself. The Document Map pane contains a list of all the headings and subheadings in your document. Simply clicking on a heading will bring you to that location in the document and places the insertion point at the beginning of the heading text. Click the **Document Map** button again to deactivate the Document Map pane.

Document Map button

Document Pane

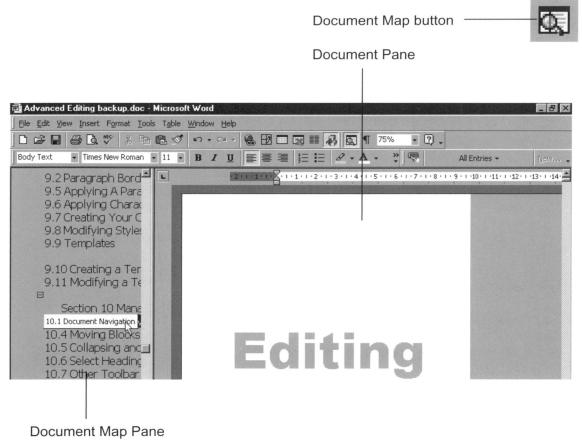

Document Map Pane

Exercise 10A

1   Open the document named "**Holidays in Bali**".

2   Check that the "screen tips" option is turned on. If you need help:

Choose **Options** in the **Tools** menu. Click on the **View** tab and check the **Screen Tips** box if it is not already turned on. Choose **OK** to return to the document. Using the vertical scroll bar, drag the slider down so that you scan through the document a page at a time with each heading being displayed in the Screen Tip box.

3   Return to the top of the document.

4   Click the **Document Map** button to display a *map* for the current document. Click on different headings to locate the various topics in the document. Click the **Document Map** button again to turn of the map panel.

5   Save the document, but do not close it.

10.3 Preparing for Outline View

If you wish to use Outline View for a document you have created using your own heading styles, you will have to reformat the document using Word's heading styles. Outline View recognises only Word's heading styles (Heading 1, Heading 2, etc). Your own heading styles are treated simply as body text. To amend your document appropriately, do the following.

- Open your document and select the first top-level heading.

- From the **Style** list on the Formatting Toolbar, select the **Heading 1** style.

- Now, continue to format the various headings in your document, using Word's heading styles in the **Style** box on the Formatting Toolbar.

- Apply the same format to the other headings of the same level by simply clicking beside each line of text. (Be careful with headings that take up more than one line of text. Each line will have to be clicked in turn)

- Having formatted all similar headings, click the Format Painter tool to cancel further formatting at the selected level.

- Repeat this sequence for each heading level.

- Choose **Outline** from the **View** menu on the **Formatting** toolbar.

- Note the text arrangement and symbols that appear.

10.4 Using Outline View (3.1.2.5)

10.4.1 Accessing Outline View

To view a document's outline choose **Outline** from the **View** menu.   Your document will appear in a slightly different format, with various symbols next to each heading or paragraph of text.

Heading with subtext   — Heading without subtext   Body text

10.4.2 Select Heading Level Display

To make your document more manageable in the Outline View, you can specify which level of heading you wish to view. For example, if you wish to see headings 1, 2 and 3, click on the **Show Heading 3** button (3) on the Outlining Toolbar. If you only wish to view heading levels 1 and 2, click on the **Show Heading 2** button (2) and so on. The screenshots below demonstrate different levels.

Level 1
Heading

Level 2
Headings

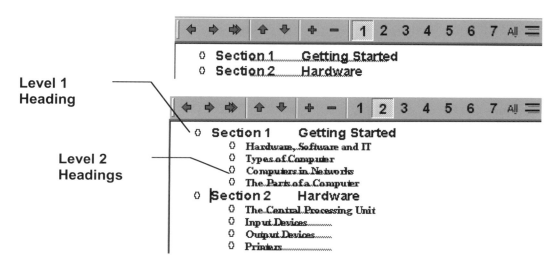

In terms of managing your document when in Outline View, there are three additional buttons on the Outlining Toolbar that are worth noting here. They are as follows.

- To display all your document text in Outline View, click the **Show All** button.

- To display the first line of body text along with the associated heading, click the **Show First Line Only** button.

- To hide all text formatting features, such as font size, style formatting, etc, click the **Show Formatting** button. Re-click to display the formatting again.

Show all text   Show formatting

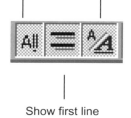

Show first line

10.4.3 Alter Heading Levels

Once your document has been created, you can easily change the level of a heading within the Outline View. For example, you may have a heading using the **Heading 2** style, which really needs to be *demoted* so that it moves to the level 3 position. You can quickly and easily change the level of headings by promoting or demoting them. To change the level of a heading:

- Place the insertion point anywhere within the heading text. (You may select more than one paragraph heading at a time.)

- Click the Promote/Demote arrow as required

- Note how Word assigns a new heading style to the text.

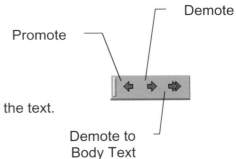

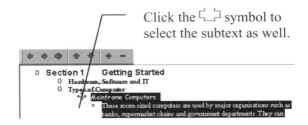

Click the ⌐⌐ symbol to select the subtext as well.

TIP

To select a heading and its subtext, click the heading symbol.

10.4.4 Moving Blocks of Text

Blocks of text may be headings of any level or the body text itself. The **Move Up** and **Move Down** options can even be used to move body text or a heading to another location in the document.   To move text within the Outline View:

- Place the insertion point anywhere within the heading text or body text. (You may select more than one paragraph heading at a time.) If you click in a heading, the body text belonging to that heading will also be moved. If you click in the body text, only the paragraph will be moved.

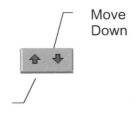

- Click the **Move Up** or **Move Down** button as required until the text is placed where you require it to be.

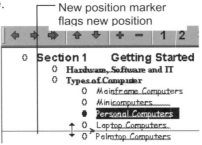

Alternatively, simply drag the paragraph or heading symbol up or down the page and drop the text in the new location. Associated text will also be moved with the main heading. Note how the new position of the dragged text is identified by the horizontal line so you can see where it will appear when you release the mouse.

Exercise 10B

1   Ensure you are working in the document named "**Holidays in Bali**".

2   Scroll through the document, noticing the heading styles that have already been applied to the headings. Return to page one.

3   Turn on Outline View. If you need help:

         You can click on the **Outline View** button in the horizontal scroll bar or choose **Outline** from the **View** menu.

4   Click on the **Show Heading 1**button on the Outlining Toolbar. Now click on the **Show Heading 2** button and then finally **Show Heading 3**. Click on the **All** button on completion and return to the top of the document.

5   Click the **Show Heading 3** button. Click on the "**Getting Around**" heading and demote it to the Heading 4 position. Now promote it to the Heading 2 position where it should originally have been placed.

6   Click on the **+** symbol next to the heading "**Currency**" so that you have selected not only the heading but any sub-text as well. Promote the heading so that it appears above "**Passports and Visas**". Now demote "**Timezone**" below "**Accommodation**".

7   Save the document but do not close it.

10.4.5 Collapsing and Expanding Text

Should you wish, you can hide or reveal different levels of text to change the amount of document detail you see while working in the Outline View.

- Place the insertion point anywhere within the heading text. (You may select more than one paragraph heading at a time.)

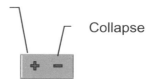

- Click the **Collapse** or the **Expand** buttons as required. Word will hide or reveal the sub-text or subheadings as appropriate.

Note that Word collapses from the lowest level and expands text from the highest level of the selected text. See the sequence in the screenshots below for collapsing a piece of text from Body Text to Heading 2 to Heading 1.

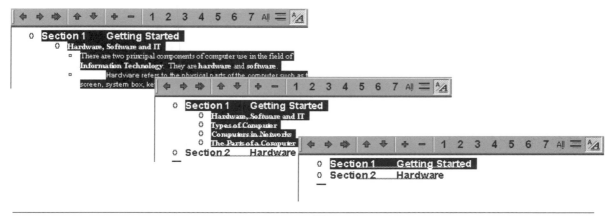

Exercise 10C

1   Ensure you are working in the document named "**Holidays in Bali**".

2   Click anywhere within the heading "**Getting There**". Click the **Expand** button to display the sub-text for this heading.   Expand the "**Currency Issues**" heading. Click on the sub-heading "**Banks**" and then collapse this heading.

3   Click the **All** button to display all of the text within the entire outline. Click the **Show First Line** button only to display only the first line of text within each sub-text paragraph.

4   Click the **Show Formatting** button to display the text without any of its formatting. Click this button again to turn the formatting back on.

5   Choose **Print Layout** in the **View** menu as we have finished working with an outline of our document.

6   Save the document, closing it on completion.

Section 11   Collaborative Editing

When a document is to be reviewed or worked on by more than one person, it is common practice for notes and comments to be exchanged regarding the content and accuracy of the document. Rather than using paper to communicate these comments and notes, you can use Word to include the notes and comments with the document itself.

11.1 Creating a Comment (3.1.4.1)

Comments can be inserted anywhere the text of a document. Comments can be viewed as either pop-up boxes or as a separate pane below the document itself. To create a comment and insert it into a document:

- Choose **Comment** from the **Insert** menu.

- The following actions take place.
    - A yellow highlight is placed over the word beside the insertion point.
    - The author's initials are placed in a *comment marker* after the highlighted word.
    - Below your document page, the Comment pane opens.

- Type the text of your comment in the Comment pane.

- Click the **Close** button on the Document pane Toolbar or leave it open if you wish to continue inserting further comments.

- When you save the document, the comments are saved also.

Highlighted comment with flagged author's initials.   Document pane

Note the dedicated Comment style.

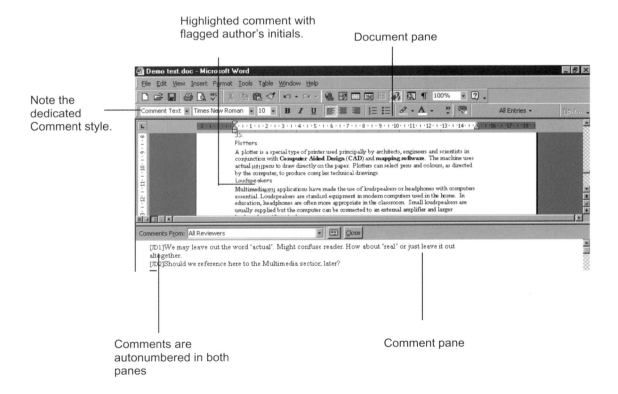

Comments are autonumbered in both panes

Comment pane

11.2 The Reviewing Toolbar

When you are working with collaborative editing features, it is a good idea to display the **Reviewing** Toolbar which includes some useful buttons which can be used with the comments and tracking features.

To turn on the Reviewing Toolbar:

- Right mouse click on any currently displayed Toolbar.

- Choose **Reviewing** from the available list.

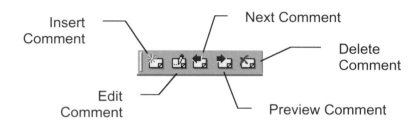

11.3 Viewing Comments

Upon opening a document, should it contain comments, highlighted markings and/or comment markers will be evident throughout the text. Should comment markers not be visible, click the Show/Hide button on the Standard Toolbar to reveal them.

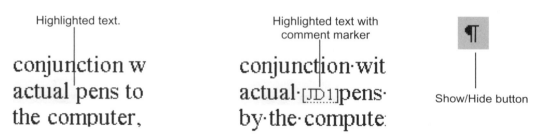

To view a particular comment, simply hold the pointer over the highlighted/flagged text. A **Notelet** icon will appear alongside the pointer and then the **ScreenTip** will appear.

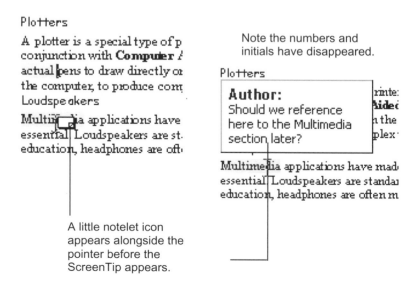

Reviewing further comments is simply done by clicking the **Previous Comment** or **Next Comment** buttons as appropriate on the Reviewing Toolbar. You can also review the comments in the Comments pane at any time. Simply choose **Comments** from the **View** menu to display the Comments pane. Selecting a comment in the Comments pane will display the line of text containing the comment as the first line on your document page.

11.4 Deleting a Comment (3.1.4.1)

You can delete a comment at any time. It will remove the marker from the document and the related text in the Comments pane.

- Click anywhere in the highlighted comment marker in the document for the comment you wish to remove.

- Click the **Delete Comment** button on the Reviewing Toolbar. Alternatively, you can right mouse click on the comment and then choose **Delete Comment**.

11.5 Edit Text Comments (3.1.4.2)

You can edit the contents of a comment at any time. Comments can be treated in much the same way as document text. To

- Place the insertion point within the highlighted comment marker within the document for the comment you wish to edit.

- Click the **Edit Comment** button on the Reviewing Toolbar. Alternatively, right mouse click on the comment and then choose **Edit Comment**. The Comment pane will be displayed at the bottom of the document.

- Amend the text as necessary.

- Click the **Close** button.

Exercise 11A

1   Open the document named "**Draft Travel Information**".

2   Turn on the Reviewing Toolbar. If you need help:

       Right mouse click on any currently displayed Toolbar. Click the **Reviewing** option.

3   Click next to the number "**25%**" in the first paragraph. Choose **Comment** in the **Insert** menu. Enter the following text in the Comment pane. Click the **Close** button on completion.

> ***Should this now be changed back to 20% in line with our new pricing policy document?***

4   Click next to the number "**7**" in the second paragraph. Click the **Insert Comment** button on the Reviewing Toolbar. Enter the following comment text, closing the Comment pane on completion.

> ***This should be changed to 10 working days.***

5   Click next to the number "**14**" in the third paragraph. Enter the following comment, closing the Comment pane on completion.

> ***Should this read "21 days before the start of your holiday"?***

6   Hover the mouse over any of the comment markers within the document so that the comment text appears.

7   Using the **Next Comment** and **Previous Comment** buttons on the Reviewing Toolbar, reviewing each of the comments.

8   Click the **Edit Comment** button and change the second comment so that it reads as follows. Close the Comment pane on completion.

> ***This should be changed to 12 working days.***

9   Click in the comment area in the third paragraph and delete this comment.

10   Save the document but do not close it.

11.6 Tracking Changes (3.1.4.3)

There may be occasions when you wish to edit a document by adding or deleting text whilst retaining the original text at the same time or someone else may wish to review the document and add or delete as well. This is often referred to as *revision marking*. Then you or another editor can the review the proposed changes and either decide to accept or reject them, individually or globally throughout the entire document.

To track your editing changes:

- Choose **Track Changes** in the **Tools** menu and then select **Highlight Changes**. The Highlight Changes window appears.

- Select the **Track changes while editing** option and **Highlight changes on screen**.

- Note the two sub-options within the window. **Highlighting changes on screen** allows you to see them as you work your way over the text. **Highlighted changes in a printed document** allows you to print the document with the changes visibly flagged.

- With **Track changes while editing** only activated, there will be no visible flagging but the tracking is still possible as is explained in the next section.

- Click the **Options** button and set your highlighting options. See the next section for more information.

- Click the **OK** button.

Display highlighted changes options

Word's response to 'Track changes while editing' and 'Highlighting changes on screen' activated.

Hardware refers to the physical parts keyboard, cables ~~which~~ that come in computer.

NOTE

An *alternative* way to activate the tracking option is simply to double click the **TRK** box on the Status Bar at the bottom of the Word screen. This box is normally greyed out until you activate it.

CHAPTER 1
Editing

11.6.1 Tracking Options

There are different highlighting or marking options for different changes you might make to a document when you are *tracking* the changes. Inserted and deleted text, changed formatting and redesigned lines and borders have different revision marks arrangements for highlighting purposes. They may be viewed as follows.

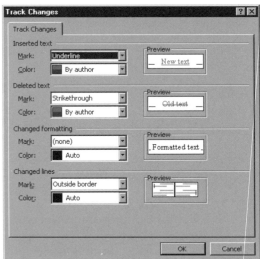

- Click the **Options** button from the **Highlight Changes** window to access the **Track Changes** box.

- Specify the formatting options you wish to use for the different types of editing action.

- Click **OK** to return to the **Highlight Changes** box.

Exercise 11B

1   Open the document named "**Draft Travel Information**".

2   Ensure you are at the top of the document.

3   Choose **Track Changes** in the **Tools** menu. Select the **Highlight Changes** option. When the Highlight Changes window appears, check the **Track changes while editing** option and **Highlight changes on screen**. Uncheck the **Highlight changes in printed document** option. Click the **Options** button to display the Track Changes window. Set the **Changed formatting** box to **Double Underline** and the **Colour** to **Bright Green**. Click **OK** to accept these changes and then **OK** again to start tracking changes.

4   In the first paragraph, highlight the first occurrence of the word "**ensure**" and delete it. Then type **guarantee**. Notice the editing marks as you made these changes.

5   Highlight the last sentence of the first paragraph "Booking forms should include…" and then make this text bold and 12 points in size.

6   In the second paragraph, click after the word "**Once**" and type "**we receive**". Then delete the words "**has been received**" later in the sentence.

7   Locate the second sentence in the third paragraph of the document. Click after the words "**The pack**" and then insert "**accompanying them**".

8   In the fourth paragraph, locate the last sentence and delete the word "**own**" so that the sentence reads "**…contact your doctor…**".

9   Highlight the sentence below the heading "**Passports for Children**". Make this text bold.

10   Save the document but do not close it.

11.6.2 Reviewing Changes (3.1.4.4)

Once the tracking option has been activated, changes made to the text will be highlighted according to the settings you have specified in the **Track Changes** window, a sample of which is shown below. IF the document passes between a number of different people, Word will identify the author of the changes by colour coding the amendments differently. (Word normally identifies the author from the details in the **User Information** tab of the **Options** window - use **Tools**, **Options** to access it if you wish to check your user name).

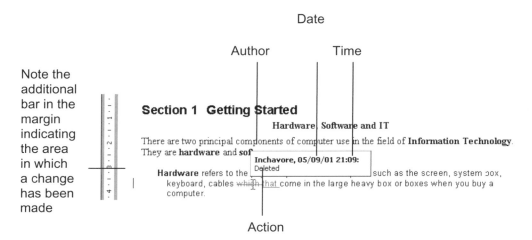

When the document has reached its final review stage, changes can be accepted or rejected. Either process converts the various types of changes into standard document text and all markings are removed.

Using the **Accept or Reject Changes** window is one way of processing the changes.

- Choose **Track Changes** in the **Tools** menu.
  Select the **Accept or Reject Changes**
  option. The Accept or Reject Change
  window will be displayed.

- Use the **Find** buttons to scan through your
  document for revision marks.

-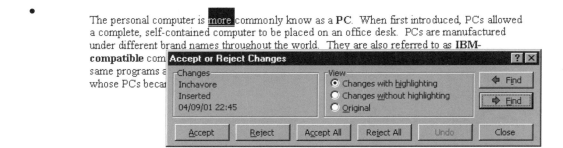

- Click the **Accept** or **Reject** buttons as appropriate. You can also accept every proposed change using the **Accept All** button or remove them all by clicking **Reject All**.

Using the Reviewing Toolbar also allows you to speedily move through the document accepting and rejecting changes. Note the button options in the screenshot below.

Enable tracking   Accept / Reject change

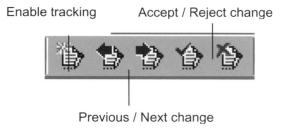

Previous / Next change

Exercise 11C

1   Open the document named "**Draft Travel Information**". Whilst you have edited this document and tracked the changes, imagine that it has been sent to you by a colleague within your organisation for your review. You will now review the suggested changes and decide whether to accept or reject them.

2   Ensure you are working at the top of the document. Choose **Track Changes** in the **Tools** menu. Select **Accept or Reject Changes**. Click the _**Find** button to locate the first change. Click the **Accept** button to confirm the deletion of the word "ensure" and then **Accept** again to confirm the insertion of the word "guarantee". Now review the remainder of the changes making your own decision as to what is accepted or rejected.

3   At the end of the process, Word will ask if you wish to search again from the beginning of the document, click **Cancel** to reject this and then **Close** to **Accept or Reject Changes** window.

4   Save the document, closing it on completion.

Chapter 2

Layout

CHAPTER 2
Layout

Syllabus

Module AM3

Word Processing – Advanced Level

Chapter Two: AM 3.2 – Layout

CHAPTER 2
Layout

Section 1   Sections

Any document that you create is usually separated into different pages.   Text flows onto the next page either when you reach the bottom of the page or when you insert your own manual page break.   Most of the page formatting commands available within Word, such as paper size, margins, headers and footers, etc, affect the entire document - that is all pages within the same document.   However, there may be times when you wish to apply different page formatting within a document and this can be achieved using *sections*.

A *section* is basically an area in your document whose page formatting is independent of the rest of your document.   Any document, particularly long documents, can be separated into different sections.   Each section can have its own unique formatting which does not affect any other section in the document, such as its own headers or footers or its own page numbering.   All new documents contain one section, even if we don't realise it.   You can then insert any new sections using what are called *section breaks*.   The Status Bar, located at the bottom of your Word screen, displays information relating to which section of a document you are working in, along with the page number for that section and the line number where your cursor is currently placed.

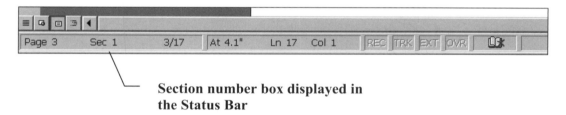

**Section number box displayed in
the Status Bar**

The formatting that is maintained within a section is as follows:

- Margins

- Paper Size and Orientation

- Paper Source for the Printer

- Page Borders

- Vertical Alignment

- Headers and Footers

- Columns

- Page Numbering

- Line Numbering

- Footnotes and Endnotes

1.1 Types of Section Breaks

There are four different types of section break that you can insert into a document. Each type controls where the section break appears and where the NEXT page will start.

Next Page Section Breaks

The **Next Page** section break is inserted at the cursor location and the new section starts on the next page. The **Next Page** section break works in much the same way as a hard page break.

Continuous Section Breaks

The **Continuous** section break inserts a break where the cursor is located and the new section starts on the same page below the break. This type of section break is most useful when you wish to mix the page formatting on the same page. For example, if you wanted to create a letterhead at the top of your page with small left and right margins, you would create the letterhead text and/or image in Section 1 of the document. When you were ready to type the main body of the text, you would insert a **continuous** section break which keeps you on the same page, but allows you to then change the margins for the body of the letter to perhaps larger widths.

Odd Page and Even Page Section Breaks

The **Odd Page** or **Even Page** section breaks insert where the cursor is located and the new section starts on either the next odd-numbered page or even-numbered page. This is particularly useful when you are creating a document that needs each new chapter to start on an odd page, so that the chapter title is displayed on the right-hand side of the book as it is read.

1.2 Creating a Section Break (3.2.3.1)

Section breaks can be inserted at any location within a document. Remember that the Status Bar displays the number of the section you are currently working in.

- Place the cursor where the new section break is to be inserted.

- Select **Break** in the **Insert** menu.

- Make an appropriate choice from the **Section break types** list.

- Click **OK** to continue.

1.3 Viewing Section Breaks

Before you can delete, move or copy a section break, you need to be able to see exactly where the break has been set. There are two main ways of displaying section breaks:

- Select **Normal** in the **View** menu to display page breaks and section breaks within your document. The Normal view does not display page formatting for your document.

    ```
    ························Section Break (Next Page)························
    ```

- If you are working in Print Layout View, Outline View or Web Layout View (all accessible in the **View** menu), click the **Show/Hide** button on the Standard Toolbar to display hidden text such as section breaks. Click this button again to turn off the display of hidden text.

Exercise 1A

1   Start in a new blank document.

2   Type the following information, centred between the left and right margins.

HOLIDAYS IN THE SUN

By

Happy Holidays International

3   Set the font size for the text to **28 pts** and use **bold** to enhance the text.

4   Ensure you have pressed ENTER a few times after the last line of the heading.

5   Insert a **Next Page** section break using **Break** in the **Insert** menu. You will now be in section 2 of the document.

6   To save time on typing, a file has been created for you for the second section. Choose **File** in the **Insert** menu. Insert the document named "**This is section two.doc**".

7   At the end of section 2, insert another **Next Page** section break.   You will now be in section 3 of the document.

8   Choose **File** in the **Insert** menu. Insert the document named "**This is section three.doc**".

9   Change to the **Normal View** and scroll through the document, noticing the change of each section and where the section breaks appear.

10   Change to the **Print Layout View** and scroll through the document. Use the Status Bar to check which section you are working in.

11   Go to page 1 of the document.

12   Select **Page Setup** in the **File** menu. Click on the **Layout** tab and select **Centre** in the **Vertical Alignment** box. Click **OK** to continue. Highlight the headings on this first page and change the font colour to blue.

13   Preview your document. Notice that the page setup change has only affected section 1.

14   Move to any page in section 2 of your document.

15   Select **Page Setup** in the **File** menu. Click on the **Margins** tab and set the **Left** and **Right** margins to 2". Click **OK** to continue.

16   Preview your document. Notice that the page setup change has only affected section 2.

17   Save your document, naming it **Sections for Holidays in the Sun**.

1.4   Copying Section Breaks

- Make sure that the section breaks are displayed within your document. See **Viewing Section Breaks** on page 96 for more information.

- Select the section break that contains the formats you want to copy. Remember that section breaks control the formatting of the text ABOVE the section break.

- Click the **Copy** button on the Standard Toolbar.

- Click where you want the copied section break to be inserted.

- Click the **Paste** button on the Standard Toolbar. The text above the newly inserted section break takes on the formatting of the original section you copied.

1.5   Deleting Section Breaks (3.2.3.2)

When you delete a section break, the formatting for the section text above it is also deleted. The text will become part of the following section and, therefore, assumes its formatting for that section.

- Make sure that the section breaks are displayed within your document. See **Viewing Section Breaks** on page 96 for more information.

- Click on the section break you wish to delete and press the DELETE key on the keyboard.

NOTE

A section break controls the formatting of the text that precedes it, until another section break is encountered. If you delete a section break, the preceding text becomes part of the following section and assumes its formatting. The last portion of a document does not have a section break, but its formatting is controlled by the last paragraph mark (¶) in the document.

Exercise 1B

1   Ensure the **Sections for Holidays in the Sun** document is open.

2   Go to the end of the document (you should be on the last page of section 3).

3   Insert an **Odd Page** section break at this point.

4   Now you are on section 4. Type the following heading:

Temperature Guide
March to October

5   In **Print Preview**, check the layout of your document. Remember that section 2 has wider margins than section 3.

6   Select **Normal View** and scroll through your document until you can see the section break at the end of section 2.

7   Select this section break and then press DELETE.   Section 2 and section 3 will now become joined and all the formatting characteristics of the original section 3 will be used for the two sections now combined. Use **Print Preview** to view these changes.

8   Undo the section break deletion so that your document is back the way it was. Check this in **Print Preview** mode if necessary.

9   In this example you will copy the formatting characteristics from section 3 into section 2. Select **Normal View** so that you can easily view your section breaks.

10   Highlight the section break at the end of section 3 by clicking to the left of the section break indicator. Click the **Copy** button on the Standard Toolbar.

11   Scroll up through the document until you can see the section break at the end of section 2. Highlight this section break and then click the **Paste** button.

12   Using **Print Preview**, view the entire document and notice the changes that have been made.

13   Save the document on completion.

1.6 Changing the Type of Section Break

Once you have inserted a section break, you can change its *type* at any time. Changing a section break type is often more preferable than deleting an existing break and inserting a new one, as the deletion process often changes the page formatting of the two sections that become joined.

To change a section break to a different type:

- Ensure that you have clicked anywhere BELOW the section break that you wish to change.

- Select **Page Setup** in the **File** menu.

- Click on the **Layout** tab.

- Make a selection from the **Section start** box.

- Ensure **Apply to** box is set to **This section**.

- Click **OK** to continue.

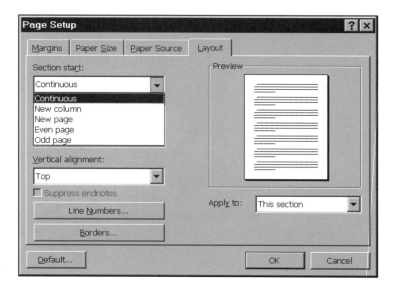

100

1.7   Headers and Footers

Headers and footers apply to the sections in your document. If you have only one section in your document, then the header and footer you create appear on every page. However, if your document is separated into more than one section, you can create different headers and footers for each of the sections independently.

- Select **Header and Footer** in the **View** menu.

- The Header or Footer boxes display the Section number for the section you are currently working in. You can use the **Show Next** and **Show Previous** buttons on the Header and Footer toolbar to move between the different sections of your document.

Displays the number of the section you are setting the header/footer for.

Displays **Same as Previous** if the header/footer is linked to the previous one.

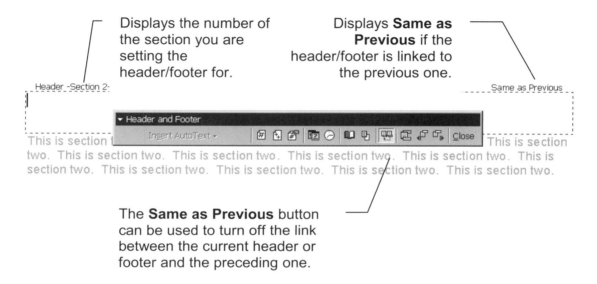

The **Same as Previous** button can be used to turn off the link between the current header or footer and the preceding one.

NOTE

The header and footer boxes from section 2 onwards are automatically linked to each previous section's header or footer. This can be useful, if either the header or footer needs to be consistent throughout the entire document. If not, you need to use the **Same as Previous** button to turn the link off.

TIP

You can print specific sections of your document rather than just selected pages or the entire document. Select **Print** in the **File** menu and then select the **Pages** option. To print specific sections, precede the section number with the letter "**s**". For example, **s3,s5** would indicate to Word that you wish to print sections 3 and 5. If you entered **p4s3-p6s5**, this would indicate to Word that you wish to print from page 4 in section 3 to page 6 in section 5.

Exercise 1C

1   Ensure the **Sections for Holidays in the Sun** document is open.

2   Imagine that you have decided that each new section starts on an odd page (that is a right-hand page as you flick through a book or manual). At the moment, all of your section breaks are *Next Page* except for the last.

3   Ensure you are working in **Normal View** so that you can easily view your section breaks.

4   Click anywhere within section 2. Remember that if you wish to change the *type* of section break used, you need to be BELOW the section break marker for the section you wish to change.

5   Whilst in section 2 choose **Page Setup** in the **File** menu. Click on the **Layout** tab and set the **Section start** box to **Odd Page**. Ensure that the **Apply to** box is set to **This section**. Click **OK** to continue.

6   If the section break at the end of section 1 does not automatically update to show the **Odd Page** indicator, go to **Print Preview** mode and then close to return to **Normal View**.

7   Scroll down until you are anywhere in section 3. Using the same instructions as steps 6 and 7 above, change the section break to an **Odd Page** break.

8   Preview your document on completion to view its overall layout. Use the **Print Layout View** and return to page 1 of the document.

9   Select **Headers and Footers** in the **View** menu.

10   Using the **Switch Between Header and Footer** button, check that both the header and footer for section 1 are blank. Switch back to the Header-Section 1 box.

11   Click the **Show Next** button to access the header for section 2. Notice that the *Same as Previous* option is displayed. This is because Word automatically links headers and footers from one section to another. Click the **Same as Next** button on the Header and Footer Toolbar to break the link. In the Header box type the following header text:

Holidays in the Sun

12   Access the footer for section 2. Enter the following footer text using automatic page numbering for the number displayed.

Section 2 - Page #

Most likely, the page number that has been inserted won't be **1**. This is because Word is counting the physical pages in the document and not in the section. To display the number **1** for the first page of section 2, do the following:

13   Whilst still in the footer for section 2 click on the Page Number Format button on the Header/Footer Toolbar. Type **1** in the **Start at** box. Click **OK**. Don't worry if the page number for section 2 now shows a **2**. This will update to **1** when you close out of Headers and Footers and next return.

14   Switch back to the header for section 2. Click the **Show Next** button to move on to section 3. This section will automatically use the *Same as Previous* setting and the preceding header text will automatically be displayed. In this case, however, you want the same heading to run through the headers for the entire manual so you don't need to turn this setting off.

15   Now switch down to the footer for section 3. This too has the *Same as Previous* setting but in this instance you don't want to use it as each section will have its own unique section number and page numbering starting from 1.

16   Click the **Same as Previous** button to turn off the link between the footer in section 2. Change the text **Section 2** so that it reads **Section 3**. Now you need to change the page numbering back to start at one. If you need some help with this:

    Choose **Page Numbers** from the **Insert** menu. Click on the **Format** button and then type **1** in the **Start at** box. Click **OK** once. Then, click **Close** to close the **Page Numbers** box.

17   Switch between the header and footer so that you return to Header-Section 2. Click the **Show Next** button to view the header for section 4. Leave this set at *Same as Previous*.

18   Switch down to the footer for section 4. Turn off the *Same as Previous* setting. Change the footer text to display **Section 4**. Update the automatic page numbering so that it starts again from 1.

19   Close out from the header and footer area and return to the document.

20   Using **Print Preview**, check the headers and footers throughout the entire document.

21   Return to the document and then choose **Print** from the **File** menu. In the **Pages** box type **s2** to print only the contents of section 2. Click **OK** to continue.

22   Save the document, closing it on completion.

CHAPTER 2
Layout

Section 2   Columns

Most of the documents you create have text that appears in one column - that is text running from the left margin across to the right margin. You can, however, create multiple columns within a document where the text flows from the bottom of one column to the top of the next. This is most useful when you are creating such documents as newsletters, brochures, flyers, etc.

2.1   Creating Multiple Column Layouts (3.2.4.1)

The easiest way to create columns is by first typing the text and then formatting the text into the number of columns you require. If you select the text and then format it into columns, Word automatically inserts section breaks before and after the text. See **Viewing Section Breaks** on page 96 for more information.

- Select the text you wish to separate into multiple columns.

- Select **Columns** in the **Format** menu.

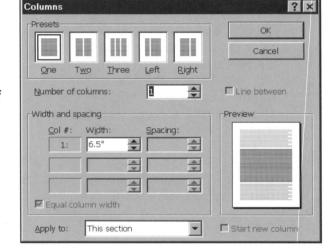

- Select the number of columns you require from the **Presets** box or specify your own number of columns using the **Number of columns** box.

- If you wish, use the **Width and spacing** panel to make any specific adjustments that you require. If the **Equal column width** box is ticked, all columns will have the same width and spacing as Column 1. If not, you can specify the individual adjustments for each column.

- Tick the **Line between** box if you want a vertical line to appear between each column.

- Use the **Preview** panel to see the effect of your choices.

- Ensure the **Apply to** box is set to *Selected text* so that only the area that you selected will be placed into columns.

- Click **OK** to continue. You will see that Word automatically balances out the length of each column.

NOTE

You can only see columns you create in the Print Layout view. In Normal View, text is simply displayed as one continuous column down the left hand margin.

2.1.1 Using the Columns Button

You can quickly create multiple columns using the **Columns** button on the Standard Toolbar.

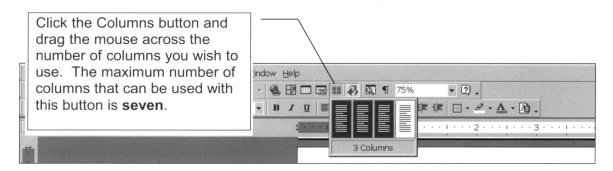

Click the Columns button and drag the mouse across the number of columns you wish to use. The maximum number of columns that can be used with this button is **seven**.

2.2 Modifying Column Layouts (3.2.4.2)

Once you have created multiple columns within a section of your document, you can easily modify the number of columns you wish to be displayed.

- Click anywhere within the columns that you wish to modify.

- Select **Columns** in the **Format** menu.

- Choose an option from the **Presets** box or use the **Number of columns** box if you wish to create more than three columns.

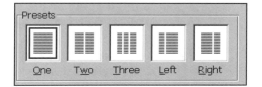

- Click **OK** to continue.

NOTE

If you wish to remove the column formatting altogether so that text flows from the left to right margins, follow the steps above but ensure that you select **One** column only.

2.3 Modifying Column Widths and Spacing (3.2.4.3)

Just as you can easily change the number of columns within an area of your document, you can also modify the formatting of those columns, such as their width or spacing.

- Click anywhere within the columns that you wish to modify.

- Select **Columns** in the **Format** menu.

- Make any necessary changes to the **Width and spacing** boxes.

- Click **OK** to continue.

Exercise 2A

1   Open the document named **Holidays in Tunisia**.

2   Highlight the text below the heading **Hammamet Yasmine** (make sure you highlight all four paragraphs).

3   Choose **Columns** in the **Format** menu.

4   From the **Presets** box select **Two** and ensure the **Equal column width** box is checked.

5   Click **OK** to continue.

6   Change the column format for the previously selected text to the preset option of **Right**. Click **OK** to return to the document. The **Right** preset uses a two-column format - the right column is half the width of the left column.

7   Change the column format again and use the **Preset** for **Three** columns. Ensure that **Equal column width** box is checked. Change the **Spacing** for the first column to **.3**. Click **OK** to return to the document.

8   Highlight the text below the second heading **Hammamet** (make sure you highlight all four paragraphs).

9   Using the Columns button on the Standard Toolbar drag across until **two** columns are selected and then release the mouse button.

10   Using the Columns button, change the selected text to a **three-column** format.

11   Select **Columns** in the **Format** menu.

12   Ensure that **Equal column width** box is checked. Set the **Spacing** for the first column to **.3**. Click **OK** to return to the document.

13   Apply the same column format to the text below the heading **Skanes**.

14   Save the document.

2.4   Inserting a Column Break (3.2.4.4)

As you have seen, the quickest and easiest method of creating columns is by first typing the text and then specifying the number of columns that are required and their relevant formatting. You can, however, also create columns as you type.

- Click where you wish to create your columns.

- Select **Columns** in the **Format** menu.

- Specify the number of columns you require and their format. See **Creating Multiple Column Layouts** on page 104 for more information.

- Click **OK** to continue.

- Type the first column of text.

- To insert a column break select **Break** in the **Insert** menu.

- Choose **Column break**.

- Click **OK** to continue.

- Repeat for each subsequent column.

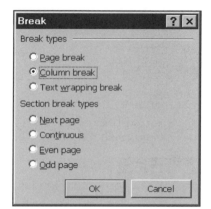

2.4.1   Returning to a Single Column Format

Once you have finished typing the column text, you may wish to return to a single column layout for the remainder of the document. You will need to insert a section break before you can change the number of columns.

- Select **Break** in the **Insert** menu.

- Choose **Continuous** if you wish to continue typing on the same page or **Next Page** if you want to start a completely new page.

- Click **OK** to continue.

- Select **Columns** in the **Format** menu.

- From the **Presets** panel select **One**.

- Click **OK** to continue.

2.5 Deleting a Column Break (3.2.4.5)

If you have manually inserted a **column break**, the subsequent text is then forced to start at the top of the next column. By deleting a column break, the natural flow of the column will be reinstated and the text from the next column will rejoin with the current column.

- Make sure that you can see where your column breaks have been inserted. The easiest way to do this is by turning on the **Show/Hide** button in the Standard Toolbar. If this button is not available on your Toolbar, you can choose **Options** from the **Tools** menu. Click on the **View** tab and then select **All** within the **Formatting Marks** section.

- Click on the Column Break marker that you wish to remove and press the DELETE key.

Exercise 2B

1   Ensure the document **Holidays in Tunisia** is open.

2   Select all of the text below the heading **About Tunisia**.

3   Format this text into two equal columns with **.3** spacing between. Check the **Line between** option to display a vertical line between the two columns.

4   To force the heading **On the Menu** into the second column, insert a column break at the beginning of this heading. If you need help:

     Click before the heading **On the Menu**. Select **Break** from the **Insert** menu. Select **Column break** and then click **OK** to return to the document.

5   You have now decided to format this text into three columns. Before doing this, remove the column break you have just inserted. If you need help:

     Click the **Show/Hide** button on the Standard Toolbar to display all hidden text. When the --------**Column Break**------------ indicator appears, click on it and press DELETE.

6   Format the text now into three columns of equal width with a line between each.

7   Finally, you have decided to return this text to a single column. Highlight all of the text and headings below **About Tunisia**. Format the text for a single column.

8   Return to the top of your document and use **Print Preview** to view the content and layout of the document. Close back to **Print Layout View**.

9   Save the document, closing it on completion.

Section 3   Table of Contents

Documents, particularly long documents such as reports, often include a table of contents to show the reader where to find information and to identify the structure and organisation of the document. A table of contents usually displays the headings used within the document and their relevant page numbers.

Sample of a Table of Contents

Using Word, you can quickly and easily create a table of contents. The table of contents can be updated to reflect any changes made by the user to the contents or structure of the document. Creating a table of contents in Word requires three main steps.

Step 1 -   You must tell Word what text within the document is to be included in your table of contents.

Step 2 -   You then need to show Word where to place the table of contents and identify what format to use for the table of contents.

Step 3 -   Lastly, you need to instruct Word to generate the table of contents.

3.1   Using Styles to Create a Table of Contents

One of the easiest ways to create a table of contents is by using the content of any *heading styles* within your document. See Chapter 1, page 59, for more information on **Styles**. Heading styles usually have an in-built hierarchy that determines the order in which they appear in your document, i.e. Heading 1, Heading 2, Heading 3, etc. This hierarchy of headings used within your document is then reflected in the table of contents once it is generated.

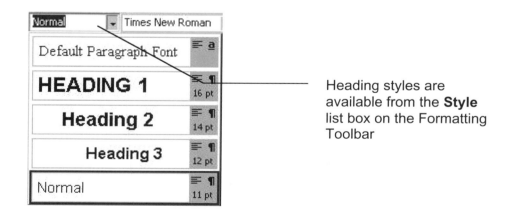

Heading styles are available from the **Style** list box on the Formatting Toolbar

3.2 Creating a Table of Contents (3.2.2.1)

A table of contents is usually placed at the front of the document, after a cover page and before the main body of the text. It should be generated once the main content of the document has been typed and formatted.

To generate a table of contents perform the following steps:

- Start on a new blank page, preferably inserted using a section break. Refer to page 96 for more information.

- Check that the page numbering for the main body of the document is correct. For example, if the first page of the main text physically starts on page 3 of your document, but you require it to display page 1 in the header or footer, you must check that the page number for that page is set correctly to start numbering at **1**. You can do this using the **Page Number Format** button on the Header/Footer Toolbar when you are working in the header or footer area. Using the **Start At** box you can control the first number you wish to display in the specified header or footer.

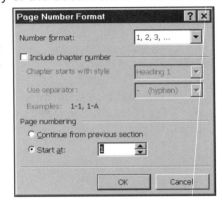

- Ensure that the cursor is located on the blank page where the table of contents is to be generated.

- Select **Index and Tables** in the **Insert** menu.

- Select the **Table of Contents** tab.

- Change any of the formatting options to suit your requirements, such as whether or not you wish to right align the page numbers or which type of tab leader you wish to use. The **Print Preview** box will display a sample of how the formatting will affect your table of contents.

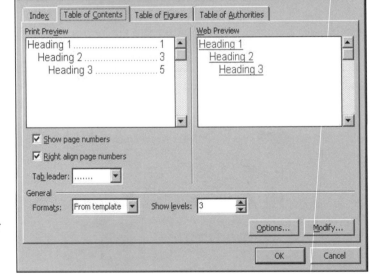

- Click **OK** to generate the table of contents.

- After a few moments the table of contents will appear starting on the blank page that you specified.

NOTE

If you are working with a particularly large document, or a document that has numerous headings to be included in the table of contents, the generation process may take a little while to complete.   The Status Bar, displayed at the bottom of your Word screen, will display an update on the table of contents generation until the process has been completed.

3.2.1 Understanding the Format of the Table of Contents

A table of contents is actually based on a series of special *field codes*. To demonstrate this you can use a keyboard combination to view the field codes temporarily.

- Press **ALT+F9** to turn on the display of field codes in your document. The **{TOC \o etc, etc, etc…}** code will be displayed on the first page of the table of contents.

- Press **ALT+F9** to turn off the display of field codes in your document.

TIP

Because your table of contents is actually based on a field code, when you click to the left of the first line of your table of contents the entire contents is selected. This selection process is useful when you wish to update the table of contents after the main body of your document has changed.

3.3   Updating and Modify an Existing Table of Contents (3.2.2.2)

A table of contents should be updated after any layout changes have been made to the document or after any additional text has been added that will affect any headings and/or page lengths.

- Click to the left of the first line of the table of contents to select its entire content.

- Press **F9** - the **Update Selected Fields** keyboard shortcut or right mouse click on the selected area and choose **Update Field**. The following window will be displayed.

Select **Update page numbers only** if you simply want to update the page numbers for the headings referred to in your table of contents.

Select **Update entire table** when you have changed the headings in your document referred to in your table of contents or when you have added new headings or text. The page numbers referenced in your table of contents will also be updated.

- Click **OK** to update the table of contents.

NOTE

If changes are made within the document that will affect the table of contents, you MUST update the table of contents field to ensure its accuracy. Do not manually make changes to a table of contents that has been generated within Word. If you do, these changes will be overwritten whenever the table of contents is updated and/or regenerated.

CHAPTER 2
Layout

3.4 Formatting a Table of Contents (3.2.2.3)

When you create a table of contents, Word automatically assigns a default format to the results based on standard settings within the document template. You can, however, select from a list of predefined formatting styles for your table of contents or create your own formatting style.

To change the format of an existing table of contents:

- Click to the left of the first line of the table of contents to select the entire table.

- Choose **Index and Tables** from the **Insert** menu. Click on the **Table of Contents** tab.

- Make any required changes to format or structure of the table of contents. Click **OK** to continue.

- A warning box will appear asking whether or not you want to replace the existing table of contents. Click **Yes** to this question, otherwise a new table of contents will appear over the top of the original one.

The **Print Preview** box shows sample formatting based on the selection you make from the **Formats** list box.

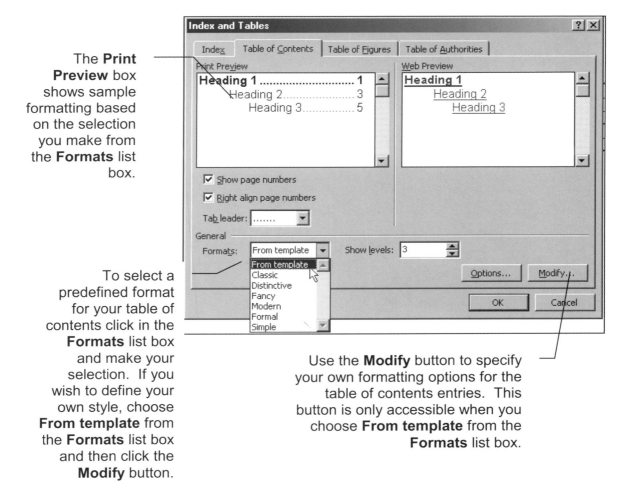

To select a predefined format for your table of contents click in the **Formats** list box and make your selection. If you wish to define your own style, choose **From template** from the **Formats** list box and then click the **Modify** button.

Use the **Modify** button to specify your own formatting options for the table of contents entries. This button is only accessible when you choose **From template** from the **Formats** list box.

CHAPTER 2
Layout

TIP

The entries in a table of contents are *links* to the actual headings in the document. You can click on a table of contents entry and you will be navigated to that particular location in your document. If you wish to return quickly to the table of contents you can click the Back button ⇐ on the **Web** Toolbar.

Exercise 3A

1   Open the document named **About Bali**.

2   Scroll through the document to view its content. Select **Document Map** from the **View** menu. Click on each of the headings in the left-hand panel to navigate through the document. Each of these headings is based on a heading style which will be used when you create a table of contents for the document. Turn the Document Map view off.

3   Return to the top of the document.

4   Insert a **Next Page** section break before the heading **Bali**. If you need help:

       Choose **Break** from the **Insert** menu. Select **Next Page** and then click **OK**.

5   Go to the top of the blank page you have just created. You will create a cover page for your document here.

6   Type the following cover page information:

Holidays in Bali

By

Happy Holidays International

7   Insert another **Next Page** section break after the cover page information.

8   Ensure you are working at the top of the new blank page.

9   Type the heading **Table of Contents** and then apply the **Title** style to the heading.

10   Press ENTER twice to leave a couple of blank lines after the heading.

11   Select **Index and Tables** from the **Insert** menu. Click on the **Table of Contents** tab.

12   From the **Formats** list select **Distinctive**. Set the **Tab Leader** to dashes (-------).

13   Click **OK** to generate the table of contents.

14   Practise clicking on the table of contents entries to "jump" to the corresponding location in the document. Remember that you can use the Back button on the Web Toolbar to return to the Table of Contents.

15   Save the document on completion but do not close it.

Exercise 3B

1   Ensure you are working in the **About Bali** document.

2   Move to the heading **Getting Around** in the body of the document.

3   Insert a new page break at this point. If you need help:

Ensure that you have clicked just in front of the heading. Press CTRL+ENTER on the keyboard to insert a hard page break.

4   Locate the heading **Getting There** on the previous page. Change this heading to read **How to Get There**.

5   Return to the Table of Contents page.

6   Select the entire Table of Contents by clicking to the left of the first line.

7   As you have made some changes to the number of pages in your document and you have modified some of the headings/text, you need to update your Table of Contents. If you need help:

Press F9 to update the Table of Contents. Select **Update entire table** and then click **OK**. Notice the changes to the Table of Contents.

8   Now that you have updated the Table of Contents, you wish to change its appearance. Select the entire Table of Contents.

9   Choose **Index and Tables** from the **Insert** menu. Click on the **Table of Contents** tab.

10   From the **Formats** box select **Formal**. Set the **Show Levels** box to **1** (this means that only headings using the **Heading 1** style will be displayed). Click **OK** to continue. Choose **Yes** to update the existing table.

11   Change the format of the current Table of Contents so that it still uses the **Formal** format but **2** levels are displayed.

12   Press **ALT+F9** to view the field codes in your document. Notice the field code for your Table of Contents. Press ALT+F9 to turn off the field codes.

13   Save the document, closing it on completion.

Section 4   Master Documents

Word will allow you to work on documents of any size, but there are a few factors to take into consideration. Large documents will always be slower to work on, they consume more memory and take longer to load and save. If a document has a lot of graphic work and embedded fields then these can often slow the document down dramatically. By breaking the document down into smaller components you will improve the speed of these functions.

A *master document* is a special type of file used to structure, organise and maintain a series of smaller, related documents, known as *subdocuments*. We could use the scenario of a book as a typical example of when a master document may be used. Rather than typing the entire book into one very large document, each chapter could be created as a smaller, individual document so that they are more easily managed and less *memory hungry*. When the time comes to put the entire book together, complete with a table of contents and index, a master document could be used to manage the whole publication.

You don't need to be working with books, however, to think of using a master document. There are various benefits to be gained even if the documents you are working with are relatively small.

Using master documents you can:

- Create a table of contents and index based on a number of documents.

- Create consistent headers/footers and page numbering across a series of documents.

- Print multiple documents consecutively.

- Create cross-references and links with other documents.

NOTE

Each subdocument has its own unique document name. It can be opened, edited and printed independently of the master document into which it is going to be placed.

4.1   Working with Outline View

To create a master document and its subdocuments, you start by working in the **Outline View**. For more information on **Outline View,** please refer to Chapter 1.

- Select **Outline View** in the **View** menu. Not only does the view change but also the Outlining Toolbar appears. The Outlining Toolbar contains special buttons specifically for the purpose of master documents.

Master Document Buttons

4.2 Creating a New Master Document from Scratch (3.2.1.1)

One way of creating a master document is to design it from scratch. Using the Outline View you can layout the main structure of your document using different heading styles and then identify to Word which headings are to become subdocuments in their own right.

To create a new master document:

- Ensure you are working in a new document.

- Select **Outline** in the **View** menu. Your document will appear in the Outline View and the Outlining Toolbar will be activated.

- Enter headings for the title of the master document and the subdocument titles. Use the Heading 1 style for all headings/titles that are going to be used as subdocuments.

All chapter headings that will become subdocuments use the Heading 1 style

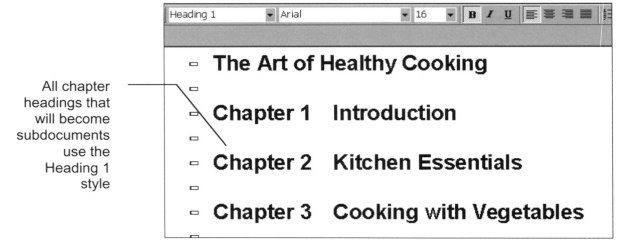

4.3 Creating Subdocuments Based on Sub Headings (3.2.1.2)

Now that you have got the main outline structure prepared, you need to identify to Word which headings are going to become subdocuments.

1. Click on the first heading you wish to create into a subdocument.

2. Click the **Create Subdocument** button on the Outlining Toolbar. This creates an outline box which will contain the subdocument. The subdocument will not, however, be created until you save the master document.

3. Repeat step 2 for all headings that you wish to create into subdocuments.

NOTE

When you create or insert a subdocument in the master document, Word places it in a separate section by inserting section breaks before and after the subdocument. By default, the section breaks that Word inserts for you are *continuous*, meaning that the next section will start on the same page as the previous section. You can change the type of section break if you wish (for example to Next Page, Odd Page or Even Page) should you wish. See **Changing the Type of Section Break** on page 100 for more information.

4.3.1 Saving a Master Document

When you save a master document, Word automatically assigns a filename to each subdocument based on the first characters in the subdocument's heading in the master document outline. For example, a subdocument that begins with the outline heading "**Section 1 Introduction**" might be named "**Section 1 Introduction.doc**".

- Click the Save button or select **Save As** in the **File** menu.

- Click **OK** to save the master document and its subdocuments.

NOTE

If you use punctuation in the subdocument headings in the master document, this will affect the filenames that Word generates. For example, if your subdocument heading is "**Chapter 1 - Introduction**", Word will name the subdocument "**Chapter 1.doc**". If your subdocment heading is "**Chapter 1 Introduction**", then Word will name that subdocument "**Chapter 1 Introduction.doc**".

TIP

It is a good idea to save all of the documents related to a master document in a new folder. This keeps all of the master and subdocuments together so if there's a chance you'll have subdocuments with the same name as already existing documents, one won't overwrite the other if they are in separate folders.

Exercise 4A

1   Create a new blank document.

2   Access the **Outline View**.

3   Enter the following headings into the document, ensuring that they are all formatted to the Heading 1 style.

        Happy Holidays - Destinations
        Bali
        Tunisia
        Thailand
        Malaysia

4   You are now going to make four subdocuments within your master document. Click the heading **Bali** and then click the **Create Subdocument** button on the Outlining Toolbar. Repeat this process for the three remaining headings.

5   Click **Master Document View** button on the Outlining Toolbar to display the section breaks within the document. Notice that each section break has been set to continuous. You will change this in a later exercise.

6   Click the **Master Document View** button again.

7   Click the **Save** button to save the master document and its related subdocuments. Firstly, create a new folder named **Holiday Destinations** where all of the documents relating to this exercise will be stored. Once this has been done, name the master document file **Happy Holidays Destinations**. Close the document on completion.

4.4 Opening a Master Document

Upon reopening a master document that has been saved and closed for the first time, you will notice that the appearance of the subdocuments is slightly different. The master document simply contains **_links_** to the subdocuments so that when you click on a **_link_** Word takes you into the individual file where you can work independently of the master file.

Click on a subdocument link to open the individual file

4.4.1 Opening a Subdocument from the Master Document

You can work in a subdocument just as you would work in any other Word document - editing, formatting, printing, and so on. Once a subdocument has been created from within the master document, you can open it as you would any other document and work within that file. You can also open a subdocument file from within the master document.

- Click on the document link to open the individual subdocument.

- You may now work within the subdocument file in the same way as you would any other Word document.

- When you have finished working on the subdocument, click the **Save** button to save the changes and then click the **Close** button. You will return to the master document window (unless, of course, you have already closed it).

4.4.2 Expanding and Collapsing Subdocuments

If you wish to view the entire contents of the master document so that you can perform any specific editing, printing, formatting, etc, you will need to display the master document with all of the subdocuments *expanded*. Remember that you should be working in Outline View to perform these tasks.

- To view all the text, headings and graphics within the entire master document (based on all of the subdocuments) click the **Expand Subdocuments** button on the Outlining Toolbar.

- If you want to display only the structure and links of a master document, click the **Collapse Subdocument** button on the Outlining Toolbar.

NOTE

If you wish to create a new subdocument into an existing master document, the existing subdocuments must first be expanded.

Exercise 4B

1   Open the **Happy Holidays Destination** document.

2   Click on the link to the **Bali** document.

3   The heading **Bali** will appear in the empty document that has already been created for you. Delete this heading. To save you time in typing information, a file has already been created for you which can be incorporated into the current document.

4   Choose **File** from the **Insert** menu. Select the file named **Bali Content** (this file will be in a different folder to the one that you created for your master document files). Once the file has been inserted, return to the top of the document. Save the current document, closing it on completion.

5   Click the **Expand Subdocuments** button in the master document to view the contents of the **Bali** document and the other subdocuments (these should still be empty). Click the **Collapse Subdocuments** button to view only the links to each subdocument file.

6   Click on the **Tunisia** document link. Delete the heading **Tunisia** in the newly created file. Insert a file named **Tunisia Content**. Return to the top of the document and then save and close. Expand the documents in your subdocument and then collapse the subdocuments again.

7   Save the document, closing it on completion.

4.4.3 Adding a Subdocument to an Existing Master Document (3.2.1.3)

In addition to creating subdocuments from scratch, you can also insert existing documents (subdocuments) into a master document.

- Ensure the master document has all subdocuments expanded.

- Click where the new subdocument is to be inserted. Ensure that you are outside of the boundaries of another subdocument otherwise you will join together two subdocuments.

- Click on the **Insert Subdocument** button on the Outlining Toolbar.

- Select an appropriate document name from the Insert Subdocument window and then click **Open**.

NOTE

> If you add a subdocument that has been saved in a different location to the other files relating to the master document, it is not automatically moved to the same folder as the master document.

4.4.4 Removing a Subdocument from within a Master Document (3.2.1.3)

You can remove a subdocument from a master document at any time. By removing the subdocument you are not physically deleting the subdocument file, rather you are simply removing the content of that subdocument from the master document structure.

- Ensure you are working in Outline View.

- Click on the subdocument icon 🖿 for the subdocument you wish to remove.

- Press the DELETE button on the keyboard.

4.5 Restructuring a Master Document

One of the greatest advantages of using a master document is the ease with which you can reorganise the sequence of the subdocuments.

- Open the existing master document.

- Ensure you are working in the Outline View.

- Click and drag the subdocument icon 🖿 for the item you wish to move. Continue to drag the icon with the mouse until you have found a new location for the subdocument. Release the mouse button. As you drag the subdocument icon, a thick indicator line moves with the mouse pointer to help you position the subdocument in its new location.

NOTE

> Ensure that the indicator line is positioned just below the subdocument that is to precede the moved subdocument. If not, Word will place the subdocument you are moving amongst another subdocument.

Exercise 4C

1   Open the **Happy Holiday Destinations** document.

2   Click the **Expand Subdocuments** button to display the entire content of each subdocument.

3   Click above the boundary for the subdocument **Tunisia** (you should be between the Bali subdocument and the Tunisia subdocument).

4   Click the **Insert Subdocument** button on the Outlining Toolbar. Select the document named **Australia Content**.

5   Once the subdocument has been inserted, click the **Collapse Subdocument** button to view the links to each of the subdocuments. Choose **Yes** to save the master document when you are prompted. Notice the new structure of the master document.

6   Imagine now that you wish to change the order of two of the subdocuments. To begin with expand the subdocuments to display their entire content. Scroll down through the document until you can see the section on **Tunisia**. Click and hold down the mouse on the Subdocument icon next to the **Tunisia** heading. Drag up with the mouse until the indicator is positioned **BELOW** the Bali subdocument boundary and then release the mouse. The subdocument should now be repositioned.

7   Collapse the subdocuments to view the document links again.

8   Click the **Print Preview** button to view the entire subdocument. When prompted choose **Yes** to open all of the subdocuments (otherwise only the structure of the master document will be previewed). As you move from page to page, notice that each new country starts on the SAME page as the previous country's information. This is because Word automatically inserts Continuous Section breaks and not Next Page section breaks. Close out of Preview mode.

9   In this step you are going to change each of the section breaks to a Next Page break. Expand all of the subdocuments and then click the **Master Document View** button to display the section break markers.

10   Click BELOW the first section break. Choose **Page Setup** in the **File** menu. Click on the **Layout** tab and then set the **Section start** to **New Page**. Click **OK** to continue. Repeat this for all section breaks within your document.

11   Preview your document to view the changes that the section breaks have made.

12   Save the document, closing it on completion.

4.6 Notes on using Templates for Master Documents and Subdocuments

You should ensure that both the master document and its related subdocuments use the same **template** file so that the final master document has a consistent look throughout, based on the global styles of the template you have used.

- To check which template is used for a document:

- Select **Templates and Add-ins** in the **Tools** menu.

- In the Document Template box, check that the template name is correct. If not, use the **Attach** button to attach the correct template file.

- Once the correct template file has been attached, it is advised that you tick the **Automatically Update Document Styles** check box so that any changes you make to the template styles, either from the master document or its subdocuments, updates all files that are dependent on that template.

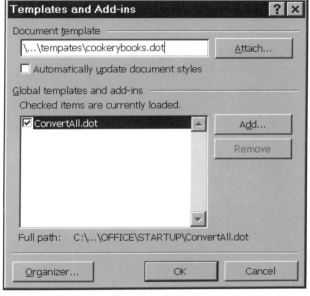

Self Check Exercises

1 How many of the following apply to the characteristics of a section break?

☐ Starts a new page on the next available page.

☐ Starts a new section which has its own unique formatting.

☐ Allows you to create different headers and footers throughout your document.

☐ Allows you to insert other documents into the existing document.

2 Which view would you use to most easily see the types of section breaks that have been inserted into your document?

☐ Page Layout View.

☐ Outline View.

☐ Normal View.

☐ Print Layout View.

3 Using the **Columns** button on the Standard Toolbar, what is the maximum number of columns that you can create?

☐ Five.

☐ Seven.

☐ Ten.

☐ An unlimited number.

4 You can update a table of contents by using which of the following?

☐ Changing the text within the document that is formatted with *Heading* styles.

☐ Highlighting the table of contents and pressing the **F9** key.

☐ Changing the text directly within the table of contents.

☐ Deleting the old table of contents and inserting a new one.

5 Where on the screen can you view the progress of the generation of a table of contents?

☐ You can't see the progress of the table of contents until it is completed.

☐ In the Status Bar.

☐ In a window that appears on the screen.

☐ In the Title Bar containing the document name.

6 What keyboard function allows you to turn on or off the display of field codes?

☐ **F9**.

☐ **ALT+F9**.

☐ **CTRL+F9**.

☐ **SHIFT+F9**.

7 Which of the following benefits relate to the use of a Master Document?

☐ You can use a consistent header or footer across the entire master document.

☐ Each sub-document can be edited and managed in its own file.

☐ Less memory intensive than having all of the text in one document.

8 Which view would you use to when you start to create a Master Document?

☐ Page Layout View.

☐ Outline View.

☐ Normal View.

☐ Print Layout View.

Practical Exercises

Please complete the following exercises as a review of the topics covered in this chapter. Should you require assistance with any of the steps within these exercises, you may refer back to the corresponding sections within this chapter.

Exercise 1

1   Open the document called "**Holidays in Greece**". Take a few moments to familiarise yourself with this document.

2   Locate the heading "**Corfu**". Insert a section break in front of this heading so that the topic on **Corfu** starts on the next page.

3   Locate the heading "**Crete**". Insert a section break in front of this heading so that the topic on **Crete** starts on the next page.

4   Locate the heading "**Getting to Greece**". Insert a section break in front of this heading so that the topic on **Getting to Greece** starts on the next odd page.

5   Preview the document to see how the section breaks have separated the different major topics.

6   Locate the heading "**Greece**". Insert a section break in front of this heading so that the topic on **Greece** starts on the next odd page.

7   Move the cursor to the top of Section 2.

8   From the **Style** box on the Formatting Toolbar, change the style from **Heading 1** to **Normal**.

9   Type the heading "**Table of Contents**" and then press **ENTER** twice.

10 Insert a table of contents that shows 3 levels of headings and uses the **Formal** format.

11 Locate the heading "**Climate**" in the body of the document. Insert two page breaks before this heading.

12 Return to the table of contents and update it so that only the page numbers are modified.

13 Highlight the five paragraphs of text under the heading "**Greece**". Format this text into two equal columns. Justify the text on completion.

14 Reformat the columns so that the spacing between the columns is **half** the current spacing amount.

15 Save the document, closing it on completion.

Exercise 2

1   Open the master document called "**Winter Holidays**".

2   Expand the documents and then preview the document to see the overall layout of the master document file.

3   Go to the end of the master document and insert a new subdocument named "**Madeira**".

4   Preview the document once again.

5   Collapse the subdocuments.

6   Move the "**Morocco**" document down below the "**Madeira**" document. Expand the subdocuments to see the changes that have been made.

7   Save the master document, closing it on completion.

Chapter 3

Document Organisation

CHAPTER 3
Document Organisation

130

Syllabus
Module AM3
Word Processing – Advanced Level

Chapter Three: AM 3.3 – Document Organisation

Section 1   Referencing

Word offers a variety of different referencing tools, helping the reader to find additional information in the document. For example, in addition to a table of contents at the beginning of the document, Word also helps you to create an *index* which identifies more specifically the individual topics and their locations within the document. Indexing is only one example of the referencing tools discussed in this chapter. Others include bookmarks and cross-referencing.

1.1   Bookmarks

A bookmark is a location in your document or a section of text that you have named for later use. Bookmarks are not part of the document text but a label for a section of text. You can "jump" to a bookmark's location or you can use it for various other referencing purposes, such as cross-referencing, index entries, etc.

1.1.1   Adding a Bookmark (3.3.1.1)

- Click where you want to place a bookmark or select the text that is to be referred to by the bookmark.

- Select **Bookmark** in the **Insert** menu.

- Enter an appropriate name for the bookmark in the **Bookmark name** box.

NOTE

Bookmark names can be a combination of letters and numbers but MUST start with a letter. You cannot include spaces in a bookmark name. However, you can use the underscore character to join words in a bookmark, such as **lowest_temperature** or **highest_temperature**.

- You can sort the bookmark names either by **Name** or **Location**. Using the **Name** option, the bookmark names are displayed in alphabetical order. Using the **Location** option, the bookmark names are displayed sequentially, starting with the last bookmark name first.

- Click the **Add** button to create the bookmark. The Bookmark window will close.

- The bookmark will be created but it is not visible unless this option is turned on (see page 136 **Viewing Bookmark Names within a Document** for more details).

1.1.2 Finding a Specific Bookmark

You can return to a specific bookmark at any time. You can also use the text or location of a bookmark for referencing purposes. See **Creating a Cross-Reference** on page 146 for more information.

- Select **Bookmark** in the **Insert** menu.

- Click on the bookmark name you wish to access.

- Click the **GoTo** button. Word will take you to the appropriate location but the Bookmark dialog box will remain open.

- Click **Close** to return to the document.

- The cursor will be positioned at the location of the bookmark.

NOTE

If a bookmark refers to a portion of text, when you go to that bookmark the corresponding text will be highlighted. Alternatively, if a bookmark was set at a location in your document, when you go to that bookmark the cursor will simply be displayed at the appropriate location.

1.1.3 Using the [F5] to Find Bookmarks

You can also use the [F5] key to access a bookmark.

- Press [F5]. The Find and Replace window appears.

- Ensure you are working in the **GoTo** tab.

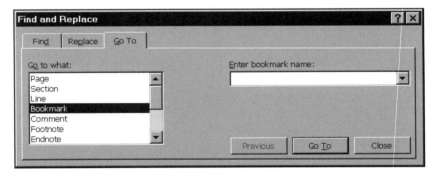

- Select **Bookmark** and then type the name you wish to access in the **Enter bookmark name** box or use the drop-down arrow to select a bookmark name from the available list.

- Click the **GoTo** button to access the bookmark and then click **Close** to return to the document.

- The cursor will be positioned at the location of the bookmark.

Exercise 1A

1   Open the document named **Spain.doc**.

2   Locate the first occurrence of the word "*peseta*" and select this word. If you need help:

        Choose **Find** in the **Edit** menu. Type **peseta** in the **Find what** box and then click **Find Next**. Click **Close** to close the Find and Replace box.

3   Bookmark the currently selected word (ie: **peseta**). Name the bookmark *currency*. Return to the document on completion. If you need help:

        Choose **Bookmark** in the **Insert** menu. Type *currency* for the **Bookmark name** and then click **Add**.

4   In this example you will create a bookmark that refers to a location and not to an actual word or phrase. Click in front of the sentence that starts "*The current rate of exchange....*". Create a bookmark called *rate_of_exchange* and then return to the document. If you need help:

        Choose **Bookmark** in the **Insert** menu. Type *rate_of_exchange* for the **Bookmark name** and then click **Add**.

5   Find the heading titled "*Medical Insurance*". Select this heading and then create a bookmark named *MedInsurance*.

6   Find the heading titled "*Major Cities*". Select the text below that reads "*Madrid and Barcelona*". Create a bookmark named *Major-cities*.

7   Go to the top of the document.

8   Find the bookmark named *currency*. If you need help:

        Select **Bookmark** in the **Insert** menu. Choose **currency** from the available bookmark list and then click **Go To**. Click **Close** once the bookmark has been located.

9   Find the bookmark named *MedInsurance*, using F5. If you need help:

        Press F5 and the Find and Replace window will be displayed. Click on the **Go To** tab. Select **Bookmark** from the **Go to what** list and then select *MedInsurance* from the **Enter bookmark name** list box. Click **Go To** to continue. Click **Close** on completion.

1.1.4 Viewing Bookmark Names within a Document

Bookmarks can be made visible within a document. The bookmarked text appears with square brackets indicating the beginning and the end of a bookmarked area. If no text was highlighted when creating a bookmark, the bookmark location is represented by an **I-beam**.

of Spain was the [peseta]. Bills of 1,000
ation. Coins are made in denominations
s may bring up to 1,000,000 pesetas
at customs. Any amount exceeding 1,00
Spain, tourists carrying more than 1,000
ncy) must declare it. [The current rat
ut it may vary from week to week. For

Bookmark name
referring to selected text.

Bookmark relating to a
location within the
document.

- Select **Options** in the **Tools** menu.

- Click on the **View** tab.

- Select the **Bookmarks** check box.

- Click **OK** to return to your document.

- Repeat this process to uncheck the **Bookmarks** box so that the display of bookmarks is turned off.

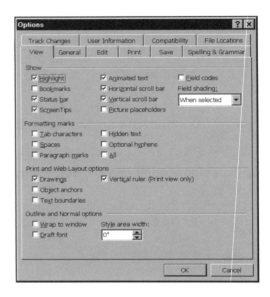

CHAPTER 3
Document Organisation

1.1.5 Deleting a Bookmark (3.3.1.1.)

A bookmark can be deleted at any time without affecting the text or location that it referred to. However, if a bookmark was referenced elsewhere in the document, such as in the case of cross-referencing or used by other field codes, the following error message will appear **"Error! Bookmark not defined"** where the bookmark had been used.

To delete a bookmark:

- Select **Bookmarks** from the **Insert** menu.

- Select the bookmark name you wish to remove.

- Click the **Delete** button.

- Click **OK** to continue.

NOTE

If you delete the bookmarked item (that is the text that was selected when the bookmark was created), then both the bookmark and bookmarked item are deleted at the same time.

Exercise 1B

1   View the bookmark locations within the document. If you need help:

Select **Options** from the **Tools** menu. Click on the **View** tab and check the **Bookmarks** box. Click **OK** to return to the document.

2   Turn off the bookmark identifiers from the current view. If you need help:

Select **Options** from the **Tools** menu. Click on the **View** tab and uncheck the **Bookmarks** box. Click **OK** to return to the document.

3   Delete the bookmark named *currency*. If you need help:

Select **Bookmark** from the **Insert** menu. Click on *currency* and then click the **Delete** button. Click **Close** to return to the document.

4   Delete the *MedInsurance* bookmark name.

5   Check that bookmarks have been deleted by accessing the Bookmark window. Click **Cancel** once you have checked that the bookmarks have been removed.

6   Save and close the current document.

1.2 Working with Indexes

Indexes help the reader to find what they're looking for quickly and easily. An index usually appears at the end of a document and consists of topics, sub-topics and their corresponding page references.

1.2.1 Planning an Index

Before you use Word to build and generate your index, it's a good idea to have a structured plan already in mind. You might like to start by jotting down a list of key words and phrases for your index. Which topics are the most important, should they include sub-topics, do they need to be cross-referenced, etc?

An example of a section from a standard index is shown below.

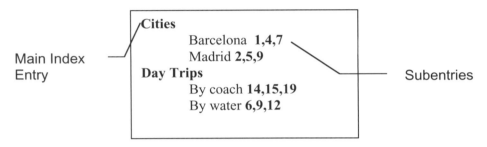

Main Index Entries are the major topics that you wish to identify to the reader in the index. *Subentries* are secondary topics that you use to refine your reading requirements. For example, you may have a main index entry named "**Insurance**". Subentries to help the reader find their specific requirements may be "**Personal**", "**Car**", "**Health**", etc.

1.2.2 Marking Index Entries

You can easily create index entries as you go or you can wait until the entire document has been typed and then set about creating your index.

The first step in building an index is to identify the words or phrases that are to be used as topics or sub-topics. The easiest way to do this is by *marking* the entry within the document. However, there may be times when you want to create an entry that does not have a corresponding word or phrase in the body of the document. You can still create the index reference, simply by clicking in the right location in the document. You then give the appropriate topic or sub-topic name to be used when you create the index using the Mark Index Entry window.

1.2.3 Creating an Index Entry (3.3.1.2)

- Highlight the text or click where the index entry is to be marked.

- Choose **Index and Tables** from the **Insert** menu.

- Click the **Mark Entry** button. The Mark Index Entry window will be displayed.

- If you have selected a portion of text, that text now appears in the **Main Entry** box.

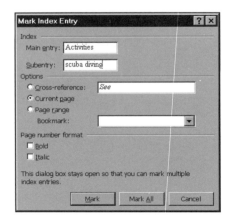

- You can edit the contents of the **Main Entry** box or you can cut and paste the contents into the **Subentry** box (you can use **CTRL+X** to cut and **CTRL+V** to paste).

- Use the **Page number format** box options to either display the page numbers for the entry in bold or italics.

  NOTE: You can also format the main entry or subentry within the Mark Index Entry window. Simply select the text and then use **CTRL+B** for bold, **CTRL+U** for underline and **CTRL+I** for italics.

- Click **Mark** to mark only the current occurrence of the word or phrase for the index. Alternatively, you can click **Mark All** which then marks every occurrence of the word or phrase throughout your document.

  NOTE: You can only use the **Mark All** option if you originally started off by highlighting text within your document before accessing the Mark Index Entry window.

- Mark another index entry or click **Close** to return to the document.

NOTE

The index itself is not visible until it is generated (see 1.2.7 - Generating an Index for more information.

TIP

You can also access the Mark Index Entry window by pressing **ALT+SHIFT+X**

NOTE

When you mark index entries within a document, Word marks each entry with a special code **{XE *Index Entry Name*}**. By default, Word displays these hidden codes within the document but you can simply turn them off by using the **Show/Hide** button on the Standard Toolbar.

{ XE· "Activities"· }The· more· active,· wanting· a· break· from· the· idyllic· beaches,· can· experience· wonderful· golf· courses· in· the· mountains· at· Bedugul· and· beachside· at· Nusa· Dua,· the· thrill· of· white· water· rafting{· XE· **"Activities:white· water· rafting"**· }· or·

CHAPTER 3
Document Organisation

Exercise 1C

1   Open the document named **About Spain with an Index**.

2   In this first exercise you will create a subentry index for the word **Madrid** with a main entry index called **Cities**. Follow these steps:

        Locate the word **Madrid** in the first paragraph and select it. Choose **Index and Tables** in the **Insert** menu. Click on the **Index** tab, if necessary, and then click **Mark Entry**. Replace the word **Madrid** in the Main entry box with **Cities** and then place the word **Madrid** in the Subentry box. If you need help:

        In the **Main entry** box press CTRL+X to cut the word **Madrid**. Instead, now type **Cities**. Highlight this word and press CTRL+B to make it bold. Click in the **subentry** box and press CTRL+V to paste in the word **Madrid**.

        In the **Page number format** box select **Bold**. Click **Mark All** so that every occurrence of the word *Madrid* is marked for your index. Click **Close** on completion.

3   Select the word **Barcelona** in the first paragraph. Press ALT+SHIFT+X to access the Mark Entry window. In this example you need to make **Cities** the **Main entry**, **Barcelona** the **subentry** and finally, make the page number format **Bold**. Mark all the entries of this word for your index and then close back to your document.

4   Click next to the heading "*Water Sports*" on page 5. Press ALT+SHIFT+X to access the Mark Entry dialog box.

        Enter **Sports** as the **Main entry**. Highlight the entry and press CTRL+B to make it bold. Enter **Water Sports** in the **subentry** box. Click the **Bold** option for the page number format. Click **Mark** to mark just the current location and then click **Close**.

5   Click next to the heading "*Outdoor Sports*" on page 5. Press ALT+SHIFT+X to access the Mark Entry dialog box.

        Enter **Sports** as the **Main entry**. You don't need to make the main entry bold once it has already been marked once. Enter **Outdoor Sports** in the **subentry** box. Click the **Bold** option for the page number format. Click **Mark** to mark just the current location and then click **Close**.

6   Now mark the index entries for the three remaining sports - hunting, golf and tennis. Use point 5 above for a guide if you need help.

7   Save the document on completion.

1.2.4 Index Entry Options

By default, when you are marking an index entry the main option is for Word to reference the **current page** number. You can, however, use cross-references or a page range instead.

1.2.5 Cross-References (3.3.1.3)

Some of your index entries will not necessarily refer to a page location but rather to another topic within the index. For example:

Cross-Referenced Index Entry

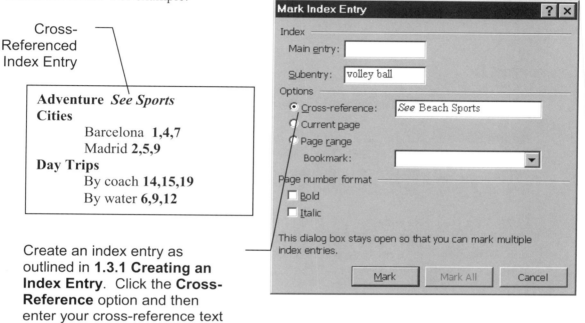

> **Adventure** *See Sports*
> **Cities**
>   Barcelona **1,4,7**
>   Madrid **2,5,9**
> **Day Trips**
>   By coach **14,15,19**
>   By water **6,9,12**

Create an index entry as outlined in **1.3.1 Creating an Index Entry**. Click the **Cross-Reference** option and then enter your cross-reference text in the available box.

1.2.6 Page Range

Instead of a single page reference for a main entry/subentry, you can also display a range of pages upon which a topic appears in the document. For example, your main topic may appear on page 5, but continues to be discussed through until page 7. The page range option will display **5-7** rather than just the current page number.

Before you can use the page range option, you need to be familiar with how to create bookmarks. See **Adding a Bookmark** on page 133 for more information.

- Highlight the full text of the topic that you wish to index, even if the topic is spread across several paragraphs or pages.

- Create a bookmark for the selected text.

- Click where the index entry is to be referenced within the document.

- Press ALT+SHIFT+X to access the Mark Entry dialog box.

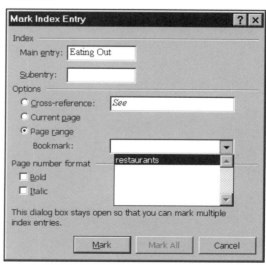

- Create the index entry in the usual way.

- Click the **Page range** option and then select an appropriate **Bookmark** from the available list.

- Click **Mark** entry to continue.

NOTE

The **Page Range** option will not work on subentries alone but must be accompanied by a main entry. You can, however, use a main entry for a page range without including a subentry.

Exercise 1D

1   Ensure the document named **About Spain with an index** is open.

2   Return to the top of the document. In the third paragraph, select the word **adventure**. Press ALT+SHIFT+X. The word **adventure** will appear in the **Main entry** box. Click on **Cross-reference** in the Options box and then type the reference *See Sports*. Click **Mark** to mark the index entry and then click **Close**.

3   In the exercise you will create a page range for an index entry. Locate the heading "**About Spain and its Locations**" on page 6. Highlight the paragraphs below the heading, over onto the next page and stop just before the next heading "**The Major Cities**". Insert a bookmark now named **Bay_of_Biscay**. If you need help:

Select **Bookmark** in the **Insert** menu. Name the bookmark **Bay_of_Biscay** and then click **Add**.

4   Move back up to the heading "**About Spain and its Locations**". In the first paragraph find the location **Bay of Biscay** and click in front of this phrase. Press ALT+SHIFT+X to access the Mark Entry window. Type **Travel Locations** for the **Main entry** and then bold these words. Click in the **Subentry** box and type **Bay of Biscay**. In the **Options** box select **Page range** and then select the bookmark **Bay_of_Biscay**. Format the page number so that it is displayed in bold. Click **Mark** to create the index entry. Click **Close** to return to the document.

5   Save the document on completion.

1.2.7 Generating an Index

Once you have marked all the index entries you wish to use, you are ready to generate the index and place it into your document.

- Click where the index is to be placed.

- Choose **Index and Tables** from the **Insert** menu.

- Click the **Index** tab.

- Select an appropriate format from the **Formats** box.

- Use the **Print Preview** box to view the effect of your settings.

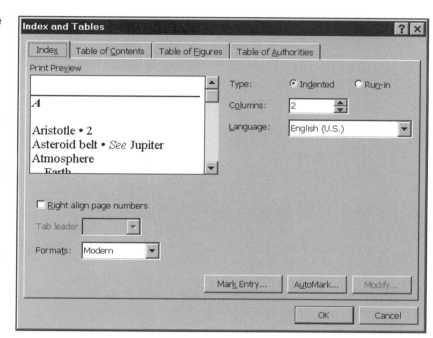

- Specify the number of columns you want to appear in the index using the **Columns** button.

- Select **Run-in** if you want subentries to appear on the same line as the main entry. Select **Indented** if you want subentries to appear **below** the main entries, slightly indented on the left.

Example of Indented Index	Example of Run-in Index
Cities Barcelona 1,3,7 Madrid 2,5,9	**Cities:** Barcelona 1,3,7;Madrid 2,5,9

- You can use the **Right align page numbers** button so that page numbers appear to the right of the column rather than next to the index entry itself. You can also set a **Tab leader** to help the reader follow from the index entry to the page number.

- Click **OK** to generate the index.

NOTE

Once an index has been generated, Word automatically places a continuous section break before it. You can, however, change it to another type of section break (such as a Next Page break), if you want to display the index within a section of its own starting at the top of a page. See **Sections** in Chapter 2 for more information.

1.2.8 Updating an Index

Whilst Word displays the generated index for you, it is actually based on a special field code *{Index}* which is part of hidden text. To display all field codes press **ALT+F9**.

To update an index:

- Click to the left of the section break line above the index to select the entire index table.

- Press **F9** to update the index.

TIP

To update index, you can right mouse click on the index and choose **Update Field** from the pop-up menu.

1.2.9 Editing an Index Entry (3.3.1.2)

To change an index entry, you need to modify the text within the index field entry. See **Inserting a Field Code** on page 150 for more information.

- Click the **Show/Hide** button on the Standard Toolbar to display hidden text within the document.

    For example: **{ XE "Cities**:Madrid" **\b }**

To edit or format an index entry, change the text inside the quotation marks.

{· XE· "Activities"· }The· more· active,· wanting· a· break· from· the· idyllic· beaches,· can· experience· wonderful· golf· courses· in· the· mountains· at· Bedugul· and· beachside· at· Nusa· Dua,· the· thrill· of· white· water· rafting{· **XE· "Activities:white· water· rafting"·** }· or·

- Click outside of the field when you have finished making changes.

1.2.10 Deleting an Index Entry

You can delete an index entry from within the body of the document.

- Click the **Show/Hide** button on the Standard Toolbar to display hidden text within the document.

- **Select the entire XE field contents and then press the** **DELETE** **key.**

    For example select the entire field including the two brace brackets:
    { XE "Cities:Madrid" **\b }**

- Turn off hidden text if you wish.

- Select the entire index table and then press F9 to update it. The deleted field will be removed from the index.

Note

If index entries are added or deleted in the document, the index table must be updated to reflect the changes.

Exercise 1E

1   Ensure the document named **About Spain with an index** is open.

2   Go to the end of the document.

3   Select **Index and Tables** from the **Insert** menu.

4   Click on the **Index** tab.

5   Select **Classic** from the **Formats** box.

6   Click **OK** to generate the index.

7   Click to the left of the section break that has been inserted by the index. Press DELETE to remove the index.

8   Now insert an index that uses the **Modern** format using **1** column. Generate the index and view the changes in the document.

9   Move back through the document until you reach the heading **Golf**. Delete the index entry used to mark this heading. Return to the end of the document. Highlight the entire index table and then press F9 to update it. The **Golf** index entry should have been removed from the **Sports** main entry.

10   Return to page 6 until you find the index entry mark for the **Bay of Biscay**. Edit the index field by removing the words "**Travel Locations**" and inserting "**Places of Interest**". Be careful not to delete the colon (:) that separates the main entry and subentry, otherwise entire phrase will be treated as a subentry.

11   Return to the end of the document and update the index.

12   Save the document, closing it on completion.

1.3 Cross-References

Cross-references can be used to point the reader to another subject within the document. You can refer to such elements as headings, footnotes and endnotes, bookmarks and captions.

1.3.1 Creating a Cross-Reference (3.3.1.3)

Cross-references can only be created within the current document. If you need to make references across multiple documents, you would need to combine all of the documents into a master document. See **Master Documents** in Chapter 2, page 117, for more information.

To create a cross-reference:

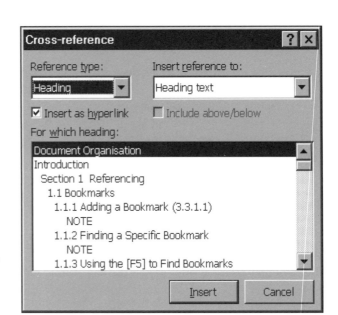

- Click where the cross-referenced information is to appear.

- Select **Cross-Reference** from the **Insert** menu. The Cross-reference window will appear.

- From the **Reference type** box make an appropriate selection. See **1.3.2** for a list of options.

- Make a choice from the **Insert reference to** box. See **1.3.3** for a list of options.

- Select which item you wish to reference from **For Which** box.

- Check the **Insert as hyperlink** if you are saving your document as a Web page and want to make the references into hyperlinks so that visitors to the page can simply click on a hyperlink to access its reference.

- Check the **Include above/below** box if appropriate. See **1.3.4** for a list of options.

- Click **Insert** to create the cross-reference.

1.3.2 Reference Types

Numbered Item	Lists all the text entries beginning with a number throughout the document.
Heading	Shows all headings based on the styles Heading 1, Heading 2, etc or outline levels.
Bookmark	Displays all the bookmarks currently available within the document.
Footnote	Shows all footnotes inserted in the document.

Endnote   Lists the endnotes you have created.

Equation   Shows any equations you have inserted into the document.

Figure   Lists all figure references.

Table   Shows all available tables within the document.

1.3.3 Insert Reference To Options

The **Insert reference to** box will change depending on which reference type you have selected. Typically, this box enables you to choose what type of resulting reference you want. For example, you may want to display a reference's page number, or paragraph number or the heading reference itself.

There are two special types of reference that can be inserted which may be confusing: **Paragraph (no context)** and **Paragraph (full context)**.

Imagine that you wish to reference a paragraph that is numbered **1. a) ii**. If you selected to insert the reference using **Paragraph (no context)** the reference for that paragraph would be **ii**. If you used **Paragraph (full context)**, the reference for that paragraph would be **1. a) ii**.

1.3.4 Include Above/Below

The **Include Above/Below** option is used to create a "relative reference" to a particular item. Imagine that you are referencing the page number of a particular heading. By checking the **Include Above/Below** option, if the referenced text appears on the same page as the reference, Word will automatically insert the word **Above** or **Below** based on the position of the reference.

1.3.5 Deleting a Cross-Reference (3.3.1.3)

Cross-references are actually special field codes that are embedded into your document. When you move the cursor over a cross-reference location, the reference usually displays with a grey background.

To delete a cross-reference:

- Highlight the cross-reference that appears in the document (remember that cross-references display with a grey background) and then press DELETE.

NOTE

If you find it difficult to highlight some of your cross-references, you may find it easier to display the entire code and then make the deletion. To turn on the display of field codes within a document, press ALT+F9.

1.3.6 Updating Cross-References

If you wish to move a cross-reference, you can simply select it and cut and paste it into a new location. As your document changes, you may also find that your cross-references need updating. For example, the number of pages in your document may change and any cross-references displaying page numbers will need to be updated.

- To update a single reference, simply highlight the cross-reference and then press **F9** to update the field.

- To update all cross-references in a document, select the entire document first (you may wish to use the mouse or **CTRL+A** to highlight the whole document) and then press **F9**.

TIP

You can request that all field codes (include cross-references) are automatically updated when you print. This can be a great safety guard if you forget to update an entire document before printing. Choose **Print** from the **File** menu. From the Print window click the **Options** button. Check the **Update Fields** box and then click **OK**.

Exercise 1F

1   Open the document named **Travel Information**.

2   Locate **3. Tickets** on the first page. You need to create a cross-reference in this paragraph to the **Passport Requirements** paragraph further down. To do this:

Click at the end of the *Tickets* paragraph. Type "*Please see*" and then choose **Cross-reference** in the **Insert** menu. Select **Heading** for the **Reference type** and **Heading text** for the **Insert reference to** box. In the **For which heading** box select **5. Passport Requirements**. Click **Insert** to insert the cross-reference. Click **Close** to return to the document.

Press **ALT+F9** to view the field code that controls the cross-reference. Press **ALT+F9** again to turn the field codes off.

Finish the cross-reference sentence off by typing "*...for more information.*".

3   Locate the heading "**Accommodation**" on page 2 of the document. Click at the end of the last sentence in point **2**. You now need to make a reference in this paragraph on how to book which is documented on page 1.

Click at the end of the paragraph for point 2. Type "*Please see*" and then choose **Cross-reference** in the **Insert** menu. Select **Numbered item** for the **Reference type** and **Paragraph number** for the **Insert reference to** box. In the **For which heading** box select **1. How to Book**. Click **Insert** to insert the cross-reference. Click **Close** to return to the document. Type a fullstop and then press the SPACEBAR. Now insert a cross-reference that inserts a reference to the paragraph heading. If you need help:

Choose **Cross-reference** in the **Insert** menu. Select **Numbered item** for the **Reference type** and **Paragraph text** for the **Insert reference to** box. In the **For which heading** box select **1. How to Book**. Click **Insert** to insert the cross-reference. Click **Close** to return to the document.

Now you need to refer to the page that this heading is on. To do this:

Choose **Cross-reference** in the **Insert** menu. Select **Numbered item** for the **Reference type** and **Page number** for the **Insert reference to** box. Check the **Include above/below** option and then in the **For which heading** box select **1. How to Book**. Click **Insert** to insert the cross-reference. Click **Close** to return to the document. Put a fullstop at the end of the sentence to complete the cross-reference.

4   Move back to the top of the document and click in front of the heading "***Booking***". Insert five page breaks so that you have changed the page sequencing of the document.

Change the heading "***How to Book***" so that it reads "***How to Complete Your Booking***". Move back down to the heading "***Accommodation***". Notice that the cross-reference has not updated. Select the entire cross-reference and then press F9 to update it.

5   Save the document, closing it on completion.

CHAPTER 3
Document Organisation

Section 2   Field Codes

Fields are special "placeholders" within a document relating to data that may change at any time. For example, you will be familiar with using automatic page numbering, usually in the header or footer of your document, and the page number is actually based on a special field called *{PAGE}*. As the document updates, so does the field code. Another common field is one that is used to display the current date by using the **Date and Time** option in the **Insert** menu. The field *{DATE}* is inserted into the document and it automatically updates as each day passes.

So as you can see, some field codes are inserted automatically when you use a particular menu option or click a particular button. One way to see field codes in your document is to use the keyboard combination **ALT+F9**. However, there are times that you wish to edit an existing field code or you wish to insert your own from scratch. Word has over 70 field codes available, each performing a different action or inserting a different reference.

2.1   Inserting a Field Code (3.3.2.1)

Fields can be added to the body of the document or to the header or footer area.

To insert a field:

- Click where you want the field to be inserted.

- Choose **Field** from the **Insert** menu.

- Select an option from the **Categories** list - the contents of the **Field names** box will change depending on your selection. If you are unsure of what a particular field does, click on the **?** Help icon (at the top right of the window) and then click on the field. A helpful description will appear.

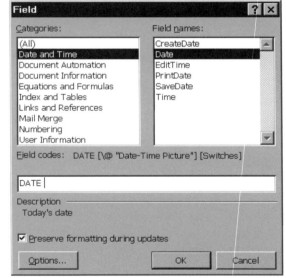

- Click on the **Options** button which takes you to a Field Options window where you can select various formatting choices from the available lists.

- Click **Preserve formatting during updates** if you wish to keep any adhoc formatting you make to a field when the field is being updated. For example, if you underline a field code once you have inserted it into your document (ie: the PrintDate), when that field is updated in the future, the underlining will remain if you have checked the **Preserve formatting during updates** option.

- Click **OK** to insert the field.

2.2.1 Elements of a Field Code

A field code generally has four basic elements:

Field identifiers - curly braces { } are used around a field that you insert using the Field window.

Field name - the name of the field, such as *Filename* or *Author*. The field name is placed within the curly braces.

Field instructions - special instructions to inform the field of other information, prompts or values that is to be inserted into the field.

Switches - options that specify the way you want the field to be displayed or formatted.

Some examples of field codes are:

{FILENAME * CAPS\p * MERGEFORMAT}

This field contains the instruction to insert the current filename of the document, in capital letters with the path (full directory) displayed. The ***Mergeformat** switch means that if the field is updated and you have added any "adhoc" formatting to it (such as underlining, italics, etc), the formatting will be retained during the update. Without the *Mergeformat switch, the formatting you applied would be lost.

NOTE

Don't worry, you won't have to remember all these special switches and instructions. Word inserts them for you when you create the field and when you use the **Options** button in the Field window.

{SECTIONPAGES * Arabic *MERGEFORMAT}

This field contains the instruction to insert a number identifying the total number of pages in the section. The number is to be in the Arabic format (that is 1, 2, 3, etc).

2.2 Editing a Field Code Entry (3.3.2.2)

You can edit a field and its formatting at any time.

- Click anywhere in the field and press **SHIFT+F9** to display the contents of that single field.

- Make changes to the field elements.

- Press **SHIFT+F9** to display the field again.

NOTE

You may find it difficult at first to edit the elements of a field so you may prefer to make a note of its elements, delete the field and then reinsert it with the new settings you require.

2.3 Updating a Field Entry

You can update the results of a field at any time or in fact all fields within the entire document.

To update a single field:

- Click in the field and press F9 to update it.

To update all fields in the document:

- Highlight the entire document with the mouse or press CTRL+A. Press F9 to update all fields.

2.4 Locking and Unlocking Fields (3.3.2.3)

You may wish to protect a field that you have created so that it cannot be easily removed or updated.

To lock a field:

- Click into the field you wish to lock.

- Press CTRL+F11 to lock the field.

To unlock a field:

- Click in the field.

- Press CTRL+SHIFT+F11 to unlock the field.

2.5 Deleting a Field Code (3.3.2.4)

You can delete a field code at any time without affecting other areas of your document.

- Highlight the entire field. If you want to ensure you have selected the whole field, press SHIFT+F9 to display the field code within its curly braces.

- Once the entire field is highlighted, press the DELETE key.

Exercise 2A

1   Open the document named **Tunisia - Field Codes**.

2   Have a look through the document. You will notice that it contains two sections - one for Holidays in Tunisia and one for Australia.

3   Return to the top of the document. In this exercise you will create, edit and update fields within the document. Whilst field codes can be placed anywhere in the body of the text, you will concentrate on adding fields to the header and footer areas of the document.

4   Ensure you are working in section 1 of the document.

5   Access the header and footer area.

6   In the left section of the header area, type the following:

Consultant:

7   Now you are going to add the field code to insert the authors name into the document. This information is retrieved from User Information tab by selecting **Options** in the **Tools** menu. You may wish to check what is currently entered on this tab now.

8   Choose **Field** from the **Insert** menu. From the **Categories** list select **Document Information**. Select **Author** from the **Field names** list. Click the **Options** button. Click on the **Uppercase** option and then click **Add to Field**. Notice the addition of *_Upper_ in the Field codes box. Click the **Undo Last** button. Now select the **Title case** option and then click **Add to Field**. Notice the use of *_Caps_ in the Field codes box. Click **OK** to return to the previous screen. Ensure that **Preserve formatting during updates** is checked and then click **OK** to insert the field into your header.

9   Press `ALT+F9` to view all field codes. Now imagine that you have changed your mind and instead of title case for the author field, you would like to use uppercase after all. Rather than deleting and then reinserting the field, you can edit it. Delete the word _Caps_ and instead type _Upper_. Press `ALT+F9` to turn off the field codes. The field has not updated. Select the entire field and then press `F9`.

10   Tab across to the right side of the header box. Type:

Printed on:

11   Insert a new field that will update with the date of printing. Use a **d-MMM-yy** format for the field. If you need help:

Choose **Field** from the **Insert** menu. From the **Categories** list select **Date and Time**. Select **PrintDate** from the **Field names** list. Click the **Options** button. Click on the **d-MMM-yy** format and then click **Add to Field**. Notice the addition of \\@_"d-MMM-yy"_ in the Field codes box. Click **OK** to return to the previous screen. Ensure that **Preserve formatting during updates** is checked and then click **OK** to insert the field into your header.

12   Toggle between displaying and then hiding field codes.

13   Switch to the footer area. On the left side of the footer, insert a field that displays the filename for this current document. Set the field options so that the filename is displayed in lowercase, with the **path** of the document included. If you need help:

Choose **Field** from the **Insert** menu. From the **Categories** list select **Document Information**. Select **FileName** from the **Field names** list. Click the **Options** button. On the **General switches** tab, click on the **lowercase** and then click **Add to Field**. Click on the **Field specific switches** tab and then select **\p** (to include the path of the document name). Click the **Add to Field** button and then click **OK** to return to the previous screen. Ensure that **Preserve formatting during updates** is checked and then click **OK** to insert the field into your header.

14   Insert page numbering on the right side of the footer. You could add automatic page numbering in the usual way (this is by using the Header and Footer Toolbar) or you could use a field code to insert the page numbering.

15   Close the header and footer to return to the document.

16   Save the document, closing it on completion.

Section 3   Footnotes and Endnotes

There may be occasions when certain topics in your document refer to other documents, individuals, companies, articles, etc, etc. The way in which we can identify the source of the information is by using a footnote or endnote. Thankfully, Word keeps track of the numbering sequence for any footnotes or endnotes you create. Should extra notations be inserted or existing ones deleted, Word renumbers the footnotes/endnotes automatically.

Footnotes appear at the bottom area of your page, usually with a line separator and a note reference mark to identify the note corresponding with a note reference mark within the body of the page.

> **delays to the flight's departure.**
>
> ---
> 1 Our standard confirmation policy is a minimum of 7 days and a maximum of 10 days.
> 2 It is recommended that children over the age of 2 have their own passport.

Endnotes work in a similar way to footnotes, except that they are all placed at the end of the document, instead of at the bottom of each page.

TIP

It's a good idea to make the length of a footnote as short as possible. Whilst Word allows you to enter as much text for each footnote, if they are too long they will take up a large amount of space at the bottom of the page. If you need to type lengthy footnote text, consider changing the footnotes to endnotes.

3.1   Creating a Footnote (3.3.3.1)

Footnotes can be inserted at any location within a document, except in the header or footer area.

To insert a footnote:

- Click where the footnote is to be inserted.

- Select **Footnote** from the **Insert** menu. The Footnote and Endnote window will be displayed.

- Select **Footnote** from the Insert panel.

- If you want to automatically number your footnotes, select **AutoNumber** in the Numbering panel. If you want to use a symbol of your choice (such as an asterisk, hash sign, etc), click **Custom mark** and then click the **Symbol** button to select which symbol you wish to use.

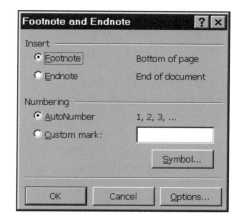

- Click the **Options** button to display the Note Options window. Use the **All Footnotes** tab to specify the placement for your footnotes, their formatting and their starting point.

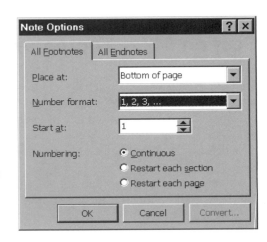

- Click **OK** to close the Note Options window and then click **OK** again to insert the footnote.

- Word adds the note reference mark where the insertion point is located.

- If you are working in **Print Layout View**, Word then places the insertion point at the bottom of the page, after the footnote identifier. Type the footnote text and then click back into the body of the document.

- If you are working in **Normal View**, Word opens a Footnote pane at the bottom of the screen and places the insertion point next to the footnote identifier. Type the footnote text and then click the **Close** button to return to the document.

Sample of the Footnote Pane displayed in Normal View

3.2 Creating Endnotes (3.3.3.1)

Creating endnotes is much the same as the process for creating footnotes, only the endnote text is displayed at the end of the document rather than at the bottom of each page.

To insert an endnote:

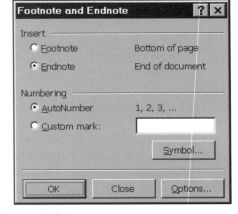

- Click where the endnote is to be inserted.

- Select **Footnote** from the **Insert** menu. The Footnote and Endnote window will be displayed.

- Select **Endnote** from the Insert panel.

- If you want to automatically number your endnotes, select **AutoNumber** in the Numbering panel. If you want to use a symbol of your choice (such as an asterisk, hash sign, etc), click **Custom mark** and then click the **Symbol** button to select which symbol you wish to use.

- Click the **Options** button to display the Note Options window. Use the **All Endnotes** tab to specify the placement for your endnotes, their formatting and their starting point.

- Click **OK** to close the Note Options window and then click **OK** again to insert the endnote.

- Word adds the note reference mark where the insertion point is located.

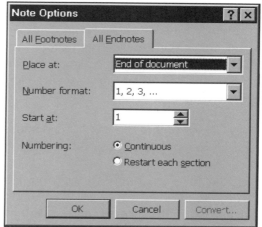

- When working in **Print Layout View**, Word then places the insertion point at the end of the page, after the endnote identifier. Type the endnote text and then click back into the body of the document.

- If you are working in **Normal View**, Word opens an Endnote pane at the bottom of the screen and places the insertion point next to the endnote identifier. Type the endnote text and then click the **Close** button to return to the document.

3.3   Viewing Footnotes and Endnotes

Footnote and endnote references are always displayed when you are working in the Print Layout View - either they are shown at the end of the page or the end of the document. If you are working in Normal View, there are various ways you can view footnote/endnote text.

1. Hover the mouse over a footnote/endnote reference marker within the document. After a few moments a **ScreenTip** box will appear, displaying the footnote or endnote text.

2. When you are working in the **Normal View**, double click a footnote/endnote reference marker within the document. The Footnote/Endnote pane will appear at the bottom of the screen, displaying the corresponding footnote/endnote text for the marker you selected.

3. To turn the Footnote/Endnote pane on without selecting a footnote/endnote marker, simply choose **Footnote** from the **View** menu. If you have both footnotes and endnotes in your document, Word will display View Footnotes window. Once you have made your selection and clicked **OK**, the appropriate pane will be displayed at the bottom of the screen. To close this pane simply click the **Close** button.

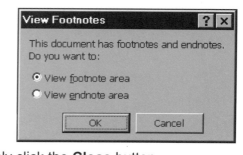

TIP

If you have the Footnote/Endnote pane displayed, you can quickly and easily switch between footnote and endnote text entries by using the options in the list box at the top of the pane.

3.4 Editing Footnotes and Endnotes (3.3.3.2)

If you are working in the Print Layout View, you can edit a footnote or endnote by simply clicking where the corresponding text is and making the appropriate changes. If, however, you are working in Normal View, you need to make changes to footnotes or endnotes using the Footnote/Endnote pane.

- Use any of the methods discussed in point **3** of the **Viewing Footnotes and Endnotes** topics on the previous page to display the Footnote or Endnote pane.

- Make any necessary changes to the note text.

- Click the **Close** button to return to the document.

3.4.1 Repositioning Footnotes and Endnotes (3.3.3.3)

If you wish to move or copy footnotes/endnotes to other locations within your document, Word will automatically renumber all notes throughout the text.

To move a footnote/endnote:

- Highlight the footnote/endnote reference mark in the body of the text. Click **Cut** on the Standard Toolbar or press **CTRL+X** to cut the note.

- Move to where the note is to be inserted and then click **Paste** or press **CTRL+V**.

To copy a footnote/endnote:

- Highlight the footnote/endnote reference mark in the body of the text. Click **Copy** on the Standard Toolbar or press **CTRL+C** to copy the note.

- Move to where the note is to be inserted and then click **Paste** or press **CTRL+V**.

Exercise 3A

1   Open the document named **Travel Information - Footnotes and Endnotes**. In this exercise you will create footnotes rather than endnotes for your document. Remember that the process is almost identical for both.

2   Ensure that you are working in **Print Layout View**.

3   Locate the ***Confirmation and Payment*** paragraph. Click at the end of the sentence "…with 7 working days.". Insert a footnote here with the following reference text:

Our standard confirmation policy is a minimum of 7 days and a maximum of 14 days.

If you need help:

Choose **Footnote** in the **Insert** menu. Click **OK** to insert the footnote. Type the footnote reference text and then click back into your document.

4   Locate the ***Health Requirements*** paragraph. Click at the end of the words "…certificate of vaccination…" and then insert a footnote with the following reference text:

You will need to travel with an original copy of the certificate and not a photocopy.

Click back in the document to continue.

5   Locate the ***Passport for Children*** paragraph. Click at the end of the sentence. Insert a footnote with the following reference text:

It is recommended that children over the age of 2 have their own passport.

Click back in the document to continue.

6   Hover your mouse pointer over any of the footnote markers in the document. A ScreenTip should appear containing the footnote reference text.

7   Switch to the **Normal View**. Double click a footnote reference to display the Footnote/Endnote pane at the bottom of the screen. Click **Close** to return to the document.

8   Save the document but do not close it.

3.4.2 Deleting Footnotes and Endnotes (3.3.3.1)

To delete a footnote or endnote:

- Locate the footnote/endnote reference mark in the document. Highlight the marker and then press DELETE. Word automatically removes the corresponding footnote/endnote reference and updates the numbering of all remaining notes in the document.

3.5 Changing the Format for Existing Footnotes or Endnote (3.3.3.3)

You can alter the formatting for your footnotes and endnotes at any time. For example, you may have used roman numerals for numbering your footnotes (ie: i, ii, iii, etc) and decide later to change to an Arabic format (ie: 1, 2, 3, etc).

- Display the footnote or endnote text either at the bottom of the page, the end of the document or within the Footnote/Endnote pane.

- Click next to the footnote/endnote marker you wish to reformat. Choose **Footnote** from the **Insert** menu. Make any formatting changes using the Footnote and Endnote window and also the Note Options window.

- Click **OK** until you return to the document. All corresponding notes will update with the new formatting you have selected.

3.5.1 Changing the Separator Line

The separator line used to show where the document text ends and the footnote/endnote text begins is usually a short solid line of approximately 5cms in length. You can, however, create a line separator of your own to divide the document from the footnote/endnote text.

- Ensure you are working in **Normal View**.

- Select **Footnotes** in the **View** menu. The Footnote/Endnote pane will be displayed at the bottom of the screen.

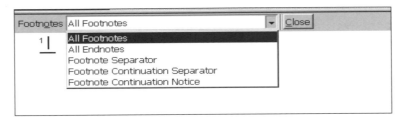

- Click on the drop-down arrow to display the items in the available list box. Select **All Footnotes** or **All Endnotes** to define which type of notes you are changing the separator line for. Once done, select the **Footnote Separator** or **Endnote Separator** from the available list.

- If you wish, you can modify the separator line to formatting of your choice. You can use dashes, borders, symbols, colours, etc, for your separator line.

- Click **Close** to return to the document. Change back to **Print Layout View** to see the new separator line.

3.5.2 Adding a Footnote Continuation Notice

If your footnotes become particularly lengthy, you may find that the footnote text continues onto the following page. Typically, the space available at the bottom of each page for footnote text is usually nine lines. If your notes require more space you can add a Footnote Continuation Separator and/or a Footnote Continuation Notice informing the reader that the footnote text continues on the next page.

NOTE

It is strongly recommended that if you have lengthy footnote text, you use endnotes instead.

To add a Footnote Continuation Notice:

- Ensure you are working in **Normal View**.

- Select **Footnotes** in the **View** menu. The Footnote/Endnote pane will be displayed at the bottom of the screen.

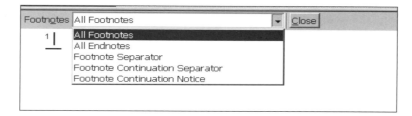

- Click on the drop-down arrow to display the items in the available list box. Select **Footnote Continuation Notice**.

- Type the notice you wish to display at the end of the footnote text when the text needs to flow onto the next page. An example of your Footnote Continuation Notice might be "**Footnotes continued on the following page**".

- Click **Close** to return to the document. Change back to **Print Layout View** to continue.

3.5.3 Adding a Footnote Continuation Separator

If you have lengthy footnote reference text and have used a Footnote Continuation Notice, you may also wish to include a Footnote Continuation Separator. This is a line that appears ABOVE the continuation footnote text on the following page. The line is usually by default a single, solid line. However, you can, if you so wish, change the line to another of your choice such as a row of asterisks, double underlining, etc.

To add a Footnote Continuation Separator:

- Ensure you are working in **Normal View**.

- Select **Footnotes** in the **View** menu. The Footnote/Endnote pane will be displayed at the bottom of the screen.

161

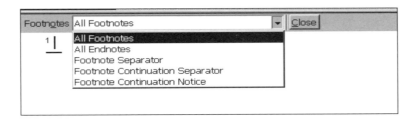

- Click on the drop-down arrow to display the items in the available list box. Select **Footnote Continuation Separator**.

- Draw the line you wish to use as the Footnote Continuation Separator. You can also use borders for this line by accessing the Borders and Shading window.

- Click **Close** to return to the document. Change back to **Print Layout View** to continue.

3.6 Converting Footnotes to Endnotes

Once you have created footnotes within your document, you may decide that you need to convert them into endnotes as the text that they reference is fairly lengthy and there are more notes which need including in the document than you originally realised.

To convert footnotes into endnotes:

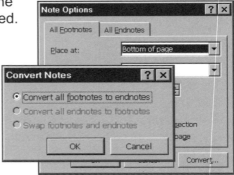

- Choose **Footnotes** from the **Insert** menu. The Footnote and Endnote window will be displayed.

- Click on the **Options** button and the Note Options box will appear. Ensure you are working on the **All Footnotes** tab.

- Click the **Convert** button. The Convert Notes window will appear.

- Ensure the **Convert all footnotes to endnotes** option is selected and then choose **OK**.

- Click **OK** again to exit the Note Options box and then **Close** to return to the document.

NOTE

Just as you can change all footnotes to endnotes, you can also change endnotes into footnotes. Follow the steps above but when you access the Note Options window, click on the **All Endnotes** tab and then click the **Convert** button. When the **Convert Notes** box appears, click the **Convert all endnotes to footnotes** option.

Exercise 3B

1   Ensure that you are working in **Normal View**.

2   Choose **Footnotes** in the **View** menu to display the Footnote/Endnote pane. For the first footnote reference, edit the text so that it reads "***...a maximum of 10 days.***" Click **Close** to return to the document.

3   Change back to the **Print Layout View**.

4   Move the footnote reference number **3** from the body of the document and paste it in the **Tickets** paragraph, following the words "...valid passport...". Use *Cut* and *Paste* for this procedure. Notice, that Word automatically renumbers the footnotes.

5   You have now decided to change the numbering sequence for your footnotes so that you use **letters** instead.

Choose **Footnote** in the **Insert** menu. Click the **Options** button and ensure the **All Footnotes** tab is selected. In the **Number format** box select the "a,b,c" format. Select the **Restart each section** numbering option so that if your document includes separate sections, each footnote reference starts at "a" for that section. Click **OK** and then **Close** (watch out for this, if you click **OK** again, you complete the formatting changes but also insert a new footnote into your document).

6   Convert all of your footnotes into endnotes. If you need help:

Choose **Footnotes** from the **Insert** menu. Click on the **Options** button and the Note Options box will appear. Ensure you are working on the **All Footnotes** tab. Click the **Convert** button. The Convert Notes window will appear. Ensure the **Convert all footnotes to endnotes** option is selected and then choose **OK**. Click **OK** again to exit the Note Options box and then **Close** to return to the document.

7   Now convert all endnotes back to footnotes.

8   Change to the **Normal View**. Display the Footnotes/Endnotes pane.   On the Footnotes Toolbar, select **Footnote Separator** from the drop-down list. Delete the existing line separator. Add a new separator of your choice. If you need help, you can use the following example:

Choose **Borders and Shading** in the **Format** menu. Select a width of your choice from the **Width** box. In the Preview panel, click on the bottom line of the sample page. Click **OK** to insert the line. Close the Footnotes/Endnotes pane and then return to the **Print Layout View**.

9   Delete the second footnote from your document. If you need help:

Highlight the "**b**" footnote marker in your document. Press <u>DELETE</u> to remove the footnote and its corresponding reference text.

10   Save the document, closing it on completion.

Section 4   Security

Word offers a password security option for documents that are confidential or for documents that can be viewed by others but not changed.

4.1   Adding a Password to a Document (3.3.4.1)

A password can be assigned to a document so that other users must enter the password code before being able to open the file or make any changes.

To assign a password to a document:

- Ensure the document is currently open.

- Choose **Save As** in the **File** menu.

- Enter a name for the file if it has not previously been named.

- Click the **Tools** button on the Save As Toolbar.

- Select **General Options** in the Tools menu. The **Save** window will be displayed.

- If you enter a password in the **Password to Open** box, the user must know the correct password to open the file, otherwise the document will remain *locked* from that user.

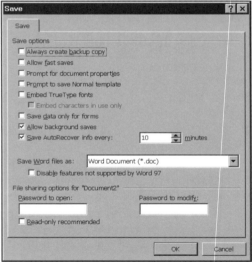

- If you enter a password in the **Password to modify** box, the user must know the correct password to make changes within the document, otherwise they can open the file but they will not be allowed to make any modifications.

- Click **OK** to continue.

- You will then need to reconfirm your password to verify that you have entered the correct code that you wish to use (to ensure complete security, asterisks appear when you are entering a password just in case someone is looking over your shoulder !!). Enter the password again and click **OK** to continue.

- Finally, click the **Save** button to save the file with the password assigned.

NOTE

Passwords may be a maximum of 15 characters long and can contain any combination of letters, numbers or symbols. If you are using letters, check whether you are entering them in uppercase or lowercase as passwords are case-sensitive.

4.2   Opening a Password-Protected Document

You, or other users must know the password of a protected document before it can be opened or modified.

- Open the document in the usual way. A Password box will appear.

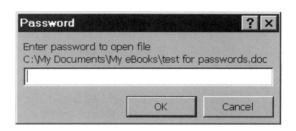

- Enter the correct password and then click **OK**. If an incorrect password is entered, Word will prompt you with a warning message. If the document you are trying to open has only a "**modify**" password and you do not know it when trying to open the file, Word will allow you in but you can only read the document, you cannot make changes.

4.3   Removing a Password from a Protected Document (3.3.4.2)

Once a password has been assigned to a document, you need to know that password before you can remove it.

- Open the document using the correct password to gain access to the file.

- When you are ready, choose **Save As** from the **File** menu.

- Click on the **Tools** button on the **Save As** Toolbar and then select **General Options**.

- Delete the password from the **Password to open** or **Password to modify** boxes.

- Click **OK** to return to the Save As window.

- Click the **Save** button to save the file.

WARNING

Passwords are an important security feature for any of your work that needs to be confidential. However, they should be used with care. If you forget the password you have allocated to a document there is nothing that can be done to open it until the correct password is entered. It is therefore, strongly recommended that you think of a password that is known only to yourself and use it consistently on all of the documents you wish to protect.   This means that you do not have multiple passwords from which to "guess" from in the future.

Exercise 4A

1   Start by working in a new, blank document.

2   Type a brief one-line sentence of your choice.

3   Save the document using the password *secret* to prevent other users from
opening the file.   Close the document on completion. If you need help:

Choose **Save As** in the **File** menu. Name the file *Policy report* and then click
the **Tools** button in the Save As window. Choose **General Options**. Click in the
Password to open box and type *secret*. Click **OK** to continue. Type *secret*
again to confirm the password and then click **OK**. Click **Save** to save the
document, closing it on completion.

4   Open the document named **Policy report** using the password we have just
allocated.

5   Save the document again using the password *secret* but this time to prevent
other users from editing the file.   Close the document on completion. If you need
help:

Choose **Save As** in the **File** menu. Keep the same name *Policy report* and then
click the **Tools** button in the Save As window. Choose **General Options**. Click
in the **Password to open** box and delete the password that was previously set.
Click in the **Password to modify** box and type *secret*. Click **OK** to continue.
Type *secret* again to confirm the password and then click **OK**. Click **Save** to
save the document, closing it on completion.

6   Open the document named **Policy report**. Imagine that you don't know the
password but instead you can click **Read-Only** to view the document. Notice,
once the document is open, the words (**Read-Only**) in the title bar. Close the
document.

7   Open the document again, but this time using the *secret* password. Now resave
the file, but remove the password at the same time so that this document is no
longer protected. Close the file and then try reopening it to ensure that the
security protection has been removed. Close the file once again on completion.

Self Check Exercises

1 What is the function of a bookmark reference?

☐ Marks the location where you were last working in the document.

☐ Marks a location spot where you want to return to when you next open the document.

☐ Marks a location in your document that you want to return to again using the bookmark reference name.

2 Which keyboard function allows you to mark an index entry within your document?

☐ **CTRL+SHIFT+X**.

☐ **ALT+X**.

☐ **ALT+SHIFT+X**.

☐ **CTRL+X**.

3 When you mark an entry for inclusion within an index, which field code is displayed within the document when you turn on the display of field codes?

☐ **{Index ....}**.

☐ **{XE ....}**.

☐ **{TC ....}**.

☐ **{Entry ....}**.

4 What would the field code **{SectionPages..}** display if included within a document?

☐ The current section number.

☐ The number of sections within the document.

☐ The number of pages within the document.

☐ The current page of the current section.

5 In which view would you see the Footnote/Endnote pane if you had included any such notes within your document?

☐ Page Layout View.

☐ Outline View.

☐ Normal View.

☐ Print Layout View.

6 Footnotes references are automatically updated within the document if you insert or delete other footnotes - true or false?

☐ True.

☐ False.

7 What is the maximum length of a password you can assign to a document to protect it?

☐ Ten characters.

☐ Fifteen characters.

☐ There is no limit to the number of characters.

8 Passwords are case-sensitive - true or false?

☐ True.

☐ False.

Practical Exercises

Please complete the following exercises as a review of the topics covered in this chapter. Should you require assistance with any of the steps within these exercises, you may refer back to the corresponding sections within this chapter.

Exercise 1

1   Open the document called "**Greece**".

2   Locate the bookmark reference named "**air_travel**". What page does this reference appear on?

3   Locate the heading "**By Sea**". Create a bookmark reference here named "**sea_travel**".

4   Locate the heading "**By Rail**". Create a bookmark reference here named "**rail_travel**".

5   Locate page 2 and display the paragraph markings in your document. A phrase has been marked for an index entry. What is the phrase that has been marked?

6   Locate any occurrence of the word "**passport**". Highlight the word and then mark all occurrences of this word as a main entry for the index you will soon create.

7   Locate any occurrence of the word "**Athens**". Highlight the word and then mark all occurrences of this word as a main entry for the index.

8   Locate any occurrence of the word "**Heraklion**". Highlight the word and then mark this entry for your index. Name the main entry "**Crete**" and the subentry "**Heraklion**". Mark all occurrences for your index.

9   Move to the end of your document and insert a section break so that the index you are about to create appears on the **next** page. Turn off the display of paragraph markings. Generate an index using the **Formal** format. Once the index has been generated you may need to turn off the display of field codes to view the actual contents of the index.

10   Save the document but do not close it.

11   Access the footer area for section 2 of the document. Turn off the **Same as Previous** option so that the footer is not linked to section 1.

12   Insert a field code into the footer that will display the filename of the document you are working on. Include a special field option that will display the **full path** of the folder in which the document is saved. Return to the document on completion.

13   Locate the heading "**Getting to Greece**". In the first sentence on this page, highlight the first question mark that appears. Insert a cross-reference here that displays the heading text for the entry "**Travel Information**". Now highlight the next question mark and insert a cross-reference here for the page number that corresponds to the heading "**Travel Information**". The end of this sentence should now read "*please refer to Travel Information on page 2*".

14   Locate the sentence "*After World War II the Dodecanissos islands were also returned to Greece*" on page 2 of the document. Insert a footnote at the end of this sentence that reads "*Formal liberation in November 1945*".

15   Return to the top of the document. Save it, closing the file on completion.

Exercise 2

1   Create a new blank document.

2   Type your name and place of birth at the top of page one.

3   Name this document "**Personal Details**" but assign the password "**Blackrock**" which must be used when someone tries to open the document. Close the document once it has been saved.

4   Open the "**Personal Details**" document using the password you have just assigned.

5   Now save the document again, using the same filename but removing the password so that there is no security assigned to this file. Close the file on completion.

6   Open the document again to ensure that the password has been successfully removed.

7   Close the file on completion.

Chapter 4

Document Elements

CHAPTER 4
Document Elements

Syllabus

Module AM3

Word Processing – Advanced Level

Chapter Four: AM 3.4 – Document Elements

CHAPTER 4
Document Elements

Section 1   Tables

In its basic form a table is simply a grid, organised into rows and columns, with each square within the table referred to as a *cell*. Tables are easy to create and work with, but Word provides powerful and flexible facilities to help you manipulate your tables and enhance their structure and functionality.

1.1   Merging Cells (3.4.1.1)

As you know, each *square* in a table grid is known as a cell. If you have 5 columns by 5 rows, effectively you have 25 cells within that table. There are times, however, when you may wish to *join* certain cells together, perhaps to enter a heading that spans across several columns, and this is known as **merging** cells.

- Select the cells you wish to merge.

- Choose **Merge Cells** in the **Table** menu.

If there is data already in the cells, this information is automatically joined; otherwise the cells are simply merged together. The joined cells can now be treated as one single cell.

	THIS IS A MERGED CELL		THIS IS A MERGED CELL	

Sample of a Table containing Merged Cells

NOTE

If your cells contained data BEFORE they were merged, you may need to do some editing to the way the information looks after the merge.

Exercise 1A

1   Open the document named **Beach Resort Hotel**.

2   Under the heading "**Accommodation Prices**", select the first two cells in the first row of the table. Choose **Merge Cells** in the **Table** menu to join these two cells together.

3   Type the heading "**Dates**" in the first joined cell.

4   Skip over the next cell in the first row and now select the four remaining cells. Merge these cells together.

5   Enter the heading "**Full Board All Inclusive**" in the newly joined cells.

6   Save the document but do not close it.

1.2   Splitting Cells (3.4.1.1)

Just as you can merge cells, you can also *split* cells into further *sub-cells* within a table.

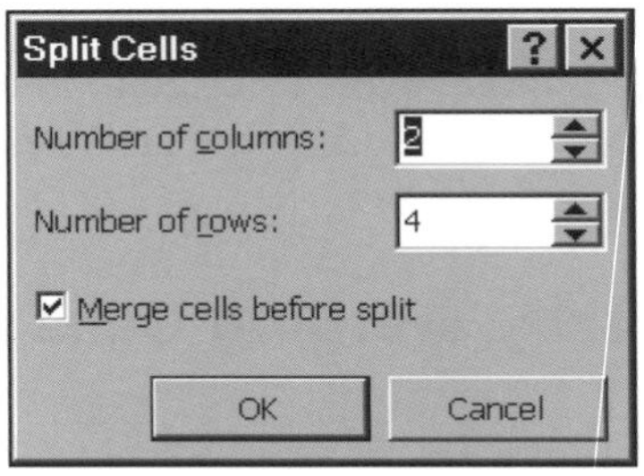

- Select the cells, row or column you wish to split.

- Choose **Split Cells** in the **Tables** menu.

- Enter the number of columns or rows over which you wish to divide the data.

- If you want to retain the basic format of the table and apply existing row and column formatting to the new columns and rows, ensure the **Merge cells before split** box is checked.

- Click **OK** to split the cells.

NOTE

After rows or columns have been split, you may need to readjust the size of the cells to suit your requirements.

Exercise 1B

1   Ensure you are working in the "**Beach Resort Hotel**" document.

2   Complete the table with the following information and apply formatting of your choice. You will need to merge a few more cells together. Select the cell containing the heading "**Dates**" and the two cells below in row 2. Merge these cells together. Select the heading "**Code**" and the cell below it and merge these cells together.

Dates		Code	Full Board All Inclusive			
			Single	Double	Twin	Extra Bed
June	July	A	532	760	680	124
August	September	B	640	890	785	150
October	November	C	490	620	590	100

3   Select all the cells in the row below the row containing the information for "**October** and **November**". Merge all of these cells.

4   Select the remaining three rows including all of the cells and split the cells into 14 columns. If you need help:

Select the row and choose **Split Cells** in the **Table** menu. Set the number of columns to **14** and the number of rows to **3**. Click **OK** to update the table.

5   Save the document but do not close it.

1.3 Converting Tabbed Text to a Table (3.4.1.2)

You may discover that you have entered columns and rows of text, simply by tabbing within the document, only to realise that the data would be better presented in a table for the purposes of formatting and data manipulation.

You can easily convert tabbed text into a table although you do need to let Word know how many columns to use and also how to handle the layout and formatting of the resulting table.

To convert tabbed text to a table:

- Select all of the text that is to be converted into a table. Ensure that the data is separated by tabs.

- Choose **Convert** in the **Table** menu and then select **Text to Table**.

- Usually, Word automatically senses how many columns are within your data and enters an appropriate number in the **Number of columns** box. Change this number, if you wish or add your own number if no number is entered by Word.

- Specify appropriate width or AutoFit settings in the **AutoFit behaviour** panel.

- Select **Tabs** in the **Separate text at** box.

- Click **OK** to create the table.

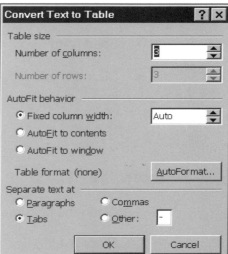

NOTE

In addition to creating tables based on "tabbed" text, you can also use text that is separated by paragraph markers, commas or other symbols or characters.

Exercise 1C

1 Ensure you are working in the "**Beach Resort Hotel**" document.

2 Select all of the text below the heading "**Flight Details - June to November**". This text has been separated by tabs. Choose **Convert** in the **Table** menu. Enter the **Number of columns** as **7** (Word did not enter a number for you as your data has a blank line separating the headings and the values below and this prevents Word from making the calculation for you). Set the **Separate text at** option to **Tabs** and then click **OK**.

3 Notice that each of the headings for the table is separated into two different cells. Select the cells containing "**Departure**" and "**Airport**" and then merge these cells. Repeat this process for all of the headings at the top of the table.

4 Delete the blank row below the **Departure Airport** row so that no blank rows exist in the table.

5 Save the document, closing it on completion.

1.3.1 Converting a Table into Text

This is really the reverse of converting text into a table. With this feature, you are using information that is already in a table and converting it back to text. For example, you may have information relating to various individuals in a table format. You need, however, to send this information to someone who is working with another program and who has requested that the data is separated by commas (often referred to as CSV - comma separated variables). Using the Convert Table to Text option, you could perform this task.

- Select all of the text within the table that you wish to convert.

- Choose **Convert** in the **Table** menu and then select **Table to Text**.

- Specify how you would like to separate the text.

- Click **OK** to convert the table.

Exercise 1D

1   Open the document named "**CSV - Confirmed Bookings**".

2   Highlight the first row of the table and delete it. If you need help:

Select the first row and then choose **Delete** in the **Table** menu, followed by **Rows**.

3   Select the remaining rows within the table.

4   Choose **Convert** in the **Table** menu. Select **Table to Text** and set the **Separate text with** option to **Commas**. Click **OK** to continue.

5   Now practise changing the data back into a table format using the **Convert** option in the **Table** menu. Remember that commas separate the data.

6   Save the document, closing it on completion.

1.4 Sorting Data in a Table (3.4.1.3)

Word provides us with several tools within a table to help us to reorganise the data in various different ways, such as in ascending or descending order for alphabetical or numerical listings.

You can sort either by using the Sort window, which gives you the greatest control over how and what you sort, or you can use the Sort buttons on the Tables and Borders Toolbar.

1.4.1 Using the Tables and Borders Toolbar to Sort

The Tables and Borders Toolbar includes a Sort button for ascending order and also one for descending order.

- Ensure that the **Tables and Borders Toolbar** is turned on. Remember that you can right mouse click on an existing Toolbar to display a Toolbar menu from which to make a selection.

- Click anywhere within the column by which you wish to sort. Click the **Sort Ascending** or **Sort Descending** button.

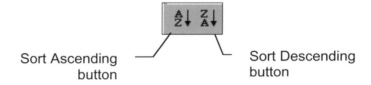

Sort Ascending button — Sort Descending button

NOTE

Using the Tables and Borders Toolbar, when you sort a column within a table, the first line of the table is not included in the sort process as it is treated as the **header row** - that is the row containing the field names for the data below. If you want to include the first row, you will need to use the Sort window instead. See the following page for more information.

Exercise 1E

1   Open the document named **"Confirmed Bookings"**.

2   Display the **Tables and Borders Toolbar**. If you need help:

Right mouse click on any Toolbar and select **Tables and Borders** from the available Toolbar list.

3   Click anywhere in the **Name** column and then click the **Sort Ascending** button.

4   Now sort in ascending order for the **Agent** column.

5   Finally, sort the table in descending order for the **Balance Due**.

6   Turn off the **Tables and Borders** Toolbar. Save the document, but do not close it.

1.4.2 Using the Sort Window

The Sort window provides a more flexible method of sorting. You can sort by multiple columns and you can also control whether or not the first row of data in a table is to be sorted.

- Click anywhere in the table upon which you wish to sort.

- Choose **Sort** in the **Table** menu. The Sort window will be displayed.

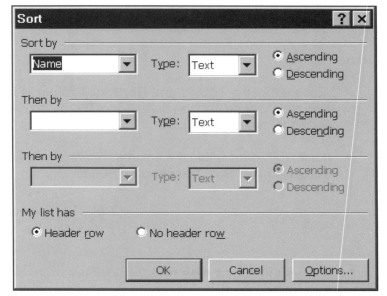

- In the **Sort by** column, use the drop-down arrow to select a field (column) upon which to sort.

- In the **Type** box, select whether the data is entered as **Text**, **Number** or **Date**.

- Select whether you wish to sort in **Ascending** or **Descending** order.

- If you wish to sort by additional columns, use the **Then by** boxes to specify the details.

- Click **Header row** if you want the first row of the table to remain unsorted or **No header row** if the first row of data is to be included in the sort process.

- Click **OK** to perform the sort.

Exercise 1F

1   Ensure you are working in the "**Confirmed Bookings**" document.

2   Click anywhere in the table. Sort the table by ascending order of the **Agent** column, as well as in descending order of the **Deposit Paid** column. If you need help:

Choose **Sort** in the **Table** menu. Select **Agent** from the **Sort by** box, with the **Type** as **Text** and the order as **Ascending**. In the **Then by** box, select **Deposit**, **Type** as **Number** and order **Descending**. Ensure you have selected **Header row** and then click **OK**.

3   Now sort the table in ascending order of the **Agent** and secondly as descending order of the **Balance**.

4   Save the document but do not close it.

1.5 Using Addition Calculations within Tables (3.4.1.4)

Some of the columns in your tables may include numerical data, perhaps revenue amounts, and salary figures, target sales values, etc. Word incorporates an AutoSum feature that allows you to add the data in a column and display the result in a particular cell in the table. If the values in the table change, so will the total.

- Click in the cell in which the answer is to be inserted. The correct location is usually BELOW a column of numbers or to the RIGHT of a row of numbers.

- Choose **Formula** in the **Table** menu. The Formula window will be displayed.

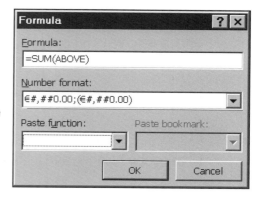

- Ensure the formula in the **Formula** box is correct. You may need to change the word "**ABOVE**" to "**LEFT**", if you wish to add up numbers in the row to the left of the cursor and not above the cursor.

- Use the **Number format** box to choose a format for the resulting calculation. If you leave this blank, a default format will be used.

- You can use the **Paste function** to insert other formulas in addition to **SUM**, such as **AVERAGE, MIN**, **MAX**, etc.

- Click **OK** to insert the formula. The cell now shows the calculated answer.

- If you change any of the values within the table, highlight the total and press [F9] to update it.

TIP

You can also add up columns or rows by using the **AutoSum** [Σ] button on the **Tables and Borders Toolbar**.

NOTE

Press ALT+F9 to display field codes within your document. You will notice that the field shows **{=SUM(ABOVE)}** if you are inserting a total below a column of numbers or **{=SUM(LEFT)}** if you are inserting a total to the right of a row of numbers.

Exercise 1G

1   Ensure you are working in the "**Confirmed Bookings**" document.

2   Select the entire last row of the table.

3   Choose **Insert** in the **Table** menu and then select **Rows Below**. A new blank row should now be displayed at the bottom of the table.

4   Click in the blank cell for the **Deposit Paid** column.

5   Choose **Formula** in the **Table** menu.   Ensure the formula is set to **=SUM(ABOVE)** and then select a Euro format from the **Number format** box. Click **OK** to add the formula to your table. The answer should be "**11,600.00**".

6   Now insert the total for the **Balance Due** column. The answer should be "**56,350.00**".

7   Locate the deposit paid by "**Ian Marshall**" and change it from **400.00** to **1000.00**. Change the balance due to **2600.00**.

8   Select the two totals at the bottom of the table and use the F9 key to update them.

9   Save the document, closing it on completion.

Section 2   Working with Forms

We are all used to filling out forms particularly paper ones and perhaps more recently online forms on the Internet. Word includes a powerful **Form Design** tool that not only helps you to create a form, but also that helps you to capture and manipulate the data that other users complete.

You may, for example, wish to create a form that is to be emailed to a group of colleagues requesting certain specific information. Once their responses are received, you may wish to "pool" their answers into one list document or table.

2.1   Planning a Form

One of the easiest ways to start a form is to begin by laying out the main body of the document, leaving space for where the various forms fields are to be inserted. Alternatively, you can build the entire document as you go. You may consider using tables within your form to make the layout of the fields easier for the reader to follow. Also you may like to include some graphics or special formatting within the form document so that it is more appealing to the reader.

NOTE

Form documents MUST be saved as templates not as standard documents otherwise the form fields will not work. See **Creating a New Template** in Chapter 1, page 69, for more information on creating templates.

2.1.2   Using the Forms Toolbar

When you are creating a form template, you will need to use the Forms Toolbar for much of the design process.

- Click anywhere on an existing Toolbar to display a list of available Toolbars. Click on the **Forms Toolbar** to turn it on.

2.1.3   Types of Form Fields

There are three types of form field within Word: **Text**, **Check Box** and **Drop-Down** fields.

- **Text Fields** allow the users to enter text, numbers, symbols or perform calculations within the designated field. You would use this type of field when there is no standard response to the field, such as someone's name, address, phone number, etc.

- **Check Box Fields** allow the user to check a particular box in response to a question. For example, you may ask for the user to respond with their age group and you could have 5 age groups all listed with a check box so that the user can "check" the appropriate group.

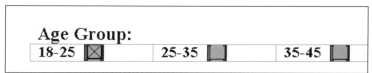

Example of a Check Box Field

- **Drop-Down Fields** allow the user to select a response from a standard list of responses.

Example of a Drop-Down Field

2.1.4 Creating a Form (3.4.2.1)

Below are the main, basic steps for form design. We will deal with each of these topics in more detail throughout this section.

- Design the layout of your form document.

- Ensure that the Forms Toolbar is turned on.

- Insert the appropriate form fields, such as Text, Check Box and Drop-Down fields.

- Specify the field *properties*.

- Protect the form.

- Save the form as a template.

2.2 Inserting a Text Field (3.4.2.2)

Text fields are usually the most commonly used. They allow the user to make "any" response to a particular field - meaning there is nothing to choose from, only free-form text to be entered.

To insert a Text field:

- Click where the field is to be inserted.

- Click the **Text Form Field** [abl] button on the **Forms Toolbar**. Word inserts the field marker **[   ]** at the cursor location. If you want to view the actual field, press **ALT+F9** - the field will be called **{FORMTEXT}**.

2.2.1 Changing Text Field Options

Once you have inserted a Text field into your form, you can change its properties to further control what type of information is inserted.

- Click in the Text field.

- Click the **Form Field Options** 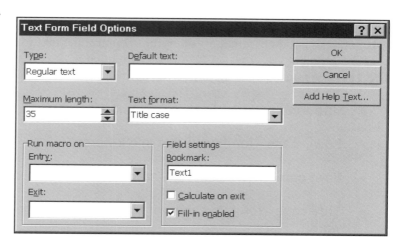 button on the **Forms Toolbar**. Alternatively, right click with the mouse and choose **Properties**.

- Make any necessary changes to the Field Options (please see below).

- Click **OK** to return to the form document.

2.2.1.1 Choosing the Field Type

From the **Type** box, you can select one of the following:

- **Regular text** - allows the user to enter text, numbers, symbols and spaces.

- **Number** - allows the user to enter only numerical values into the field.

- **Date** - allows the user to enter a recognised date value.

- **Time** - allows the user to enter a recognised time value.

- **Current Date** - inserts the current date automatically for the user.

- **Current Time** - inserts the current time automatically for the user.

- **Calculation** - performs a calculation of your choice, the contents of which cannot be changed by the user.

2.2.1.2 Default Text

Word provides a **Default text** option that appears automatically in the field when the user opens the form. This text is usually the most common response that could be made. Users can either leave the text as it is (if it applies) or change it to a response of their choice.

2.2.1.3 Maximum Length

Use the **Maximum Length** box to enter in the number of characters that you wish to limit the response to. You can leave the box set to **Unlimited** - so that the response can be as long as necessary, or you can use the up and down arrows to specify a value of your choice. Be careful not to underestimate the maximum length of a field. For example, setting a **Name** field to only 25 characters would be restrictive to people with longer names.

2.2.1.4 Text Format

To ensure a consistent look and feel to your completed forms, and to the data that you may "extract" into another format, it is helpful to control the text format for Text fields.

The **Text Format** box has the following options from which you can choose:

- **Uppercase** - formats all text into uppercase.

- **Lowercase** - formats all text into lowercase.

- **First capital** - formats all characters in lowercase, except for the first.

- **Title case** - formats each word in lowercase, except for the first character of each word.

2.2.1.5 Running Macros within Forms

Forms can include macros that run on a certain entry action within a field. This is a very powerful feature within Word but not within the scope of this syllabus. If you require more information, you can use Word Help.

2.2.1.6 Field Settings

If you would like to allocate a bookmark name to the field you are creating, enter an appropriate name in the **Bookmark** box. Please see Referencing in Chapter 3 for more information on Bookmarks.

If you would like Word to calculate the fields in your form each time you exit the form, you can check the **Calculate on exit** box. Each time you exit the form, Word updates the numeric fields and recalculates any calculations in the form.

If you have entered a standard response in the **Default text** box, check the **Fill-in enabled** box so that the text is automatically displayed in the field when the user clicks in the field, rather than when the form is initially opened.

Exercise 2A

1   Open the document named "**Holiday Enquiry Form**". This document contains a table that will be used as the basis for our form.

2   Turn on the **Forms Toolbar**.

3   Click anywhere in the blank cell to the right of the **Name** field. Click the **Text Form Field** [abl] button on the **Forms Toolbar**. Select the field and then click the **Form Field Options** [icon] button. Set the **Type** for the field to **Regular Text** and the **Maximum Length** to **30** characters. Change the **Text format** to **Title Case** and then click **OK** to return to the document.

4   Click anywhere in the blank cell to the right of the **Address** field. Insert a Text field at this location. For now, we will not worry about changing the field options for this field as it is appropriate to leave them at the defaults - which is regular text, unlimited length and no special formatting.

5   Click anywhere in the blank cell to the right of the **Contact Number** field. Click the **Text Form Field** [abl] button on the **Forms Toolbar**. Select the field and then click the **Form Field Options** [icon] button. Set the **Type** for the field to **Regular text** and the **Maximum Length** to **15** characters. Click **OK** to return to the document.

6   Click anywhere in the blank cell to the right of the **Agent Name** field. Click the **Text Form Field** [abl] button on the **Forms Toolbar**. Select the field and then click the **Form Field Options** [icon] button. Set the **Type** for the field to **Regular text** and the **Default text** to your full name. As you will be the person most regularly filling out this particular form, it would save time if your name automatically appeared, rather than typing it in each time. Change the **Maximum Length** to **30** characters and the **Text format** to **Uppercase**. Click **OK** to return to the document.

7   Create a text form field in the box containing the word "**From**". Change the options for this field so that its **Type** is set to **Date** and the **Date format** is set to "**d-MMM-yy**". Click **OK** to return to the document. Now create another text form field with the same options for the "**To**" box.

8   Save the document, but do not close it.

2.3 Inserting a Check Box Field

Check Box fields are used when you need the user to make a choice on a form. For example, you could have a check box for different age categories, and the user then simply needs to click the one that corresponds to their own age.

To insert a Check Box field:

- Click where the field is to be inserted.

- Click the **Check Box Form Field** ☑ button on the **Forms Toolbar**. Word inserts the field marker ☐ at the cursor location. If you want to view the actual field, press **ALT+F9** - the field will be called **{FORMCHECKBOX}**.

2.3.1 Changing Check Box Field Options

Once you have inserted a Check Box field into your form, you can change its properties to give you further control about what type of information is inserted.

- Click in the Check Box field.

- Click the **Form Field Options** 🖳 button on the **Forms Toolbar**.

- Make any necessary changes to the Field Options (please see below).

- Click **OK** to return to the form document.

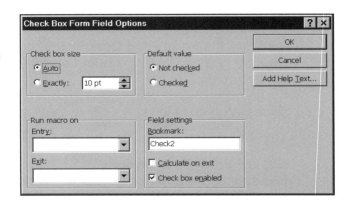

TIP

When you wish to change the properties for any field within a form template, you can double click on the field to open the appropriate Field Options window, rather than using the **Form Field Options** button.

2.3.1.1 Choosing the Check Box Size

You can use the **Exactly** option to set a specific size in **points** for the Check Box. Alternatively, you can leave the setting at **Auto**, so that the Check Box is sized to Word's default.

2.3.1.2 Default Value

If you would like the Check Box to be empty when the form is first opened, choose the **Not checked** option. Alternatively, if you select **Checked**, the Check Box will automatically be selected when the form is opened.

2.3.1.3 Running Macros within Forms

Forms can include macros that run on a certain entry action within a field. This is a very powerful feature within Word but not within the scope of this syllabus.

2.3.1.4 Field Settings

If you would like to allocate a bookmark name to the field you are creating, enter an appropriate name in the **Bookmark** box. Please see Referencing in Chapter 3 for more information on Bookmarks.

If you would like Word to calculate the fields in your form each time you exit the form, you can check the **Calculate on exit** box. Each time you exit the form, Word updates the numeric fields and recalculates any calculations in the form.

If you want to lock a Check Box field so that users are unable to alter it, select the **Check box enabled** option. For example, if you have defaulted a check box field to be automatically checked and you don't wish to give the users an opportunity to uncheck the field, turn the **Check box enabled** option on.

Exercise 2B

1   Ensure you are working in the "**Holiday Enquiry Form**" document.

2   Click in the box that contains the word "**Full**". Click the **Check Box Form Field** ☑ button on the **Forms Toolbar** to insert a check box at this location. Double click the check box field so that you can change its options. Change the size of the check box to **Exactly 16pt** and ensure the **Default value** is set to **Not checked**. Click **OK** to return to the document.

3   Create another check box for both the "**Half**" field and the "**None**" field using the same options as those above for the "**Full**" field.

4   Save the document, but do not close it.

2.4   Inserting a Drop-Down Field

A Drop-Down field allows you to create a list of choices from which the user can make one selection. For example, you may have a drop-down field to display a list of travel destinations, or months during which the holiday is to take place.

To insert a Drop-Down field:

- Click where the field is to be inserted.

- Click the **Drop-Down Form Field** 🔽 button on the **Forms Toolbar**. Word inserts the field marker **[　]** at the cursor location. If you want to view the actual field, press **ALT+F9** - the field will be called **{FORMDROPDOWN}**.

2.4.1 Changing Drop-Down Field Options

Once you have inserted a Drop-Down field into your form, you can change its properties to give you further control about what type of information is inserted.

- Click in the Drop-Down field.

- Click the **Form Field Options** 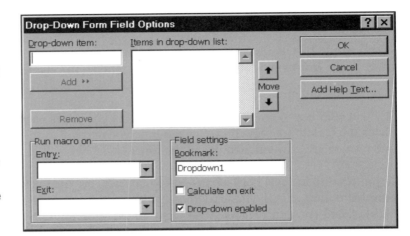 button on the **Forms Toolbar**.

- Make any necessary changes to the Field Options. Please see below for more information.

- Click **OK** to return to the form document.

2.4.1.1 Setting the Drop-Down Items

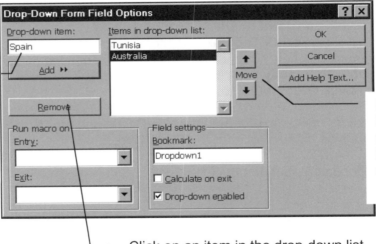

Enter a new item in this box and then click **Add** to include it in the list.

Use the **Move** buttons to rearrange the items in the drop-down list.

Click on an item in the drop-down list box and click **Remove** to delete it from the list.

2.4.1.2 Running Macros within Forms

Forms can include macros that run on a certain entry action within a field. This is a very powerful feature within Word but not within the scope of this syllabus.

2.4.1.3 Field Settings

If you would like to allocate a bookmark name to the field you are creating, enter an appropriate name in the **Bookmark** box. Please see Referencing in Chapter 3 for more information on Bookmarks.

If you would like Word to calculate the fields in your form each time you exit the form, you can check the **Calculate on exit** box. Each time you exit the form, Word updates the numeric fields and recalculates any calculations in the form.

If you want to lock a Check Box field so that users are unable to alter it, select the **Drop-down enabled** option.

Exercise 2C

1   Ensure you are working in the "**Holiday Enquiry Form**" document.

2   Click anywhere in the blank cell to the right of the **Destination** field. Click the
        Drop-Down Form Field 🖾 button on the **Forms Toolbar**. Double click the box
        to access the Drop-Down Form Field Options. Add the following destinations to
        the **Items in drop-down list** box:

                   Spain, Italy, France, Portugal, Greece

3   Use the **Move** buttons to change the order of the destinations so that they are
        listed alphabetically. Click **OK** to return to the document.

4   Click anywhere in the blank cell to the right of the **No of Travellers** field. Insert a
        drop-down form field here. Change its options so that it includes the following
        numbers in the **Items in drop-down list** box:

                   1, 2, 3, 4, 5, 6

5   Click **OK** to return to the document.

6   Save the document, but do not close it.

2.5   Adding Help to Forms

You may wish to provide customised help messages for the users of your forms, assisting them with specific details for each field. You can add help information when you are working in any of the Field Options windows. To add help to your form:

- Double click the field you wish to add help to, or click on the field and use the **Form Field Options** button on the Forms **Toolbar**. The appropriate Field Options window will open.

- Click the [Add Help Text...] button to open the Form Field Help Text window.

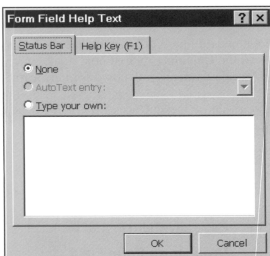

- You can display help text either in the Status Bar at the bottom of the screen or when the user presses the [F1] key, or both. The help becomes available when the user has clicked or tabbed into the specific field.   Use the **Status Bar** and **Help Key (F1)** tabs to enter your appropriate help text.

- Click on the **Type your own** option and enter your text in the box provided. Alternatively, you can select an **AutoText entry** from the available list, if an AutoText entry contains the help text you wish to use.

- Click **OK** to return to the form.

2.6   Using Field Shading

You can toggle the display of form field shading using the **Form Field Shading** button. When the shading is *on*, a grey shade appears in the box, making it slightly easier to identify than when the shading is turned off.

Exercise 2D

1   Ensure you are working in the "**Holiday Enquiry Form**" document.

2   Double click the text field for the **Name** box so that you can access its options. Click the **Add Help Text** button. Select the **Status Bar** tab and **Type your own**. Enter the following help text:

Type the first and last name only. Do not worry what case you use to type in the text as Word will change it to title case automatically.

3   Click **OK** twice to return to the document.

4   Double click the text field for the **Contact Number** box so that you can access its options. Click the **Add Help Text** button. Select the **Status Bar** tab and **Type your own**. Enter the following help text:

You can use spaces or dashes to separate sections of the phone number.

5   Click **OK** twice to return to the document.

6   Turn the field shading off using the **Form Field Shading** button. Now turn the field shading back on again.

7   Save the document, but do not close it.

2.7   Protecting a Form (3.4.2.4)

Before you can "publish" a form so that a user can work with it, the form must be **protected**. When you protect a form, you effectively lock the fields in place so that no further changes can be made to their format or properties. A protect form will then appear as the user will see it.

To protect a form:

- Click on the Protect Form 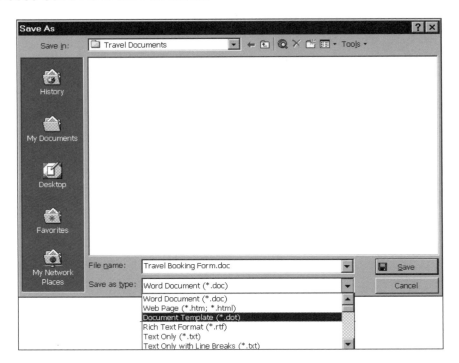 button on the **Forms Toolbar**.

If you are now ready for the form to be available to other users, remember that it must be protected and then saved as a template for the form to work.

2.7.1 Saving a Protected Form

To save a form as a template:

- Choose **Save As** in the **File** menu.

- Enter an appropriate name for the form in the **File name** box.

- Select **Document Template (*.dot)** from the **Save as type** box.

- Click the **Save** button to save the file.

2.8 Using a Form

To fill in a form, you must base the new document on a form template:

- Choose **New** from the **File** menu and then select **More Word Templates**. (If you are using a previous version of Word, simply choosing **File**, **New** will display the available templates from which you can make your selection).

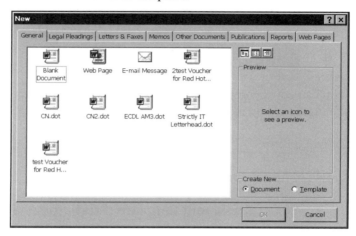

- Click on the appropriate tab and then double click the template name you wish to use.

- The mouse pointer will be located in the first field of the form. Use the mouse or the TAB key to move around through the fields in the form.

- When you have finished with the form, save it in the usual way (the form will be saved as a document and not as a template). In addition, you can save a blank form if you wish so that it can be passed on to others for completion.

NOTE

When you are working in a Check Box field, you can either use the mouse to check or uncheck the box or you can use the SPACEBAR. When you are working in a Drop-Down field, you can click on the drop-down arrow ⬇ to select form the list, or you can use the keyboard combination ALT+↓.

Exercise 2E

1. Ensure you are working in the "**Holiday Enquiry Form**" document.

2. You are now ready to protect the form and save it as a template so that it can be filled-in by yourself or another user. Click the **Protect Form** 🔒 button on the **Forms Toolbar**. Choose **Save As** in the **File** menu. Select **Document Template (*.dot)** from the **Save as type** box and then ensure the filename is set to **Holiday Enquiry Form.dot**. Click **Save** to save the document and then close it.

3. To access the form for the purposes of filling it in, you need to base a new document on the template you have just created. Choose **New** in the **File** menu and select **More Word Templates**. Click on the appropriate tab until you find the **Holiday Enquiry Form** template and then click **OK** to use it.

4. When you are in the **Name** field, notice the help text that appears in the Status Bar. Click in the **Contact Number** field and view the help text for this field. Click back in **Name**.

5   Fill in a name of your choice in the **Name** field using lowercase - when you press the TAB key to leave the field, Word will automatically change it to title case. Complete the form using TAB to move from one field to another.

6   Save the document as "**My first enquiry**", closing it on completion.

2.9   Editing a Form (3.4.2.1)

You can edit a form at any time. However, it is important to note that you must open the original template file and not a document, based on the template.

To edit a form:

- Choose **Open** from the **File** menu.

- Select **Document template (*.dot)** from the **Files of type** box.

- Locate the file in the appropriate folder and then click the **Open** button.

- You may now edit the text surrounding the form fields or the general layout of the document.

2.9.1 Unprotecting a Form

Before you can make any changes to the fields themselves, you must unprotect the form first.

To unprotect a form:

- Click the **Protect Form** 🔒 button on the **Forms Toolbar**.

- Make any necessary changes and then protect the form again before saving it and closing it.

2.9.2 Deleting a Field (3.4.2.3)

Should you wish to delete a field from a form, you must ensure first that the form is unprotected.

- Highlight the entire field that is to be removed.

- Press the DELETE button on the keyboard.

Exercise 2F

1   Open the template named "**Holiday Enquiry Form.dot**".

2   Turn on the **Forms Toolbar** if it is not already displayed.

3   Unprotect the form so that you can make some changes.

4   Delete the entire contents of the box containing the word "**None**" and the check box as well.

5   Protect the form once again.

6   Save the form template, closing it on completion.

Section 3   Text Boxes

Text boxes are free-floating containers, independent of the other text in your document, that you can use to enclose information.   These boxes can help you to create interesting page layouts and designs. You may want to use text boxes to add special types of information to your documents, such as quotations, tips, instructions, etc. Or, you may wish to use text boxes to create a more specific document, such as a newsletter.   Whichever it is, Word provides easy-to-use tools for the creation and manipulation of text boxes.

3.1   Inserting a Text Box (3.4.3.1)

Before you can create a text box it is essential that you are working in the Print Layout View. In this view you can create and manipulate as many text boxes as you want.

To insert a text box:

- Choose **Text Box** in the **Insert** menu. When you hover the mouse pointer over an area of the page, it changes shape to a *cross-hair* **+**.

- Drag the mouse pointer on your page to create a text box and then release the mouse.

- The text box will appear as well as the **Text Box Toolbar**.

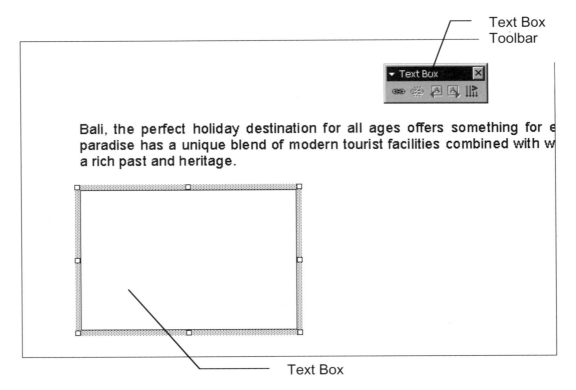

Text Box Toolbar

Bali, the perfect holiday destination for all ages offers something for e
paradise has a unique blend of modern tourist facilities combined with w
a rich past and heritage.

Text Box

TIP

You can also insert a text box using the **Text Box** button on the **Drawing Toolbar**.

3.1.1 Selecting a Text Box

To select a text box, simply click on any of its borders. When a text box has been selected, a shaded selection frame surrounds it and the Text Box Toolbar automatically appears. If you click away from the text box, it becomes unselected and the Text Box Toolbar disappears.

3.1.2 Entering Text into a Text Box

Once a text box has been created, it is ready for you to add text and to format the box if appropriate.

To enter text into a text box:

- Click anywhere within the text box. The text entry border will appear around the selected box. Begin typing. You can format the text in a text box in the same way as you would for any other text in your document.

TIP

You can also paste information into a text box if the information has already been typed.

3.1.3 Resizing Text Boxes (3.4.3.2)

Once a text box has been created, you can change its size at any time.

To resize a text box:

- Position the mouse over any of the *sizing handles* on the selection frame. Drag until you have reached the appropriate size and then release the mouse.

Sizing handles are represented by the white squares surrounding the selection frame.

3.1.4 Moving a Text Box (3.4.3.2)

You can move a text box to another location within a document.

To move a text box:

- Click on the text box to select it.

- Hover the mouse over any border of the selection frame. The mouse pointer changes to include a four-arrow headed selection pointer. Click and drag with the mouse until you have reached the new location. Release the mouse button.

Exercise 3A

1   Open the document called "**Holiday Brochure**".

2   Create a text box similar to the example below.

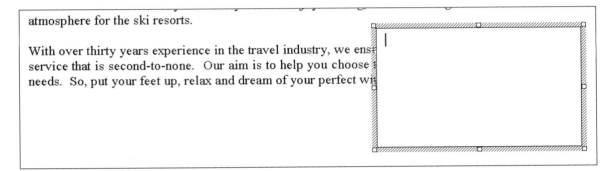

atmosphere for the ski resorts.

With over thirty years experience in the travel industry, we ens[...]
service that is second-to-none. Our aim is to help you choose [...]
needs. So, put your feet up, relax and dream of your perfect w[...]

3   Enter the following text into the text box:

> **BOOK EARLY**
> **SAVE €100**
> **GUARANTEED**
> Book before the 31st July and save
> €100 per adult couple on all winter
> brochure holiday prices.

4   Format the text within the text box to enhance the information and resize the box if necessary.

5   Save the document, but do not close it.

3.2 Formatting Text Boxes (3.4.3.3)

When you create a text box, by default it is formatted to a rectangle shape with a .75 point black line surrounding it. You can, however, change the formatting of the text box to suit your own requirements.

To format a text box:

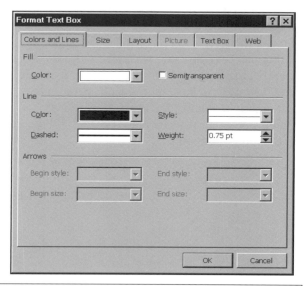

- Select the text box and then choose **Text Box** in the **Format** menu.   The Format Text Box window will be displayed.

- Use the various tabs to make changes to the layout and format of the text box. For an overview of the main options within the Format Text Box, see 3.2.1 below.

- Click **OK** to return to the document.

NOTE

You can also access the Format Text Box window by double-clicking the border of a selection frame for the text box you wish to modify.

3.2.1 Format Text Box Options

Colours and Lines

The **Colour and Lines** tab can be used to choose a particular "fill" colour, shade or pattern for the text box you are modifying. You can also use the Line options to control the outside line of the box, including the colour of the line, its weight and style. If you wish to remove the outside lines altogether, choose the **No Line** option.

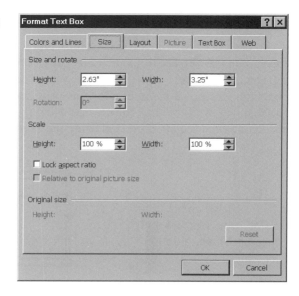

Size

Using the **Size** tab you can set exact height and width dimensions for the text box. Alternatively, you can adjust the height and width using the **Scale** percentages so that the text box increases or decreases by the specified percentage, based on the original box.

If you check the **Lock aspect ratio** box, both height and width are changed in proportionate ratio when you change only one setting such as the height or width.

Layout

Using the **Layout** tab, you can control how the text box aligns with text and how the text wraps around the box itself. For an explanation of each layout wrapping style, click on the Help question mark (**?**) in the right corner of the window and then click on the style you wish to learn about.

Text Box

Using the **Text Box** tab, you can control the margins inside the text box object. For example, you may want to have more blank space on the left and right sides of the box so that the text stands out, or perhaps increased space at the top or bottom.

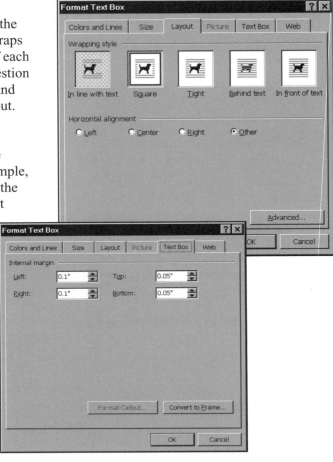

3.2.2 Borders and Shading (3.4.3.3)

In addition to adding lines or fill effects using the Format Text Box settings, you can also use borders and shading. However, it is important to understand that there is a distinct difference between the two.

If you use the Format Text Box, **Colour and Lines** settings to add a line to a text box, the line appears on the **outside** of the text box. If you use the Borders and Shading option, the line appears on the **inside** of the text box. Whilst there may be occasions when you wish to mix the two, in most cases it is preferable to use one and not the other. The example below shows a text box that has two borders - one created using the Borders and Shading option (that is the dashed inside line) and the other created using the Format Text Box option (that is the outside solid line).

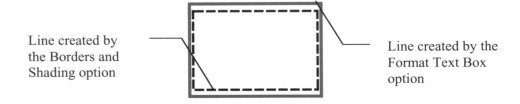

Line created by the Borders and Shading option

Line created by the Format Text Box option

To add lines or shading:

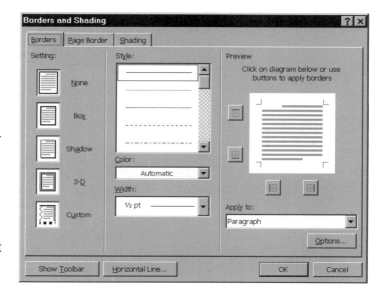

- Select the text box and then choose **Borders and Shading** in the **Format** menu. The Borders and Shading window will be displayed.

- Use the various tabs to make changes to the layout and format of the text box. For an overview of the main options within the Format Text Box, see 3.2.1 above.

- Click **OK** to return to the document.

Exercise 3B

1   Ensure you are working in the "**Holiday Brochure**" document.

2   Select the text box you created in Exercise 3A.

3   Choose **Text Box** in the **Format** menu or double click the text box to access the Format Text Box options.

4   Click on the **Layout** tab and select **Square** as the **Wrapping style**. Set the **Horizontal alignment** to **Right** and then click **OK** to return to the document. Move the text box further over to the right, using the mouse, so that it partly sits in the blank right margin.

sorts.

xperience in the travel industry, we ensure
vel of service that is second-to-none. Our
e the best holiday to suit all of your needs.
relax and dream of your perfect winter

**BOOK EARLY
SAVE €100
GUARANTEED**
Book before the 31st July and
save €100 per adult couple on all
winter brochure holiday prices.

5   Access the **Format Text Box** window again and click on the **Colours and Lines** tab. Set the **Fill Colour** to a light grey shade. Click the **Semi-transparent** option to fade the fill colour further. Set the **Line Colour** to **red** and choose the last option on the **Line Style** list which is **6pt** with two thin lines and one thick. Click **OK** to continue.

6   Save the document, but do not close it.

3.3   Linking Text Boxes (3.4.3.4)

Word allows you to *link* text boxes together so that the information in one box automatically flows into another box when the first one is full. This is useful when you want to create multiple text boxes all of which are to contain a continuous "story". If you edit the text in any of the boxes, Word again automatically adjusts the text between the boxes to accommodate the remaining amount of text. Linking text boxes is often useful when you are creating such documents as newsletters. You may wish to create a text box on the first page that contains a particular article which then flows into another linked text box on page two to complete the article.

NOTE

The maximum number of text boxes that can be linked in one document is **32**.

To link two or more text boxes:

- Ensure that the text boxes that you wish to link are empty.

- Click on the first text box that is to start the link.

- Click the **Create Text Box Link** button on the **Text Box Toolbar**. The mouse pointer changes to display a *pitcher pointer*.

- Move the mouse to the text box you want to link to the first box. The mouse pointer changes to a *pouring pitcher*. Click in the text box to create the link.

- If you want to link to another text box, select the box you have just linked to and begin the process again.

TIP

If you have clicked the **Create Text Box Link** button and then decide you don't want to create a link, simply press the **ESC** key to return the mouse pointer to its normal shape.

3.3.1   Inserting Text into Linked Text Boxes

Once you have linked together two or more text boxes you can either type information into them or paste information that you have previously copied.

- Click in the first text box to contain the data. Either type or paste into this box. Once the first text box becomes full, the text will flow into the next text box and so on until you finish entering text.

3.3.2   Moving Between Linked Text Boxes

You can easily move from one linked text box to another to read, edit or format information in the boxes.

- Use the **Next Text Box** and **Previous Text Box** buttons on the **Text Box Toolbar**.

Previous Text   Next Text Box
Box button   button

NOTE

You can also use move between linked text boxes using the cursor direction keys. At the end of the text in a linked box, click the ⟶ key to move to the next text box. At the start of a text box, click the ⟵ key to move to the previous text box.

3.3.3 Unlinking Text Boxes

You can easily remove the link between two text boxes without deleting any of the data they contain. When you remove the link, information in the second box, returns to the first box which you may need to resize to see all of the data. The second text box will be empty. If you have linked more than one text box together, when you break a link, subsequent links are not affected.

- Select the text box containing the information you want to prevent from flowing into another linked box.

- Click on the **Break Forward Link** button on the **Text Box Toolbar**.

- The text flows back into the selected box and the linked box becomes empty.

3.3.4 Deleting Linked and Unlinked Text Boxes (3.4.3.1)

To delete an unlinked text box:

- Click on the text box you want to delete to ensure that it is selected.

- Press the **DELETE** key on keyboard. The text box and the text it contained are both deleted simultaneously.

To delete a linked text box:

- Click on the text box you want to delete to ensure that it is selected.

- Press the **DELETE** key on keyboard. The text box is deleted and the text it contained flows on to the next text box in the link.

Exercise 3C

1   Ensure you are working in the "**Holiday Brochure**" document.

2   Below the existing text, type the following heading, formatting it to 14pt and bold.

This Month's Special Feature - Tenerife

3   Add three more text boxes as per the example below. As a tip, a quick way of creating two or more text boxes of the same dimensions, is to create the first box, select it and then hold down the CTRL key and drag a copy of the selected box to another location on the page. Alternatively, you can copy the first box and paste it twice to create the three boxes you require.

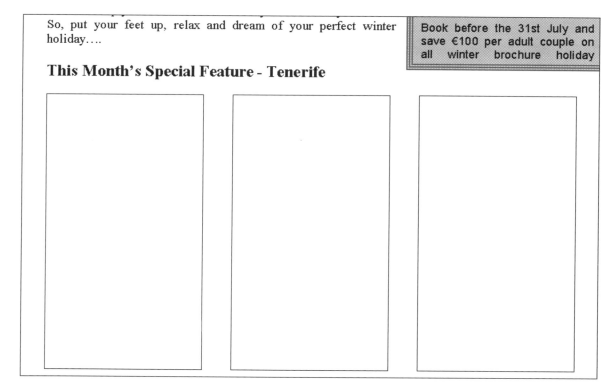

4   Link the three newly created text boxes together. If you need help:

Click on the first text box and then click the **Create Text Box Link** button on the **Text Box Toolbar**. Move the mouse over to the second text box and the mouse pointer will change to a *pouring pitcher*. Click to create the link. Now select the second text box and link it with the third.

5   Click in the first text box in the group of three. To save typing, you can insert an existing file into the text boxes rather than typing in from scratch. Choose **File** from the **Insert** menu. Select the document named "**Tenerife Information**" and then click **Open**. Notice how the text flows between the linked text boxes.

6   Use the **Next Text Box** and **Previous Text Box** buttons on the **Text Box Toolbar** to move from one text box to another.

7   Break the link between the second and third text boxes. If you need help:

Select the second text box and then click the **Break Forward Link** button on the **Text Box Toolbar**.

8   Notice that the text flows back into the second text box and leaves the third box empty. Relink the second and third text boxes.

9   Select the first text box and choose **Borders and Shading** in the **Format** menu. Select the **Shadow** setting and then click **OK** to return to the document. Notice that the border appears around the paragraph text and not around the box itself. Click the **Undo** button to reverse this action.

10   Double click the borders of the first text box to access the **Format Text Box** window. Select the **Colours and Lines** tab. Use the **Lines** settings to place a border around the text box. Apply the same formatting to the two remaining boxes.

11   Save the document, closing it on completion.

Section 4   Spreadsheets

One of the most powerful features of a word processing program is its ability to handle information created in another program, such as a spreadsheet, database, chart or picture. Word gives you the capability to work with such data from other programs, either by *linking* the information or by *embedding* it into a document.

Whilst linking and embedding initially appear to be very similar, they are in fact, two very different processes.

Linking
Linking data from one program into another establishes a **link** between the original file (known as the source) and the destination file. When the information is changed in the source file, the information in the destination file is automatically updated (or updated when the user confirms it).

Embedding
The action of embedding data into a document places an intact copy of the source information into the destination file. If you change the source data, the changes are not reflected in the destination file. You can, however, edit the data in the destination file without having to exit Word, using the functionality of the original source program.

Objects
The term **object** applies to the data that is placed in the destination file, whether you are linking or embedding. For the purpose of this chapter we will only be working with embedding objects and not linking.

4.1   Embedding an Existing Worksheet

One of the easiest ways of embedding an object, such as a worksheet, is to use an existing file that has already been created.

- Click where the object is to be embedded.

- Choose **Object** in the **Insert** menu. The Object window appears.

- Click the **Create from File** tab.

- Enter the correct path and file name in the **File name** box or use the **Browse** button to locate the appropriate file.

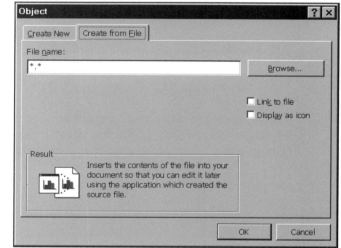

- Click **OK** to continue.

NOTE

Do not click the **Link to file** box as this would *link* the object into your document rather than simply embedding it.

4.1.1 Modifying an Embedded Worksheet (3.4.4.1)

Once a worksheet has been embedded within a document, the data can be edited at any time, using the functionality of the source program, such as Excel.

- Double click the embedded worksheet object you wish to modify. The menu bar and toolbars will change to that of the source program.

- Make any changes to the source data that you wish.

- Click outside of the object to exit the program and return to Word's normal functionality.

Exercise 4A

1   Open the document named "**More on Tenerife**".

2   Click in the blank space below the heading and paragraph referring to "**Hotel Accommodation**".

3   Insert an existing spreadsheet called "**Beach Resort Hotel Rates**" that has been created in Excel. If you need help:

   Choose **Object** in the **Insert** menu. Click on the **Create from File** tab and then **Browse** for the file named "**Beach Resort Hotel Rates.xls**". Click **OK** to insert the file once you have located it.

4   Click on the newly inserted worksheet object to select it. Click on the **Centre** button on the **Formatting Toolbar** to centre it between the left and right margins.

5   Change the following values in the worksheet object:

   Change the June to July Double figure from **760** to **790**
   Change the June to July Twin figure from **680** to **695**

   If you need help:

   Double click the worksheet object so that you are working in Excel but from within the Word document. Make the appropriate changes and then click outside of the object to return to Word's normal functionality.

6   Save the document, but do not close it.

4.2 Embedding a New Worksheet

Embedding an existing file, such as a worksheet, is probably the most common method of embedding data into a document. However, you can also create an embedded object on the fly. Perhaps you are creating a document and decide that a table of figures would be best presented in a worksheet format rather than using a table format. Word lets you create the worksheet and embed it at the same time.

- Click where the embedded object is to be placed.

- Choose **Object** in the **Insert** menu. The Object window will be displayed.

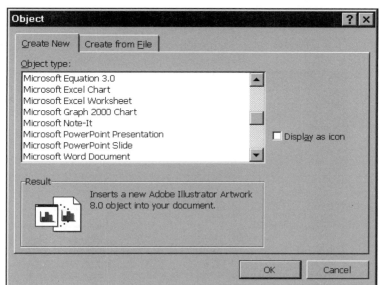

- Click on the **Create New** tab.

- From the **Object type** list, select the program that is to be the source program for the data you are about to enter.

- Click **OK** to continue.

- An object will appear in your document, ready for you to enter your data. The toolbars and menu bar will be that of the source program you have previously specified.

- When you have finished entering your data, click outside of the object to return to Word's normal functionality.

Exercise 4B

1   Ensure you are working in the "**More on Tenerife**" document.

2   Click in the blank space below the heading and paragraph referring to "**Temperatures**".

3   Insert a newly created Excel worksheet object. If you need help:

      Choose **Object** in the **Insert** menu. Click the **Create New** tab and then select the **Microsoft Excel Worksheet** object type and click **OK**.

4   Enter the data as shown in the example below and centre and bold the headings.

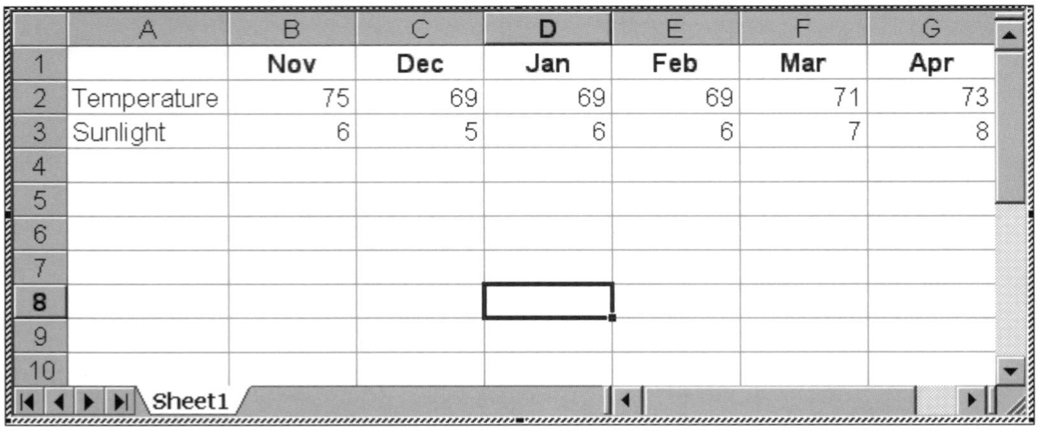

	A	B	C	D	E	F	G
1		**Nov**	**Dec**	**Jan**	**Feb**	**Mar**	**Apr**
2	Temperature	75	69	69	69	71	73
3	Sunlight	6	5	6	6	7	8
4							
5							
6							
7							
8							
9							
10							

Sheet1

5   Select all of the data (from A1 to G3) and then choose **AutoFormat** in the **Format** menu. Click the **Options** button and then uncheck **Width/Height** at the bottom of the AutoFormat window (this will prevent the AutoFormat changing the width or height of your worksheet cells). Select the **Classic 2** format and then click **OK** to return to the worksheet object.

6   Resize the worksheet by dragging the right corner of the sheet, so that only rows 1 to 3 are visible (the embedded object must be open when you perform the resizing). Click outside of the worksheet object to return to Word's normal functionality. Select the worksheet and then centre it between the left and right margins.

7   Save the document, closing it on completion.

4.3 Creating a Chart (3.4.4.2)

If you are familiar with using Excel, you will know how quickly and easily you can create a chart (also known as a graph) from worksheet data. Using Word, you can also create charts either based on the data in a table, or from data that has been pasted from a worksheet that was originally created in Excel. It is important to note, however, that you cannot create a chart based on linked or embedded data from Excel. If you want to use information that already exists in an Excel spreadsheet you would need to copy and paste the data into the document without creating any link.

- Click in the table or pasted worksheet data that contains the data you wish to display in a chart. Highlight all of the data that is to be included in the chart.

- Select **Picture** in the **Insert** menu and then select the **Chart** sub-option. Microsoft Graph is now launched and it creates a default chart based on the information you have selected. Two new boxes are displayed, one containing the default chart and the other containing a datasheet which displays the data you previously selected.

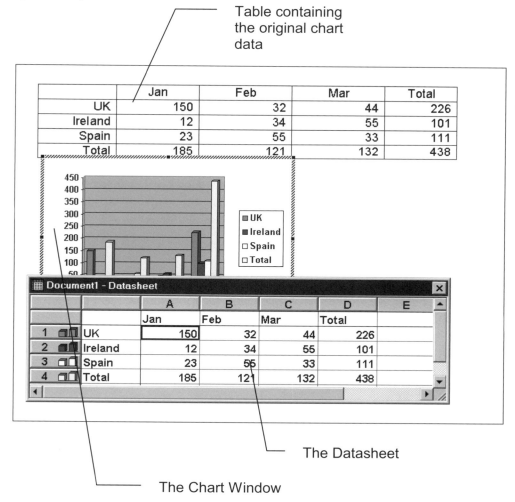

Table containing the original chart data

The Datasheet

The Chart Window

4.3.1 The Microsoft Graph Window

The Microsoft Graph window includes several key elements when you insert a chart based on data contained within a Word document. Firstly, a datasheet window appears as well as a chart window. In addition, when you are working within either of these two windows, the menu bar changes as well as some of the buttons on the Standard and Formatting Toolbars.

The Datasheet Window - the information you selected within your Word document is shown in a datasheet window. The datasheet is organised in the same way as a worksheet - with columns and rows, the junction of which is referred to as a cell. Within the datasheet window, you can change some of the information, if you wish, to customise the information shown in the chart.

The Chart Window - the chart window displays a default chart based on the information you originally selected. As you make formatting or data changes, the chart in the chart window updates automatically.

4.3.2 Exiting Microsoft Graph

When you have finished working with a chart and/or its datasheet, you can return to Word's normal functionality, simply by clicking outside of the chart area. The menu bar and Toolbars return to their normal settings.

If you wish to return to the Microsoft Graph window to make further changes or enhancements to a chart simply double click the chart object within the document. The menu bar and Toolbars will once again change.

4.3.3 Changing the Data in the Datasheet Window

You can easily make changes to the data in the datasheet window at any time and these changes will automatically update your chart in the chart window. However, changes that you make to the original table where the data was selected, will not automatically update the chart. Therefore, you may need to update the datasheet with the same changes so that both the table and the chart reflect the same information.

To make changes in the datasheet window:

- Ensure that you are working in a Microsoft Graph window (you can simply double click a chart object to access this window).

- Make any necessary changes to the chart and these changes will be reflected in the chart window.

- Click outside of the chart area to exit from Microsoft Graph.

Exercise 4C

1   Open the document named "**Bali Climate**".

2   Select the table under the heading *Climate*.

3   Create a new chart based on the table data. If you need help:

Select the entire table and then choose **Picture** in the **Insert** menu. Choose **Chart** and the chart window and datasheet will be displayed.

4   Click outside of the chart to place the default chart within the document.

5   Within the table, change the number of sunshine hours for **October** to **9** and for **November** to **8**.

6   Double click the chart object so that you can make changes to it. Update the sunshine hours for **October** and **November**. Click outside of the chart on completion.

7   Save the document, but do not close it.

4.4   Formatting a Chart (3.4.4.3)

Once a chart has been created within a Word document, you can make extensive formatting changes to its appearance. For those of you who have experience of working in Microsoft Excel, all of the formatting functionality that you would use in that program is available to be used in Word. For the purpose of this chapter, we will concentrate on some of the main chart formatting options.

4.4.1   Chart Types

When you first create a chart based on data within a document, Word automatically uses a 3D column chart as its default. There are, however, many other chart types that you can use.

To change the chart type:

- Ensure you are working in a Microsoft Graph window.

- Choose **Chart Type** in the **Chart** menu. The Chart Type window will be displayed.

Choose an appropriate style from the **Chart type** list

Once you have selected a main type from the Chart type list, select an option from the **Chart sub-type** box

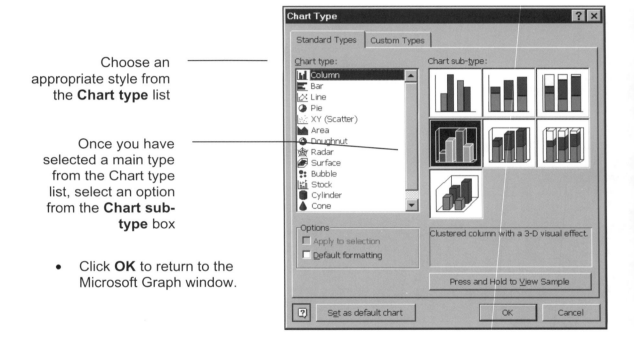

- Click **OK** to return to the Microsoft Graph window.

TIP

If you want to quickly change the chart type, you can also use the **Chart Type** button on the Standard Toolbar.

4.4.2   Chart Options

Once you've decided on the main chart type, you can further modify the chart's appearance using the Chart Options window.

Ensure you are working in a Microsoft Graph window.

- Choose **Chart Options** in the **Chart** menu. The Chart Options window will be displayed.

- Use the various tabs to make changes to the contents and/or appearance of your chart.

- Click **OK** to return to the Microsoft Graph window.

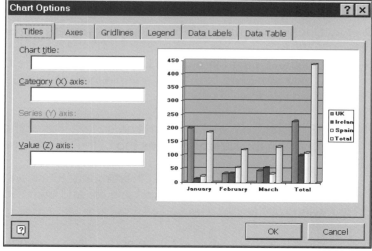

4.4.3 Formatting Specific Chart Elements

One of the easiest ways to make changes to the different elements within a chart window is simply by double-clicking the element you wish to change. For example, if you double-click a Legend box within the chart window, the Format Legend window will appear.

Using the double-click method is a quick way of formatting within a chart window, without using the menu options or Toolbars.

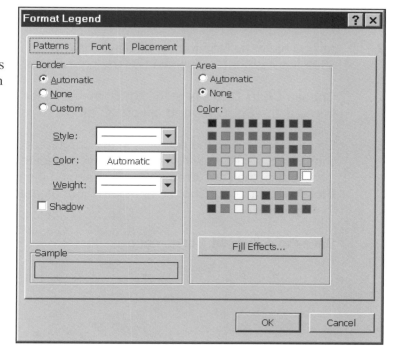

Exercise 4D

1   Ensure you are working in the "**Bali Climate**" document.

2   Double click the chart object so that you are working in Microsoft Graph.

3   Choose **Chart Type** in the **Chart** menu. Set the **Chart type** to **Line** and the **Chart sub-type** to the first sample in the available list. Click **OK** to return to the chart window.

4   This time, change the chart type so that it uses the **Line - Column** type which is found on the **Custom Types** tab of the Chart Type window. If you need help:

   Choose **Chart Type** in the **Chart** menu. Click on the **Custom Types** tab. Select **Line - Column** from the available list and then click **OK** to return to the chart window.

5   With the chart window still selected, drag the right side of the chart across to the right margin so that you can see all months displayed for the climate chart.

6   Add a data table to the chart to make it a little more readable. If you need help:

   Choose **Chart Options** in the **Chart** menu. Click on the **Data Table** tab and then click the **Show data table** option. Click **OK** to return to the chart window.

7   As you have the legend now displayed in the data table, you can now turn off the other legend (that is displayed on the right side of the chart). If you need help:

   Choose **Chart Options** in the **Chart** menu. Click on the **Legend** tab and then uncheck the **Show legend** option. Click **OK** to return to the chart window.

8   Double click any of the columns in the chart to access the **Format Data Series** window. Select a new **Area** colour of your choice and then click **OK**.   Now double click the **Plot Area** (the colour behind the columns) to access the **Format Plot Area** window. Choose another colour of your choice and click **OK** to return to the chart.

9   Save the document, but do not close it.

4.5 Positioning a Chart within a Document (3.4.4.4)

Once you have created a chart based on data within your document, the chart appears as an object where your insertion point was initially located. To have greater flexibility to position the chart window, it is often easiest to format the layout of the chart object.

Click on the chart to ensure it is selected (don't double click or you will be taken into Microsoft Graph mode).

- Choose **Object** in the **Format** menu. The Format Object window will be displayed.

- Click on the **Layout** tab.

- Select a **Wrapping style** and a **Horizontal alignment** position. In most cases, you will have greater flexibility if you choose any of the wrapping styles except **In line with text**.

- Click **OK** to return to the document.

- Use the mouse to drag the chart to a new location in the document, if you so wish.

Exercise 4E

1 Ensure you are working in the "**Bali Climate**" document.

2 Resize the chart so that it is not taking up the entire width of the page but so that you can still see all twelve months in the chart.

3 Click once on the chart object to select it and then choose **Object** in the **Format** menu to access the Format Object window. Change the **Wrapping style** for the chart to **Square** and the **Horizontal alignment** to **Centre**. Click **OK** to return to the document. Use the mouse to reposition the chart on the page at a location of your choice. Be careful if you move the chart up as it will join into the table from which it was created. You can drag the chart back out of the table area, but sometimes this can take a number of attempts before the chart is outside of the table area.

4 Save the document, closing it on completion.

Section 5   Images/Drawing

Word provides a whole range of drawing and image control features that enable it to be used as a publishing tool as well as a word processing program. For example, you can insert graphics, scanned images, photographs, sound files, video clips and all sorts of drawings and shapes that you create yourself.

5.1   Modifying Image Borders (3.4.5.1)

When you insert an image into a document, be it a clipart object, a picture from a saved file on disk, etc, etc, you can change the borders around the image to enhance its appearance within the document. The process of changing the borders of an image apply also to other types of objects in your document, such as tables, text boxes, etc.

- Select the image or object for which you wish to modify the borders.

- Choose **Borders and Shading** from the **Format** menu. The Borders and Shading window appears.

- To set a standard border, select an option from the **Settings** box. A sample of effects will appear in the Preview box.

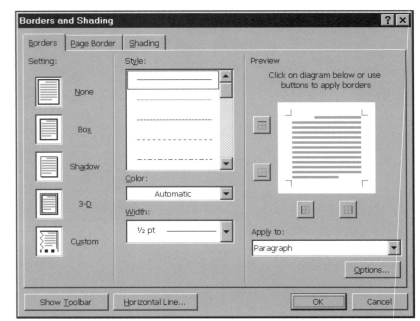

- Use the remaining boxes to further enhance your image. Please see below for details.

- Click **OK** to return to your document.

5.1.1 Border Settings

In addition to the standard settings on the **Borders** tab, you can also further enhance the borders of your selected image or object.

Style
Use the **Style** box to select a different type of line for your border. Use the scroll bar to look through the available samples and then click one of your choice.

Colour
Click on the arrow next to the **Colour** box to display a palette of available colours. Click a colour of your choice.

Width

Click on the arrow next to the **Width** box to select a thickness for your border lines.

Applying Border Settings to Different Sides of an Object

In the Preview box, you will notice that there are four buttons each representing one edge of the border. If you make appropriate selections from the Style, Colour and Width boxes, you can then click on one of these buttons to apply the settings to the edge of your choice. You could then, if you wished, make other selections for another edge of the image.

5.2   Shading (3.4.5.3)

Using the Borders and Shading window, you can also change the shading of a selected object. It is important to note, however, that not all objects or images will give you access to the **Shading** tab, such as in the instance of a clipart image.

- Use the **Fill** palette to select a background shade for the selected image (in this case we have chosen a table). Click the **More Colours** button if you wish to view a more extensive list of colours.

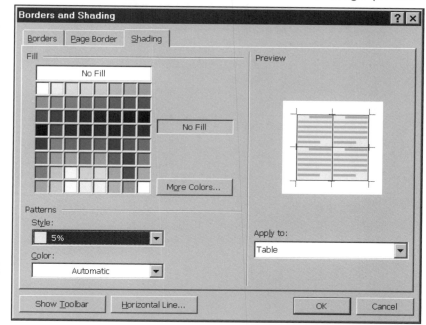

- Alternatively, in the **Patterns** area, you can click on the **Style** arrow to select a style pattern for the background and also an appropriate **Colour**.

- Click **OK** to return to your document.

NOTE

Take care when using shading for your images within a document as they may not look quite as you expected when you print. If in doubt, preview the document after applying a shading option or print just a small portion of the document that includes the formatted object before you continue with any others.

NOTE

If you have changed the *text wrapping* for any inserted object from "In Line with Text", in the Format Object window, then when you choose **Borders and** Shading from the **Format** menu, you will be presented with the **Colours and Lines** tab on the Format Object window where you can then make any necessary changes. The Borders and Shading window will not be displayed.

For more information, please see **Paragraph Borders** in Chapter One, page 57.

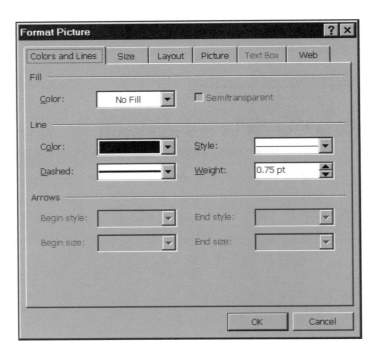

Exercise 5A

1   Open the document called "**Bali - Borders and Shading**".

2   Select the image at the top of the first page. This is a clipart image that has been inserted but still remains "in line with text".

3   Click on the image to select it and then click the **Centre** button on the Formatting Toolbar to place it between the left and right margins.

4   Choose **Borders and Shading** in the **Format** menu. Select the **Shadow** setting and change the **Colour** to blue. Click **OK** to return to the document.

5   With the image still selected, return to the **Borders and Shading** window. Select the **Box** setting and choose a line **Style** of your choice. Change the **Colour** to red and the line **Width** to **3pts**. Notice that you cannot click the **Shading** tab for this image. Click **OK** to return to the document.

6   Select the image and the right mouse click on it and choose **Format Picture**. Click on the **Layout** tab and select **Square** for the wrapping style and **Left** for the horizontal alignment. Click **OK** to return to your document. Notice that the border has now been removed. With the image still selected, choose **Borders and Shading** in the **Format** menu. Notice that the **Colours and Lines** tab appears in the Format Picture window. Click **Cancel** to close out of the window as we do not wish to use it at this stage.

7   Highlight the table that is on page 1.

8   Access the **Borders and Shading** window. Set the **Colour** to red, the **Width** to **1 _ pts** and choose **Grid** from the Settings. Click on the **Shading** tab. Select the **Grey, 15%** option and then click **OK**.

9   Save the document, closing it on completion.

5.3 Creating a Simple Drawing Using the Drawing Options
(3.4.5.2)

Using Word, you can create drawings by combining objects such as *AutoShapes*, *freeform shapes*, *curves*, *lines, arrows* and *text*.

To create a drawing:

- Click the **Drawing** ⊡ button on the **Standard Toolbar**. The **Drawing Toolbar** will be displayed (usually at the bottom of the Word screen, above the Status Bar). If you click the **Drawing** button again, the **Drawing Toolbar** will be removed.

Drawing Menu

Drawing and AutoShapes Buttons

AutoShapes and Drawing Options

- Use the Drawing and AutoShapes buttons to create a drawing on your page.

- Once you have clicked an appropriate Drawing or AutoShape button (e.g. a line or square, etc), position the mouse where you want the drawing to appear. The mouse pointer changes to a **crosshair** shape.

- Hold down the mouse button and drag until the drawing or shape is the size you require. Release the mouse button.

NOTE

The **AutoShapes** ⎡AutoShapes ▾⎤ button, will display a pop-up menu listing the main categories of AutoShapes. Select a category and then select an AutoShape from those available.

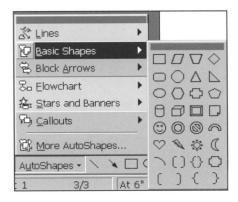

5.3.1 Resizing a Drawing Object or AutoShape

You can change the size of a drawing object or AutoShape once it has been placed on the page.

- Click on the object you wish to resize to select it. Small white squares, known as **selection handles** appear around the object.

- Click and drag on any selection handle to resize the object. The mouse pointer changes to include a two-arrow headed selection pointer when you are positioned over a selection handle.

TIP

If the graphic is distorted when you drag a corner handle, hold down the SHIFT key while you drag to keep the proportions of the object correct.

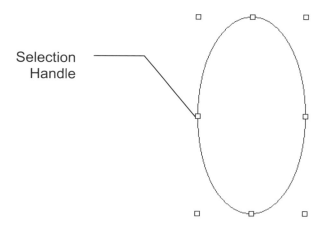

Selection
Handle

5.3.2 Moving a Drawing Object or AutoShape

You can move an AutoShape or drawing object to another location within your document.

- Position the mouse pointer inside the object. The mouse pointer will change to include a four-arrow symbol.

- Click and drag with the mouse to a new location in your document and then release the mouse button.

Exercise 5B

1   Ensure you are working in a new blank document.

2   Using the buttons on the Drawing Toolbar, practice drawing a rectangle, oval, arrow and line. If you are not happy with any object that you have drawn, simply click on it to select it and then press DELETE to remove it from the page.

3   Use the AutoShapes button to practice drawing some AutoShapes of your choice.

4   Practice resizing and move the objects you have drawn on the page.

5.4 Using Pre-Defined Shape Options (3.4.5.3)

The right-hand side of the Drawing Toolbar provides a number of buttons to help you change the appearance of AutoShapes and drawing objects.

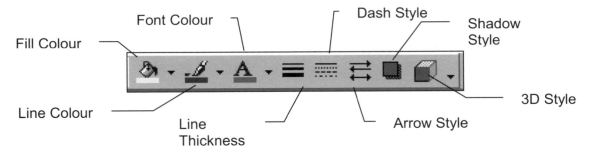

- Click on the drawing or AutoShape object that you wish to change.

- Click on any of the formatting buttons on the right-hand side of the **Drawing Toolbar**, such as the Line Thickness, the Fill Colour, etc.

Exercise 5C

1   Using the objects you previously created in Exercise 5A, practise changing their appearance using the buttons shown in 5.3 above.

2   Save the document as "**Drawings**" and then close it.

5.5   Setting the Order of Drawing and Shape Objects
(3.4.5.4 and 3.4.5.5)

There may be times when you create a drawing that consists of a number of different drawing objects or AutoShapes. Each of the objects is *layered* one on top of the other, in the order that they are drawn. However, using the *Order* function, you can change the position of an object within the layers of a drawing.

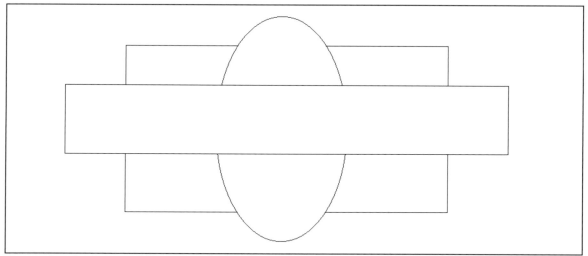

Example of a Layered Drawing Object in Word

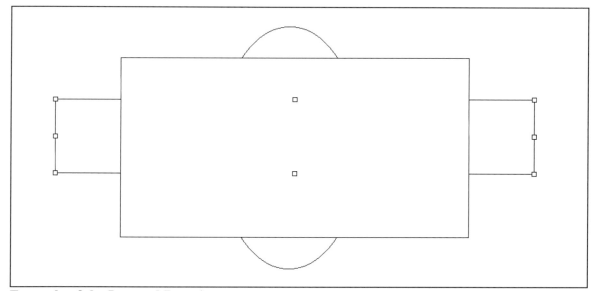

Example of the Layered Drawing once the shapes have been reordered

To change the order of an object within a layered sequence:

- Click on the object that you wish to move within the layered structure of the drawing.

- Click the **Draw** button on the **Drawing Toolbar** and then select **Order**.

- Choose an appropriate option from the pop-up menu. See below for more information.

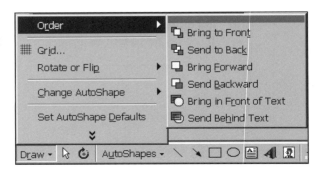

5.5.1 Drawing Order Options

Bring to Front - brings the selected object to the top of the layered structure.

Send to Back - takes the selected object to the very back of the layered structure.

Bring Forward - brings the selected object forward once place in the layered structure. For example, if you had a drawing composed of ten objects and you selected the eighth object, by choosing **Bring Forward** the object would then appear in the seventh position.

Send Backward - takes the selected object back one position in the layered structure.

Bring in Front of Text - the object sits on top of any text so that the text flows behind the object.

Send Behind Text - the object sits behind any text, so that the text shows through the object.

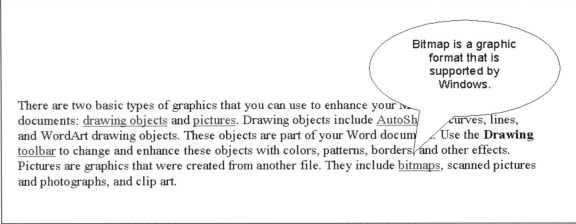

Example of a "Bring in Front of Text" order position

CHAPTER 4
Document Elements

Exercise 5D

1   In this example we are going to design a basic logo for our "Happy Holidays" company. Create the following drawing objects layered one on top of each other. The first object is a *bevel*, the second is a *sun* and the third is a *rounded rectangle*; all of which can be found in the **Basic Shapes** option under the **AutoShapes** menu.

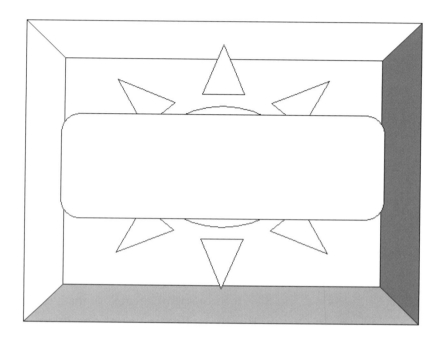

2   Select the *bevel* and change its order so that it appears at the front. Change the position again so that it is at the very back of the other objects.

3   Send the *rectangle* back one level. The drawing objects should now appear as shown in the example below.

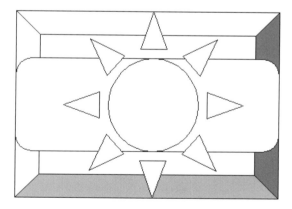

4   Save the document as "**Happy Holidays Logo**" but do not close it.

5.5.2 Rotating an Object

In addition to resizing and reshaping objects, you can also rotate them.

- Click on the object you wish to rotate to ensure that it is selected.

- Click on the **Rotate** 🔄 button on the **Drawing Toolbar**. Rotation handles will appear at specific locations on the object.

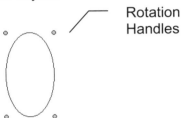

Rotation Handles

- Hover the mouse over any of the rotation handles and then click and hold down the mouse button.

- With the mouse button still held down, move the mouse to rotate the object. Release the mouse button when the object is in the correct position.

- Click the **Rotate** 🔄 button again to end the rotation.

Exercise 5E

1   Ensure you are working in the "**Happy Holidays Logo**" document.

2   Select the *rectangle* object in our logo and rotate it so that it appears as per the example below. Remember to click the **Rotate** button at the end of the rotation process to turn the rotating feature off.

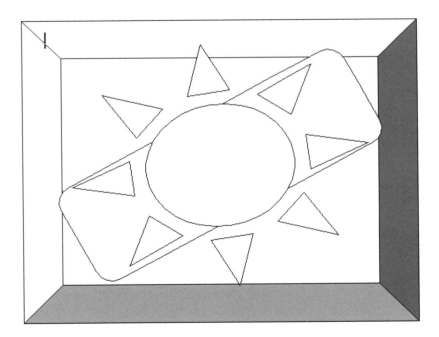

5.6   Grouping Drawing Objects (3.4.5.6)

If a drawing consists of many different objects, you may find it easier to *group* all of the objects together when you have finished, so that they are treated as a single drawing object. Grouped drawing objects can be moved, rotated, flipped and resized as a single unit. For example, you may wish to draw a circle and then add a text box inside that contains some text. The circle and the text may need to be treated as one object when you wish to move or resize the objects. Grouping the circle and the text box together would bind them as one object.

To group two or more objects together:

- Click on the first object to select it.

- Hold down the SHIFT key and then click on all subsequent objects to be included.

- Once all of the objects have been selected, click on the **Draw** button on the **Drawing Toolbar** and select the **Group** option. Selection handles will now appear around the single drawing object.

TIP

If you have a very complex combination of individual drawings that you wish to group into one, it can sometimes be quite difficult to use the SHIFT and click method to select every individual object. An easier way is to use the **Select Objects** button on the **Drawing Toolbar**. Click this button and then draw a rectangular selection shape around all of the objects to be included for grouping. When you release the mouse button, all objects that were within the selection shape will be selected. Click the **Select Objects** button again to turn off this feature. You can now group the objects using the **Draw** button on the **Drawing Toolbar**.

5.6.1   Ungrouping a Drawing Object

Once a series of individual objects have been grouped into a single object, you may need to ungroup it again so that you can make changes to any of the individual objects.

- Click on the grouped object you wish to ungroup.

- Click the **Draw** button on the **Drawing Toolbar** and select **Ungroup**. All of the individual objects will be selected. Click away from the objects to unselect them all. Now make any necessary modifications that you wish.

TIP

Once you have finished modifying an ungrouped series of objects, you can group them again using the *regroup* option, rather than selecting all the objects again and choosing **Group**. Simply click on the **Draw** button on the **Drawing Toolbar** and select **Regroup**.

Exercise 5F

1   Ensure you are working in the "**Happy Holidays Logo**" document.

2   Select all three objects that make up our logo.

3   Using the **Draw** button, group the objects together to form one object.

4   Move the logo now to another location on the page.

5   Using the **Draw** button, ungroup the object so that it returns to three individual objects.

6   Rotate the *rectangle* back to its original position.

7   Using the **Draw** button, regroup the objects back into one.

8   Save the document, closing it on completion.

5.7   Adding a Watermark to a Document (3.4.5.7)

A *watermark* is a faded piece of text or a pale picture that appears behind the main document text, usually appearing on every page of the document.

Watermarks are often used to identify the status of a document - such as using the word *Confidential* or *Draft* as the watermark across the page. In addition, watermarks can also add visual appeal to a document. For example, you may have created a menu in Word and want to use a pale picture of some food or a bottle of wine as the watermark to further enhance the menu's presentation.

NOTE

One of the most important things to remember when adding a watermark to your document or a section of your document is that you must use the HEADER area to create the watermark and not the main body of the document.

To create a watermark:

- Choose **Header and Footer** from the **Insert** menu.

- If your document has multiple sections and you want to create a different watermark for each section, ensure that you are working in the correct header section before you continue.

- Click the **Show/Hide Document Text** button on the **Header and Footer Toolbar** so that the main body of the document is hidden. This is an optional step but often makes it easier for you to place the watermark on the page without the interference of the actual document itself.

- Insert a graphic, a drawing or a WordArt object into the header. Position the object anywhere on the page.

NOTE

If you are inserting an image as your watermark, you must ensure that its wrapping layout is set to *Behind text*, so that the image sits behind the text on your page. To change the text wrapping for the image, right mouse click on it and choose **Format Picture**. Click on the **Layout** tab and select the **Wrapping style Behind text**.

In addition, for images, you can also set the colour control for an image to *watermark* so that it is more faded behind the text than the usual image. Right mouse click on the image in the header view and choose **Format Picture**. Click on the **Picture** tab and click on the **Colour** option. Select **Watermark** from the list and then click **OK** to return to the header area.

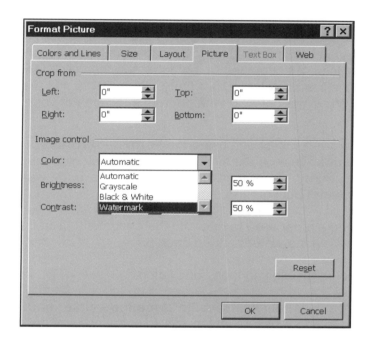

- Click the **Show/Hide Document Text** button on the **Header and Footer Toolbar** so that the main body of the document is now visible. You may wish to make some last minute changes to the size or positioning of the watermark object at this time.

- Click the **Close** button on the **Header and Footer Toolbar** to return to the document.

TIP

Depending on what object you use for a watermark, you may find that it can slightly interfere with the legibility of the document text. You may need to lighten the object either by changing its fill or text colour.

CHAPTER 4
Document Elements

Exercise 5G

1   Open the document named "**Tunisia - watermark**". In this document we are going to insert a watermark that reads "**Draft Only**" on every page.

2   Access the header area for section 1.

3   Turn off the document text so that you can concentrate on the entire page without the body text being displayed. If you need help:

Click on the **Show/Hide Document Text** button on the **Header and Footer Toolbar**.

4   Click the **WordArt** button on the **Drawing Toolbar** to insert a WordArt object. Select the second style in the first row for the available WordArt styles (this style slants upwards from bottom left to top right) and then click **OK**. Set the font to **54** and then in the **Text** box type **Draft Only**. Click **OK** to add the WordArt object to your page. Move the object on the page to a location of your choice.

5   Select the WordArt object and using the **Format WordArt** button on the **WordArt Toolbar** change the fill colour and the line colour so that they are the same shade of grey, rather than black. This will make the watermark slightly more faded on the background of each page.

6   Close from the header area to return to the document. Scroll through the document to view the watermark on each page.

7   Save the document, closing it on completion.

8   Open the document named "**Travel Information - watermark**". In this example we are going to add a picture watermark to every page of the document.

9   Access the header area and turn off the display of the document text. Insert a clip art image of your choice. If you need help:

Choose **Picture** from the **Insert** menu and then select **Clip Art**. Locate a clip art image of your choice, click on it and then click the **Insert clip** button to add it to your header. Close the **Insert Clip** window.

10   Select the clip art image and then choose **Picture** in the **Insert** menu. Click on the **Layout** tab and select **Behind text** and then **Centre** for the layout style. Now click on the **Picture** tab and set the **Colour** to **Watermark**. Click **OK** to return to the document. Move the clip art image to a location in the centre of your document and then close the header. View the pages of your document. If your watermark is too light, you will need to return to the header and change its colour back to **Automatic**. Do this by selecting the object and choosing **Picture** in the **Format** menu. Click the **Picture** tab and set the **Colour** to **Automatic**. Click **OK** and then close the header.

11   Save the document, closing it on completion.

Section 6   Captions

A *caption* is a numbered label, such as "Figure 1," that you can add to a table, figure, equation, or similar item within your document. You can vary the caption label and number format for different types of items — for example, "Table I" and "Equation 1-A." If you later add, delete, or move captions, you can easily update the caption numbers all at once.

There are two ways of adding a caption, either manually or automatically. To use the automatic facility, you simply inform Word of what type of insertion you wish to automatically caption and how you want the insertions labeled. For example, you may instruct Word to automatically add a caption to any table that is inserted into the document, using the numbering system Table 1, Table 2, etc.

To manually add a caption to an item within your document, you simply insert the item, such as a table, picture, equation, chart, worksheet, etc, and then use Word to insert a caption to be associated with that item.

Whether you use the manual or automatic method for adding captions, Word renumbers all captions if you add or remove any items that have previously been inserted with a caption.

6.1   Adding a Caption to an Item within a Document
(3.4.6.1 and 3.4.6.2)

To manually add a caption to an item within your document, you must insert the item first.

- Select the item to which the caption is to be associated.

- Choose **Caption** in the **Insert** menu. The Caption window will be displayed.

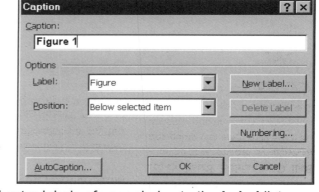

- From the **Label** box, select the label you wish to use for the caption. The default settings are **Figure**, **Equation** and **Table**. If none of these are appropriate, use the **New Label** button to add extra labels of your choice to the **Label** list.

- From the **Position** list, select whether you wish to insert the caption above or below the currently selected item.

- The numbering for your caption will appear automatically, based on other captions you have used within the document. By default, Word uses the Arabic numbering system (1, 2, 3, etc), but you can use the **Numbering** button to apply a different numbering style if you wish.

- In the **Caption** box, type the description of your selected item, next to the label and number that appears, such as **Figure 1**. It's a good idea to leave a space or two before you type your description. Note, however, that it is not compulsory for you to add a description; some captions simply use a label and numbering sequence.

- Click **OK** to insert the caption and return to your document.

Exercise 6A

1   Open the document called "**All about Sydney**".

2   Select the climate table that is displayed under the heading "**Climate**". Insert a table caption that is to appear below the table which has the description : "**Average Temperatures - Bureau of Meteorology**". If you need help:

Ensure the table is selected. Choose **Caption** in the **Insert** menu. Type the description next to the label (ensure that you leave a space between the number and the description). Select **Below selected item** and then click **OK**.

3   Add a caption to the table that appears under the "**Public Transport**" heading. Use a table label that is to appear below the selected item. The label description should be: "**Public Transport Web Sites**". Notice when you return to the document that the new caption is now **Table 1** and the climate table is **Table 2**. You may need to move the caption below the public transport table to make it in line with the table itself.

Bus and Ferry Services	**www.busandferry.com.au**
City Rail Train Services	**www.cityrail.com.au**
Country Link Rail Services	www.countrylink.com.au

Table 1 Public Transport Web Sites

4   Save the document, but do not close it.

6.1.1   Editing a Caption's Description

If you want to change the text you have used to identify the caption. You can either use the Caption window to make the changes or edit directly into the document.

To edit a caption using the Caption window:

- Select the entire caption and then choose **Caption** in the **Insert** menu. The Caption window will be displayed.

- Change the description in the **Caption** box and then click **OK**.

To manually edit a caption:

- Click anywhere within the caption text.

- Make any necessary changes you wish to the description.

NOTE

Captions actually use field codes to create the numbering sequence as each one is added to your document. To view the field codes within your document, use **ALT+F9**.

6.1.2 Deleting a Caption

You can easily remove a caption from an item within your document.

- Select the caption you wish to remove (ensure that the entire caption line is highlighted).

- Press the DELETE key.

6.1.3 Updating Captions

If you edit your document and insert new items with associated captions, Word will automatically update the numbering for subsequent captions within your document. However, Word will not automatically update captions if you have deleted or moved a captioned item within your document.

To update the numbering sequence of all captions within a document:

- Highlight the entire document.

- Press F9 to update all field codes within your document.

Exercise 6B

1   Ensure you are working in the "**All about Sydney**" document.

2   Select the entire caption for **Table 2** and then choose **Caption** from the **Insert** menu. Edit the caption description so that it reads ""**Average Daily Temperatures - Bureau of Meteorology**" and the click **OK** to return to the document.

3   Manually edit the caption description for **Table 1** so that it reads "**Sydney Public Transport Web Sites**".

4   Highlight the entire caption for **Table 1** and then delete it. Update the remaining captions in the document. If you need help:

Press CTRL+A to highlight the entire document. Press F9 to update all field codes. The **Table 2** caption, should now be renumbered to **Table 1**.

5   Save the document, but do not close it.

6.1.4 Changing the Label for Captions

If you have used a particular label throughout your document for a specific type of item, such as **Figure 1**, **Figure 2**, etc, there may be occasions when you may need to change the label globally, updating all captions using that particular label.

- Select a caption that uses the label you wish to change globally throughout your document.

- Choose **Caption** in the **Insert** menu.

- Select a different choice from the **Label** list. Remember that you can use **New Label** to add other labels to the Label list.

- Click **OK** to return to the document. Word automatically updates all captions that used the label of the selected caption.

NOTE

If you only wish to change the label for one caption within your document, you need to delete it and create a new caption from scratch.

6.2   Using Automatic Captions (3.4.6.3)

As we identified at the beginning of this section, Word can be used to automatically add captions to specific types of item that are inserted into your document. For example, you may wish to use a **Figure** caption for all pictures that are inserted and a **Table** caption for all tables that you create.

To create automatic captions:

- Choose **Caption** in the **Insert** menu. The Caption window will be displayed.

- Click the **AutoCaption** button. The AutoCaption window appears.

- Click next to an item you wish to automatically create a caption for in the **Add caption when inserting** list.

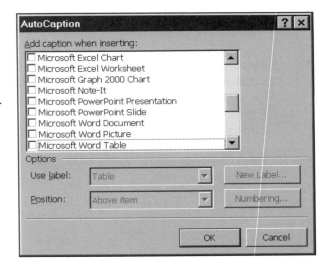

- Use the **Options** to control the label to be used and its position. You can use the **New Label** button to add new labels of your choice and the **Numbering** button to control the numbering for the captions.

- Select another item from the **Add caption when inserting** list if you wish to automatically add captions to another type of item within your document. Use the **Options** box to control the label and its position.

- Click **OK** to return to the document.

NOTE

If you wish to turn off any of the automatic captioning options, simply retrace the steps above but uncheck the items you wish to remove auto-captioning for.

6.2.1 Inserting an Item with an Automatic Caption

Once you have identified to Word which items are to have automatic captions, you are ready to insert the items within your document. Simply insert an item, such as a table, a worksheet, etc and the caption will appear, displaying its label and number. Simply click after the number to type a description of your choice.

Exercise 6C

1   Ensure you are working in the "**All about Sydney**" document.

2   In this example you have decided to set automatic captions for when you insert a Word picture or a Word table. If you need help:

Choose **Caption** from the **Insert** menu. Click on the **AutoCaption** button. Scroll through the available list of items and check the "**Microsoft Word Picture**" option. Ensure **Use label** is set to **Figure** and the **Position** is set to **Below**. Now click the "**Microsoft Word Table**" option and set the label to **Table**. Click the **Numbering** button and change the **Format** to **I, II, III** and then click **OK**. Click **OK** again to return to the document.

3   Locate the text under the heading "**Accommodation**". Click in the blank space below the **Hotel Isis** paragraph. Insert the following two-column table into the document (do not worry about entering any data into the table at this point).

4   Type the table caption description as "**Hotel Isis Rates**".

5   Click in the blank space below the **Newton Hotel** paragraph. Insert another two-column table into the document (again do not worry about entering any data into the table at this point).

6   Type the table caption description as "**Newton Hotel Rates**".

7   Insert another two-column table below the "**Hyde Park Place**" paragraph. Type the table caption description as "**Hyde Park Place Hotel Rates**".

8   Go to the end of the document and create a page break.

9   Insert a clip art picture of your choice. Once inserted, the **Figure** caption should appear. Enter in a description of your choice.

10   Return to the top of the document and locate the first table caption below the "**Climate**" heading. In this example, you have decided to change all the **Table** captions so that they read "**Reference**". If you need help:

Select the entire caption and then choose **Caption** in the **Insert** menu. Click on the **New Label** button and enter **Reference**. Click **OK** and then **OK** again to

CHAPTER 4
Document Elements

return to your document. Scroll through the document to ensure all the captions have updated.

11 Before we finish this exercise, we need to turn off the automatic caption facility, otherwise all subsequent documents will use this feature for the insertion of tables and pictures.

Choose **Caption** in the **Insert** menu. Click the **AutoCaption** button. Uncheck the two items that were previously selected for the AutoCaption feature. Click **OK** and then **OK** again to return to the document.

12 Save the current document, closing it on completion.

Self Check Exercises

1 If you are using the Sort Ascending button on the Tables and Borders Toolbar to sort a column of text, the first row of data is also included in the sort - True or False?

☐ True.

☐ False.

2 When you are using the Sort window to sort a number of columns at the same time, what is the maximum number of columns you can sort?

☐ Unlimited number of columns.

☐ Five columns.

☐ Three columns.

☐ One column.

3 If you are creating a form that can be completed "online" what type of field would the ▭ **ab|** button on the Forms Toolbar allow you to insert?

☐ Check Box Form field.

☐ Text Box Form field.

☐ Drop-Down Form field.

4 Before you can "publish" a form so that it can be completed by other users, what must you do to the form?

☐ Save it as a template.

☐ Shade all of the fields in the form.

☐ Protect the form.

5 If you embed a spreadsheet file into your document and change the source data, the embedded information automatically updates - True or False?

☐ True.

☐ False.

6 You can create a chart within a document based on what type of data?

☐ An embedded Excel object.

☐ Data within a table.

☐ Data copied and pasted from Excel.

☐ A linked Excel object.

7 To position a chart within a document, which tab do you choose to select a wrapping style?

☐ Colors and Lines

☐ Picture

☐ Size

☐ Layout

8 Name the five shading options below.

241

Practical Exercises

Please complete the following exercises as a review of the topics covered in this chapter. Should you require assistance with any of the steps within these exercises, you may refer back to the corresponding sections within this chapter.

Exercise 1

1   Open the document called "**Plaza Hotel Morocco**". Take a few moments to familiarise yourself with the contents of this document.

2   Select the first two cells in the first row of the table and merge them together. Select the last four cells in the first row and merge them together as well.

3   Select the last row of the table and split the row into **10** columns and **4** rows.

4   Select the tabbed data under the heading "**Flight Details**" and convert this text into a table. Sort the data in the newly created table so that it is in ascending order of the first column.

5   View the table under the heading "**Morocco Platinum Extras**". Add formulas into the last two cells of the table that calculate the total extras for an adult and a child. Format both totals so that they align on the right of the cells.

6   Select all rows in the table except for the **first** and the **last** (this means that you are excluding the totals row and the row containing the word "**Per**"). Create a chart based on this data. Change the chart type to a "**cylinder**" format instead of a "**column**" format. Click back into the document once the chart has been created. Resize the chart object so that it appears below the table and takes up the width of the page.

7   Save the document but do not close it.

8   Click below the heading "**Car Rental**". Insert a spreadsheet object based on the existing file named "**Car Rental Rates**".

9   Select the spreadsheet object and insert a caption for it. Set the label to "**Figure 1**" and type the caption description as "**U-Drive Car Rental Rates**".

10   Save the document, closing it on completion.

Exercise 2

1 Open the document named "**Telephone Message Form**". This document contains a form that needs to be completed before it is saved as a template.

2 Select the empty cell to the right of the "**Date**" field. Insert a Text Form Field at this location. Change the properties for this field so that the field type is "**Current Date**" and the field format is "**d-MMM-yy**".

3 Select the text field to the right of the "**Taken By**" field. Change the properties of this field so that your name is entered as the default text.

4 Protect the form and then save it as a template named "**Telephone Message Form**". Close the document on completion.

5 Create a new document based on the **Telephone Message Form** template. Fill in the form with some sample data of your own choice. Once the form has been completed, save it as "**Test Message**". Close the document on completion.

Exercise 3

1 Open the document named "**Consultant Newsletter**".

2 Create a text box that appears to the right of the second paragraph which contains the following text:

> **BEST of the BEST**
> Win a TWO-WEEK, all expenses paid holiday in Malta for making bookings 20% over target within the next two months.

3 Format the text box so that text can wrap squarely around the box and also so it appears on the right-side of the page.

4 Save the document, but do not close it.

5 Insert two text boxes next to each other under the heading "**This Month's Special…**". Link the two text boxes together. Insert the file named "**All about Malta**" into the first text box. Resize the text boxes so that the entire *story* about Malta is displayed evenly across the two boxes.

6 Select the image to the left of the text "**Dear Consultant**". Format this picture so that it has a fill effect of your choice and has a black border around the outside.

7 Save the document, closing it on completion.

CHAPTER 4
Document Elements

Chapter 5

Special Tools

Syllabus
Module AM3
Word Processing – Advanced Level

Chapter Five: AM 3.5 – Special Tools

CHAPTER 5
Special Tools

CHAPTER 5
Special Tools

Section 1   Mail Merge Refresher

Mail merge is used to join or *merge* two sources of information into a single document. Its most common uses are for producing form letters and mailing labels.

A form letter is a letter with standard information to be sent to many people but where each one must have some individual information, such as their name, company, address, etc.

The source of this individual information is known as the ***data file*** or ***data source***. A data file contains individual details for each person that you want to send a letter to. These individual details are known as ***records***. The records in a data file are merged with a form letter to produce personalised letters.

1.1   Using the Mail Merge Helper

One of the easiest ways to work with the mail merge process is by using the Mail Merge Helper. The Helper window steps you through the necessary tasks needed to create or edit form letters, data files and mailing labels.

To start the Mail Merge Helper:

- Select **Mail Merge** in the **Tools** menu.

- Choose **Options**. The Mail Merge Helper window appears.

- Use the available buttons to perform the various mail merge steps.

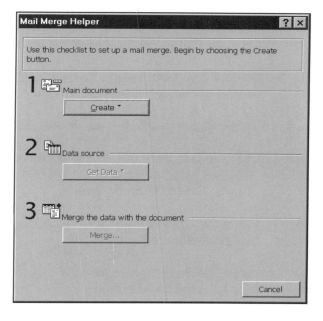

Exercise 1A

This exercise is designed as a refresher for the basic mail merge procedure.

In the first part of this exercise you will create a simple form letter.

1   Start a new blank document and type the following letter.

Ref: TR1/73

Dear

Please find enclosed our latest corporate travel brochure, including the latest revisions for flight schedules for all major airlines.

As you know, etc, etc…..

2   Save the document as **Corporate Travel Letter**. Do not close the letter.

In this part of the exercise you will use the Mail Merge Helper to create the form letter from the contents of the current document.

3   Select **Mail Merge** from the **Tools** menu.

4   Click the **Create** button under the **Main Document** heading.

5   Select **Form Letters** and then choose **Active Window** to show Word that the current document contains the content for your form letter.

In this part of the exercise you will use the Mail Merge Helper to create your data file.

6   Click the **Get Data** button under the **Data Source** heading.

7   Choose **Create Data Source**.

8   When the **Create Data Source** window appears, click **OK** to accept the default field names provided by Word.

9   When the **Save As** window appears, name your data file **Corporate Clients** and then click the **Save** button.

In this part of the exercise you will enter some details into your data file.

10   Click the **Edit Data Source** button.

11   Enter the following details for the first record.

Title:	Mr
FirstName:	Jack
LastName:	O'Neill
JobTitle:	Human Resources Manager
Company:	Finlay, Smith and Wilson
Address1:	2 Pembroke Street
City:	Dublin 2

12   Click the **Add New** button to create another record.

13   Enter the following details for record 2.

Title:	Miss
FirstName:	Helen
LastName:	Kelly
JobTitle:	Business Manager
Company:	Retext International
Address1:	25 Belfield Road
City:	Dublin 4

14   Click **OK** to close the Data Form window.

In this part of the exercise you will insert the merge fields from the data file into the form letter.

15   Use the **Insert Merge Field** button on the Mail Merge Toolbar to add the following merge fields into your letter.

Ref: TR1/73

«Title» «FirstName» «LastName»
«JobTitle»
«Company»
«Address1»
«City»

Dear «Title» «LastName»

Please find enclosed our latest corporate travel brochure, including the latest revisions for flight schedules for all major airlines.

As you know, etc, etc…..

In this part of the exercise you will merge the data file with the form letter to create two personalised letters.

16   Click the **Mail Merge Helper** button on the Mail Merge Toolbar.

17   Click the **Merge** button. Ensure the **Merge to** box is set to **New Document**.

18   Click the **Merge** button.

19   Check through the results document which should contain the two personalised letters.

20   Save the results document as **Corporate Travel Brochure**. Close the document on completion.

21   Save and then close the **Corporate Travel Letter** document. When you are prompted to save the data file, **Corporate Clients**, click **Yes**.

1.2 Editing a Mail Merge Data File (3.5.1.1)

A data file can be opened in the same way as for any other document. You can make changes to the document simply by editing the existing data or by inserting additional records. In addition, you can also edit the data source from the Mail Merge Helper window or when the data has been merged (but before it is sent to the printer).

To edit a data file from the Mail Merge Helper window:

- Open the form letter you wish to use for merging.

- Click on the Mail Merge Helper button on the Mail Merge Toolbar. The Mail Merge Helper window appears.

- Click the **Get Data** button and then select **Open Data Source**. Choose the appropriate data file document and then click **OK** to return to the Mail Merge Helper.

- Click the **Edit** button and then click the data file from the list that appears. The data file will open and the **Database** Toolbar will appear at the top of the document. The buttons on this Toolbar will help you to work with your data file. Please see the Database Toolbar below.

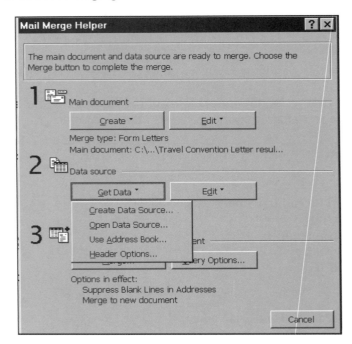

1.2.1 The Data Form Button

You can use the **Data Form** button to access a special window that helps you to add, edit or delete records within your data file.

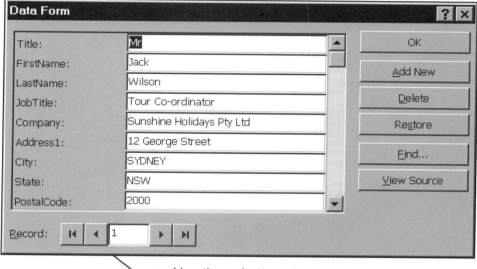

Use these buttons to move amongst the records within your data file.

1.2.2 Managing Fields

Use the **Manage Fields** button to add, remove or rename field names in your data file.

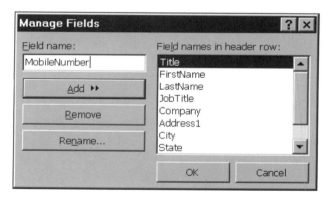

1.2.3 Adding/Deleting Records

Use the **Add New Record** or **Delete Record** buttons to update your data file.

1.2.4 Sorting Records (3.5.1.2)

You can use the **Sort Ascending** and **Sort Descending** buttons to rearrange records in a particular order. Simply click in the column by which you wish to sort and then use the appropriate **Sort** button.

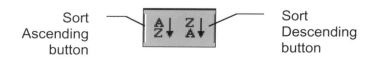

Sort Ascending button

Sort Descending button

CHAPTER 5
Special Tools

1.2.5 Finding a Record

If you are working with a particularly large number of records, you may find it easier to locate a particular record using the **Find Record** 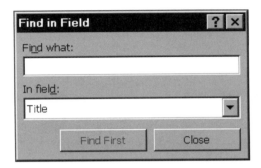 button, rather than scrolling through the records yourself.

- Click the **Find Record** button. Enter the information you are searching for in the **Find what** box and select the appropriate field to search in from the **In field** box. Click **Find First** to continue.

- Use the **Find Next** button to continue searching and then click **Close** on completion.

1.2.6 Returning to the Main Document

Click the **Mail Merge Main Document button** to return to the main form letter.

NOTE

You can also click the **Edit Data Source** button within the main document, if you want to make changes to the data without returning to the data source file.

CHAPTER 5
Special Tools

Exercise 1B

In this first part of the exercise you will attach a data file to a form letter that will be used for merging.

1   Open the document named **Travel Convention Letter**. This is the form letter for our merge exercise.

2   Click **Mail Merge** in the **Tools** menu.

3   Click on the **Create** button and then choose **Form Letters**. When the next window appears, click on the **Active Window** button to show Word that the current window contains the form letter you wish to use for merging.

In this part of the exercise you will attach the data file you wish to use for merging with the form letter. The data file has already been created for you.

4   Click the **Get Data** button.

5   Choose **Open Data Source**. Select the file named **Travel Consultants** and then click **Open**.

In this part of the exercise you will add the merge fields you wish to use from your data file into your form letter.

6   Click the **Edit Main Document** button to return to the form letter.

7   Using the **Insert Merge Field** button on the Mail Merge Toolbar, add the following merge fields to the start of the letter.

«Title» «FirstName» «LastName»
«JobTitle»
«Company»
«Address1»
«City» «State» «PostalCode»
«Country»

Dear «FirstName»

In this part of the exercise you will edit the data file to update the existing records.

8   Click on the **Mail Merge Helper** button on the Mail Merge Toolbar.

9   Click on the **Edit** button in the **Data Source** section.

10   Click on the data file name **Travel Consultants** to view the data records in the Data Form window. Take a few moments to familiarise yourself with the records in the Data Form.

11   Click **OK** to close the Data Form.

In this part of the exercise you will edit the records in your data file directly in the document in which they reside.

12   Click the **Edit Data Source** button on the Mail Merge Toolbar. When the Data Form window appears, click **View Source** to open the data file document.

13   Click the **Add New Record** button and insert the following details:

Title	Mrs
Firstname	Angela
Lastname	Connor
JobTitle	Senior Travel Consultant
Company	Mount Travel Ltd
Address1	2 Merrion Square
City	DUBLIN
State	
PostalCode	2
Country	Ireland

14   When you have finished entering the new record, click the **View Data Source** button to view your records in the document in which they are stored.

15   Click anywhere in the "**Karen Kelly**" record and then use the **Delete Record** button to remove it from the data file. Click Undo to reverse the deletion.

16   Use the **Manage Fields** button to add a new field named "**MobileNumber**". Click **OK** to return to the data file document.

17   Click in the **Company** field and then click the **Sort Ascending** button to reorder the records according to their company name.

18   Click in the **LastName** field and then click the **Sort Descending** button to reorder the records according to the consultants' surnames.

19   Use the **Data Form** button to view the records in a form view. Locate the "**Viva Holidays**" record and change their street address to "**119 Plaza Nova**". Click **OK** to return to the document.

In this part of the exercise you will return to the form letter and perform the merge.

20   Click the **Mail Merge Main Document** button to return to the form letter.

21   Use the **Merge to New Document** button to create an individual letter for each person in your data file. Look through the resulting letters but then close the document without saving it.

1.3 Using Query Options (3.5.1.3)

Whether you have only a few records in your data source file or many, you may occasionally wish to limit the number of records that are used within the merge based on specific *criteria*. For example, you may only wish to send the letter to people in a certain location (such as a City or Country) or you may only wish to send to people with a particular job title or company name. The type of criteria you use is unlimited - it simply depends on what types of fields you have used in your data source file. To specify your query options:

- Click the **Mail Merge Helper** button to access the Mail Merge Helper window.

- Click on the **Query Options** button to display the Query Options window.

- Click on the **Filter Records** tab.

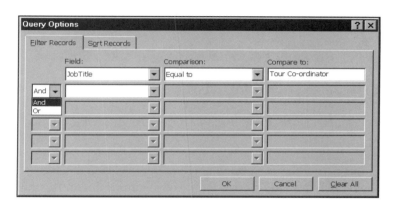

- Use the **Field**, **Comparison** and **Compare to** boxes to specify your criteria. If you have more than one criteria item, you can use the join **And** or **Or** and then specify your next criteria item. Use **And** if you want the records that match BOTH pieces of criteria. You can use **Or**, however, when you want the resulting records to match either pieces of criteria that you specify.

- Click **OK** when you are ready to continue. You will be returned to the Mail Merge Helper window where you can either continue with the merge, or you can close back to your document.

1.4 Sorting Records during a Merge (3.5.1.2)

You can sort records when you are editing the data file or when you are using the Query Options window.

- Click the **Mail Merge Helper** button to access the Mail Merge Helper window.

- Click on the **Query Options** button to display the Query Options window. Click on the **Sort Records** tab.

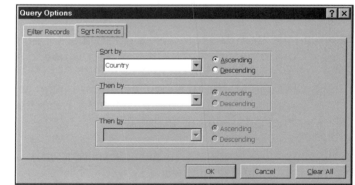

- Specify the fields you wish to sort by and whether they are to be ascending or descending.

- Click **OK** to continue. You will be returned to the Mail Merge Helper window where you can either continue with the merge, or you can close back to your document.

Exercise 1C

In this first part of the exercise you will create a letter for only those consultants who live in Australia.

1   Click the Mail Merge Helper button.

2   Click the **Query Options** button. Ensure the **Filter Records** tab is selected.

3   Use the arrow for the **Field** box and select the field named **Country**.

4   Ensure the **Comparison** box is set to **Equal to**.

5   In the **Compare to** box type **Australia**.

6   Click **OK** to close the Query Options window and then click **Close** to return to the form letter.

In this part of the exercise you will merge the form letter to a new document. The resulting letters should only be addressed to those consultants living in Australia.

7   Click the **Merge to New Document** button to perform the merge. Look through the results - there should be three letters, each addressed to a company in Australia. Close the document on completion, without saving it.

In this part of the exercise you will include another query option for when you perform the next merge. In addition to writing to contacts living in Australia you also only want to send the letter to *Tour Co-ordinators*.

8   Click the **Mail Merge Helper** button.

9   Click on the **Query Options** button and then click on the **Filter Records** tab.

10   Leave the first criteria line and ensure the "join" for our two criteria statements is **And**.

11   Use the arrow for the **Field** box to select the **JobTitle** field.

12   In the **Comparison** box select "**Equal to**" and in the **Compare to** box type "**Tour Co-ordinator**". Click **OK** and then **Close** to return to the document.

13   Click the **Merge to New Document** button to create the individual letters. Look through the results - there should be two letters. Close the document on completion, without saving it.

In this part of the exercise we are going to create a query so that we can send a letter to all of our contacts except those in Australia.

14   Click on the **Mail Merge Helper** button.

15   Click on the **Query Options** button.

16   Click on the **Filter Records** tab.

17   Click on the **Clear All** button to clear the previous criteria settings.

18   Click on the arrow for the **Field** box and select **Country**.

19   Click on the arrow for the **Comparison** box and select **Not Equal To**.

20   In the **Compare To** box type **Australia**.

In this part of the exercise you will specify that you would like to sort the merged letters first by country and then by company.

21   Click on the **Sort Records** tab.

22   In the first sort box select **Country**, in the "**then by**" box select **Company**. Ensure both are set to ascending order.

23   Click **OK** and then **Close** to return to the document.

In this part of the exercise you will merge the form letters.

24   Click the **Merge to New Document** button. Scroll through the resulting records. Check that there are no letters addressed to Australia. The letters should be in sorted by country and company. Close the document on completion without saving.

25   Save the **Travel Convention Letter**, closing it on completion. Save and close the data source file named **Travel Consultants**.

2.1 Macros

A macro is simply a series of commands and instructions that you group together to accomplish a particular task. Macros allow you to automate tasks that you perform on a regular basis. Instead of manually performing a series of repetitive actions, you can create a single macro that accomplishes all the actions for you. For example, you may regularly format pictures in a certain way, perhaps entailing five or more mouse actions or windows. One macro could perform all five actions with one mouse click or keystroke.

Using a macro you can:

- Combine multiple commands (such as inserting and formatting a table) with a single command.

- Speed up formatting and editing procedures.

- Automate a more complex series of tasks.

Word offers two ways for you to create a macro: the **Macro Recorder** or the **Visual Basic Editor**.

2.1.1 Recording a Macro

The easiest way to create a macro is to *record* it. Once you have started recording your macro, Word captures all the keyboard instructions and mouse actions that you make. When you stop recording the macro, the instructions you have captured are stored in a macro under a name of your choice. The macro can then be replayed as many times as you wish.

2.1.2 The Visual Basic Editor

Visual Basic is a powerful programming tool that enables you to create very flexible and often complex macro routines. In fact, when you record a macro, Word writes the instructions using Visual Basic but this happens in the background and you don't need to know about what is being written if you are using the recorder to create basic macros.

For the purpose of this syllabus, we will concentrate on the process of recording a macro and not the more complex issue of working with Visual Basic.

2.2 Recording a Simple Macro (3.5.2.1)

Before you start recording a macro, it's a good idea to think through exactly what you want the macro to do. Often it helps to go through the process manually first, so that you are confident with all of the steps that need to be recorded.

To record a macro:

- Select **Macro** in the **Tools** menu. Select **Record New Macro**. The Record Macro window will be displayed.

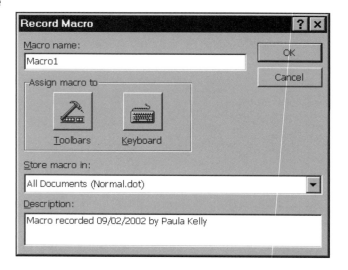

- By default, Word provides a name for your macro, such as *Macro1*, *Macro2*, etc. Enter a name of your choice for the macro you are creating. See **Naming a Macro** below for more information.

- Select an appropriate location for your macro to be stored in the **Store macro in** box. See **Storing a Macro** below for more information.

- Enter a description for the macro. This information will help you, or other users, identify the nature of the macro at a later date.

- You can select to assign a macro to the **Toolbars** or a **Keyboard** function, by selecting an appropriate button in the **Assign macro to** panel. Refer to **Assigning a Macro to a Keyboard Shortcut** on page 266 and **Assigning a Macro to a Button on a Toolbar** on page 268 for more information.

- Click **OK** to start recording the macro.

When the Macro Recorder starts, the Record Macro window closes, and the **Stop Recording** Toolbar appears. **REC** also appears in the Status Bar to show you that you are in Record Mode. Word will now start recording all of your actions.

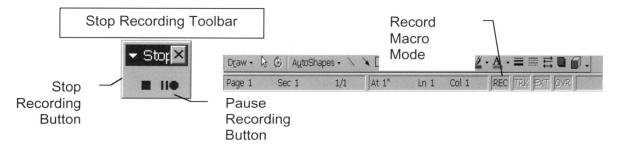

- When you have finished recording, click the **Stop** Recording button. See 2.4 Stopping the Macro Recorder for more information.

Naming a Macro

The name you give to a macro helps you to identify it later on when you need to run it, or when you want to copy or move it to another document or template.

- A macro name must begin with a letter.

- A macro name can contain numbers.

- A macro name can't include spaces or symbols.

- A macro name can be a maximum of 80 characters long.

Storing a Macro

The location where you store a macro is important as it controls when and where the macro can be run. There are three main locations for storing a macro:

- **Active Document**: you can store the macro in the active document so that it will only run when the document is open.

- **All Documents (Normal.dot)**: you can store the macro in the Normal.dot template so that it is available to be run within any document that is open.

- **Template**: you can store a macro in a specific template (other than Normal.dot). However, the template needs to be attached to the current document for this choice to be available within the **Store macro in** box.

2.3 Pausing a Macro

If you need to, you can pause the Macro Recorder at any time by clicking the **Pause Recording** button. You can then perform as many actions as you wish without affecting your macro. Click the **Resume Recording** button to continue recording.

2.4 Stopping the Macro Recorder

When you have finished recording your macro you must stop the Macro Recorder. There are two ways to do this:

1. Select **Macro** in the **Tools** menu and then select **Stop Recording**.

or

2. Press the **Stop Recording** button.

2.5 Running a Named Macro (3.5.2.3)

Remember that a macro can either reside in an individual document, within a specific template or in the Normal.dot template. If the macro you wish to run is in the Normal.dot template, you can use it within any document. If the macro is in another template or document, you need to ensure that the document is open or the appropriate template is attached before the macro can be run.

To run a macro:

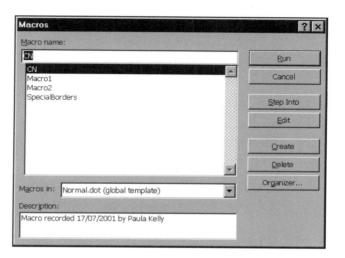

- Select **Macro** in the **Tools** menu.

- Choose **Macros** and the Macros window will be displayed.

- Select an appropriate name from the **Macro name** box. If you need to look in another document or template, select the appropriate file from the **Macros in** box.

- Click **Run** to replay the macro.

Exercise 2A

Imagine that you regularly work on large documents that often include a section that is formatted to the landscape paper size amongst other sections that are typed in portrait mode. You have decided to record a macro that performs this formatting process, rather than performing the steps manually each time.

In this first part of the exercise you will start the macro recorder as well as naming the macro for later use.

1   Ensure you are working in a new, blank document.

2   Choose **Macro** in the **Tools** menu. Select **Record New Macro**.

3   Name the macro: **LandscapeSection** and ensure that it is stored in the **All Documents (Normal.dot)** template. In the **Description** box, add the following details that will help you to identify this macro later on.

      "This macro inserts a section that is formatted to landscape and then inserts another section that returns to portrait mode."

4   Click **OK** to start recording. You should see the Stop Recording Toolbar and also the abbreviation **REC** in the Status Bar. Perform the following steps:

In this part of the exercise you will record the steps you would usually perform manually to insert a section break and change the paper orientation to landscape.

5   Choose **Break** from the **Insert** menu and then select **Next** Page.

6   Choose **Page Setup** in the **File** menu. Select the **Paper Size** tab and then click on **Landscape**. Click **OK** to continue.

7   Press the **ENTER** key once to insert a blank line.

In this part of the exercise you record the steps you would usually perform manually to insert another section break, changing the page orientation back to portrait.

8   Choose **Break** again from the **Insert** menu and then select **Next Page**.

9   Choose **Page Setup** in the **File** menu. Select the **Paper Size** tab and then click on **Portrait**. Click **OK** to continue.

In this part of the exercise you will stop recording for the current macro.

10   Click the **Stop Recording** button to end the macro.

11   Close the current document without saving it. Note that the macro has been saved with the Normal document template.

In this part of the exercise you will run the macro you have just created.

12   Create a new, blank document. On the first page type "*This is a portrait section.*".

13   Select **Macro** in the **Tools** menu.

14   Choose **Macros** and then select the macro named **LandscapeSection**.

15   Click **Run** to replay the macro.

16   When the macro has finished, go to Print Preview mode and view the changes in your document. The second section of the document should be formatted for landscape and the next section should return to portrait mode.

17   Close the document on completion, without saving the changes.

CHAPTER 5
Special Tools

2.6 Assigning a Macro to a Keyboard Shortcut

In addition to giving a macro a specific name, you can also assign a macro to a keyboard shortcut so that it can be easily replayed once the keyboard combination is pressed.

The steps to create the macro are the same as those in **Recording a Simple Macro** on page 260. Once the macro has been named, you can then click the **Keyboard** button if you want to assign the macro to a keyboard shortcut.

Click the Keyboard button to assign the macro to a keyboard shortcut.

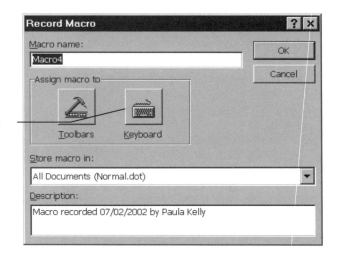

The Customise Keyboard window will be displayed.

Press the keyboard combination you wish to use. Word places the shortcut in this box and then shows below what the shortcut is already assigned to or if the shortcut is unassigned.

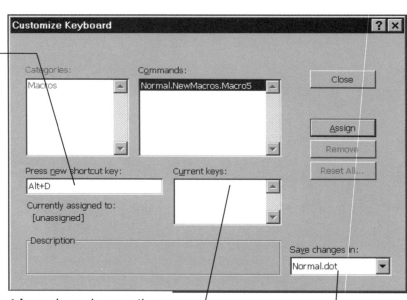

The **Current keys** box shows other customized keyboard assignments for the current template or document.

Use this box to select the template or document where the shortcut is to be stored.

NOTE

Be careful when you are assigning shortcut keys to your macros. If you reassign a keyboard shortcut that is used for another function (such as **CTRL+X** for **Cut**) then that function will no longer be available to you using that keyboard shortcut - the macro will have overwritten it.

Exercise 2B

As you are working on long documents on a regular basis and you use section breaks frequently, you have decided to create a macro that inserts a Next Page section break when a specific keyboard shortcut is pressed.

In this part of the exercise you will record the new macro.

1   Ensure you are working in a new, blank document.

2   Choose **Macro** in the **Tools** menu and then choose **Record New Macro**.

3   Name the macro **NextPageSectionBreak** and ensure it is stored in the **All Document (Normal.dot)** template.

4   Click on the **Keyboard** button to access the Customise Keyboard window.

5   Press CTRL+B - notice that this shortcut combination is assigned already to **Bold** function. Backspace out the shortcut combination and press ALT+B - this combination should be unassigned. (If not, keep trying with ALT+ a keyboard letter until you find one that is not already assigned).

6   Click **Assign** and then **Close**. You will now be in Record Mode.

In this part of the exercise you will record the steps you would usually perform manually to create a next page section break.

7   Choose **Break** in the **Insert** menu and then select **Next Page**.

8   Click the Stop Recording button to end the macro.

9   Close the document without saving the changes.

In this part of the exercise you will run the macro you have just created within a new document.

10   Start a new blank document.

11   Type "*This is section 1*" and then press ALT+B or whatever you used as your keyboard shortcut.

12   Now type "*This is section 2*" and then press the keyboard shortcut again to insert another section break.

13   Close the current document, without saving the changes.

2.7 Assigning a Macro to a Button on a Toolbar (3.5.2.4)

In addition to assigning macros to keyboard shortcuts, you can also assign a macro to a button on any Toolbar. Buttons are easier to remember perhaps than keyboard shortcuts. Not only can you use a picture on the button, which will help users identify with its function, but also you can include text as well.

The steps to create the macro are the same as those in **Recording a Simple Macro** on page 260. Once the macro has been named, you can then click the **Toolbars** button if you want to assign the macro to a Toolbar.

It is important to ensure that the Toolbar to which you wish to assign a macro is already displayed before you assign the recorded macro.

Click the Toolbars button to assign the macro to a Toolbar.

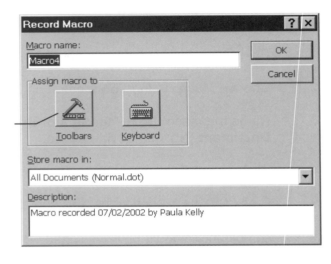

The Customise window will be displayed.

- Ensure the **Commands** tab is selected and the **Categories** list is set to **Macros**.

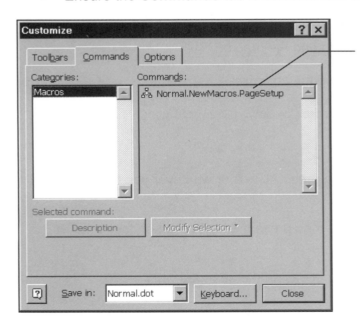

Click on the name of the macro you are recording and then drag the macro onto the appropriate Toolbar.

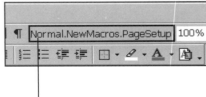

The Macro button appears in a text format on the Toolbar of your choice.

2.7.1 Customising a Macro Button

After you have added a macro to a Toolbar, you can customise its appearance by right-clicking on the button and using the shortcut menu.

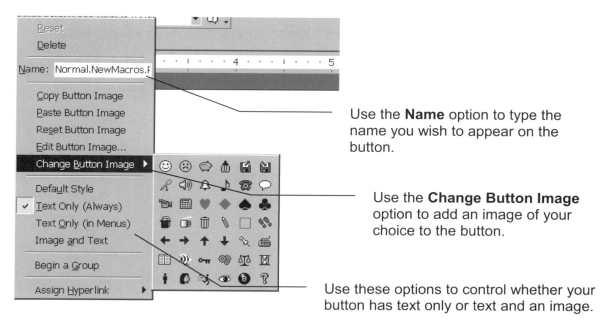

Use the **Name** option to type the name you wish to appear on the button.

Use the **Change Button Image** option to add an image of your choice to the button.

Use these options to control whether your button has text only or text and an image.

When you have finished customising your button, click **Close** in the **Customise** window. You will now be in Record Mode, ready to start working through the steps for your macro.

NOTE

> If you have recorded a macro without assigning it to a Toolbar button, you can always make the assignment at a later stage. Simply right-click on any Toolbar and then select **Customise**. Select **Macros** from the **Categories** list and then drag the appropriate macro onto a Toolbar of your choice. You can then customise the button in the usual way. See the previous topic for more information.

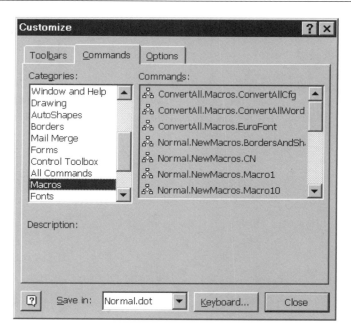

NOTE

When you customise the buttons on a Toolbar, you can also remove a button that is no longer needed. Simply click on the button on the Toolbar, whilst the Customise window is open and then drag the button off the Toolbar and onto the main area of the screen. When you release the mouse the button will disappear from the mouse pointer and will have been removed from the Toolbar.

Exercise 2C

You find that you regularly insert a special type of table into your documents and have decided to create a macro to insert the table and apply the formatting. For this macro, you would like to assign it to a Toolbar so that it can be run at the click of a button.

In this part of the exercise you create a customised button for your new macro.

1   Ensure you are working in a new, blank document.

2   Choose **Macro** in the **Tools** menu and then choose **Record New Macro**.

3   Name the macro **ReportTable** and ensure it is stored in the **All Document (Normal.dot)** template.

4   Click on the **Toolbars** button to access the Customise window. Ensure the **Commands** tab is selected.

5   Drag the new macro name up onto the Formatting Toolbar. Move the mouse until you are happy with the button location and then release the mouse to insert the button.

6   Right mouse click on the new button and highlight the existing macro name in the **Name** box. Type **Table** as the new name.

7   Change the style for the button to **Image and Text**. Right mouse click again on the new button. This time select **Change Button Image**. Select an image of your choice and view the changes in the Toolbar. Click **Close** to close the Customise window. You are now in Record Mode.

In this part of the exercise you will record the steps you would usually perform manually to insert a table.

8   Choose **Insert** from the **Table** menu.

9   Click the **Table** option to access the Insert Table window.

10   Specify **7** for the number of columns and **10** for the number of rows.

11   Click the **AutoFormat** button and select the format **Columns1**.

12   Click **OK** to continue and **OK** to insert the table into the document.

13   Click the **Stop Recording** button. Close the current document without saving.

In this part of the exercise you will run your new macro in a new document.

14   Start a new blank document.

15   Click the **Table** button on the Formatting Toolbar.

16   When the table has been inserted, click below it and press **ENTER** a few times.

17   Now insert another table using the **Table** button.

CHAPTER 5
Special Tools

18   Close the document without saving.

In this part of the exercise you will remove the newly created macro button from the Formatting Toolbar.

19   Right mouse click anywhere on the Toolbar.

20   Select **Customise** from the menu.

21   When the **Customise** window appears, drag the **Table** button off the Formatting Toolbar until you are within the document area.

22   When you release the mouse the button will be removed. Click **Close** to return to the document.

2.7 Copying a Macro to other Documents or Templates (3.5.2.2)

When you create macros in a document or template, Word automatically stores the macros in a *single macro project*. A macro project is a collection of macros, grouped together under one name and stored as a single entity. When you record macros, by default Word stores the macros in a project named **NewMacros**. You can copy the **NewMacros** project from one document/template to another document/template using the *Organiser*. You may wish to copy macros from one template to another to save time in recreating those macros that would be useful to the new template as well as the original one.

- Select **Macro** in the **Tools** menu.

- Select **Macros** to open the Macros window.

- Any macro name containing the phrase **NewMacros** means that it belongs to the NewMacros project. These are the macros that will be copied or moved using the Organiser.

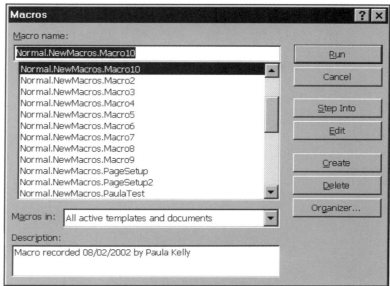

- Click the **Organiser** button. The Organiser window will be displayed. Ensure the **Macro Project Items** tab is selected.

- Use the **Copy** button to copy the **NewMacros** project from one file or template to another. You can use the **Macro Project Items available in** boxes to select the appropriate document or template where the project is to be copied, if it is not already displayed in the **To:** section.

- Click **Close** once the project has been copied.

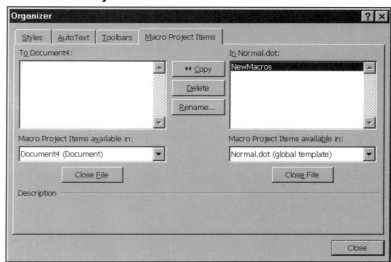

CHAPTER 5
Special Tools

Exercise 2D

In this exercise you will copy the NewMacros project from the Normal.dot template, to another document.

1   Ensure ALL documents are closed within Word.

2   Create a new, blank document.

3   Choose **Macro** in the **Tools** menu. Select **Macros** and then click the **Organiser** button in the window.

4   Click the **NewMacros** project **In Normal.dot**. Click the **COPY** button to copy the project into the currently open document.

5   Click **Close** to return to the blank document.

6   Save the document as **Our Special Macros**, closing it on completion.

Self Check Exercises

1. Name the three buttons that appear when you first open the Mail Merge Helper?

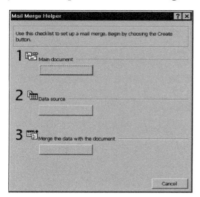

2. Match the following buttons to the titles..

   Delete Record

   Data Form

   Manage fields

   Find Record

3. Which of these functions should be chosen to sort records?

   ☐ Query Option

   ☐ Manage Fields

   ☐ Data Form

   ☐ Find Records

4. Which of these statements apply to use of a macro?

   ☐ Combine multiple commands.

   ☐ Automate a series of tasks.

   ☐ Speed up formatting procedures.

   ☐ Activated by keystrokes.

5. Tick the true statement(s)

   ☐ A macro can only reside in a specific template.

   ☐ A macro can run in the Normal template.

6. Name the following windows:

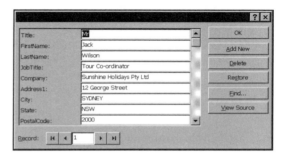

   ☐ Data Form

   ☐ Query Option

   ☐ Find a Record

   ☐ Manage Fields

CHAPTER 5
Special Tools

Practical Exercises

Please complete the following exercises as a review of the topics covered in this chapter. Should you require assistance with any of the steps within these exercises, you may refer back to the corresponding sections within this chapter.

Exercise 1

1   Open the document called "**Convention Followup Letter**". Take a few moments to familiarise yourself with the contents of this document.

2   Create this letter into a main document for mail merging using the Mail Merge Helper window. Do not close the window yet.

3   Open the data source that will be merged into your main document. The name of the data source is "**Travel Consultants List**". Once this has been attached to the main document, edit the main document so that you are working in the actual body of the letter.

4   Within the main document, insert the following merge fields below the name fields (ie: Title, Firstname, Lastname).

     «JobTitle»
     «Company»
     «Address1»
     «City» «State» «PostalCode»
     «Country»

     Also insert the <<Firstname>> field after the word "**Dear**".

5   Use the Edit Data Source button to view the data records in the Data Form window. Using the Data Form box, view the data source so that you can see all of the records in the data file in the document into which they were typed. Sort the records in ascending order of their country.

6   Return to the main document.

7   Using the Mail Merge Helper window set the query options for your merge so that only consultants in **England** are included in the merge results. Now perform the merge to a new document - there should only be three letters created. Close this new document without saving it.

8   Save any document that is now currently open, closing it on completion.

Exercise 2

1 Ensure you are working in a new blank document.

2 Record a new macro named **GuaranteeBox** and store it in the Normal.dot template.

3 Once the recorder has started, insert a file named **Price Guarantee** and then stop the recorder. Close the document on completion without saving it.

4 Create a new blank document.

5 Run the **GuaranteeBox** macro to check that it has been successfully recorded.

6 Delete the text box once it has been inserted.

7 Using the Customise window, add the **GuaranteeBox** macro to the Standard Toolbar. Edit the button once it has been placed on the Toolbar. Change the button image so that it includes a "smiley face" picture and change the name of the macro to "**Guarantee**".   Close the Customise window and try running your macro using the button on the Standard Toolbar.

8 Return to the Customise window and remove the button from the Standard Toolbar.

9 Access the Macros window and delete the **GuaranteeBox** macro. Return to the document on completion.

10 Close the document without saving it.

Chapter 6

Printing

CHAPTER 6
Printing

Syllabus
Module AM3
Word Processing – Advanced Level

Chapter Six: AM 3.6 – Printing

CHAPTER 6
Printing

Section 1   Preparing to Print

Printing can often be a simple matter of clicking the Print button on the Standard Toolbar for all pages within the document to be sent to the printer. However, there may be times when you wish to have greater control over the output of your document. You may wish to print only pages within a particular section or odd or even pages only. This chapter deals with some of the more selective ways of printing your documents.

1.1   Printing Odd Number Pages Only (3.6.1.1)

You can specify that you wish to print only the odd pages within a document. This could be particularly useful if you wanted to produce a double-sided document. You could print all the odd pages out first, then return the paper to the printer so that the even pages can be printed on the blank side.

To print odd pages:

- Choose **Print** in the **File** menu or press CTRL+P. The Print window will be displayed.

- Make any necessary changes within the Print window, such as changing the number of copies to be printed or the page range.

- Select **Odd Pages** from the **Print** list.

- Click **OK** to continue.

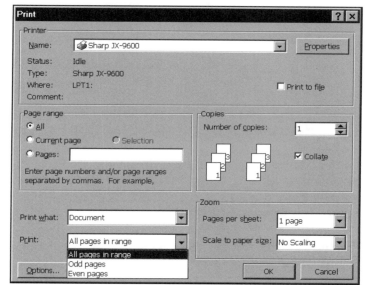

NOTE

If you want to print only the odd pages within a particular range, specify the range of pages within the **Pages** box. For example, you could enter **110-200** in the Pages box and then select Odd Pages from the Print box. Only the odd pages within the range of pages 110 to 200 will be printed.

CHAPTER 6
Printing

1.2   Printing Even Number Pages Only (3.6.1.2)

Printing even pages is much the same as printing odd pages. Again, you can specify that you want to print all even pages in your document or just those from a selected range.

To print even pages:

- Choose **Print** in the **File** menu or press CTRL+P. The Print window will be displayed.

- Make any necessary changes within the Print window.

- Select **Even Pages** from the **Print** list.

- Click **OK** to continue.

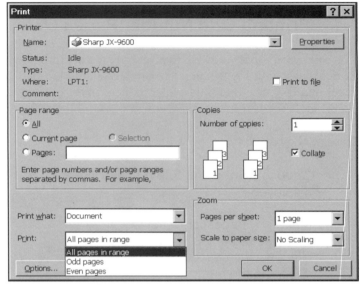

1.3   Printing a Defined Selection (3.6.1.3)

You can print a defined selection within your document - perhaps only a few paragraphs or a range of pages or even a single section within a longer document.

1.3.1   Printing a Selection

Printing a selection means that the text you wish to print does not fall into a standard page range. For example, you may wish to print only a few paragraphs or from the middle of one page to the middle of another.

- Select the text you wish to print.

- Choose **Print** in the **File** menu or press CTRL+P.

- Choose **Selection** in the Page Range box.

- Click **OK** to print the selection.

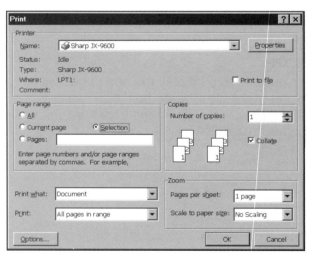

1.3.2 Printing a Section

If your document is separated into different sections, you can print one or more specific sections in the document rather than the entire file.

- Choose **Print** in the **File** menu or press CTRL+P.

- Choose **Pages** in the Page Range box.   Enter the section or sections you wish to print eg: **s3** or **s3,s5,s9**. You can also specify pages within a section such as **p3s4-p2s6**.

- Click **OK** to print the selection.

1.4   Printing Several Pages per Sheet (3.6.1.4)

The ability to print several pages per sheet allows you to see in a concise manner the layout of a document and how the information is presented. Word shrinks the pages to the appropriate size for printing purposes.

- Choose **Print** in the **File** menu or press CTRL+P.

- Make any necessary changes in the Print window.

- Select the number of pages from the **Pages per sheet** list in the Zoom box.

- Click **OK** to print the selection.

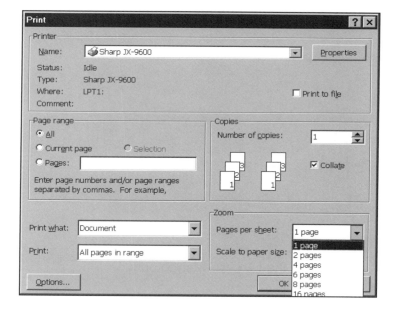

Practical Exercises

Exercise 1

1   Open the document named "**Greece - Printing**".

2   Print only section 3 of the document. The printout should contain the pages relating to the section on **Corfu**.

3   Print only the odd pages of the entire document.

4   Locate the heading "**Travelling Formalities**". Highlight this heading and the related text below. Print only this selection to your printer.

5   Print the entire document specifying that you want four pages per sheet. The resulting printout will give you an overall representation of the layout of the document.

6   Save the document, closing it on completion.

Index

Accept

In *Editing:* AutoFormat changes, 30; edit changes, 88

Alignment

In Editing: WordArt, 52

Amending

In *Editing:* AutoCorrect entries, 18

Apply

In *Editing:* apply as you type options, 21–22; borders, 22; bulleted lists, 23; character, 61; headings, 22; numbered lists, 23; paragraph styles, 60; tables, 23

Aspect

In *Editing:* ratio, 48; aspect ratio and text boxes, 201

AutoComplete

In *Editing:* insert AutoText entry, 35

AutoCorrect

In *Editing:* adding entries, 17; AutoCorrect, 16–17; adding shortcuts, 18; amending entries, 17; tools, 19

AutoFormat

In *Editing:* accept, 30; always AutoFormat plain text e-mail, 29; amend, 30; as you type, 21; finished document, 28; reject, 30; review, 30; running, 29; setting options, 28; text, 21

Automated

In *Editing:* correction, 16; text procedures, 16

Automatic

In *Editing:* caption*, 238;* colour, 7; text formatting, 21; text entry, 33

In *Layout*: update document styles, 125

AutoShapes

In *Document* Elements: AutoShapes, 224; grouping, 231; moving, 225; options, 224; pre-defined options, 226; order options, 228; resizing, 225; rotating, 230; setting order, 227; ungroup, 231

AutoText

In *Editing:* creating your own, 33; editing entry, 37; inserting, 35; inserting predefined, 33; managing entries, 36; toolbar, 36; using AutoComplete, 35

Blocks

In *Editing:* moving blocks of text, 78

Bookmark

In *Document Organisation*: adding, 133; bookmarks, 133; deleting, 137; error, 137; finding a, 134; names, 136

Border

In *Editing:* apply as you type, 22

Border

In *Editing:* apply as you type, 22; dimensions, 58; line style, 57; paragraph, 56; setting, 57

In *Document Elements*: colour, 220; different

sides, 221; paragraphs, 56; settings, 220; shading, 221; style, 220; width, 221

Breaks

In *Editing*: line, 59; page, 59

Breaks

In *Layout*: column 107; continuous, 96; changing type, 100; copying section breaks, 98; creating section breaks, 96; deleting section breaks, 98; deleting column, 108; footers, 101; headers, 101; next page, 96; even, 96; odd, 96; viewing, 96

Bullet

In *Editing:* automatic bulleted lists, 23; AutoFormat in finished document, 28

Capitalise

In *Editing:* names of days, 17; first letters of sentences, 17

CapsLock

In *Editing:* accidental usage of, 17

Caption

In *Document Elements*: automatic, 238; adding to an item, 235; changing label for, 238; inserting an item with, 239

Case

In *Editing:* changing case, 14

Cells

In *Document Elements*: merging, 175; splitting, 176

Character

In *Editing:* style, 60–61

Charts

In *Document Elements*: changing datasheet, 214; chart window, 214; creating, 213; datasheet window, 214; elements, 217; formatting, 216; graph window, 214; options, 217; positioning, 219; types, 216

Check Box

In *Document Elements*: default value, 188; drop-down field, 189; field, options, 188; 188; settings, 188; size, 188

Colour

In *Editing:* automatic option, 7; font, 5, 7; palette, 7; WordArt, 47; text boxes, 202

Columns

In *Layout*: button, 105; creating multiple, 104; deleting column break, 108; inserting break, 107; modify layout; 105; returning to single, 107; spacing, 105; widths; 105

Comments

In *Editing:* creating, 81; deleting, 83; editing, 83; viewing, 82; reviewing changes, 87

Correct

In *Editing:* AutoCorrect, 16–17; initial capitals, 17

Cross-references

In *Document Organisation*: creating a, 146;

cross-references, 141; deleting, 147; include above/below, 147; updating, 147

Data Form

In *Special Tools*: data form, 253

Datasheet

In *Document Elements*: changing data, 214

Dimensions

In *Editing*: altering border, 58

Document

In *Editing*: AutoFormat, 28; caption, 237; content management 74–79; email documents, 29; modify style within, 67; navigation, 75; outline view, 74; template, 69; positioning a chart within 219; watermark, 232

In *Document Organisation*: adding a password to a, 164; opening password protected document, 165; removing password from a document, 165

In *Special Tools*: copying a macro to a, 273

Drawing

In *Document Elements*: AutoShapes, 224; border settings, 220; create, 224; grouping, 231; modify borders, 220; moving, 225; options, 224; order options, 228; resizing, 225; rotating, 230; setting order, 227; ungroup, 231

Drop

In *Editing*: drop capital, 13; position, 13

Drop-Down

In *Document Elements*: changing field options, 190; inserting in a form, 189

Editing

In *Editing*: collaborative, 81–88; comment, 81–83; tracking changes, 85; reviewing toolbar, 82

Effects

In *Editing*: animated, 9; font, 8; text, 9

Email

In *Editing*: AutoFormat plain text in email documents, 29

Endnotes

In *Document Organisation*: adding to continuation separator, 161; AutoNumber, 156; changing format, 160; converting to footnote, 164; custom mark, 156; deleting, 160; editing, 158; endnotes, 155–162; creating 156; repositioning, 158; separator, 160; symbol, 156

Exceptions

In *Editing*: AutoCorrect exceptions, 19

Field

In *Document Organisation*: categories, 150; codes, 150–152; deleting code, 152; editing code, 151; elements of, 151; locking field, 152; names, 150; identifiers, 151; inserting, 150; instructions, 151; switches, 151; options,

150; preserve formatting, 150; unlocking field, 152; updates, 150

Fields

In *Document Elements*: changing text field options, 185; choosing field type, 184; deleting, 196; drop-down, 184; inserting text field, 184; protecting, 194; saving protected form, 194; settings, 186; shading, 192; template, 195; text format, 186

In Special Tools: managing fields in data forms, 253

Font

In *Editing*: choosing, 6; colour, 5; option, 5; effects, 8; position, 6; properties, 6; size 6

Footers

In *Layout*: footers, 101

Footnotes

In *Document Organisation*: adding to continuation notice, 161; changing format, 160; converting to endnote, 162; deleting, 160; editing, 158; footnotes, 155–162; creating 155; print layout view, 156; normal view, 156; repositioning, 158; separator, 160

Format

In *Editing*: menu, 5, WordArt, 48

In *Layout*: format of table of contents, 111

Formatting

In *Editing*: formatting text, 5; formatting options, 5; list item, 26; styles based on, 26; text boxes, 201; text box options, 201

Forms

In *Document Elements*: creating, 184; choosing field type, 184; editing, 196; fields, 183–185; forms, 183–196; help, 192; macros, 186; planning, 183; toolbar, 183; unprotecting; 196

Fraction

In *Editing*: character, 22

Galleries

In *Editing*: WordArt 44

Grammar

In *Editing*: errors, 16

Headers

In *Layout*: headers, 101

Heading

In *Editing*: alter levels, 78; demote, 78; level, 77; promote, 78; style, 80

Headings

In *Editing*: apply as you type, 22; AutoFormat in finished document, 28

Height

In *Editing*: same letter in WordArt, 51

Highlighter

In *Editing*: button, 7; using the, 7

Images

See Drawing

Indexes

In *Document Organisation*: creating, 138; cross-references, 141; deleting entry, 144; entry, 139; entry options, 141; generating,

294

mountain bike rides to the south east

rough ride guide ltd publishing

First published in 2005 by:

Rough Ride Guide Ltd
Walnut Tree Offices
The Old Road
Pishill
Henley-on-Thames
Oxon
RG9 6HS

ISBN 0-9548829-0-3

The maps in this book have been reproduced by permission of Ordnance Survey on behalf of the Controller of Her Majesty's Stationery Office, © Crown Copyright 100037674.

Printed by Orien Cards, U.K.

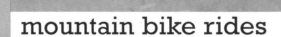

mountain bike rides to the south east

SPECIAL THANKS TO:

My wife Sarah who has inspired and supported
me throughout this project.
My friends & family for their help and support.
Mark Harris for his advice.
Fisher Outdoor for providing me with lots of great
bicycle products.
Madison for loaning us the superb Rocky
Mountain ETS-X bikes.
'Bike (UK) Bristol' in Bristol for their help with
parts and photos.
The riders, clubs and bike shops who have
showed us their best local trails.
Ken Williams for his technical advice and help.

You for buying this book, I hope you find it
educating, motivating, and inspiring.

EDITORS
Max Darkins
Richard Sanders
Vicky Trapmore
Sarah Darkins

DESIGNER
Kate Lester

PHOTOGRAPHS
Max Darkins
Richard Sanders
Sarah Darkins
Ken Williams
Rocky Mountain
Race Face
What MTB
Specialized

foreword by the author

Since having the idea to produce this book 4 years ago it has not always been easy seeing my dream (or pub talk) through to reality. I had wanted access to a comprehensive book that would show me where to ride good off-road routes that were exciting and challenging; routes that would take me on new adventures, and let me explore the countryside far and wide. Not being convinced that such a publication existed, I started on the long and exciting task of writing this monster.

It hasn't always been fun grovelling for finances, putting on frozen socks, going out in the pouring rain, and peering at computer screens for months on end. However, travelling the country and riding some beautiful new trails in the fresh air has to beat my previous office job. I hope that this book will enhance your enjoyment, understanding and love of the sport, and teach you new skills. I also hope that the new trails will create great adventures for you and inspire you to get out and ride your bike whatever your level.

Mountain bikers are generally a friendly bunch, who will stop and chat, admire each others bikes and assist with breakdowns so lets keep it that way. It is a sport that anyone can enjoy, so do make the effort to make everyone feel welcome, whatever their age, sex or ability. Also, bear in mind that we are not the only people out enjoying the trails, we are actually (at the moment!) the minority, and racing around the bridleways in large groups can be intimidating for other people. Everyone has a right to enjoy the countryside, so slow down when passing other trail users, be polite and be friendly - the future of our sport may depend on it....

Max Darkins

Sort those annoying sounds and get your bike running smoothly; let riding, the trails, the people, the laughs be what you remember in years to come

GENERAL

all the 'stuff' associated with mountain biking

GENERAL
SECTION

This first section contains all the general information we
thought would be useful to mountain bikers of all levels.
With so many mountain bike products available, decisions
about what to buy, especially when you're getting started,
can be daunting to say the least. This section will give you
a sound overview of all aspects of mountain biking from
clothing and buying a bike to more specialist information
such as bike geometry and suspension.

■ NOTE: 'Clunkers' (see right) are making a come back, and new ones are available from ATB Sales, see www.electrabike.co.uk

WHERE IT ALL BEGAN........

The evolution of mountain biking is a little shrouded in mystery. The classic American story is that, some time back in the seventies in Marin, California, a bunch of roadies and Grateful Dead fans looking for kicks decided to take their bikes off-road. The only models of bikes remotely up to the task at the time were old beach cruisers, called Clunkers or Klunkers, which had big fat 'balloon' tyres, one gear, and back pedal brakes on the rear wheel. Things like mudguard's, lights, false fuel tanks etc were stripped off to save weight, and the bikes were pushed uphill then ridden back down at great speed. As you'd expect they were not ideal - breaking frequently and weighing upwards of 50lbs.

Californian riders including Gary Fisher, Joe Breeze, Tom Ritchey and Charles Kelly saw a future for their new activity; they set up the Clunkers and held a downhill race called Repack. They started to adapt old bikes with parts from the world of motor biking and road cycling. The scale was small at first; Joe Breeze introduced cantilever brakes, flat bars and a triangular frame in 1976, then Tom Richey built some frames for Gary Fisher, and with Charles Kelly, they formed a company called Mountain bikes in 1979. It wasn't until 1981 however, that the first mass produced MTB, the Specialized Stumpjumper was born. This sold in thousands, and was the beginning of the MTB boom that swept the world.

WHERE IT IS TODAY........

Today the bikes are refined, parts are numerous, advertising is slick and mountain biking has become an Olympic sport. Competitive riding has encouraged the evolution of specialist bikes and riding styles as diverse as can be within one sport.

The mountain bike has made cycling less of an endurance activity and more of an adventure sport, enabling riders to sample many terrains and extreme gradients. Although the technology behind mountain biking has changed tremendously since the 1970's, the original vision is still very much the same; to get off-road, explore new trails, and have some fun. You do not need the latest design or bounciest bike around to get off-road and enjoy yourself, so don't be put off by the complexity and expensiveness of gear around, just get out and enjoy yourself.

Buying a Bike

Buying a new bike can be a daunting prospect with so many different styles and sizes to choose from, not to mention whether to opt for suspension or disc brakes. The deciding factor at the end of the day will be your wallet, but there will still be many options within each price range. Answering the following questions may help you decide:

1 What type of riding will I be doing? Different types of riding require different types of bikes. Will you be racing all-day cross country epics, flying downhill and walking back up, or something between? See the 'types of bikes' on page 4 for further information.

2 How much money should I spend? A good basic entry level, off-road mountain bike can be bought for around £300. Alternatively you could spend up to £5,000 for a state of the art machine. Buying last year's model, or even this year's model just before the new models comes out (around July to October) can yield good discounts especially on less well-known makes and models.

■ **NOTE:** Remember to keep some of your budget aside for other MTB items: You will need the right equipment e.g. helmet, basic tools, MTB specific clothing, SPD shoes, hydration pack.

3 Should I get a full suspension bike? A much asked question. It is not essential, but it does make riding easier and more comfortable. However full suspension bikes cost more to purchase, require more maintenance, and you will need to search out more technical trails for a challenging ride. See the suspension section on pages 34 and 35 for more information on different suspension designs.

4 What frame material should I get? Most bikes are made of aluminium but steel, titanium and carbon fibre frames offer different qualities (prices) - see the 'frame materials' on pages 29 for more information.

5 Where should I buy my bike? Good high street *bike shops* will let you test ride bikes, give one-on-one advice, and provide after-sales service. *Mail order* can be cheaper, but you need to know exactly what you want. If you are getting a bike *second hand* you may pick up a bargain, or a costly mistake, as replacement costs for a few worn parts may make the purchase uneconomical. You won't get a warranty with a 2nd hand bike either, so check the frame for cracks or bends and that it isn't stolen - see right for more information.

6 Are disc brakes worth it? Yes, especially if you ride through the winter as they are not affected by the wet and mud like V-brakes are. Upgrading from rim brakes to disc brakes can be expensive (if not impossibe) though.

Buying a 2nd Hand Bike

If you are buying a 2nd hand bike check it over thoroughly. If you need to replace too many parts it will soon become uneconomical. We have provided rough replacement costs for basic entry level parts, but you can spend much more i.e. a basic headset may cost £10 while a top of the range one will be over £100.

Frame: Check the frame for cracks (ripples in the paint may indicate a crack underneath) or dents.

Cost: Don't buy it.

Suspension: Check the suspension compresses and rebounds smoothly and that there isn't any unwanted 'play' in rear suspension pivots and fork bushings.

Cost: Servicing from £25, new suspension forks from £70 and rear shocks from £100.

Wheels: Check the wheels spin smoothly with no rumbling noise or play in the hubs. Check the wheel rims on rim brakes are straight and not overly worn (concave). Check the tyres are suitable for what you want them for. Look for cracks and tears and the amount of tread left on them.

Cost: Wheels from £90 a pair and tyres from £10 each.

Gears: Test ride the bike and check the gears click into position accurately. Check for wear on the chainrings and sprockets, and any play in the mechs. Check the chain is clean and rust free.

Cost: Cables £10 a pair, Chain £10, Cassette £15, Cranks and Chainrings £30, Front and rear mechs from £20.

Headset and Bottom bracket: These should turn smoothly with no play.

Cost: Headsets from £10 and bottom brackets from £15. Labour costs are around £15 for each.

Contact points: Check the saddle for tears or bent rails, the stem, bars and seat post for bends or cracks and that the pedals are the type you want.

Cost: Grips £5, Saddle from £15, Bars, stems, seat posts from £10 each, pedals £10 a pair.

TOP TIP:
If you are thinking of buying a 2nd hand bike, we recommend you purchase our MTB maintenance supplement. This will tell you how to check, repair or replace the parts that need attention.

Mountain biking has evolved, and today there are many different types of mountain bikes: each one designed to perform well in a particular situation.

Here are six of the most popular designs around today.

COMMUTING OR TOURING

The upright riding position and sturdiness of a mountain bike makes it an excellent machine for commuting or touring. Mountain bikes have smaller wheels than road bikes, making them stronger and more stable when loaded up with luggage.

Fitting a mountain bike with slick tyres, rigid fork, a rack for luggage and mudguard's converts it to a sturdy and reliable urban machine.

CROSS COUNTRY (XC) TRAIL BIKE

At the heart of mountain biking is the trail bike - tough and competent in going up and down hills and tough, but lightweight. This is the standard cross country mountain bike and is suitable for the majority of riders and general riding.

Technology for these bikes comes largely from the race circuit, and the bike design adapts to meet criteria of cost, durability, comfort and weight for most riders. Many trail bikes have front and rear suspension (3-6 inches of travel), to provide greater traction, comfort, and control.

CROSS COUNTRY (XC) RACE BIKE

As the name suggests these bikes are ultra-lightweight with a long riding position to ensure the most efficient power transfer. They have lightweight wheels and tyres, low handlebars and bar-ends to aid climbing.

Front suspension is usually about 2-3 inches, and some highly efficient rear suspension designs may have around 1-3 inches of travel on the back as well.

ENDURO/ FREERIDE / OUT OF BOUNDS

These bikes will 'go anywhere and do anything'. They are tough and have the performance of a downhill bike, but also the ability to get back up the hills.

They have a full range of gears, 4+ inches of suspension front and back (and maybe even a 'lock out' on the suspension), are lighter than a downhill bike, but heavier than a cross country.

DOWNHILL (DH) RACE BIKE

To cope with the rigours of downhill racing, a DH bike needs long travel full suspension (6+ inches front and back), super strength and a high standover height.

It will have one chainring, powerful disc brakes, wide tyres, a low saddle, wide riser bars, and a short & high stem for greater control when pointed steeply downhill (not designed for going uphill).

JUMP / SLALOM / BSX BIKES

These bikes need to have tough compact frames, and bombproof components for the repeated abuse. Long travel forks, a high front end, very strong wheels, flat pedals and a low, out of the way saddle.

don't leave

valuables

in your

car

BIKE SIZING & SET-UP GUIDE

An incorrectly fitting bike will feel uncomfortable and difficult to ride, so it is worth spending some time to make sure that you adjust it correctly, especially if you are not an 'average' sized person or are a woman using a bike designed for a man. The following two pages are a guide on how to adjust and change your bike, so it suits you perfectly. Women should also see page 10 for information on woman specific design bikes.

■ NOTE: These are general guidelines and that in the end, your personal preferences are the most important thing.

01 SADDLE HEIGHT: For maximum power, your leg should be almost straight when your foot is at the bottom of the pedal stroke i.e. in the 6 o'clock position.

If the saddle is too high your hips will rock when you pedal, too low and you won't achieve maximum power (but this will help when going downhill).

■ NOTE: Don't extend the seat post past the limit line or it will snap.

SADDLE ANGLE: Most people prefer the saddle to be flat. A forward tilt will put pressure on your arms, while a backward tilt will put pressure on your privates.

SADDLE SET-BACK: For maximum power your knee should be directly over the pedal axle when you are pushing down and the crank is horizontal. To achieve this, move the seatpost clamp along the saddle rails (but not too close to either end of the rail or they could bend or break).

■ NOTE: If your seat will not slide back far enough on the rails, you can get a seatpost with some lay-back i.e. the seatpost bends backwards or the clamp is set back behind the top of the seatpost.

02 PEDALS: For maximum power the ball of your foot should be over the pedals axle, when the foot is horizontal. The foot should also be at it's natural angle, and as close to the crank as possible. If you use 'clipless' pedals please see the next page for more information.

TOP TIP: Upgrading to clipless pedals is probably the easiest, cheapest and most effective way of improving your riding in terms of efficiency and control.

03 CRANKS: The typical crank arm length is 175mm, but different lengths are available.

The longer 177.5 or 180mm may suit long legged people, or those wanting extra leverage e.g. singlespeeders, but be aware of the reduced ground clearance. The shorter 170 or 165mm cranks may suit shorter (legged) riders and women.

04 HANDLEBARS: These should (usually) be set about 1-2 inches below the height of the saddle, and their length be approximately the same width as your shoulders.

05 STEM: These come in different lengths and height / rise. Changing the stem length will affect your reach, weight distribution, and the handling / steering characteristics of the bike.

New riders generally prefer a short, upright position as it is more comfortable, and takes the strain off your arms and onto your bum. A long and low riding position is more efficient and aids climbing as it brings your weight forward.

06 BRAKE LEVERS: The brake levers should be in-line with your arms, and the levers close enough to the bars, so that you do not have to move your hands to apply the brakes.

■ NOTE: The lever reach can usually be adjusted via a small screw on the lever.

07 WHEELS: Most bikes come with 26 inch wheels which are suitable for most people; however smaller (24 inch) and larger wheels (29 inch) wheels are available (see over).

■ NOTE: The measurements 24, 26, and 29 inches include the tyre; the actual rims measure 20.5, 22.5 or 25.5 inches.

FRAME SIZE
When standing with both feet flat on the floor you need at least 2 inches of standover height (space between the frames top tube, and your private parts) and be long enough so your knees don't hit the handlebars when turning the bars sharply.

■ NOTE: The frame size is measured along the seat tube from the bottom bracket, but ends at different places depending on the manufacturer e.g. the centre of the top tube or top of the seat tube, making it very difficult to compare frame sizes between different companies. Another useful measurement to look out for (and compare) is the top tube length.

TOP TIP: If you can't find a frame size small enough to give you 2 inches of standover height, try using the smaller 24 inch wheels.

Making small adjustments and tweaks to the components on your bike isn't just something the professionals should do. Mountain bikes will rarely fit someone perfectly and we all have our own personal preferences. Making adjustments where necessary will make you feel a lot more comfortable and confident.

WHEELS:

Most bikes use 26 inch wheels, while some small, jump, dual, and freeride bikes may use 24 inch wheels, and some e.g. Gary Fisher bikes, may use 29 inch wheels (a.k.a. 700C's by roadies).

Smaller wheels may be suitable for a small frame or rider, but also freeride and jump bikes, as they are lighter, accelerate faster and are stronger.

Larger wheels may suit larger bike frames and riders and are good for long rides. These will roll over objects better and have more grip, but will be heavier, and have slower handling and acceleration.

■ NOTE: 24 and 29 inch wheels have a more limited range of parts i.e. rims and tyres.

SADDLES

Saddles come in all different shapes and sizes, because everyone's bum is a different shape and size. The only real way to tell if a saddle suits your bum is to test it out, which decent bike shops will allow you to do. Some features to consider include the following:

Nose: Thin noses do not obstruct pedalling, while rounded noses reduce the chance of snagging baggy shorts.

Shape: rounded shoulders enable you to slide over the back more easily, and a raised rear end gives you something to push against. A shorter saddle with a wide back often suit women, as their pelvic bones are wider.

Length: long saddles allow you to shift your weight around (popular on DH bikes), while short saddles stay out of the way (popular on jump bikes).

Hole / Groove / Gel: these are used down the central section of the saddle to relieve the pressure on your privates (and works for both men and women).

Kevlar Shoulders: Harder wearing.

Rails: a long flat rail enables you to adjust the saddle in relation to the seatpost clamp. Titanium seat rails are more expensive, but are lighter and springy, taking some of the 'buzz' out of the trail.

SADDLE POSITION

While moving the saddle back or forth on it's rails will affect your reach it will also affect the position of your knee over the pedal. Therefore it is better to adjust other parts of the bike to alter your reach.

TOP TIP: Make a mental note of where you sit on the saddle when out riding. If you are sitting on the nose or back a lot, adjust the saddle position accordingly.

■ NOTE: Having your knee directly over the axle will give smooth high speed pedalling, whilst slightly behind the axle gives greater leverage and powerful seated climbing. Slightly forward will keep the front end of the bike down on steep climbs.

REACH

The amount your arms are extended forward can be altered by changing the stem height or length, the handlebar height (or the saddle position).

■ NOTE: A rough guide to the 'right' amount of reach: with your elbow on the tip of the saddle, your longest finger should reach the centre of the stem top cap.

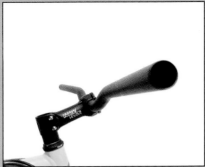

STEMS

The stem length is measured (in mm) from centre of bar clamp to centre of steerer tube clamp. XC bikes usually have stems around 100+mm, while DH bikes have stems around 70-mm (due to their geometry, see page G24).

A longer stem brings your weight forward which helps keep the front wheel down on climbs and gives a more stretched and efficient riding position. Too long however and the steering can be heavy and un-subtle.

A shorter stem will put your weight back, giving faster and lighter steering, but too short and the riding position may be cramped, the steering too 'twitchy' and the front wheel may lift on climbs.

■ NOTE: Manufacturers choose the stem length to match the geometry of the bike, so it's best to stay within +/- 10mm of the original length.

Stems can also be used to alter the height of the handlebars as they have different amounts of 'rise' (measured as degrees from horizontal). The height of old style 'threaded' stems can be adjusted, while the more common 'threadless' (Aheadset) stems (see above) only enable a small amount of height adjustment by placing spacers above or below the stem.

HANDLEBARS

The handlebars are usually set at 1-2 inches below the saddle height. A higher front end will provide a more comfortable riding position, but it is less efficient and the front wheel may lift up. Most general XC riders opt for wide, 'riser' bars (kinked to raise the two ends, as above) as they provide greater leverage and give better control and comfort. 'Flat' bars (no rise) give a lower, more streamline riding position, but also un-subtle slow speed steering.

RISE: This curve is measured in inches or millimetres, from the top of the flat central section of the bars, to the highest raised section.

BACKSWEEP / LAYBACK: This bend (usually between 4-10 degrees) puts the riders arms in a more comfortable position.

UPSWEEP: The upward slop (usually 3-4 degrees) is the upward angle of the bar along the straight section.

■ NOTE: Bar ends (on flat bars only) give alternative hand positions. An angle around 15 degrees gives a strong standing and climbing position, while 45 degrees is for more casual and relaxed seated riding.

CLIPLESS PEDALS (SPDs)

Also known as Spud or SPD (Shimano pedalling dynamics), these pedals use a system similar to a ski binding, where a cleat in a (specialist cycling) shoe attaches to the pedal. The shoe is then fastened to the pedal until you twist your heel outwards to un-clip. This enables you to lift the bike, pull up on the pedal (resulting in circular pedal stroke), and stops your foot sliding off the pedal.

There are basically three types of pedal; Shimano (see pic above), Time and Egg Beater (see right), each of which needs to be used with their own specific cleat design (the majority of pedals e.g. Scott, VP, Wellgo, Bontrager, and Ritchey accommodate the Shimano style cleat). Time and Egg Beater pedals have more float (movement before the cleat releases from the pedal) than SPD pedals i.e. about 10-15 degrees rather than 6.

POSITIONING CLEATS

Sit on a ledge and dangle your legs and make a note of the (natural) angle they hang at. Now angle the cleats on the shoes so your foot can sit on the pedal like this i.e. if your toes point inward, point the cleat inward. Also position the cleat so that the ball of your foot is over the pedal's axle.

■ NOTE: It is important to position the cleats correctly to avoid knee pain (although the float allows some room for misalignment).

SPD RELEASE TENSION

Shimano (and similar) design pedals allow you to adjust the engagement and release tension of the pedal on the cleat (Time and Egg Beater designs have a pre-set release tension).

A higher tension will usually means more security i.e. fewer accidental releases, but makes the pedal harder to get in and out of, and loosening them has the opposite effects. You can also choose between a tight 'single release' or looser 'multi release' design.

TOP TIP: Start with the SPD pedal release tension set low, so they are easy to get out of, until you get used to unclipping from them.

To adjust the SPD pedal entry and release tension, turn the small hex key on the rear of the pedal as above (one click at a time) anti-clockwise to reduce the tension and clockwise to increase it - get the tension the same for each side of the pedal (look from above the pedal, towards the back, for a little tab in the slot of the pedal body which indicates it's tightness).

■ NOTE: Increasing the tension can reduce the float on some pedals e.g. Ritchey, Wellgo.

■ NOTE: Some people suffer knee strain due to 'forefoot Varus' where the foot tilts inward, causing the knee to roll inward, or 'forefoot Valgus' where the foot tilts to the outside. Check with your doctor, and see about getting custom made wedges that fit under the SPD cleat on the shoe - available from www.lemondfitness.com/bf/forefoot.htm.

■ NOTE: Grease the cleat bolts when fitting them, and remove and re-grease them regularly to stop them from seizing in. Also check the cleat for wear and loose bolts, or you will find it hard to engage and release.

■ NOTE: Egg Beater pedals (see above) offer superb mud clearance, 4-sided entry, a large degree of float and are lightweight yet robust.

9

GENERAL

A Woman's Needs...

It may come as a shocking revelation, but men and women aren't quite built the same. Apart from the obvious a typical male rider is taller, heavier, has a stronger upper body and proportionally shorter legs with long femurs. Women on the other hand are shorter, lighter, have a weaker upper body, proportionally longer legs, but shorter femurs, and a wider pelvis. These differences mean that some women riding a standard bike (which are generally set-up for men) may find it uncomfortable and difficult to ride. Women specific design (WSD) bikes have been designed to take these physical differences into consideration, and may be worth a try.

FEATURES OF A WOMEN SPECIFIC BIKE:

01 A ladies saddle has a shorter nose and is wider at the back, to comfortably support the wider pelvic bones.

02 Narrower handlebars, smaller grips, and brake controls closer to the bars for smaller hands.

03 A shorter top tube and/or stem will reduce the weight put on the arms when riding, and make steering easier.

04 A shorter head tube, to enable the full use of front suspension forks, without lifting the front of the bike up. Also, a slacker head tube angle e.g. 70 degrees, rather than 71 will move the front wheel farther away from the feet and lengthen the wheelbase to provide better handling.

05 Smaller 24 inch wheels (may already be fitted to some small frame bikes) will be better proportioned with the bike, provide better handling, faster acceleration and a greater standover.

06 A larger seat tube angle e.g. 74-5 degrees, to place the feet and knees over the pedals for efficient pedalling.

07 A smaller frame will give a greater standover height, use smaller diameter and thinner tubing, to save weight (as ladies are lighter so don't require such a strong, and heavy frame) and not give such a harsh ride.

08 Shorter cranks may be better suited for shorter legs and will also give greater ground clearance. The normal length is 175mm, which is suitable for 5ft 6in to 6ft 2in, so 170 or even 165mm cranks may be better suited to people shorter than 5ft 6in.

D.I.Y. SEX CHANGE

If you already have a regular bike i.e. one designed for a bloke, or you can't find a suitable WSD, you can make some alterations yourself to make the bike infinitely more comfortable.

10 easy ways to customise your bike 'lady style'

1 ▸ Fit smaller (24inch diameter) and lighter wheels if standover height is less than 2 inches clear of the top tube.
2 ▸ Fit a women's specific saddle.
3 ▸ Move the saddle forwards on it's rails.
4 ▸ Fit a shorter (possibly higher angled) stem.
5 ▸ Fit riser handlebars.
6 ▸ Reduce handlebar width to shoulder width (it's OK to saw most bars down with a hacksaw).
7 ▸ Fit smaller handlebar grips.
8 ▸ Bring the brake levers (reach) closer to the handlebars.
9 ▸ Fit shorter length cranks i.e. less than 175mm if under 5ft 6in.
10 ▸ Fit a wider gear ratio cassette on the rear e.g. 11-32 or 12-34.

■ NOTE: These changes are especially important if the female (or male) rider is under 5ft 6in.

You may need to do all of the above things or only a couple of them to customise your bike; the important thing is that you are not over-stretched, it feels comfortable, and that you feel confident riding on it.

EQUIPMENT

For pretty much any ride, it is advisable to take water and prepare yourself for a puncture, broken chain or loose bolt. There is a tendency not to want to carry much equipment, but on longer rides it is only responsible to be prepared for the unfortunate. Rides may go on longer than you have anticipated, the weather may change and things break, so taking extra clothing, food, tools, and spare parts may save you a long, cold, hungry walk back home.

ESSENTIAL ITEMS:

Chain tool *
Compass
First aid kit (see survival page)
Food and drink (see next page)
Gaffer Tape - wrap some around your pump to save space.
Hex keys (a.k.a. Allen keys) in sizes 3,4,5,6 and 8mm*
Knife *
Light - of some kind
Map
Mobile Phone
Money, credit card (doubles as ID)
Needle, thread, and a strip of toothpaste tube - for tyre repairs.
Pump
Puncture Repair Kit
Screwdrivers (to adjust the brakes) *
Shimano Black Pin (if you are using a Shimano chain)
Spare Inner Tube(s)
Spoke Key
Tyre levers *
Whistle
Wind/Waterproof Coat
Zip Ties - for emergency repairs.

* These items can be often be found together in a good multi tool.

LONGER RIDES:

Tissue - leaves just don't work.
Extra food
Extra water (or water purifying tablets)
GPS
Matches
Penknife
Shock pump
Spare top
Survival bag
Thermos Flask
(metal types are bump proof).

USEFUL ITEMS

01: MULTI TOOL

There are various designs of multi tools, all with varying amounts of gadgets and gizmos on them. These range from just the bare essential hex keys, to one with hex keys, a chain tool, knife, spanners, etc, all in one easy to use and hard to lose package that saves valuable space while out on a ride.

02: GPS (Global Positioning System)

These electronic hand held gadgets are great if you are prone to getting lost, or like to cycle in unknown territories. They can provide a grid reference (to see where you are on an OS map), or be programmed with grid references (which we have supplied with our routes), so that the GPS points you around the route - we still suggest you take a map though.

RUCKSACK & HYDRATION PACKS:

To carry all this you will require a bag of some sorts. Panniers are not suitable for mountain biking so a rucksack is the obvious choice. Many riders these days use hydration packs (such as the market leaders, Camelbak), which can carry large volumes of fluid, as well as all your tools, spares, food, etc. They are basically a rucksack with a special bag (bladder) to hold your water, with a hose to enable drinking whilst on the move. There are various different sizes of these from ones that carry just the bladder to full-on day rucksack with a compartment for the bladder and room to carry a whole heap of other stuff.

03: If you are going for a short ride then a slender backpack should suit your needs, with 2 litres of water and room for a few tools, food, and spare tube.

04: If you are planning on going out for a longer ride you will need something with a bit more space, which will allow you to carry extra clothing, food, water, tools, etc. Some designs may also have a zip that enables the bag to be expanded to fit more things in, or reduced to keep things snug.

TOP TIPS:

You should clean and dry out your bladder after use (especially if you are using anything other than water in it) as it will start to go smelly and taste disgusting.

If your bladder has started to fester, try washing with some bicarbonate of soda or dissolving denture tablets in the bladder to take the nasty taste away.

When packing the rucksack spread the weight around the rucksack and put the heavier items nearer the bottom and centre to avoid muscle strains.

If the word bonking conjures up images of a night down the local nightclub then read on. This page explains how your body metabolises food and what food and fluids to take out riding with you.

TOP TIP: Simple sports drinks can easily be made; dilute fruit juice with an equal quantity of water and add a pinch of salt. Squash diluted between four and six equal parts of water also makes a reasonable fluid replacement drink.

■ **NOTE**: Foods with a high glycemic index (GI) e.g. wine gums, lucozade and baguettes provide an excellent quick 'fix' when eaten in moderation. A high GI means that the glucose they contain will quickly find it's way into your blood. However, be aware that if eaten in large quantities they could leave you feeling lethargic, due to a sugar rush.

EATING; THE SCIENCE...

Energy that the body needs for things like moving comes from the metabolism of certain food groups e.g. carbohydrate, fat and to some extent protein. As an energy source they differ in their calorific value, e.g. 1g of fat yields 9 kcals of energy, whereas 1g of carbohydrate yields 4 kcals.

Carbohydrates are the best energy source as they yield lots of energy without being bad for you in large amounts. There are different forms of carbohydrate; simple sugars like sucrose and glucose (found in honey, fruit, sweets etc), through to complex carbohydrates like starch and glycogen (found in pasta, potatoes, bread, rice, etc). Simple carbohydrates are easily absorbed into the blood where they can be metabolised to release energy, whereas complex carbohydrates require more digestion to be broken up into simple sugars before they can be absorbed.

When doing a lot of exercise you need to eat a balanced diet, but with more carbohydrates than usual i.e. aim for around 60-70% carbohydrates, 15-20% protein, and 10-20% fat, of your calorie intake. Also vitally important, but needed in smaller amounts are vitamins, minerals and fibre (found in plentiful supplies in fruit and vegetables)

■ **NOTE**: Try to avoid processed foods i.e. anything that has been ready made, as they normally contain artificial colours, preservatives, flavours, and lots of salt and fat.

HYDRATION

During exercise, the body looses water through water vapour in our breath and sweating. The average water loss is around 1 litre of fluid per hour of exercise, which can be closer to 2 litres if training hard or on a hot day. Excessive loss of water (dehydration) quickly produces side effects, such as dramatically reducing the ability to exercise, blurred vision and headaches. At the risk of stating the obvious, the way of preventing dehydration is to drink plenty, but little and often, before, during and after exercising. Try to drink before you get thirsty, as this is a sign that you have already started to become dehydrated - 'prevention is better than cure'. Also, try to avoid alcohol and caffeine when doing exercise as they are diuretics (make you wee more), so can lead to dehydration.

■ **NOTE**: If your urine is yellow it means you are not drinking enough - it should be a pale straw colour.

Water is the number one choice for most riders, as it is cheap and easy to get, doesn't rot your teeth or gunk up the bladder quickly and can be used to clean wounds (if you crash).

Sports drinks are designed to increase the speed of water absorption and replace the salt lost from sweat. They do this by having a mixture of sugars and salts with a lower concentration than the body's own fluids, so absorption is fast. Isotonic drinks contain roughly the same concentration so get absorbed as fast as water but also contain fuel for the muscles (good for long rides requiring fluid and energy).

WHAT TO EAT

BEFORE THE RIDE...

Try to eat a meal high in both simple and complex carbohydrates around 1-2 hours before riding. This is because after eating a meal, the level of glucose rises in the blood stream and if it is not used immediately, the body stores the glucose in the form of glycogen (a branched chain of connected glucose sugars). This glycogen gets stored in the liver and muscles where it remains ready to be broken into glucose units for energy. Once riding, if you were to eat nothing, after about 2-3 hours your glycogen stores would be diminished and you would experience 'bonking' i.e. your legs would feel like jelly. It is therefore important to eat snacks during a ride, (especially a long one) and a snack within an hour of finishing a ride to restock those glycogen levels - see below.

ON THE RIDE.....

Most people won't feel like eating much on a ride so if you are cycling over 2-3 hours, snack on little bits frequently. This way you will keep your blood glucose levels topped up without getting huge sugar highs or bonking. Choose small snacks that are high in carbohydrates e.g. cereal or energy bars, dried fruit and nuts, malt loaf, bananas, and fig rolls. Don't forget that sports drinks are also a good source of glucose and salts and will of course keep you hydrated.

■ **NOTE**: To use fat as energy, your body requires carbohydrates; it is therefore important that you keep your carbohydrates topped up and don't just eat eat less carbohydrates in an attempt to burn off that big belly!!

TOP TIP: Sports drinks and energy bars such as the ones pictured are a great way to keep your energy levels up on a long ride.

CYCLE SPECIFIC CLOTHING

Mountain biking is a difficult sport to dress for, with long sweaty climbs, fast windy descents (creating a draft on your chest, but not on your back), let alone changing weather conditions, and trying not to look silly at the pub afterwards. Therefore the best way to dress is by wearing various layers i.e. a base layer, mid-layer, and an outer layer, which can be added or removed as required.

TOPS

You will always need a base layer, which should be breathable and wick away any sweat, then depending on the weather you may need additional layers to go over this - see the summer and winter pages for more information.

TOP TIP: Don't skimp on the base layer and use a cotton top, as these absorb sweat, and will make you cold.

USEFUL CYCLE TOP FEATURES:

* Strategically located mesh panels e.g. under the armpits.
* Breathable fabric.
* Chunky zips for ease of use with gloves.
* Close fitting designs - to reduce bulk, snagging & wind resistance, but not your movement.
* Draw-cords - to keep the bad weather out.
* Flat stitching in key areas e.g. shoulders, for comfort.
* Lightweight material.
* Longer back and arms to account for the stretched forward riding position.
* Moisture wicking fabric.
* Quick drying fabric.
* Rear storage pockets.
* Reinforced shoulders & elbows for crash and rucksack protection.
* Rip-stop material.
* Reflective piping.
* Stretchable panels e.g. on the shoulders.
* Zip baffle (backing to zip to make it waterproof).

GLASSES

If you need glasses to drive you need them to ride. However, sunglasses are also very useful out on the trail to keep mud, bugs and branches out of your eyes, and stop them becoming sore and tired due to the wind and U.V. light.

■ NOTE: Buy glasses that meet the EU and British safety standards (BS) with regards to UV and impact protection.

TOP TIP: If the lenses steam up (caused by lack of clearance between face and lenses), use "anti-fog" or washing up liquid on the lenses.

■ NOTE: Glasses with interchangeable lenses (like these from BLOC) enable you to buy just one pair glasses for all types of conditions.

GLOVES

Often over-looked, but very useful in providing protection to your hands in both summer and winter. Make sure they fit snuggly, and have an absorbent sweat / snot wipe on the back.

HELMET

Wearing a helmet will give you more confidence (as you feel safer), which makes you ride faster. It could also save your life.

When choosing a helmet, make sure it fits snuggly, not too tight, or so loose it moves around - the fit can vary between manufacturers, so do try different brands. A visor will help to keep the sun, rain and branches from hitting your face, and more vents increase the air flow over your head (which can actually be cooler than not wearing a helmet). Also, VAT has been knocked off the price, and some manufacturers offer a crash replacement policy (so keep your receipt).

■ NOTE: Helmets can be road or MTB specific (to do with the air vents working better at different speeds), so make sure you get the right type and look for the (European standard) CE or EN1078 safety marks.

TOP TIP: Remove the pads in the helmet (attached by velcro) and wash them regularly, or your helmet will stink.

SHOES

Old trainers with flat-soles provide a good grip on flat pedals; a fairly stiff sole will transfer the power from your legs efficiently. Cycle specific shoes with cleats in the sole of the shoe (see pic above), clip into SPD pedals and have stiff soles. The soles get stiffer the more race orientated the shoes, while casual trail shoes have a softer front and back section to make walking easier. Look for shoes that use a secure fastening system, are easy to adjust, and keep clear of the chain e.g. velcro straps rather than laces.

SHORTS

Classic lycra shorts are the best leg-wear for cycling. They don't have any loose material to catch and pull, and are lined with a chamois pad to prevent chaffing, add comfort and wick away sweat. They are made up of panels, and generally the more panels, the better the fit. A basic short may use 4 panels, the average 6, while top quality ones use around 10.

■ NOTE: You're not meant to wear underwear under lycra shorts - cyclists go commando!

■ NOTE: The shape of shoes differ between manufacturers and designs: 'race' type shoes tend to be narrower, and casual shoes wider.

Uniform?

Don't think you have to squeeze into tight lycra to go riding. Although comfortable and efficient for cycling, not everyone feels comfortable or looks good in it i.e. men.

Most trail riders prefer looser fitting attire, so that they (and others around them) feel more comfortable, when enjoying that well deserved post-ride pint in the pub.

Although summer weather may be warmer you still need to be prepared for changing conditions in the UK, or especially in the mountains.

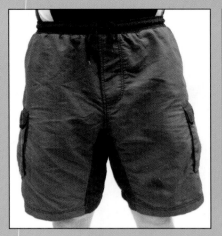

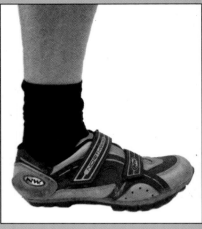

Use a sports specific suncream, as this should stay on sweaty skin better than the normal stuff. Decant some into a smaller vessel to take with you so you can re-apply it later on as well.

It might sound silly, but wearing a (thin) bandanna under your helmet can actually keep you cooler. It stops the sun beating down directly onto your head as well as absorbing sweat.

GLASSES & GLOVES

In the summer glasses keep out dust and bugs as well as the sun. Smoked lenses are good in bright sunshine and amber lenses are better for changing conditions (e.g. dappled light under the trees).

Even on warm summer days gloves are useful to provide some crash protection and stop sweating palms from slipping on the grips. Choose short-fingered lightweight gloves with a mesh back which should still be relatively cool to wear.

TOPS

In the summer you can get pretty sweaty, so it's important that your clothing is breathable and wicks sweat away to cool you down. On very warm days a single (cycle specific) top may be enough. The likes of a (bike specific) vest underneath can help move sweat away even quicker, as well as trapping a layer of air to keep you warmer when it cools down a bit. On cooler days, a thin mid-layer with venting, or a gilet (body warmer) is a useful and versatile top.

■ **NOTE**: You should also carry a wind / showerproof top (especially on long rides), as the weather in the UK is very fickle.

SHORTS

Lycra shorts are the best for cycling, but blokes don't look good in them (especially in the pub). You could wear a pair of normal shorts over the top, but this can get hot. Cycling 'baggies' are normal looking 'baggy' shorts which have a concealed lycra lining (with a chamois) sewn inside them. These shorts may also have the seams sewn on the outside of the lycra, making them more comfortable.

SHOES & SOCKS

In the summer, your feet are likely to get hot, so choose a light, breathable shoe with some space for your toes to breathe. There are also cycle (or sport) specific socks available, which can help keep your feet cool and dry.

■ **NOTE**: Race-type shoes are usually cooler than casual style shoes.

SHAVING LEGS: WHY?

Some keen cyclists shave their legs because it stops scarring, cuts are easier to clean, it is more aerodynamic, sweat evaporates quicker, massaging is easier. The real reason is probably because it looks good; muscle definition is enhanced (especially with a tan), and it shows everyone you are a dedicated cyclist (or you bat for the other team). Whatever your reason, expect your friends to laugh and gossip about you, as mince around in the bathroom with your lady shave.

In the winter the cold windy descents and hot sweaty climbs will be even more noticeable than in the summer. The best way to tackle these extreme changes in temperature is to wear a number of thin layers.

GLASSES & GLOVES

In the darker winter months, wear glasses with clear lenses to maintain visibility and keep all that wet spray and mud from blinding you.

Full-length or even thermal gloves keep the cold off (but don't go too thick, or you won't be able to feel the bars and brakes).

■ **NOTE:** In wet conditions, waterproof gloves e.g. Sealskinz keep your hands dry and warm, while still offering enough feel on the bars and controls.

TOPS

The winter will probably be colder and wetter than the summer so you will probably need a base layer (that will wick away the sweat) and a warm, thin, breathable long sleeved top e.g. a Roubaix micro fleece. You should also take or wear an outer shell that is wind and/or waterproof.

Waterproofs have the added benefit of keeping the rain out, but they are usually bulkier and won't breath as well as windproofs.

■**NOTE:** Read the washing instructions and use a re-proofing product (available from most outdoor shops) when the garment losses it's waterproof qualities.

TIGHTS / TROUSERS

In the winter you will want to keep knobbly knees warm, so wear a pair of cycle specific trousers with draw-cords at the bottom and padded inners. If it is cold, wet and muddy, the best thing to wear are lycra tights. These avoid excess material flapping around the chainrings and pedals and dry quicker than trousers. They may have a chamois in them or require cycling shorts to be worn underneath them.

■ **NOTE:** 'Bib' tights have a higher front and back, with shoulder straps, to keep out draughts.

SHOES & SOCKS

In the winter, you want shoes with good protection and treads (and even studs by your toes, for traction when you have to get off and push). Look for synthetic materials (rather than natural ones like suede), as these should dry quicker and endure more abuse. Few cycling shoes are truly waterproof, so investing in some 100% waterproof socks e.g. Sealskinz, will help keep your feet warm and dry.

■ **NOTE:** On very wet days, water can collect in waterproof socks, so use neoprene over-shoes that slip on over your cycle shoes to stop this from happening.

TOP TIPS:

Buy winter shoes slightly on the larger size to accommodate 2 pairs of socks or the thicker waterproof socks (having tight shoes on restricts the blood flow and your tootsies will cool very quickly).

If water gets in around the shoe cleat, use bathroom silicone to fill the holes.

TOP TIP:

All those vents in your helmet that keep you cool in summer will probably make you cold in the winter! Wear something underneath the helmet e.g. a skull cap, beanie, or warm bandanna to stop ice-cream headaches. A buff or neck warmer stops those nasty cold draughts down your neck. Cover your mouth too, to stop you gulping down cold air (which can cause damage to your respiratory system).

WINDCHILL FACTOR
It is especially important to consider the windchill factor in the winter. For every 5mph of wind speed or cycling speed, the temperature will effectively reduce by 2-3°C. Therefore a temperature of +5°C (cold, but not uncomfortable), when cycling at 10mph, in a wind speed of 10mph will effectively drop the temperature down to around -5°C, which is very cold and uncomfortable.

REMOVE MUDDY FOOTWEAR

BEFORE ENTERING THE BAR

Ok it's time to pack the bike away and get the turbo trainer out for the cold winter months.................like hell it is.

Think about it! There are less people out on the trails - their loss (bear with me here), no insects to fly into your eyes or mouth, and lots of slippery trails to really hone your skills and fitness levels, while your counterparts are watching crap tv and stuffing their faces - all you need to do is follow the next ten points on winterising your bike, and get some winter clothes (see previous page). Remember that in the winter it gets dark earlier, so unless you are only riding at the weekend you will most probably end up riding in the dark - but this is no bad thing, in fact it is a great thing - see the night-riding page.

TOP TIP:
If the muddy weather is causing your gears to skip and chain to suck consider running just one chainring or going singlespeed.

01: Grease the seatpost to avoid it seizing in, and to stop water getting into the frame. Water may still find its way into the frame, so drain it by removing the seatpost and turning the bike upside down.

02: Cover vulnerable parts like the upper and lower headset, and seat clamp, with neoprene covers or use some old inner tubes (thin road ones usually fit better), but remember to take the covers off after a ride to let it dry underneath.

03: Fit mud guards - Don't use the skinny metal type, get the big chunky plastic motor-cross style ones. This will save your bike and you from getting filthy (especially that embarrassing brown spray up your backside).

04: Loosen your SPD (pedal) springs, as mud can make them become stiffer and jam up. Also try spraying a light lube on your shoe cleats to stop mud from sticking to them so easily. Alternatively use Egg Beater or Time pedals, which don't tend to clog up (see page 9).

05: Fit mud tyres - there are two schools of thought on mud tyres; one is to use thin tyres e.g. 1.8" pumped up hard, to cut through the mud and provide good tyre clearance (good for sticky mud). The other is to use a wide tyre, with less air, to 'float' over the mud (better for sloppy mud and rocky terrain). Both designs use long pointy, widely spaced knobs, so the mud falls off the tyre easily. You may see racers using slick tyres so the mud has nothing to hold on to, but this is probably not suitable for your needs.

06: Handlebar grips can slip around if water gets underneath them, so either glue them down, use zip-ties on the ends, or fit bolt-on grips.

07: Disc brakes are much more efficient than rim brakes in winter weather as their braking surface stays clean.

If you can't fit or afford disc brakes on your bike, using sealed cables e.g. XTR, Gore-tex, or Avid flak-jackets, will keep the cables clean and moving smoothly for longer.

■ **NOTE:** Hydraulic Magura rim brakes are also a good winter rim brake option.

08: Plug wheel rim holes. If you use Presta inner tube valves in Schraeder sized wheel rim holes, get some rubber grommets to fill the gap around the valve, to stop water getting into the tyre.

09: Use wet weather chain lube that won't get washed off as easily as a lighter lube, and may even need to re-lube while out on the ride. Don't over lubricate the bike though, as this can just attract more dirt and create an abrasive gunk that wears parts even quicker and cause chainsuck.

10: Clean and lube the bike properly after a muddy ride.

WINTER AND NIGHT RIDING

In the winter it can be completely dark by 5pm, so riding in the dark will probably be the only option for weekday rides - but what an option.

If you thought singletrack was as good as it gets, think again - at night it's even better. The trails become more fun than you ever thought possible: your reflexes, skills and nerves will be tested to the max. Even fire roads can seem technical! You will see all sorts of wildlife as you twist through the night. This is why you still find riders waiting until after dark to go riding on the dry, empty trails on warm summer nights.

THE SET-UP:

You will need to get a good set of lights, with at least 10watts of power, a halogen bulb and a rechargeable battery. Some designs use one lamp, while others may use two (one wide flood light, and one narrow, focused beam). See www.fisher outdoor.co.uk for Smart lights.

■ NOTES:

Don't just limit yourself to riding in the dark at night, as early morning rides in the dark and seeing the sun rise is also a fantastic experience.

When riding at night you will ride slower and lights fade quickly, so always carry some form of back-up light. This can also be useful if you have to carry out any bike repairs on the trail in the dark.

As watts of halogen isn't as bright as the same watts of halide bulbs, the best method of measuring the brightness output of a light is by 'Lumens' rather than watts.

It is difficult to navigate at night, so go somewhere you know well, with at least one other person.

TOP TIP: When a car approaches, close one eye then open it back up once the car has passed. This will stop the pupil in the closed eye from contracting, so you should still have some of your night vision.

THE BATTERY:

The battery pack will usually pop into the water bottle cage, or strap to the frame. More important is the type of battery.

Sealed Lead Acid (SLA): provide the least power, but are cheap and have a long lifespan, and don't require special care when being recharged.

NiCad (nickle cadmium): 25% more power density than lead acid, but flatten suddenly and should be recharged only after being run down. Cadmium is also a nasty pollutant, so needs to be disposed of properly when they finally die.

NiMh (nickel metal hydride): 40% more power density than the lead acid, have a longer burn time, but will still fade suddenly and cost more. Read the manufacturer's charging recommendations, as they don't like being over-charged.

Lithium-Ion (Li-ion): very lightweight, but also very expensive.

BATTERY CHARGERS:

Completely discharging a battery may damage it. Bike lights use a lot of charge and fade quickly so when they start to dim, turn them off asap, and recharge them. Even when you aren't using the lights / battery, they will slowly discharge, so recharge it every month or so.

Dumb chargers: typically take over 10hrs to recharge a battery, but don't monitor its state of charge, so you need to monitor the amount of time you've used the lights for, then work out the time required to recharge them. Remember that overcharging can damage NiCad and NiMh batteries.

TOP TIP: Use a plug timer (like the ones used for timing lamps to go on and off) so you don't over-charge the battery.

Smart Chargers: These monitor the state of battery charge, and change to a 'trickle' charge, so as not to overcharge and damage battery. They are often used with a fast charger to speed up charging.

BULBS:

Halogen bulbs: use a tungsten filament inside a bubble of halogen gas, to produce a light. They are probably the most common type of bulb as they are bright and inexpensive.

Metal halide HID (high intensity discharge): use halide gas and 2 electrodes, which spark to produce a white light. This method produces about 4 times more light than a halogen bulb i.e. a 10w halide bulb is about as bright as a 40w halogen bulb. A replacement metal halide bulb is much more expensive than a halogen bulb.

■ NOTE: Some manufacturers achieve a brighter (and whiter) light by applying more voltage to a bulb than recommended. This makes the battery run down quicker, and shortens the life of the bulb, but the % increase of light is around twice that of the % increase of power required, and a bulbs life is long anyway.

LIGHT MOUNTINGS:

Helmet Mounted Lights: These will shine the way you are looking, which is useful when twisting through the woods. However they can make the trail look 2-D, move around a lot, and be heavy on the neck.

Bar Mounted Lights: These will shine where the bike is pointed, which can make corners hard to negotiate, and cast out of proportion shadows.

■ NOTE: British standard BS6102-3 requires them to be visible from the side, which most night riding lights aren't. This could cause a problem regarding insurance if you are involved in an accident. Therefore having a set of commuter lights is a good idea, they will also save using your off-road lights battery before you even get off-road, and act as a back-up set of lights.

IT HAPPENS TO THE BEST OF US

(and me).

I once went on a ride with four mates in the Mendips. We set out typically late at around 2pm, which wasn't the best idea as it was winter. Someone got a puncture, someone else injured their eye, we got lost and it started getting dark. The path we decided on shortly disappeared and I have this memory of all five of us walking through thick gorse whilst carrying our bikes above our heads.

By the time we found the main path it was completely dark (no-one had lights of course) and someone had hypothermia. To top it all off, when we returned to my van it had been broken into and my Tunnocks caramel wafers (my reason for carrying on in the face of adversity) had been stolen.

Unless very lucky, we all experience some form of nightmare ride. The key thing is to 'be prepared' like the scouts say. These pages have been compiled from my extensive mountain biking incidents, so hopefully once read you will be able to avoid such things happening - or at least know what to do when they do...

TOP TIP: Try to use a good quality D-lock (like this one from Squire) and another design of lock e.g. a cable to deter those well prepared bike thieves.

ANIMALS

Dogs can be unpredictable - they may be a man's best friend, but they aren't a cyclists. They don't like things moving quickly, and some bike noises (which our ears can't always hear) can set them off, so be wary of them biting or running out in front of you at the last minute and be ready to lift your feet if they go in for the nip.

TOP TIP: If you are particularly scared of dogs, a dog dazzler (ultrasonic) deterrent should scare the dog away - not to be confused with a dog whistle!

Horses (like dogs) can hear high pitch noises from your bike, which can be why cyclists freak them out for 'no apparent reason'. So stop and let them go by, and if you are approaching from behind, call out to the rider, asking for permission to pass - but still keep your distance, as they can kick very hard (the horse that is).

■ **NOTE:** The law states that cyclists are required to give way to all other trail users.

Wild Things: watch out for stags during mating season (winter time) as they may stand their ground and use their antlers to protect their ladies from you (not a nice thought either way). Snakes will usually slither away before you even notice them, but be aware of adders (brown, yellow or white, with black diamonds down the back), which are pretty rare; a love bite from one of these will leave you pretty sick.

■ **NOTE:** It is illegal for landowners to have dangerous animals on public rights of way e.g. most varieties of bull.

THIEVES

Thieves are opportunists, so don't give them the opportunity. Park your car in a busy place, preferably a protected car park, pack everything out of sight, and get back before it gets dark.

When leaving your bike, remove all quick release components and secure the bike with a lock (two different types if possible) to something immovable in a busy well-sighted position. D-locks are probably the best, but position it so the lock is difficult to reach and minimise the empty space in the D area (as thieves can use a bar in here to twist it open).

TOP TIP: If you have to leave your bike for a short while, and you don't have a lock, wind the brake barrel adjusters out, to lock the brakes on, or disconnect the brakes, leave it in a big gear, take the chain off, and undo the quick release skewers, to slow them down a bit.

Insuring your bike (and yourself) is a good idea, as bikes are easy to steal and sell, and their value can be in the £000s. For that reason the insurance is costly, usually around 10% of the bikes value for specialist insurance (who may also include third party public liability). If you have your own house, it may be cheaper to get the bike(s) covered (as sports / expensive items) under house insurance, but read the small print carefully and keep all receipts to prove the value of the bike.

TOP TIP: Most police stations are able to 'tag', number or post code the frame, so you can be reunited if it is found after being stolen. This may get you a discount from your insurer.

LOST

We recommend that you carry a map, compass, and even a GPS, and check them all regularly. It is also advisable to take a mobile phone, light, a whistle, and let someone back at home know where and when you expect to return.

■ **NOTE:** A map and compass are not much use if you don't know how to use them, so make sure you read the map reading and (OS) map key pages in the route section.

■ **NOTE:** The international distress signal is 6 blasts or flashes then wait for 1 minute and repeat. The reply is 3 blasts or flashes with 1 minute pauses.

BIKE BREAK DOWNS

Prevention is better than cure, so make sure you maintain your bike and do a pre-ride check, and carry a selection of useful tools and spares (see the equipment page).

You should be able to carry out most bridleway-side repairs (see 'trail bodges' in the maintenance supplement), but for those occasions where you can't, a mobile phone could save you a long walk.

CARS

Roads are getting more and more dangerous, with more cars and more aggro drivers, which is another reason to get off them and onto the bridleways.

■ **NOTE:** Watch out for car doors opening on parked cars or queuing traffic, they hurt - a lot.

WARMING UP & DOWN

-10 minutes of easy riding (spinning your legs with little muscular effort) before and after a ride pumps blood around the muscles. This will warm them up and reduce risk of injury.

Warming down will flush out waste products (e.g. lactic acid) and bring in fresh nutrient-rich blood to help prevent DOMS (delayed onset muscle soreness).

STRETCHING

When you exercise muscles you damage the fibres', these then grow back stronger, but also shorter and less flexible. You therefore need to make an effort to stretch, to keep your muscles at their maximum length and strength.

A classic example of shortened muscles in cyclists are tight hamstrings and calves, which can lead to lower back pain. One way to stretch your hamstrings is to sit on the floor with your legs out straight in front of you and gently lean forwards, trying to touch your toes.

When stretching, make sure the muscles are warm to avoid straining them, and do each stretch 2-3 times, holding for 10-15 seconds - don't bounce or rock during the stretch, as this can damage the muscle.

ACHES & PAINS

This is your body telling you there is something wrong, so don't ignore them and take pain killers as you are likely to aggravate the injury even more. The same thing goes for simple illnesses like colds; if you continue as normal you will make things a lot worse.

1ST AID

mountain biking is a relatively safe sport, but we like to take risks and push our limits to get that extra 'kick' and this is usually when we get injured. Excessive risk taking and lack of concentration are the main culprits of accidents, which are mostly just minor ones. You should however be prepared for more serious problems as well. Carry a first aid kit with you and have some knowledge of what to do in an emergency. Perhaps the best piece of kit to carry is a mobile phone - so if anything serious happens you can get the emergency services on the case ASAP (signal permitting).

The following items could be useful in your first aid pack:

* Antiseptic wipes
* Bandages
* Cold pack (activated by squeezing)
* Foil blanket
* Pain killers
* Plasters (please be aware that some people are allergic to plasters)
* Scissors or knife
* Sterile gauze pads
* Tape
* Tweezers

Also carry some form of ID, name, address, telephone number and any specific medical details about yourself, just in case you are the one who has had the accident.

INJURIES

It is difficult to give decent advise about serious injuries as they are varied and obviously more complicated. Therefore we suggest you do a proper first aid course to be better prepared, more confident, and less panicky when faced with a serious situation.

The most common injury will be a graze or cut, which should be rinsed with water and (if you have them) wiped with anti-septic wipes, and if it is bleeding a lot, put a plaster or bandage on it. If the bleeding is heavy, cover the wound with a (sterile) dressing, press down firmly, and elevate the injured area to above the heart (to slow bleeding). It may also be necessary to press on the nearest artery to stop very heavy bleeding - these are found on the inside of the arm, in between the biceps and triceps, and against the front of leg where hip bends - use the heel of your hand for this one.

■NOTE: After a ride, any swelling from an injury can be reduced by an ice pack, keeping the injured part elevated, and taking anti-inflammatories e.g. Ibuprofen.

BLOWS TO THE HEAD

Immobilise the patients' head and neck and send for medical assistance immediately. You should keep the patient still, warm and reassured, and if they are unconscious, check they are breathing, their airway is not blocked (by their tongue or food), and that they have a pulse (at their wrist).

After calling for help, if they are not breathing, or don't have a pulse you will have to use CPR (cardiopulmonary resuscitation), which is 2 breaths to 15 compressions of the (bottom middle of the) chest.

■NOTE: If a helmet has taken a big knock, it will need replacing, which should be done even if you can't see any visible damage.

STINGS:

Insect Stings: Antihistamine cream or pills such as Piriton reduce your body's allergic response to the sting. If you don't have any and get stung by a bee (they leave their sting in you), remove the sting and relieve the pain by using an alkaline solution (to neutralise the sting), such as soapy water or a bi-carbonate of soda solution (as their sting is acidic). A wasp sting (doesn't stay in you) is alkaline, so it is best treated with a weak acid such as citrus juice or vinegar.

Stinging Nettles: Probably the most likely pain is going to be dealt by the stinging nettle. The tiny hairs on the underside of the leaves are like minute needles of acid - you should not scratch when stung, or you will just aggravate the area. Use an alkaline solution, such as bicarbonate of soda, soap, or dock leaves (see picture below) to help reduce the tingling itch.

TOP TIPS:

By cross-training (e.g. swimming, rowing, weights) you will strengthen non-cycling muscles, which will help support and prevent twisting injuries from crashes.

If you can persuade your partner to give you a massage, this will speed up and aid the muscle recovery. Some gyms also offer a massage service.

For more 1st aid information view these websites:
www.redcross.org.uk
www.sja.gov.uk
www.thebmc.co.uk

Most work places need a qualified first-aider, so volunteer and get your (free) training this way (and get the day off work as well).

ACHE OR PAIN	POSSIBLE CAUSES	REMEDY
HEAD ACHE	Dehydration or over exertion Tight helmet or glasses	Ensure enough water is drunk Ensure both items fit correctly
LIGHT HEADED	Low blood sugar Sunstroke	Take food on the ride Avoid prolonged sun exposure
SORE OR TIRED EYES	Mud, branches, flies, dust etc in eyes Eyes 'tired' from sunlight and warm air	Wear glasses or fix mudguard's to stop debris flying from tyres Use sunglasses. Rest eyes from computer screen at work
STIFF OR PAINFUL NECK	Stationary head position for long period Low / long riding position	Move head during ride + stretch after Raise bars with higher or shorter stem
SHOULDERS SORE	Locked elbows when riding. Incorrect handlebar width. Incorrect handlebar height	Bend elbows to absorb shock Handlebars should be approximately the width of shoulders + hands Raise bars with higher stem or riser bars
TRICEPS PAINFUL	Overly stretched riding position	Try a shorter, more upright stem or riser bar to decrease stretch
HANDS NUMB / COLD **BLISTERS** **HANDS/WRISTS ACHE**	Not moving hands enough Loose fitting gloves Hands are at an unnatural angle Fingers over-stretched for brakes Gripping too tight or grips too small	Change hand position, shake hands, or use thicker gloves Wear tighter gloves. Rub hands with surgical spirit to harden skin Line up gear and brake controls with your arms Move brake lever closer to the bar with reach adjustment screw Loosen grip, move hands, and / or try larger grips
LOWER BACK PAIN	Poor flexibility (back, hamstrings, calves) Weak abdominals not supporting back Weak lower back muscles Vibration transmitted through back Too long / low riding position	Improve flexibility with stretching exercises mountain biking uses but doesn't build the abdomen, so do crunches / sit-ups Do hyper-extensions (backward sit ups) to build up lower back muscles Try suspension seat-post or full suspension bike Modify riding position e.g. shorter or higher stem or riser bar
HIPS ACHE	Saddle too high Different leg lengths Excessively high gears	Adjust seat height to stop hips rocking Insert layer in to shoe of shorter leg Try using lower gears and increasing cadence
PAIN IN THE ARSE	Bottom not accustomed to riding Saddle incorrect shape Saddle at incorrect angle Chaffed skin on legs Poor hygiene causing soreness Improper clothing Front of saddle causes pain for women	More time in / better padded saddle, or use nappy rash cream Try several designs of saddle Adjust saddle angle Use saddle with thinner front end. Use Nivea handcream on sores Wash shorts after every ride - get 2nd pair if riding frequently Wear lycra shorts with a chamois (& use chamois cream) Point saddle downwards slightly

ACHE OR PAIN	POSSIBLE CAUSES	REMEDY
PAINFUL KNEES	Saddle too high or low	Try lowering or raising the saddle
	Excessively high gears	Use lower gears and increased cadence
	Insufficient 'float' (lets foot rotate)	Try different pedal system (e.g. Time pedals have greater float)
	Flat foot - rolls inward putting pressure on the inside and twisting the leg / knee	Use custom made shoe inserts to re-align the foot - see www.cyclefit.co.uk
PAIN IN SIDE	Cleats not aligned	Reposition cleats on shoes so the knee can move naturally
	Excessively high cleat tension	Reduce cleat tension on pedals
STIFF	Cold	Cover knees with knee / leg warmers or tights
PAINFUL LEGS	Hard and long rides	Increase intensity & length of rids gradually
	Not warming up and down	Start & finish rides gently
	Muscle cramp	Stretch the muscle, consume (salty) fluid, ease up, and keep warm
LOWER LEG PAIN	High foot arches (inflexible foot)	Use custom made shoe inserts to re-align the foot - see www.cyclefit.co.uk
ANKLE PAIN	Not correctly warmed up	Warm up & stretching
	Climbing in too high a gear	Use lower gears + alternate between sitting and standing
	Incorrect saddle height	Reposition saddle
	Incorrect cleat position	Reposition cleats
PAINFUL FEET	Tight shoes, especially later in summer & end of day as feet get hot and swollen	Ensure shoes accommodate swelling (buy them in the afternoon if possible - as your feet are largest / swollen at this time)
	Hard soles	Install cushioned shoe liner
	Blisters caused by friction	Reduce friction with plaster + 2nd layer of slippery material / sock
	Incorrect cleat position	Reduce pressure on the foot by adjusting cleat so that ball of foot is slightly in front of pedal axle
NUMB FEET	Cold, trapped nerve or poor blood flow	Move feet, wiggle toes. Could be Raynaud's syndrome - see doc
	Shoes are stiff	Use softer inner soles or more flexible shoes
SKIN	Sunburn due to UV exposure	Use SPF 15+ sunscreen, and reapply frequently, as you sweat it off
		Cover sunburn with clothing and apply moisturiser to burnt areas

■ NOTE: Cycling will improve your lung power, strengthen your heart, muscles, de-stress you, leave you happier, healthier and energised, while the varying terrain and challenges will take your mind off the effort required.

TOP TIP: A 'Turbo Trainer' is an indoor apparatus that enables you to pedal your bike indoors. This enables controlled training and a ride in the warm and dry. Tacx trainers are available from www.fisheroutdoor.co.uk

■ NOTE: The easiest way to train by using your HR is to get a heart rate monitor (HRM) watch, which displays your HR which it reads from a strap that fits around your chest.

Everyone will have different reasons and targets for their fitness levels, and opinions of what is fit and what isn't will vary. Some people are naturally fitter, faster, stronger, have more time, reasons, or less commitments, so don't judge yourself on others, concentrate on your objectives and enjoy yourself. This page is just a simple guide to fitness, which should be suitable for most people, but if you want to get ultra competitive, you have an endless supply of books out there to read.

AEROBIC V's ANAEROBIC

In simple terms, muscles get their energy from splitting sugary molecules stored in the body. If there is enough oxygen, the fuel in your body is broken down into energy, water and carbon dioxide, you are working aerobically. If you are working too fast / hard for the lungs to provide enough oxygen however, glucose gets broken down less efficiently and lactic acid (which makes your muscles ache) is the by-product of the energy generated, you are working anaerobically.

To make your body stronger and fitter you need to push or 'overload' it. This can be done by either increasing training frequency, duration, or intensity. More frequent training will decrease the time the body needs to recover from exercise, while increasing training session duration (time) will increase stamina, and higher intensity training will increase power.

RECOVERY

Do not underestimate the importance of letting your body recover from exercise. If you start your next session too soon your body will not have had sufficient time to recover ('over training') and you won't benefit from the previous exercise. If you wait too long (under training) however, and the body starts to regress, losing the increase in performance you has just worked so hard to achieve. This time period is usually around a few days, but it will depend things like your body, diet, intensity of training etc, so you will have to find out what suits your needs through trial and error - listen to your body.

■ NOTE: Too much hard exercise can depress your immune system and make you ill, so if you are not feeling 100%, rest and recover or you could make it a whole lot worse.

HEART RATE TRAINING (HRT)

An effective way to train is to listen to your heart. This is because your heart rate (measured in beats per minute or BPM) indicates the intensity of exercise you are undertaking.

A typical adults resting heart rate (HR) is around 70 BPM; maximum heart rate is approximately 220 minus your age (this is an estimate: getting a sports lab to take it, or pushing yourself until you are totally and utterly exhausted is more accurate).

A more useful comparison between people is the % of maximum heart rate (MHR) at which you are exercising e.g. if someone had a MHR of 200 BPM, and was exercising at 150 BPM, they would be exercising at 75% of their MHR.

■ NOTE: As you get fitter, your resting heart rate (RHR) will decrease. It can therefore be used as a guide as to how your fitness is improving.

DIETING

Muscle weighs more than fat, so aim to lose fat, NOT weight. Often 'dieters' will eat too little, causing their metabolism to slow down, making the body store energy as fat. This can also lead to binge eating of unhealthy foods, muscle wastage and lethargy.

The best way to lose excess fat is gradually over a long period of time, so that it can be sustained. Exercise regularl for long gentle periods (about 50-60% o your MHR) and consume regular, small, balanced meals that make up slightly less calories than you are burning off.

MHR %	EXERCISE INTENSITY	HEALTH BENEFIT	ENERGY
Level 1 50-60%	EASY. A gentle ride where conversation is easy. Exercise can be sustained for several hours of riding.	Weight loss. Lowers blood pressure. Develops stamina.	Aerobic activity: oxygen can be carried around the body at a sufficient enough rate to maintain long periods of exertion in this zone (provided fluid and glucose levels are maintained). These levels of exercise are the most beneficial to the majority of people.
Level 2 60-75%	MODERATE. A more intense ride where only minimal conversation is comfortable. Exercise can be sustained for over two hours of riding.	Increases aerobic capacity. Burns high proportion of fat.	
Level 3 80-90%	HARD. Full-on riding where you are pushing yourself hard. Heavy breathing makes it very difficult to talk. Exercise is sustainable for less than 1hr.	Increases aerobic capacity. Increases your lung capacity. Develops your stamina for hard exercise.	On border between an/aerobic activity i.e. oxygen for muscles is limited.
Level 4 90-100%	VERY HARD. Pushing yourself to your absolute limit. This is only sustainable for under 1 minute.	Increases sprinting power.	Creatine phosphate is used as energy, but is in very short supply.

WANT TO TRY SOMETHING NEW?

Bored of occasional rides with a friend? Perhaps you need some variety in your riding to stimulate that faded enthusiasm. Here are a few ideas that might motivate you to get out and ride a bit more.....

GROUP RIDES

If you want to make cycling a sociable occasion, meet new people, ride new routes, and motivate yourself to get out and ride, group rides are perfect. They also give you the opportunity to learn new skills and bike knowledge from other riders. Ask your local bike shop if they have (or know of) any groups that you could possibly join, or have a look on www.bikemagic.com, or www.ctc.org.uk (cyclists touring club), which has easy going, social, off-road club rides.

CHARITY RIDES

Why not combine cycling with raising money for charity? These rides usually involve mass participation on non-technical trails, which are aimed at being fun and friendly.

Examples: Over 25,000 people take part in the annual London to Brighton bike ride to raise money for The British Heart Foundation (BHF).

RANDONEES

These are mass participation rides on long courses that are non-competitive.

GAMES

There are other things you can do on a bike without entering an organised event. We like the Poop challenge to see who can bunny-hop the largest pile of horse manure, Puddle Splashing where you soak your mates or Bike tag to keep you warm while someone fixes a puncture.

RACING

If you think you're a bit tasty on your bike or maybe you just want to set yourself a personal challenge and have some fun, get yourself along to a mountain bike race. Look for race information in specialist mountain bike magazines e.g. MBR, What MTB, MBUK.

Most races have a range of categories and different age groups. There are also lots of different types of races within XC (see below), as well as the other specialist disciplines e.g. downhill, slalom, X4 (like slalom but with 4 riders), and trials events.

Cross Country (Classic)

This is what most people will recognise as MTB racing. Riders will race around a set circuit (and usually complete a set number of laps), as fast as they can. These races last around 2-3 hours and are often highly competitive.

Examples: Cheddar challenge.

■**NOTE**: Riders who want to overtake you will probably call 'to your right / left' to indicate the side THEY want to pass by on. You should try and move over if it is safe to do so, enabling them to pass.

Endurance Races

These races usually involve laps of a set course, to be done in a time limit. They are usually fun-based challenges that encourage taking part in a big event without the win/lose attitude of racing. The name 'Enduro' is usually given to races lasting between 6-24. These can be attempted in a team or done solo. Teams generally work in shifts to sleep, eat and get as many laps in as possible. They may sound like hard work, but are actually very rewarding and great fun.

Examples: Enduro 6, Dawn till Dusk, Thetford Enduro, Mountain Mayhem (24hr), Sleepless in the Saddle (24hr).

If you get bored with beating everyone in the UK, there are similar races abroad as well, including bigger scale stage races.

Examples: Grand raid Cristalp (marathon race) in Switzerland, and the Trans Alp (multi-stage) from Germany to Italy.

Marathons

These are races over a set distance, usually 100KM, although shorter options are usually offered as well. The numbers of riders competing in these races is high, with most just aiming to complete the distance and have fun.

Examples: Kona 100 and Schwinn 100.

MTB-O'S and TrailQuest

MTB-O's (orienteering) require you to visit certain check points in a fixed order within a set time. However, racing on bridleways is illegal in the UK, so Trailquests are more common over here.

Trailquests give you a set time and a map to try and amass as many points as possible by visiting checkpoints and punching a check-sheet. It can be done alone or in a team and taken as seriously as you want - either charging around chasing the prizes (not usually that big), or enjoying the course and challenge with friends.

Examples: Trailquest or Polaris (a 2-day challenge where you usually carry all of your gear).

'Alternative Trailquest'

This is when you and friends award yourselves points for finding or spotting peculiar objects whilst out riding e.g. discarded pants, jazz-mags and randy couples in car parks.

■**NOTE**: You are not allowed to race on bridleways. However, racing is defined as the winner being the fastest person over a fixed route. Trailquest can therefore use bridleways, as they allow all the competitors the same amount of time to find as many checkpoints as they can.

PACKING A BIKE BAG:

01: Remove the pedals (remembering that the driveside pedal unscrews anti-clockwise and the non-driveside unscrews clockwise).

02: Remove both wheels (place in wheel bags if you have them) and put them either side of the bike frame. If you have disc brakes, put a spacer between the callipers to stop them closing together if the lever accidentally gets squeezed.

03: Ask your local bike shop for any spare drop-out spacers or remove the wheel skewers from the hubs and put these between the fork and rear drop-outs to stop the frame and forks getting bent.

04: Remove the rear mech and thread the skewer through it so the mech is between the drop-outs.

05: Remove the bars from the stem, and tape them to the top tube.

06: Use plumber's pipe lagging on the frame, extra cardboard under the chainrings, over the sprockets, down the side of the bag, and any clothing to fill the gaps in the bag.

TOP TIP: Lock or zip-tie the zips together, and remember a spare zip-tie for the return journey.

01

02

03

04

05

06

AUTOMOBILES

The car boot is the simplest, safest, most aerodynamic, and cheap method of transporting your bike. Take measures to stop the bikes scratching each other or the car, and getting the boot muddy.

When attaching the bike on the outside of the car, ensure it is fixed on securely with nylon buckle straps, bungees or rope. Check they are still secure over long journeys. Avoid having any bikes touching one another or the car, and make sure that the bikes do not protrude from the side of the car by more than 12 inches, or obscure the number plate or rear lights (as these are fineable offenses). This may involve removing the wheels, and buying another number plate (from a garage), or buying a trailer board, which houses the number plate and lights.

Roof racks are cheap, but specific to certain cars and are cumbersome. They also put the bike up high, causing drag (slows the car down and increases the running costs). Furthermore, the added height means that you won't get under some height restriction bars, and while it's out of sight, it may also be out of mind.

Rear / boot racks allow easy mounting and dismounting and cause less drag than roof racks. However they can scratch the car paint, obscure your rear view, lights and number plate, or protrude from the side of the car by more than 12 inches which are all fineable offenses. They are also easy prey for thieves.

Tow ball carriers fix on to the car's towbar, giving a platform on which the bikes stand upright. This keeps the bikes and car apart (so no scratches), and leaves your view, lights and number plate visible, but if you don't already have a towbar they can be expensive to fit.

TRAINS

Trains can be an economical (especially if booked early), environmentally friendly, and a relaxing (in theory) way to travel. They are also perfect for one-way rides. Be prepared for the delays, over-crowding and hit and miss chance of actually getting your bike on the train. This will depend greatly on the guard on duty, how busy the train is and the time of day. You can just try your luck and turn up with your bike (seems to work in most cases), or pay a booking charge for the bike - although this bizarrely does not guarantee you and your bike a place.

■ **NOTE:** To contact railway enquiries about train times, costs, routes, etc phone 0845 7484950.

PLANES

Check with your airline before booking, and inform them your pride and joy (bike) will be accompanying you. It is usually free (except on charter flights) to take your bike on the plane, as long as you don't exceed the baggage allowance. Pack your bike well to avoid it getting damaged. You can get an old cardboard bike box from your local bike shop or we recommend a bike bag - especially if you intend to travel again with your bike in the future.

BIKE BAGS

Hard box bike bags are expensive and heavy, but are very safe, while the more common, soft bag, should be suitable for most uses. Look for wheels on the bottom, so you can drag the bag along, covers for your wheels and zipped compartments inside to carry spares and tools.

■ **NOTE:** The superb Neil Pryde bike bag (as seen above left) has all the features you should need, is well mde and looks very professional, see www.ultrasporteu. com for more details.

if you go down to

the woods today

be sure to have a good ride

discover new horizons

ALUMINIUM (Yankee=Aluminum)

In the last few years, aluminium has become the most popular frame material for quality mountain bikes. It is mixed with small amounts of other metals to make alloys (for some reason 'alloy' usually means an aluminium alloy in the bike world).

Aluminium is light (frame weigh around 2.5-4.5lbs), inexpensive (between £150-£1,000), won't corrode as it has a tough layer of oxide, and is easy to work with. However, it has a low tensile strength so will break easily if bent. To combat flexibility, a lot of it is used, typically by having large diameter tubes or thick walls; this gives tubes sufficient strength and stiffness whilst remaining lightweight.

The combination of being easy to shape, and stiff when used correctly, make aluminium alloy the usual choice for suspension bikes, regardless of overall bike cost.

Aluminium bikes have a reputation for giving a 'harsh' or bumpy ride, and transmitting the shock to the rider, rather than absorbing it. This was the experiences with early frames, where excessively large and thick tubes were used. As the material has come of age, most manufacturers have learnt how to engineer the frames to perform as required, giving comfort or stiffness where it's needed.

Advantages: Makes for a comfortable, strong and lightweight frame.

Disadvantages: Cheaper frames can feel bumpy or harsh.

STEEL

Until recently, steel ruled in the bike frame world. Everything from department store kids bikes to the handcrafted Italian masterpieces that won the Tour de France were made from various types of steel. Today, steel has mostly been pushed out of the mid-market to either the very low or fairly high-end.

Steel is stiff and strong, but heavy, with frames typically weighting between 3.5-5.5lbs. To be lighter, better grade steel with thin walled tubing is used, but there is a limit to how thin a tube can be made before the quality of the join or strength of the tube is affected. The usual result is that steel frames are heavier than their similar priced aluminium counterparts.

The old dog has tricks up its sleeve however. Steel has a unique springy ride quality that many riders love, and is still a top choice for a lively trail bike. It is very resistant to damage, making it an ideal material for high-abuse jump bikes. Steel is also easily reparable - making it the only frame that could be fixed up a thousand miles from home by someone with a welding torch and basic knowledge. However it will rust if exposed.

Advantages: Stiff, strong and repairable frame. Gives a 'springy' feel to the ride.

Disadvantages: Slightly heavier than aluminium, will rust if scratched.

CARBON FIBRE

On paper, carbon fibre frames should be the lightest (often below 3lbs), the strongest and most shock absorbing. Due to the way it is made carbon fibre can be stiff in one direction and compliant in another, which makes it ideal for fine-tuning the ride of a bike. So why isn't every top-end mountain bike made of carbon fibre?

Some early frames & components were prone to failure, which made riders distrustful of the material. Frames were frequently not as light as expected, difficult to bond metals parts to, and expensive. Component manufacturers have had greater success making super-light and reliable handlebars and seatposts of carbon fibre, but now faith is also returning in carbon frames with various successful designs.

Advantages: Light, strong and with some shock absorbent qualities.

Disadvantages: Suffers fatigue and will fail if it exceeds it's stress limits or receives external damage. Expensive.

TITANIUM

The 'wonder metal', titanium is in many ways the ideal mountain bike material. It is as strong as steel but only half the weight (typical frame is around 2.5lbs), while being stiffer than aluminium. It is also very resistant to corrosion and fatigue so can last for years and not look old.

It is however incredibly difficult and time consuming to work with, and so titanium frames are expensive and their evolution has been fairly slow. Technology is now at the point where the high-end frames are becoming increasingly more sophisticated, mixing low weight and strength with a comfortable springy ride while simple frames are becoming affordable (from £600).

Advantages: Corrosion and fatigue resistant, and strong yet lightweight. Springy feel. Lifetime warrantee.

Disadvantages: Very difficult and dangerous to work with, making it expensive.

When choosing a bike to buy, the main factors that determine how the bike feels to ride are the bike geometry (shape) and suspension. Frame material will subtly contribute to the 'feel' of the bike and will determine the weight, strength or life of the frame. Having said that, once you've decided on how much money to spend, you will probably find the choice of materials limited (around 80% of bikes are made of aluminium these days). For those occasions where there is a choice of material available in your price range, here is a brief guide to the most common materials around.

TOP TIP: It is usually advisable to avoid getting the latest exotic frame materials, as they may have an uncertain lifespan, short warranty, and be expensive (but their price will usually drop quickly).

■ NOTE: Butting means that the tube is thinner in the middle, than at the ends, in order to save weight.

The geometry of a bike refers to the length and angle of the frames tubes. This varies between bikes, and goes some way to deciding how it steers, how your weight is distributed, and to some extent the comfort. These measurements are readily available from manufacturers and help you compare bikes, but there is more to it than just frame angles, as component properties e.g. fork length and stem length will also affect the geometry and handling of the bike.

■NOTE: A headtube angle of 71 degrees and a seat angle of 73 degrees are the most common on XC bikes and provide an efficient, and responsive yet stable ride, while DH bikes have smaller angles to give more stable steering at high speeds.

BOTTOM BRACKET HEIGHT

This affects the bikes stability, as it changes the bikes centre of gravity, as well as the rider's height from the ground - a high BB will result in a higher seat, and therefore a higher centre of gravity.

Lower: Stable as the centre of gravity is low, but pedal clearance is poor.
Higher: Good pedal clearance, but the bike is less stable and will also feel big as the saddle will be up high.

TRAIL

The trail determines how the steering handles. If there were no trail the steering would feel very twitchy. The factors determining the trail length are the head tube angle, wheel diameter, fork length, and rake (offset of the pivot line from the axle).

Shorter: More responsive steering.
Longer: Increase the bikes tendency to steer straight ahead, therefore making it more stable, but the steering less responsive.

■ NOTE: A compressed fork will reduce the bikes trail.

TOP TUBE

If all other angles remain the same, a longer top tube increases the wheelbase. Most modern MTBs tend to have top tubes that slope down from the front to the back. This gives a greater standover height, and makes the frame triangles smaller and stronger.

Shorter: More maneuverable and comfortable, but less efficient (if it is too short the rider will feel cramped and their knees may get in the way of the handlebars when turned).
Longer: Generally on 'sportier' bikes, as it provides a low, efficient riding position, but too if too long, the rider will be stretched and the steering slow.

WHEEL BASE

Normally about 41 inches for a hard tail and 43 inches for full-suspension bike.

Shorter: More responsive and maneuverable, but can feel cramped.
Longer: Tracks straight ahead better, is more comfortable, feels safe, good on long rolling descents at high speed, but at the cost of steering responsiveness (especially twisty singletrack), and the front end may lift on climbs.

CHAINSTAY LENGTH

Chainstay length has decreased since early off-road models, putting the rear wheel further underneath the rider.

Shorter: Quick acceleration and turning, increased traction when pedalling standing up on steep climbs, but there may be tyre clearance problems and harsh feel on rough terrain.
Longer: More stable and comfortable (especially downhill).

SEAT TUBE ANGLE

The normal angle is 73°-74° and affects the traction & power transfer to the wheels.

Smaller Angle: Gives better climbing traction, but is less comfortable, reduces power transfer efficiency, and effectively makes the bike longer the higher the saddle is put up.
Greater Angle: Allows better power transfer due to the rider's weight being more directly over the pedals.

■ NOTE: A 'laid back' seat post (the saddle clamp is back, not directly above the seatpost) positions the saddle further back, which has a similar affect to reducing the seat tube angle.

HEAD TUBE ANGLE

This angle is usually 70°-72° for a XC bike or 65°-67° for DH bikes, and will effect the steering in a similar way to the trail.

Smaller Angle: The bike is more stable in a straight line, and at high speeds, but harder to steer (especially up-hill).
Greater Angle: This will shorten the wheelbase, and make the steering more responsive.

■ NOTE: A longer (travel) fork will decrease the head tube angle by about 1 degree for every extra 20mm of travel - thus slowing the steering down.

TYPES OF SUSPENSION BIKES:

There are basically 3 types of bikes when it comes to suspension:

1 'Rigid' which has no suspension.
2 'Hardtail' with front suspension.
3 'Full suspension' which has front and rear suspension.

'Hardtails' are the most common, and are suitable for most riders. However, if you don't mind the loss of power transfer, greater cost and weight, and want to ride rougher trails in more comfort, then you will want a full suspension bike.

Most people think of a 'spring' as a coil spring, but in mounain biking compressed air or elastomer stacks can also be used to create the spring.

TOP TIP: To ride a full suspension bike without 'bobbing' use smooth circular pedalling strokes, and move your weight forwards when pedalling standing up.

ADVANTAGES OF SUSPENSION:

* Greater comfort - reduces fatigue and riders can stay seated on rough terrain.
* Ride rougher terrain - soaks up bumps and enables you to pick the best line rather than the smoothest.
* Better traction - wheels 'hug' the ground improving grip on rough ground, corners, technical climbs, and when braking.
* Aid jumping - compressing the suspension just before jumping gives some springback to boost your jump.

DISADVANTAGES OF SUSPENSION:

* Compresses when not wanted - Front suspension may compress/dip when you brake (sending your weight forwards), and rear suspension can compress and sap your energy when you pedal.
* Handling - can be less responsive due to rotational deflection in the fork.
* Heavy - It will add weight to your bike.
* Expensive - It is more expensive to buy, maintain and replace.

■ NOTE: As suspension technology develops many of the disadvantages are being dealt with i.e. today a full suspension bike (can) have very little pedal 'bob' and brake feedback, stiff forks, good lateral stiffness, weigh around 20lbs and not cost the earth.

AIR

These designs use compressed air to provide the 'spring'. This design enables riders of various weights to use the same unit, as they simply change the spring rate by changing the pressure (measured in pounds per square inch) in the shock, by using a specialist 'shock' pump - don't try using standard pumps as they aren't made to reach the high pressure that the shocks require, and will break - honest, I've done it!

Pros: Light, easily adjustable for any rider weight, and can be almost as good as a coil spring, without the inertia drawbacks.

Cons: Less responsive than coils, can blow, and they leak gradually (meaning they need regular re-setting).

■ NOTE: Additional drawbacks with air springs can be addressed as follows:

* Tight seals increase friction, but using negative springs overcomes this.
* The air can warm up with high activity, making it expand and the pressure increase , but using a gas e.g. nitrogen in the shock design reduces this.
* A constant volume of air in the shock results in a progressive spring rate i.e. it gets stiffer towards the end of the stroke. However, by having two chambers this can be overcome to a degree.

COIL

This is made of a wound piece of steel or sometimes titanium (lightweight, but expensive). Springs come in different lengths and strengths to take into account the suspension design and the rider's body-weight.

Suspension fork spring strength is usually classified as soft, medium or hard, while rear suspension spring strength is expressed in lbs / inch or Newtons / mm. This figure is usually printed on the spring, along with it's length. For example 500 X 3 means that 500lbs is required to compress the spring 1 inch, and it has 3 inches of travel. Therefore it will take a force of 1,500lbs to fully compress this (linear) spring.

Pro's: Long life, sensitive, reliable, smooth, plush travel, and are naturally linear, but can be wound to be progressive.

Con's: Heavy and require different strengths depending on the riders weight.

ELASTOMERS OR MCUs

These look like cylindrical bits of rubber, and have bubbles of nitrogen inside to provide the spring. They were common in early suspension designs, but are not used much today. Like coil springs, they need to be chosen to suit the weight of the rider, and are usually colour coded to indicate their strength.

Pro's: Cheap, simple and light.

Con's: Not very responsive and can be affected by changes in temperature i.e. go harder in the cold and softer in the heat. The 'stack' may rot over time and the nitrogen bubbles will slowly escape, leaving you with duff suspension.

■ NOTES:

See page 32 for an explanation of suspension jargon.

By staying relaxed and focused on the trail ahead your body will react accordingly to the terrain, providing the best (and cheapest) suspension.

Any suspension will increase comfort, but keeping it active, efficient, light and the brake and pedal feedback low, is the ultimate aim.

Most people (even racers) are convinced that the benefits of full suspension outweigh the drawbacks and are generally more fun to ride.

Adjustable travel suspension designs let you customise your bike, to various different terrain and styles of riding - but be aware that this can affect the geometry and therefore the handling or 'feel' of the bike.

As if suspension wasn't hard enough to understand already, everyone seems to use a whole variety of foreign words when talking about it. Worry no more, this page should enable you to understand and talk (or at least listen) about it with some degree of confidence.

AXLE PATH: is the path the rear wheel axle moves between the suspension being extended and compressed.

BIO-PACING: is when the chain tension increases from pedalling forces.

BLOW-OFF VALVE: emergency valve that opens when damping is overloaded.

BOBBING: unwanted suspension movement caused by the rider bouncing up and down on the seat due to an un-even pedal stroke or because the suspension design causes the chain tension to alter when it compresses or extends.

BOTTOM OUT: is when the suspension thuds as you reach maximum travel.

BRAKE FEEDBACK: is when applying the brakes affects the rear suspension, by compressing or extending, or a combination of the two depending on where you are in the travel.

TOP TIP: To test a bike for brake feedback: hold the rear brake on and push down on the rear suspension while watching the front wheel: the more it rolls the more the feedback.

BRAKE FORCES: is the force created by the rider applying the brakes.

BRAKE JACK: is when the rotational forces created by disc brakes cause the swingarm to extend (lifting the rear end of the bike).

BUSHING: smooth bearing surface.

CHAINLINE: is the line from the top of the chosen chainring to the chosen sprocket. Pedalling forces go along this line and affect the suspension (unless the main pivot linkage is level with this line).

CHAINGROWTH: refers to increased tension on the chain caused by the distance between the rear axle and bottom bracket changing when the

suspension compresses. Too little chain tension and the bike will 'bob' and have poor traction, too much and the bike will rise on the pedal stroke which has the effect of pulling back on the chain / pedals and make the pedals feel like they are locked - see pedal feedback.

CAVITATION: air mixing with damping oil causing a change in the viscosity of the oil and therefore the performance.

COMPRESSION DAMPING (CD): controls the speed at which the suspension compresses, by taking away some of the energy.

DAMPING: controls the speed at which the shock can move - without it, the suspension will compress and rebound at top speed - see compression and rebound damping.

DRIVETRAIN INDUCED SHOCK COMPRESSION (DISC): suspension is compressed due to pedalling forces.

LEVERAGE RATIO: the ratio between the movement of the rear wheel and the movement of the shock e.g. a 2:1 ratio means that the rear wheel moves 2 inches to every 1 inch the shock moves.

LINEAR / FLAT / CONSTANT RATE: the force required to compress the suspension stays constant throughout the whole travel.

LINKAGE: part of a rear suspension lever design.

LOCKOUT: stops the suspension from compressing (or returning) - usually by increasing either the compression or rebound damping.

NEGATIVE SPRINGS: a springs that work against the main suspension spring, to compress the suspension, making the initial spring rate more linear and 'plush', and also stop top-out.

PEDAL FEEDBACK: is when the pedal stroke stiffens due to changes in the chain tension caused by pedalling and suspension movement affecting one another - see chaingrowth for more information.

TOP TIP: To test for pedal feedback, push down on the suspension and see how much the pedals rotate backwards (do this in each chainring as results will differ).

PEDAL FORCES: the force created by the rider pedalling, which pulls on the rear axle, via the chain.

PIVOT: a pin about which a part rotates through a bushing or bearing.

(Stable) PLATFORM SHOCK: a suspension that attempts to stop the suspension compressing under pedalling forces, but compress for bumps in the trail.

OPEN BATH DAMPER: free floating oil in the suspension fork legs.

PRELOAD: the amount the spring is compressed when at rest - used to determines the initial force required to start compressing the suspension.

PROGRESSIVE RATE: the force required to compress the suspension increase as you go through the travel (air shocks are naturally rising / progressive).

REBOUND DAMPING (RD): controls the speed at which the suspension returns to it's uncompressed state.

SAG: is the compression of the suspension, caused by riders weight - this enables the suspension to extend / float up and down over ripples in the terrain.

SHOCK STROKE: is the distance the shock moves between extended & compressed.

SPRINGS: absorb the shock and return the fork or frame to its original position. 'Coils' are what most people understand as being a spring, although there are other forms e.g. air or elastomers.
Spring Rate / Strength: the amount of force (usually expressed in lbs) needed to compress the actual spring 1 inch.

Fork springs indicate their spring rate e.g. 60lbs with one number, while rear shocks have 2 numbers; one for the spring rate e.g. 500lbs (higher than forks due to the mechanical leverage) and another to indicate it's movement (usually in inches).

■ **NOTE:** To alter the spring rate of a coil or elastomer spring you need change it, while with air shocks you increase or decrease the pressure of air in the shock.

SPRUNG MASS: see unsprung mass (opposite of).

SPRING WEIGHT: refers to the strength of the spring e.g. a 'heavier' or 'harder' spring will require more force to compress it.

STICTION: is the static friction, which needs to be overcome to start the shock moving.

SWINGARM: is the 'arm' near or instead of the chainstay, joining the main pivot and the rear axle on a single-pivot bike.

TRAVEL: is the distance the wheel moves between extended and compressed.

TOP OUT: is when the fork returns to it's extended position with a thump - rebound damping and negative springs help overcome this.

UNSPRUNG MASS: is anything that is not suspended by the suspension (e.g. wheels, fork lowers, disc brakes, swingarm, etc). A low unsprung mass will enable the suspension to react quicker and work more efficiently.

FRONT SUSPENSION DESIGNS

Most front suspension forks will be the 'telescopic' design - where the upper set of legs (stanchions) slide into another set of (larger) legs. The travel on these forks is the same as the distance the fork legs move over one another - easy! Well not quite, as there are variations of the telescopic fork and other design to choose from, as well as all the choice between air, elastomer or coil springs, and different set-up adjustments, travel options and more.

TOP TIP: Don't just look at the maximum travel, check out the forks adjustment knobs e.g. preload, rebound, compression damping, and even threshold damping. These will enable you to tune the suspension to your personal preferences.

TELESCOPIC	UP-SIDE-DOWN TELESCOPIC	TRIPLE CLAMP	LINKAGE	USE	LEFTY	HEADSHOCK

TELESCOPIC

Pros: Light, wide range of prices, fit on most bikes. A rear arch is lower and broader, to try and make the fork stiffer.

Cons: Friction as tubes slide over each other. Prone to flexing. Limited mud clearance.

UP-SIDE-DOWN TELESCOPIC

Pros: Lower unsuspended weight and improved mud clearance.

Cons: Can be flexible and are only compatible with disc brakes.

TRIPLE CLAMP

Pros: Allow longer travel on forks (4+ inches) and keeps them strong and stiff.

Cons: Heavy, reduce steering lock, and need a strong headtube joint on the frame to combat increased stress.

■ **NOTE:** Triple clamp forks may invalidate the warranty on some frames.

LINKAGE

Pros: Bump efficient axle path and doesn't compress / dive when the front brake is applied.

Cons: More pivots add more weight and maintenance. Is also bike specific.

USE

Pros: Anti-dive design when braking, lightweight, and head turning design.

Cons: Expensive, and can stiffen up when braking over rough terrain.

LEFTY

Pros: Turns heads on the trail, quick and easy to change inner tubes and tyres, is light and stiff.

Cons: Expensive, and will you feel safe?

■ **NOTE:** Cannondale bikes use their in-house lefty or Headshock suspension designs, which use a 1.5inch (fork) steerer tube, rather than the standard 1 1/8inch. Reducer cups are available if you want to fit a conventional fork.

HEADSHOCK

Pros: Lightweight and stiff with good mud clearance.

Cons: Have limited travel and only fit on certain bikes e.g. Cannondales.

■ **NOTE:** A bike frames geometry is designed for a particular length of suspension fork. Fitting longer travel forks will raise the front of the bike, pushing your weight further back, raising your centre of gravity, and increasing the trail of the bike which will slow down the steering - therefore check with the bike manufacturer as to the amount of travel they recommend before buying a new fork.

■ **NOTE:** Some forks have adjustable travel (external dials / knobs are the most convenient), which adds versatility. Use the short setting to aid climbing, or for responsive steering, the mid setting for general use, or crank it up to full travel for bashing over stuff and riding downhill. There may also be a 'lock out' option which stops the suspension from compressing and is useful for smooth climbs.

Rear suspension is more complicated than front suspension; for a start the rear wheel moves further than the shock travels (due to the 'leverage ratio'). mountain biking has seen various rear suspension designs over the years e.g. URT (unified rear triangle), no pivot, parallelogram, monolink, single pivot, 4-bar or multi link pivot and virtual pivots - of which it is the latter three that make up the main types of rear suspension designs in today's market.

■ NOTE: There is a balance to be struck between the (most suspension efficient) axle path and chain length (which affects pedal feedback).

The key to minimising pedal (and brake) feedback is to control the chaingrowth. This can be done by having either a straight axle path or a suspension design where the chain and pedalling are independent from the suspension.

SUSPENSION SEATPOSTS

If you already have a 'hardtail' bike, the cheapest and simplest way to take some of the sting out of the tail is with a suspension seatpost. There are basically two designs, the telescopic and the parallel link (see pics at bottom of page).

The Telescopic design is the most common design, and works by one section sliding into another, which is supported by a spring. The drawbacks are that it only works well when the rider is sitting in the middle of the saddle, and the distance from the saddle and pedals change when it compresses.

The Parallel link design uses pivots to provide the travel. This design generally has more travel, and when it compresses, the distance between the saddle and the handlebars changes, which is actually quite good as your weight shifts backwards and downwards. However, this can take some getting used to, and this design is usually more expensive.

Pros: Cheap and lightweight.

Cons: Doesn't work when you are standing up, and it suspends the rider not the bike, so the wheels don't track the ground any better.

Telescopic

Parallel link

SINGLE PIVOT

This design has a swingarm with the wheel at one end and a pivot at the other, resulting in an axle path in the shape of an arc. The problem with this is that when the suspension compresses or extends, the distance between the sprockets and chainrings will change, which means that you may feel big hits through the pedals. More importantly, pedalling pulls on the top run of the chain, which pulls the rear wheel towards the bottom bracket. Depending on the position of the pivot to the chainline, this can make the suspension extend or compress. Ideally the pivot position wants to be level with the chainline for the best results but this is not possible on bikes with three chainrings.

Mid pivot point slightly above the middle chainring (the most popular position), makes the chain extend the suspension, but the pedal force counteracts it by compressing the suspension. This is only the case in the middle chainring however - in the small ring it will behave like a high pivot bike and the suspension will stiffen (the Orange Sub5 pictured, is an example of a mid pivot design that works very well).

Low pivot point causes the suspension to compress under pedalling, which lifts the wheel. This provides good traction and plush, active suspension, although the pedalling will feel soft, as the suspension 'squats' (compresses) if the pedalling action is not smooth.

High pivot point increases the chain tension when pedalling, which pulls the wheel into the ground, thus extending and locking out the suspension. This will give a rough ride and the pedals will 'kickback' (pull back), when you hit something.

Pros: Simple, laterally stiff, sturdy, light, low maintenance, and works well on bikes with just one chainring e.g. downhill bikes.

Cons: Braking & pedalling can adversely effect the suspension, and increasing the travel steepens the head angle (which is generally not wanted). These cons will increase the longer the travel is.

■ NOTE: This may sound like a hampered design, but done correctly (or by using 'stable platform' shocks) it provides a simple, dependable and effective suspension action, that is liked by many riders.

■ NOTE: A floating / independent drivetrain e.g. Maverick / Klein's monolink or GT's I-drive (eccentrically revolving bottom bracket) isolate the suspension from the drivetrain to minimise chaingrowth (and therefore 'bobbing' and pedal 'kickback'). This aims to provide a rear suspension design that has the advantages of a single-pivot and the activeness of 4-bar.

Horst link

TOP TIP: Don't get bogged
down in all the physics and
claims of rear suspension
designs, just try some out and
go with what you like best!

4-BAR

The name comes from the 4 independent 'bars' in the suspension design: main frame / shock, chainstays, seatstays, and a linkage/rocker.

The two main 'true' 4-bar designs are the FSR and the Rocker. These are usually recognised by the 'Horst link' (named after it's inventor Horst Leitner) pivot on the chainstay. This allows the rear wheel to pivot forward as the suspension goes through its travel (effectively changing the position of the main pivot), and enabling the axle path to be more vertical (thus minimising chaingrowth).

■ NOTE: The 'Horst link' has been patented by Specialized to protect their FSR design, although it is licensed out to others to use e.g. Giant, Ellsworth, Schwinn, Turner, Intense and others. The patent only covers bikes made within Taiwan and the USA, so some manufacturers e.g. Bianchi can use the design without having to pay the fee.

Pros: The suspension is active at all times. Achieves long travel from a short travel shock. Designers can set the responsiveness of the suspension (for small or big bumps). The travel can be adjusted without effecting the head angle.

Cons: The numerous linkages and pivots will increase the weight, cost, and maintenance and cause some lateral play. The rear mech may also hit the Horst link (more annoying than anything else).

■ NOTE: Designs that use multiple linkages but don't have any pivots between the main pivot and the wheel will have an axle path of an arc. These are basically single pivot designs with a linkage activated shock - and are sometimes known as 'faux bars'. However, there are some 'true' 4-bar designs, that don't use the 'Horst link' e.g. Rocky Mountain's ETS-X and Marin's Quad design.

VIRTUAL PIVOT POINT (VPP)

These designs create a 'virtual' pivot point somewhere off the bikes frame, which can move position through the travel (a feature of 'true' 4-bar designs). The VPP aims to create a changeable axle path that a single or multi-pivot design cannot achieve.

The 'virtual' pivot point away from the bike enables the axle path to go up, down, back and forth and change direction through its travel. This enables a variety of axle paths to be created in an attempt to find the best compromise between bump responses and chain tension changes (to minimise the wheels reaction to pedalling forces), and provide different ride characteristics and suspension movement at different points in the travel.

Pros: Smooth, active, suspension with no 'bob'. The axle path can be manipulated through its travel, to change the properties of the suspension.

Cons: More weight and maintenance in the form of all those pivots and links.

■ NOTE: Outland have patented the VPP design, but they sell the rights to other manufacturers to use e.g. Santa Cruz and Intense.

GENERAL

35

SAG

DAMPING

SHOCK DEVELOPMENTS

NEGATIVE SPRINGS

It's a crying shame that after spending lots of money on suspension, many riders don't take the time to set it up properly.

Suspension is usually set at the factory to fit an 'average' rider i.e. around 70 kg, cycling at an average speed on average terrain. Therefore if you are above or below this weight by 10%, or do more extreme or sedate riding than the 'average' rider you will probably need to change the springs and twiddle some knobs and dials to get the best performance from your suspension.

When setting up your suspension, you should start with the sag, then go on to the rebound damping, then the compression damping, if you have them. As a general rule, the suspension should 'bottom out' or use all of its travel about once or twice a ride - that way you know you are making the most of it.

Suspension compression caused by rider's weight; enables the suspension to extend as well as compress. This results in a smoother ride as the wheel extends into dips as well as rising over bumps.

To alter the sag, coil springs use a preload dial, while air springs will have a valve for the shock pump to fix onto - on suspension forks both of these are usually found on the top of the fork leg. Increasing the preload (on a spring or elastomer) reduces the sag - this increases the the initial amount of force required to activate the suspension, it doesn't stiffen the suspension action.

■ **NOTE**: DO NOT use lots of turns of the preload to set the sag on coil springs, as preloading the spring compresses it and keeps it compressed. This will put the spring under continual stress shortening it's life, could cause spring failure, reduces the overall travel, might cause 'top out', and stiffens the suspension up faster through its travel (on progressive springs e.g. elastomer).

This controls the energy absorbed by the spring to stop it compressing and rebounding too quickly and easily. This is usually done by restricting the movement of oil (although air and friction can be used), by using holes or valves to create some resistance. The amount of damping will therefore be dependant on the speed the shock compresses, the size of the holes, and the viscosity of the oil. The faster the suspension moves, the smaller the holes, and the thicker the oil, the more the damping (resistance).

Rebound damping

This controls the speed the suspension rebounds (to its uncompressed state) after it has been compressed - this is important on coil springs, as they have no frictional energy loss, so will return with almost the same energy that they've just absorbed. It wants to be fast enough that it is ready for the next bump, but not so fast it bucks you around and the tyre loses traction. It is pretty common to have rebound damping knobs on suspension but even if you don't have any you can change the weight of the oil to affect the damping (see page 38 for more information). Rebound damping is where most riders can make the biggest improvements to their suspension performance. Ideally you want to use as little rebound damping as possible, so that the suspension rebounds as fast as possible, ready for the next bump. However, you don't want it to spring back so fast that it throws you around, tops out, and causes the wheel to lose traction.

Compression damping

This controls the speed the suspension compresses, stops it from bottoming out harshly on high-speed hits and allows a softer spring to be used (as it takes more and more load off the spring as the speed increases). This makes the suspension more reactive over small bumps and low speed hits, and allows a wider range of performance.

Some (front and rear) suspension designs aim to create a shock that doesn't compress due to rider's movements like pedalling, but will still compress over bumps in the trail. This can be done in different ways:

Speed sensitive compression damping - because the rider's movements are slow and terrain bumps are fast, increasing the low speed compression damping should provide a more stable shock.

Threshold damping - by restricting or preventing the suspension moving until a certain threshold / is reached all the small movements will be removed, providing a more stable ride, but at the loss of small bump sensitivity. Some shock designs may also use another threshold limit near the end of the travel, to stop bottoming out harshly.

Spring loaded valves - by using valves that only open from forces below and not from above, the suspension only compresses at trail bumps, rather than at rider's movements.

■**NOTE**: Probably the most important thing about these shocks is that you have the ability to adjust them.

■**NOTE**: 'Platform' shocks can transform over-active suspension designs, but also make already well-performing suspension designs too stiff, especially on small bumps.

Some suspension designs use a 'negative' spring (air or coil) which works against the main spring, to make the initial spring rate more more active / plush, sensitive and responsive on consecutive small bumps, and stop topping out. Negative springs are not required on rear coil shocks, as they have a linear spring rate.

■ **NOTE**: Some rear shocks e.g. Rock Shox may have a + and - valve, while others e.g. Fox may have only the one positive valve, but a groove on the air canister of the shock that automatically lets air pass from the + to the - chamber (making the set-up easier).

CALCULATING THE SAG:

Unwind the preload, rebound and compression damping (the suspension should compress and rebound easily and quickly), and if you have adjustable travel, set it at the maximum travel. Now, wearing your cycling clothes and rucksack follow these sag measuring techniques.

FRONT FORKS

01 With the bike unweighted, tie a zip-tie around one of the forks stanchions (inner leg, that the outer leg slides over) by the seal.

02 Now gently get on the bike, in your riding position, then dismount and measure how much the zip-tie has moved. Divide this measurement by the total travel of the suspension and multiply by 100 for the sag %.

■ **NOTE:** If you don't know the maximum travel, measure the stanchions from the top of the seal to the bottom of the crown and minus 21mm from this measurement to get the maximum travel.

REAR SHOCKS

03 Measure the vertical distance from the ground to a fixed point on the bike e.g. top of the saddle. Now gently get on the bike, in your riding position and re-measure the distance again.

04 Alternatively, measure the distance between the centre of the two shock mounts, or use a zip-tie (or there may already be a rubber O-ring) on the shock body. This is not as accurate though, as there isn't necessarily a linear relationship between the shock travel and wheel travel.

The difference between the first and second measurements is the sag. Divide this by the shock stroke (see note below), then multiply that by 100 to get the sag as a %.

■ **NOTE:** If the shock stroke isn't written on the shock, unwind the preload collar fully and measure the length of the shock body.

Eyes

ADJUSTING THE SAG:

COIL AND ELASTOMER SPRINGS:

Ideally you want to get the correct sag using the softest springs, with as little preload as possible. Starting with the preload fully unwound increase it (clockwise) until you get the correct sag. If you need to use several turns on the preload you should really get a firmer spring fitted. If you can't get enough sag even with the preload fully unwound you need to fit a softer/lighter spring.

The preload dial is usually on the top of the fork (pic **01**) and only offers quite small adjustments. The rear shock springs (pic **02**) can be fully compressed but the gaps between the coils should add up to (10%) more than the shock stroke to avoid spring failure.

TOP TIP: Ask for the correct strength spring to be fitted on a new bike.

AIR SPRINGS

You will need a specialist shock pump (normal pumps aren't strong enough) to add air to the shock. Gently screw the pump adaptor onto the valve; on top of the fork leg (pic 03) or shock body (pic 04). Stop half a turn after the pump starts to read the pressure or you can damage the valve.

Now reduce the sag to the desired amount by adding air to the shock (thus increasing the air pressure / spring rate). Most pumps have a button on them to release small amounts of air if you have put in too much and now need to increase the sag.

Negative Springs

If you have a + and a - value, you usually set them within +/- 20psi of one another - but check the manufacturers recommendations if possible.

■ **NOTE:** Air pumps can be inaccurate, and you may also lose some air when detaching the pump from the valve (especially Schrader valves), so add an extra 5-10psi to compensate for this, and always do the sag test. The recommended psi varies between shocks and suspension designs, so consult your owners manual.

HOW MUCH SAG?

The 'right' amount of sag will depend on various factors e.g. terrain, bike design, personal preferences. Generally, a XC rider would have around 10-25%, a freerider around 25-40%, and a downhiller around 40-50%. Therefore a general cross-country rider with a 100mm travel suspension fork, should set their sag with between 10-25mm. Less sag gives a firmer and faster ride, while more sag gives an active ride and greater traction on corners and braking. Too much and you lose some (+) travel and it can feel wallowy.

■ **NOTE:** Shorter travel and air suspension should be set up with less sag than longer travel and coil suspension (because air shocks have a naturally high preload due to their tight seals, so require less sag than coils).

■ **NOTE:** When you unscrew the pump the hiss is air escaping from the pump & hose (not the shock) if the seals are ok. When attaching the pump it is air leaving the shock and entering the pump & hose that you hear.

REBOUND DAMPING

COMPRESSION DAMPING

ADVANCED DAMPING CONTROLS

Once you have set the sag you can set the rebound damping and then the compression damping (if you have it / them). First, make sure both the rebound damping and compression damping dials/knobs are both wound all the way out (anti-clockwise).

TOP TIPS:

Most rebound damping systems use oil, so even if you don't have a rebound damping dial or it's not making enough difference, you can use an oil with a different viscosity (weight) to make adjustments.

Adding (extra) oil to inside the fork has a similar affect as preloading a coil spring i.e. the fork will stiffen up quicker. This is useful for when an air pressure is working well, but it bottoms out a lot.

When making changes to the rebound damping and compression damping, only ever make small adjustments and do them one at a time, so you can tell what does what, and even make notes.

Do not mess with the piggy back chamber as it is under very high pressure and should be left to the specialists.

This controls the speed the suspension rebounds. Ideally you want to use as little rebound damping as possible, so that the suspension rebounds as fast as possible, ready for the next bump. However, you don't want it to spring back so fast that it throws you around, tops out, and cause the wheel to loose traction.

■ NOTE: If the rebound damping isn't set up fast enough, the sag will be useless as the wheel won't rebound fast enough to use it.

Start with the adjuster knob turned all the way out / open (anticlockwise), and ride (while seated) over some repetitive bumps and see how well the suspension reacts.

* If it starts getting stiff / harsh, the suspension is rebounding too slowly, causing it to 'pack down' as it isn't able to extend before the next bump, so you need to reduce the rebound damping (anti-clockwise).

* If it springs up off the bumps quickly, and skips along the top, increase the rebound damping (clockwise) to slow it down.

Now, ride (seated) at an average speed over a single, bigger bump e.g. a kerb, that will compress the suspension nearly all the way, and see how it reacts. As a rough guide, the suspension should compress, rebound and compress halfway before coming to a rest.

* If it feels more like two bumps, it is returning too quickly and you need to increase the rebound damping.

* If it feels slow or returns to it's uncompressed state without rebounding past this position first, decrease the rebound damping.

* If your suspension doesn't have any rebound damping knob (or it's not making enough difference) but uses oil for the rebound damping (most do) you can change the viscosity i.e. weight of the damping oil.

The thicker, heavier oil e.g. 10wt will increase damping rebound i.e. slow it down, which might suit heavy riders, while a thinner oil is better for lighter riders, as it will decrease the damping i.e. quicken it, but it will also have less range of adjustment. Find out what weight oil is already in the shock and go up or down about 2.5wt, or more if you think you need it.

Manufacturers will recommended the volume of oil in open bath forks. However, if an air pressure is working well, but the forks bottom out you could increase the volume of oil by a few mms. This has a similar affect as preloading a coil spring, increasing the spring rate / progressiveness of the fork, making it harder to compress near the end of the travel.

* If there is too much oil in the system you won't be able to use all the travel, too little and you will bottom out harshly.

This controls the speed the suspension compresses and stops it bottoming out harshly on high speed hits. It also allows a softer spring to be used (as it takes more and more load off the spring as the speed increases), which makes the suspension more reactive over small bumps and low speed hits, and allows a wider range of performance. Ideally, you want the use as little compression damping as possible, as it will give a harsher ride, may stop you using all of the available travel, or slow the compression stroke down suddenly.

Start with the adjuster knob turned all the way out / open and increase it as required - you want to use all of the available travel once or twice a ride, in a smooth and controlled manner, without bottoming out harshly.

* If it compresses quickly, easily and bottoms out harshly, increase the compression damping. If it compresses slowly, but you are still bottoming out, you may need a heavier spring. If the spring is ok, you could add heavier oil.

* If it seems harsh, rarely bottoms out, and you aren't using all of the travel, reduce the compression damping (if it is totally unwound check the oil isn't over-filled, and reduce the spring rate).

* If you are bottoming out easily and the spring rate is ok, you could use a heavier oil. However this will also slow down the rebound damping, so if the rebound damping is ok, you could increase the volume of oil in the forks to make the suspension action progressive i.e. harder to compress at the end of the travel. Make small adjustments e.g. 5mms at a time (too much will stop you using all of the travel). This technique is useful on air forks when the air pressure is working well, but still bottoming out.

Some high end suspension may have adjustable threshold and speed sensitive damping.

* Increasing the threshold will make the suspension less active, while decreasing it increases activity.

* Increasing the slow speed damping compression damping will result in a more stable / stiffer suspension which pedals better.

* Increasing the high speed compression damping will stop you bottoming out easily, but will also make the shock feel harsher.

■ NOTE: Position sensitive compression damping can be set at different levels for the start and end of the shocks movement e.g. soft at the beginning, and stiffening up towards the end, to provide a plush ride without bottoming out on big hits.

PROBLEM	POSSIBLE CAUSE	REMEDY
Fork has too much sag	Spring rate is too soft.	Reduce the sag by increasing the preload (clockwise), or increase the air pressure. If the preload knob is wound fully clockwise, fit a stiffer / heavier spring.
Fork doesn't have enough sag	Spring rate is too hard.	Increase the sag by reducing the preload (anti-clockwise), or decrease the air pressure. If the preload knob is wound fully anti-clockwise, fit a softer / lighter spring.
Fork 'bottoms out' regularly and needs more than the maximum preload to get proper sag. Suspension compresses and 'bottoms out' easily, but has the recommended sag	Spring rate is too soft or fork oil is too low. / Not enough compression damping.	Get stiffer spring, or add air, and check the oil height. / Change oil level to increase the compression damping.
Not getting full travel or the fork rarely bottoms out	Spring is too heavy/stiff or the oil is too high.	Decrease the compression damping or reduce the spring rate, check the oil height.
Compression is slow but still bottoms out	The spring is too soft.	Fit a stiffer spring and reduce the compression damping.
Fork springs back slowly, 'packs up' over multiple bumps, and feels harsh	If compression damping and spring rate are ok, there is too much rebound damping.	Reduce rebound damping / use lower oil viscosity.
Fork becomes hard and front end lowers on multiple bumps and / or the front wheel wants to tuck under in corners	Too much rebound damping - the fork cannot recover from hits fast enough or spring rate is too soft.	Reduce rebound damping or increase spring rate.
Feels harsh and rarely bottoms out despite soft spring and/or little preload	Too much compression damping.	Reduce the compression damping.
Fork action is slow / unsensitive if rebound damping and compression damping are not too high	Rebound and compression damping are too high. / Fork neglected / seals dry or worn. / Dirty oil or damaged seals / internals. / Very cold weather can affect fork oil or the action of elastomer springs.	Reduce rebound damping and / or compression damping. / Apply teflon lube to seals & cycle fork. / Change the oil / service the fork. / Use lighter fork oil. / Use lighter elastomers.
Forks springs back too quickly	Not enough rebound damping.	Increase rebound damping or use a higher oil viscosity.
Fork dives when braking	Too little compression damping. / A quirk of some linkage forks.	Increase compression damping. / Ain't much you can do about it!
Knocks during rebound, but doesn't top out	Too much rebound damping.	Decrease rebound damping.
Suspension is poor on small bumps	Compression and rebound damping are too high, or the the spring rate might be too high.	Decrease compression damping and/or rebound damping, spring rate, and / or increase negative spring.

■ NOTES:

If the fork feels hard, try decreasing one or more of the following:
Compression damping
Rebound damping
Spring rate
Oil viscosity

If the fork feels soft, try increasing one or more of the following:
Compression damping
Rebound damping
Spring rate
Oil viscosity

A spring that is too soft may fool you into thinking it is too stiff. This is because you have used up all the travel before you even start (and if a progressive spring) it may will be working in a stiffer spring rate range on small bumps.

SKILLS

have confidence in yourself, relax, focus and breathe

SKILLS
SECTION

This section takes you through basic mountain bike skills such as pedalling and braking through to advanced techniques such as bunny hopping and wheelies.

Just as play is important in the development of a child, you will find that mucking around in car parks, riding down steps and practicing simple manoeuvres can simulate extreme trail conditions in a relatively controlled environment. Use the advice here as a starting point to develop your skills, but remember; practice practice practice is what it is all about...

Weight shifting, pedalling and gear changing are key skills in mountain biking that once mastered, allow you to tackle a range of varying terrains. There are also many technical aspects to mountain bike riding such as basic climbing, descending and cornering, not to mention the more advanced techniques: bunnyhops, wheelies, endo-turns. By understanding and developing your basic skills, you will develop your confidence to tackle a range of situations.

On the following three pages we have summarised what we think to be the basic skills fundamental to successful, smooth riding. and technique.

PEDALLING

Pedalling? We know what you're thinking - what is there to know about? You push your legs down and the pedals go round: simple. However, being aware of ways to maximise your pedalling efficiency will make it a whole lot easier next time you are slogging uphill (or might take your mind off of it anyhow).

Think smooth, steady, round pedal strokes (not stomping up and down) to improve your riding, muscle efficiency, and power. Practice at a slow cadence (revolutions of the pedals per minute), at moderate pressure, in smooth circles, using a relaxed cycling style to avoid any jerkiness. If you have clipless pedals try cycling one legged; it will feel jerky at first until you smooth it out (advance to a slight uphill slope to perfect it).

The (theoretical) average person achieves peak performance and most efficient use of energy at a steady cadence of 80-90rpm on the flat, and 70-80 on climbs. Between these speeds you will be exercising aerobically and making the best use of your energy - above 100rpm wastes energy and is unproductive, while below 60rpm uses more muscle strength (an-aerobically) and tires you out more quickly. Don't become obsessed with hitting the right cadence, just try and keep a comfortable and steady rate, using your gears to shift down when you are pushing hard or up when your legs start spinning too fast.

■ *Calculate cadence (rpm) by counting the number of times a foot reaches the 6 o'clock position in 15 seconds then multiplying it by 4.*

THE PEDAL STROKE.....

1 - Through the 12 o'clock position, drop the heel and push forward.

2 - Push downward on the pedal with the ball of the foot (foot flat).

3 - At the 6 o'clock position, pull your heel backwards as if you scraping mud off the bottom of your shoe.

4 - At the 9 o'clock position start pulling upwards and forward (as if trying to touch your knees on the handlebars) to even the stroke power. *(now go back to step 1 and repeat about 5,000 times per hour).*

BRAKING

Braking is intended to slow you down, not to skid; skids are for kids. Keep the brake levers covered by two fingers and squeeze them (don't pull or you may lock the wheels and skid). Skidding means that the brakes are no longer effective, and you may loose control of the bike and damage the trail. If the wheels do lock up, release the levers and gently re-apply them.

The key to controlled braking is to slow the bike when it is going to respond predictably i.e. on straight, even sections - not in corners. This may seem like impractical advice when flying down a terrifying descent, but remember that tyres have a difficult enough job gripping the terrain when they are rolling smoothly and braking makes them fight the trail for traction rather than complying with obstacles.

The front brake has more stopping power, but (especially on corners) is more likely to loose traction and slide out. It becomes more sensitive the more weight is put on it - so ease off on downhills or you may end up over the bars.

The rear brake gives less stopping power, but is safer to use. You will however need to keep your weight back over it when descending steeply or the rear tyre will loose traction, lock up and the brake become ineffective. If this happens bring your weight over the rear wheel to restore some control, ease off on the brakes and re-apply them again gently.

STEERING

Surprisingly, turning the bike, especially as the speed increases, is little about turning the handlebar, and more about subtle weight shifts. An experienced rider can steer a bike 'no handed' by leaning their weight to control the bikes direction.

Mountain bikers frequently talk about 'picking lines' through the trail. The ability to find the fastest, smoothest line, over which the rider can elegantly glide is an important skill and is developed by experience. The key is to achieve a relaxed upper body, with slightly bent arms and smooth movements.

■ NOTE: Look at where you want to go, not the object you want to avoid, as the bike will tend to go where your eyes are looking.

attack...

THE 'ATTACK' POSITION

This is a useful position to adopt when going fast on an unfamiliar trail, as it enables you to react quickly to obstacles.

* Relax your upper body.

* Bend your arms and legs slightly to absorb bumps and perform quick weight shifts to de-weight the wheels.

* Hover your bum just over the saddle to allow the bike to move up and down.

* Look ahead at the line that you want to ride rather then at obstacles you want to avoid as you tend to steer towards where you are looking.

* Have your brake levers covered by at least two fingers for faster braking.

* Keep your pedals level as this allows better ground clearance and aids balance.

GEARS

Firstly, the lever on the right shifts the chain on the rear sprockets, while the lever on the left shifts the chain on the front chain-ring. The purpose of these gears is so that you do not have to perform one revolution with your legs to achieve one revolution of the wheel.

Gear selection is an important skill in mountain biking and as you become more experienced you will develop the ability to pre-select gears to be in the correct one for the terrain ahead. When your legs are pushing hard you are in too high a gear, likewise if your legs are racing round, it is already time you changed up the gear. When accelerating, increase the speed of your legs before changing to a higher gear, as this is more efficient and easier on your joints and muscles.

When changing gear, ease off on the power slightly and try to shift gears on an easy section of the trail rather than when you are mashing down on the pedals with all your strength. Not only is the latter bad for the components, but it can cause the chain to jump, making you to lurch forwards and get a handlebar stem where it hurts. Any mud on the chain and worn or slightly mismatched components will mean that gear shifting is unreliable (especially when under load i.e. pedalling hard).

When the tyres have poor traction, too much power will make the back wheel spin. Mountain bikes have a wide ratio of gears for this reason - use low gears so that you don't have to push with lots of power (even on very steep hills), thus providing better traction.

■ **NOTE:** When changing gears you need to change down one at a time, but you can change up in multiples.

	GEAR	
	LOW	**HIGH**
BIKE SPEED	Slow	Fast
FRONT CHAINRING	Small	Big
REAR SPROCKETS	Big	Small
GEAR RATIO*	Low	High
*Calculated by front chainring teeth / rear cog teeth	e.g. 0.69	e.g. 3.5

■**NOTE:** Avoid using the gears that cause the chain to sit diagonally i.e. on the large chainring and large cogs, or small chainring and small cogs, as this causes additiona stress and wear on the chain.

WEIGHT DISTRIBUTION

Deciding where to distribute your weight over the bike will effect traction, braking, pedalling efficiency, balance, steering and the ease with which you can lift up the front and back of the bike. It is therefore important to be aware of how subtle weight changes can make life easier when tackling the wide array of terrain, gradient and obstacles you will be faced with when out riding. To alter your weight distribution subtly, simply move your body into a more upright position to transfer your weight back, or lean forwards to the handlebars to transfer it forwards.

A skillful rider can descend the impossibly steep, glide up over loose rocky ascents and seemingly float over challenging terrain, where tyre grip to the mere mortal seems as scarce as men at a Tom Jones concert.......

On the flat, weight distribution should be approximately 40% over the front wheel to allow sufficient traction to steer accurately and 60% over the rear wheel to allow for maximum traction and pedalling efficiency. This will have to change depending on the terrain and angle of the slope. When ascending, move your weight forwards, and when descending move it further back. Also, when entering a muddy, sandy or water-logged section you should shift your weight back and lighten the front wheel to avoid the front wheel 'digging in' which may send you over the top.

Riding over obstacles such as logs, will require shifts in your weight distribution. Below we have outlined the main points to practice.

▲ Lifting the Front Wheel:

Lean back on the bike and accelerate slightly, pulling up on the bars. Learn how hard you can pull back without falling over backwards.

Remember that pulling the rear brake will send the front wheel back to earth.

▲ Lifting the Rear Wheel:

Move the body weight up and slightly forward while lifting up the back end of the bike with the pedals.

Stand up and brace your feet against the pedals. Push back and up (a scooping action)

PHYSICAL & PSYCHOLOGICAL

Cornering requires overcoming both physical and psychological fear.

Trust your tyres, the side knobbles are (usually) in better condition than the central ones. Brake before the corner while you are still going in a straight line and have maximum traction, as braking in the corner will pull the bike upright and drag it off in to a straight line. Enter the corner slowly and accelerate out (enter too fast and you may have to use the brakes in the corner, lose control and risk 'washing out' in the turn).

At higher speeds the bike will need tilting into the corner, however this will reduce tyre grip (as the centre of gravity is shifted away from the centre of the tyres). So you need to keep your weight upright and low; pushing weight down on the outside pedal will help.

Experience (we don't necessarily mean injury) will teach you how fast you can take each corner - start slow and speed up as your confidence increases. Remember, in wet, muddy conditions, there will be less traction, so corner less aggressively with less speed and try to stay more upright. Use the trailing foot on the inside of the corner to help get your weight low and save your balance if the tyres start to slide.

RACING LINE

The best line to take in a corner is the straightest.

By approaching the bend from out wide not only can you see around the corner, but you can then steer into the apex (inside) of the corner. On the exit, let yourself drift out wide as you put the power back down, and accelerate out of the corner.

SPEEDWAY STYLE

You can purposefully slide the rear wheel if you have over-shot the corner and need to get the bike pointing in the right direction.

Do this by applying the rear brake hard, and moving your weight forwards slightly (un-weighting the rear wheel). Use your body and feet to help push the the rear end around and when it is facing the correct direction, release the brake.

■ NOTE: Only do this on hard-pack surfaces and only when totally necessary.

SWITCHBACKS

These are very sharp corners i.e.180 degree turns. Approach them slowly and cut in sharply towards the apex of the bend. Keep the outside pedal hard down to help the bike turn, and lean your weight backwards or the front wheel may dig in.

An alternative technique to use on slow steep switchbacks is to 'endo' the bike forwards so that the rear wheel leaves the ground and can be swung around, pointing the bike in the correct direction. This is effective and looks good, but is also pretty difficult (see page 17).

TOP TIP: Being able to do a trackstand (see S16) will help you do switchbacks.

Apex

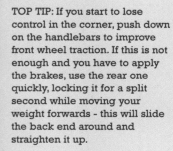

Approach the bend on the opposite side to the way the trail turns. (e.g. approach a right hand bend on the left of the trail).
Then cut in, aiming for the apex of the bend. Angle the inside knee outward and lean your bike (not your body) into the bend. Keep some weight over the front end to stop it drifting out.

TOP TIP: When tackling multiple corners, approach at a speed at which you can take all the corners on the straightest possible line through all the apexes.

IN THE CORNER

As the bend gets tighter push the outside pedal down and transfer your weight onto it (this also gets the inside pedal up and out the way of the ground).

Lift yourself off the saddle slightly (resting the inner thigh of the 'outside' leg on the nose of the saddle) to control the bike.

Drop your inside shoulder and shift your weight forward and outward taking the bike with you.

TOP TIP: If you start to lose control in the corner, push down on the handlebars to improve front wheel traction. If this is not enough and you have to apply the brakes, use the rear one quickly, locking it for a split second while moving your weight forwards - this will slide the back end around and straighten it up.

EXIT

As you pass through the apex, aim for the outside edge of the trail.

Move your shoulders and bike into their usual position and as the corner straightens out, push down with your inside leg and accelerate out of the turn.

The bike should pull itself back upright, and (without noticing) you will have your bum on the saddle and be pedalling off looking ahead for the next obstacle.

CLIMBING may not be the highlight of your ride (unless of course you are a masochist), but it is none the less inevitable on a cross country ride. Climbing is tiring, but it shouldn't hurt; if it does you are pushing too hard, ease off and pace yourself. Aim to get past the top with enough energy to carry on and enjoy the descent, not to collapse in a painful heap whilst coughing up your lungs. The key to coping with climbing is to take it steadily and smoothly, so as to keep your momentum going. In order to achieve this consider the following:

■ NOTE: On a full suspension bike, stay seated to get more traction, and keep the upper body relaxed and still to avoid bouncing.

TOP TIP: When you are going up a very steep incline, pull up on the handlebars on the same side as the leg which is putting the power down (pull up on the left side of the bar, as the left pedal goes down and vice versa), to help stop the wheels from spinning.

GEARS: Select a gear in good time, that will enable you to pedal at a steady rate throughout the climb. Having too high a gear is better than too low, as changing up is always difficult. Pedal in smooth circles, pushing forwards, down, back and then pulling up, to keep the power even throughout the stroke.

WEIGHT DISTRIBUTION: Lean forward over the handlebars (keeping your elbows below the level of your hands) to allow your weight to be distributed over the pedals. This will give maximum power and will stop the front wheel from lifting up (don't go too far forward or you will start to loose rear wheel traction).

Although sitting creates more traction, it is sometimes a good plan to stand up on the pedals when the ground is firm, to use different muscles and to get more power. If the ground doesn't have enough traction try coming forwards on to the saddles nose

POSTURE: Keep your upper body relaxed and still, back straight, loose grip and arms relaxed. You can use your arms to pull forwards on each pedal stroke, but make sure you keep a smooth and constant effort through the pedals - remember pedal in circles.

For steep sections where the front wheel may loose traction, keep your weight low, move forwards on to the nose of the saddle. Dropping your wrists will lower your elbows, and bring your forearms parallel to the ground, so you pull back on the bars rather than up, (which would lift the front wheel and make steering difficult).

CHOOSING A LINE: Using your common sense to select a decent path is probably the most important thing to make climbing easier. By avoiding slippery patches, loose rocks, excessively steep bits, you should be able to keep it all flowing nicely and avoid stalling. Over tricky, poor traction sections, a quick bust of speed while traction is still good may allow sufficient momentum to carry the bike through the section.

BIKE SET-UP: A low tyre pressure will give more traction - but is probably only worth doing when the surface is difficult and you have a long climb ahead of you. Using bar ends (on flat bars) will allow you to use your upper body for climbing without loosing traction.

STARTING ON A HILL:

Start off diagonally or perpendicular to the slope of the hill to lessen the gradient, with the 'downhill' foot on the pedal (at the top i.e.11 o'clock position) and the 'uphill' foot on the ground.

Push your weight forward while pushing down on the pedal, then bring your other foot up and get in to a rhythm quickly, and clip in with the second foot once you have got some momentum.

OFF CAMBER CLIMBS:

With off-camber climbs the front wheel wants to slip down the slope. Therefore you must keep it pointing upwards of where you actually want to go, so it slips down to the direction you want.

Lean the bike into the slope, whilst leaving your body position vertical. This will help stop the bike from slipping out from under you.

DESCENDING has to be one of the most exhilarating aspects of mountain biking. It can also be the most daunting if you lack confidence, be it due to inexperience or bad experience. Confidence is the single biggest factor in getting the best out of DH's (not to be confused with over-confidence which will help you get the best out of the NHS). It is actually harder to keep the bike stable the slower you are going, but don't let this goad you into getting up too much speed and losing control of the bike - you should always be able to stop as there could be hidden danger ahead.

GEARS: Select a reasonably high gear to prevent you from spinning the cranks too fast, which can upset balance and draw attention away from the terrain ahead (it will also stop the chain from slapping around).

WEIGHT DISTRIBUTION: You will need to get your weight over the saddle - further back the steeper the descent. Be aware that lightening the weight on the front wheel will reduce steering control, but it's safer to fall off the back than go over the front of the bike. Shift your weight around, depending on the gradient, obstacles and ground surface and try to avoid braking hard. Keep your centre of gravity low and try to use your body to steer the bike.

POSTURE: Have your arms and legs relaxed and slightly bent to flex for bumps or dips, as even on a suspension bike, it is still your arms and legs that provide the majority of the shock absorption. Also with your weight being pushed forwards onto your arms, a nervous and tense body with locked arms will act as a pivot from the bars in a arc, over the handlebars, if you have to brake or hit an obstacle.

Pedals should be level, saddle gripped between the legs, two or three fingers covering the brakes, and your head up. Keep eyes ahead on where you want to go, remember you will tend to steer toward what you are looking at.

CHOOSING A LINE: Choose a line and be committed to it - hesitating or trying to change line will cause you to slow down or lose control. Approach rocky sections with enough rolling momentum to clear any obstacles, whilst keeping the body and bike as light as possible (especially the front wheel to allow it to be lifted easily), so you can take a more direct line, over the obstacles.

BRAKING: Try and use your momentum to carry you over obstacles, only using the front brake very gently, as sudden hard breaking will make the bike lunge forward and compress the front suspension. The front brake has more stopping power (but if descending steeply with your weight not low and back far enough you will find yourself over the bars). The rear can be used to 'dab' off speed, but you need to keep your weight back to stop the brakes from locking the wheel and causing it to skid.

TOP TIPS:

* Get yourself a bike bell (or even a cow-bell) to ping as you fly down a trail. This will warn others of your approach

* Don't grip the bars too tightly, stay relaxed, be confident, use your momentum, shift your weight around and enjoy it.

* If you are unconfident or nervous, try lowering the saddle & unclipping SPD pedals (or use flat pedals), to make you feel safer on descents.

DOWNHILL SET-UP:

Downhill bikes are set up differently to cross country bikes, to make descending easier.

* High, short stem and/or riser handlebars will make it easier to keep your weight further back and still steer comfortably.
* Low saddle keeps your centre of gravity low and enables you to get your bum over the back of the saddle, to get your weight even further back.
* Big wide tyres, run at low pressures e.g. 35-45psi increases the surface area of tyre on the ground, and therefore improve grip.
* Flat pedals will give you more confidence and enable you to quickly dab your foot out to balance yourself when/if needed (or just unclip SPD shoes).

OK, so you won't be able to make many of these changes out on the trail. But by not having an overly stretched riding position, using riser bars, lowering your saddle, and unclipping SPD pedals you should find very steep declines easier to tackle.

SKILLS

What makes mountain biking so good is that you can ride just about anywhere and on any surface: grass, leaves, rocks, gravel, hard-pack, sand, water, stones, roots, tarmac and of course mud. Each surface has it's own properties that require different skills and techniques to master.

TOP TIP: The key to riding in mud (and other terrain where the traction is poor) is to make smooth pedal strokes, so the rear wheel doesn't lose traction and spin.

MUD

Mud is something that you will be very familiar with if you live in the UK. It sticks to the tyres, is slippery and causes loss of control, makes you dirty and cold, and clogs the rear derailleur, V-brakes and clipless pedals. It will also take a lot more effort to pedal than normal. Furthermore mud will eventually grind down all those expensive components into shapeless rubbish.

Protection: After a muddy ride you need to wash your bike thoroughly as mud can get into lots of places and wear down parts. There are various anti-mud devices available to protect your bike from this nasty stuff, for example:

* Big moto-cross style mudguard's.
* Neoprene covers for fork sliders, shocks and headsets.
* Plug stops (fits on the underside of steerer tube).

Remember to remove neoprene covers when the bike is home, so it can dry out; any moisture can corrode the parts - see the 'Winterising your bike' in the general section for more info.

TOP TIP: Loosen the mud on the bike by riding through water when possible.

■ Sloppy mud can make changing direction difficult so approach on a line that avoids having to steer whilst in it - if steering is necessary try not to turn the bars, instead use your upper body to lean the bike.

■ Approach as fast as is safe, so your momentum carries you through the mud; aim for existing tracks as these will be slightly compacted, and firmer to ride.

■ Change down a couple of gears in anticipation; the gears are less likely to slip on a larger cog as the chain is in contact with more teeth and load on the drivetrain is reduced. Also being in too high a gear may lead you to stall and get a muddy foot.

■ Keep your weight back, de-weight or lift the front wheel slightly to avoid front wheel drag (which would slow it down more than the rear and could send you over the bars).

■ Be ready to pedal in smooth, powerful strokes once in the mud. Slow down, move your weight back and ease up on the front end, then push the pedals down firmly and smoothly, while pushing forwards (not down) on the handlebars, and before the next pedal stroke, gently move back again ready for the next surge.

SAND

This is similar to riding in mud, but even worse for the moving parts on bikes; sand is incredibly abrasive. It is therefore not advisable to ride in sand on a regular basis, as it will soon make metal dust of the expensive moving parts of a bike.

■ When riding in sand, adopt the same tactics as mud riding i.e. straight line, aim for a shallow looking section, keep your momentum, keep the front end light, don't steer or use your body to do so and make wide turns as the wheel will tend to dig in. If you are stalling or digging-in on a turn, sit back and turn the wheel the other way.

■ Moving between standing and sitting will give you a balance between power and traction; when wheels grip, put on the power by standing slightly, but keep weight low to keep traction. Also keep your upper body loose and ready, as sand is unpredictable.

WATER

The trouble with riding through water is that you probably won't be able to see what lies beneath. There may be rocks, big holes, piranha and most probably some mud. In the likely event that the area surrounding the puddle is muddy, go through the puddle as this will stop further erosion of the path. A pool of water usually means there is also a fairly hard packed surface underneath anyway.

■ If you want to cross a short section of water quickly and don't mind a splash of water on your feet and bum pull a manual wheelie. If the water crossing longer and will require pedalling which will result in your feet going into the water, select a relatively high gear, approach the water at a good speed and use your momentum and 1/4 pedal stokes (12 to 3 o'clock) to get you through without getting your feet wet.

■ NOTE: Remember that that rim brakes become less effective when the rims are wet, so give them a gentle pull to check and dry them.

ICE & SNOW

Fair play for getting out in this weather. Ice and snow can provide some tricky conditions to ride in, so be aware of what to do.

■ Snow hides obstacles so keep your weight back off the front wheel.

■ Ice is dangerous and braking should be forgotten about or done very lightly. Never lock the brakes, as you will lose traction and find it difficult or impossible to get back again. Steer with your body, keep your weight back, and stay on the saddle to keep some of that elusive traction.

TREE ROOTS

Roots (especially when wet) are the slipperiest obstacles regularly encountered on the trail, felling even experienced riders.

■ They should be approached square-on (90 degrees) if possible, and every effort should be made to keep weight off the wheel in contact with the root.

■ To get over large logs, you will probably need to stop and lift the bike, so as not to damage the chainrings. If you feel confident enough however, you can lift the front over as usual, then using your pedals, lift the rear wheel up and surge forwards with your upper body, so that the chainrings clear the log.

■ **NOTE:** Don't try jumping roots if you are not sure you can clear them; if the wheel lands on them, they make for a very tricky (and painful) landing.

GRASS

On a fine dry day, grass will do little more than slow you down. Add some British rain, however and it becomes extremely slippery, making going up and downhill difficult.

■ Stay seated and pedal smoothly and consistently to keep rear wheel traction, and make only small movements when steering (keeping your weight off the front end).

■ **NOTE:** Cut grass can invade every part of the drive train, quickly smothering sprockets and seizing jockey wheels, which will stop the bike from shifting or freewheeling. It can be a nightmare to remove, so every effort should be made to avoid it.

ROCKS & GRAVEL

Rocks become slippery when wet, and can go from a welcome challenge to an outright menace.

■ Their irregular shape and size requires more body movement than other surfaces, especially downhill - keep your weight back and poise yourself over the bike to soak up any bumps the suspension doesn't. Brake carefully to avoid locking / skidding the tyres on loose rocks.

■ **NOTE:** Speed and momentum will help you over rocky sections, but too much and you risk wiping out.

■ Cycling over small stones should not cause too much difficulty. Deep gravel however is much like sand in that steering is difficult, as the front wheel likes to dig in, so maintain a straight line and light front wheel.

■ Gravel on hard surfaces is more like riding on ice or ball bearings, as the stones will slip and slide over the surface giving you little control. Stay off the brakes and keep your weight over the rear wheel

TOP TIP:

Choose tyres to match the terrain you are riding

General Riding: 1.9-2.1 inch tyres for a reasonable volume of air for comfort, while still offering speed and traction in the dry on loose ground.

Mud: 1.9 inch and less, with long knobs, wide spaces and inflated to a high pressure to shed mud quickly and offer good frame clearance. Avoid riding these tyres on tarmac as they will wear down quickly.

Rocks: 2+ inch tyres with square edged knobs, and pumped up hard to protect against pinch punctures.

FALLING!!

There is no excuse for not wearing a helmet when riding. No-one plans to crash, but when you do a helmet can save your life.

A helmet will also give you more confidence when riding - which will in turn will help you perform better and ride faster.

Getting too hot is no excuse as good helmets (like the MET 5th Element below) have lots of vents that channel air over your head, keeping you nice and cool ▾

TOP TIP: Keep the receipt for your helmet as many manufacturers offer a crash replacement warranty e.g. MET helmets offer a discount on a new helmet within 3 years of your original purchase (see www.fisheroutdoor.co.uk).

Yes this is a skill, and can save you from a bad injury and embarrassment. Most riders come off their bikes fairly frequently, but being able to control a fall can make the difference between a spell in casualty and a story in the pub.

We all take risks when mountain biking, it's what makes it exciting. However, excessive risk taking can lead to a loss of control and probably a wipeout. By avoiding such circumstances you are less likely to crash and you won't have to ever implement the following advice.

▴ Tuck your limbs and head away to create a ball when you fall - be careful of low speed crashes as these often result in the full impact being concentrated in one area.

GOING OVER THE TOP:

This is the most dangerous fall. If you know you are destined for the air unclip your feet from the pedals and keep one hand on the handlebars (to keep some control over the bike and ensure the bar ends don't end up where the sun doesn't shine) and leap frog the bike.

BIKE SLIPS SIDEWAYS:

When the bike slips sideways from under you, stay with the bike, keeping your feet on the pedals and the bike pushed away from you slightly. This helps stop the top tube going somewhere painful if the bike suddenly stops.

BASIC FALLING GUIDE LINES

If you can't avoid a crash, try to stop the falling action as soon as possible. If you start to lose control and know you are going to fall, try and slip off the back of the bike. As you gather speed it becomes harder to dismount in a controlled and pain free manner - get ready for some stuntman antics!

Fight the natural urge to use your hands to break your fall. Complex bones in your hands and wrists are easily injured or collarbone easily broken. Keep your limbs and head tucked into your body to create a ball and go with the momentum (try not a fall directly on your shoulder this could result in a broken collarbone).

Let yourself roll along the ground until you come to stop rather than using your arms or legs to stop you. Also, allow the bike to absorb some of the impact.

DUST DOWN

After 'ahem' a miscalculation, dust yourself down (smile and grin, no matter how much you hurt) whilst you check yourself for any damage.

Pick your bike out of the hedge and inspect it for any damage (whilst asking if anyone else saw that kamikaze rabbit). Check that: the bars are straight, brakes work, wheels are not buckled, the seat is straight and the seatpost is not cracked as the bike will often land on the saddle in a crash.

If your helmet receives a large knock in a crash it should be replaced - even if you can't see any damage yourself as it may be internally damaged and useless for any future gravity-defying antics.

TOP TIP: Once home, check the forks aren't twisted or bent, then take them off the bike and check the join between the steerer and the stanchions for any cracks. Other parts worth checking damage for are the frame welds (especially the seatpost), rear mech, bars, and wheels.

relax

stay focused

believe in yourself

enjoy...

The wheelie and coaster wheelie (wheelie without pedalling) form the basic element to many MTB skills: getting the front wheel over an obstacle, getting out of a rut, going over a drop-off, going through water or mud. Most importantly though, they are great for showing off when going down the street.

Because of their wide array of uses, wheelies should be one of the first (advanced) skills you acquire, but they will probably take quite some time and patience (and maybe a few bumps and bruises) before you learn how to do them well. However, only being able to lift the front wheel slightly for a short period of time will still help you out while on the trail.

TOP TIPS:

* Keep the back brake covered and use it to stop you falling over backwards.

* Find a slight incline on a smooth surface, be relaxed, select a low-ish gear (i.e. middle front and low rear) as this will give you the power and acceleration to pull away.

* Believe in yourself and lean back.

* To make it easier and give you more confidence when starting out, use flat pedals (to get your feet down quickly - if necessary), lower the saddle, start on a incline and on a soft surface (for landing), away from the eyes of others.

■ NOTE: Wheelies are good for getting you out of a rut (of the MTB variety). If you are in a rut, wheelie the front wheel out and over the rut, then push your weight forwards and onto the bars to de-weight the rear wheel and let your momentum pull the rear wheel out it.

Deeper ruts may require you to use your feet to 'lift' the rear wheel so it doesn't just slide along the rut.

01 Ride slowly and push your weight forwards, bending your arms over the bars, with fingers covering the brakes.

02 Now you have to do several things all at once: sit on the saddle, push your weight backwards and pull up on the bars, and push down with your leading foot at the top of the pedal stroke to accelerate. Do all of this quickly in one smooth motion, but not too aggressively as you'll just end up on your back.

03 To keep the wheel up, look forwards and keep calm with your bum on the seat and weight central. The balancing point is quite far back, and at first you will feel like you are over balancing.

One finger on the rear brake is all that is required: a light touch will give enough reduction in speed to send the front wheel down and stop you going over the back.

If the front wheel is falling push a little harder on the pedals to bring it back up.

04 Once you find the balancing point and got used to it, you can work on the steering and smooth pedalling. This will require sitting well back with your arms straight and careful weight-positioning to balance, while keeping the pull on the bar. Be careful of your stronger arm and leg, as they may cause you to veer off to that side.

Pick a target destination and use your wheel to balance and steer the bike that direction.

When cycling off-road (or even on road) you will come across many obstacles e.g. logs, holes, poop, bunny rabbits, that are too big, smelly or cute to be ridden over at full speed with the wheels on the ground. However, you don't want to get off the bike every time, so you need to learn how to jump the bike so your riding can stay a lot more fluid, faster and enjoyable. The type of jump required will depend on the circumstances, see below:

SPEED JUMP	BUNNY HOP	PRE-JUMP	JUMP

TOP TIPS:

* Practice jumping over cardboard boxes or sticks rested on objects, as these won't damage your bike and show how high you can get.

* Be wary of your stronger arm pulling the wheel around to one side. If you start falling to one side, dip the opposite shoulder.

* Avoid lifting too much with the pedals as it tips the bike forwards.

* When going over obstacles, look out for ones 6-12 inches high as they could catch the chainrings.

* Once the front wheel is over the object you can simply bounce / bash the rear wheel over, by leaning forwards to de-weight the rear wheel.

SPEED JUMP
Lift the front and rear wheels simultaneously. Used to jump over objects or avoid a bump / jump in the ground. This move requires a good amount of speed, and good timing.

BUNNY HOP
Lift the front wheel first and then the rear wheel. It is harder to get the timing right than the speed jump, but it can be done at any speed.

PRE-JUMP
Basically a bunny-hop to get over the lip of a steep drop in the trail, to minimise time in the air. This is faster and safer than jumping off the lip of a steep drop, as you can keep pedalling, steering & braking.

JUMP
Show off and feel good as you leap off a ramp or lip, high into the air.

01 The Approach. The initial preparation for all these jumps is the same. Approach in the 'attack' position i.e. crouched, with arms and legs slightly bent, on the line you want to take, with enough speed so that your momentum can carry you over, and stay focused on the obstacle (before you get to it).

02 Keep your pedals level, and just before the object compress the suspension (if you have it) and spring upwards, raising your body. Pull upwards on the bars and pedals (if using clipless) or scoop the pedals back and upwards.

03 Once over the object, extend your arms and legs to lower the bike and absorb the landing. Try to land on both wheels, and stay off the front brake until you are firmly back on the round and under control.

02 Just before the object compress the front suspension, then in an explosive but smooth action, launch yourself upwards and forwards, by pulling up on the bars (not by leaning backwards). For higher jumps, use half a pedal stroke as you pull up on the bars for some extra height.

03 Once the front wheel is at the required height you need to bring the rear wheel up. To do this push forwards on the bars, twist the handlebar grips forwards and move your weight forward while pulling up with your feet with SPDs or scoop the flat pedals back and up (more tricky). Now the bike is level, look at the landing and pull up slightly on the bars, shift your weight back a bit to try and land on both wheels together (or the rear one first).

02 Lift the front wheel before the top of the crest to the down slope, and bend your knees (or lift the rear end) so that the rear of the bike comes up underneath you. Keep your weight back and the rear brake covered.

■ NOTE: Aim to keep your head at the same height throughout the jump, by using your arms and legs to push and pull the bike from your body.

03 With the front wheel over the crest, straighten your arms and push the front wheel back down the other side. As the rear end comes over, push your legs out into the down slope to stop the back end kicking up and tilting you forwards.

02 Keep your pedals level, compress the suspension, and as you hit the bump, explode upwards, bending your arms and legs so that the bike can move up towards you (keep your weight back so that the saddle has space to move towards your stomach area).

03 When airborne, push the bike away from you (but keep your arms and legs slightly bent to absorb the landing). Land the bike on the rear wheel first, then when both wheels are on the ground, land yourself onto the bike, using your arms and legs to cushion the impact.

DROPPING IN

This is a technique for rolling down steep slopes where there is enough of the slope that the front wheel can roll down without getting stuck in a ditch or obstruction, or putting the bike at too great an angle.

1 Look for the best line and approach in a roll, arms and legs slightly bent and pedals level. As the front wheel goes over the edge, move your weight back, and off the saddle.

2 Feather the rear brake only (careful not to lock it up) and extend your arms to push the front wheel down. As the slope levels out, move your weight forward over the saddle.

■ NOTE: Do not use this technique on very steep almost vertical drop offs.

DROPPING OFF

This is a technique for wheeling off the edge of a drop or step in the trail, that simply riding down would put the bike at such a great angle that when the front wheel hits the bottom, might cause you to go over the top . It is daunting to start with, so practice on kerbs or small drops by letting the front wheel roll over, then as the drops get bigger, give the front wheel more of a lift.

01 Approach with enough speed to get over comfortably. Scan ahead down the track and aim for a clean entry at the top and a safe exit. Stand up with your arms and legs slightly bent and pedals level (don't pedal as you go over the top, as you might catch the lip), and keep the rear brake lever covered. Just as the front wheel reaches the lip, pull back on the bars and do a small wheelie (don't lift the front wheel too high or leave it too late).

02 When the rear wheel reaches the lip, push forwards with your arms, extend your legs slightly ready for the landing and apply the rear brake slightly to drop the front wheel back down. Keep your weight over the back wheel (even more so if you are going down hill) to stop the front digging in on the landing. Use your arms and legs to absorb and compress the bike on the landing and release the rear brake as the front wheel comes down (don't use the front brake until you are under control again).

■ NOTE: If you are approaching the drop too slowly, bring your leading foot to the top (12 o'clock position) of the pedal stroke and put in a quarter of a pedal stroke (pedals end up horizontal) as you pull up on the bars at the edge of the drop.

DESCENDING STEPS

This is not just for cycling around town, as natural and man-made steps are a feature of many trails. They can be daunting at the first, but if ridden correctly they are quite easy and it looks impressive.

■ NOTE: It will be hard to keep your speed down because the tyres will have very little and short contact with the ground and will probably just lock up - so scrub your speed off before the steps and let your tyres roll.

01 Approach slowly. If you need to slow down use the rear brake, and pick a central line, avoiding the edges. Lean well back over the bike to get the weight off the front wheel and let the front tyre roll down the first step.

02 When the front tyre hits the flat of the step, if the steps are close together there may be times at which both wheels are on a lip at once. If so use the brakes sparingly to slow down, being careful not to lock the wheels or stop the bike completely. If the steps are bike length or more apart, use the front brake gently to lower the rear wheel on to the step.

TOP TIPS:

* Use the large chainring to keep the chain tensioned and stop it slapping about or becoming derailed.

* If you are unsure about the gradient, but don't want to be beaten by the drop, get off and roll the bike down to see what angle and line to take.

* Don't panic or apply your brakes just before the drop as this will shift your body weight forwards and cause the front end to dive, and probably end with you (not your bike) getting some air-time.

* Avoid going too slowly and using the front brake - if you need to slow down use the rear brake or both brakes together or the front wheel will dig in and send you over the top.

SKILLS

15

Not all MTB skills involve speed. There will be times when you are riding very slowly, even stopping still, yet still need to turn the bike so read on...

TRACKSTANDS

This is a tactic developed by track riders and employed by cycle couriers to save unclipping and be first away from the lights. It is also incredibly useful for mountain biking. It involves stopping and maintaining a stationary position without putting your feet down, which can save time, as you stay clipped in and have pressure on the pedals ready to go.

Becoming accustomed to accelerating from a trackstand will mean you become better at recovering from a stall, and can continue riding where other riders are cursing their clips on SPD pedals and fighting to start their bikes.

SIDEWAYS HOPS

Hopping your bike sideways can be very useful for getting out of sticky situations e.g. ruts while stationary or on the move (it's easier to learn from a stationary position, but the technique is the same for on the move).

You will need to be able to trackstand and bunny hop. Practice on the flat, over an imaginary line, then progress to on and off a raised surface.

SHUFFLE TURNS

The shuffle turn involves turning the bike to face a different direction on the spot without your feet touching the ground. This can help you get out of a sticky situation when you need to turn in a restricted area, and there isn't enough room to steer the bike around.

This may seem like a trials trick, but it will save you unclipping and clipping your feet back into the pedals, which can be awkward and waste time.

01

01

01

02

02

PERFORMING A TRACKSTAND

01 Find a very gradual slope and set off at a slow pace. Slow down to a stop, and use the brakes to steady yourself. Keep your arms straight and stand up on the pedals, which should be level with your favoured leg forwards, and turn the front wheel about 45 degrees.

Maintain your balance by easing off pressure on the front pedal to inch the bike backwards and increasing pressure to inch forwards - if you start to loose your balance ease off the brakes to roll forward slightly to recover it. Moving your weight forwards, using a gentle rocking motion or using a different gear may also help you keep your balance.

Keep practicing this until you can balance for as long as possible without needing to roll forward. If you roll back too far you will not get enough leverage to control the bike.

PERFORMING A SIDEWAYS HOP

01 Trackstand (or ride), parallel to the desired location, have the pedals level and choose the point you are going to hop to. Compress the bikes suspension, then pull up on the bars (more the higher you need to get) and scoop back and upwards with your feet (or just pull your feet up if you use clipless pedals), as if doing a bunny hop.

02 As the bike leaves the ground, use your thighs and some hip movement to push the bike and your weight sideways. Use your arms and legs as shock absorbers to take the sting out of the landing.

■ NOTE: Try to land straight (i.e. vertical): it's safer and reduces the sideways impact on the wheels. If on the move, allow the bike to carry on moving forwards.

PERFORMING A SHUFFLE TURN

01 Follow the basics of the sideways hop i.e. pedals level, favoured foot forward, both brakes applied, legs and arms bent, and balanced on the spot. Spring up, taking the bike with you.

02 On the upward movement, pull the front end around with the handlebars, using your body and turning your shoulders to do so. At the same time use your feet to push the rear of the bike around (use as much or as little force that confident allows) and move your bum in the same direction.

When you land, crouch and compress the suspension again and keep repeating the move until you are facing the direction you want. Release the brakes and pedal away.

endo turns

Endo turns involve locking the front brake and moving your weight forwards to lift the rear wheel up and swing it around. They are useful for very tight hair pin bends, especially when on descents, as the rear end is already higher than the front (therefore requiring less weight shift). More importantly(!) they look good.

▲ 01 Find a level (and soft) surface, ride at a slow pace in an easy gear. Use flat pedals or clip out of your SPDs. With your pedals level, cover the brakes and focus on the turning spot; when you get there, start to turn the front wheel in the direction you wish to go.

Pull smoothly and firmly, locking the front brake (keeping it pulled throughout the turn) and push forward on the bars, leaning your weight forwards (pull up on clipless pedals if worn). Let your feet and legs come up underneath you and turn the bars, head and body in the direction you want to go.

It will seem odd at first so get a feel for the movement a few times, getting the rear wheel further off the ground each time, before progressing further.

▲ 02 Keep your weight central and gently push on the bars to keep the rear end up. Look ahead at where you want to go (your body and bike will follow). Use your hips to swing the bike around (push the inside pedal down and back slightly to keep control of the bike).

As the rear end is approaching the desired position, let it start to fall by moving your weight backwards (be ready for rear wheel impact). Release the front brake, put your bum on the saddle and pedal away.

■ **NOTE:** You will probably have a favourite side to do this on, but practice both, as you can't choose which way the trail takes you.

ROUTES

experience new adventures...   southeast

ROUTES
SECTION

Here are 51 quality rides including 2 epics, the Ridgeway and the South Downs Way. It may be an effort to put your bike in the car, but think of the benefits you'll receive: a memorable adventure, a change from the routine, a sense of achievement, and a chance to develop your riding skills. So stop making excuses, get organised and get out on some decent new rides. If you enjoy them half as much as we enjoyed researching them you won't be disappointed.

The south east is blessed with areas such as the Chilterns, South Downs and North Downs (all of which are within an hour from the big smoke), which all provide miles and miles of the classic South East woodland singletrack (and country pubs). Rides that we thoroughly recommend you should try and cycle at some point in your life include: the Epping Forest and Canterburys unmarked singletracks, Friston Forest, Bramber, Box Hill, Westcott, Whiteways, Freshwater, Selborne, Alton, Bracknell, Woodcote, Watlington, Ibstone, Stokenchurch, Princes Risborough and of course the Ridgeway and South Downs Way.

As with most sports it is easy to like your fellow sportsmen and easier still to slate those in a similar but slightly different sport (why is it so enjoyable yelling 'Roadie' from the safety of the car as we overtake a lycra clad road rider?). It's nothing new; think of surfers V's body boarders, skiers V's Snowboarders, rugby league V's rugby union.

So why does this antagonism exist? Probably from the two parties having to share a common ground and each sport feeling it is more justified than the other to be there. This mentality can be seen on bridleways, where walkers, mountain bike riders, and horse riders have to share the trails alike.

So why does it have to be that way? Largely it's not; like with all things, quite often images are formed based on the behaviour of a minority. Mountain bikers that tear around blind corners as fast as possible give the sport a bad reputation, just as a few awkward ramblers can give them all a miserable image. With the risk of sounding like a child of the sixties, lets accept the fact that we all share a passion for the outdoor trails and just get on with enjoying it together.

If everyone takes the opportunity to be friendly and courteous when they pass a fellow trail user the countryside would be a better place to be in.

COUNTRYSIDE CODE:

Only ride on open trails
Be in control of your bike at all times
Slow down or stop and let people pass by
Warn people of your presence by calling or ringing a bell,
pass by slowly and thank them
Don't scare any animals
Don't leave any rubbish
Look ahead and be aware
Be kind & courteous to other trail users
Shut gates behind you

TRAIL ETIQUETTE

Be aware of the fact that of all the trail traffic, we probably go the fastest, make the most noise, and appear the most intimidating. So go out of your way to smile and thank people if they step out of your way - they deserve it, especially seeing that as cyclists we are legally the ones required to stop and let people past us.

TOP TIP: Fix a bell to your bike to politely warn others of your presence. Alternatively, get a cow bell attached to your bike or ruck-sack as this will allow you to keep your hands on the brakes.

WHERE TO RIDE

In the UK we have pretty good access to off-road trails. In England and Wales there are over 50,000 miles of paths open to cyclists. Scotland doesn't have footpaths, etc as such, but basically, if there is a path on the ground you are usually allowed to cycle it.

As mountain bikers we are allowed to ride on bridleways, BOAT's (By-way Open to All Traffic), and RUPP's (roads used as public paths). Further to these we are sometimes allowed to cycle on old railway tracks, old carriageways / roads, permissive R.O.W's, park land, commons, canal paths, around reservoirs, and open access Forestry Commission forests and National Trust land.

■ NOTE: You can usually push your bike along footpaths, but some counties may prohibit even this.

BLOCKED RIGHT OF WAYS

If a R.O.W. is obviously blocked in some way e.g. a locked gate, speak to the councils right of way section and / or the 'Right to Ride' on 0870 8730060. You are perfectly within your rights to continue along the path (or where it should be), by passing around or climbing over the obstacle.

The police should also be informed of an aggressive dog stopping you from progressing on a public ROW.

■ NOTES:

We have made every effort to ensure that these routes only use legal paths, but access rights can change. If you are ever unsure, please walk your bike to avoid confrontation.

If you want to represent mountain bikers at the 'Countryside Rights of Way Forum' contact the CTC (tel: 0870 8730060).

Red flags (usually on military ranges, or posh people shooting at things) indicate that there is live firing and you should stay away.

The CroW (Countryside Rights of Way) right to roam act allows people on foot to wander off footpaths onto mountain, moor, heath, down and common land (marked on new OS Explorer maps), but NOT mountain bikers.

ROUTE INTRO

M3

Gone are the days of wrestling with an A1 map in the wind.

TOP TIP: The brown (contour) lines on a map show the height of the land, and the closer they are together, the steeper the gradient.

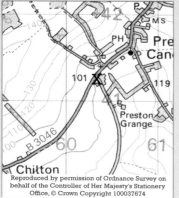

Reproduced by permission of Ordnance Survey on behalf of the Controller of Her Majesty's Stationery Office, © Crown Copyright 100037674

X marks the grid reference 603/412

TOP TIP: By dividing each side of a square on an OS map into tenths (creating 100 tiny 'imaginary' squares) and allocating it a number from 0 to 9, and putting this number behind the first two figures creates a six figure grid reference which will be accurate to 100 meters, see the example above.

Reading maps is easy if you know how. Ordnance Survey maps are some of the best maps in the world and we are privileged in the UK to have our country mapped out to such a high standard. This page provides information on basic map reading skills, to enable you to follow as easily as possible your way around our routes.

USING MAPS

Make sure you are familiar with the OS map key (see next page), and always take a compass with you.

The best advice to give when following a route is to look where you are about to go on the map and search for any distinguishing features e.g. the path crossing a stream, a road on your left, a pond on your right. Visualise those features and then look out for them as you ride. Stopping frequently can be annoying (but at times is unavoidable) so try and aim for a particular place on the map to stop at. This should ideally be some point where your journey changes direction e.g. at a T-junction.

TAKING A GRID REFERENCE

Grid references allow you to locate a particular point on a OS map (see left). This is done by using the numbers allocated to the lines of the grid which are found on the maps. These lines are 1Km apart and are allocated two numbers, of which the ones going across the page from West to East (i.e. the lines going up) are known as 'eastings' and the numbers going from South to North (i.e. lines going across) are known as the 'Northings'. When reading a grid reference you always read the eastings first, then northings i.e. across the up.

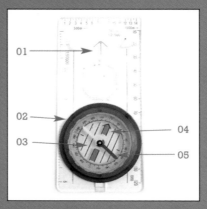

EXPLAINING YOUR COMPASS

01 DIRECTION ARROW: The arrow drawn on the base plate, is the arrow you follow when taking and travelling along a bearing.

02 ROTATING BEZEL: This dial has 2 degree marks on it's circumference and will rotate.

03 MERIDIAN LINES: The parallel lines inside the rotating bezel are for lining up with the vertical grid lines on the map, when taking a bearing.

04 NORTH MARKER: The red arrow with chevrons on the bezel (this should be lined up with the compass pointer when taking a bearing).

05 POINTER: The red arrow inside the compass that will always points to magnetic north.

■ **NOTE:** Keep the compass away from any form of magnetic interference e.g. electrical equipment, electricity pylons, iron, etc.

TAKING A BEARING FROM A MAP

Use this method if you can't see where you want to get to.

01 Line up the following with each other:
* OS map vertical grid lines
* North marker
* The red pointer (this should hover over the north marker).

02 Identify on the map a landmark or path you want to follow and keeping the bezel north facing, turn the base plate in the direction you want to go in.

03 After the map has been put away, simply keep the red pointer over the north marker and follow the direction arrow on the base plate.

TAKING A BEARING FROM A LANDMARK

Use this method when you can see where you want to aim for.

01 Line up the following with each other:
* OS map vertical lines
* North marker
* The red pointer (this should hover over the north marker).

02 Identify a landmark or direction you want to follow and keeping the bezel north facing, turn the base plate in the direction you want to go in.

03 Keeping the red pointer over the north marker, follow the direction arrow on the base plate.

FINDING WHERE YOU ARE

Unsure where you are on your map? If you can see 2 identifiable features on the ground and map you can find your location:

Point the arrow on the baseplate of the compass to one landmark and rotate the bezel so the red pointer hovers over the north marker.

Keeping the red pointer over the north marker line these up with the OS maps vertical grid lines. Keeping this orientation, move the compass so one edge goes through the landmark.

Repeat this with another landmark, and where the lines cross is your position.

■ **NOTE:** This ignores the variation between magnetic and grid north.

There are actually 3 norths:
Magnetic North: The direction a compass points to.
Grid North: The direction the of a grid line parallel to the central meridian on the National grid.
True North: The direction of a meridian of longitude which coverges on the North pole.

The angle difference between True north and Grid North is called Convergence.

The angle difference between True North and Magnetic North is called Magnetic Variation.

TOP TIP: If you've forgotten your compass; hold an analogue watch horizontal and point the hour hand at the sun (in winter, minus 1 hour from the time before you start). Cut the angle between the hour and minute hand in half - this is your north-south line (north behind you).

Confused? Just remember the sun rises in the east and sets in the west.

The routes in this book are aimed at a wide variety of mountain bikers. Our main aim has been to provide a bank of decent off-road routes that are fun and challenging to ride. Because all of the routes have the option to be lengthened or shortened, we hope that a wide selection of riders will be encouraged to try these rides.

The routes use a (blue) main route, based on a circular loop with a distance of around 20 miles, which will be suitable for most competent and fit mountain bikers. We have also included shortcuts (yellow) for riders wanting a shorter and easier ride, and extensions (red) for riders wanting a tougher challenge, making the distance of the ride closer to 10 miles, or 30 miles respectively.

■ NOTE: The emboldened directions provide the 'must know' information and the ordinary directions provide greater detail for when you may be unsure.

(RRG) ABBREVIATIONS

To reduce the amount of text you have to read through, we have abbreviated the frequently used words. It looks a long list, but most are very simple and obvious, but make sure you know what they stand for before you go riding.

L = Left
R = Right
SA = Straight ahead / across
Bear = A bend of less than 90 degrees
T-J = T-Junction (track splits in two directions at around 180 degrees)
Fork = Track splits in two directions (less than 180 degrees)
X-rds = Cross roads (4 road junction)
X-tracks = As X-rds, but tracks not roads
DH = Downhill
UH = Uphill
FP = Footpath
BW = Bridleway
ByW = By-Way
(P)ROW = (Public) Right of Way
RUPP = Road used as public path
BOAT = By-way open to all traffic
DT = Double track (wide enough for a car or two bikes)
ST = Single track (narrow trail only wide enough for one bike).

DISTANCE & HEIGHT

The main (blue) route shows the distance and amount of climbing. The extension or shortcut will have a + or - figure, to show the change in distance and climbing from the main route. For example, if the main route is 20 miles with 500 meters of climbing, and you ride this and the extension which reads +7 miles and +150 meters of climbing, you will ride a total of 27 miles with 650 meters of climbing.

It is very useful to have a bike computer, to show exactly how far you have gone, so you can follow the distances we provide between points on the trail.

■ NOTE: Our distances are pretty accurate, but be aware that we all weave, etc differently while riding, so some slight discrepancies may occur between your bike computer and our distances - use them as a guide, not gospel.

The climbing on the route is probably as important as the distance - generally, 300+ meters of climbing over 10 miles is strenuous. Therefore any ride of 30 miles with over 900 meters of climbing is going to be very tough. Also look at the route profiles to see the gradient.

We have measured distances in miles instead of kilometres as although the OS maps use 1km (0.62 miles) squares, road signs are in miles and most of us have grown up using, and thinking in miles.

ROUTE PROFILE

In the bottom right hand corner of the route maps we have provided a profile (cross section) of the main route, to show you where the climbs and descents are.

■ NOTE: The numbers above the profile correlate to the route text numbering.

GPS (Global Positioning System)

These use (a minimum of 3) satellites to determine your position (as well as speed and height) to an accuracy of a few metres.

■ NOTE: Trees, buildings, etc can interfere with the signal and it may take a few minutes to find your position from when it is switched on.

You can also programme routes into a GPS by entering various grid references (as waypoints) for the ride (which we have supplied), and the GPS will point you from one waypoint to the next.

■ NOTE: GPS's are an aid, rather than a replacement for traditional paper maps. The maps within the GPS is probably very limited, with just villages as dots, etc, offering nothing like the detail that a paper map offers.

OTHER INFORMATION

We have included further information on each map such as how to get there, where to park, places to stay, nearby bike shops and most importantly pub stops.

■ NOTE: For further information on accommodation phone the tourist information offices (numbers provided), www.cycleweb.co.uk for a list of bike shops in the UK, and www.met-office.gov.uk for a weather report.

TOP TIPS:

* When taking the route page on a ride, place them inside a freezer bag (available from the super market) to keep them in good condition. These are cheap, re-useable and water-tight.

* When following a new route for the first time, allow plenty of time for stopping to read the map. With practice your map reading skills should improve to a stage where you won't need to refer to our written instructions as much / at all.

* Map holders that fit onto the bikes handlebars are a very useful aid when you are following a map - just don't try reading them as you are riding along though.

* Be aware that new roads, housing estates, and tracks (especially in working forests), may appear over time to try and confuse you.

ORDNANCE SURVEY (LANDRANGER) MAP KEY

TOURIST INFORMATION

🅸 ⓘ	Information centre, all year/seasonal
▨	Selected places of tourist interest
⚛	Viewpoint
Ⓟ	Parking
▲	Youth hostel
⌐	Golf course or links
⬌	Bus or coach station

✕	Picnic site
⚑	Camp site
⛺	Caravan site
✆	Public telephone
✆	Motoring organisation telephone
PC	Public convenience (in rural areas)

ABBREVIATIONS

P — Post office
PH — Public house
MS — Milestone
MP — Milepost
CH — Clubhouse
PC — Public convenience (in rural areas)
TH — Town Hall, Guildhall or equivalent
CG — Coastguard

ANTIQUITIES

+ Site of monument
• □ Stone monument
VILLA Roman
Castle Non-Roman
✕ Battlefield (with date)
☆ ⸱⸱ Visible earthwork

Information provided by the Royal Commissions on Historical Monuments for England and Ancient and Historical Monuments for Scotland and Wales

BOUNDARIES

National
District
National Park or Forest Park
County, Unitary Authority, Metropolitan District or London Borough

  Forestry Commission access land · National Trust – limited access, observe local signs

  National Trust – always open · National Trust for Scotland

NOTE: The * above, is next to the forestry commission symbol that indicates that the forest is an open access forest. This means that you are allowed to cycle any of the tracks within the forest, as long it isn't specifically set aside for walkers only.

GENERAL FEATURES

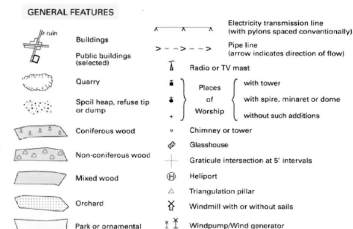

ruin — Buildings
Public buildings (selected)
Quarry
Spoil heap, refuse tip or dump
Coniferous wood
Non-coniferous wood
Mixed wood
Orchard
Park or ornamental grounds

Electricity transmission line (with pylons spaced conventionally)
Pipe line (arrow indicates direction of flow)
Radio or TV mast

Places of Worship { with tower / with spire, minaret or dome / without such additions }

○ Chimney or tower
◇ Glasshouse
+ Graticule intersection at 5' intervals
Ⓗ Heliport
△ Triangulation pillar
✗ Windmill with or without sails
Windpump/Wind generator

WATER FEATURES

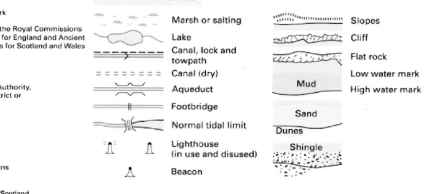

Marsh or salting
Lake
Canal, lock and towpath
Canal (dry)
Aqueduct
Footbridge
Normal tidal limit
Lighthouse (in use and disused)
Beacon

Slopes
Cliff
Flat rock
Low water mark
High water mark
Mud
Sand
Dunes
Shingle

ROCK FEATURES

outcrop
cliff
scree

HEIGHTS

— 50 — Contours are at 10 metres vertical interval
· 144 Heights are to the nearest metre above mean sea level

Heights shown close to a triangulation pillar refer to the station height at ground level and not necessarily to the summit.

1 metre = 3.2808 feet

ROADS AND PATHS — Not necessarily rights of way

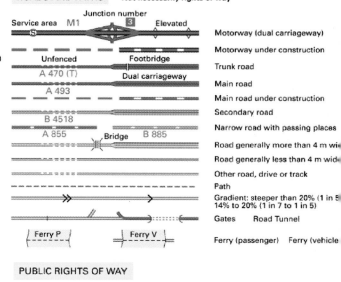

Service area M1 — Junction number ③ — Elevated
Unfenced — Footbridge
A 470 (T) — Dual carriageway
A 493
B 4518
A 855 — Bridge — B 885

Motorway (dual carriageway)
Motorway under construction
Trunk road
Main road
Main road under construction
Secondary road
Narrow road with passing places
Road generally more than 4 m wide
Road generally less than 4 m wide
Other road, drive or track
Path
Gradient: steeper than 20% (1 in 5), 14% to 20% (1 in 7 to 1 in 5)
Gates   Road Tunnel

Ferry P   Ferry V

Ferry (passenger)   Ferry (vehicle)

PUBLIC RIGHTS OF WAY

Footpath — Road used as public path
Bridleway — Byway open to all traffic

Public rights of way shown on this map have been taken from local authority definitive maps and later amendments. The map includes changes notified to Ordnance Survey by (date). The symbols show the defined route so far as the scale of mapping will allow.
Rights of way are not shown on maps of Scotland.

Rights of way are liable to change and may not be clearly defined on the ground. Please check with the relevant local authority for the latest information.

The representation on this map of any other road, track or path is no evidence of the existence of a right of way.

Danger Area — Firing and Test Ranges in the area. Danger! Observe warning notices.

OTHER PUBLIC ACCESS

• • • Other route with public access

The exact nature of the rights on these routes and the existence of any restrictions may be checked with the local highway authority. Alignments are based on the best information available. These routes are not shown on maps of Scotland.

◆—◆ National Trail, Long Distance Route, selected Recreational Paths
●—● National/Regional Cycle Network
— Surfaced cycle route
④ National Cycle Network number
⑧ Regional Cycle Network number

RAILWAYS

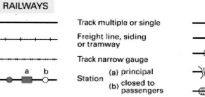

Track multiple or single
Freight line, siding or tramway
Track narrow gauge
a b — Station (a) principal (b) closed to passengers

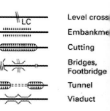

LC — Level crossing
Embankment
Cutting
Bridges, Footbridge
Tunnel
Viaduct

THE SKY

IS THE

LIMIT...

ROUTESINTRO

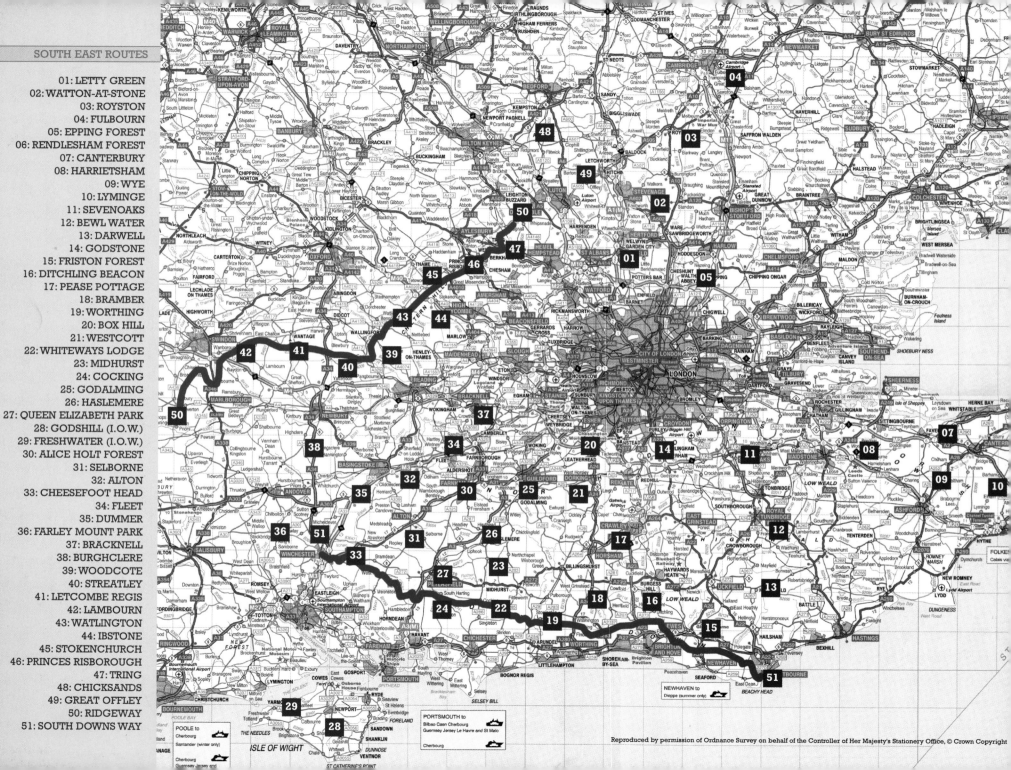

another
day

another
ride

go on...

DO IT!

■ **MAIN ROUTE:** 20.5 miles
(425 metres of climbing)

■ **SHORTCUTS:** -12.5 & -6.2 miles

■ **EXTENSIONS:** +2.5 miles

THE RIDE

SUITABILITY

A pretty easy to follow, non-technical, route with gentle climbs, plenty of bail-out options and is close to facilities, making it a ride suitable for all abilities.

TECHNICAL RATING

In general the ride isn't very technical, but the woods of Wormley, Derry's, Home, and Cowheath all have some nice unmarked singletrack that can provide some exciting trails.

TERRAIN

Mainly off-road on good trails that generally fair well in bad weather, although some sections can hold the water.

■ **NOTE:** Greatwood Country Park is out of bounds to mountain bikers, but I did pick up some high scoring points for the 'alternative' trailquest game, by spotting a randy couple who were getting 'jiggy with it' in their car, in full view of everyone, one busy lunchtime.

■ MAIN ROUTE

20.5 miles & 425 meters of climbing

1 START. Head (east) away from car park entrance on the wide track. After 1.6m turn R immediately after crossing a bridge, following the horseshoe signs to a rd (309/116). Turn L on the rd, UH for 0.1m, then R on a B W (signposted as a FP) for 0.75m to a driveway (302/104) by a farmhouse.

2 Turn L on the drive, which bears R, and follow this for 0.6m, past a quarry and bear L over a bridge, to a rd (298/096). Go SA (slight L) on a B W, joining a drive (301/089) and keep SA to a rd. T urn L on the rd for 0.25m, then L on Bucks Alley (BW no.3) (294/080) or see shortcut 1.

3 0.8m (down and up a dip) to a T - J and turn R, then after 0.4m turn L on White stubbs lane (302/070). 0.4m, along this turn L on the Chain Walk ByW (308/071) into the woods or see shortcut 2.

4 Keep SA to a rd (311/083), and turn R on this for 0.85m to the Farmers Boy pub and turn L on a B W (Fanshaws lane) (322/080). 0.85m to a rd (325/093) and turn R on this for 0.2m, then bear L on a ByW shortly after a farm and keep SA for 0.5m through a farm, becoming a rd.

5 After 0.1m keep SA/R on the B W as the rd bears L (335/085) and follow this for 0.9m (DH then UH). Joins a drive by some houses and turn R on the B W, after Bramble wood house, before a rd (343/075).

6 Follow this through the woods to a DT and turn L on this, to a rd (340/070). Turn R on the rd for about 0.6m then R on the permissive path next to the rd. K eep L through the car park (with picnic tables), staying close to the rd, to a fork and bear L to the rd (324/070).

7 Turn R on the rd for 0.15m, then L on a BW (322/072) for 0.5m to a rd (317/067). Turn R on the rd for 0.4m, then turn L on a ByW (not signposted), opposite Claypits farm (311/068).

8 Keep SA for 1.45m (becomes tarmac, and passes houses and a hotel) to a rd (302/049) and turn R on this (past a pub). After 0.1m bear L off the rd onto New park rd (LHS of Nelito's restaurant) (300/050). Follow this DT , becoming off-road, for 1m bearing sharp R, and keep SA on the DT to the rd or see the extension.

9 Turn L on the rd for 0.05m then turn R (284/058) on Cucumber lane rd for 1.1m, to a fork in the rd (276/072).

10 Turn R on Berkhamsted Lane, for 0.9m then turn L on a B W, through the white gates (288/076).

11 Follow this for 0.6m, then take the 2nd R (just before the metal gates to the farm) (282/084). 0.9m, to a rd (282/098) and go SA on the rd (Letty Green) for 0.65m then turn L on a DT (unsuitable for motors) (284/108) by the green, as the rd bears R

12 Follow this for 0.55m close to the duel carriageway then turn R on the permissive path (276/108). 0.15m to a T - J and turn R (276/109) on a good wide track. Follow this for 0.6m, back to the car park (285/111) on your L.

SHORTCUT 1:

-12.5 miles & -270 meters of climbing

1 Keep SA, 0.2m into the village and bear R at the fork on Berhamsted lane . After 0.25m turn R on a B W through the white gates (288/076), and rejoin the main route at no.11 .

SHORTCUT 2:

-6.2 miles & -130 meters of climbing

A Keep SA on the rd for another 0.25m, then turn R (opposite Claypits farm) (311/068) on a ByW (no signpost), and rejoin the main route at no.8.

EXTENSION:

+2.5 miles & 50 meters of climbing

1 Shortly after the DT turns hard R, turn L on a B W, for 1.35m, past a farm, to a rd (265/056) (Grubbs lane opposite). Turn R on this rd , but use the path along the side for your safety.

2 After 0.85 then turn R on a (Tylers Causeway) BW (270/067) and follow this for 0.9m to a rd (280/060). Turn L on this for 0.8m to a fork (276/072) and rejoin the main route at no.10 .

ROUTES

01

The lovely tree lined Chain Walk trail provides a lovely start to this ride.

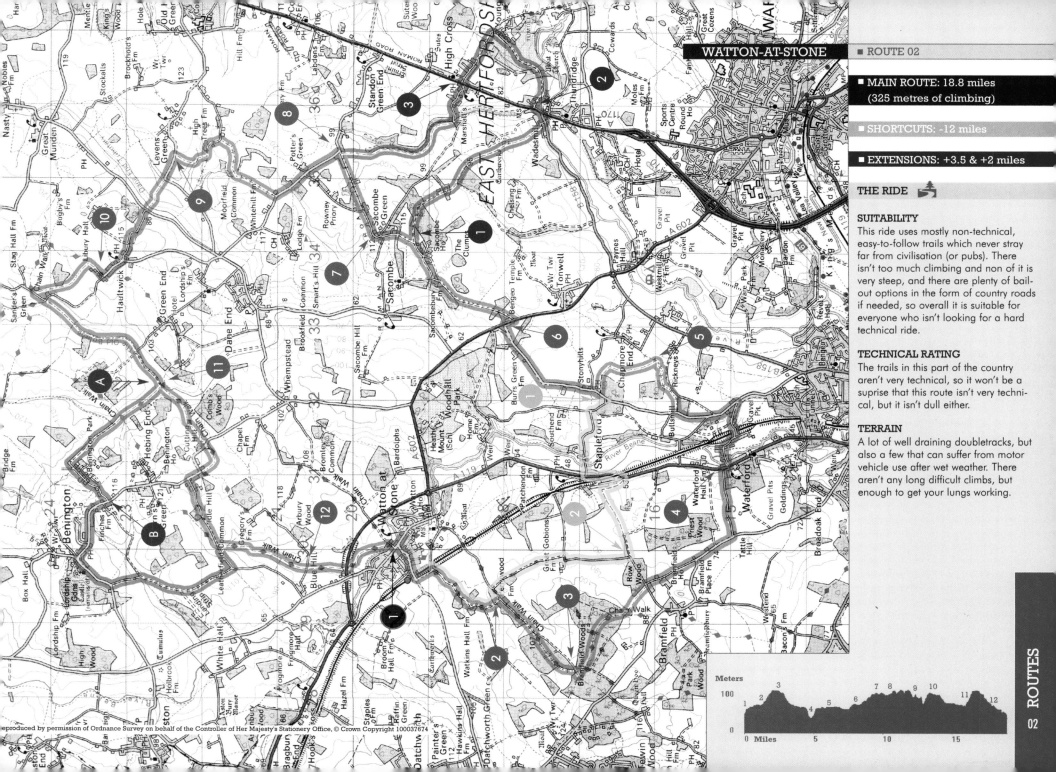

■ **MAIN ROUTE:** 18.8 miles
(325 metres of climbing)

■ SHORTCUTS: -12 miles

■ EXTENSIONS: +3.5 & +2 miles

THE RIDE

SUITABILITY

This ride uses mostly non-technical, easy-to-follow trails which never stray far from civilisation (or pubs). There isn't too much climbing and non of it is very steep, and there are plenty of bail-out options in the form of country roads if needed, so overall it is suitable for everyone who isn't looking for a hard technical ride.

TECHNICAL RATING

The trails in this part of the country aren't very technical, so it won't be a suprise that this route isn't very technical, but it isn't dull either.

TERRAIN

A lot of well draining doubletracks, but also a few that can suffer from motor vehicle use after wet weather. There aren't any long difficult climbs, but enough to get your lungs working.

ROUTES

18.8 miles & 325 metres of climbing

GETTING THERE

This ride starts in the village of Watton-at-stone, which is on the A602 between Hertford and Stevenage (junction 7 of the A1). Follow the public toilet signs to the (free) car park (302/192) near the playing fields (opposite the Bull pub), near the school. There is also a railway station in Watton-at-Stone.

ACCOMMODATION

B&B in Dane end on: 01920 438320
B&B's in Hertford on 01992 302538 or 582487
Camping & Caravanning near Hertford on tel: 01992 586696.
Hertford T.I. on 01992 584322

BICYCLE SHOPS

Marshalls bike shop in Hertford on: 01992 503868 and also in Stevenage and Welwyn Garden City on: 01707 393322and a Halfords in Hertford on: 01432 356442

REFRESHMENTS

There are some pubs and a shop in Watton-at-Stone and pubs in Chapmore End, Stonyhills and Haultwick. Also on the extensions in Wadesmill and Bennington, and Stapleford on the shortcut.

1 START. Back at the high street, turn L, for 0.15m then L on Station road (300/194). After 0.35m turn L on a rd immediately after going over the railway bridge (295/191). 0.15m to a fork and go R (297/189) on a farm rd (BW), keeping L at the farm to a fork and turn L, UH to the woods.

2 0.15m, through the woods to a T-J on the other side (293/180) and turn R, past a farm, becoming a ByW. After 0.4m bear R into the woods by the Forestry commission sign. After 0.5m bear R (on the only ROW) to some X-tracks (all 4 are rights of way) (283/170) and turn L on the Bramfield BW.

3 Follow this for 0.7m (over two DT's) to a fork (as the track bears R) and bear L on the ST (291/164) - easy to miss. DH to a rd (295/161) and go SA on the BW, past a farm, back to a rd. Keep SA/L on this rd for 0.35m, then turn L on a rd to Waterford (301/149), DH, to a main rd.

4 Turn R then immediately L on Vicarage lane (311/150), over a bridge, UH, (over a railway) for 0.65m to T-J (319/149). Turn L on the rd for 0.55m then turn R on the Chapmore end ByW (318/157). Go SA on the DT as you exit the trees, through a field to the far corner (325/159).

5 Bear L on the BW along a field edge (not SA on the ByW), for 0.7m, bearing L, on the RHS of a wood. DH to a rd and turn R on this (320/167) or see the shortcut.

6 1m to a fork and bear R, this bears R parallel and then to the main rd (330/178). Go SA, over the main rd into Sacombe Park

(Private drive), for 0.7m to a fork (by a cottage). Bear L then shortly R at the next fork (336/189), past a green cottage, to a fork (341/192) and turn L or see extension 1.

7 0.25m to some X-rds in Sacombe green (342/196), and go SA on Lowgate lane, bearing R. After 0.3m keep SA on a ByW as the rd bears L (by the building). Follow this for 0.5m to a rd (353/201) by lowgate lodge and turn L on the rd.

8 After 0.65m turn R on the (Levens Green) ByW (347/210) just past a house. 0.4m to a fork and bear R (staying on the ByW), to a tarmac track (355/217) and turn L on this towards a farm. Just past the farm turn R at the fork, on a BW, to a rd (353/223).

9 L on the rd, for 0.2m, then keep SA on a BW as the rd bears sharp L. DH, over a stream, to a rd (345/227) and go SA on Giffords lane (Haultwick). 0.5m into the village and bear R, on The Street, for 0.2m then R on the (Chain walk) BW (336/233).

10 After 0.2m bear L on a BW (338/235) leaving the Chain walk, DH to a rd and turn L on this. DH for 0.1m then turn R as the rd bears L (333/240), over a bridge and turn immediately L on a DT (P.R.U.P). Keep SA on this DT for 1.3m to a (BW) X-tracks (321/225) and keep SA on the Chain walk path or see extension 2.

11 0.6m, UH to a rd (314/219) and keep SA on the BW, which bears R back to the rd. Keep SA/L on the rd for 0.1 then turn L on the (High Elms lane) rd (309/221). After 0.6m at the dip in the rd, turn L on the

Chain walk BW (300/218), and keep SA through a field (at the feint X-tracks after 0.05m). Note: This can get very muddy.

12 Keep SA, DH, for 1.15m to and (carefully) over a duel carriageway (297/201). Bear L on a BW for 0.4m to a lane and turn R on this. To the High street in Watton at Stone (300/194) and turn L for 0.2m, then turn R back to the car park (302/192).

SHORTCUT:

-12 miles & -185 meters of climbing

1 Turn L on the rd, then shortly R at the triangle on the rd (Stapleford), over a bridge to the main rd in Stapleford (309/169). Turn L on this rd for 0.3m, just under the railway bridge and turn R on a BW (309/164). Follow this bearing L, and keeping SA as it joins a track, to a rd (299/163).

2 Turn R on the rd for 0.55m, bearing sharp R by the farm, then immediately turn L onto a BW (299/172). 0.75m to a farm rd (294/181) and turn L on this for 0.1m then turn R on a BW by a farm (been here before). Retrace your earlier steps, back to the car park in Watton-at-Stone (302/192).

EXTENSION 1:

+3.5 miles & +90 meters of climbing

1 Bear R/SA at the fork, for 0.7m, past a high wall and through some woods, DH, to a X-tracks (349/186). Turn L and follow this for 0.95m, following the woods, past an allotment, to rd (357/174) and turn L on this. to a T-J by the Anchor Beefeater pub.

2 Turn L then shortly R on Youngsbury lane, by the Feather Inn pub (359/176). Keep SA on the BW, through a gate, onto a drive. Bear L, UH, through the park for 0.75m to a X-crds (370/181), past some houses then L to a rd (petrol station on R).

3 Turn L, then immediately R, opposite the White Horse pub (362/185) on a rd to Sacombe. After 0.35m in a dip, turn R opposite a green hut (358/187) on a BW. Follow this for 1.1m to Lowgate lodge (353/201) and turn R to the rd then turn L on this, and rejoin the main route at no.8.

EXTENSION 2:

+2 miles & +45 meters of climbing

A Turn R on the BW, through a gate and keep SA on this for 1m (just past a barn on the L) and turn L, UH on a DT (311/237) (as the BW SA is usually poor). Through the farm to a T-J by a house (308233) and turn R to a rd T-J (306/232) and turn R on this.

B After 0.6m bear L at a fork (298/236) by the green, DH on the rd for 0.35m, past a church, then turn L on a ByW (295/232). Keep SA for 1m to a rd (297/216) and turn L for 0.2m, then turn R on a BW in the dip (300/217). Shortly turn R at the (feint) X-tracks, and rejoin the main route at no.12.

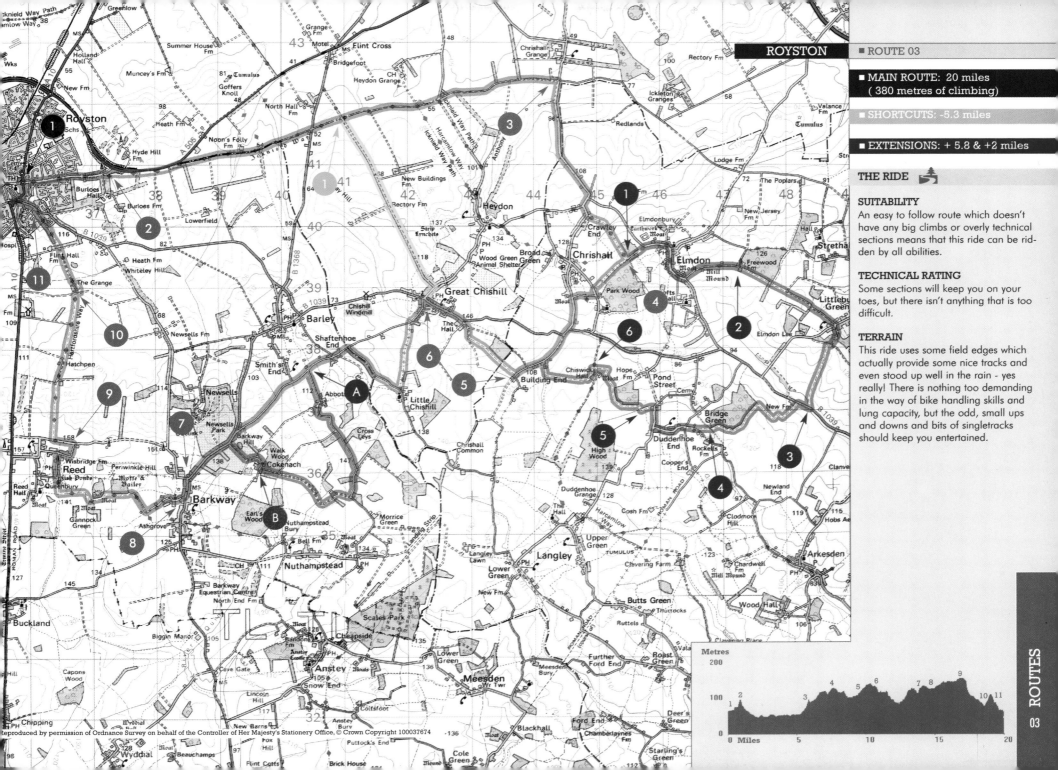

■ **MAIN ROUTE: 20 miles**
(380 metres of climbing)

■ SHORTCUTS: -5.3 miles

■ EXTENSIONS: + 5.8 & +2 miles

THE RIDE

SUITABILITY

An easy to follow route which doesn't have any big climbs or overly technical sections means that this ride can be ridden by all abilities.

TECHNICAL RATING

Some sections will keep you on your toes, but there isn't anything that is too difficult.

TERRAIN

This ride uses some field edges which actually provide some nice tracks and even stood up well in the rain - yes really! There is nothing too demanding in the way of bike handling skills and lung capacity, but the odd, small ups and downs and bits of singletracks should keep you entertained.

ROUTES

03

■ MAIN ROUTE

20 miles & 380 metres of climbing

① START. Exit the car park and turn R to the roundabout (359/407), then turn L at this, on Newmarket rd. UH for 0.8m, then turn R past a black gate with a 'Private' sign, then immediately L on the (Icknield way) ST BW (371/408).

2 Keep SA/L, DH on this for 2.15m, on the RHS of the A505 for a while, to a rd and go SA for 0.3m to another rd (409/417) and go SA or see the shortcut. Follow this Icknield way BW for 1m to a rd and go SA, for another 1.25m to a 3-way rd junction (444/423).

3 Turn R on the rd for 1.3m to a fork just after a RHB, and keep SA/R for 0.1m to another fork (447/403). Bear L (Chrishall) for 0.1m then bear L onto a ByW just after the first house (448/401). 0.65m alongside a field, through some trees, to a T-J in a clearing (454/394) and turn R or see extension 1.

4 0.45m to a rd and turn L, for 0.05m then turn R on (Chalky lane) rd (449/388), 0.25m to a T-J (446/388). Turn L for 0.3m to the main B1039 rd and keep SA/R on this 0.1m, then keep SA on a minor rd (Building end), as the B1039 bears R (445/382). After 0.6m turn R on a BW (437/375) opposite a black barn.

5 After 0.4m at the end on the wood, keep SA, across a field for another 0.2m to a T-J with a DT (429/381) and turn R on this to a rd (428/384). Turn L on the rd, for 0.45m to a X-rds (422/388) in Great Chrishall, by a church, and turn L on May street.

6 After 0.3m bear L on a ByW (420/384) through a tunnel of trees (no signpost). Follow this for 0.7m to a rd (418/373) in Little Chishill and turn R on the rd for 0.7m to a T-J (410/380). Turn L on this rd and keep SA for 1.45m to the main B3168 rd (392/366) or see extension 2.

7 Turn L and follow this rd for 0.9m into Barkway village and turn R on Church lane, by the church (384/356).

8 After 0.45m bear R with the DT on the Hertfordshire way, and follow this for 1.2m (bears L by the woods (376/357) to some X-tracks (364/356), and turn R, becoming a rd. Keep SA through Reed village, for 0.25m to a T-J (364/363) and turn R on the rd, which bears L, to a T-J (366/364).

9 Turn L on the rd for 0.2m then turn R on a BW (Royston) (363/365), for 0.6m, DH, joining a DT by some farm buildings, and keep SA on this. After 0.25m keep SA across a field as the track bears sharp L, for 0.65m to a DT (367/389) with a house SA.

10 Bear R then immediately L (effectively SA) on the RHS of the house, for 0.2m to a X-tracks and go SA on the BW. Through a field, DH, to a cul-de-sac, and keep SA to a T-J. Turn R on Beldam Av, to a T-J with Barkway rd (360/402) and L on this rd.

11 DH, for 0.2m and bear L on the A10 (Barkway st), then immediately R at the fork (357/404), onto Market Hill rd. Follow this (A10) rd for 0.25m to a roundabout and go SA, and immediately L, back into the car park (358/408).

SHORTCUT:

-5.3 miles & -80 metres of climbing

1 Turn R on this rd (409/417) and follow it for 1.95m to a T-J in Great Chishill and turn R for 0.15m to a X-rds (422/388) by the church. Go SA on May street and rejoin the main route at no.6.

EXTENSION 1:

+5.8 miles & 110 metres of climbing

1 Turn L at the T-J to a rd (457/396), and turn R on this for 0.3m to a fork by a church in Elmdon village and bear R. After 0.4m, DH then UH, turn L on the (Icknield way) BW (463/391), and follow this for 0.55m to a farmyard (472/393).

2 Keep SA onto a grassy track, keeping SA, for 1.15m to a rd (487/383), and go SA onto a drive (BW). Bearing R onto a concrete track, to a T-J and turn R then immediately L on a BW (486/380). DH for 0.7m, bearing L at the bottom, to a rd (483/370).

3 Turn R on the rd for 0.15m, then turn L on a BW (481/371), through a farm. Bear R at a fork at the top of the field, following a line of trees, for 0.35m to the woods and turn L on a BW (475/370). Follow this BW for 0.8m, bearing R after the FP crosses you, to a DT (465/367).

4 Bear R on the DT, past a farm, keeping SA on the gravel drive, to a 3-way rd junction and go SA. 0.3m, through Duddenhoe end village, to a T-J (458/367) and turn R for 0.2m then turn L on a BW (459/370), by the houses.

5 (Can get rough) After 0.15m bear R

over a small bridge, across a field to the woods on the other side (456/370). Turn L alongside the woods, and bear R with it, for 0.45m, then keep SA as the woods bear R again, over a small bridge (452/374), UH towards a yellow house at the top.

6 To a drive (449/376) and go SA, bearing L on the BW, by the RHS of the house, and bearing R. Turning R on the BW by a stream, DH, to a rd (441/377) and turn L on this. After 0.3m turn R on a BW (437/375) opposite a black barn and rejoin the main route at no.5.

EXTENSION 2:

+2 miles & +15 metres of climbing

A Turn L on the rd for 0.5m then turn L on Nuthampstead rd (404/376), for 1.5m the R on a BW, as rd bears sharp L (410/355). Follow this track for 1.1m to a farm.

B Turn R, behind the big green tanks, to a drive and bear L on this (396/362), to the B1368 rd (391/365) and turn L. After 0.75m on this rd into Brakway village, turn R on Church lane, by the church (384/356) and rejoin the main route at no.8.

🚗 GETTING THERE

This ride starts from the King James car park in central Royston, off the A10 (Melbourn Road). Follow the car park signs from the A10 to the (King James) car park (358/408) which costs £1.50 for the whole day. There is also a railway in Royston.

📦 ACCOMMODATION

B&B in Great Chishall at Hall farm (working farm) on: 01763 838263. **YHA** in Saffron Walden on: 0870 7706014 or Cambridge on: 7705742 **Camping** in Fowlmere, at Apple acre park on tel: 01763 208 229 or 353 **Letchworth T.I.** on: 01462 487868 **Cambridge TI** on: 01223 322640

🚲 BICYCLE SHOPS

Newdales on the high street in Royston on: 01763 247911

🍴 REFRESHMENTS

There is lots of choice in Roysten and there are pubs on the route in Chrishall, Great Chrishall, Barkway and Reed. There is also a pub in Elmdon on extension 1

ROUTES

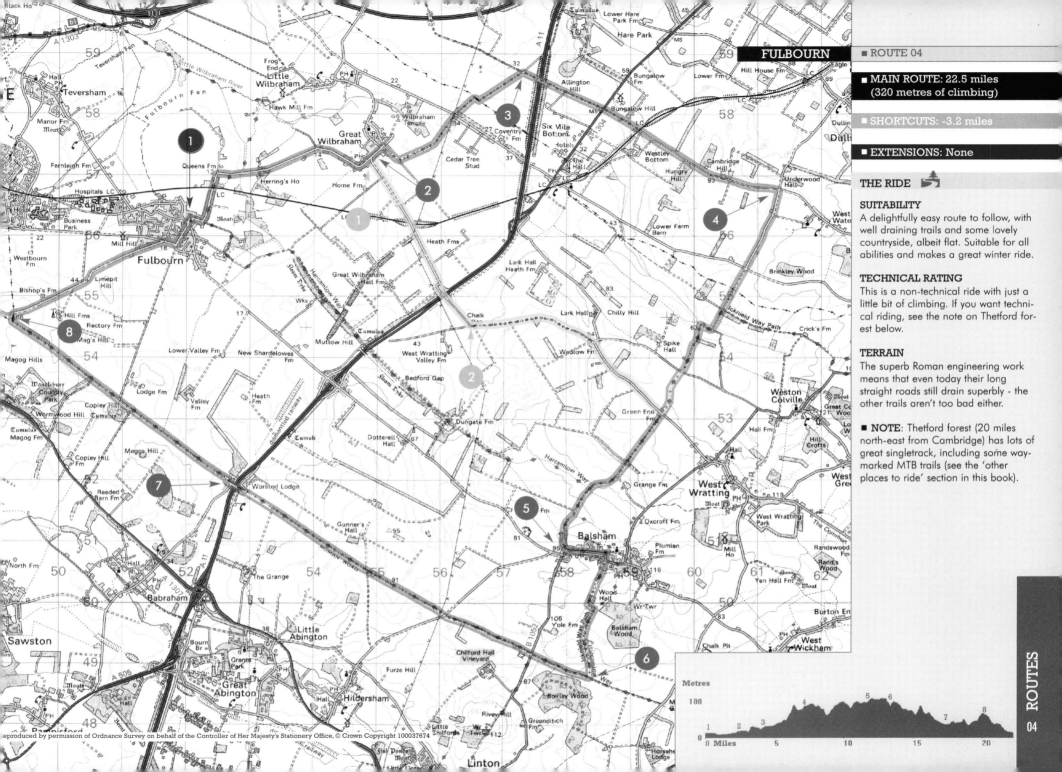

ROUTE 04

■ **MAIN ROUTE: 22.5 miles**
(320 metres of climbing)

■ **SHORTCUTS: -3.2 miles**

■ **EXTENSIONS: None**

THE RIDE 🏕

SUITABILITY
A delightfully easy route to follow, with well draining trails and some lovely countryside, albeit flat. Suitable for all abilities and makes a great winter ride.

TECHNICAL RATING
This is a non-technical ride with just a little bit of climbing. If you want technical riding, see the note on Thetford forest below.

TERRAIN
The superb Roman engineering work means that even today their long straight roads still drain superbly - the other trails aren't too bad either.

■ **NOTE:** Thetford forest (20 miles north-east from Cambridge) has lots of great singletrack, including some waymarked MTB trails (see the 'other places to ride' section in this book).

ROUTES

04

GETTING THERE

This ride starts the village of Fulbourn, which is on the south-east edge of Cambridge. Most people will probably be best using Balsham road from the roundabout off the A11, into Fulbourn and find somewhere sensible to park e.g. near the church (520/562). There is a railway station in Cambridge.

ACCOMMODATION

B&B in Cambridge at Ashtrees guesthouse on tel: 01223 411233
B&B in Cambridge at Assisi guesthouse on tel: 01223 246648
YHA in Cambridge on tel: 0870 7705742
Camping at Great Shelford on tel: 01223 841185.
Cambridge TI on tel: 01223 322640

BICYCLE SHOPS

Ben Hayward cycles on: 01223 352294, Cambridge Recycles ltd on: 01223 506035, and The Bike Shop on: 01223 316 596, all in Cambridge

REFRESHMENTS

Two pubs in Fulbourn, and more in Great Wilbraham and Blasham and a tea shop just off the route between Balsham and Linton at Chilford Hall Vineyard.

22.5 miles & 320 metres of climbing

① START. Head north on the main rd, (Church lane, becoming Station rd), **over a railway line** (523/567), **out of the village. Follow this rd to the next village** (Great Wilbraham), **and go SA through the village** or see the shortcut.

② Keep SA (on the High st) **as the main rd bears sharp L** (becoming Church st) just past a pub. **Turn R immediately on Butt lane** (550/574), **which becomes a BW and forks after 0.2m** (553/572). **Bear L, for 0.75m to a rd and keep SA on the ByW for another 0.85m to a X-tracks** (572/586).

③ Turn R on the DT for 0.9m, on a bridge over the A11 rd, **to the A1304 rd and go SA on the ByW** (can see a windmill on the L). **To a railway line and go over this, to a rd and go SA/L on this for 1.55m to a X-rds** (613/567) **and turn R** (Linton).

④ 0.9m to a X-rds and go SA, on the rd for another 0.7m and turn R on a ByW (Icknield way), **as the rd bears sharp L** (602/544). **Follow this for 3 miles,** bearing L by the big blue tanks, over 2 roads, **to a rd in Balsham village** (579/508).

⑤ Turn L on the rd for 0.45m, into the village, then just after going around a RHB, **keep SA on Woodhall lane** /Icknield ByW, as the rd bears L (585/506). **Follow this ByW for 1.35m to a T-J** (583/487) **and turn R here.**

⑥ Keep SA on this (Icknield way) **ByW for 3.85m,** over 2 roads, **to the corner of a hairpin bend in the rd,** (529/518). **Bear L (SA) on the rd, over the A11 rd, keep SA** (Mount farm/dead end) **as the rd bears sharp R, then bear L** (effectively SA) **as the track bears R.**

⑦ Keep SA on this (Icknield) **ByW for another 2.7m,** bearing R through a car park, **to a rd** (492/547).

⑧ Turn R on the rd, for 1.65m to a T-J (516/558) in Fulbourn **and turn R on Cambridge road. After 0.15m turn L on School lane,** as the rd bears R, **for 0.25m to the X-rds by the church** (520/562), and go back to where you parked your car.

① 0.15m after bearing L into the village, turn R on Mill road (548/572) **at the grass triangle. Follow this rd for 1.45m to a fork and bear R,** going over the A11 rd. **After 0.4m from the bridge, turn L on a ByW** (564/545), **as the rd bears sharp R** (West Wratting farm).

② Follow this ByW track keeping L, for **1.3m to corner of a rd** by Wadlow farm (584/542). **Turn R on the rd for 1m, then turn R on the** (Icknield way) **ByW** (594/530) **by Green end farm. Follow this for 1.8m to a rd in Balsham village** (579/508) **and rejoin the main route at no.5.**

A great ride for the winter as the tracks drain well and the route is very easy to navigate which will keep you moving (and warm).

HIGHLY RECOMMENDED

■ ROUTE 05

■ **MAIN ROUTE:** 22.7 miles
(455 metres of climbing)

■ **SHORTCUTS:** Variable

■ **EXTENSIONS:** +2.9 miles

THE RIDE

SUITABILITY
There is something here for EVERY-ONE. Forest tracks, canal side cycle-ways, or unmarked forest singletrack.

TECHNICAL RATING
The route itself doesn't use very techni-cal trails, so everyone will feel comfort-able riding it. However, the forest is famous (with London MTB'ers) for it's miles and miles of technical singletrack.

TERRAIN
The 6,000 acre forest has loads of sin-gletrack and a good network of wide, well draining, hard-pack forest tracks, with a few short sharp climbs and descents.

■ **NOTE:** Most of the forest is open to cyclists, but please stay out of areas where there are signs saying otherwise.

TOP TIP: Local bike (shop) clubs cycle here most weekends, so you might like to tag along (see www.epping-forest-mbc-co.uk). There is also a 2 mile man-made off-road course for cyclists near Leyton / Hackney, see www.leevalley-park.com for more information.

ROUTES

05

GETTING THERE

Exit the M26 at junction 26 on the A121 (Loughton) for 0.3m then turn right on Clay Pit Hill by a thatched hut, then immediately left into the (free) car park (412/996). There are lots more car parks e.g. at High Beach, where there is also a public toilet, a pub, and a cafe. There are railway stations at Wanstead park and Forest Gate.

ACCOMMODATION

B&B's in Waltham Abbey on: 01992 764892, 787413 & 717174
B&B in Epping on: 01992 619959
YHAs at High Beach on: 0870 7705822 & Cheshunt on: 7706118
Camping at Cheshunt on: 0870 770 8868, Loughton on: 0208 5083008 & Chingford on: 0208 5295689
Waltham Abbey TI: 01992 652295

BICYCLE SHOPS

Bikes etc in Loughton on: 0208 5081048, Wades cycles in Buckhurst hill on: 5045033, Heales cycles on: 5271592 & Top Banana on: 5590170

REFRESHMENTS

Two pubs near the start / end of the ride, a cafe by the canal (nr Waltham Abbey). A pub, cafe and snack shop at High Beach, and a restaurant at the round-about by Jack's hill.

22.7 miles and 455 metres of climbing

1 START. Cross the main road onto Woodgreen rd, north of the car park. **After 0.3m turn R on a ST** (no sign)), just after going under the M25. **0.2m along this** parallel to rd, **to a T-J** (412/004) **and turn R, UH, for 0.1m, then L at the fork** (414/004).

2 After 0.15m bear L at a fork, joining a drive, and shortly leave it again by keeping SA as the drive bears R. Go across the grass, **to the rd** (410/010) **and go SA on the BW** (drive to 'Warlies'). **After 0.3m turn L on a DT** just after the car park.

3 Keep R at the fork by the Clock house, **to a rd** (416/017) **and turn L on this. After 0.4m turn L at Fernhall farm, for 0.3m to Maynards farm, and keep SA on a rough DT. UH, for 0.3m to a fork** (417/032) **and bear L,** or see the extension.

4 After 0.4m turn R on a (rough) **BW** (412/034) opposite the houses, **for 0.6m to a farm, and go SA,** past the house on the L, DH, for 0.45m on the drive, **to the rd at the bottom** (410/050).

5 Turn L on this rd for 0.1m to a round-about (408/050), **and turn L again on** Bumbles green lane. Follow this for 1.65m, becomes off-road, DH, **to a drive** (395/029), opposite 'Black cottage'. **Turn R, for 30 meters to a fork** (house SA) **and bear R on the** (Holyfield) **BW.**

6 NOTE: Rough DH, with a ditch by the drive. Turn R on the drive, to the rd (386/030), **and turn L on this for 0.3m then turn R on Stubbins hall lane** (Hayes hill fm). **Bear L after 0.1m to the car park** (380/030)

7 Go through the car park, and turn L (visitors centre on the R) following the National grid sign. **After 0.05m turn L on the foot/cycle track** (376/032), **just before a bridge. Go over a bridge to a T-J** with the lake in front of you **and turn L and follow the Waltham Abbey cycle trail.**

8 Keep SA/R through a car park, onto the DT at the far L end of the car park, and follow this along the RHS of the river, to the A121 rd (375/005), (there is now a river on your RHS). **Turn R on the rd/bridge,** over the water, **then R again,** back down to the water and turn sharp R (180 degrees).

9 Follow the river (on your LHS) for 1.2m (under the M25, past a cafe which is popular with cyclists) **to a rd,** by the Greyhound pub, just past the 2nd bridge (371/987). **Go SA, keeping alongside the river for 0.25m,** then bear L over the water, towards Rifles pub.

10 Turn R back alongside the river as soon as you've crossed it (371/983), **and follow it for 1.95m up to a rd** by the lock (363/954). **Turn L on the rd** to some lights at a duel carriageway, **and turn R on this rd for 0.75m, to some** lights at a X-rds (375/949), **and turn L.**

11 After 0.75m turn R on the (easy to miss) High Beach BW in the bus stop lay-by (377/960). Steep UH, **keeping L, for 0.7m** to a drive by the Scouts activity centre, **and turn R on this. To a rd** (389/963) **and turn R on an off-road ST,** parallel to the rd, which later joins the rd.

12 After 0.4m (of the ST and the rd), **bear L onto a** good, wide **forest track,** parallel to the rd. **After 0.25m on this DT, turn L** (by a black barrier on the R) on another forest track (393/953). **Keep SA at the X-tracks, for 0.25m to a fork and bear L,** to another fork and bear R at this one.

13 To a ST rd and go SA over this, on a good track, to the main rd (409/963) and go SA on the track opposite. Bear L, following the white posts with a horse shoe, behind the car park, **to a fork, and bear R,** (leaving the horse track), UH, to a pond.

14 Bear L and join a wide forest track, to a rd and car park (415/967), **and go SA,** back on the forest track. Keep SA on this, past a black barrier, **into an opening** (white post on R), **and go SA, to a fork and bear R,** to a rd (428/985).

15 Go SA on the forest track, keeping L on this for 0.8m to a rd (435/995) (Jack's hill), and go SA, through the car park. After 0.4m on this forest track, bear L at the fork, to a rd (433/000). Go over the rd onto a forest track and immediately bear L (parallel to the rd).

16 Keep SA over an old ST rd, for 0.4m to the edge of the woods, (barrier and rd SA) **and bear R on the forest track** (425/994). **Keep bearing L on the forest tracks, to a rd** (420/994), **and go SA** past a black barrier, on the Three forests way (Loughton 3m).

17 After 0.6m turn R at a fork (414/989), DH, for 0.45m to a rd and turn R on this, then shortly R, into the car park (412/997).

1 Turn R at the fork, and follow this DT, which becomes a rd at Parvills farm, **keeping SA for 1m to the** B181 rd (437/044), just past Chambers Manor farm. Turn L on the rd for 0.75m, in to Epping Green, **then turn L on the** (Harolds park farm) **BW,** just after the Cock & Magpie pub (434/055).

2 Keep SA on this BW for 1.6m (leaving the Forest way which turns L, after 0.8m), **to a** farm/stables. Turn R, DH, on the drive just before the house (412/043), **for 0.45m, DH, to a rd** (410/050) and rejoin the main route at no.5.

SHORTCUT:

Various

There are good forest paths and lots of singletrack within Epping forests 6,000 acres. There are some areas which are out of bounds to cyclists, but apart from that, just go where you fancy.

A choice of woodland singletrack, or wide cycletracks on this ride.

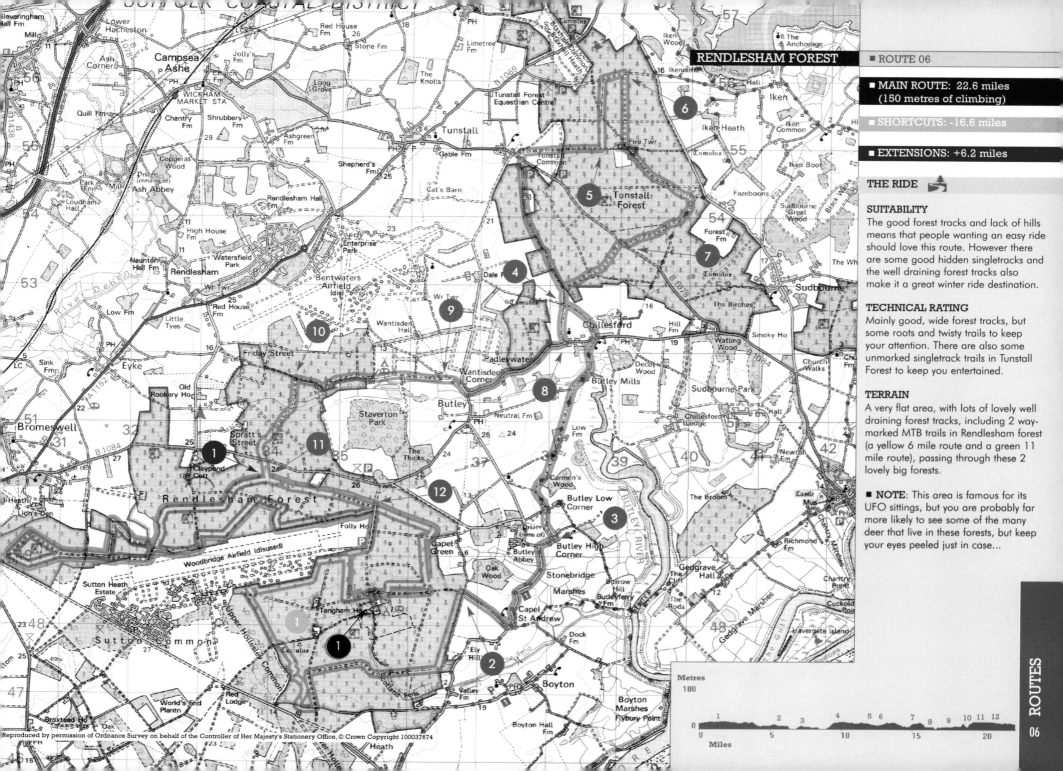

ROUTE 06

- **MAIN ROUTE:** 22.6 miles (150 metres of climbing)
- **SHORTCUTS:** -16.6 miles
- **EXTENSIONS:** +6.2 miles

THE RIDE

SUITABILITY

The good forest tracks and lack of hills means that people wanting an easy ride should love this route. However there are some good hidden singletracks and the well draining forest tracks also make it a great winter ride destination.

TECHNICAL RATING

Mainly good, wide forest tracks, but some roots and twisty trails to keep your attention. There are also some unmarked singletrack trails in Tunstall Forest to keep you entertained.

TERRAIN

A very flat area, with lots of lovely well draining forest tracks, including 2 way-marked MTB trails in Rendlesham forest (a yellow 6 mile route and a green 11 mile route), passing through these 2 lovely big forests.

■ **NOTE:** This area is famous for its UFO sittings, but you are probably for more likely to see some of the many deer that live in these forests, but keep your eyes peeled just in case...

ROUTES

06

■ MAIN ROUTE

22.6 miles & 150 metres of climbing

+6.2 miles & +20 metres of climbing

🚗 GETTING THERE

This ride starts from the Tangham car park in Rendlesham forest, which costs £1 for the day. Exit the A12 on the A1152, by Woodbridge, through Melton, and follow the Rendlesham forest signs. Bear right on the B1084, for just over 3 miles, then turn right into Rendlesham forest, for 1 mile to the car park (353/484). There is a railway station in Melton.

🛏 ACCOMMODATION

B&B in the Ship Inn, Blaxhall (nr Tunstall forest) on: 01728 688316
B&B in Aldeburgh on the coast, on tel: 01728 602149
YHA in Blaxhall on: 0870 7705702
Campsite in Rendlesham forest by the car park, on tel: 01394 450707
Woodbridge TI on : 01394 382240

🚲 BICYCLE SHOPS

Thomas's Cycle Revolution on tel: 01473 716 604, and Ranelagh Cycle Warehouse on: 01473 250610 in Ipswich.

🍴 REFRESHMENTS

Cafe and campsite shop at the start / end, pubs at Butley and Chillesford, a tea shop in Butley, a campsite shop in Rendlesham forest (near Butley) and a tea shop and two pubs in Snape.

1 **START**. Head west from the car park, following the yellow cycle track signs. Stay on this waymarked track, which bears north, before going around the southern part of the forest, **for 5.5 miles** (at the end of a 0.7m stretch of singletrack, along the edge of the forest) **where the cycle trail bears L, by a gate, near the corner of a rd (367/484).**

2 **Turn R to the rd, and go SA/R on this for 0.5m to a X-rds (374/479)** at Capel St Andrew, **and turn L** (Butley). **After 0.85m** on this rd, **turn R** (Butley high corner) (378/491) on the dead end rd, **for 0.15m, then turn L on a ROW (380/492).**

3 After 0.25m go SA at the rd, for another 0.2m to a fork (378/499), by the power lines, and turn R. Keep SA on this main track for 1m to a rd and turn R on this, for 0.5m to a T-J in Chillsford village. **Turn R then immediately L on a BW (386/522)** by a post box, **for 0.4m to a X-tracks (381/527).**

4 **Turn R and keep SA on this DT, for 1.45** to a rd and go SA on a ST (bird sign) for 0.1m to a sandy DT (375/549) and turn R on this (leaving the bird trail). **Enter the forest after 0.3m, and keep SA on the DT for another 0.35m then turn L (387/550)** following a signpost with a bicycle on it.

5 0.25m to a X-tracks and go SA for another 0.05m to another X-tracks and go SA (L then R), on a ST (not the bird trail on L). Keep SA on this track for 0.35m to a rd (387/560) and turn R on this rd for 0.2m then turn R past a green barrier (by a 2/4 sign) **on a wide forest track (390/561).**

6 Follow this main track, for 0.75m, which bears L to a X-tracks (390/550) and go SA, past a house on the LHS. **Keep SA over 2 X-tracks, for 0.75m to a T-J (399/543) and turn R. Keep SA on this forest track for 0.8m** (under some power cables), **to a rd (390/536).**

7 Go SA, past a barrier, **on another wide forest track, by a no.32 sign, and keep SA** (at X-tracks after 0.45m) **for a total of 0.7,** past a barrier, **to a T-J at the edge of the woods (381529)** (been here before). **Turn L, for 0.15m to a X-tracks and go SA** (not been down here before), **to a rd (382/521).**

8 Turn R on this rd, for 1.05m into Butley village, **then turn R** (Tunstall, Camping) as the rd bears L (368/514). **Bear L immediately at the fork, for 0.15m and bear L on a (grassy DT) BW,** just past a house on the L. Follow the telegraph poles, through a farm, **to a good DT track, and go SA/L on this.**

9 Keep SA after 0.25m on a grassy DT (BW), as the good track bears L. Keep SA, becoming a ST, **to a good DT (354/516) and keep SA on this** into the trees (the campsite on L sells food). **Keep SA on this DT for 0.75m** (alongside the telegraph poles) **to a wide forest track on the L** in an open area (343/516).

10 Turn L (following the bird sign) past a green barrier, **and keep SA,** DH, (over a X-tracks with red topped posts) **bearing R. To a fork and bear L at this, to a X-tracks and keep SA,** following the bird sign **to a rd. Go SA for 0.2m to a (DT) T-J (340/501) and turn L** (bird sign) or see the extension.

11 0.3m to a T-J and turn L (there are some old shipping containers on the L), **and join a good, wide forest track. Keep SA on this,** following the (green) bike signs **to a rd (355/497).**

12 Go SA, and follow the (green) cycle trail **for 1.2m, to a (small) X-tracks in the trees** (362/486). **Turn R on the yellow cycle trail** (signs on other side of the wooden post), **leaving the green cycle track, and follow the yellow signs, to a tarmac rd** (under power cables) **and keep SA on this, back to the car park** at the start/end (353/484).

A great ride for all abilities, which works well in the winter.

1 Turn R and follow the (green) cycle trail signs (going to the western edge of the forest, then back east, using some of the same tracks), for 7.2 miles, to a rd (355/497), and rejoin the main route at no.12.

SHORT ROUTE:

6 miles & 30 metres of climbing

1 Follow the 'yellow' cycle trail markers.

■ **NOTE:** There is also an 11 mile 'green' waymarked cycle trail, which we have marked on the map in red, as we have used it as an extension. Both trails start from the car park and can be cycled in either direction.

TOP TIP: Still take a map and compass on the marked cycle routes as new tracks appear, signposting is not always wonderful, and there are plenty more tracks you might like to explore in these open access forests.

HIGHLY RECOMMENDED

- **ROUTE 07**

- **MAIN ROUTE: 17 miles**
  (370 metres of climbing)

- **SHORTCUTS: -6.9 miles**

- **EXTENSIONS: Various**

THE RIDE

SUITABILITY
This ride is great for all abilities of riders as there are wide forests tracks and twisty woodland singletracks.

TECHNICAL RATING
The main route isn't very technical, but it's the superb network of the unmarked twisty woodland singletrack that really makes this a great place to ride - see the extensions for more information.

TERRAIN
Mostly good woodland trails with a bit of climbing - nothing too severe. There are miles and miles of great singletrack trails in the woods, but it can get slippery and damaged by horses and over-use in bad weather.

- **NOTE:** Not all of the woodland is necessarily open to cyclists (see over the page). Also, see www.kent-trails.co.uk for information on group rides.

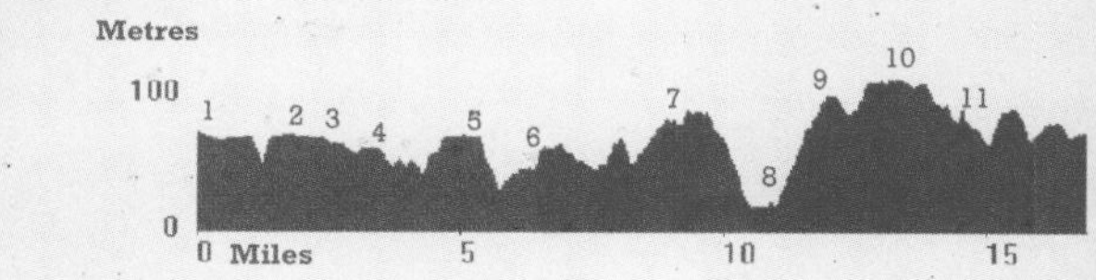

ROUTES

07

GETTING THERE

The ride starts from the (free) Rough common nature reserve car park (121/594), which has a height restriction. Follow the Blean woods nature reserve signs off Rough common road (which goes between the A290 and the A2050/A2.

ACCOMMODATION

B&B at Cathedral gate hotel in Canterbury on tel: 01227 464381
B&B in Whitstable on: 01227 263506
YHA in Canterbury on: 0870 7705744
Camping in Canterbury, just off the A257 on tel: 01227 463216
Canterbury TI on tel: 01227 378100

BICYCLE SHOPS

Cycle Mart in Canterbury (Lower bridge street) on tel: 01227 761488

REFRESHMENTS

A pub and shop on the road before the car park track, and lots of choice in Canterbury. On the ride there is the The Dove pub in Dargate and at Dunkirk (just off the route) .

ROUTES

07

17 miles & 370 metres of climbing

1 START. Go back down the drive to Rough common road (126/592), and turn L, to a T-J. Turn R for 0.05m then turn L on the Crab and winkle/Whitstable cycleway, (130/594). Keep SA on this for 0.85m to a rd and go SA for 0.1m and turn R on a ST (no sign) before the style (128/609).

2 After 0.45m, exit the trees and turn R (129/615) on a feint (BW) track (no sign), between 2 fields and parallel to the power lines, on your LHS. 0.4m to some X-tracks by the commercial green houses, and go SA past the willow tree, for 0.05m to the edge of a field SA (135/619).

3 Bear L on the grassy DT, for 0.05m then turn R and go along the RHS edge of the field (can get rough). Keep SA through the trees to a rd (138/625) and turn L for 0.1m to a fork (138/626). Keep L (or turn R to Thorden woods), for 0.25m then turn L past a barrier into Clowes wood (136/630), as the rd bears sharp R.

4 Turn R on the fire road, DH, for 0.85m and bear L (125/636) back UH, for another 0.65m to a fork (126/626) and turn R on the wide (Canterbury cycleway) track. After 0.35m keep SA on the rough DT, as the cycle track bears sharp L.

5 Follow this DT (or use the ST on the RHS after 0.25m) for 0.4m and keep SA on the ST, past a style, into a field, DH, to a rd (114/621). Turn R on the rd for 0.4m, then turn L on Fox cross rd and immediately L on a BW (109/625).

6 Keep bearing R to get to the far end of the woods after 0.65m (100/626) and turn sharp L on the BW. DH, to a rd (101/618) and turn R on this for 1.7m to a fork (082/602), or see the shortcut.

7 Turn R, UH, for another 0.5m then turn R on a DT (075/599), for 0.1m to a fork and bear R, through a farm (079/604) and keep SA into the woods, DH, for 0.8m to a rd (080/613). The 'Dove' pub is 0.1m SA/R on the rd.

8 Turn L on the rd, for 0.65m to a fork and bear L, for 0.25m then turn L on a BW in the lay-by (072/606). Go UH to the start of the woods (073/605) and bear L on a ST between the field and woods.

9 Keep bearing R at any forks (079/607), UH, for 0.7m to a DT (by a house), and keep SA. DH, to the rd (075/599) you've been here before and go SA on the BW for 0.65m, through a gate by a secluded cottage, to a rd (074/590) by Courtney house.

10 Turn L on the rd, and keep SA on this for 0.5m, then turn L past a wooden barrier into the woods (082/589) on an unsignposted ST (shortly after Dunkirk cars). 0.7m to a T-J (084/596) and turn R on this, then turn L just past a wooden barrier (089/599).

11 Go DH on this wide grassy track, between the trees, for 0.5m to a DT (093/605) and turn R. Keep SA on this main DT for 2m, back to the car park (121/594).

-6.9 miles & -195 metres of climbing

1 After 0.6m turn L on a BW (096/610) opposite Denstroude farm, and stay on this main DT for 2.35m back to the car park (121/594):

Various

Clowes wood - An open access Forestry Commission wood with a wide doubletrack, and a few nice singletracks in places.

Rough common / Church wood / North Bishopden wood - A few well surfaced doubletracks, and lots of singletrack - although some of it is (signposted) no-go for MTB's.

Thorden / West Blean wood - This woodland recently changed ownership over to Kent Wildlife Trust, who hadn't confirmed the access rights for users when we went to print. There is a good surfaced doubletrack going through the centre of the woods, with lots and lots of superb twisty singletracks all through these woods.

The woodland around Canterbury is home to miles of sweet singletrack.

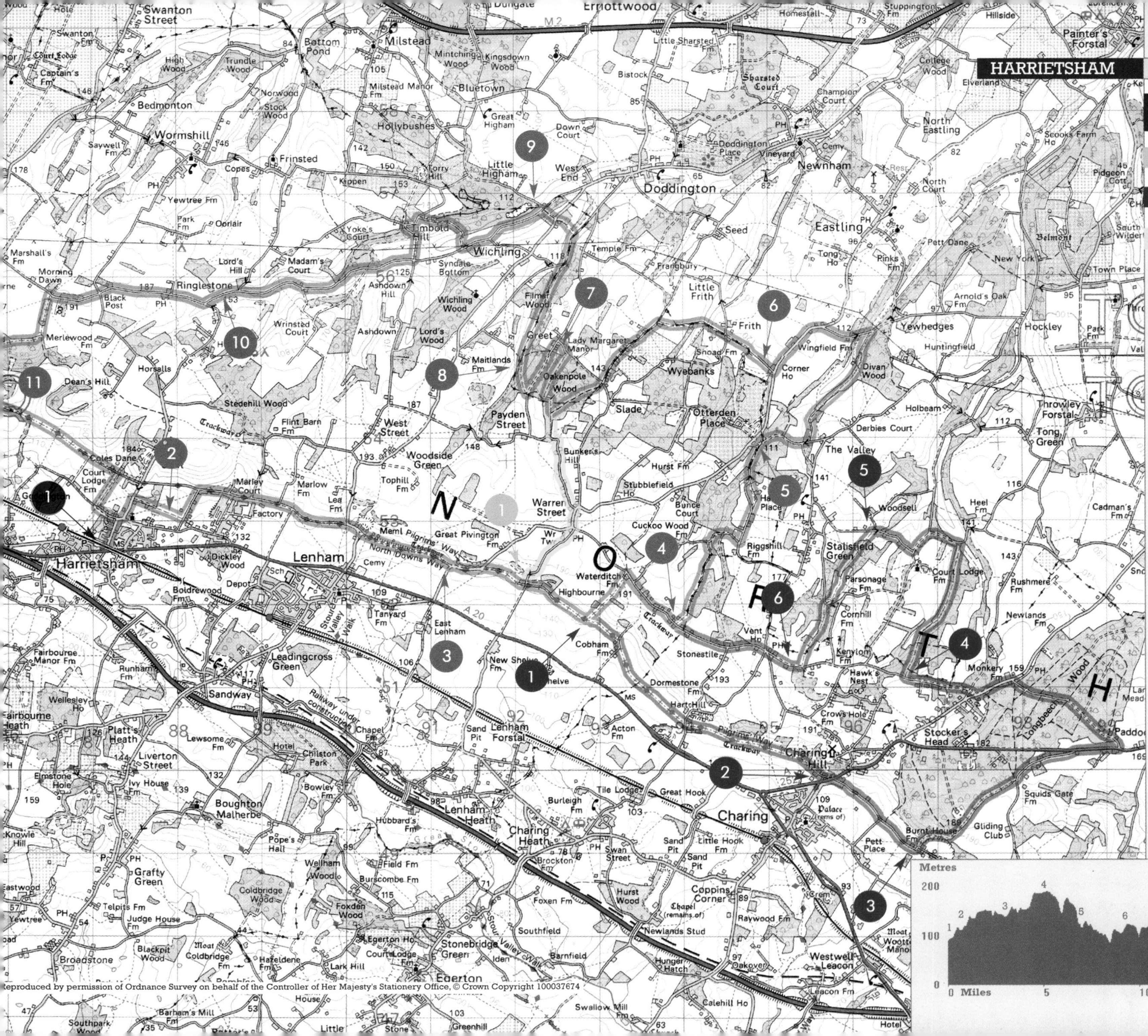

HARRIETSHAM

■ **MAIN ROUTE: 22.1 miles**
(650 metres of climbing)

■ SHORTCUTS: -6.25 miles

■ **EXTENSIONS: +9.8 miles**

THE RIDE

SUITABILITY
Thanks to the singletrack just getting more technical the faster you ride it, and the fact that the route can be chopped and changed to make a variety of lengths (the extension on it's own makes a good 11 mile ride), it is suitable for all abilities.

TECHNICAL RATING
There is more singletrack than you might think thanks to sections of the North Downs Way (Pilgrims way) being overgrown to become singletrack. The northern part of the ride also has it's fair share of singletrack and hills, which makes this a fairly challenging ride.

TERRAIN
Lots of good tracks which will be very fast in the dry, but can get slippy in the wet and may be over-grown in places. A few short steep ups and downs, with a big climb left to near the end of the ride, but it is on the road.

ROUTES

08

Reproduced by permission of Ordnance Survey on behalf of the Controller of Her Majesty's Stationery Office, © Crown Copyright 100037674

GETTING THERE

This ride starts in Harrietsham, which is on the A20. You will probably use junction 8 off the M20 (by the service station), and follow the A20 (past Leeds castle) for just over 3 miles to Harrietsham. Park with consideration in the village e.g. by the train station (on Station rd, off west street), or by the church (on church rd).

ACCOMMODATION

B&B in Hollingbourne on: 01622 880594
B&B in Charing at the Royal Oak Inn on: 01233 712612
B&B at the Dog & Bear hotel in Lenham on: 01622 858219
Campsite in Hogbarn (near Harrietsham) on: 01622 859648
Maidstone TI on: 01622 739029

BICYCLE SHOPS

Cycle Mart on tel: 01622 752 226 and Senacre Cycles & Spares on tel: 01622 752 695, both in Maidstone.

REFRESHMENTS

A pub and a post office shop in Harrietsham and a pub in Ringlestone. A pub on the short-cut in Warren Street, and more pubs & shops in Charing and near the end of the extension.

MAIN ROUTE

22.1 miles & 650 metres of climbing

1 START. Go north on Church rd off the A20, by a school (871/526) (Campsite and Frinsted). Under a bridge, **bearing R after 0.25m then bearing L** in front of the church, on Stede hill. 0.2m past the church, UH, **turn R** through a gate, **onto a BW** (874/532), **for 0.4m to a rd** (880/530).

2 Turn L, UH, to a T-J (882/533) and turn R on this rd (Pilgrims way) **for 0.7m, then keep SA on the ByW**, as the rd bears R. 0.45m to a rd and bear R on this for 0.1m then **go SA/L** (901/528) **back off-road, for 0.7m** to another rd and **go SA/L** on this.

3 After 0.25m turn R/SA back off-road (916/524) onto the Pilgrims way, **for 0.35m to a rd** (921/522) **and go SA** or see the shortcut. **After another 0.55m** on the Pilgrims way **turn L** on a ByW (928/518) or see the extension. **UH for 0.5m** through the farm **to a rd** (933/523) **and turn R** on this **for 0.6m, then turn L** on a ByW (938/517).

4 Past the old cars and junk, **for 0.7m, DH, to a T-J and turn R, UH** to a rd (946/527). **Turn L** on the rd for 0.25m then **keep SA** on a BW, as the rd bears L. **Bear L** (948/532) past a house, **to the rd and bear R** on this, DH, **for 0.3m to a grass triangle** (949/539).

5 Turn R on the rd (Stalisfield green), **for 0.35m to a fork and turn L**, UH, **for 0.05m to the top and turn L** on a BW (954/539). DH, **for 1m to the rd** (962/553) **and turn L** on this for 0.4m to a T-J (956/553). **Turn L on the rd** for 0.55m to a grass triangle and post box **and turn R** (950/548).

6 After 0.5m keep SA on a BW (just after rd on the L to Wyebanks) as the rd bears R, **DH** in the trees. **Into the open at the bottom and go SA**, UH, (track disappears), **joining a DT, to a rd** (937/554). **Turn L** on this for 0.65m to a T-J, and go SA into the woods. **Bear R at a fork**, to some X-tracks (924/543) **and turn R**, DH, **and keep SA for 0.6m to a rd** (926/550).

7 Turn L on the rd for 0.1m to a T-J (925/552) **at Ellans court and turn L** (Lenham). **Go UH** for 0.5m, **then turn sharp R** (by the end of the wood) **into the woods**, by the Oakenpole woods sign (921/545). **Go DH on the ST** for 0.3m to valley bottom.

8 Keep SA through a gate (920/550), on a grassy BW, **along the valley bottom**, between the ROW markers. **Back into the woods and keep SA** to a rd, and go R/SA on this. After 0.25m turn L on a BW by brick hut, UH, (track improves) **to a rd and turn R, then immediately L** on a DT, DH, to a rd (923/568).

9 After 0.7m on this rd **turn R** on a ByW (913/563) just after a electricity pylon). UH, **for 0.5m to a rd**, and turn L for 0.15m then **turn L on a ByW** (906/566), DH for 0.3m, to a X-rds (908/561). **Turn R** on the rd, for 1.4m to a fork and keep L.

10 Keep R after 0.25m, **for 0.8m, through Ringlestone** (pub here), **to some X-rds and go SA** (Hollingbourne). After 0.4m turn L on a ByW (865/557) **and follow this** DH, for 1.15m to a T-J with a DT (Pilgrims way) (853/546) **and turn L** on this.

11 After 1.4m just after joining a driveway, **turn R** on a ST (873/535) (faded sign on a post). **Go DH for 0.3m** to a T-J with a driveway (870/531) **and turn L** on this, back to Church rd (872/531) by Court lodge. Now make your way back to your car, wherever you parked it (the church is SA and the village of Harrietsham is on the R).

SHORTCUT:

-6.25 miles & -190 metres of climbing

1 Turn L on the rd, UH, **for 0.6m to a T-J and turn L**, to another T-J and **turn R** on Warren st. After 0.15m **turn L** on Payden street (927/531) **and 0.6m** along this, after a LHB, **turn R** on a BW (924/540). **Go DH on this for 0.75m**, to a rd (926/550), **and rejoin the main route at no.7.**

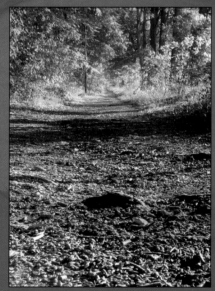

EXTENSION:

+9.8 miles & +270 metres of climbing

1 Keep SA (Pilgrims way), **for 0.3m, joining a DT** by Cobham farm, **and bear R** for 0.05m then **keep SA/L** leaving the DT (Pilgrims way). **0.75m to a rd** (940/505) and **go SA** (R then L) (Pilgrims way), **for another 1.2m to the A252 rd** (957/498).

2 Turn L, then immediately R, over the rd, on the Pilgrims way rd, **for 0.85m** just around a sharp LHB by Burnt house farm, then **bear L/SA** into the trees on a DT ByW (no sign) as the rd bears R (967/490).

3 1m, UH, **R then L**, DH, **to a rd** (979/498) **and turn L** on this. **0.5m to the A252 rd** and **turn R** on this for 0.3m then **turn L** on Monkery lane. 1m to a T-J (978/510) **and turn L, then R** after 0.3m (974/509), **to a X-rds and keep SA** for 0.55m **then turn R** on a BW (966/511) in the woods.

4 DH, on this BW **for 1.2m to a rd** (972/527), **and turn L** on this for 0.25m and **bear L** at the fork. **0.2m to another for** (967/526) **and turn R** (Stalisfield Green) **for 0.35m then turn L** through a wooden gate on a BW (962/528) into the woods.

5 Keep SA, **exit the woods, across a field, through a gate, to a rd** (956/520) **and turn R** on this, then immediately (sharp) **L on a BW** (can get overgrown, so you may want to use the rd). **Keep SA**, UH, for 0.55m, along the field edges, **to a rd** (953/512).

6 Turn R on the rd **for 0.3m to a X-rds** by the 'Bowl' pub, **and go SA** (Warren street). After 0.7m **turn R** on a ByW (939/517) and **rejoin the main route at no.4.**

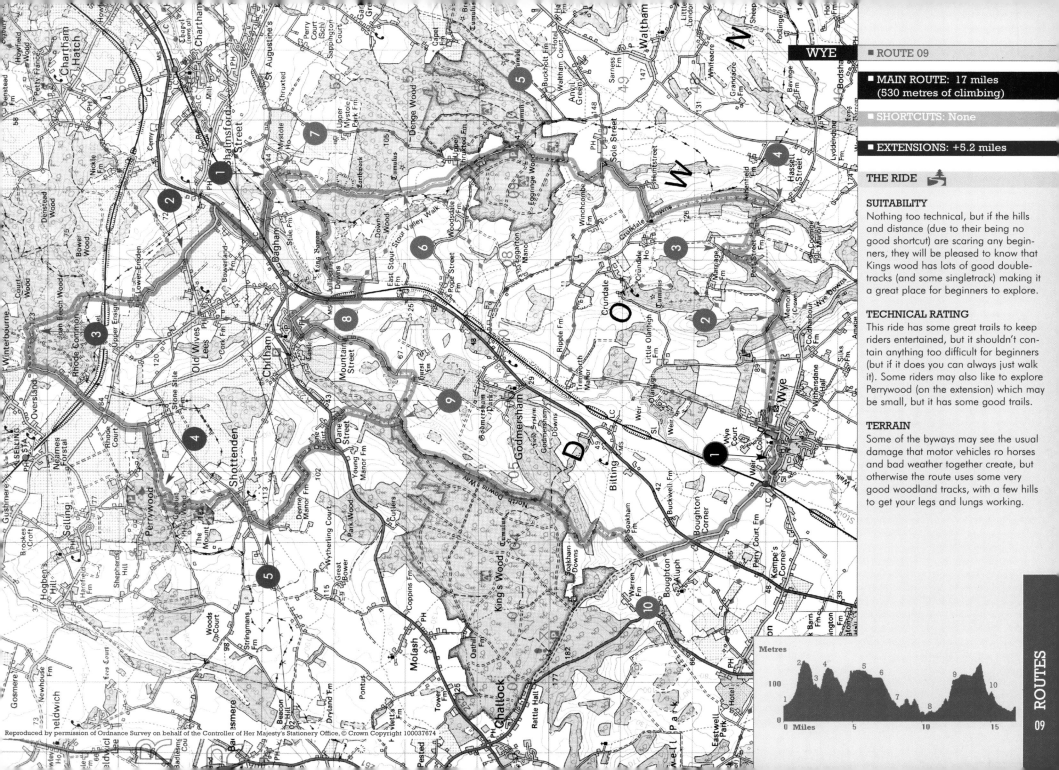

▪ ROUTE 09

▪ **MAIN ROUTE:** 17 miles
(530 metres of climbing)

▪ **SHORTCUTS:** None

▪ **EXTENSIONS:** +5.2 miles

THE RIDE

SUITABILITY

Nothing too technical, but if the hills
and distance (due to their being no
good shortcut) are scaring any beginners, they will be pleased to know that
Kings wood has lots of good doubletracks (and some singletrack) making it
a great place for beginners to explore.

TECHNICAL RATING

This ride has some great trails to keep
riders entertained, but it shouldn't contain anything too difficult for beginners
(but if it does you can always just walk
it). Some riders may also like to explore
Perrywood (on the extension) which may
be small, but it has some good trails.

TERRAIN

Some of the byways may see the usual
damage that motor vehicles ro horses
and bad weather together create, but
otherwise the route uses some very
good woodland tracks, with a few hills
to get your legs and lungs working.

ROUTES

09

GETTING THERE

This ride starts in the town of Wye in Kent. Exit the M20 at junction 9 and go north on the A28 (Canterbury) for just over 3 miles then turn R (Harville road) to Wye. Go over the railway and a bridge then turn left on Churchfield rd (after the 'The Tickled Trout' pub) and follow the parking signs to the (free) car park (052/468). There is also a railway station in Wye.

ACCOMMODATION

B&B's in Wye on: 01233 813011 and 813098
B&B in Chilham, at the Woolpack (pub) on: 01233 730208
YHA in Canterbury on: 08707705744
Camping in Petham at the Yew tree park on: 01227 700306 or Ashfield farm on: 01227 700624
Ashford TI on: 01233 629165
Canterbury T.I. on: 01227 378100

BICYCLE SHOPS

Cycle Mart in Ashford on: 01233 622800 and in Canterbury on: 01227 761488 and Trev's cycles in Canterbury on: 01227 787880

REFRESHMENTS

There is a shop, pubs and toilets in Wye. On the route there are 2 pubs in Sole street, pubs and tea shops in Chilham, and a shop in Bagham.

MAIN ROUTE

17 miles & 530 metres of climbing

1 **START.** Back at the rd, turn R on this for 0.2m, past the church and turn L on Olantigh rd (055/468), for 0.15m then turn R on the (North Downs Way) BW (056/469). 0.6m to a rd and go SA, on a ST, UH through some woods to a rd (069/469).

2 Turn R on the rd for 0.3m then go SA through a gate, as the track bears L, by the house. Go through another gate (075/467) and bear L for 0.65m, along the edge of the woods, though a field, then DH, on a rocky track, to a T-J at the bottom (081/475).

3 Turn sharp R, following the blue arrows, through a tunnel of trees, bearing L, for 0.35m to a drive. Go SA (between the hedges) on a ST, DH, to a DT and bear L, past a farm, UH on a DT, which bears R, for 0.25m and turn L at a metal gate (Kent CC sign) on a ByW (087/468).

4 Follow this for 1.25m to a rd, (085/486) by a church, and turn R on this for 0.75m, DH then UH, to a T-J (094/493). Turn L for 0.1m then R (on a FP) for 0.1m to a X-tracks (091/495) and turn R and follow this main forest track for 0.75m to a minor rd (096/504).

5 Turn L on the rd for 0.5m, past a factory on the L, then keep SA on a BW, as the rd bears R (094/512). Just inside the woods keep SA on a ST as the DT goes R, keeping SA through the fields and gates, (cables overhead), for 0.65m, to the edge of the wood (089/520), and bear to the L of them (not on the ST FP into them) (089/520).

6 0.2m and go through a gate and into the woods, following the blue BW arrows, DH, for 1.15m to a drive, by a farm. Turn L, to the corner of a rd (092/538) and turn immediately L on the (Stour valley walk) ByW or see the extension.

7 Keep SA on this ByW for 1.5m to a X-tracks by a wooden signpost (077/526), and turn R on the main track. DH, over the railway, to the A28 rd (074/526) and turn R on this. After 0.4m turn L on Branch rd, UH, for 0.25m to a T-J (071/536) and turn L (towards the castle).

8 To the square and bear L, then R (effectively SA) on Hambrook lane, to a T-J (069/534) and turn L (on Mountain street). After 1.05m keep SA on the ByW (NDW) (063/521), as the rd bears sharp L. Bearing R, UH, for 0.4m, to the top (057/521), and turn L through a gate on the NDW.

9 Follow the red arrows, on the NDW for 3m, on a good track along the edge of Kings wood, through a farm, to a rd (038/486).

10 Turn L on the rd, for 0.45m to some off-set X-rds and go SA on Bramble lane (Wye), for 0.9m to a fork by the train station. Turn L, over the railway, and a bridge, then immediately turn L on Churchfield rd (049/469), and follow this rd back to the car park (052/468).

EXTENSION

+5.2 miles & +140 metres of climbing

1 Go SA/L on the rd, DH, over a railway track, to the A28 rd (081/540). Turn R (use the path parallel to the rd) for 0.6m then turn L on Shalmsford rd (Old wives Lees) (088/546). After 0.6m on this rd, turn R at the fork (Lower Ensden).

2 After 0.6m, turn R on a BW, by a black barn (no sign) (074/556). After 0.45m, just over a railway bridge, keep SA into the woods, on a ST BW (towards the Private sign) as the DT track bears R (074/564). Keep L at the fork on the BW to some X-tracks (070/572) at the edge of the woods.

3 Turn L for 0.1m then bear R by a house, onto a DT and bear L, DH to a rd (064/572) and turn L on this for 0.8m to a X-rds (058/562). Go SA (Shottenden) for 0.4m then turn R on a rd (056/556). 0.25m to a fork and bear L for another 0.25m then turn L on the BW (048/554) (easy to miss).

4 Through the trees and gates for 0.35m to a T-J (045/553) and turn L for another 0.4m, then turn L on a ST, by a big tree (045/547). DH, joining a track and keep SA to a T-J with a rd (047/544) and turn R on the rd. Keep R for 0.25m to a X-rds (043/542) and turn L on Denne Manor lane (no through rd) for 0.2m then turn L on a ByW (042/539).

5 Follow this for 1.15m, DH to a to rd (052/529) and turn L on this for 0.3m, then turn R on Dane Street (ByW) by a house (057/530). 0.45m UH and bear L at the fork (057/521), for another 0.1m then turn R through a gate, on the NDW (057/521) and rejoin the main route at no.9.

The early rider, catches the empty trail.

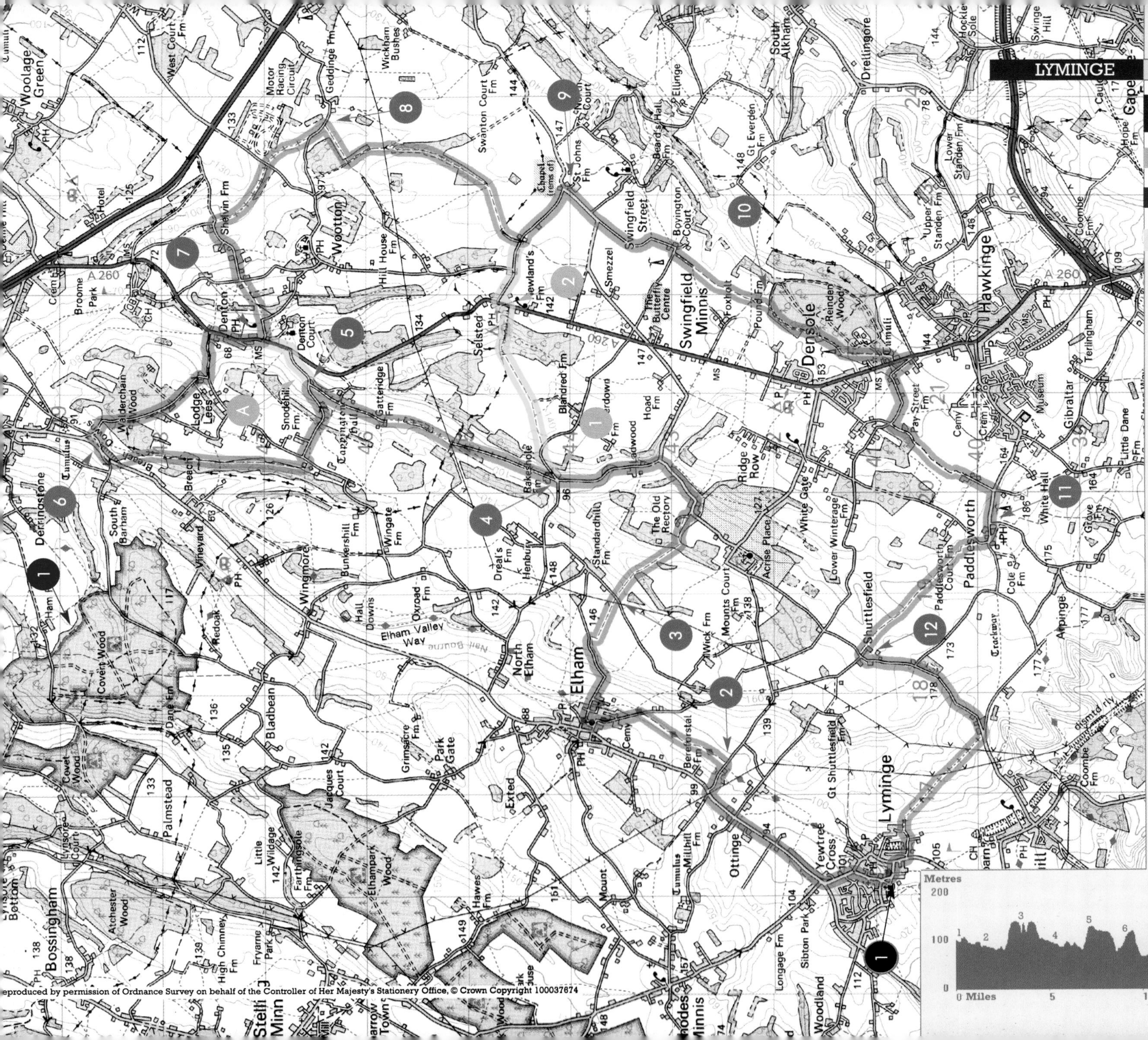

ROUTE 10

- **MAIN ROUTE:** 21.8 miles
  (555 metres of climbing)

- **SHORTCUTS:** -7 & -3.2 miles

- **EXTENSIONS:** Various

THE RIDE

SUITABILITY

This ride is suitable for all rider abilities, as there isn't anything too technical, and there are a couple of shortcut options. However, be cautious when it's been raining as the mud around here can get really sticky.

TECHNICAL RATING

Although it's not a particularly technical ride, the extension to Covert wood will certainly spice things up with it's network of superb twisty singletrack.

TERRAIN

A fast ride in the dry, which slows down significantly in the wet as the mud gets very sticky.

- **NOTE:** We haven't made any recommendations as to the tracks to ride in Covert wood as there are far too many. Just go along, explore and enjoy this singletrack haven.

ROUTES

10

🚗 GETTING THERE

The ride starts in Lyminge, which is north-east of Folkestone. Exit the M20 at juntion 11 and take the B2068 north for 2 miles then bear right to Lyminge. There is parking in the village hall car park (158/408) by the bend in the road where Woodlands rd joins the High St. There is a railway station at Shepherdswell 3 miles from the route.

🛏 ACCOMMODATION

B&B at Harbour side Hotel in Folkestone on: 01303 256258
B&B Beachborough park in Newington (Folkestone) on: 01303 275432
YHA in Dover on: 0870 7705798
Campsites at Selsted, Densole, near Covert wood, and Capel Le Ferne on the coast on: 01303 251188.
Folkestone TI on: 01303 258594

🚲 BICYCLE SHOPS

Renhams cycles in Folkestone (nr the library) on: 01303 241884

🍽 REFRESHMENTS

There is a pub in Lyminge and on the route in Elham, Denton, and Paddlesworth. There are also pubs in Wootton, Densole, and Selsted on the shortcut.

ROUTES

10

21.8 miles & 555 metres of climbing

1 START. Back on the rd, turn R on the High street for 0.15m, then turn L on Church rd (161/409), to a T-J at the other end. Turn L (Canterbury rd) for 0.2m to a X-rds (161/415) and turn R (Elham), keep for 0.9m to the (2nd) X-rds (under elec cables) and turn R (Acrise Place) (170/426), for just 0.2m (just over a bridge) and turn L on a BW (173/425).

2 0.65m to a rd (178/433) and turn L on this for 0.3m then turn R on Pound lane (176/437). Shortly turn R on Duck st, UH, for 0.6m to the top and turn R on a BW (185/438), keeping L across the field to a rd (189/435).

3 Keep SA on the BW for 0.75m , to the Old Rectory's drive and bear R to the corner of a rd (198/428). Bear L on the rd, DH past some houses, for 0.4m to the bottom of the hill and bear L as the rd bears sharp R (Ladwood) (203/431). After 0.65m at a T-J (201/441), go SA through Rakenshole farm or see shortcut 1.

4 Keep SA on this ByW for 1.75m to a rd (211/466) and turn L on this rd (UH) or see shortcut 2.

5 Climb UH for 0.5m to a T-J (204/466) and turn L for just 100m, then R on a BW (between some buildings), into the woods. After about 50m, at some X-tracks with a stone marker (203/466) turn R and keep SA on this trail, and as you exit the woods bear L on a feint DT through a field to a gate by a rd (203/485). Turn R on this rd, for 0.1m and bear R on Derringstone Downs rd or see the extension.

6 Shortly turn R again (206/487), UH (Lodge Lees) and keep L at the fork after 0.5m, for another 0.4m to a T-J (212/475). Turn L here, going DH to the main rd (216/475) and turn R for 0.35m through Denton (*Jack Daw pub*), then L on a rd (Wootton) (216/470).

7 After about 100m keep SA on a BW/FP as the rd bears sharp R, climbing UH to the top (222/472). Go SA on the rd for 0.4m (DH past farm, then UH) and turn R on a ByW (opposite a rd on the L) (227/475). Follow this to a rd and go SA on the ByW to another rd and keep SA (L) on this rd for around 100m before turning R on a BW (237/464).

8 Follow the edge of the woods for 0.3m to a X-tracks (233/462) and turn L for 1.4m (alongside some trees, across a field, into some woods) to a rd (225/445) and turn L on the rd for 0.4m to a T-J (231/441).

9 Turn R for 0.3m (ignore L to Swingwood street) and keep SA (L) as the rd bears sharp R. After 0.6m (just after the rd bears sharp R by some houses) turn L on BW (driveway) (224/430). Keep SA on this BW for 0.7m to a fork at the (Reinden) woods and bear R (219/420).

10 Keep SA on this trail for 0.9m to the A260 rd (213/408), and turn L on this, for about 100m then turn R on Pay street (214/406). After 0.5m turn L on a track (opposite a rd on the R) (207/408), for 0.8m to a rd (200/398). Turn R and keep R for 0.3m, then turn R just past the 'Cat & Custard pot' pub (195/399).

11 After about 100m on the rd, turn L on a BW, through a field, following the blue signposts to the edge of the field. Turn L between the hedge and the fence (with gate SA), and keep SA, to the farm (gate) on the other side of the field, to the rd (184/412).

12 Turn L on the rd for 1m, then R on a ByW (as rd joins on L), passing under some electricity lines. This joins a drive and bears L to a rd (164/407). Turn R on this rd, then shortly L on Mayfield rd, leading back to the church in Lyminge (161/409).

EXTENSION:

Various

1 Turn L off the main rd, and keep L for 1m, DH over the water, through south Barham, UH, into Covert wood. There are some great trails around these woods with all sorts of challenges, so go and play.

-7 miles & -190 metres of climbing

1 Turn R for 0.25m (steep UH, then levels out) and turn L on a BW (205/443) and keep SA (L) on this for 0.95m (bears R and DH through the woods) to rd (219/446).

2 Turn L on the rd then shortly R on another rd (opposite the pub) and keep R on this rd for 0.85m to a T-J (231/441) and rejoin the main route at no. 9.

SHORTCUT 2:

-3.2 miles & -100 metres of climbing

A Turn R on the rd for 0.25m to the A260 rd. Turn L on this for 0.2m then turn R on another rd (216/470) (Wootton) just after the lane to the church and rejoin the main route at No.7.

Covert woods has some great singletrack.

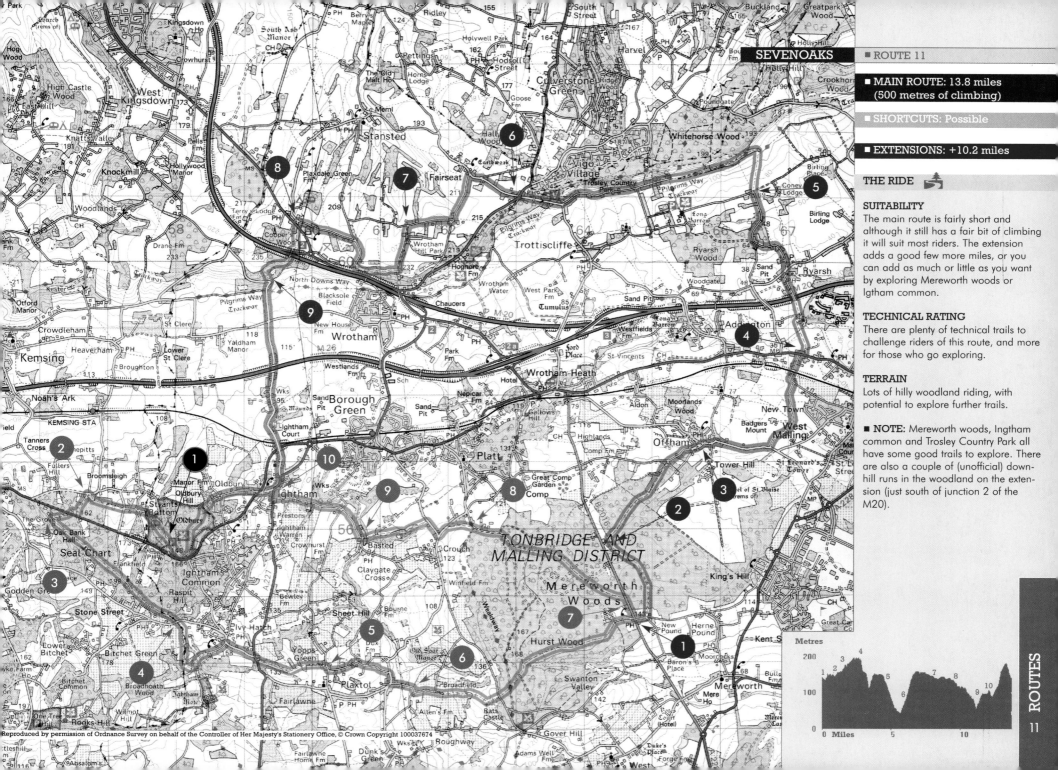

■ **MAIN ROUTE: 13.8 miles**
(500 metres of climbing)

■ **SHORTCUTS: Possible**

■ **EXTENSIONS: +10.2 miles**

THE RIDE

SUITABILITY
The main route is fairly short and although it still has a fair bit of climbing it will suit most riders. The extension adds a good few more miles, or you can add as much or little as you want by exploring Mereworth woods or Igtham common.

TECHNICAL RATING
There are plenty of technical trails to challenge riders of this route, and more for those who go exploring.

TERRAIN
Lots of hilly woodland riding, with potential to explore further trails.

■ **NOTE:** Mereworth woods, Ingtham common and Trosley Country Park all have some good trails to explore. There are also a couple of (unofficial) downhill runs in the woodland on the extension (just south of junction 2 of the M20).

Metres
200

100

0 Miles   5   10

GETTING THERE

This ride starts from the free woodland car park in Ightham common. Exit the A25 between Seal and Ingtham (near the Crown pub), and head north on a road to Styants bottom (picnic and camping sign) and the car park is shortly on the left up here (578/559).

ACCOMMODATION

B&B in Sevenoaks on: 01732 465262.
B&B (Moorings Hotel) in Sevenoaks, on: 01732 452589
YHA in Kemsing (just north of the M26), on: 0870 7705890
Camping at Styants bottom (nr the start) on: 01732 762728
Sevenoaks TI on: 01732 450305

BICYCLE SHOPS

Bikes, Bikes, Bikes in Sevenoaks on tel: 01732 464 997 or see www.bikes-bikesbikes.co.uk

REFRESHMENTS

A pub on the A25 near the start / end of the ride, and in Ivyhatch, Plaxtol, Mereworth woods (by the B2016), Basted and Ightham. Also in Offham, Ryarsh, and Vigo village on the extension.

MAIN ROUTE

13.8 miles & 500 metres of climbing

1 START. At the exit of the car park (578 /559) turn L on a BW (just before the rd), UH for 0.3m. Bear L at the fork, and join a tarmac rd (575/562), DH then UH, to a grass triangle and keep SA over the rd, onto a BW, through the trees for 0.4m to a rd (567/565).

2 Turn L and L again immediately on another rd towards the A25 rd, for 0.2m then turn R on a ST rd just before the A25 rd. After 0.05m turn L on a FP to the A25 rd, and go SA on a BW (but a FP sign, for 0.15m to a DT and turn L and L again on a ST (561/561).

3 0.4m to a rd and go SA, for another 0.5m to another rd (572/552) and bear R on this towards a 30mph sign and a church. After 0.1m bear L on a BW just past a school, for 0.45m (good ST to side of the main track) to a fork and bear R, DH, to a rd (580/546).

4 Go SA on the BW for 0.4m, bearing L and DH to a rd (582/539)and turn L on this. UH, for 0.4m to a T-J (587/542) in Ivy Hatch and turn R, to the A272 rd (591/540). Go SA on a BW, for 0.3m as you exit the woods, then bear L and keep SA to a rd

5 Turn R on the rd, then immediately L at the grass triangle on Grange hill (602/538). 0.3m to a fork and bear L on Dux hill and keep L on this, DH, to a T-J and turn R on Long mill lane. After 0.1m turn L on Brook lane (611/536) for 0.25m to a T-J and turn L (Old saw manor).

6 After 0.2m, keep SA on a ByW, (618/535) as the rd bears L, UH, for 0.5m to a T-J, and bear L to a rd (627/534). Go SA into Mereworth woods, and keep SA on this BW, for 1.5m to the B2016 rd (647/546) by the Old beech Inn pub, and turn L on this rd or see the extension.

7 After 0.25m, turn L on a BW (645/549), back into the woods, and follow this SA, following the blue arrows, for 1.35m to a DT/drive at the edge of the woods. Follow this for 0.25m and keep SA on the BW , as the track bears R (623/560), not on the Wealdway path on the L.

8 0.25m to a rd and turn L on this for 0.1m then turn R on Crouch lane (618/559), for 0.2m then turn L onto a BW (616/561). Go DH, for 0.6m, to a X-rds in Basted village, and go SA, which immediately bears R, on Basted lane (607/558).

9 0.35m to X-rds and go SA on Mill lane (Ightham), for 0.7m to the A227 rd. Turn R on this rd for 0.1m, then turn L on Sevenoaks rd (Seal) (594/565).

10 0.1m to the A25, and go SA on Oldbury lane, keeping SA after 0.5m, as the rd bears L, and keep SA on the BW at the side of a house (585/564). UH, to a big 5-way junction and take the 2nd L (BW), DH, bearing R by the A25 rd (581/555), DH, back to the rd by the car park (578/558).

EXTENSION:

+10.2 miles & 270 metres of climbing

1 Go SA on Beech rd, for 0.1m then turn L on a (quiet lane) BW (Stone sign) by a barn, (649/546). Keep SA after 0.4m (in the clearing) on the ST as the DT bears R, back into the woods. Keep SA/L to a fork by a suspended electricity box, nr the main rd (643/558).

2 Bear R on a (hard to see) ST BW, for 0.5m to a X-tracks (648/564) and go SA, becoming a ST, with the woods on the R and a fence on the L. 0.45m to a rd and turn R on this into Offham village (657/572) and turn R on Teston rd, past the Kings Arms pub, on the cycle lane.

3 After 0.65m turn L on Fartherwell rd, where the cycle lane ends (667/572), for 0.7m to a T-J (670/581). Turn L, on Sandy lane, under a bridge to the A20 rd. Turn R on this for 0.05m, then turn L on a BW (672/586) for 0.05m and keep SA on the BW, as the DT bears R.

4 0.3m to a church (671/591) and turn L on a path, over the M25, past a factory, to some (off-set) X-rds (669/598) in the village and the Duke of Wellington pub on the R. Go SA on Chapel street (dead end), for 0.5m to a T-J and turn R on Park farm rd, for 0.5m to a T-J (664/610).

5 Go SA on the BW (RHS of the barn), UH, to the NDW at the top (665/616), and turn L on this. Keep SA on this, becoming a DT by some houses, for 1.95m to a rd (636/608). Turn R, steep UH, (Vigo/Trosley country park), for 0.5m to the A227 rd.

6 Go SA on Vigo rd, for 0.5m to a grass triangle (623/613), and bear L on Platt house lane (Wrotham). 0.5m to a fork (620/606) and bear R on Rotham hill rd (Labour in vain), then after 0.4m turn L towards Hilton park farm (private rd sign) (613/605).

7 After 0.45m turn R through a green gate, on a BW (before the house) (612/598). DH, (with the M20 on the L below), to the bottom (606/599) and bear R, becoming a rd, to a fork (606/603). Bear L (Labour in vain rd), for 0.6m (just past the elec. cables) then turn L to the A20 rd (597/605).

8 Go SA onto a BW, through a gate, on a DT, and keep SA across the field, as the DT disappears, to a silver gate. Go through this and over the M20, to a fork in the woods. The BW is on the L, but is usually overgrown, although there are some great trails if you bear R (which bears L and DH), and all trails lead to a green barrier by a rd, at the bottom (593/597).

■ NOTE: Turning R, UH, on the rd for 0.25m, then R into the trees, takes you back to the top of these DH runs.

9 Turn L on the rd, for 1.9m to a T-J with the A227, and go R on this, into Ightham village. After 0.15m turn R on Sevenoaks rd (Seal), just past the George & Dragon and Olde Chequers Inn (594/565) and rejoin the main route at no.10.

■ **MAIN ROUTE: 21.4 miles**
(465 metres of climbing)

■ **SHORTCUTS: -8.5 miles**

■ **EXTENSIONS: None**

THE RIDE

SUITABILITY
This is a very easy route to follow (nearly all waymarked), and the flat 13 mile loop of the lake is perfect for beginners. The lake loop is still great fun for advanced riders (just ride it faster), and Bedbury forest provides some steeper gradients.

TECHNICAL RATING
The twisty lake side trails get more technical the faster you go. There is also some singletrack worth exploring in Bedbury forest if you desire.

TERRAIN
This ride follows a nice waymarked cycle track around the largest lake in the south east. This section is obviously quite flat, but it them climbs and descends some hills as it follows another cycletrack through Bedbury forest.

■ **NOTE:** The Bewl water cycle track is only open to cyclists between May and October. There are also lots of other activities to do here e.g. boat rides, windsurfing, sailing, fishing.

ROUTES 12

GETTING THERE

This ride starts from the Bewl water visitors centre car park (675/337). Head south from Lamberhurst on the A21 for 1 mile, then turn right, and follow the brown 'Bewl Water' signs to the car park, which costs £4.50 (for weekends in season). The nearest train stations is at Stonegate (see bottom left of map).

ACCOMMODATION

B&B at the Cherry tree inn in Ticehurst on: 01580201229
B&B in Wadhurst on: 01892 783896
B&B in the 'Best beach Inn' in Wadhurst, on: 01892 782046
Camping (on the north of Bewl water) off the A21, on: 01892 890566.
Tunbridge wells TI on: 01892 515675 or www.heartofkent.org.uk

BICYCLE SHOPS

Bewl Water bike hire (open in the summer) on: 07801 670999

REFRESHMENTS

There is a cafe at the Bewl Water visitors centre at the start/end of the ride, a pub in Flimwell and a cafe at the Pinetum, in Bedgebury forest.

21.4 miles & 465 metres of climbing

1 **START**. Follow the 'Bewl water route' signs, heading **west**, for 0.75m to the lake and turn R (669/333).

2 **Follow the lake** (on your LHS) **for 3.15m, then turn R through some gates** (661/324) by a hut, **following the BW sign**. Short UH, **to a DT and turn R on this**, following the BW signs **to a rd** (665/322).

3 **Turn R on this rd**, for 0.6m to a fork (663/314) and **bear L**, following the brown signs. 1.2m to a T-J (676/306) **and turn L**, on Burnt lodge lane.

4 After 0.45m, keep SA on Lower Hazlehurst, **for 0.3m then through a** 'Bewl water' **gate** (678/318). **Follow the Bewl water signs for 3.3m** alongside the water, **to a T-J with a rd** (700/318) **and turn R on this rd**, or see the shortcut.

5 **UH, for 0.65m to a T-J** with the B2087 (702/310) **and turn L on this rd, for 0.8m to a X-rds** with the A21 (714/312). **Turn L,** along the A21 (or cross it and walk on the pavement, to avoid cycling on the busy rd).

6 After 0.25m turn R on a BW (715/315), just past 'The Snail' pub, **for 0.2m to the start of 'Bedgebury Forest'** (717/318), **and go SA, following the green MTB signs.** After 1.55m turn L (731/336), still on the green MTB trail to 'Sugarloaf Hill', **for 0.4m to a T-J** (733/342).

7 Turn R, on the green MTB trail, **for 0.7m to a T-J** (739/334) by Louisa Lodge (a house with lots of chimneys), **and turn R.** After 0.25m turn L (734/334) on the green MTB trail.

8 Follow the green MTB trail signs for **2m back to where you** entered the forest and **joined the green MTB trail** (717/318). **Turn L, back to the A21** (715/315) and retrace your steps, back to Bewl water.

9 **Turn L** on the A21 **for 0.25m to a X-rds** (714/312) **and turn R,** on the B2087, **for 0.8m,** then **turn R** on Rosemary lane (702/310). **After 0.8m** (0.15m past the BW you came earlier), over the bridge, **turn L** back **onto the Bewl water track** (700/320).

10 Follow the signposts alongside Bewl water, **for 3.2m, back** to the visitors centre (677/338).

1 Turn L, over the bridge, **for 0.15m** then turn L back onto the Bewl water track (700/320), and rejoin the main route at no 10.

With such an easy route to navigate you will have plenty of time to stop and refresh yourself.

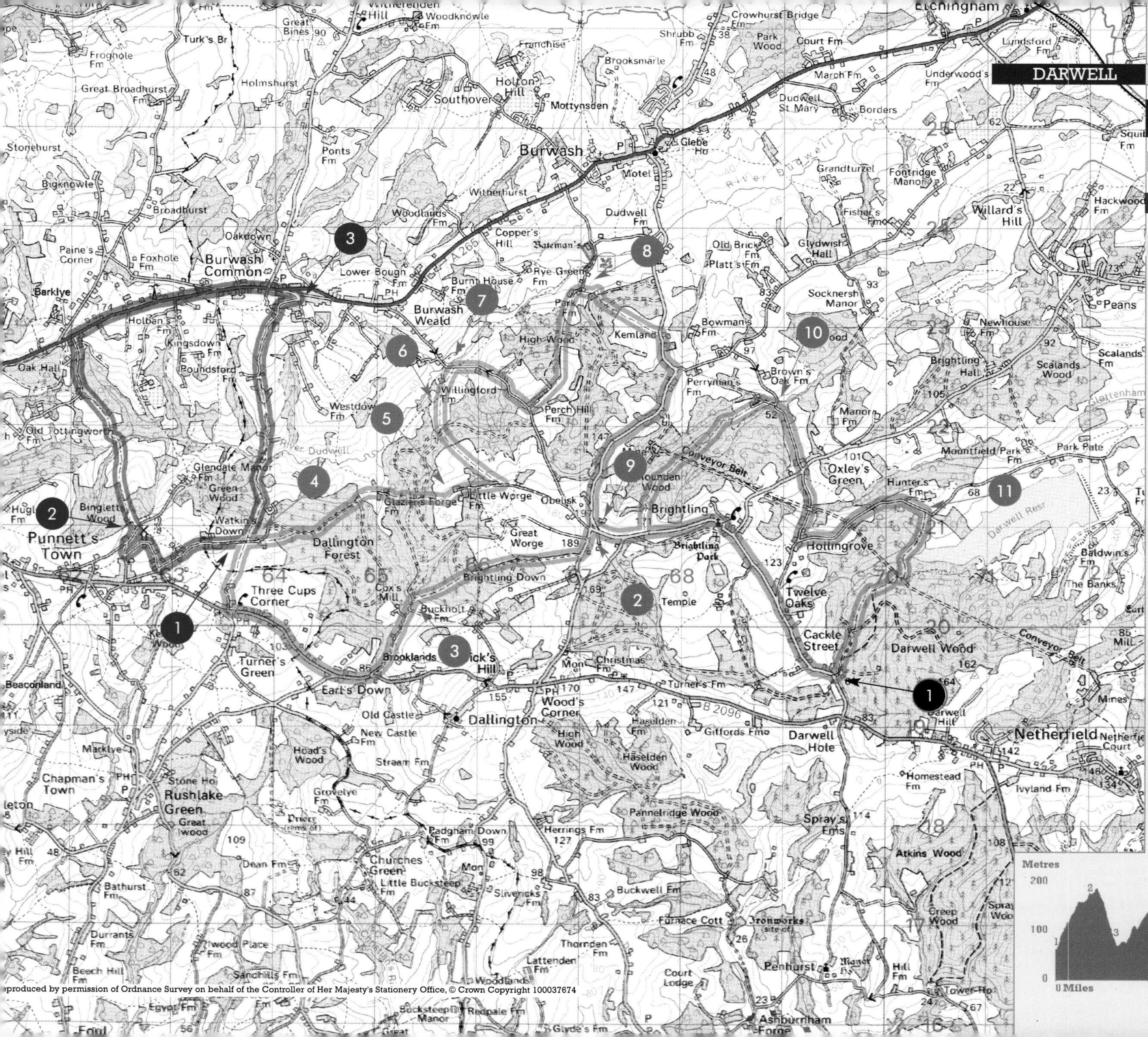

■ **MAIN ROUTE:** 16.4 miles
(740 metres of climbing)

■ **SHORTCUTS:** Various

■ **EXTENSIONS:** +5.7 miles

THE RIDE

SUITABILITY

The steep terrain with little or no rest between going up before coming back down makes this route physically, mentally and technically demanding. However, we have been able to design the route so that it is very easy to cut the ride short at various points (we haven't marked these on the map, but they are pretty obvious).

TECHNICAL RATING

The steep terrain, mixed with a bit of rough ground and exhaustion makes this quite a technically demanding route.

TERRAIN

There are constant ups and downs on this ride, and some parts can suffer from damage, especially in bad weather, which can make things very tiring, so we recommend attempting it in good weather.

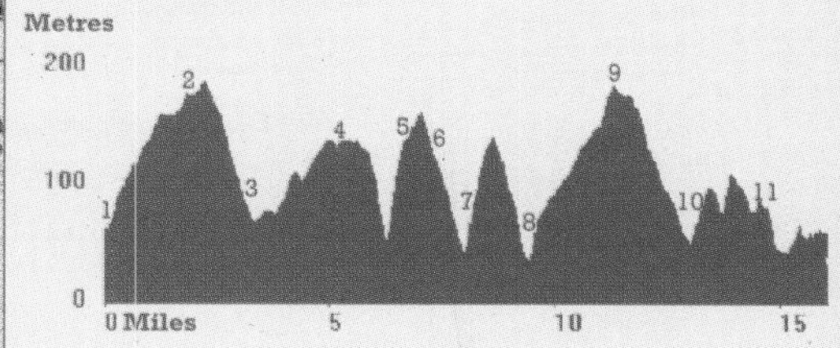

GETTING THERE

This ride starts from a (free) car park in Darwell wood, just off the B2096 (which runs between Battle and Heathfield). Turn north at the cross roads (Cackle Street) 0.7 miles west of Netherfield village, then right after 1/4 mile to the car park (695/195).

ACCOMMODATION

B&B in Battle at Moons hill farm on: 01424 892645
B&B in Hastings on: 01424 812528
YHA in Guestling (nr Hastings) on: 0870 770 5850
Camping in Catsfield at Senlac wood (pool, laundry, shop, paintball) on: 01424 773969 or 752590.
Battle T.I. on: 01424 773721

BICYCLE SHOPS

Cycle Revival in Heathfield (Hailsham Road), tel: 01435 866118

REFRESHMENTS

There is only a pub in Three Cups Corner, and in Burwash Weald on the extension. Otherwise there is a pub just down the road from the start / end of the ride, in Netherfield.

ROUTES

13

16.4 miles & 740 metres of climbing

1 START. Go back to the rd and turn R on this, UH, for 0.65m to a fork and bear L. 0.45m to another fork (685/209) and bear L, through Brightling village, for 0.75m to a fork and bear R (Burwash). 0.15m to another fork and bear L to a X-rds (671/209).

2 Turn L (Woods corner), UH, for 0.15m then turn R on a BW through a silver gate (670/207) just past an antenna. After 0.4m keep SA on a ST BW as the main DT bears L, for 0.3m to a DT. Go SA, back in to the trees, DH, on a ST for 0.4m (can get rough), through a small stream, to a DT (653/202).

3 Go L/SA on the DT, for 0.6m, to a rd (649/195) and turn R, for 1m to Three cups corner village, and turn R on a BW (opposite the pub) (635/201). Bear R after 0.15m, to the LHS of a barn, on a ST, over a wooden bridge and alongside a field, for 0.3m to a DT and BW X-tracks (637/208), and turn R on the DT, or see the extension.

4 After 0.1m keep SA on the ST BW, as the DT bears L, into the woods, and follow this for 0.95m, to just past a big wooden shed, then turn L on a BW, leaving the DT (651/213) steep UH, over some firetracks.

■ **NOTE:** Going L on the firetrack to Perch hill farm will miss out the rough/bumpy BW from Little worge farm to Willingford farm, but we couldn't find out it's legal status, so we can't recommend it.

5 Keep SA, out of the trees, and bear L towards a farm house (658/213). Go SA past the houses for 0.3m then turn sharp L

on a BW (662/214) 0.1m after a cattlegrid. Through the middle of a field, aiming for a tree in the middle of the hedge halfway through field, **and keep SA to a** small silver **gate,** back in to the trees.

6 Keep SA, over a DT, to and gate and out of the woods (656/219). Bear R towards a house (can just see the top of it), DH, to the RHS of the house, and LHS of the barn, bearing R into a dip between the hedges, to a rd (657/225).

7 Turn R on the rd, steep UH, for 0.6m then turn L on a DT (665/221) just before the farm. Keep SA on this for 0.65m to a T-J in a clearing and turn L then immediately R on ST (BW). DH, to a farm and turn R on a permissive BW just over a bridge (669/233), through a gate.

8 UH, through the field to a single gate into the woods, and keep SA, over the firetrack, out of the woods, and keep SA to a rd (677/229). Turn R on the rd on this rd for 1.45m, UH, to a fork (671/210) and turn L (Brightling).

9 0.05m to a T-J and turn L (been here before) and keep L on this rd for 0.35m, then turn L through a big gap in the hedge on a DT (BW but no sign) (676/209). DH, into the woods, and keep SA on this for 1.2m to a T-J with a DT and turn R on this.

10 0.1m to a rd (689/222), and turn R, UH, for 0.45m to X-rds and go SA for 0.5m to a junction in Hollingrove (691/208). Turn L on the rd for 0.9m, then turn R on a feint track into the woods (BW, but no sign)

(703/211) just before the rd bears L.

■ **NOTE:** New tracks can appear in these woods, making navigation confusing.

11 Go DH, for 0.5m to a gravel T-J and turn L to the (underground) **conveyor belt** (701/204). Go over this and immediately turn R on a track (BW), which bears L and UH. 0.25m to a DT. Bear L on this, UH, to a fork and bear R, to a T-J with a gravel DT. Turn R on a grassy DT, DH, past a metal barrier **into the car park** and your car (695/195).

1 Turn L on the DT for 0.6m, becoming a rd, **to some X-rds** (628/205), and turn R for 0.35m, bearing L, to a T-J. Turn R on Greenwoods lane, bearing R as Upper Greenwoods lane joins from the L, for 0.2m then turn L on a BW (626/209), opposite the windmill.

2 DH, for 0.6m, and go across a stream (624/218), UH, on the BW opposite, 0.4m to a drive. Turn R on this, UH, to the main A265 rd (620/228) and turn R on this. After 1.35m, in Burwash village, turn R on Vicarage rd to a fork and turn R on Westdown lane, **then immediately R again** on Vicarage lane (642/232).

3 After 0.6m keep SA on the BW, as the track bears R to Poundsford farm. DH, for 0.55m, keeping L, **over the river** (638/216), back UH, **on the BW for another 0.55m to a DT** BW X-tracks (637/208) (been here before) **and turn L and rejoin the main route at no.4.**

This ride has a very remote feel to it ..... for the south east anyway.

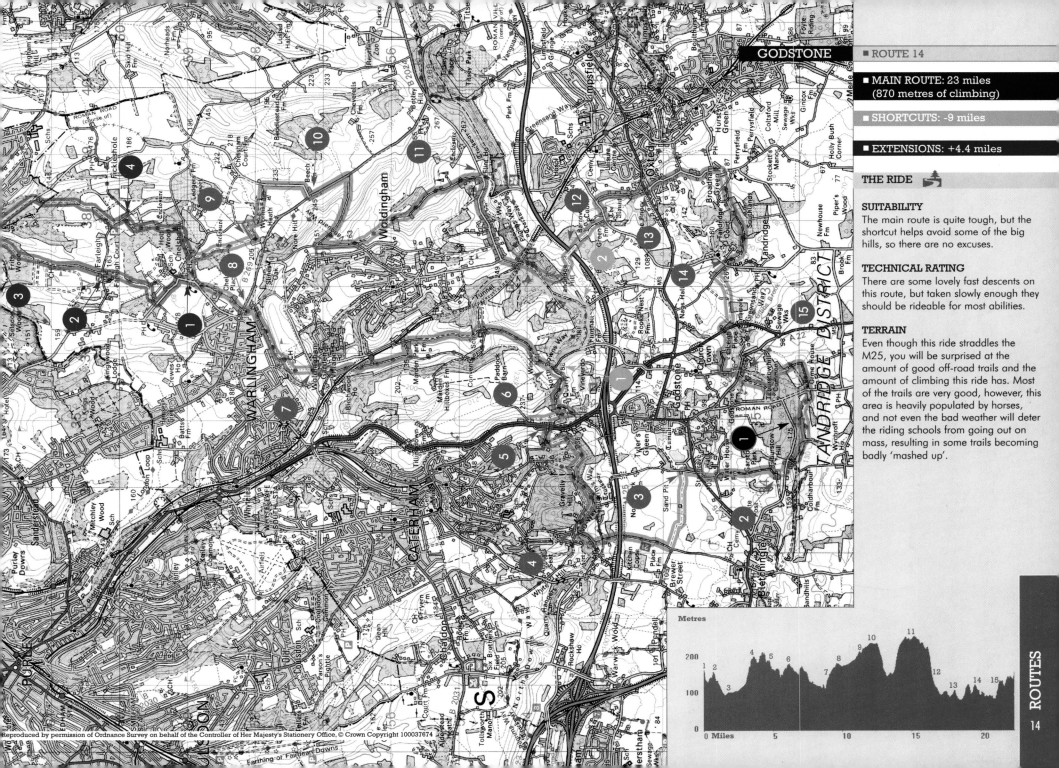

■ **MAIN ROUTE:** 23 miles
(870 metres of climbing)

■ **SHORTCUTS:** -9 miles

■ **EXTENSIONS:** +4.4 miles

THE RIDE

SUITABILITY
The main route is quite tough, but the shortcut helps avoid some of the big hills, so there are no excuses.

TECHNICAL RATING
There are some lovely fast descents on this route, but taken slowly enough they should be rideable for most abilities.

TERRAIN
Even though this ride straddles the M25, you will be surprised at the amount of good off-road trails and the amount of climbing this ride has. Most of the trails are very good, however, this area is heavily populated by horses, and not even the bad weather will deter the riding schools from going out on mass, resulting in some trails becoming badly 'mashed up'.

■ MAIN ROUTE

23 miles & 870 metres of climbing

① START. Exit through the back of the car park on the FP, DH, to a (track) T-J (350/499) and turn R on this. After 0.25m bear R (FP only SA), then immediately L (effectively SA), for another 0.25m to a rd (343/501). Turn R, UH, to a T-J and turn L for 0.1m then turn R on a DT (BW, but no sign) with a post in the middle of it (341/502).

② Follow this for 0.65m bearing R by the buildings, to a rd (341/512), and turn L on this to a T-J. Bear R on Waterhouse lane to the A25 and go SA over this on North park lane. After 0.15m turn L on to a BW (opposite some old, large machinery) (342/517).

③ Keep SA/R for 0.8m to a gate near the corner of a rd and parking area (330/519) and turn R on the Cycleway 21 (BW). 0.65m, under the M25m, to a X-tracks and keep SA, UH, to a T-J with a DT (331/530) and turn R. UH, for 0.2m to a 3-way rd junction and turn R on Gravely hill rd and immediately R on a BW (333/532).

④ Keep L, for 0.6m to rd and turn R on this for 0.1m, to the other side of the green - water tap here, **and turn R on the BW (342/533)** - be careful of the steps along here. 0.65m to a rd (346/537) and turn R on this, and keep SA immediately, over a bridge, as the rd bears L.

⑤ Turn L, parallel to the rd, for 0.15m then sharp R on Gatwick red hill ByW (349/539), DH, for 0.4m to a rd (350/533). Turn L on this, bearing R, and keep SA as it becomes a BW/cycleway. Bear R, then immediately L at the fork by South lodge house, towards the school, (357/536) or see the shortcut.

⑥ 0.75m to a fork, (363/546) just past some large gates and bear R. Keep L on this track for 0.8m, then turn L through Marden park farm, for 0.15m to a T-J (359/557) with a minor rd. Turn R on this for 0.7m (under a bridge) then turn R onto a BW (357/568) just before entering the trees.

⑦ To a rd and go SA on a BW, UH, to a DT and turn L on this, DH to a rd (357/571) and cross this and go SA on the gravel cycle track, bearing R, behind the golf clubhouse. Join a dirt track by the trees (359/575), going UH, for 0.6m to a T-J (366/580) with High lane and turn L, to the B269 rd.

⑧ Go SA on the (Gatwick red hill cyclepath) BW for 0.5m to a rd, and turn R on this to a fork (370/588), and bear R or see the extension. After 0.25m turn R on a BW, just before the X-rds (374/589).
8a - Through a green gate and keep SA for 0.65m, past a barrier, to a rd (377/580).

⑨ Turn L on the rd, for 0.2m then R on a ByW (379/581) by a gate, for 0.1m to a X-tracks (379/579) and turn L on a ST BW. Becomes a good track, past a silver gate, to the rd (385/578), and turn R on this. 0.4m to a T-J (383/572) with the main rd and turn L on path next to the rd.

⑩ After 0.4m turn R over the rd (386/566) onto a BW, and follow this DT, DH for 0.8m to a rd by Warren barn farm (376/571). Turn L on rd for 0.35m then keep SA/L onto a BW as rd bears R (376/565). Keep SA on this BW, UH, for 1.4m, to a rd (386/546).

⑪ Turn R on the rd for 0.85m to a fork (374/543) and bear L on Gangers hill rd, for 0.35m then turn L on a BW (372/538). NOTE: This track can get messed up in bad weather, but a better draining (FP) track 0.15m further along and on the L, going steeply DH, avoids some of this.

⑫ Follow this BW, DH, and over the motorway, for another 0.4m to a rd (380/528) by Barrow green farmhouse. Turn L on the rd for 0.2m, then turn R on Sandy lane (382/529), UH, and keep SA on Brook hill, under a bridge to a X-rds (384/522) by the old Bell pub, in Oxted.

⑬ Go SA on Beadles lane, for 0.35m to a fork and bear R on Hall hill for another 0.4m, then turn R on the Greensand way BW (387/511). After 0.3m having joined a drive, keep SA/L on the BW, as the drive bears R, for 0.75m past Tandridge court farm shop to a rd (373/510).

⑭ Turn L, then immediately R at a grass triangle, DH, on a rd for 0.15m then turn L on a BW (371/512) opposite the Dairy. After 0.6m turn L under a bridge (363/511) and keep SA on the BW for 0.45m to a rd (356/511). Turn L on this, to a T-J with the main rd and turn R then immediately L on Enterdent rd (356/508).

⑮ Go UH, for 0.35m then turn L on a BW (354/504) just past a green barrier. Follow this BW, bearing R and UH (358/499), for 0.7m to a rd (354/498) and go SA on the BW, for 0.25m, and turn R, UH, on the FP, back to the car park (349/500).

SHORTCUT:

-9 miles & -270 metres of climbing

① Bear R at the fork, for 0.3m to a rd (360/532), and turn L on this, UH. After 0.2m keep SA on a DT (NDW) BW as the rd bears L, for 0.2m on another rd (366/531).

② Turn L, UH, on the rd, for 0.3m to a T-J, and turn R. After 0.2m turn R (372/538) on a BW and rejoin the main route at no.12.

EXTENSION:

+4.4 miles & +90 metres of climbing

① Keep L/SA, on Chelsham rd, for 0.15m to some X-rds (371/591) (school SA), and turn L on Harrow rd for 0.3m, then turn R on Daniels lane (367/594). To the end and bear R on the BW, and follow this (2nd L at X-tracks after 0.15m) for 0.65m to a rd by Farleigh court riding centre (372/602).

② Go SA onto a BW, through the golf course, for 0.65m, and keep SA into the woods as the track bears L. Follow the yellow arrows, R/SA, DH, for 0.5m to a rd (377/619) and turn R on this. Turn L immediately on a drive, then immediately again, on to a BW, parallel to the rd.

③ After 0.6m bear R through a gap in the hedge to the rd (careful as it comes out onto the rd) (383/612). Cross the rd, and go SA, past Pear Tree farm, on the BW for 0.8m, UH, to a rd and turn L for 0.15m then R on Greenwich cycle way (380/599).

④ 0.6m to a rd (378/590) and turn R on this rd for 0.25m to a X-rds (374/589). Go SA then immediately L on the BW, and rejoin the main route at no.8a.

Sidebar

🚗 **GETTING THERE**

This ride starts from a free (but height restricted) car park just south of the village Godstone. Exit the M25 at junction 6, into Godstone, (joining the A25), then bear L on the B2236. After 0.2m bear R at a fork (brown Godstone farm sign) on Tilburstow hill rd, for 0.6m, then turn R on Rabies Heath rd (off-set X-rds) for 0.25m to the car park on the left (349/500). There is a railway station in Woldingham and Oxted.

🛏 **ACCOMMODATION**

B&B in Oxted at Arawa, on: 01883 714104 or 0800 298 5732
B&B in Oxted, at the New Bungalow on: 01342 892508
Camping at Lingfield (6 miles down the A22) on: 01342 833205
Sevenoaks TI on: 01732 450305

🚲 **BICYCLE SHOPS**

Finch & Sons in Reigate (on Bell Street) on: 01737 242163

🍴 **REFRESHMENTS**

There is a pub etc in Godstone near the start/end, another pub half-way around the route in Chelsham and a choice of pubs and shops Oxted. There is also a water tap at GR 342/533.

ROUTES

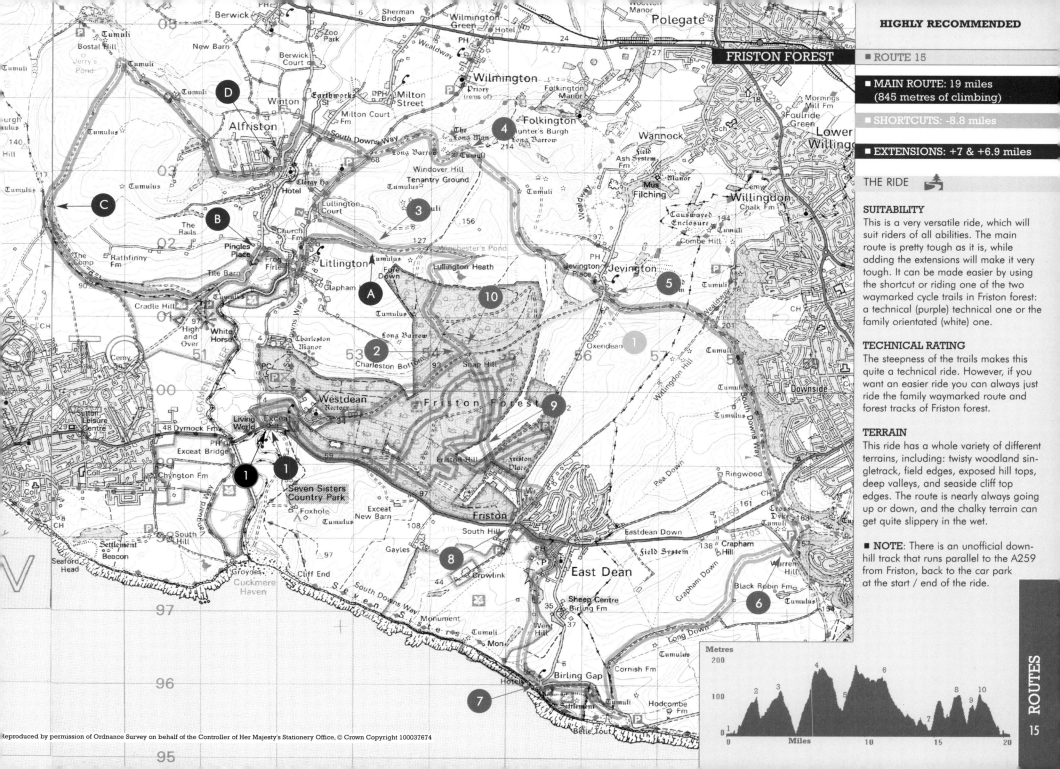

FRISTON FOREST

■ ■ ROUTE 15

- ■ **MAIN ROUTE: 19 miles** (845 metres of climbing)
- ■ **SHORTCUTS: -8.8 miles**
- ■ **EXTENSIONS: +7 & +6.9 miles**

THE RIDE

SUITABILITY

This is a very versatile ride, which will suit riders of all abilities. The main route is pretty tough as it is, while adding the extensions will make it very tough. It can be made easier by using the shortcut or riding one of the two waymarked cycle trails in Friston forest: a technical (purple) technical one or the family orientated (white) one.

TECHNICAL RATING

The steepness of the trails makes this quite a technical ride. However, if you want an easier ride you can always just ride the family waymarked route and forest tracks of Friston forest.

TERRAIN

This ride has a whole variety of different terrains, including: twisty woodland singletrack, field edges, exposed hill tops, deep valleys, and seaside cliff top edges. The route is nearly always going up or down, and the chalky terrain can get quite slippery in the wet.

■ **NOTE:** There is an unofficial downhill track that runs parallel to the A259 from Friston, back to the car park at the start / end of the ride.

ROUTES

15

GETTING THERE

The ride starts from the Exceat / Friston Forest National Trust car park (518/995). This is a pay& display which gets locked at dusk and is situated between Seaford and Eastbourne, on the A259 by a narrow bridge over Cuckmere river. There is also a good long stay car park in Alfriston, and a railway stations at in Seaford and Eastbourne.

ACCOMMODATION

B&B's at Exceat farmhouse on: 01323 870218, the George Inn on: 870319, Dean's barn on: 870319, and the Giants Rest pub in Wilmington on: 870207 **YHA** in Alfriston on: 0870 8705666 **Camping** in Alfriston on: 01323 870560 or the Sussex Ox (nr Alfriston) on: 01323 870840 **Eastbourne TI** on: 01323 411400

BICYCLE SHOPS

Nevada bikes on: 01323 411549 and Phoenix cycles on: 729060 in Eastbourne. Cuckmere cycles at the car park hire bikes tel: 870310.

REFRESHMENTS

A cafe at the start/end of the ride and a pub just over the bridge. A pub in Jevington, cafe at Birling gap, shops and pub in East Dean, and pubs, tea gardens, etc in Alfriston.

ROUTES

15

MAIN ROUTE

19 miles & 845 metres of climbing

1 START. Go through a gate at the north end of the car park, onto a BW and follow this, around the bottom of the wooded hill. After 0.6m, at the houses, turn L then immediately R on a narrow lane, UH. Follow this main track for 1.4m, becomes a gravel surface, through a field, back into the woods, to a X-tracks (544/005), by Snap hill.

2 Turn L (Lullington heath), DH, keeping R at a fork after 0.1m, for another 0.2m to a multiple (7) junction (541/007). Bear R (Lullington heath), UH, going through a gate into the nature reserve, and follow the BW to a gate and T-J (545/018). Turn L on the (DT) BW, (Litlington), UH, for 0.4m to a X-rds, at Winchester's pond.

3 Keep SA, for 0.4m to a fork (532/019) and bear R, or see extension 2. 0.65m, DH, to the rd (525/025) and turn R on this, and keep SA, UH, for 0.6m, then turn R on the SDW (532/032).
3a - Up Wendover hill, for 0.55m to a fork (540/035) and bear R (L is a FP), along the top of a valley, to the summit (544/033).

4 Keep following the blue SDW signs, along, then down the hill, alongside, then into some woods after 1.2m (553/018). Keep R then SA, DH, on a steep and technical track, to a (St Andrews) church and keep SA on the rd. To a T-J in Jevington, and turn R then immediately L on Eastbourne Lane (BW), (562/013) or see the shortcut.

5 UH, rejoining the SDW, for 0.95m to a X-tracks (576/009), and keep SA on the SDW. 1.65m to the A259 rd (585/985). Go SA on the SDW, to a trig point and keep R, to

the B2013 rd. Cross the rd, into a car park and turn R for 0.05m, to a gate, and follow the BW (586/979), DH, into the valley.

6 Keep SA for 1.9m and bear L, on a drive, just past the farm (563/963), for 0.4m to a rd (564/956). Turn L on the rd, then shortly R, through a gate, on a BW, parallel to the rd (heading west). Later, rejoin the rd, and turn L on this for 0.15, then keep SA on the SDW, as the rd bears sharp R.

7 UH, for 0.2m then bear R (552/962), on the BW, up Went hill, joining a good track. After 0.2m bear R, DH, to a rd (West way), then bearing L on Lower street, then R on Upper street (nr the Tiger Inn), to a T-J (557/979) in East dean. Turn L on the A259, UH, for 0.45m, then turn R on Old Wilmington rd (Jevington) (550/982).

8 After 0.15m bear R at a fork, for 0.25m then turn L (554/986), through a gate, on a BW, steep DH, to a rd. Turn R on this for 0.05m then turn L (552/988) on a BW (dirt track on the RHS of the drive). After 0.3m, keep SA on a BW, into the trees, as the drive bears L, UH, across a field, back into Friston forest.

9 Follow this forest track (or the purple cycle trail, for a longer, more technical finish to the ride) for 0.8m, through a clearing, SA over a path, up, then down some of Snap hill, to a X-tracks (544/005) and turn L.

10 Follow this track (you came along at the start) for 1.4m (keeping R after 0.15m), back to the houses in Westdean, and turn L on the BW, back to the car park (518/995).

EXTENSION 1:

+7 miles & +390 metres of climbing

1 Follow the purple (MTB) markers around the forest, for 7m, in a full circle, back to the car park.

EXTENSION 2:

+6.9 miles & +310 metres of climbing

A Keep SA/L, (Litlington), DH, through a farm, to a rd, (523/019), and turn L on this. After 0.3m, through Litlington, after the rd bears R then L, turn R (522/016) on a BW (Frog Firle) opposite a thatched cottage. Go over a bridge, to a rd (517/019) by the YHA, and turn L on the rd.

B After 0.55m, DH then UH, turn R, through a gate, on a grassy BW, into the trees (512/014). Keep L on the BW (R is a FP), UH, out of the trees, and turn R, over a field, following a fence on the RHS. Join a track, and follow this for 0.9m to a X-tracks (488/024), by a bench 'In loving memory of Paul Earle'.

C Turn R through a small gate, DH to a gate, then UH for 1.15m to a X-tracks (499/044), and turn R on the SDW. Follow the SDW, for 1.8m, DH, keeping SA as it joins Kings ride rd (520/030), to a T-J in Alfriston (520/030).

D Turn L on North street, going out of Alfriston, towards the A27 rd, for 0.4m then turn R over a bridge (522/036). To a T-J and go SA onto the SDW opposite, UH, for 0.45m to a rd (532/032). Keep SA, UH, on the SDW, and rejoin the main route at no. 3a.

SHORTCUT:

-8.8 miles & -395 metres of climbing

1 Stay SA on the rd for another 0.05m and turn R on a BW (562/012), UH, for 0.55m, into Friston forest. Keep SA on this BW forest track, DH, for 0.65m to a X-tracks (544/005), and go SA, and rejoin the main route at no.10.

This is a ride that has a bit of everything, for every type of rider.

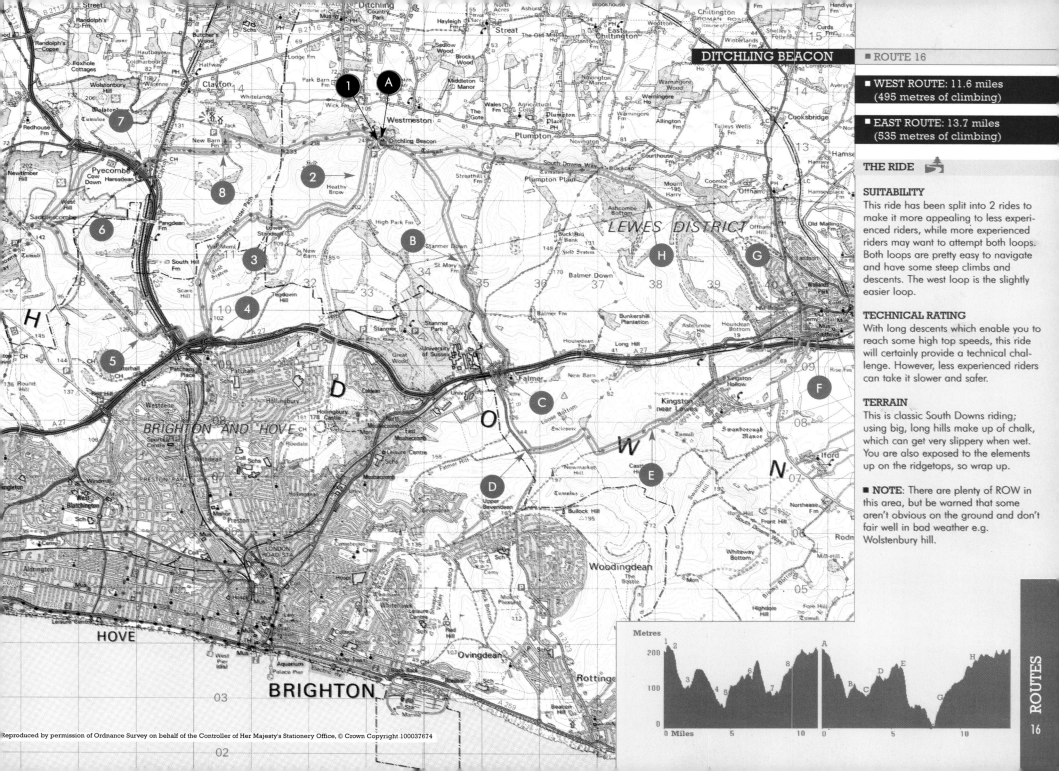

■ **WEST ROUTE:** 11.6 miles
(495 metres of climbing)

■ **EAST ROUTE:** 13.7 miles
(535 metres of climbing)

THE RIDE

SUITABILITY

This ride has been split into 2 rides to make it more appealing to less experienced riders, while more experienced riders may want to attempt both loops. Both loops are pretty easy to navigate and have some steep climbs and descents. The west loop is the slightly easier loop.

TECHNICAL RATING

With long descents which enable you to reach some high top speeds, this ride will certainly provide a technical challenge. However, less experienced riders can take it slower and safer.

TERRAIN

This is classic South Downs riding; using big, long hills make up of chalk, which can get very slippery when wet. You are also exposed to the elements up on the ridgetops, so wrap up.

■ **NOTE:** There are plenty of ROW in this area, but be warned that some aren't obvious on the ground and don't fair well in bad weather e.g. Wolstenbury hill.

■ **WEST LOOP**

■ **EAST LOOP**

GETTING THERE

Both rides start from the car park at Ditchling Beacon (333/130). This is south of Ditchling village, at the top of the hill, off Ditchling road. There are railway stations at Sussex university, Keymer (nr Ditchling) and Lewes.

ACCOMMODATION

B&B at Poynings Manor farm on: 01273 857371
B&B in Kingston near Lewes on: 01273 472295
YHA in Brighton on: 0870 7705724
Brighton backpackers on: 01273 777717
Brighton T.I. (premium rate) on: 0906 7112255
Worthing T.I. on: 01903 210022.

BICYCLE SHOPS

Action Bikes in Brighton (on London rd) on: 01273 605160
The Bicycleworks in Lewes (on Western rd) on: 01273 483 399

REFRESHMENTS

There is often an ice-cream van at the start/end. West loop: a pub and tea shop in Pyecombe. East loop: a pub in Falmer, Kingston near Lewes, and lots of shops etc in Lewes.

11.6 miles & 495 metres of climbing

1 **START.** Head west away from the rd, through a gate, on BW no.13 (main SDW track) for 0.2m, just around a LHB then turn L (330/131) off the main/SDW track, through a gate, on BW no.16 (Heathy brow). Go DH, for 0.7m to a fork , just past a gate and bear R on Lower Standean BW (328/128).

2 DH, into the valley, through a gate by the trees, on BW no.37, through a field and bear R to a single wooden gate. Immediately through this turn L on BW no.38, for 0.1m to a fork and bear R, on BW no.39. Keep L to a DT (315/115) and turn R on BW no.21.

3 Keep SA at BW no.20, to a gate and turn L on BW no.19, UH, to some X-tracks (309/117). Turn L, through a gate onto the West Sussex border path, and keep SA on this as the ST gets very feint, for 1.6m on the RHS of the field, through a gate to a rd (302/095).

4 Turn R, to a T-J (A27 just ahead), and turn R, keeping SA at the roundabout for 0.35m, bears R, then turn L on the (Waterhall) BW (297/096). Over the A23 and railway, and turn R, bearing L, UH, on a DT, to a T-J (291/095) by a barn.

5 Turn R, UH, for 1m to some X-tracks (280/107) where the main track bears R, and go SA through a silver gate on a ST. After 0.6m go through a gate and bear L, DH, through a tunnel of trees for 0.1m then turn R through a gate before the houses and a drive, and immediately sharp R again, UH, on a DT (273/115).

6 Keep SA, to a gate by some trees (New Timber hill), and go SA, DH, on the grass, to the A23 rd. Go over the bridge (over the A23) and to a rd (284/129) and turn R on this. Joining the slip rd off the A23, and keep SA (Pyecombe/A273) for 0.25m then turn L on Church lane (291/124) into Pyecombe.

7 Bear R by the church, on School lane, to the A273 rd and turn L on this for 0.15m, then turn R over this rd (294/129).On the SDW, through the golf club for 0.7m, through a gate, to some X-tracks (305/128)

8 Turn L on the SDW, towards the windmills for 0.25m to a T-J (305/132) and turn R on the SDW. Keep SA on the main track (SDW) for 2m, all the way back to the car park (333/130).

A short but demanding route, with some great views.

13.7 miles & 535 metres of climbing

A **START.** Cross the rd from the car park, going east, on the (SDW) BW for 0.35m then turn R (post but no BW sign), (338/128). Through some trees, to a single gate and bear R on BW no.11, on a feint track through the field, for 1.4m to the farm rd (347/108).

B Bear R/SA on this for 0.7m to a rd (350/098). Go R/SA on the rd, DH, and keep SA for 0.6m, then bearing R by the A27 rd SA. After 0.05m turn L over bridge, opposite the Swan inn pub (353/089).

C Turn R on the other side of the bridge, then L on Park street, past a pond on the L, bearing R to a T-J with the B2123 rd (352/086). Turn L on the rd, UH, going through a gap in the hedge on the L, parallel to the rd, for a total of 0.8m and turn L on a BW (358/075).

D After 0.65m, at a corner of some woods, bear R to a gate, through this, and turn immediately R through another gate onto the SDW (367/078). UH, to a T-J with a good track (369/074) and turn L on this for 0.7m to a fork (379/079) and keep L/SA, leaving the SDW.

E DH, on a rutty DT for 0.9m, becoming Kingston ridge rd, to a rd in Kingston near Lewes, (390/087). Go SA on the BW for 1.1m, over the A27 rd, bearing R, on Juggs rd, and keep SA to the B2193 rd. Turn L on this rd (Southover High st), then immediately L on Bell lane (408/095).

■ **NOTE:** There are shops, pubs, bike shops etc in Lewes if required

F Follow this rd bearing R, becoming Winterbourne Hollow, for 0.4m UH, to a X-rds with the A277 rd. Go SA on Nevill rd for 0.1m then turn L on a BW (405/101) opposite Spital rd.

G Keep SA, UH, on this main track (bear to the RHS of the pylon after 2m, at the Blackcap hill sign, through a gate) for 2.4m to a fork (377/122) and bear L around the bottom of the hill.

H Through a gate after 0.5, to a X-tracks (369/125), and keep SA on the SDW. Keep SA on this for 2.4m, past Dews pond, to a rd and go SA back to the car park at the end/start (333/130).

A classic, exposed ridgetop ride along the South Downs Way.

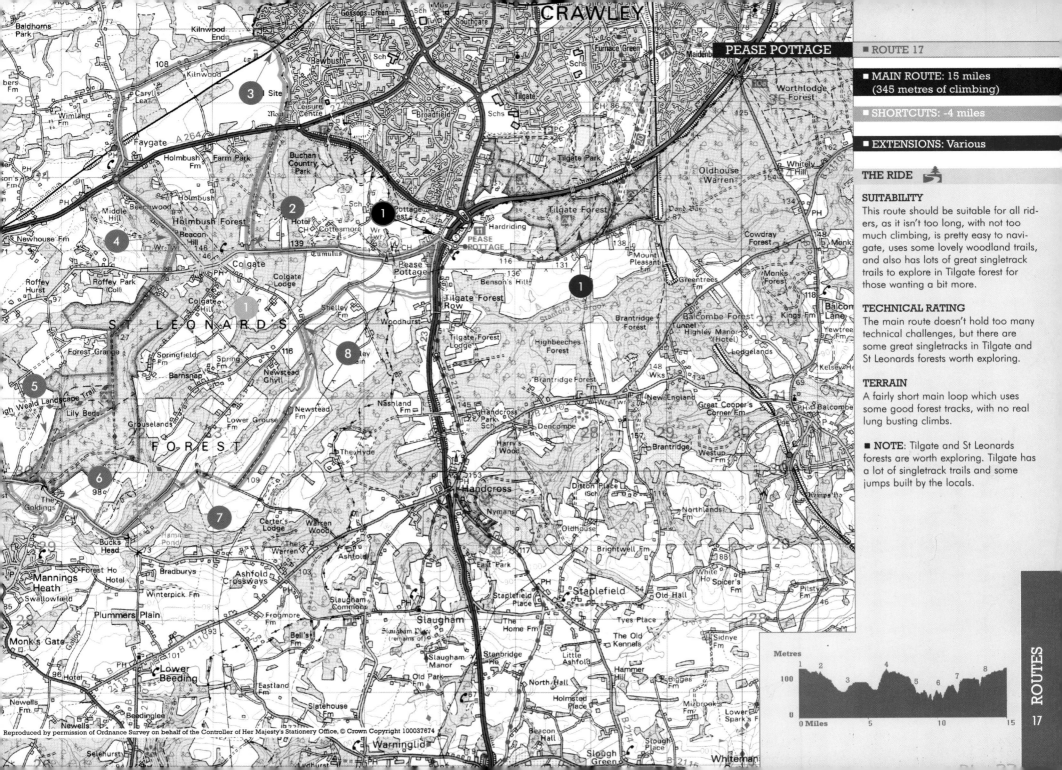

ROUTE 17

- **MAIN ROUTE: 15 miles**
  (345 metres of climbing)

- **SHORTCUTS: -4 miles**

- **EXTENSIONS: Various**

THE RIDE

SUITABILITY

This route should be suitable for all riders, as it isn't too long, with not too much climbing, is pretty easy to navigate, uses some lovely woodland trails, and also has lots of great singletrack trails to explore in Tilgate forest for those wanting a bit more.

TECHNICAL RATING

The main route doesn't hold too many technical challenges, but there are some great singletracks in Tilgate and St Leonards forests worth exploring.

TERRAIN

A fairly short main loop which uses some good forest tracks, with no real lung busting climbs.

■ **NOTE:** Tilgate and St Leonards forests are worth exploring. Tilgate has a lot of singletrack trails and some jumps built by the locals.

ROUTES

17

🚗 GETTING THERE

This ride starts in Pease pottage, which is just off junction 11, where the M23 becomes the A23. As soon as you enter Pease pottage village, turn right on Old Brighton road north (before the Black swan restaurant) and park down here (GR 260/331).

🛏 ACCOMMODATION

B&B in Ardingly on: 01342 715372
B&B in Crawley on: 01293 520002
Camping in Southwater on: 01403 730218
Crawley T.I. on: 01293 545322 or Horsham T.I. on: 01403 211661

🚲 BICYCLE SHOPS

Action Bikes in Crawley on: 01293 539395
C&N Cycles in Crawley on tel: 01403 251206

🍽 REFRESHMENTS

The Black Swan restaurant at the start/end of the ride in Pease Pottage. On the route there are pubs in Colgate and Faygate.

MAIN ROUTE

15 miles & 345 metres of climbing

1 START. Head **west** on Horsham rd (towards Colgate/Horsham), past the Black swan **for 1.6m , then turn R** (by the 'Slow' rd marking) into the woods, **on a BW** (234/330) or see the shortcut.

2 0.5m to some X-tracks and keep SA, then shortly **bear R at a fork** (235/338). To a driveway and bear L on this, to the A264 rd (238/346) and carefully **cross this. Go SA on the BW** opposite to a (BW) fork and bear L, to a railway line (238/357).

3 Cross the railway line (carefully), and follow the BW as it bears L, for 1.5m (keeping L at the house with pond), to a rd (217/351). **Turn L on the rd**, DH, (past Holmbush Inn) for 0.7m to a roundabout (217/340). Go SA on the rd (Colgate 2m), UH, for 0.7m then R on a BW (225/331).

4 DH, to a rd and keep SA onto the forestry DT (BW), for 1.3m to a X-tracks (216/304), and **turn R**, leaving the main DT. DH, **into the woods**, for 0.6m to a T-J and stream at the bottom (209/304), and bear L.

5 Follow this track to a rd and **turn R on this**, for 0.2m then **turn L on a BW** (202/298). Follow this BW for 0.5m to a rd (207/292) and **turn L on this rd**, UH, for 0.3m to a T-J (210/295).

6 Turn R and follow this rd for 0.55m to a fork (217/291) and **bear L on Grouse rd**, for 0.65m then **turn R on a BW** (224/298). After 0.1m **bear L (FP only SA)** across a field towards some trees (228/300), **to a DT** (227/300).

7 Bear R on the e DT, through the water, UH, **for 0.35m to a tarmac track** at the top (232/297) **and turn L on this.** Follow this farm track for 0.8m to the farm and keep **SA on the BW**, this bears L, DH, after 0.45m, to a 3-way rd junction (241/319).

8 Turn R on the rd for 0.6m, then turn R on a BW (249/325) and follow this for 0.65m, under the electricity lines, **to a rd** (258/323). **Turn L on this rd**, alongside the A23 rd, for 0.45m back to Pease Pottage, and your car is SA.

SHORTCUT:

-4 miles & -70 metres of climbing

1 Keep SA on the rd for 0.4m, into and through Colgate village, to a X-rds (228/327) **and turn R** on Tower rd. **After 0.35m** on this rd, **turn L on a BW** (225/332) **and rejoin the main route at no.4.**

EXTENSION:

Various

1 Tilgate forest has lots of (singletrack) trails, which are well worth exploring. Go east from Pease Pottage, over the A34 rd, and keep SA at the roundabout, and the forest is on the left, less than 1 mile down this road.

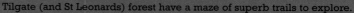

Tilgate (and St Leonards) forest have a maze of superb trails to explore.

HIGHLY RECOMMENDED

■ ROUTE 18

- ■ **WEST LOOP: 14.8 miles** (570 metres of climbing)
- ■ **SHORTCUTS: -3.75 miles**
- ■ **EXTENSIONS: +3.5 & 1 miles**
- ■ **EAST LOOP: 11.5 miles** (505 metres of climbing)
- ■ **SHORTCUTS: None**
- ■ **EXTENSIONS: +3.2 miles**

THE RIDE

SUITABILITY

Both loops have some big climbs and descents that need to be ridden with care (and good brakes). However, this does not make them unsuitable for inexperienced riders, but they should stay clear of the extensions which are quite technical. One loop should be enough for most riders, but both could be done together for a very tough ride.

TECHNICAL RATING

Both routes have some good technical challenges, be they long fast, bumpy, rutted doubletracks or tight twisty singletracks. The extensions also provide some more fast, furious and technical descents (and climbs back up) for those who want a bit more.

TERRAIN

The chalky terrain can get slippy in the wet and you will be exposed up on the ridgetops, so wrap up warm.

GETTING THERE

This ride starts from the village of Bramber, which is on the river Adur, between Steyning and Upper Beeding. Follow the A283 which runs between the A24 and A27 and park in the (free) car park (GR 187/106) or sensibly off the road. The nearest railway stations are along the coast e.g. Shoreham-By-Sea.

ACCOMMODATION

B&B in Steyning on: 01903 812286
B&B at Poynings Manor farm (Brighton) on: 01273 857371
YHA at Truliegh Hill (Tottington barn) on: 0870 7706078
Brighton Backpackers on: 01273 777717
Brighton T.I. (premium rate) on: 0906 7112255
Worthing T.I. on: 01903 210022.

BICYCLE SHOPS

Life Cycle on: 01273 697617 and Baker Street Bikes on: 01273 675754, both in Brighton.

REFRESHMENTS

Good choice in Bramber / Upper Beeding. West loop: a cafe, pub and shop in Findon (just off the route). East loop: Pub and sometime an ice-cream van on the extension.

ROUTES

18

■ WEST LOOP

14.7 miles & 555 metres of climbing

1 **START.** Head West on 'The Street' to the A283 roundabout (185/105) and go SA (2nd L) on Maudlin lane. 0.4m to a T-J and turn R then immediate L on Sopers lane (180/103). UH for 1.4m, through Maudalin farm, keeping L at a Private rd sign, to a rd at the top (162/094).

2 Turn R on the rd for 0.1m then keep SA on the SDW, as the rd bears R, to a DT. Bear R/SA to a X-tracks (162/099) and go SA (bearing L) on the SDW or see the shortcut or extension 1. Follow this for 2.1m to a fork past Chanctonbury ring (138/120), and bear L on the SDW, or see extension 2.

3 Follow this DT, for 0.6m, over a cattle grid, and bear L at a grass triangle (130/116), leaving the SDW.
3a - DH, for 1m to some X-tracks (121/103). Turn L for 0.3m then bear R through a gate on a BW (126/101), bearing L, UH, to a rd.

4 Go SA through a gate into a field, and go SA, UH, to another gate (127/098) and turn L. Past a farm, becoming a ST for 0.3m to a fork and bear L, to a DT, and turn L. To a grass triangle (139/094) and turn R on a DT for 0.6m to a X-tracks (or turn R after 0.4m on the Monarch's way BW, DH, to Findon, for refreshments.

5 Go SA through the gate (to Cissbury ring) and immediately bear L on a BW (139/084) by a National Trust sign. 0.35m to a fork (142/081) and bear L, before a wooden gate. Good ST, DH, to a gate and bear R, then shortly L through another gate (149/079).

6 Through the field for 0.95m to (not through) a silver gate at the end (158/068), and turn L through a wooden gate, to a T-J. Turn L onto a grassy ST, to a farm, and bear R on the concrete track (past houses) to a rd (161/072), and turn L on this. 0.55m UH, and turn R on a BW (opposite a car park) (162/080) for 0.3m to a fork and bear L.

7 0.1m to a X-tracks (elec. pylon on the R) (168/079) and turn L and follow this alongside a fence, and keep SA this ends, to a rd. Keep SA/R on the rd for 0.05m then turn R on the SDW (ST, BW) (165/089), across a field (away from the rd). Keep SA as the trail fades, to the R of some trees, to, and through a wooden gate.

8 Bear R alongside a fence, DH onto a DT, and just after this bears sharp L, turn R on steep gravel track (186/092). Through a gate and bear R on the field edge for 0.4m, through gate and turn R, steep UH, bearing L to a rd (191/087) by a electricity pylon.

9 Turn L on the rd for 0.45m, past a church and LHB, then turn R on the SDW (by a parking area), to a X-tracks (193/094). Turn L on the Downs link, and keep SA on this (signposted) to a rd. Cross the rd, following the downs link (parallel to rd) to a roundabout (185/105) and turn R, on the rd back into Bramber (187/106).

SHORTCUT:

-3.8 miles & -105 metres of climbing

1 Turn L on the Monarch's way, for 1.8m DH, then UH, to a DT (138/088) and turn L for 0.2m to a X-tracks and rejoin the main route at 5.

EXTENSION 1:

+3.6 miles & +200 metres of climbing

1 Go SA, and immediately bear R on a BW, leaving the SDW, for 0.2m to a fork (163/102) and bear L for 0.35m to another fork (159/106). Bear R, steeply DH for 1m through the woods, to a DT X-tracks (168/117). Turn R (Mouse lane) for 0.35m and bear R on the High street for 0.3m to a X-rds (177/111).

2 Turn R on Sheep pen lane, becoming Newham lane for 0.8m to Bostal rd (169/103), and turn R on this, steep UH. After 0.4m bear R on a DT, for 0.15m back to the X-tracks (162/099) you were at earlier, and turn R to rejoin the main route at 3.

EXTENSION 2:

+1 miles & +150 metres of climbing

A Bear R, steep DH, for 0.5m to a T-J at the bottom & edge of the woods (131/124), and turn L. Back UH, for 0.5m to the SDW (DT) (125/120), and turn L on this, UH for another 0.5m to a grass triangle at the top (130/166). Turn R here, leaving the SDW, and rejoin the main route at no.3a.

EAST LOOP

11.5 miles & 505 meters of climbing

A **START.** Head east on 'The street', through Upper Beeding, to a roundabout (196/103) by the Sun Inn, and turn L on the A2037. After 0.3m turn R on Bostal rd BW, as the rd and bears L, (200/101).

B 0.6m steep UH on this DT to a rd at the top, and turn L on this (SDW). Keep SA (off-road) on this main DT (SDW) for 3.3m then turn R (253/107) by some gates, on the Sussex Border path or see the extension.

C DH for 0.7m to a T-J (247/097) and turn L, for 0.4m to a DT (249/091) under the elec cables and turn R on this. Follow this (main) track DH for 1m (leaving the SB path) through a gate and go SA/L to Mile oak farm (242/079).

D Turn R by the farm on a steep UH, BW, bearing L, over the A27 tunnel, then bear R (under the elec cables). UH, to and through a gate in the fence (241/074), and turn R on the DT. Follow this UH, for 1.5m and turn L on a ST, by some animal pens (227/091).

E DH, through a gate, UH then DH again, for 1.3m to a rd (208/096). Go SA, DH for 0.6m on the rutted BW you came up earlier, to the rd (200/101) and turn L. To a roundabout and turn R on the High street and back to the car park (187/106).

EXTENSION:

+3.2 miles & +200 meters of climbing

Y Keep SA (on the SDW) for 0.3m to a rd (258/107) and go SA on the BW. Keep bearing L, steeply DH the RHS of the valley, to a gate at the bottom (266/116). Go through the gate into the trees, bearing R at the fork, to a rd (265/120).

Z Turn L on the rd, then L again by the church, for 0.2m and turn L on a BW (261/119). Follow this BW, UH, for 1m, keeping SA to a rd and turn L on this for 0.1m then turn R on the SDW (258/107) (you came from earlier). 0.3m back to the X-tracks and turn L on the Sussex border path and rejoin the main route at C.

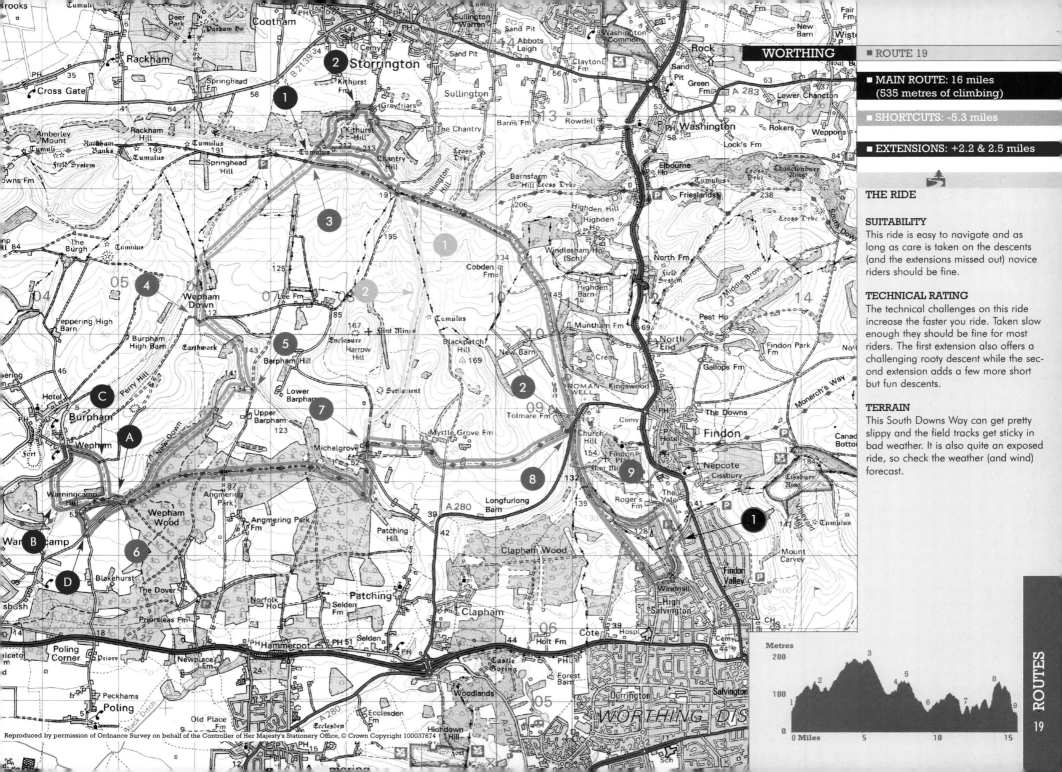

▪ **MAIN ROUTE:** 16 miles
(535 metres of climbing)

▪ **SHORTCUTS:** -5.3 miles

▪ **EXTENSIONS:** +2.2 & 2.5 miles

THE RIDE

SUITABILITY

This ride is easy to navigate and as long as care is taken on the descents (and the extensions missed out) novice riders should be fine.

TECHNICAL RATING

The technical challenges on this ride increase the faster you ride. Taken slow enough they should be fine for most riders. The first extension also offers a challenging rooty descent while the second extension adds a few more short but fun descents.

TERRAIN

This South Downs Way can get pretty slippy and the field tracks get sticky in bad weather. It is also quite an exposed ride, so check the weather (and wind) forecast.

GETTING THERE

This ride starts on the edge of Worthing, in High Salvington. Exit the A24 on Bost hill (windmill sign) for 0.3m to a (free) car park in the park at the bottom of the hill (GR 123/072). From the A27 turn off on Salvington hill rd (windmill sign), becoming Furze rd, down the hill on Bost hill to the car park. There is another car park (with a height restriction) at the top of the hill on Honeysuckle lane, which is off Furze rd (GR 119/068).

ACCOMMODATION

B&B in Worthing on: 01903 233002
B&B in Worthing at Woodlands guest house on: 01903 233557
YHA in Arundel on: 0870 7705676
Camping in Crossbush (nr Arundel) at Maynards on: 01903 882075.
Arundel TI on: 01903 882268

BICYCLE SHOPS

The Bike store in Worthing (on Brighton Road) on: 01903 206311

REFRESHMENTS

A shop on Furze rd at the start / end of the ride, and lots of choice in Worthing. There is nothing on the main route, but there are pubs off the extensions in Storrington and Burpham.

16 miles & 535 metres of climbing

① **START**. Turn R on the rd, going steeply UH, for 0.45m (past the windmill), **and turn R on Honeysuckle lane,** (120/066) as the rd bears sharp L. Keep SA as it becomes a BW, on this main track, for 1.45m, DH, to the A280 rd (110/088).

② Cross the rd (very carefully), and go SA on the ST BW opposite. Joins a better track after 0.75m, and follow this for 0.9m to a fork (102/113)and bear L. After 0.45m at a barn (095/116), turn L on the SDW and keep SA on this for 1.35m to a (feint) X-rds (075/123) or see the shortcut.

③ Turn L on a (feint) ST through a field or see extension 1.
3a - Keep SA, DH, for 1.2m to the fields edge (061/110) and turn L towards the woods. 0.15m to a X-tracks (060/108) and turn L, UH, for 0.45m to a good track.

④ Turn L on this (ignore the DT, BW SA) for 0.07m then turn R on a BW, through a gate (061/102). After 0.7m, UH, across the field, between some trees, at a DT at the end of the field (067/092). Turn very hard R (almost back on yourself) staying in the same field, following the LHS.

⑤ After 0.15m, turn L (064/092), alongside the trees for 0.2m, then into the woods. Keep SA on this DT for 1.15m to a X-tracks with good forest roads (050/077). Turn sharp L, almost back on yourself, on the good wide forest track or see extension 2.

⑥ Follow this main track (Monarch's way) SA, for 2.2m to a X-tracks (082/077) and turn L, DH on a loose stoney DT, to a rd.

Turn L on the rd for 0.25m, then R on a BW just after the buildings (082/085).

⑦ 0.5m to Myrtle grove farm and go SA on the track opposite, bearing R, up to a rd (093/082) and go SA on the BW. Keep SA on this main track, across the fields, for 1m and bear R at a fork, back to the A280 rd (110/088).

⑧ Cross the rd (very carefully) and go UH (came down here earlier) for 0.9m then turn L on a ST BW (114/075). DH for 0.55m to a X-tracks (122/076).

⑨ Turn R, for 0.3m back to the rd and the car park (123/072).

① After 0.55m from the barn, turn L on a BW (087/119) before (and NOT on) the DT BW, and a rd on the R. **DH,** for 0.85m to a fork (090/106) (shortly after a BW joins from the L) and bear R.

② Keep SA, DH for 1.4m to a good track (083/088), and turn L on this for 0.15m, then turn L on the (Monarchs way) BW (082/085) by some buildings, and rejoin the main route at no.7.

If the Romans made singletrack....

① Turn R, for 0.1m to some X-tracks and keep SA, into the trees, DH, on a rooty ST BW. 0.2m to a fork (easy to miss, but you can use either track) and bear L on a thin ST. To a DT and turn L on this for 0.05m then turn R on another DT (081/131).

② After 0.1m turn R on a BW (by Greyfriars) (083/130), on a steep and difficult UH (becoming a DT), for 0.7m to a T-J at the top (085/121). Turn R, through a gate, for 0.7m to some X-tracks (076/125) you were at earlier. Turn L, for 0.1m to the X-tracks with the SDW (075/123), and go SA, and rejoin the main route at no.3a.

EXTENSION 2:

+2.5 miles & +130 metres of climbing

A Bear R (not sharp R on the DT), then keep SA on a BW, DH, to a DT at the bottom. Turn L on this for 0.05m to a fork (048/077) and bear L, then immediately R at another fork. Along the valley bottom, in the field, for 0.35m to a X-tracks and turn R.

B Steep UH, then DH on a ST through the trees, to a rd, and turn R on this. After 0.1m turn R on a driveway (043/084), UH. After 0.3m at the top, keep SA on a BW (047/082), as the main track bears L.

C DH, for 0.3m to a T-J (048/077), you were at earlier, and turn R then immediately L at the fork on the DT this time, UH, for 0.45m to a X-rds (045/073).

D Turn L for 0.4m to the wide forests roads a X-rds (050/077) you were at earlier and go SA, rejoining the main route at no.6.

HIGHLY RECOMMENDED

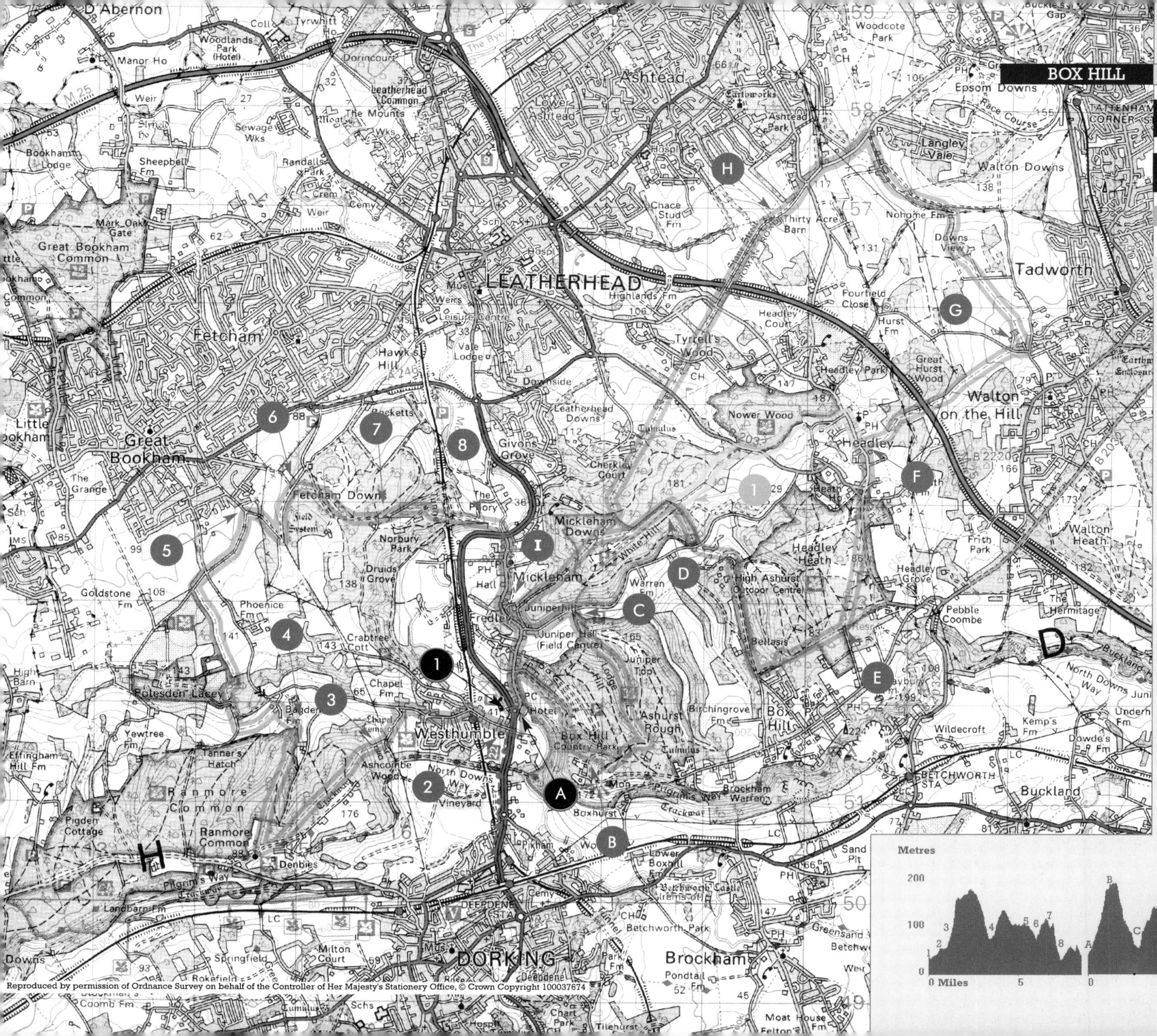

- **ROUTE 20**

- **WEST LOOP: 8.6 miles**
  (345 metres of climbing)

- **EAST LOOP: 14.6 miles**
  (630 metres of climbing)

- **SHORTCUT: -1.5 miles**

THE RIDE

SUITABILITY

The West loop is the easier of the two loops, as it is shorter, has less climbing and shallower gradients, so is suitable for most riders. The East loop is a lovely challenging ride, as it tackles some long steep climbs, steep and fast descents, and has some good singletrack that advanced riders will love.

TECHNICAL RATING

The West loop is the less technical, but still holds some challenges, especially if taken at speed. The East loop is defiantely for more advanced riders as there are some very steep climbs, descents, and technical singletrack.

TERRAIN

There are lots of very steep hills on this ride (which may have you walking) and some tree roots and loose rocks to be aware of. The trails drain pretty well, but be aware of slippery roots and soft patches as you fly down the hills.

- **NOTE:** Box hill is very popular with walkers so please ride with care.

■ WEST LOOP

■ EAST LOOP

GETTING THERE

This ride starts from the large car park (171/521) near Burford hotel, just off a roundabout on the A24, near Westhumble. This is a well known meeting place for (motor) bikers, and has a cafe / burger bar and toilets.

ACCOMMODATION

B&B in Dorking on: 01306 888337
B&B in Denbies on: 01306 876777
Burford bridge hotel at the start of the ride on: 0870 4008283
YHA (Tanners Hatch) on: 0870 7706060.
Camping at East Horsley on: 01483 283273
Guilford T.I. on: 01483 444333 or **Dorking TI** on: 01306 879327

BICYCLE SHOPS

Nirvana Cycles in Westcott on: 01306 740300

REFRESHMENTS

A cafe at the start/end of both the loops. East loop: a pub in Headley and a cafe in the car park just south of Headley. West loop: a pub near the end of the ride in Mickleham.

WEST LOOP

8.6 miles & 345 metres of climbing

1 START. Exit the car park and turn R, to the A24 roundabout, and turn L on the path alongside the A24 rd. After 0.1m bear L on a path which bears R, under the A24, to the other side and turn L, to a rd and turn R on this (170/517), into Westhumble.

2 After 0.3m (just over the railway line) bear L at a fork (166/519), on Chapel lane, for 0.5m then turn L on a BW (159/519), by Chapel ruins. UH, for 0.25m then bear R on a ST BW as the rd bears L (158/516).

3 Keep SA , UH, track widens, to the top, SA over a minor rd, for 0.15m to the (same) rd (148/505). Turn R on this rd for 0.1m, then turn R on a BW (opposite a church) (146/505). DH, for 1m, nr Bagden farm, and turn L onto a BW, (148/519).

4 0.3m across a field, through a gate to a DT (144/517) and turn R on this. Follow this BW for 1m, UH, under a bridge, to a rd (139/531) and turn R on this. After 0.1m go SA on a ByW, as the rd bears L, for 0.5m to a X-tracks (144/538) and turn R on a BW.

5 To the top (under the elec. pylons) and go keep SA on the DT, (or the twisty ST just inside the woods on the RHS), DH, for 0.25m to an off-set X-tracks (148/536). Turn L on a DT, for 0.35m then turn R, UH, on a BW (149/541) opposite a farm house.

6 0.15m, UH then DH, to a X-tracks with a DT (151/540) and keep SA, UH. Follow the edge of the trees. Keep SA on the BW, joining a DT and keep SA/L on this to a large grass triangle (with a play area) and bear R/SA on the Mickleham BW (157/538).

7 Keep SA on this BW, over the railway tunnel, **out of the trees** (by a radio mast) (165/538) and keep SA, **DH**. Go past a barrier and join a well surfaced track, going SA/R on this, then shortly keep SA on a BW, as the track bears L.

8 DH, to a drive (169/537) and turn R on this to the main rd (170/537). Cross the rd carefully, **going SA on the B2209 rd opposite, through Mickleham. Keep SA on this** for 1.1m then turn R, back to the car park (171/521).

A hilly and rocky ride.

EAST LOOP

14.6 miles & 630 metres of climbing

A START. Exit the car park and turn L on the rd for 0.2m, then turn R on a BW (171/523) just by Zig Zag rd. Steep UH for 0.8m to a rd at the top and go SA through a gap into a car park (180/515).

B Keep SA on the BW (by the trees) along the LHS of an open area, then bear L by a medieval hut (180/513). After 0.4m turn L on a BW (184/516), DH, for 1m to a small car park and rd at the bottom (177/529).

C Turn L on the rd for 0.35m then turn R on a ByW at Juniper hill (the L of the two DT's) (172/527) just before the B2209 rd. After 0.8m turn R at a X-tracks (178/536), on a BW. After 0.55m turn R or see the shortcut, onto another BW (186/540), going very steeply DH to a rd.

D Go SA on a BW, by a house, going very steep UH, for 0.25m, bearing R, to a drive (by High Ashurst Outdoor centre) (192/533). Turn L on this drive for 0.75m then turn L on a BW (195/522) just before the rd forks, for 0.65m, to 3-way BW junction (DT on the R) (204/528)

E Turn L on a BW for 0.65m to a rd and keep SA/L on this (cafe in the car park on L), for 0.15m, then bear R off this main rd (206/541) on another rd. 0.35m on this rd, turn R on a BW in Headley (205/546).

F Going under the M25 after 0.5m, for another 0.2m to a fork (214/551) and bear L. UH, on a grey sandy track for 0.5m to a rd and turn R on this for 0.1m, then L on a drive (221/555). Keep SA at the end of this drive, onto a stoney ST BW.

G After 1m (just past a farmhouse) bear L (214/569) and follow this for 0.8m, becoming a concrete track, through another farm, to a rd (205/577). Turn L on the path parallel to the rd, UH, for 0.5m to the X-rds and go SA, to Thirty acre farm (196/569).

H Keep SA on the Stane street ByW and stay on this for 3.2m (over the M25, across 2 roads, back into Mickleham downs woods and back along the track you came along earlier) to a rd (172/527).

I Turn R to the main B2209 rd, and turn L on this for 0.45m then turn R back into the car park (172/521) to finish.

SHORTCUT:

-1.5 miles & -90 metres of climbing

1 Keep SA on the BW for 0.55m to a T-J by a rd, and turn R for 0.15m to the rd (195/545). Go SA on the ByW, for 0.4m to a rd (200/547) and turn L on this for 0.25m to a T-J. Turn R on this rd for 0.2m then turn L on a BW (205/546) in between the houses, and rejoin the main route at F.

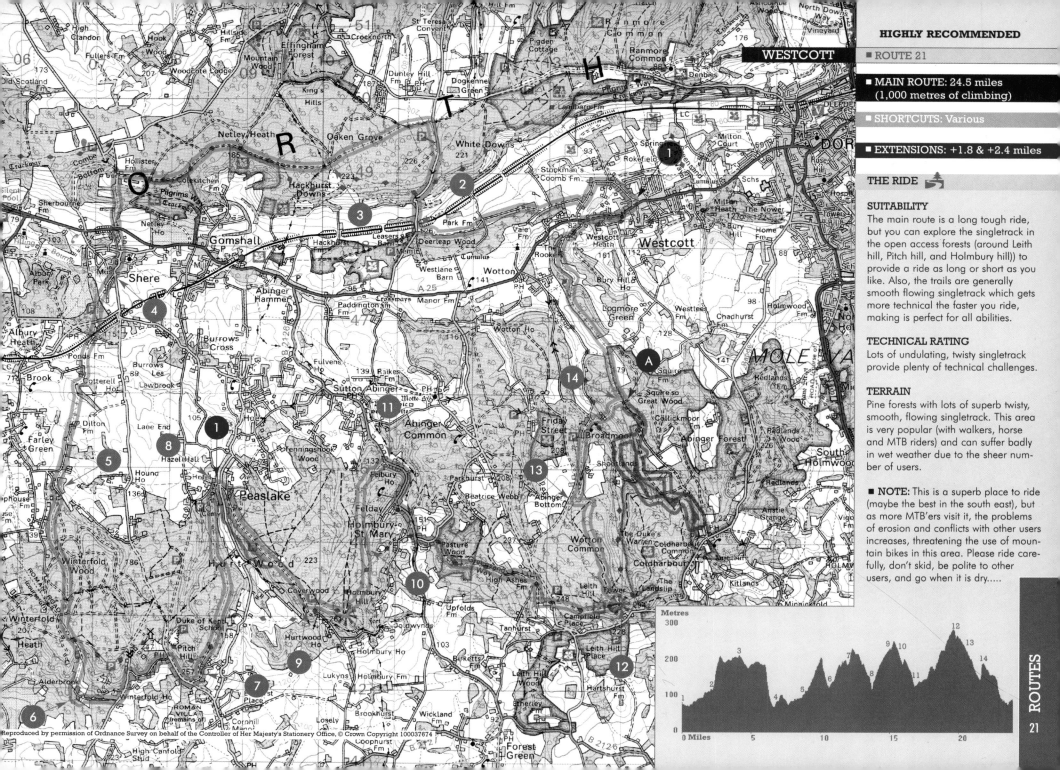

HIGHLY RECOMMENDED

- ■ ROUTE 21

- ■ **MAIN ROUTE: 24.5 miles**
  (1,000 metres of climbing)

- ■ **SHORTCUTS: Various**

- ■ **EXTENSIONS: +1.8 & +2.4 miles**

THE RIDE

SUITABILITY

The main route is a long tough ride, but you can explore the singletrack in the open access forests (around Leith hill, Pitch hill, and Holmbury hill)) to provide a ride as long or short as you like. Also, the trails are generally smooth flowing singletrack which gets more technical the faster you ride, making is perfect for all abilities.

TECHNICAL RATING

Lots of undulating, twisty singletrack provide plenty of technical challenges.

TERRAIN

Pine forests with lots of superb twisty, smooth, flowing singletrack. This area is very popular (with walkers, horse and MTB riders) and can suffer badly in wet weather due to the sheer number of users.

■ **NOTE:** This is a superb place to ride (maybe the best in the south east), but as more MTB'ers visit it, the problems of erosion and conflicts with other users increases, threatening the use of mountain bikes in this area. Please ride carefully, don't skid, be polite to other users, and go when it is dry.....

■ MAIN ROUTE

24.5 miles & 1,000 metres of climbing

1 **START**. Carry along Westcott street to a fork (137/489) and bear L on Balchins lane for 0.3m then turn R a BW (134/486). **Keep SA on this for 0.4m to a fork (128/485) and bear R, for 0.5m to a DT** by a farm (121/483). **Bear L then R between the barns** (effectively SA) and follow this alongside the woods, **for 0.6m to a rd** (112/482).

2 Turn R on the rd, steep UH, for 0.7m then turn L off the rd onto a ST (known as Blind terror) (115/492) near a FP and BW on the R. 0.3m, parallel to the rd, **to a DT and turn L on this** (ByW) (113/497). 0.25m to a fork and bear L, on a DT ByW and keep SA for 0.7m, SA at the X-tracks, **to a fork** (100/491) **and bear R, on the NDW.**

3 Follow this main DT for 1.65m to a T-J (077/489), and turn R for 0.05m then L at a 3-way split. After 0.35m, just past a farm, **turn L on a BW** as the rd bears sharp R (072/489). **DH, under the A25 to a rd,** in Shere, **and go SA (Middle street) for 0.2m, then turn R (Pathfields cul-d-sac)** (072/476).

4 Keep SA on the BW, into the woods and bear L, then R at the first a fork, then very shortly L at another fork, **to a rd. Go SA on the BW, to a T-J and turn L to a railway crossing** (069/467), **and cross this** (carefully). Turn R on the ByW, for 1.2m, becoming a rd, **and keep SA over a log, on a BW,** when the rd bears sharp R, (065/449).

5 0.15m to a rd and turn L on this, then R at a (just before the houses), **on a BW**, into the woods. **Follow the BW signs for 1.35m to a T-J with another BW**, and turn L, UH, to a rd (067/426). **Turn R on the rd, then**

immediately L, on a BW. 0.55m DH then L on a BW (just past a house) (067/418).

6 To a drive and go R on this to a rd (073/418), and turn L on this, for 0.25m, then turn R on a BW (074/422), for 0.4m to a rd (080/424). **Turn R on this rd** (or there's a Quarry for playing in, on the L), for 0.3m, past the Windmill pub, **and bear L** off the main rd, for 0.1m then turn L on a (Private drive) BW, UH (084/421).

7 0.5m to a fork and bear R, for 0.55m to another fork and bear L, for 0.25m to yet another fork, **and bear R. After 0.3m, by the cemetery, turn R just after the green barrier**, on a rutted BW, **DH to Peaslake church and go SA to a rd** (086/447).

8 Turn R, past Hurtwood Inn, to a X-rds with a bus stop and Peaslake village shop SA. Turn R, then shortly L on Radnor rd (086/447), **UH, for 1.25m** or see extension 1.

9 Turn L (098/431) on bumpy track, UH, into a car park, and go SA **past the metal barriers, to a fork and bear R.** Past some stagnant water, **to the top** (viewpoint on the R - the BW going steep DH here is known as Widow maker) **and turn L on a DT** (103/430). After 0.15m, turn R on a ST (known as Parklife) (103/431) **and follow this to a DT** (the end of the ST) (105/435).

10 Turn R on the DT to some X-tracks, and bear L on a feint ST (known as Telegraph road) (in between the DT's going SA and L), under the telegraph lines. **Keep SA** on this over other tracks **for 0.75m to a slight clear**

ing and turn R on a ST (known as Mutiny) (104/448), **DH to a rd** (108/451).

11 Turn R on the rd, for 0.85m, then turn L on Pasture wood rd (112/440), for 0.15m and go SA on the Greensand way (GSW) BW, as the rd bears L. After 1.15m turn R at the T-J, on the GSW, bearing L, **to a rd and SA on the BW, UH to Leith tower** (139/432).

12 Turn L on the good BW track just before the tower (with a snack shop inside it) (steep BW DH on the R is known as Cliff Richard), keeping SA for 0.25m, then bear R on a ST (137/434). **To a fork and bear L on a ST** (known as Caspers, the ST on the R is known as Trout mask replica) DH, for 0.6m to a T-J with a FP (136/445) and turn L.

13 0.2m to a X-tracks (133/445), then turn R on a BW (133/445). **Keep SA, DH, on the BW** (becoming a drive) for 0.75m, then **keep SA on a BW** (not R, on the DT BW), as the rd bears sharp L by the stables (135/456). **To a DT and go SA**, past the houses, **UH on a ST, to a X-tracks at the top** (140/459) **and turn L** or see extension 2.

14 Follow this sandy ByW (or on the better ST on the sides) **for 1m, then turn R on a BW**, by a wooden post (easy to miss) (132/473). **To a drive and turn R, to the A25 rd, and turn R on this, back into Westcott** and your car (141/485).

+1.8 miles & +100 metres of climbing

1 0.8m UH on the rd, then turn R (opposite a worksite entrance) (094/437), **to a feint ST fork and bear L** (wooden posts on R ST). **Follow this twisty ST** (known as Golden Birdies) **to a rd** (087/443) **and turn R.** Back into Peaslake village **and turn R back UH on Radnor road** (086/447), UH, for 1.25m, **and rejoin the main route at no.9.**

EXTENSION 2:

+2.4 miles & +75 metres of climbing

A Turn R on the DT for 0.3m to a clearing and join the 'Summer lightening' MTB trail here. Follow this circular waymarked trail all the way around back to here, and turn L back to the X-tracks and go SA, rejoining the main route at no. 14.

SHORTCUT:

Rather than suggesting a shortcut to the main route, park at Holmbury hill car park (GR 098/431) and explore the numerous singletracks in here, Leith hill and Pitch Hill.

With so many superb pine forest singletrack trails, this is a mountainbiking mecca.

This ride starts in Westcott (although there are other car parks on the route) which is west of Dorking. Park (considerately) on Westcott street by the green, opposite Nirvana Cycles bike shop (GR 141/486). There are railway stations in Dorking and Gomshall.

ACCOMMODATION

B&B in Lockhurst Hatch farm on: 01483 202689
B&B at the Royal Oak on: 01306 730120 or Hurtwood Inn on: 01306 730851, both in Peaslake.
YHA in Holmbury St Mary on: 0870 7705868
Camping & Caravanning at Horsley on: 01483 283273
Guilford T.I. on: 01483 444333
Dorking T.I. on: 01306 879327

BICYCLE SHOPS

Nirvana Cycles bike shop in Westcott on: 01306 740300. They also do regular (free) guided group rides.

REFRESHMENTS

Shop at Westcott, a snack shop at Leith hill tower, (tea) shop at Peaslake village stores (popular with cyclists). There are also pubs at Shere, Pitch hill, and Holmbury St Mary.

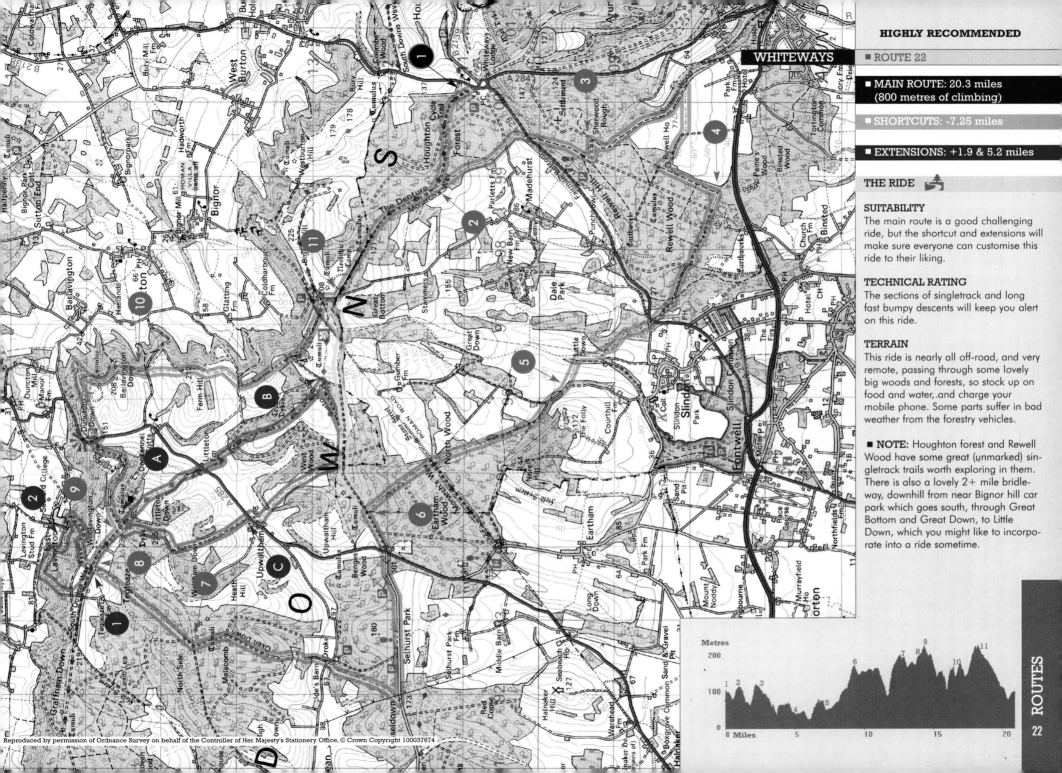

HIGHLY RECOMMENDED

■ ROUTE 22

■ **MAIN ROUTE: 20.3 miles**
(800 metres of climbing)

■ SHORTCUTS: -7.25 miles

■ EXTENSIONS: +1.9 & 5.2 miles

THE RIDE 🌲

SUITABILITY

The main route is a good challenging ride, but the shortcut and extensions will make sure everyone can customise this ride to their liking.

TECHNICAL RATING

The sections of singletrack and long fast bumpy descents will keep you alert on this ride.

TERRAIN

This ride is nearly all off-road, and very remote, passing through some lovely big woods and forests, so stock up on food and water, and charge your mobile phone. Some parts suffer in bad weather from the forestry vehicles.

■ **NOTE:** Houghton forest and Rewell Wood have some great (unmarked) singletrack trails worth exploring in them. There is also a lovely 2+ mile bridleway, downhill from near Bignor hill car park which goes south, through Great Bottom and Great Down, to Little Down, which you might like to incorporate into a ride sometime.

ROUTES

22

■ MAIN ROUTE

20.3 miles & 800 metres of climbing

1 START. With you back to the rd, cafe / hut on L, go past the orange gate (001/108), DH on a DT, following the blue BW signs, then the green cycleway signs. After 0.5m keep SA/L, leaving the DT, for another 0.5m, out of the woods, **to a grassy DT T-J (988/113) and turn sharp L on a BW.**

2 DH, on a ST, keeping SA/R, to a rd and go SA on the BW to the A29 rd (955/102). Cross the rd (carefully) and bear R on a track, UH, into the woods, for 0.5m to a 3-way split (by a FP) and keep L. Shortly coming to the corner of a DT (992/093), turn sharp L on this for 0.15m then R off this track (995/093), just after the FP.

3 0.2m to a fork (just past a FP), and turn L on a good track, along the edge of the woods, **for 0.9m then turn R through a gate (002/080).** To a gate, across the hill, bearing to the RHS of Rewell house, through a gate, **to a X-tracks (991/084). Turn L, DH,** and **keep SA/L for 0.5m to a T-J at the bottom (987/076).**

4 Turn R on this DT BW, for 0.7m to X-tracks (in the trees) and take the 2nd R (i.e. SA) and follow this to a rd. Go SA on the rd (LHS of the triangle), **bearing L, then immediately turn R on a BW (969/085). 0.5m to a X-tracks and go SA/R** (not through a gate on the R to Bignor) **on a DT,** along the edge of a field, **bearing L, DH to a rd (961/096).**

5 Turn R on the rd, for 0.2m to a fork, and bear L on a BW (NT woods), for 0.2m to another fork and bear R, on the main track. Keep SA on this for 0.9m to a X-tracks (951/114) **and go SA/L on the Easting BW.**

After 0.7m, UH, to a T-J with a DT (944/122) **and turn L** or see the shortcut.

6 DH on the DT, to a rd, and go SA on the rd (Goodwood) for 1.3m then turn R on a BW, just past the elec. pylons (919/118). DH for 0.7m, **to a rd and go SA on the BW,** UH, for 0.9m to a T-J and turn L, on the BW, for 0.3m to a X-tracks (926/145).

7 Go SA, bearing R, for 0.1m then keep SA/R on the BW, leaving the DT, and follow this for 1m to a X-tracks with the SDW (937/159) and turn R or see extension 1.

8 UH, on the SDW for 0.5m to a X-tracks (942/155), and turn L on a ROW (leaving the SDW) to Duncton or see extension 2.

9 1m to the A285 rd and turn R on this, then immediately L on a BW (954/158. After 0.65m (through fields, back into the woods) to a X-tracks, as you start going DH, and turn sharp R on a BW (964/161) (easy to miss). UH on this BW for 0.7m, bearing R, then steeply DH to X-rds (963/151).

10 Go SA on the DT, through the fields, for 0.85m to a T-J (962/139) and turn R, then immediate L onto a chalky DT, UH. Keep SA/L at the top near the top and masts, for 1.1m, to a car park (973/129), and go on the 2nd BW on the R, to a X-tracks (973/126) and L on the Monarch's way.

11 Keep SA/R on this grassy descent for 1.25m to a fork (988/113) (been here before) and bear L, and retrace your tracks from earlier, back to the car park i.e. follow the green cycle signs, UH, (001/108).

-7.25 miles & -385 metres of climbing

1 Turn R at the T-J, and keep SA for 0.7m to a fork (954/126), and bear R, and keep SA on this BW for 0.8m to a X-tracks. Go SA, on and staying on the Monarchs way (by bearing L, R and R again at the forks) to a X-tracks (973/126). Go SA (still on Monarchs way), and rejoin the main route at no.11.

This ride is nearly always going through one lovely wood or another.

+1.9 miles & +150 metres of climbing

1 Turn L on the SDW for 0.15m then bear R on a BW, to some X-tracks (FP SA) (933/161) and turn R. DH for 0.4m to a T-J (936/165) at the edge of the woods and turn R on this BW for 0.55m, and keep SA/R on the DT by some buildings on the L.

2 After 0.1m bear sharp R on the DT, steep UH, (944/162), for 0.55m, back to X-rds (937/159) with the SDW, and turn L, rejoining the main route at no.8.

EXTENSION 2:

+5.2 miles & +275 metres of climbing

A Go SA at the X-tracks (on the SDW), DH for 0.85m to a rd (950/144) and go SA on the SDW. UH for 1.35m to a X-tracks (962/128) masts on the L, and turn sharp R (leaving the SDW).

B After 0.5m bear R, as a track joins you from the L, for another 0.1m and turn R at the fork, for another 0.15m to a X-tracks (950/126). Turn R and follow this BW, DH, to a farm and turn R on the DT, and follow this to the rd (944/138).

C Go SA on the BW, UH, for 0.7m, then bear R off this DT, on the BW going across a field, and back into the woods. Turn R at a T-J, back to the X-tracks (942/155) with the SDW and go SA, rejoining the main route at no.9.

🚗 GETTING THERE

The ride starts from the Whiteways Lodge (free) car park (001/108). This is 3 miles north of Arundel, by the roundabout, where the A29, B2139 and A284 roads all meet. There are toilets and a hot and cold snack shop here. There is a railway station at Arundel, close to the ride.

🛏 ACCOMMODATION

B&B at Arundel house on: 01903 882136
B&B in Charlton in 'The Fox goes free' on: 01243 811461
YHA in Arundel on: 0870 7705676
Camping at Gumber Bothy farm (GR 961/118), tel: 01243 814484 but has no road access
Chichester T.I. on: 01243 775888
Arundel T.I. on: 01903 882268

🚲 BICYCLE SHOPS

Chain Reaction in North Bersted (Bogner Regis) on tel: 01243 841114

🍴 REFRESHMENTS

There is a snack bar in the car park at the start / end of the ride and a couple of pubs in Slindon, but other than that there aren't any refreshment stops on the route.

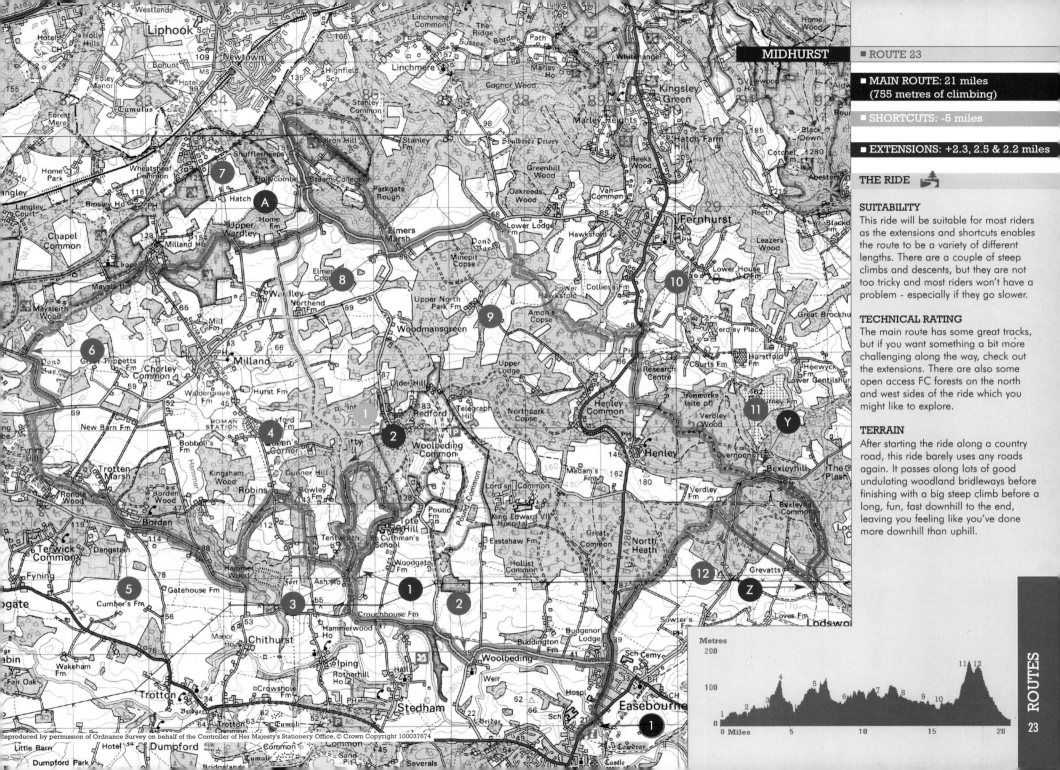

■ **MAIN ROUTE: 21 miles**
(755 metres of climbing)

■ **SHORTCUTS: -5 miles**

■ **EXTENSIONS: +2.3, 2.5 & 2.2 miles**

THE RIDE

SUITABILITY
This ride will be suitable for most riders as the extensions and shortcuts enables the route to be a variety of different lengths. There are a couple of steep climbs and descents, but they are not too tricky and most riders won't have a problem - especially if they go slower.

TECHNICAL RATING
The main route has some great tracks, but if you want something a bit more challenging along the way, check out the extensions. There are also some open access FC forests on the north and west sides of the ride which you might like to explore.

TERRAIN
After starting the ride along a country road, this ride barely uses any roads again. It passes along lots of good undulating woodland bridleways before finishing with a big steep climb before a long, fun, fast downhill to the end, leaving you feeling like you've done more downhill than uphill.

■ **MAIN ROUTE**

🚗 GETTING THERE

The ride starts from a (free) large car park in the town of Midhurst, where the A286 (going north to south) and the A272 (going east to west) roads cross. The car park is situated at the north end of the town, behind the Tourist Information office (GR 887/218), close to the shops.

🛏 ACCOMMODATION

B&B in Midhurst on: 01730 814858
B&B at The Elsted Inn, in Elsted Marsh on: 01730 813662 .
Gumber farm barn accommodation on: 01243 65313
YHA (Hinehead), north of Haslemere on: 0870 7705864
Midhurst T.I. on: 01730 817322
Petersfield T.I. on: 01730 268829

🚲 BICYCLE SHOPS

Midhurst sports shop has a few basic bike bits, otherwise try The Sensible Bicycle Co. in Petersfield (on the A3) on: 01730 266 554.

🍴 REFRESHMENTS

Shops, pubs, bakery, take-aways, etc in Midhurst. There is a pub just off the route at Wheatsheaf common (on the B2070), and the 'King's Arms' in Henley (on the A286).

21 miles & 755 metres of climbing

1 **START**. Exit the car park, and turn R on the rd, over a bridge, to a roundabout (in Easebourne), and turn L (889/221) on the A286. After 0.8m turn L at the X-rds (891/228) (Woolbedding), for 1.25m to a T-J (873/229) by a church and houses.

2 After 0.45m bear L at a fork, on a small rd, and keep SA (rd bears R by Crouchhouse farm) for 0.7m to a fork (857/235), and turn R/SA on a ST rd (dead end), as the rd bears L. Shortly along here, bear R into the woods on a BW. Bear L at the first fork, to another fork (856/241) and L again, or see extension 1 or the shortcut.

3 Over a bridge and bear L, UH on a BW. 3a - To the top and keep SA to a rd, and go L/SA on this for 0.2m and turn R on a BW (851/243) opposite a rd on the L, UH for 0.4m, through a gate at the top by a house and bear L in front of a hut (851/249).

4 Shortly, bear L on the BW, into the woods, DH, past some houses to a rd (846/251) and go SA (R then L) on the BW. Keep SA, DH for 1m to a rd (842/238) and turn R on this, for 0.5m, then bear L on a DT BW (before the rd goes DH). Keep SA on this DT for 0.6m to a 3-way rd junction (827/247).

5 Turn R (Borden wood), for 0.2m then bear L, as the rd bears sharp R, for 0.1m and turn L, UH, on a BW, by the fork in the rd (824/250). Keep SA at the X-tracks, on the main track, bearing R, over a small bridge, to a rd (814/262). Turn R on this, for 0.2m, then turn L on a ST rd (818/263).

6 After 0.6m, turn R on a BW (813/270), on a DT by a house, and follow this for 1.4m, past a farm, to a rd (830/282). Turn R on the rd for 0.1m then L by a house, on a drive, and keep SA/R after 0.1m on a BW, as the drive bears L (832/281).

7 Follow this BW for 0.7m to a rd (841/285), and bear R on the rd for 0.1m then turn L on a BW (842/284). Keep SA for 0.5m, past Home farm to a rd and join this, going SA/L, for 0.3m, UH, to a T-J (852/289) and turn R or see extension 2.

8 After 0.8m to a fork (861/283) and turn L on a rd (Fernhurst), and follow this for 1m (877/288) to Lower lodge farm.
8a - Bear R off the rd, through the farm, as the rd bears L, through a gate onto a BW. Bear L through a field, by the trees, to a fork and bear L, then R at a fork by some water, to a T-J (878/281).

9 Turn L on the BW, along the LHS of the field, to the end, then bear R, then immediately L, through some gate posts. DH, then UH to some X-tracks and keep SA, through a field, along the RHS of the stream to a rd (895/273).

10 Turn R on the rd, then bear L, off the main rd, just past the King's Arms pub. 0.1m to a rd and keep SA/L on this, for another 0.3m then turn L on a (Private) rd (894/263), (this is a FP until the X-tracks). Go SA at the X-tracks, and follow this main track for 1.35m to a rd (910/253), and turn R on this or see extension 3.

11 After 0.5m on the rd, turn R (907/246) on another rd (opposite a forest entrance on the L).

12 After 0.2, turn L on a R.O.W. (904/248), following the Green arrows (main DT) for 1m, to a (DT) XT-tracks (no quarry traffic sign and under elec cables). Bear L, DH, to a rd (891/232), and go L on this, DH into Easebourne. To a roundabout and turn R, over the bridge, into Midhurst and L back to the car park (887/218).

SHORTCUT:

-5 miles & -240 metres of climbing

1 Follow extension 1 and note 1 to the T-J at the end of note 1 and turn R here. Follow this DT (past houses on the L) for 0.8m, to a rd and join this going SA. 0.45m to a X-rds (848/275) and go SA, for 1.1m, UH, to a T-J (852/289) and turn R and rejoin the main route at no.8.

+2.3 miles & +100 metres of climbing

1 R at the fork, UH, for 0.8m to a T-J (862/248) with a DT and turn L, then short bear L at a fork. Shortly after the farm build-ing bear L on a BW, off the DT (861/250). 0.75m, bearing L, to a T-J (855/253) with a DT (the shortcut leaves the extension here).

2 Turn L and follow the green arrows, bear ing R, then turn sharp L on a BW (FP only S and keep L, DH to the bottom. Turn R on a BW (just before a small bridge) (856/241) a rejoin main route at no.3a.

EXTENSION 2:

+2.5 miles & +100 metres of climbing

A Turn L on the rd for 0.85m, then turn R (848/302) (shortly after electricity cables ov head) and follow this DT to the R for 0.85m T-J and turn R the shortly L on BW (opposite building) into the woods and steeply DH to rd (863/284). Turn L on the rd for 0.9m an rejoin main route at no.8a.

EXTENSION 3:

+2.2 miles & +100 metres of climbing

Y Turn L on the rd for 0.25m, then turn R a BW (on the L of Nightingales drive) (914/252). Keep R/SA for 0.7m to a fork (919/243) and bear R, UH, then steep DH, the bottom and bear L, UH to a sandy DT (918/238) with electricity cables overhead.

Z Turn R on the DT, for 0.25m then keep SA/L (no signs), leaving the DT as it bears R Go SA, into the woods, keeping SA on this (main) track to a 3-way rd junction. Go SA the rd and rejoin main route at no.12.

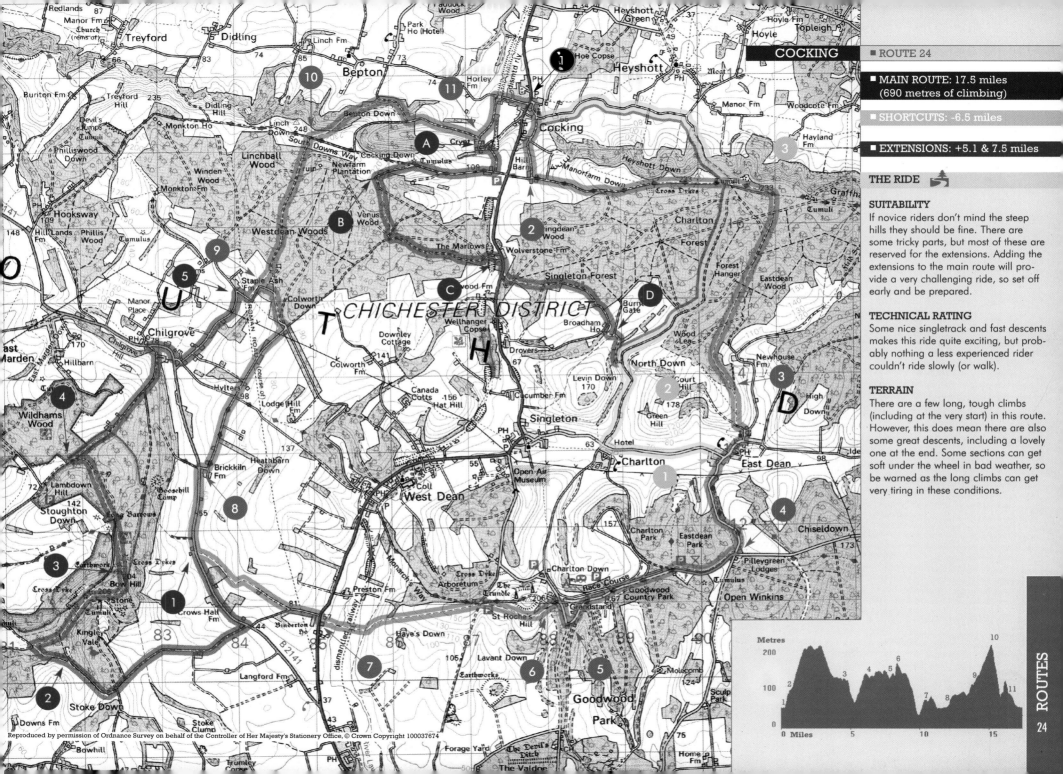

■ MAIN ROUTE: 17.5 miles
(690 metres of climbing)

■ SHORTCUTS: -6.5 miles

■ EXTENSIONS: +5.1 & 7.5 miles

THE RIDE

SUITABILITY

If novice riders don't mind the steep
hills they should be fine. There are
some tricky parts, but most of these are
reserved for the extensions. Adding the
extensions to the main route will provide a very challenging ride, so set off
early and be prepared.

TECHNICAL RATING

Some nice singletrack and fast descents
makes this ride quite exciting, but probably nothing a less experienced rider
couldn't ride slowly (or walk).

TERRAIN

There are a few long, tough climbs
(including at the very start) in this route.
However, this does mean there are also
some great descents, including a lovely
one at the end. Some sections can get
soft under the wheel in bad weather, so
be warned as the long climbs can get
very tiring in these conditions.

ROUTES

24

GETTING THERE

The ride starts in Cocking village, on the A286, south of Midhurst (where the A272 crosses the A286). Parking is limited within the village, but there is a car park just outside the village, south on the A286, at the top of the hill, on the right (by the Bepton organics sign). The nearest railway is in Chichester (5 miles away).

ACCOMMODATION

B&B at 'The Fox goes free' in Charlton on: 01243 811461
B&B at 'Lodge Hill Farm' in West Dean on: 01243 535245
Camping & caravanning near Graffham on: 01798 867476 or Goodwood on: 01243 755 033/022.
Chichester T.I. on: 01243 775888

BICYCLE SHOPS

Midhurst sports shop has a few basic bike bits, otherwise try The Sensible Bicycle Co. in Petersfield (on the A3) on: 01730 266 554.

REFRESHMENTS

A pub and post office shop in Cocking at the start / end of the ride and a pub in East Dean. Also a pub in Chilgrove on extension 1, and a pub in Charlton on the shortcut.

ROUTES

24

17.5 miles & 690 metres of climbing

1 START. At the post office (opposite the Blue Bell pub) (878/176), **turn onto Mill lane, then bear R immediately,** behind the back of the PO. **After 0.15m**, past the church, and **keep SA/L on a BW,** as the rd bears L, and follow this SA, UH, for 0.5m to a T-J by Hill farm (878/166).

2 Turn L, for a tough UH on the (SDW) DT, **for 2.1m, then turn R on a BW,** off the SDW (910/164) (before the this track starts going DH). **After 0.5m keep R/SA at a fork, then shortly keep L/SA on a BW,** leaving the DT which bears R (907/154).

3 Exit the woods through a wooden gate, through some more gates, **DH,** to a DT and **turn L** to a rd. **Turn R on the rd,** DH to a T-J (906/131) (by Droke farm) **and turn R.** 0.2m to a fork and **bear L** on Eastdean hill (Goodwood) or the shortcut.

4 After 0.9m **turn R on a BW** just before a T-J (904/116), running parallel **then rejoining the rd after 0.55m. Keep SA/R on the rd for 1m** (alongside the Goodwood horse race track) **to a T-J** (882/107) **and turn R on the rd, UH.**

5 After 0.15m **turn L** through car park no.6 **on a BW** (881/110) **bearing L and UH.** To the (Seven points) car park (871/110) **and go SA on a gravel track, shortly to a fork and bear L on a BW,** and follow this DH through the fields.

6 1m on a fast, grass ST, steep DH, to some X-tracks (by a gate at the bottom of the field) (856/107). **Go SA,** over a brick bridge, then a wooden bridge, **and keep SA to a rd.**

---

7 Turn R on the cycleway on the RHS of the rd for 50 meters then **turn L over the rd onto Binderton lane** (850/108). **After 0.25m keep SA,** as the rd bears L, **onto a DT and keep SA on this to the rd** (834/117) **and turn R** or see extension 1.

8 After 0.7m **turn R** (Brickkiln farm) (835/128) **on a rd and follow this for 0.7m to a X-rds and keep SA for another 0.7m to a T-J** (846/146) (BW, SA). **Turn L on the rd for 0.45m** (843/152) **then keep SA** as the rd bears sharp L, **dropping down onto a BW, and turn R on this.**

9 Keep SA on this main DT to a T-J with the SDW (849/171) by a water tank. **Go SA over the DT, bearing R through a field** (feint track) **down to the trees and through a small entrance into the woods** (852/172).

10 DH, to a DT (859/176) **and turn R, UH for 0.35m to a T-J** (862/174). **Turn L** out of the woods, DH for 0.65m to a T-J (871/171) **and turn L** or see extension 2.

11 0.4m to a rd (873/177) **and turn R,** under a bridge, **back into Cocking** by the Blue Bell pub and PO (878/176).

SHORTCUT:

-6.5 miles & -275 metres of climbing

1 Keep R at the fork (Charlton) **for 1m to a X-rds** (887/130) **and turn R on North lane** (by Woodstock house hotel). **Keep SA on this for 0.75m to a fork** (890/141) **and keep R on North lane.**

---

2 Keep SA on this track for another 0.9m to a fork (900/149) shortly after a X-tracks by a building, **and bear L. Keep SA, UH, for 1m to a X-tracks** with the SDW (904/165) (came past here earlier).

3 Go SA on the BW opposite, DH for 0.75m to a fork (899/174) with two better DT's **and bear L.** 0.45m to a rd and **keep SA/L on this,** for another 1m, into Cocking (878/176), by the PO and pub.

EXTENSION 1:

+5.1 miles & +260 metres of climbing

1 Turn L on the rd for 0.75m then turn R on a BW (just past the farm buildings) (841/107). **Keep SA on this for 1.35m,** then **turn R on a BW** (823/098), UH, keeping the woods close on your RHS.

2 0.65m to a fork and **bear R on the cycleway** (not the DT just before), UH to a DT (813/105) as you exit the woods. **Turn R on the DT,** in then back out of the woods **and keep SA across the top** on the RHS of the mounds, **back into the woods.**

3 After 0.3m back in the woods, **turn L** at the X-tracks (825/112) just after a trig point on the L, **and keep R at the fork.** To a DT and **go R/SA on this** then very shortly **bear off it again on a BW** (824/121). **DH for 0.45m** joining a DT, and **keep SA/L on this for 0.2m** then turn **sharp R on a grassy DT** (818/129).

4 Keep SA, DH on a stoney DT to a rd (828/144) with the White horse pub opposite, **and turn R on the rd.** After

---

0.25m bear L on a lane after the common, **to some X-rds** (833/142) **and turn L** towards Staple Ash farm.

5 After 0.8m at a T-J (840/151) by the farm, **turn R for 0.1m, then L on a BW,** UH **and rejoin the main route at no.9** (843/152).

EXTENSION 2:

+7.5 miles & +395 metres of climbing

A Turn R at the T-J and follow the green arrows, to the farm buildings and **bear L** then **keep R,** UH. To a T-J with the good farm track (SDW) (873/167) **and turn R** on this for 0.65m, then **turn L off this,** on a DT, (863/168) UH into the woods.

B After 0.3m **bear L on the DT** (ignore the BW SA), then shortly **bear R off the DT on a BW.** Go DH for 0.5m to a T-J with a DT (860/159) **and turn R,** to an off-set X-tracks and **turn L** then shortly **R at the fork** (by a tower). **Follow this for 1m** on a grassy DH, **to the rd** (875/155).

C Turn R on the rd for 0.15m, then L on a driveway (Singleton Oil field), **and immediately L again on a BW** (874/153). **Keep SA** (L then R) **on the BW at the rd,** through the woods. **Join a DT and keep SA/L on this,** on the the RHS of the wood.

D To some X-tracks (888/146) **and keep SA** (to the L of the house, then bear R behind it), **to a fork and bear R. DH on this for 0.3m** (bearing sharp L) **to a T-J** (890/141) **and turn L** follow the shortcut directions from no.2, back into Cocking.

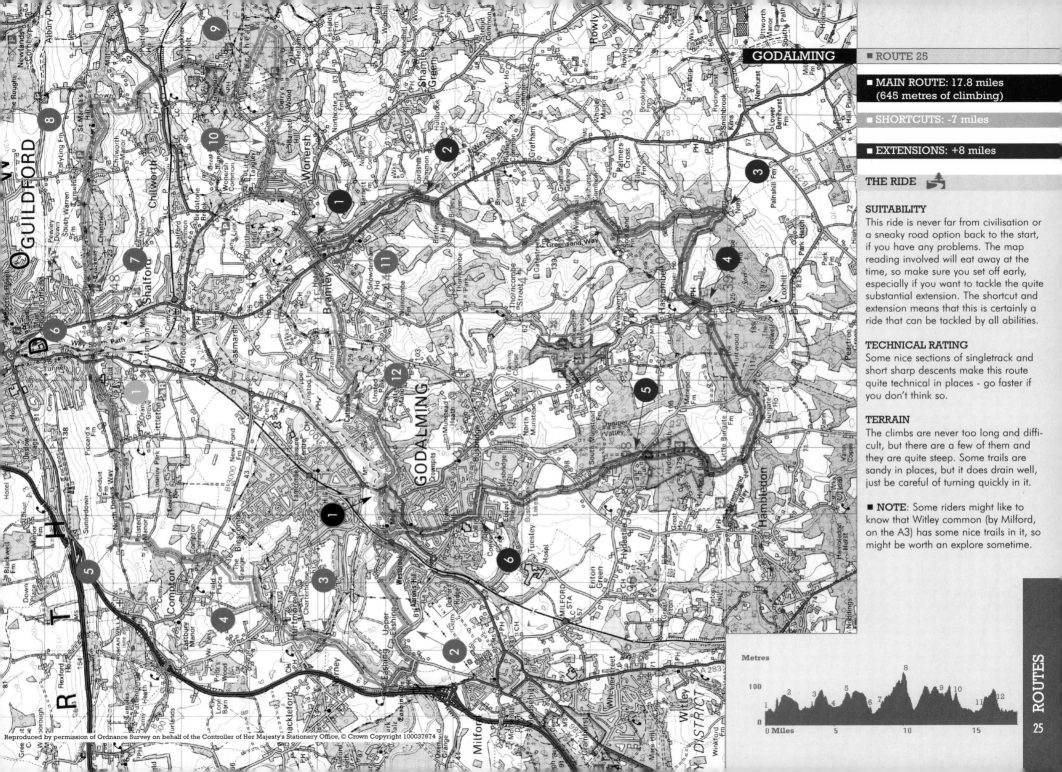

ROUTE 25

- **MAIN ROUTE: 17.8 miles** (645 metres of climbing)
- **SHORTCUTS: -7 miles**
- **EXTENSIONS: +8 miles**

THE RIDE

SUITABILITY
This ride is never far from civilisation or a sneaky road option back to the start, if you have any problems. The map reading involved will eat away at the time, so make sure you set off early, especially if you want to tackle the quite substantial extension. The shortcut and extension means that this is certainly a ride that can be tackled by all abilities.

TECHNICAL RATING
Some nice sections of singletrack and short sharp descents make this route quite technical in places - go faster if you don't think so.

TERRAIN
The climbs are never too long and difficult, but there are a few of them and they are quite steep. Some trails are sandy in places, but it does drain well, just be careful of turning quickly in it.

- **NOTE:** Some riders might like to know that Witley common (by Milford, on the A3) has some nice trails in it, so might be worth an explore sometime.

25

Reproduced by permission of Ordnance Survey on behalf of the Controller of Her Majesty's Stationery Office, © Crown Copyright 100037674

■ MAIN ROUTE

17.8 miles & 645 metres of climbing

① START. Go back to the Burys rd and follow this (west), keeping SA/R (on Moss lane), to the High street and turn R on this. 0.2m to a T-J with Station rd (967/437) and turn R for 0.15m then bear R on Station approach then immediately L on Westbrook rd. Go under the railway, then immediately turn L on the (New way) BW (966/441) and follow this for 1.15m to a rd (953/436).

② Turn R on the rd for 0.45m, then R on The Hollow rd (948/435) (Eashing). 0.4m, past the Stagg pub, over a bridge, **and turn R on a BW** (between the Old farm stable and The Cottage) (944/439), before the A3, and follow this for 0.75m to a X-tracks.

③ Go SA, UH, for 0.3m and bear R at a fork (no signs) to a rd (953/455) and go SA on a BW to another rd and go SA on the BW (R of the house gates). DH for 0.2m (by a field) and bear R, to the far end and turn sharp L on a ST and follow this to a rd and turn L on this to a X-rds (963/466).

④ Go SA (R then L) on Withies lane for 0.3m to a T-J (963/470) and turn R. After 0.4m, at the end, go SA by Polsted Manor house on the BW, for 0.25m to a X-tracks (966/478) and turn R on the NDW.

⑤ After 0.4m bear R on the BW into the woods, for another 0.45m to the corner of a rd (980/479). Go SA/L on this rd for 0.85m to a T-J with the A3100 rd, and turn R on this, then immediately L back on the NDW (992/482), DH to the river. Turn R to and over a bridge, or see the shortcut.

⑥ Turn L on the other side, then shortly R

through some gates. heading away from the river. Keep SA, across the playing fields to a rd (998/483), and go SA on the Pilgrims Way rd. After 0.25m bear R off the rd on Guilford Nature trail BW (002/484).

⑦ Follow this for 1.15m to a rd (020/483) and turn L on this, then immediately R on a BW. After 0.25m, UH on the sand, bear R at a fork onto a narrower track (no sign) and follow this for 0.5m to a Downs link sign (031/483) and turn R at this.

⑧ DH for 0.5m to a T-J (030/476), and turn L on the (Downs Link) driveway, over a rd for 0.5m to a fork (037/466). Bear R (on the downs link, through the woods) for 0.35m to a rd (032/463). Turn L on this to a X-rds and turn L then immediately R on a BW (033/462). After 0.75m turn R on a BW (042/457), before the UH to some houses.

⑨ Follow this BW, bearing R, along the deep rut, UH, to a rd (034/456) and go SA on a BW. Bear L at the barriers, and keep L, on a steep DH, to an old farm (FP on L) and keep SA, UH. Past a cemetery to a track and bear R to a rd (026/457).

⑩ Turn L on this rd, for 0.55m, through a village, to a T-J (017/458) and turn L for 0.4m to another T-J (016/452) (opposite a pub). Turn R on this rd for 0.7m to a T-J with the A281 or see the extension.

⑪ Turn R for 0.1m then L on Clockhouse lane (007/450) and keep SA on the BW, to a rd (997/446). Go SA on the BW for 0.5m to a T-J (989/444), and turn R for 0.2m to a DT (986/446) and turn L on the BW.

⑫ Keep SA as this becomes Catteshall lane, joining Wharf Street (982/441) and keep SA/L on this. 0.5m to a roundabout. and bear L to a T-J and turn R to another roundabout. Turn L on Bridge street, then immediately R on The Burys, (973/440) back to the car park.

-7 miles & -400 metres of climbing

① Keep SA on the path alongside the RHS of the river Wey for 3.5m all the way back to the A3100 rd (973/441) in Godalming (NOT the Wey-south path). Turn L on this rd to a roundabout and go SA/R on Bridge street, then immediately R on The Burys, and back to the car park.

EXTENSION:

+8 miles & +285 metres of climbing

① After 0.55m (i.e. before the T-J with the A281) turn L on the Riverside trail (Downs link) (009/450). Follow this good track for 1.15m to a bridge (018/435) and bear R, up to the top. Turn R at the top to the (A281) rd and turn L on this, DH for 0.15m, then turn R on a BW (before Briteley Nursing home) (016/432).

② Follow this for 0.6m, bearing R by a farmhouse, to a T-J (010/427) and turn L. After 0.25m, at a T-J, turn R and follow this, which becomes a drive, and keep SA to a rd T-J (016/408). Turn R on the rd for 0.3m, then turn L on a BW, and keep SA on this DT for 1m to a T-J (015/930).

③ Turn sharp R on a BW, as the DT bears sharp L, UH, for 0.2m bear R at a fork, for another 0.15m, then fork L (012/394), DH for 0.7m to a rd (002/396) in Hascombe. Turn L on the rd for 0.15m to the main rd, by the pub, and turn L on this for 0.1m, then turn R on a BW (000/392).

④ Go 0.1m to a X-tracks (999/393) and turn L on Greensands way, and follow this for 0.85m to a rd (988/387). Go SA on the BW, bearing L, UH to the edge of the field and along the woods edge, to a T-J and turn R, then L to a rd (978/387). Turn R, UH, becoming sandy, for 0.35m to a hut and bear R, UH, on this BW for 0.75m, to a car park (978/402).

⑤ Go SA, over the main rd onto Clock barn lane for 0.3m then turn L on a (drive) BW (976/407) after a nursery. After 0.1m bear R off the drive, on the BW, DH, to a rd (974/411) and go SA on a BW. Go past Busbridge lakes, UH to a rd (973/426) and turn L on this for 0.25m to a T-J (969/426) and turn R (Tuesley rd).

⑥ Follow this rd (R at the fork), becoming Holloway hill, to some X-rds (lights) with the A3100 rd (967/436). Go SA on the High street, bearing bears R, for 0.2m then turn L on Moss lane and follow this back to the car park (971/440).

🚗 GETTING THERE

This ride starts from the Crown Court car park (971/440) in the town of Godalming. Exit the A3 and follow the A3100 road into Godalming to the a roundabout by the river and turn left on Bridge street, then shortly right on The Burys, and the car park is off this. There is also a railway station in Godalming, right near the start.

🛏 ACCOMMODATION

B&B in Shalford on: 01483 202685
B&B in Godalming on: 01428 682808
YHA in Hinehead (nr Haslemere) on tel: 0870 7705864 or Tanner hatch (nr Dorking) on: 0870 7706060
Guildford T.I. on: 01483 444333

🚲 BICYCLE SHOPS

Guilford cycles (in Guildford of course) on tel: 01483 300380
Beyond mountain bikes in Cranleigh on: 01483 267676

🍴 REFRESHMENTS

Plenty of choice in Godalming, and pubs in Eashing, Hurtmorem, Compton, Blackheath and Wonersh. Also in Hascombe on the extension, and in Shalford on the shortcut.

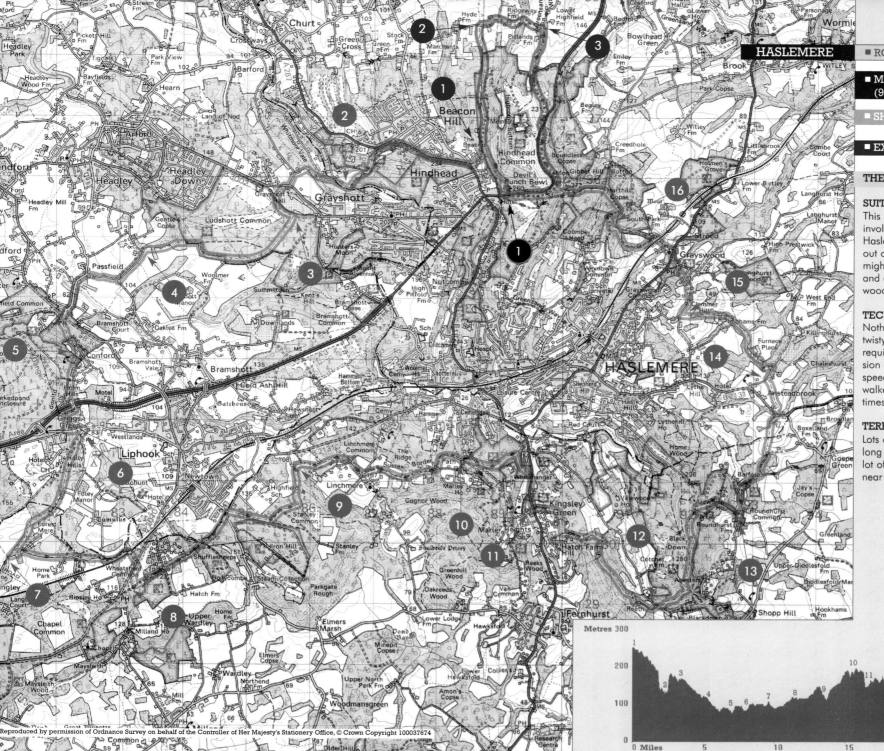

■ ROUTE 26

■ MAIN ROUTE: 26.6 miles
(935 metres of climbing)

■ SHORTCUTS: Possible

■ EXTENSIONS: +4.9 miles

THE RIDE

SUITABILITY

This is a long route with lots of climbing involved, but it does circle the town of Haslemere, so there are various bail-out options. Less experienced riders are might prefer to just ride the extension and check out the (open access) FC woods around here.

TECHNICAL RATING

Nothing too dangerous, but the long, twisty, steep, woodland singletracks will require your full attention. The extension also offers a lovely long, high speed descent, but be very careful of walkers (best attempted at off-peak times).

TERRAIN

Lots of woodland singletrack, along this long undulating ride, which has quite a lot of climbing, with two very steep ones near the end - so reserve your energy.

ROUTES

26

GETTING THERE

This ride starts from the in Devil's Punch Bowl (National Trust) car park on Hindhead common (890/357). This is just off the A3, north of Haslemere, by the Devil's bowl cafe. There is a train station in Haslemere and Liphook, close to the route.

ACCOMMODATION

B&B's on: 01428 653120 and 658023, both in Haslemere.
YHA at the Devils punchbowl, on: 0870 7705864
Camping at Liphook, on: Haslemere (museum) information desk on: 01428 645425

BICYCLE SHOPS

Nothing in Haslemere, but there is Liphook cycles in Liphook on: 01428 727858, Cycleworks in Guildford on: 01483 300380 , The Sensible Bicycle Co. in Petersfield on: 01730 266 554 and Beyond mountain bikes in Cranleigh on: 01483 267676

REFRESHMENTS

A National trust cafe at the start / end of the ride, and pubs in Conford, Griggs Green, Wheatsheaf common, Grayswood and lots of choice in Haslemere.

ROUTES

26.6 miles & 935 metres of climbing

1 START. Head north across the grass, to a BW, and turn L on this, for 0.5m, to a X-tracks (887/364), and turn L on a BW, or see the extension. Go past a car park, joining a drive, to the A287 rd (885/362) and turn R on this rd. After 1m, turn L on a ByW (870/364), after the shops, DH, for 0.5m to a rd (866/358).

2 Turn R on this for 0.15m to a fork and bear L (Whitmoor vale), UH, for 0.15m then turn L on a ByW (861/359). 0.3m, UH, along the edge of the woods, to a rd, and turn L on this to a T-J with the B3002. Turn R on this for 0.05m then turn L on a BW into Ludshott common, for 0.2m to a X-tracks (854/355).

3 Turn L, for 0.2m then turn R (857/353) on a BW. Keep SA on this for 0.8m (SA at some X-tracks, for another 0.1m), to a fork (847/349) and bear R (847/346). 0.45m to another fork and bear L, which becomes a ByW, for 0.55m to a rd (833/347).

4 Turn L on this (Gentles lane) rd, for 0.4m, DH, to a T-J (829/342), and turn R. Keep L, through Passfield on Passfield rd, to the B3004 rd, and go SA on a track, then immediately L on a BW (820/336). Through some woods, joining a rd in Conford, for 0.05m then turn R on a BW (823/330), back into the woods.

5 Over a footbridge, UH, on the (main track) BW, for 0.55m to a bridge over the A3 (821/322). Go over this, into the wood, to a rd, by a gate. Turn L on the rd for 0.0.15m then turn R on a ByW (824/318) (Campsite & hotel), to a 3-way junction.

6 Take the central BW, UH, bearing L into the woods, and keep SA over some X-tracks, joining a track. Keep SA at the end of the track, on the BW, to a fork (818/304), and bear R. Keep SA on this for 0.65m, along the edge of the woods, to a X-tracks (812/297), and turn sharp L on the Sussex border path (SBP).

7 Follow the SBP, bearing R at the tarmac after 0.15m, past a lake on the LHS, for 0.5m to a fork (just past Home park estate on the R). Bear L, leaving the SBP which goes R), on a ST BW, which joins a rd, and bears R, over the railway, to the B2020 rd. Cross the rd and turn R on a BW, along the golf course, to a X-tracks (832/292).

8 Turn L, on the SBP for 1.2m to a 3-way rd junction, and go SA then immediately R (847/305)on the SBP. 0.8m to some X-tracks (858/306) and turn L on a BW (the SBP, SA is a FP). 0.4m to a house (857/312), and turn R, back on the SBP.

9 Keep SA on the (grassy) SBP at a X-tracks R into the woods, for 0.05m then L following the fence to a rd (866/313). Turn R on the rd for 0.2m then turn L on Linchmere rd, then immediately R at a fork, on the SBP (868/311). After 0.75m, join a drive, bear L at the fork (880/312), (leaving the SBP), on a BW, to a rd (884/313).

10 Go SA on a BW, into the woods, for 0.55m (rejoins the SBP) to a fork (892/314) and turn R on a ST BW, leaving the SBP. Along the hill, then DH to the A286 rd, and turn R on this, UH, for 0.35m, then turn L on a BW, (895/305) on Hatch lane.

11 Keep SA/L on the BW, for 0.5m to a T-J (with a FP) and turn L on the BW. 0.25m, to the side of a house, to a T-J, and turn L. UH, on this ByW for 0.15m, to a (track) T-J (906/300). Turn R and follow the BW for 0.8m to a fork and bear R, joining a track and bearing L on this, to a rd (914/289).
■ **NOTE:** There are a lot more trails in Black Down, than the map shows.

12 Go SA (on the LHS) BW, going steeply UH, to a view point (919/292). Head north, along the ridge, joining the SBP after 0.75m, and turn R on this, and follow it, past a couple of car parks, and bearing R, steeply DH on a ST, to a rd (927/304).

13 Turn L on the rd for 0.3m to a fork and bear R, DH, on Jays lane, for 0.25m then turn L on a BW (931/311). Follow this BW for 0.65m, through the woods and a stream, joining a track and keep SA, to a rd (933/321). Go SA on the BW opposite, UH, along the field edge, to a tarmac track and turn L on this, to a rd.

14 Turn R on the rd for 0.15m then turn L on a BW (drive) (933/329), and keep SA on the BW, by a big house (Furnace place). After 0.35m, past some ponds, to a junction and keep SA, through a farm, UH, to the top of a hill, then DH, to a rd (918/337).

15 Turn R on the rd, for 0.35m to a fork and bear L (Grayswood), for 0.3m to the A286 rd. Turn R on this for 0.1m, then L on a BW (917/348), after the church. UH, for 0.3m, (under a railway bridge) to a T-J (914/350) and turn L on the BW, UH, for 0.6m to a T-J in the woods (907/351).

16 Turn R on the BW (forest track), and keep SA on this BW, UH, bearing L at a (BW) fork, to a X-tracks (900/358) with a ByW. Turn L, UH, to a X-tracks with the Greensands way, and go SA on the ByW. Keep SA on this ByW, for 0.5m, parallel with, then to the A3 rd, and (carefully) cross this rd, back to the cafe and car park (890/357).

EXTENSION:

+4.9 miles & +225 metres of climbing

1 Go SA on a good BW track, (not R on the BW going steeply DH), for 0.3m to a fork (by a memorial) and bear L, leaving the DT (887/369). DH, for 0.5m and bear L at the fork (easy to miss), DH, on a ST, for 0.5m to a rd at the bottom (886/384).

2 Turn R on the rd, for 0.2m, then keep SA on a ByW, as the rd bears sharp L. Past a farm, onto a dark track, DH, over the footbridge at the bottom, and bear R, UH, on the ByW. Turn L at the tarmac drive, to a. grass triangle (896/384) and turn R on the Greensands way (GSW) ByW.

3 Follow this, UH, for 1.1m to the A3 rd (896/368) and go SA on the (GSW) ByW. Follow this ByW track for another 1.25m, (bearing R after 0.7m, leaving the GSW (989/358)), parallel, then to the A3 rd. Cross the A3 rd (carefully), back to the cafe and car park (890/357) and rejoin the main route at no1.

HIGHLY RECOMMENDED

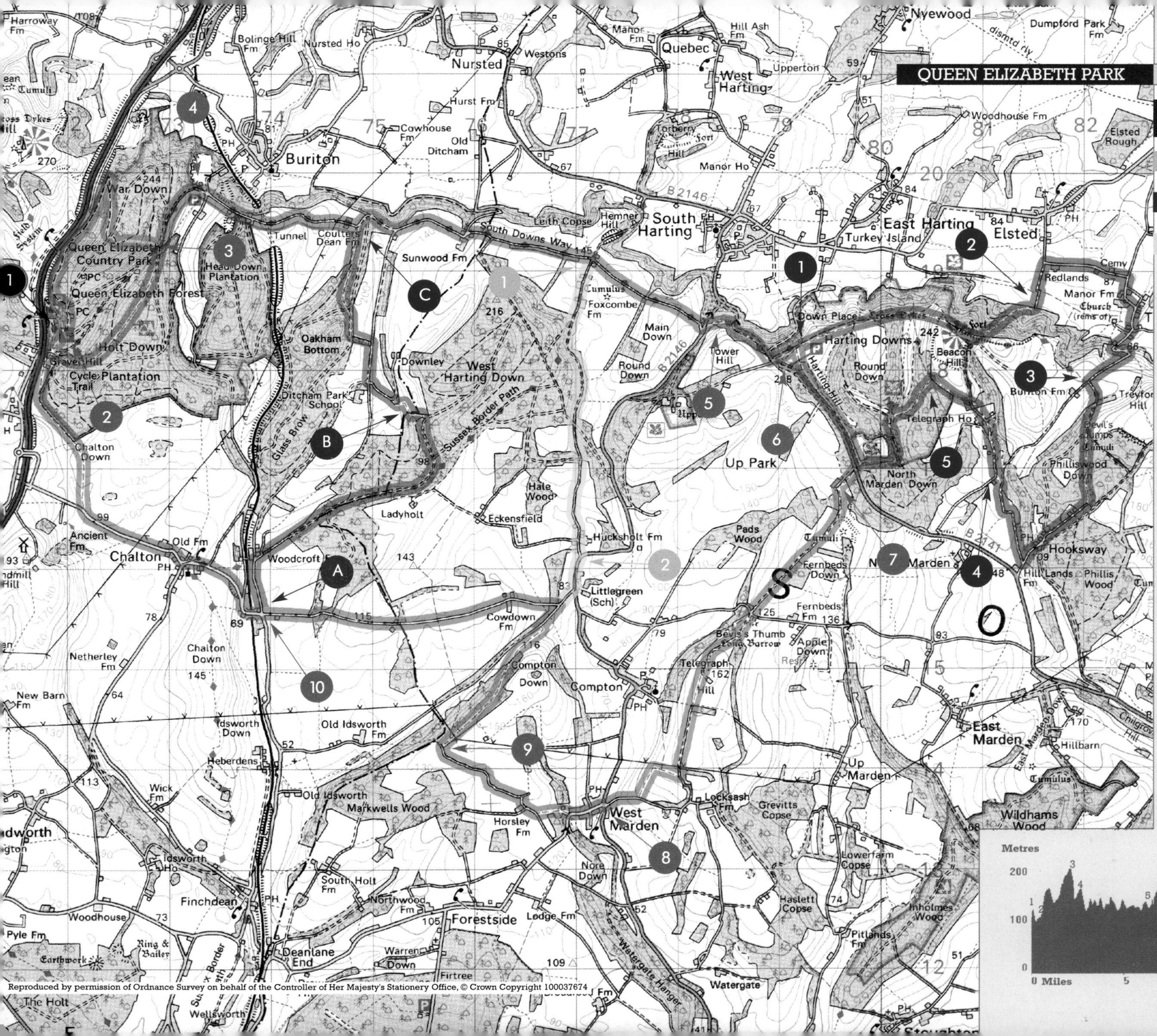

■ ROUTE 27

■ **MAIN ROUTE: 17.5 miles** (745 metres of climbing)

■ **SHORTCUTS: -5.7 miles**

■ **EXTENSIONS: +6.3 & 3.6 miles**

THE RIDE

SUITABILITY

This is a pretty hilly route, with lots of small ups and downs, but it is easy to navigate so you can just get on with it all. There are a few challenging parts to the ride (and more on the extensions), but less experienced riders should be able to cope. There is also a family and advanced MTB'er waymarked cycle trail in the QECP forest.

TECHNICAL RATING

This ride has a good amount of technical and flowing singletrack and fast downhills to challenge your skills.

TERRAIN

There is some great woodland (or tree lined) singletrack and a long section of the South Downs Way. This can get slippery (especially tree roots) in places when wet, but generally drains well.

■ **NOTE:** The QECP has 2 MTB trails: an advanced (orange) 3 mile MTB trail and a 3 mile family gravel track. There are also over 500 acres of open access FC woodland to explore here, and a cafe, information centre, adventure playground, and B-B-Q's for hire.

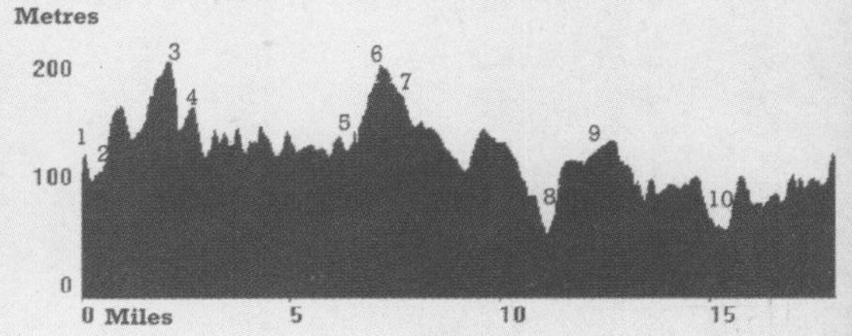

ROUTES

27

■ MAIN ROUTE

EXTENSION 1:

EXTENSION 2:

GETTING THERE

The ride starts from the Queens Elizabeth Country park car park which is just south of Petersfield (nr Clanfield), off the A3. Follow the brown signs for the QECP, to the visitors centre and car park (GR 718/185) which costs £1 or £1.50 on Sunday, for the whole day. There is a railway at Petersfield (but you'll need to head south on the B2070, to Buriton and join the main route around there).

ACCOMMODATION

B&B at Heath Farmhouse on: 01730 264709
B&B in Petersfield on: 01730 268829
Petersfield T.I. on: 01730 268829

BICYCLE SHOPS

The Sensible Bicycle Co. on: 01730 266 554 and Owens Cycles on: 01730 260446, both in Petersfield.

REFRESHMENTS

There is a café, B-B-Q's for hire, toilet, etc at the visitors centre, tel: 023 92595040. There are pubs on the route in West Marden, Charlton, and on extension 1 in Hooksway.

MAIN ROUTE

17.5 miles & 745 metres of climbing

1 START. From the visitor centre, go to the Woodland area sign (719/185), and turn R, following the orange wooden posts. After 0.25m turn L, UH on a DT, just before a rd and Gravel hill car park just ahead.

2 To a minor rd and turn L on this, then L again at the 2nd orange post, into the woods. Follow the orange markers (parallel to the A3 rd), bearing sharp R, then L, DH across a track, and keep SA, UH to a T-J with a DT (792/192).

3 Turn L on this DT (South downs way), leaving the cycle trail and QECP, and keep SA on this DT, bearing R and DH. Go through the car park to the 3-way rd junction (733/198), and go SA on the rd (SDW).

4 Keep SA for 1.75m (rd changes to off-road, then rd again) then bear R off the rd, between some buildings, just after a sharp LH bend by Sundown farm (759/193). Follow the SDW for 0.8m to a X-tracks (771/191) and keep SA or see the shortcut.

5 0.8m to the B2146 rd, and go SA on the SDW, parallel to rd, for another 0.5m, then bear L, over the rd (789/181). After 0.15m (on Harting Downs), turn R on the BW (791/182) or see extension 1.

6 Follow this BW for 0.85m, parallel to the rd, to a T-J and turn R to the rd (797/170), and cross this, onto the BW opposite.

7 Go past the horse jumps, then R through a rusty gate, and keep SA to a rd (787/155). Go SA, over the rd, then immediately keep L/SA at the fork, on a DT for

1.15m to a T-J (780/139) just after going under the elec.cables. Turn R, off the DT, and keep/bear L, DH to a rd and turn R on this to a X-rds (772/136) into West Marden.

8 Go SA on the rd for 0.2m then keep SA on a BW, as rd bears sharp L, 0.2m UH to a T-J (766/135). Turn R on the track and shortly R at fork (by houses), to a T-J and turn L, for 0.6m to the wood (756/142).

9 Turn R on a BW (FP only SA), then immediately R at a fork, DH through the woods, to a rd. Turn R on this, for 0.15m then turn L on track (to Cowdown farm) (768/156). 9a - Keep SA, becoming nice track between the trees, for 1.9m, to a 3-way rd junction (739/155), and go SA or see extension 2.

10 Over a railway bridge, bearing R, then keep L, UH, into Chalton and keep R at the fork (Clanfield / A3) by the Red Lion pub. After 0.7m, turn R on a BW (721/166), and keep SA on this, past Gravel hill car park, to the visitor centre (718/185).

SHORTCUT:

-5.7 miles & -125 metres of climbing

1 Turn R at the X-tracks for 0.4m (past Foxcombe farm) to a fork and bear L, along the LHS of the woods, for 0.7m to a X-tracks (769/174). Keep SA on this SA/L for 0.85m, past Hucksholt farm to a rd.

2 Go SA/R on this rd for 0.2m then turn R on a track (770/157) opposite a school, (769/157), past Cowdown farm and rejoin the main route at no.9a.

EXTENSION 1:

+6.3 miles & +400 metres of climbing

1 Keep SA on the feint grassy (SDW) track, for 0.75m, DH, to the bottom of Beacon Hill, and keep SA, to and over the top. DH, to the X-tracks at the bottom (809/183), and turn L, going steeply DH in the woods.

2 After 0.4m, at the edge of the woods, turn L on a DT, and keep SA on this for 0.3m to a rd (816/190) and turn R on this. After 0.5m turn R at the T-J, into Treyford, over the stream and turn R on a (dead end) rd (824/184). Go steeply, UH, for 0.65m, levels out, and turn L on a BW coming across the DT (821/179), back on the SDW.

3 After 0.35m, bear R at a feint fork (easy to miss) on a BW (820/174) (leaving the SDW, DT), into the woods. DH, for 0.4m and bear R on a DT past the houses, joining a rd. Follow this for 0.15m past the Royal Oak pub, then R on a R.O.W. (814/160).

4 After 0.55m bear L at a fork, on a BW, down a drive, to another DT (811/169) and turn R on this. After 0.5m, past a posh house, to a fork and bear L. After 0.4m on this, turn L on a grassy BW (shortly after going through a gate) (805/179).

5 Go DH to a T-J at the bottom (by a wooden circular fence) and turn L and follow this BW, bearing R to a rd (797/170) and go SA on a BW, rejoining the main route at no.7.

EXTENSION 2:

+3.6 miles & +180 metres of climbing

A Turn R on the rd for 0.35m to Woodcroft farm and bear R on the Sussex Border Path. After 1.25m, UH, bear L on the DT, (755/169) leaving the SBP (FP only, SA), for 0.35m, then keep SA/L on the BW, leaving the DT as it bears R.

B Steep UH, for 0.5m to a T-J by Ditcham park school, and turn R on this for 0.25m then turn L on a BW (750/182) into the woods. After 0.15m bear R, for another 0.2m then keep SA on the BW, as the DT bears L, and follow this for 0.55m to a DT (SDW) (748/194) (been here before).

C Turn L and retrace your earlier tracks i.e. keep SA for 1m and go SA through the car park (733/198), bearing L, UH, to where you left the Orange trail (729/192) on the R. Follow the orange markers SA/L just inside the woods (haven't ridden this before) back to the visitor centre (719/185).

This route will provide a great day out for riders of all abilities.

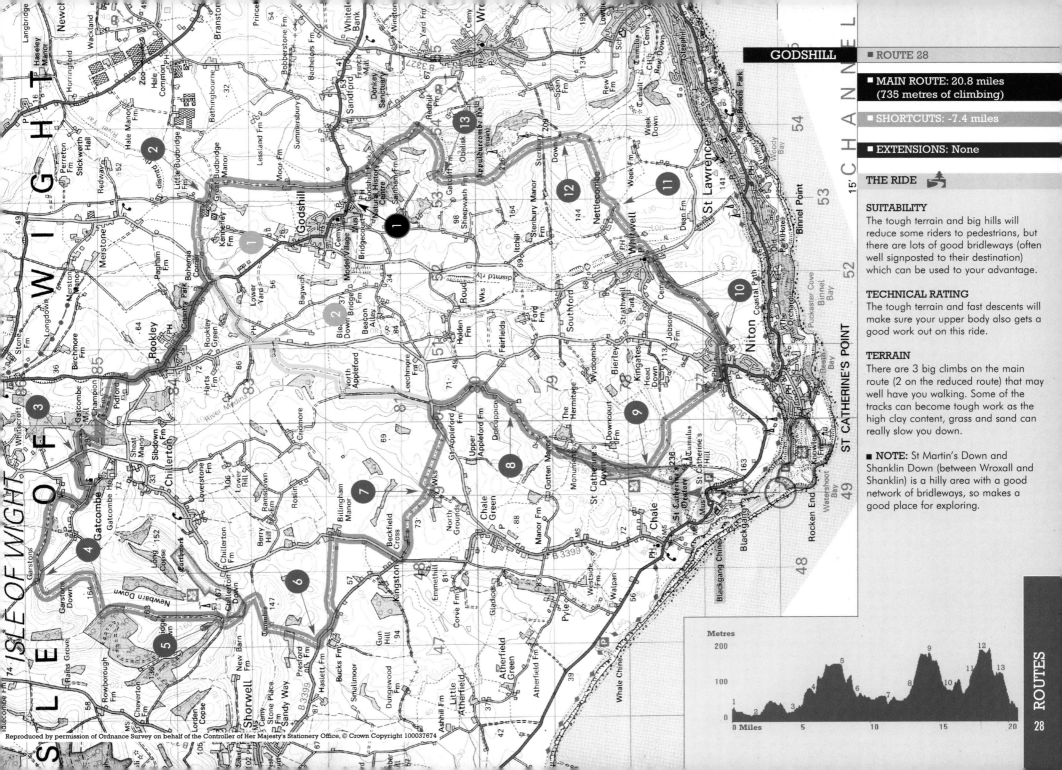

■ MAIN ROUTE: 20.8 miles
(735 metres of climbing)

■ SHORTCUTS: -7.4 miles

■ EXTENSIONS: None

THE RIDE

SUITABILITY
The tough terrain and big hills will reduce some riders to pedestrians, but there are lots of good bridleways (often well signposted to their destination) which can be used to your advantage.

TECHNICAL RATING
The tough terrain and fast descents will make sure your upper body also gets a good work out on this ride.

TERRAIN
There are 3 big climbs on the main route (2 on the reduced route) that may well have you walking. Some of the tracks can become tough work as the high clay content, grass and sand can really slow you down.

■ **NOTE:** St Martin's Down and Shanklin Down (between Wroxall and Shanklin) is a hilly area with a good network of bridleways, so makes a good place for exploring.

ROUTES

28

ROUTES

28

🚗 GETTING THERE

Get a ferry to the Isle of Wight (WightLink ferries on: 0870 582 7744, 0239 2751751or www.wightlink.co.uk or Hovertravel on: 01983 811000, 0239 2811000 or www.hovertravel.co.uk) then follow signs to Newport, then keep on to Godshill, south on the A3020 for 6 miles and find a place to park.

🛏 ACCOMMODATION

B&B in Whitwell on: 01983 731242
Hotel (Palmerston) in Shanklin is bike friendly, and on: 01983 865547
YHA in Sandown (on the east coast) on: 0870 7706020.
Camping at Sandown on tel: 01983 403432, Shanklin on: 01983 867028 and Wroxall on: 01983 852597
Newport T.I. on: 01983 813818

🚲 BICYCLE SHOPS

Offshore Sports in Shanklin on: 01983 866 269, and First gear on: 01983 521417 and Wight Mountain on: 01983 520530, both in Newport.

🍴 REFRESHMENTS

There is a cafe, shops, and pubs in Godshill. On the route there are some pubs and shops in Rookley, Niton, and Whitwell. There is also a pub on the shortcut, just south of Rookley.

20.8 miles & 735 metres of climbing

① **START.** Go east on the A3020 rd, towards Shanklin, **and shortly after leaving Godshill, turn L on the (GL46) Great Budbridge Manor BW (532/817).** Follow this sandy track for 1.1m to a T-J (532/834), and turn L, bearing R with the DT, by the manor, then immediately **turn L on a BW** (farm track through the fields), (530/837).

② Keep SA to a rd and turn L on this to a T-J, with the A3020 rd (519/835) and **turn R on this,** or see the shortcut. Follow this rd for 1.25m (through Rookley village), then turn L on a BW (506/848). Join a DT and follow the BW, to the RHS of the house, through the woods, **bearing R, to a house, then L on a drive, to a rd.**

③ Turn R on rd, for 0.05m then L on a minor **rd** (Gatcombe) (495/853) for **0.55m, bearing R by the church, to a fork** (489/852) **and turn R, UH. After 0.2m turn L on a good DT, BW** (Garstons), as rd bears sharp R (490/855), **and keep SA on this for 0.7m to a rd.**

④ Go SA/R on the rd for 0.05m, just past the house on the R, **and turn L** (478/858) on the (Downs, Shorwell) BW, around a chalk pit. Steep UH, **through a gate and keep SA,** around the side of the hill, **to a tree** (478/850), **and turn R. Go through a gate,** to the woods, **and turn L** (south) **just past a barn** (474/849).

⑤ Follow this for 1m, past a radar mast, and **go SA at the concrete rd** (BW, X-tracks) (474/834), steeply DH. **Keep SA/L on this BW for 0.4m to a T-J** (476/829)

and turn R, UH. 0.3m to a fork (472/827) and bear L, going DH, past some woods, to the B3399 rd (470/821).

⑥ Turn L on this rd, for 0.3m then turn L on a BW (474/819) and follow this for 0.7m to a rd (484/819) opposite Billingham Manor. Turn R on the rd, for 0.6m to the B3399 rd (482/810). Turn L on the tarmac (SW41) ByW, which becomes a grassy DH, for 0.7m to the sewage works.

⑦ Go over a cattle grid and turn L on a track for 0.1m, which then bears R, UH, for 0.45m to a (Appleford) rd (498/804). Turn L on this rd, for 0.25m then turn R on a minor rd (502/806), opposite a track on the L.
7a - 0.5m to a fork (504/799) and bear R (dead end), bearing R after 0.3m on the BW (502/795), just before a house.

⑧ 0.4m to a 3-way and go SA on the BW, in between the DT's which go either side, for 0.2m to a BW fork (495/789), shortly after a BW on the R. Bear L on the BW, then immediately R at another (BW) fork (L goes to a monument), and go (south) along the ridge, for 0.3m to a fork (493/777) and bear L on the BW (FP goes R) at the base of a hill SA.

⑨ Go along the hillside for 0.5m to a X-tracks (500/774) and bear R, DH, on the BW to Niton. Join Pan lane in Niton, and keep SA to the A3055 rd (505/767), and turn L, on Church street, for 0.1m to the X-rds. Go SA on Rectory rd (Godshill), for 0.15m, then turn R then immediately L on

Allotment road, by the playground sign (510/767).

⑩ Keep SA at the end of this drive, on the BW, which becomes Ashknowle lane BW, for 0.7m to a rd. Go SA (slight L) on the (Wroxall) BW (522/777), grassy DH, over a bridge, and turn R then L over an old railway. Stay on the BW, UH along the field edge, to a stoney track by a small lake, and turn R on this, for 0.05m then L on the (Wroxhall) BW (529/781).

⑪ Tough UH, bearing R after 0.25m along the field edge, for 0.05m then turn L through a (metal) gate (532/783). 0.45m, UH, to the top of the hill (538/786) (posts, but no signs on them), on a feint track across a field. Bear L (north) through some gates towards some masts, on the Wroxall BW (GL48), going to the LHS of the masts, becoming a ST.

⑫ UH, then DH to a (BW) fork (533/797) and bear R (north) along the LHS of the hillside (with an obelisk at the top). 0.5m, bearing R, to a junction (533/805) with some tall gates.

⑬ Keep SA on the (GL49) BW (Godshill & Wroxall). 0.5m, DH, to a X-tracks (540/807) and turn L, DH on a better track, for 0.8m to the A3020 rd and turn L on this rd, back into Godshill (529/816).

---

① Turn L on the A3020 rd, for 0.05m then turn R (519/834) on Chequers Inn road (Chale). After 0.4m keep R at a fork for 0.3m to a X-rds (511/829) by a pub. Take the 2nd L (main rd, not Bagwich lane), for 0.2m then R on the (GL9) BW (Wilderness & Gridmore) (510/826).

② 0.3m to a fork (507/824) and bear L, for 0.4m then turn R on the BW, UH, to a DT, by a building (503/817). Turn L on this DT, for 0.75m to a 3-way rd junction (502/806) and go SA on the rd opposite, and rejoin the main route at no.7a.

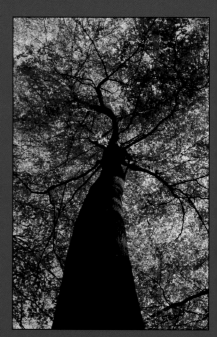

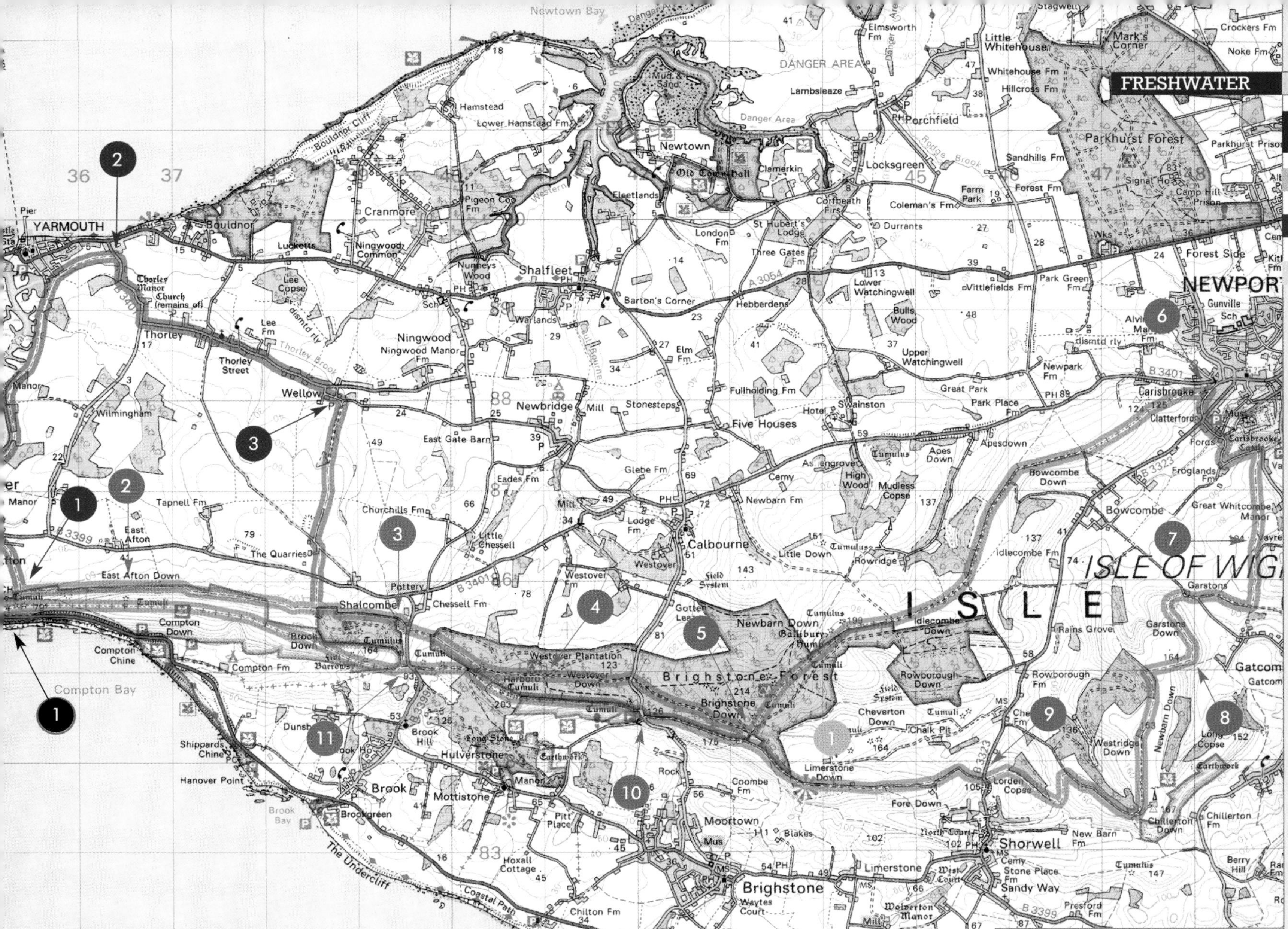

FRESHWATER

■ ROUTE 29

■ **MAIN ROUTE: 23 miles** (870 metres of climbing)

■ SHORTCUTS: -11.7 miles

■ EXTENSIONS: +4.5 miles

THE RIDE

SUITABILITY

A tough 'classic' Isle of Wight MTB ride, but the shortcut halves the distance and almost halves the climbing to make it more appealing to less experienced riders.

TECHNICAL RATING

There are numerous good descents and challenging terrain that will test your skills and require you full attention.

TERRAIN

Hilly, quiet, remote, downland, forest, field edge, and singletrack riding, which doesn't see to many mountain bikers.

■ **NOTE:** Brighstone forest is an open access FC forest which has some good trails in it, (including a downhill course at grid reference 434/851).

TOP TIP: If you are just going for the day it will be cheaper to go as a foot passenger from Lymington to Yarmouth and join the ride on the extension.

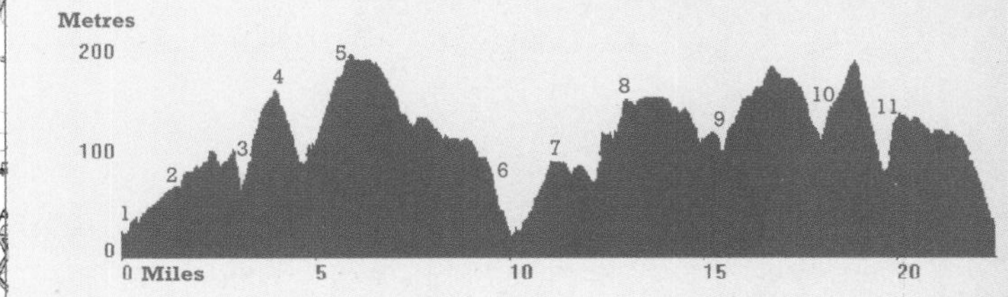

ROUTES

29

■ MAIN ROUTE

GETTING THERE

Get a ferry to the Isle of Wight (WightLink ferries on: 0870 582 7744, 0239 2751751or www.wight link.co.uk or Hovertravel on: 01983 811000, 0239 2811000 or www.hov-ertravel.co.uk then head for Freshwater and park in the (cliff side) car park (351/856), off the A3055.

ACCOMMODATION

B&B in Freshwater on: 01983 753723
B&B's in Carisbrooke on: 01983 524359/522173 and 523463.
Palmerston Hotel on: 01983 865547
Campsites at Grange farm, Brighstone on: 01983 740296, Stoats farm, Totland bay on: 01983 755258 & Compton farm on: 01983 740215
YHA in Totland Bay (on the West coast) on: 0870 7706070
Yarmouth T.I. on: 01983 813818

BICYCLE SHOPS

First gear on: 01983 521417 and Wight mountain on: 520530 in Newport and Isle cycle hire in Yarmouth on: 01983 760219

REFRESHMENTS

There aren't any pubs actually on the route, but there are some just off them in: Freshwater, Yarmouth, Carisbrooke, and Shorwell.

23 miles & 870 metres of climbing

1 START. Go towards Freshwater on the A3055 rd, after 0.1m turn R on Southdown rd (349/857), and shortly R again on the Old Highway, Carisbrooke **BW** towards the Golf club. After 0.45m bear L at the fork, **DH** on the (F32 Freshwater way) **BW**, then shortly R on the Pilgrims way, along the edge of the golf course or see the extension.

2 After 0.8m, at the end of the golf course, go through some gates onto a grassy track, along the bottom, (east). After 1.35m, go through a gate, and bear R into the woods (386/857).

3 Follow this BW to a T-J and turn R on the farm track, DH, to the rd (395/855). Cross the rd onto the (Bridgestone forest) **BW SA**, for 0.3m through a gate, and R at the fork, UH, for 0.4m to a DT (403/851), and turn L on this, for 0.45m to multiple X-tracks.

4 Keep SA on the main track, DH, for 0.6m to a rd (419/849) and keep SA on the BW. Keep SA at X-tracks on the (BS9 Carisbrooke) BW, keeping R, on the lower track, for 0.9m, to Bridgestone down five lane ends (432/843) and turn L on the Tennyson trail (N139) or see the shortcut.

5 Keep SA on this ByW (SA at some X-tracks, through a gate on the N136a, bearing R on the main track Old Highway N128 Carisbrooke, and SA at the X-tracks on the N123) for 4.2m, DH to a tarmac T-J (481/881).

6 Turn sharp R to the rd and go SA (R then L) at the off-set X-rds onto Clatterford Shute (481/877). After 0.4m, through 2 fords,

bear L at Froglands triangle (483/872). After 0.25m, (castle on your L), turn R on the (Gatcombe N108) **BW** (486/874), before Whitcombe rd on the R.

7 0.65m to a fork and bear L on (Gatcombe G6) **BW** (486/863), for 0.4m.to a X-tracks (486/857). Turn R and follow this for 0.5m then turn L on the (Downs, Shorwell) **BW**, just past a house on the R (478/858). Around a chalk pit, steep UH, through a gate, and keep SA around the side of the hill **for 0.5m to a tree (478/850).**

8 Turn R at the tree, through a gate **to a T-J** in the woods (474/849) and turn L, to a barn. After 1m bear R by the radar mast and keep bearing R at the X-tracks **onto a con-crete rd** (474/834). **After 0.6m turn L on BW** (blue arrow) (466/838), **to gate and keep R through more gates and R again** along the edge of the woods, follow this **DH to a rd** (457/838).

9 Go SA on the (SW51 Freshwater) **BW**, and keep SA on this for 1.25m (surface changes) to the viewpoint at the top of Limerstone down (438/837). Keep SA on the main (BS10 Tennyson trail, Lynch lane) **track**, through some gates, keeping the wood on the RHS, **for 1.2m to a rd.**

10 Turn R on the rd, for 0.05m then L through a car park (420/845), on a ByW (Mottistone Down, Freshwater). After 1.3m keep SA at some X-tracks with a dirt road, through a gate into a field (402/850) and bear L on the DT, through the fields, **for 0.4m to a rd** (395/850).

11 Go SA on the track opposite, turning L at the bottom of the chalk pit, to some gates and bear R at the fork, UH on a chalk track. Follow this ByW for 2.8m along the ridge top (Brook Down), through a golf course, to a fork (359/857). Go L/SA on the (Tennyson Trail, old highway) ByW, to the A3055 rd and turn L back to the car park (351/856).

EXTENSION:

+4.5 miles & +45 metres of climbing

1 Stay on the (Freshwater) F32 BW, for 0.4m, DH to a rd and bear R on this to the main B3399 rd (350/865). Go SA/L on the (Causeway) rd, for 0.45m, then turn R on a (cycle path) BW (348/871). Follow this for 2m along the riverside, bearing to the R of Yarmouth, to the B3401 rd (364/896).

2 Turn R on this rd, staying L on this after 0.55m (366/888), through Thorley village. After another 1.35m, turn R, in Wellow village, on the round island cycle route (386/881), for 0.15m then turn R on the (S19 Hamstead Trail) BW, (388/880), by the brook.

3 UH for 1m to a rd (by a thatched cottage) and turn L then immediately R on a driveway (The Quarries) (385/863). Keep SA on the BW, to the B3399 rd and go SA on the BW opposite, UH for 0.25m, to a X-tracks (386/857) and turn L, and rejoin main route at No.3.

-11.7 miles & -375 metres of climbing

1 Turn R at the X-tracks, to another X-tracks (FP only SA) and turn R on a DT ByW , and follow this for 0.75m to a rd (421/845), and rejoin the main route at no.10.

At the heart of this ride is the lovely Brighstone forest, which is home to some great trails.

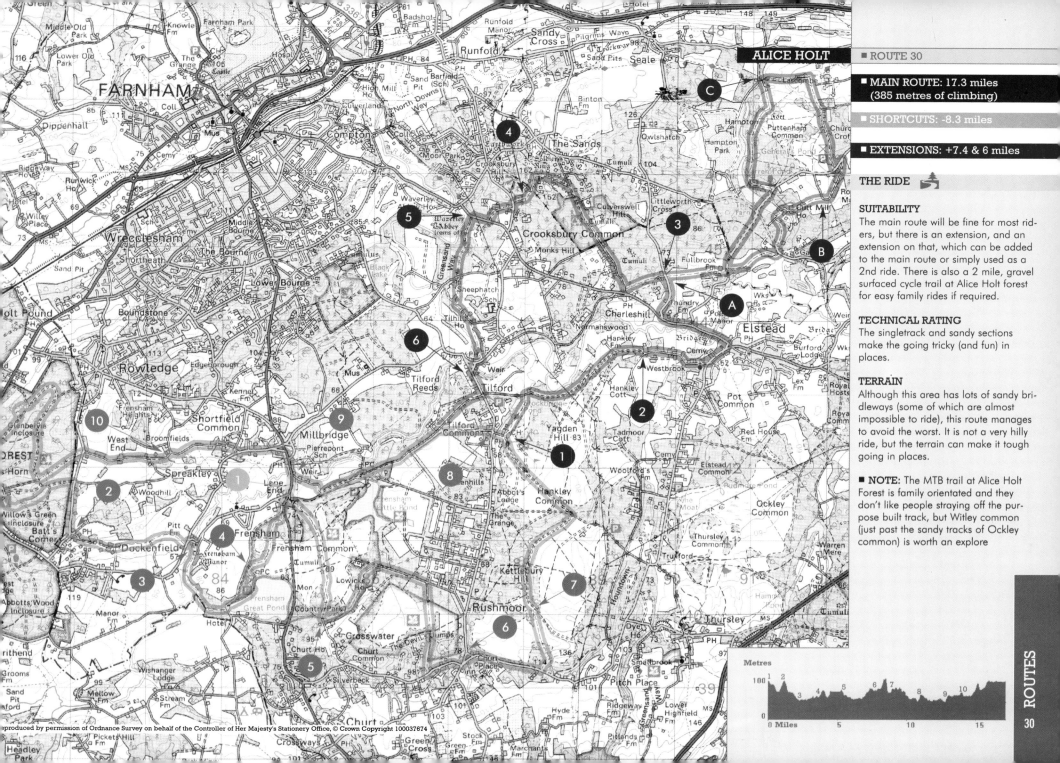

ALICE HOLT

■ **MAIN ROUTE:** 17.3 miles
(385 metres of climbing)

■ **SHORTCUTS:** -8.3 miles

■ **EXTENSIONS:** +7.4 & 6 miles

THE RIDE

SUITABILITY
The main route will be fine for most rid-ers, but there is an extension, and an extension on that, which can be added to the main route or simply used as a 2nd ride. There is also a 2 mile, gravel surfaced cycle trail at Alice Holt forest for easy family rides if required.

TECHNICAL RATING
The singletrack and sandy sections make the going tricky (and fun) in places.

TERRAIN
Although this area has lots of sandy bri-dleways (some of which are almost impossible to ride), this route manages to avoid the worst. It is not a very hilly ride, but the terrain can make it tough going in places.

■ **NOTE:** The MTB trail at Alice Holt Forest is family orientated and they don't like people straying off the pur-pose built track, but Witley common (just past the sandy tracks of Ockley common) is worth an explore

Metres

0 Miles   5   10   15

ROUTES

30

Reproduced by permission of Ordnance Survey on behalf of the Controller of Her Majesty's Stationery Office, © Crown Copyright 100037674

GETTING THERE

This ride starts in the Alice Holt Forest car park, which is easy to find and to get to, but there are plenty more car parks on or close to the route. Exit the A31 and go south on the A325, following the signs to the Alice Holt visitors centre (about 3 miles) car park (811/416). Parking costs £2 for the day, and there are toilets and a shop here. There is a train station in Bentley, on the west side of Alice Holt forest (less than 2 miles away).

ACCOMMODATION

B&B at South Lodge (nr Alice holt forest), on: 01420 520960
B&B in Tilford on: 01252 792009
YHA in Hindhead on: 0870 7705864
Camping nr Churt on: 01428712090
Farnham T.I. on: 01252 715109

BICYCLE SHOPS

Robin Cycles in Lindford (nr Bordon) on: 01420 476612 and
Pedalabikeaway cycle hire at Alice Holt Forest on: 07775 840807.

REFRESHMENTS

A shop at the visitors centre, or pubs on the route in Batt's corner, Churt Place, Tilford, and Millbridge. There are also pubs at Elstead, Charleshill, and Tilford on extension 1.

MAIN ROUTE

17.3 miles & 385 metres of climbing

1 **START**. At the cycle hire hut (811/416), and follow the (3 mile) family cycle route, for 0.5m to the 3rd X-tracks. Turn R, to a 3-way rd junction (820/417) Woodhall lane opposite, and turn R on the rd, for 0.45m then turn L (820/411), by the Bluebell pub.

2 Keep SA/R, joining a BW (just past the FP) and follow this (bear L at a fork) for 0.9m to a rd (835/409). Turn L on the rd then immediately R over the river (Frensham), then immediately R through a gate, past Mill house, on a BW (836/409).

3 0.8m to a rd (with a lake SA), and turn L on the rd for 0.05m, then turn R on a BW (840/401). Follow the cycle / horse track, bearing L, UH, to, then parallel to a rd. To a (minor) tarmac rd (843/406) and turn R on this, then immediately L, on BW no.45.

4 Keep SA, to a rd, and join the A287 rd, for 0.15m then turn R on the cycle track/BW no.44 (848/416) or see the shortcut. UH, to a X-tracks at the top of the hill and keep SA on the cycle track/BW no. 44, DH, for 0.7m and bear L on BW no.42 (853/399).

5 Follow this to a good track (860/406), and turn R on this, for 0.4m then turn R on a BW (867/404) opposite Packman's house. Keep SA (R then L at X-tracks) for 0.8m, to a rd (867/392) and turn L on this for 0.35m to a X-rds, by the Pride of the Valley pub.

6 Go SA, on Thursley rd, for 0.7m, UH, then turn L on a BW (882/392). 0.15m to some X-tracks (883/393) and turn L, DH, and keep SA (over 2 X-tracks - not on the map), for 0.45m, UH, to some X-tracks with a good DT (881/400), and turn L.

7 0.5m to a fork and bear R, for 0.4m to some X-tracks (886/413) (looks like a T-J with a DT, but a BW goes SA). Turn L on a DT, then bear R at a fork, and keep SA, through a golf course, for 0.85m to a feint fork (877/424) and keep SA/L to a rd (by Hankley pub), or see extension 1.

8 Turn R on the rd, then immediately L on a BW (875/424), keeping L after 0.5 (868/425) for another 0.8m, to a rd. Keep SA/R on the rd for 0.65m to the A287 rd (849/418) and turn R on this (Farnham).

9 After 0.25m (over a bridge and shortly after the Mariners pub), turn L (848/422) on Wirecap rd. After 0.4m bear R at the fork (842/442) (by a telephone box on the L), and follow this rd for 0.6m to another fork (833/421) by Broomfields house, and bear L on West end street.

10 Keep SA, for 0.75m to a T-J (821/422), and go SA, UH, on a gravel BW, for 0.45m to a well surfaced gravel (cycle) track (815/418). Turn R on this track (or for a shortcut, keep SA on the BW to the car park), and follow it for 2m, back to car park (811/416).

SHORTCUT:

-8.3 miles & -180 metres of climbing

1 Keep SA on the A287 rd for 0.2m to a bridge (849/419) and rejoin the main route at no.9.

+7.4 miles & +175 metres of climbing

1 Bear R at a fork (before the rd), between some buildings, on Greensands way (GSW) BW, for 0.4m to a T-J (879/429). Turn R, 0.15m to a fork and bear L, and follow this BW for 1m, under some power lines, past Hankley farm, to some X-tracks (895/435).

2 Turn L (Westbrook hill rd), for 0.55m to a triangle, in Elstead (904/434) and turn L (Thursley rd) for 0.2m to a large triangle (906/436). Turn L on the B3001 for 0.65m then turn R on Seale rd (898/440) , for 0.4m then turn L on a BW/driveway (898/446), or see extension 2.

3 Keep SA/R on the BW, into the woods, for 0.35m to a minor rd/BW (893/444) and turn R on this. 0.45m to a X-tracks, and keep SA on the BW, for 0.55m through the woods, to a (BW) fork (885/458 and bear L. 0.3m to a rd (881/459), by a transmitter, and turn L, for 0.15m, and keep SA on a ByW, as the rd ends/bears R.

4 After 0.1m, bear R at the fork, on a BW, to a rd and turn L on this for 0.05m then turn R on a BW/drive (878/455). 0.25m to the B3001 rd and turn R on this, for 0.15m then turn L on the (GSW) ByW (872/454).

5 Follow this (R at a fork) for 0.55m to a rd, and go SA on the GSW, for 0.25m to a T-J. Turn L, for 0.2m (joining a drive, then leaving it), and bear R, on the GSW (872/439). Alongside the river, to a rd (874/434), and turn R, over a bridge and bear L at the triangle.

6 To a T-J, and turn L on Tilgate rd, for 0.2m then turn R (874/429) leaving the

GSW, on a ByW. Join a rd after 1.3m, and keep SA/R on this for 0.65m to a T-J with the A287 (849/418). Turn R (Farnham) on the rd, and rejoin the main route at no.9.

EXTENSION 2:

+6 miles & +170 metres of climbing

A Turn R on a BW, for 0.5m to a rd, past Fullbrook farm, and keep SA on the BW, for 0.5m to a rd. Turn L on this rd for 0.05m then turn R on a BW (913/450), through the woods to Cutt mill ponds. Follow this BW around the ponds and house, UH, to a minor rd (919/456).

B Keep SA/R on this rd, past Rodsall manor, to a T-J (921/462) and turn L on this rd. After 0.1m, turn R (920/460) and keep SA (north), through a car park, on the BW for 0.85m, to a T-J, with the North downs way (917/473). Turn L on the NDW for 0.4m, then turn L on a BW (911/473), just before a stream.

C 0.25m to a X-tracks and turn R, to the top, and keep R, on the LHS of the ponds, for 0.95m, through a car park, to a rd (912/458). Turn R, to a X-rds, and go SA, for 0.6m then turn R on a BW, by Fullbrook farm (906/446), which you came along earlier. 0.5m to a rd and go SA on the BW, and rejoin extension 1, at no.3.

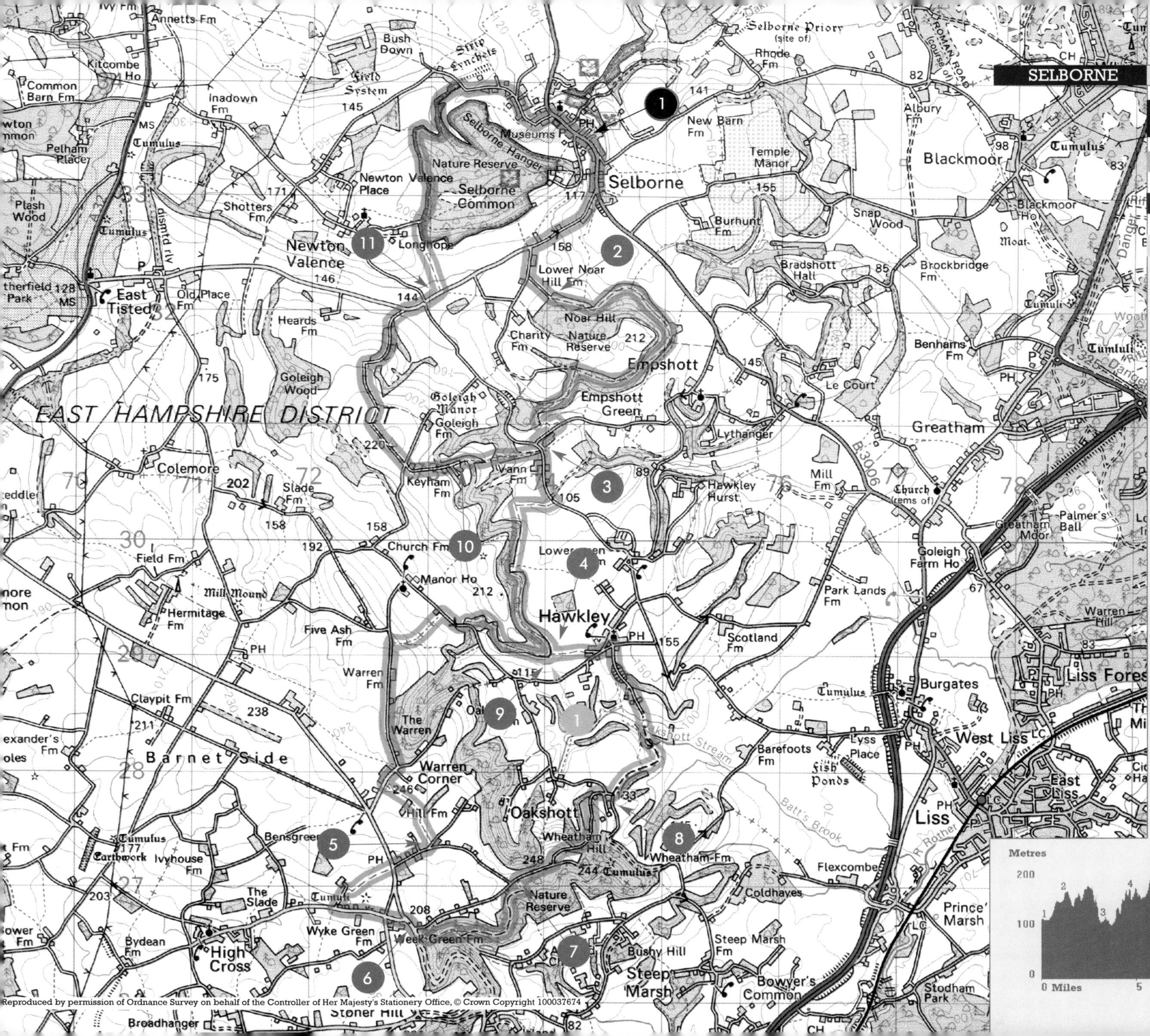

HIGHLY RECOMMENDED

■ ROUTE 31

■ **MAIN ROUTE:** 16.9 miles
(900 metres of climbing)

■ **SHORTCUTS:** -6.5 miles

■ **EXTENSIONS:** None

THE RIDE

SUITABILITY

The southern loop of the ride is very hilly, with some pretty technical secions, which won't suit novices. However, the shortcut avoids all this, leaving you with a beautiful ride, with an optional pub stop at Hawkley before the return leg.

TECHNICAL RATING

The reduced ride offers a lovely ride without anything too technical, while the southern loop has steep hills with rocks, roots, drop-offs and ruts, and will keep you battling for control of the bike.

TERRAIN

Superb woodland riding, with great single-track, but be careful of the roots in wet weather. A lovely descent brings you back to the quaint village of Selborne, where the cyclist friendly pubs will happily pull you a well deserved pint.

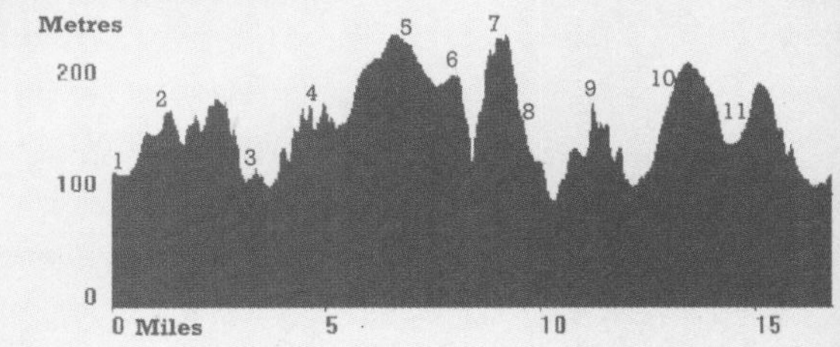

ROUTES

31

GETTING THERE

16.9 miles & 900 metres of climbing

This ride starts in the lovely village of Selborne, which lies between Alton (on the A31) and Petersfield (on the A3), on the B3006. Park in the (free) car park in Selborne (742/335), which also has toilets and is close to the post office / shop.

ACCOMMODATION

B&B in Selborne on: 01420 511285
B&B in Selborne on: 01420 473464
There are no campsites or YHAs close to this route.
Alton T.I. on: 01420 88448

BICYCLE SHOPS

1st Gear Cycles in Alton on: 01420 543 922 or The Sensible bicycle co. in Petersfield on: 01730 266 554

REFRESHMENTS

There are a couple of pubs and a post office shop in Selborne. There is also a pub in Warren Corner, and another in Hawkley which is a good half-way point.

1 START. Go back to the B3006 rd and turn R on this for 0.4m, then turn R off this main rd, **on another rd** (East Tisted) (744/330). **Go UH, for 0.5m and turn L** on another rd (Lower Noar hill farm) (738/325) **for 0.15m then turn L on a DT BW. UH, for 0.15m then turn L on a BW** (easy to miss) (740/321).

2 0.85m to a fork and bear R (staying in the woods), **and keep SA on this** (BW joins from the R) **for 0.6m to a X-tracks** (742/314). **Turn L on a BW**, steep DH, **bearing L at a fork, then L at a T-J, to a rd and turn R on this to a T-J** (739/308).

3 Turn L on this rd for 0.35m (just over a small bridge) **and turn R on a BW** (740/303). **Keep SA for 0.2m**, along the field edge, **to a** (BW) **T-J**, by some trees (737/303) **and turn L, UH on the BW. 0.95m to a fork** (740/290), **and bear R on the main track** or see the shortcut.

4 After 0.65m at the rd, turn R on this for 0.1m then turn L on a ByW (731/293), **UH, for 0.35m to a rd** (726/291). **Turn L on the rd for 0.8m** (0.1m after Warren lane on your L), **then turn L on a BW** (726/278), **across a field, for 0.45m to a rd** (730/273).

5 Turn R on the rd and keep SA on this for 0.25m to a busy rd, and go SA on a BW, and follow this **onto a driveway and turn L on this, to a rd** (722/268). **Turn L on this rd, keeping SA** at the X-rds after 0.25m, for another 0.1m **to the main rd** (728/267).

6 Turn R on the main rd for 0.1m then turn L on a BW (729/265) just after Cockshott lane, on a steep, technical, DH for 0.3m to a fork (733/265). **Bear L,** steeply UH, for 0.55m to a fork and bear L to a DT (737/270).

7 Turn R on this for 0.25m, then turn L on a DT (it's a ByW but there is no sign) (740/271). **Go DH,** getting very rutty, **for 0.6m to a rd, and bear R/SA on this for 0.05m then turn L on a ROW** (745/278), as the rd bears R.

8 Keep SA on this track which becomes a drive, **for 1m to a X-rds in Hawkley** (745/290), **and turn L on the rd** (or R to the pub). **0.05m to another rd and bear L** on this, then immediately **turn R on a drive, which becomes a BW,** across a field, **to a T-J just inside the wood** (740/290) **and turn R.**

9 You came from this way earlier. **After 0.95m turn R,** back across the field, **to the rd** (740/303) **and turn L on this,** over the bridge. **After 0.3m turn L on the ByW** (739/307) near the lay-by, very steeply **UH,** but gets rideable, (you haven't been here before).

10 Join a driveway and keep SA/R on this to a rd (728/306) and go SA on the ByW. Short UH, then **DH for 1m to a rd and turn R on this for 0.2m** (0.1m to a X-rds and go SA for another 0.1m) **then turn L on a BW** (730/321).

11 UH for 0.4m and go SA, bearing slight R on the BW into and along the LHS of the woods. **Follow the BW signs,** DH, on the LHS of the woods, **for 1.1m to a rd** (732/339) **and turn R on this. 0.6m to a T-J with the B3006** (740/337) **and turn R,** into Selborne and back to the car park (742/335).

Short, steep and very sweet..

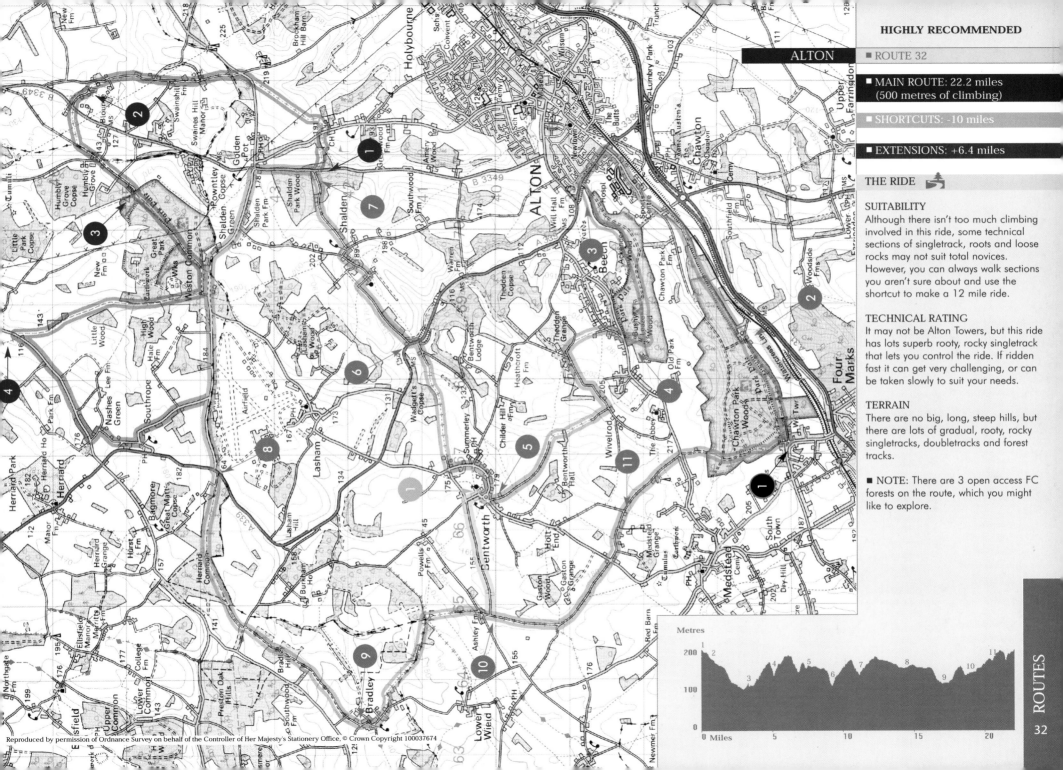

HIGHLY RECOMMENDED

■ ROUTE 32

ALTON

■ **MAIN ROUTE: 22.2 miles**
(500 metres of climbing)

■ **SHORTCUTS: -10 miles**

■ **EXTENSIONS: +6.4 miles**

THE RIDE

SUITABILITY
Although there isn't too much climbing involved in this ride, some technical sections of singletrack, roots and loose rocks may not suit total novices. However, you can always walk sections you aren't sure about and use the shortcut to make a 12 mile ride.

TECHNICAL RATING
It may not be Alton Towers, but this ride has lots superb rooty, rocky singletrack that lets you control the ride. If ridden fast it can get very challenging, or can be taken slowly to suit your needs.

TERRAIN
There are no big, long, steep hills, but there are lots of gradual, rooty, rocky singletracks, doubletracks and forest tracks.

■ NOTE: There are 3 open access FC forests on the route, which you might like to explore.

ROUTES

32

■ **MAIN ROUTE**

GETTING THERE

This ride starts in the (forestry commission) Chawton park wood car park (672/361) near a place called Four marks, nr Alton. Exit the A31 at Four Marks, going north on Boyneswood rd, for 0.4m and go straight ahead/right to the car park, as the rd bears left.

ACCOMMODATION

B&B in Lower Farringdon on: 01420 587076
B&B in East Worldham on: 01420 82392
No campsites or YHAs close by.
Alton T.I. on: 01420 88448

BICYCLE SHOPS

1st Gear Cycles in Alton on the High Street, tel: 01420 543 922

REFRESHMENTS

There are lots of pubs, shops in Alton and pubs in Bentworth, and Golden pot on the main route and also in Southrope on extension 2.

22.2 miles & 500 metres of climbing

1 **START**. Exit the car park and turn L for 0.05m then L again on a ByW (671/360). When possible, bear L on the better ST, parallel to the ByW, and keep SA on this for 1m to a driveway. Keep SA past the houses, to a fork and keep SA/L, on a rough track. Bear R then L (effectively SA) on a ST (by the entrance to a stockcar track), along the edge of the woods.

2 Turn L (effectively SA) on a ST on the RHS of the woods, and follow this, DH, for over 1.25m to a rd (702/377). Turn L on the rd, which bears R immediately, for 0.75m, past a sports centre and hospital, to a T-J (710/385). Turn L on the A339 rd (Beech/Basingstoke) for 0.4m then turn L on a BW (705/388).

3 Follow this good ST on the RHS of the wood, for 0.7m to a fork (697/382) and turn L onto a wider track. Keep SA for 0.85m ignoring any L and R turns, to a DT, and bear R, DH, on this (684/379), for 0.2m to a clearing and keep SA to the rd (685/382).

4 Go SA, steeply UH on a BW, for 0.15m to a fork at the top and bear L on the BW to a rd (685/389). Turn L on this rd for 0.75m then turn R on a ByW (no signpost), opposite a house (676/384). Follow this for 1.35m to a rd/roundabout (663/400) and turn R on this, or see the shortcut.

5 After 0.6m through the village, turn R on a ByW (668/406), DH, for 1m, to a minor rd, and keep SA/L to the A339 rd. Turn L on this for 0.07m then turn R on a rd to Shalden (684/411).

6 UH, for 1.05m to a fork in Shalden and bear R on this rd for 0.07m then turn L onto a ByW (697/420) opposite the telephone and go DH, to the B3349 rd (707/424) and turn L on this rd or see the extension.

7 UH, for 0.5m to a X-rds (708/432) and turn L and follow this rd for 2.65m, past the gliding club, to the A339 rd (668/438).

8 Turn L on this rd for 0.02m then turn R on a BW, UH, into the woods. Keep SA for 1.5m on the main track, which bears L, becoming a ST, to a rd (646/434). Go SA (L then R) on the Three castles BW, for 1.15m to a X-rds and go SA for 0.15m to a (rd) T-J (633/418).

9 Turn L on the rd for 0.3m into Bradley village, then bear L on a ByW (636/414). UH, for 0.85m to a ByW X-tracks (648/409) and go SA on a ByW, DH, to Ashley farm. Bear R to the rd (648/401) and turn L on this for 0.05m then keep SA/R on a ByW, as the rd bears L.

10 After 0.6m bear L at a fork (647/391), on the DT, for 0.7m to a 3-way rd junction (655/384) and go SA on the rd. Keep SA after 0.45 as this becomes a ByW.

11 UH, past a mast, to a rd (669/374) and go SA on the BW, DH, through the woods, to a X-tracks at the bottom (669/369). Go SA and keep SA for 0.6m, back to the car park entrance (672/361).

-10 miles & -195 metres of climbing

1 Turn L at the roundabout, for 0.2m, past the church, to a X-rds (663/404) and turn L. After 1m on this rd turn L on a ByW (648/400) as the rd bears sharp R (to Ashley farm), and rejoin the main route at no.10.

EXTENSION:

+6.4 miles & +180 metres of climbing

1 Go SA on the ByW, steep UH, to a rd (712/423) and turn R then immediately L, on the ByW. 0.75m to a rd and turn R on this for 0.1m to a X-rds (720/434) and turn L on a ByW. DH, joining a rd after 0.65m, and keep SA for another 0.6m, then turn L on a ByW (719/453).

2 DH, to a rd and turn L then immediately R on a ByW, UH, for 0.35m to a T-J (711/456) and turn L for 0.25m to a 5-way junction. Go SA on the (RHS) ByW, for 0.4m to the end of the drive, and go SA to some X-tracks at the start of the forest (704/448).

3 Go SA on the main wide, grassy track through the woods, for 1.05m through a gate to a minor rd/drive (691/439). Go SA on the DT BW, which bears sharp R, DH, in the woods. 0.6m to a fork and keep R, DH, for 1m to a rd (686/464).

4 Turn L on the rd, for 1.1m to a X-rds (672/454) and turn L, for 0.1m then turn R at the fork, to Southrope. 0.35m to a fork in Southrope (671/448) and bear L (Back lane) for 0.75m to a T-J (677/438). Turn R on this rd for 0.6m to the A339 rd (668/438), and rejoin the main route at no.8.

Fairlytale forest singletrack

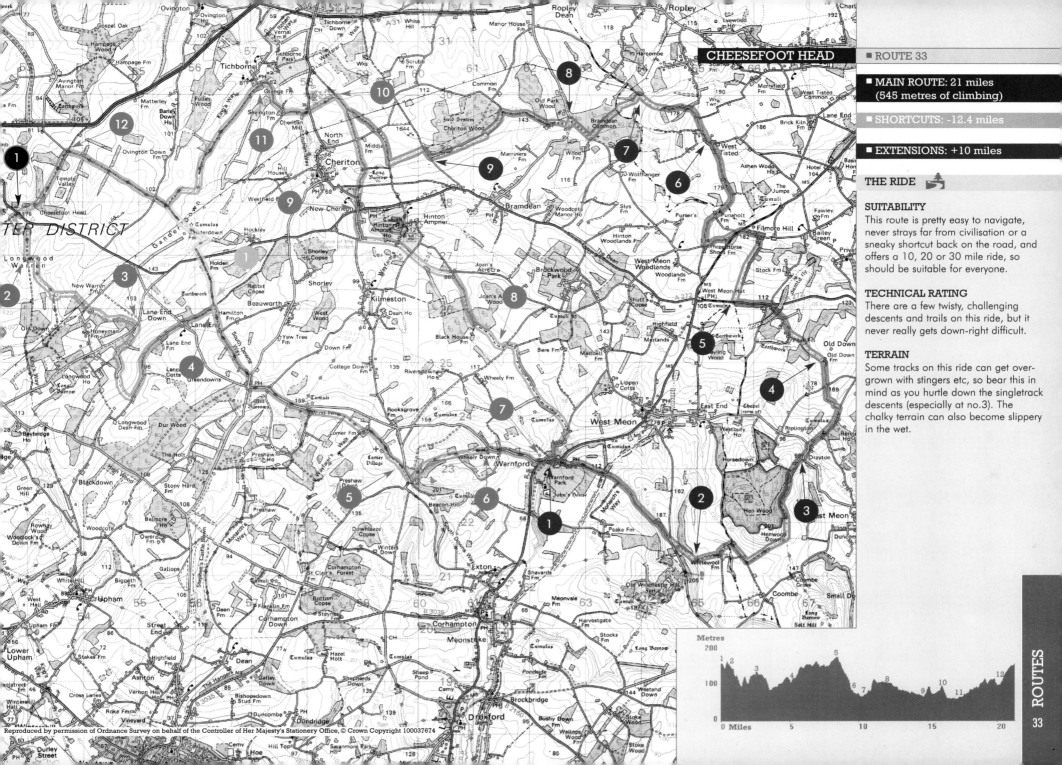

■ ROUTE 33

■ **MAIN ROUTE: 21 miles**
(545 metres of climbing)

■ **SHORTCUTS: -12.4 miles**

■ **EXTENSIONS: +10 miles**

THE RIDE

SUITABILITY

This route is pretty easy to navigate, never strays far from civilisation or a sneaky shortcut back on the road, and offers a 10, 20 or 30 mile ride, so should be suitable for everyone.

TECHNICAL RATING

There are a few twisty, challenging descents and trails on this ride, but it never really gets down-right difficult.

TERRAIN

Some tracks on this ride can get overgrown with stingers etc, so bear this in mind as you hurtle down the singletrack descents (especially at no.3). The chalky terrain can also become slippery in the wet.

ROUTES

33

■ MAIN ROUTE

21 miles & 545 metres of climbing

① **START**. Turn R on the rd and immediately L on a BW (SDW), 0.05m to a X-rd (527/277) and turn L. Bears L, UH, becoming a DT, to a T-J (530/274) by a big green container. Turn R on the DT, for 0.35m then L on a (easy to miss) BW (530/269).

② 0.6m, DH, to the edge of a wood and turn L on a BW (534/262), UH, past an old yellow container, DH. Keep SA over a track, UH, for 0.65m to a rd (549/256). Go SA over the rd, through a gate then immediately R (no signpost).

③ After 0.45m bear L at a slight clearing (grassy DT, SA) (546/251) back into the trees. 0.6m, DH, to a rd (548/243) and turn L on this for 1.1m to a X-rds. Go SA on a stony track into the trees, UH then DH, to a big wide X-rds (563/260) in the open, and turn R or see the shortcut.

④ 0.3m, UH, to a rd and keep SA/R on this for 0.6m to a T-J. Turn R to a X-rds (569/245) and turn L on the rd for 0.75m then turn R as the rd bears L, into Wind farm on the SDW (579/241). Follow the SDW signs through the farm, for 0.7m to another farm and bear L then R, on the SDW, to a rd.

⑤ Keep SA/R on the rd for 0.2m then turn L by the parking area, on a (temporary SDW route for cyclists) BW (598/227). Through 2 gates into a grassy field and turn R shortly on a DT, through a silver gate and then L, DH, on a stoney DT, to a rd (612/233).

⑥ Turn R on the rd for 0.6m to a T-J with the main rd in Wanford (621/231). Turn

L on this main rd for 0.1m then turn L on another rd before the bridge, into Warnford, or see the extension.

⑦ After 0.5m as you exit the village, turn L (626/237) on a R.O.W. and keep SA on this for 1.2m to a fork and bear L to a rd. Turn L on the rd, then immediately R on another R.O.W. (615/252).

⑧ Keep SA/R after 0.4m as you join a driveway, for another 0.65m to a rd junction (606/266) and turn L on a BW just before the rd. 0.55m to a rd and go SA on the BW for 0.6m to the corner of a rd (589/273), and turn R, to the A272 and go SA.

⑨ After 0.15m keep SA on the BW, as the rd bears L, to a X-tracks (589/283). Go SA, keeping SA/L at a fork after 0.2m, to a rd and go SA on the BW. After 0.35m, under some elec. cables, bear L at a fork, for 0.2m and turn L on the Wayfarers walk BW (585/299).

⑩ Go DH, along the fields edge, to a rd (580/297) and go SA on the rd opposite (Tichbourne). After 0.8m keep SA on the wide DT BW, as the rd bears R into the village, by a farm (571/301).

⑪ Follow this BW for 1.5m to a T-J and turn R, through a gate and bear L to a (DT) T-J by a barn (555/279). Turn R on the DT, to a rd, and go SA on the BW for 1.1m to some X-tracks (537/289).

⑫ Turn L on the SDW, UH, for 1m to the A272 rd and turn L, then L again back into the car park (529/277).

SHORTCUT:

-12.4 miles & -285 metres of climbing

① Turn L on the SDW, for 0.6m past a farm to a rd and go SA, UH, for 0.15m, through a gate and turn R (560/271). 0.2m to a T-J (562/272) and turn L, for 0.6m, DH then UH, to a fork by a barn. Keep SA/L to a rd (552/280) and rejoin the main route at no.12.

EXTENSION:

+10 miles & +345 metres of climbing

① Stay on the main rd for another 0.15m and turn R on Old winchester hill lane (Clamfield) just over the bridge (625/231). UH, for 1.65m to a junction at the top, and go SA/L through a gate on the (SDW) BW (645/216). DH, through a double silver gate and turn L on the DT (649/212).

② To the farm and bear L on the drive, to a rd (656/216) and turn R on this for 0.3m, then turn L on the SDW (658/212). Go UH on this for 0.55m to a X-rds (666/216) and turn L on the ByW, for 1m DH, past Hen wood to a rd (by Treaton cottage B&B).

③ Turn L on the rd for 0.2m then turn R on a minor rd (Privett) as the rd bears L (670/234). Keep L at a fork after 0.25m for another 0.3m to a fork (675/241) and turn L. 0.35m to some X-rds and go SA for 0.25m, then bear L on the ByW by the Old down farm building (672/250).

④ Through a silver gate, heading towards a yellow house on the grass, to a driveway. Turn R on this, to the A272 rd (663/260) and turn L on this, for 0.4m,

then turn R on a BW (in the lay-by), on the LHS of the trees, (656/261). NOTE: This can get overgrown.

⑤ UH, for 0.85m to a rd (661/273) and turn L on this to a main rd and turn L on this for 0.1m then turn R on a ST rd (the drive on the R cuts the rd DH then UH out, but is private). Go DH, for 0.35m to some X-rds (651/271) and turn R, UH, on this rd for 1.35m to a fork.

⑥ Turn L for 0.45m, through the village, turn L on a DT (ByW, but no sign) as rd bears R (648/297). Into the woods, DH, on a rocky track with steps, for 0.6m then turn L through a single wooden gate (20 meters after a BW on R) (639/299).

⑦ Through another gate and go SA to the other side of the field, and bear R to some X-tracks and turn L into the woods. Keep SA, using the ST on the R of the DT when possible, to a rd (631/291) and turn R on this for 0.3m to a T-J.

⑧ Turn L for 0.05m then turn R on a DT (627/294) for 0.8m to a T-J (614/296) (Private sign SA). Turn L for 0.35m, exiting the wood, to a (ST) T-J (612/292) and turn L, which then bears R, and follow this for 0.75m to a DT.

⑨ Turn R on the DT for 0.15m then L on a BW (600/289) for 0.45m to another DT (594/287). Turn R on this, to a minor rd and go SA on the BW for 0.6m (under the elec. lines), then turn L on the Wayfarers Walk BW (585/299), and rejoin the main route at no.10.

🚗 GETTING THERE

This ride starts from remote Cheesefoot Head car park, off the A272. Exit the M3 (at junction 9 or 10) and head east on the A31, shortly turning right on the A272 and the (free) car park is 1 mile on the left.

🛏 ACCOMMODATION

B&B in Cheriton at the Flower pots Inn on: 01962 771318
B&B at Milburys pub (on the route) near Beauworth on: 01962 771248
YHA in Winchester on: 0870 7706092
Camping in No Man's Land (near where the A272 leaves the A31) on: 01962 869877
Winchester T.I. on: 01962 840500

🚲 BICYCLE SHOPS

Peter Hargroves cycles in Winchester, on Jewry Street, on: 01962 860005

🍴 REFRESHMENTS

There are pubs on the main route south of Beauworth, in Warnford, New Cheriton, Cheriton, and Tichborne. There is also a pub in West Meon Hut on the extension.

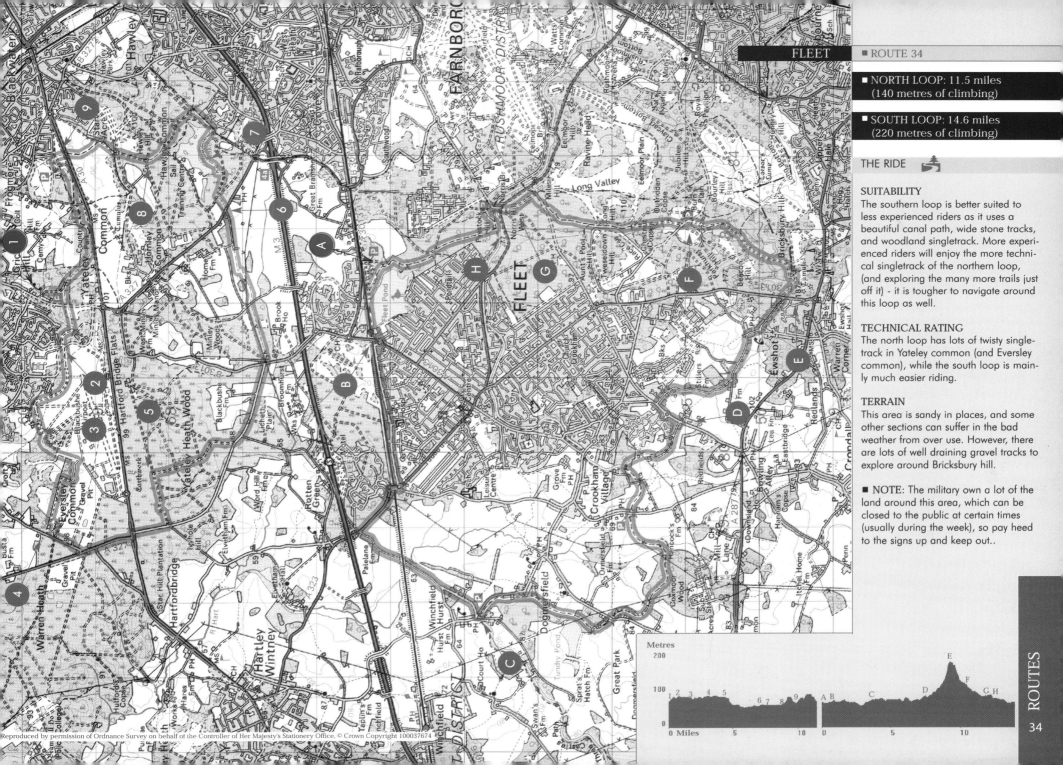

■ **NORTH LOOP: 11.5 miles**
(140 metres of climbing)

■ **SOUTH LOOP: 14.6 miles**
(220 metres of climbing)

THE RIDE

SUITABILITY
The southern loop is better suited to less experienced riders as it uses a beautiful canal path, wide stone tracks, and woodland singletrack. More experienced riders will enjoy the more technical singletrack of the northern loop, (and exploring the many more trails just off it) - it is tougher to navigate around this loop as well.

TECHNICAL RATING
The north loop has lots of twisty singletrack in Yateley common (and Eversley common), while the south loop is mainly much easier riding.

TERRAIN
This area is sandy in places, and some other sections can suffer in the bad weather from over use. However, there are lots of well draining gravel tracks to explore around Bricksbury hill.

■ **NOTE:** The military own a lot of the land around this area, which can be closed to the public at certain times (usually during the week), so pay heed to the signs up and keep out..

ROUTES
34

GETTING THERE

Exit the M4 at junction 4a, or there is a train station in Fleet.
North loop: Go north on the A327 to a roundabout with the A30 and go straight ahead (Cricket hill lane) for 1/2 mile then turn right (by a telephone box) on a rough track bearing left at the fork, into the (free) Yateley common car park (821/596).
South loop: Go south on the A327, then right on the A3013. Follow the (brown) Fleet pond signs, turning left off this road, then bearing right on a bumpy track to the (free) height restricted car park (824/553).

ACCOMMODATION

B&B's in Fleet on: 01252 816924 and 623755.
Camping in Finchampstead on: 0118 9733928
Fleet T.I. on: 01252 811151

BICYCLE SHOPS

Cycle Kingdom in Fleet on: 01252 624136

REFRESHMENTS

North loop: A pub near the start / end of the ride or shops, pubs, take-aways in Yateley.
South loop: Pubs in Winchfield Hurst, Crookham, Ewshot and Fleet.

NORTH LOOP

11.5 miles & 140 metres of climbing

1 START. Go back to the fork in the rough DT (entrance to the car park), and turn L. After 0.1m keep SA on a ST, leaving the DT as it bears L (by a house) and go SA. To a better track, at the edge of the trees (821/594) and turn R on this, to a rd. Go SA on the BW, for 0.2m to an old (disused) tarmac rd (816/593), and bear R on this, to a rd (814/594) (Dungells rd on the R).

2 Turn L over the main (Vigo) rd, onto an off-road ST (no sign), and keep SA on this to an old runway. Keep SA on the runway (or the ST to the RHS), bearing R, to some houses at the end (806/598), and turn L on a better (newer) runway. After 0.3m turn R off the runway, as it bears L (before some old, large metal gates) to face the airport, on a ST, into the trees (802/596).

3 To a T-J, by a fence, and turn L, alongside the fence, for 0.3m to a (dirty) sign and turn R on the stoney (permissive BW) track. Follow this around the quarry, then R on the BW into the woods. Emerge by a barrier, by a rd (788/595) and keep SA on a permissive path, parallel to the rd on your RHS.

4 Exit by a quarry entrance, and go SA/L on the rd to a T-J (786/591) with the A327. Turn L on this rd for 0.4m to the A30 and go SA (L then R) on Blackbushes rd. After 0.3m turn L into Yateley Heath wood (opposite Ivyhill hole rd), for 0.5m on the main track then R on the (3rd) track (797/582).

5 Keep SA on this forest track for 0.8m to a rd (801/571), and turn L on this for 0.75m to a T-J with the B3013 (811/567). Go SA, over the rd, past an old arch gate house on the L, onto a BW. Keep SA (R then L) over a

DT after 0.5m, for another 0.3m, past a pylon, and turn L then shortly R (east) on a DT (no signs), to the A327 rd.

6 Cross the rd into the woods, and keep SA on the BW for 0.15m to some X-tracks (834/573) with a grassy DT SA. Turn R on a BW, to a for and bear L, for 0.2m then turn L on the (DT) BW (837/572) (lake on your LHS). Just before you exit the trees to the sandy lake side, turn R over a small (hidden) wooden bridge, into the woods.

7 Follow this ST, keeping L, to the southeast edge of the lake. Turn L over a small bridge, then immediately turn R on a BW, to a (BW) T-J (843/574) and turn L, for 0.25m to a (BW) X-tracks (846/576). Turn L on the wide BW track, which joins a tarmac rd, then leaves it at a T-J (after 0.4m), as you keep SA (off-road) on the BW.

8 0.2m to a multiple X-tracks and turn L then immediately R (effectively SA), UH. 0.25m to an off-set X-tracks, and go SA (L then R) to a T-J (840/587) and turn R. After 0.15m turn L on a DT, following the telegraph poles, DH, and keep SA to the duel carriageway at the bottom (840/593).

■ **NOTE:** There are lots of tracks in Yateley Common. We have provided rough directions so you can ride what you want - it isn't too big so you shouldn't get too lost.

9 Cross the rd (carefully) and go SA on the BW opposite, and shortly turn L on the first ST you see. Stay parallel to the A30 rd on your LHS, for about 1.2m, then turn R (north) for 0.4m to some houses and a track back to the car park (821/596).

SOUTH LOOP

14.6 miles & 220 metres of climbing

A START. Head west, alongside the railway line, to the pond. Keep SA between the pond and the railway for 0.2m then turn R, up some steps (816/552), as the path bears L alongside the lake, into a train station car park. Turn L, through the car park, to a roundabout (815/553), and go SA (west) on Elvetham rd, alongside the railway.

B Keep SA on this rd for 1.2m to a roundabout (795/549) and turn R on the A323 rd, to another roundabout and go L (staying on the A323). After 0.45m turn L on Pale lane (789/554), and stay on this for 1.25m (L at a fork after 0.85m) to a junction by the Barley Mow pub.

C Go into the car park, to the river (778/537) and turn L along the towpath, for 3.25m (0.18m after going under the 4the bridge), then turn R (798/518) over a white, foot bridge, into Zebon Copse. Emerge by some houses and stay on the BW (between the cycle path and Albany farm), to a rd (803/510) and turn L on this.

D 0.1m to a roundabout and keep SA for another 0.1m, then turn R on Ewshot lane (806/513). Follow this rd for 1.15m to a fork (815/501) and bear R on church lane (Ewshot), for 0.15m then bear L onto a BW track, as the rd bears R, and follow this for 0.3m to the B3013 rd (820/496).

E Go SA, over the rd, and follow the main track SA, for 0.25m then turn L (824/495) and follow this track (north), DH, for 1.2m to a rd. Turn L on the rd for 0.1m then bear R, over the rd, off-road on a DT (830/510) by a 'No access when in Military use' sign, just past a wide track (UH, to a car park).

F Keep SA (north) as you join a gravel, then a sandy track, across an open area, for 1.1m to a fork. Bear L, off the main track as it bears R, by a yellow 'test traffic' sign) to a rd (833/529) and turn R on this. After 0.1m bear L onto a DT that goes SA, parallel with the rd, UH, and follow this DT as it bears L, to a T-J with some wide forest tracks.

G Turn R, DH, to a large roundabout and turn L at this, over a bridge then shortly turn sharp L, off-road on a feint track (832/536), DH, to the river. Turn R on the path alongside the river, then shortly turn R by a metal fence on your L, on a feint track (before crossing stream) (830/535).

H 0.6m to some X-tracks and turn L over a wooden bridge ('no horses' sign), for 0.2m and bear R at a fork. Follow the blue and yellow signposts to a viewpoint of the lake and a picnic area (825/551). Keep following (any of) the coloured signposts to the (north east side of the) lake, then turn R, back to the car park (824/553).

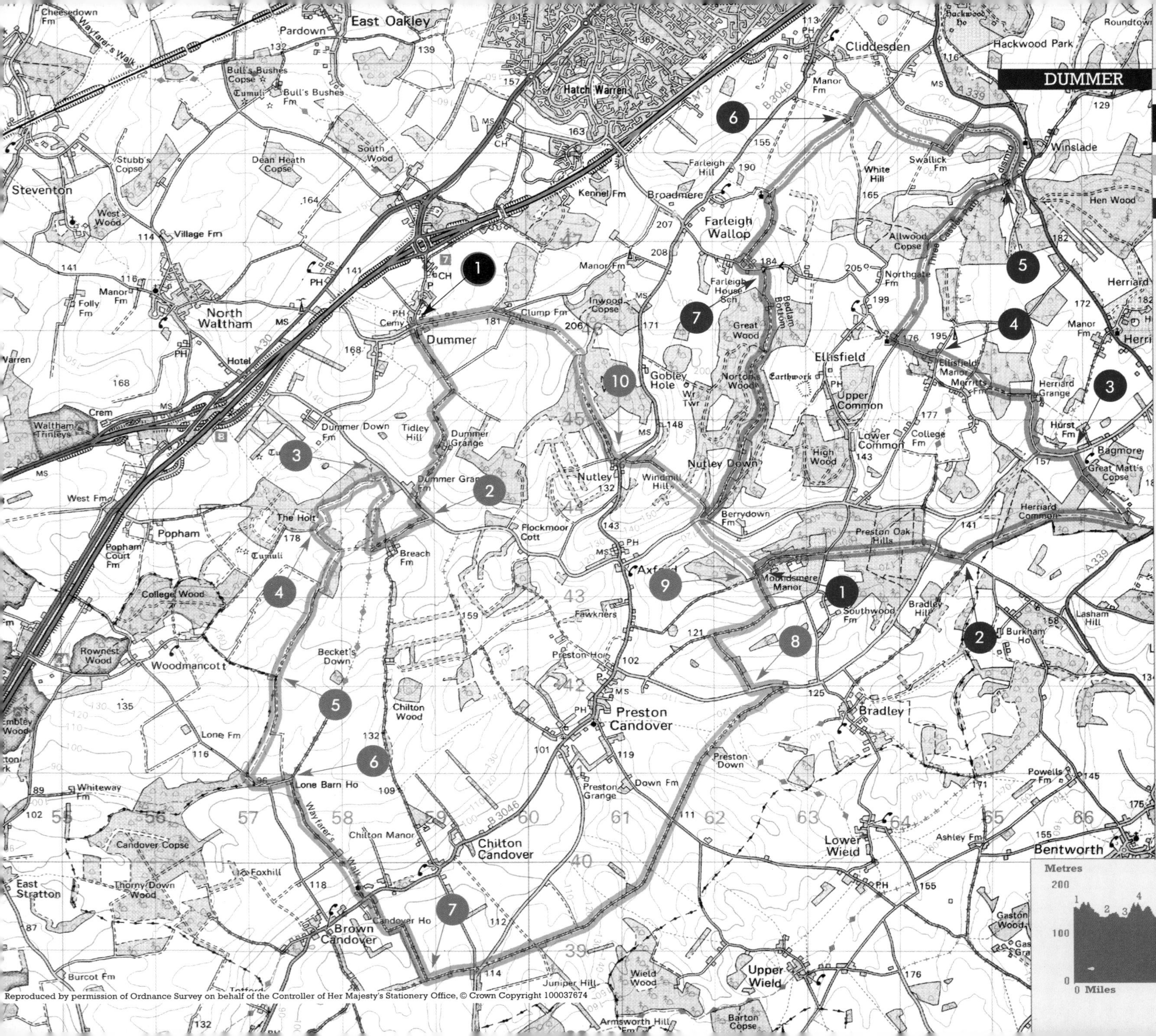

MAIN ROUTE: 15.7 miles
(400 metres of climbing)

SHORTCUTS: None

EXTENSIONS: +11 miles

THE RIDE

SUITABILITY
The main route should be fine for all riders, and although there aren't any shortcuts, there are some alternative routes back to the start if required. The extension is always there for more experienced riders wanting a few more miles of lovely trails in this great countryside.

TECHNICAL RATING
There are a few sections of singletrack on the main route to keep you alert (and more on the extension), but otherwise it's the challenge of (some good) doubletrack, which can be ridden at a good speed to liven things up.

TERRAIN
The route uses mostly well surfaced tracks which (although they may hold some water on the surface) stand up well in bad weather. This area does see its fair share of horses, so things can get messy in the wet.

NOTE: Black wood (just over the M3, by Micheldever train station) is open access Foresrty Commission land and has some good singletrack in it, which you might like to explore.

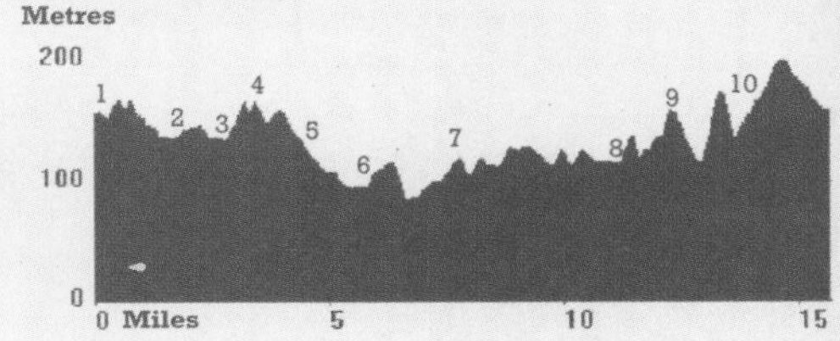

ROUTES

35

GETTING THERE

This ride starts in the small, idyllic village of Dummer, just 1/2/ a mile south of junction 7 of the M3. Parking is limited in this small village, so park considerately on the roadside (near the church (588/460) is probably a good place). There is a railway in Basingstoke or Micheldever (west of Dummer) just over the M3 near Black Wood, which is closer to the route.

ACCOMMODATION

B&B in Dummer at Oakdown farm bungalow on: 01256 397218
B&B near Oakley on: 01256 780949
No YHAs or campsites nearby
Basingstoke T.I. on: 01256 817618

BICYCLE SHOPS

Action Bikes in Basingstoke (on Winchester st.) on: 01256 465266 and Basingstoke cycle works (on Station approach) on: 01256 814138

REFRESHMENTS

There is a pub in Dummer, but nothing on the route. There are pubs in Preston Candover and Axford just off the route and on the extension in Ellisfield.

■ MAIN ROUTE

15.7 miles & 400 metres of climbing

1 START. From the church, **go west** on Up street **for 0.05m** then **turn L on the Wayfarers Walk (BW)** (588/460). After 0.5m bear R (592/453), for another 1m to a rd (588/441). **Turn L** on this **for 0.15m** then **turn R** on a track (Breach farm) (588/441).

2 0.45m to a X-tracks (583/435) (SA private) and **turn R** into the woods, **to a T-J** with a DT. **Turn L** on this, out of the woods, and **bearing R** around the edge of the field, then **bearing L** by the woods on the other side of the field (584/443).

3 Go alongside the woods, on the DT, slight UH, ignore the ROW on the R into the woods, for 0.5m (from the ROW on the R) and **keep SA on the BW** across the grass, when the woods on the R end, **for 0.1m to a T-J** by some trees (577/437).

4 Turn L alongside a wood, **for 0.25m**, exit the wood, to another wood and **bear R** into these (479/434). After 0.3m at the far side of the woods **bear R to a DT** (577/431). **Turn L** on this DT **for 0.65m** to a fork (573/421) and **keep SA** (to the L of the house).

5 After 0.4m **keep SA** between the trees, as the DT bears L, **to a rd** (570/410) and **turn L** on this. After 0.15m keep SA/L (dead end) as the rd bears R, **for another 0.15m to a house** (574/409), and **turn R** on their drive (BW), on the LHS of the house.

6 Go through a wooden gate and **keep SA for 0.9m**, over a style and past the church, and **keep SA to the rd**.. **Turn L** on this then immediately **R on a BW** (582/396)

through a farm. After 0.3m **turn L**, following the line of trees, bearing R (586/392), **for 0.4m to a T-J** (588/386).

7 Turn L, **for 0.35m** to a rd and **go SA**, to another rd and **go SA on the ByW** (595/388). After 1.7m at a rd (615/404), **go SA on the ByW, UH, for another 1.25m to a rd** (627/419). **Turn L** on this rd for 0.25m past the Keepers cottage **and turn** then **turn R on a BW** (623/419), through the wooden gate (by a silver gate).

8 After 0.45m, UH then DH, **at a T-J** (619/425) **turn R on a ByW, UH, for 0.45m to a fork** (626/428) and **bear L**. UH, **for 0.25m to** Moundsmore Manor drive (gates on R) (624/432). **Go SA**, over the drive **and keep SA immediately**, leaving the DT which bears R, **through a** (single) **gate**, or see the extension.

9 DH, **for 0.6m to a rd and turn R** then immediately **L** (618/438) **on a BW**, just before the thatch cottage.
9a - UH, **for 0.8m to a rd and bear L**, then immediately **R on a BW** (609/445), keeping to the RHS of the farm buildings.

10 After 0.45m at a (DT) **T-J, go SA on the grass** (leaving the DT), becoming a DT again, **for 1m**, past some houses **to a rd** (597/461). **Turn L** on this rd and follow it **for 0.6m, into Dummer** by the church (588/460), and back to wherever you left your car.

EXTENSION:

+11 miles & +240 metres of climbing

1 Stay on the DT as it bears R, past the barns, **for 0.5m to a rd** (632/434) and **go SA on the BW**. Keep SA for 0.75m, out of the woods, **to a 3-way rd junction and go SA** (Burkham). After 0.2m **turn L on a BW** (646/434) into the woods.

2 After 0.3m at a (feint) X-tracks (650/436) with a DT on the L, **keep SA on the ST** (can get overgrown). Along the RHS of the wood, **for 0.5m to a DT** in a clearing, and **go SA**. After 0.5m **turn L on a DT** (664/438) (before a green barrier across the DT), DH, **to a rd** (658/446).

3 Turn L on the rd for 0.2m, then **turn R on a drive** (655/446) (Grange farm), UH, **to a T-J** (654/452) by a barn conversion. **Turn L and keep SA for 0.7m**, through the woods, a wooden gate, and some X-tracks, **to a 3-way rd junction**, by some houses (644/457).

4 Go SA on Church lane, **for 0.3m** then **turn R on a BW** (639/459) by the Church (just after Furzen lane on the L). After 1.1m (through a grassy conservation area) **at a T-J** with a DT (647/474) **turn R**. 0.4m to a (silver) **gate**, **bear L** on the (permissive) **BW**, past a hut, **steep UH, to a T-J** (652/477).

5 Turn L on this old railway track, **for 0.7m to a rd** (647/482) and **turn L, UH, for 0.2m** and **bear R on the ByW** (645/480) by the houses. DH, **for 0.65m to a rd** (636/485) and **turn L to a T-J** and **turn L on the rd**.

6 After 0.15m **bear R on a BW** (634/483) just after the school, UH, **for 0.75m to a fork** and **keep SA/L** by the church. 0.6m to a rd (623/467) and **turn L** on this, for

0.15m, then **turn R on a BW** (625/466).

7 Follow this main track **for 2m**, to a rd and **turn R** on this for 0.05m and **turn R on a DT BW** just past the thatch cottage (618/438), **and rejoin main route at no.9a**.

Look out for the wild deer.

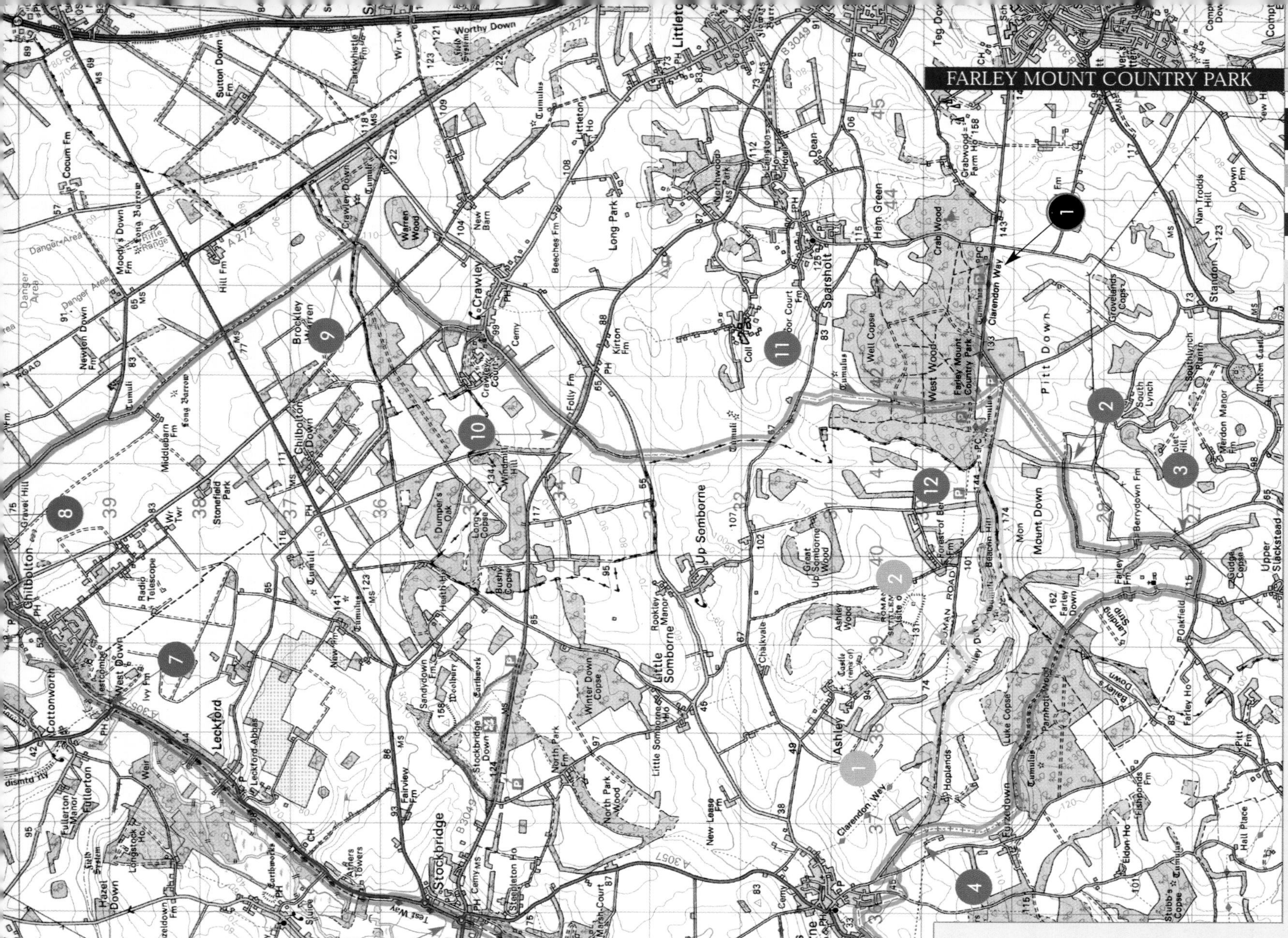

■ **MAIN ROUTE:** 26.2 miles
(475 metres of climbing)

■ **SHORTCUTS:** -15 miles

■ **EXTENSIONS:** None

THE RIDE

SUITABILITY

This is a long ride, but it isn't very hilly, is easy to navigate, and there is a shortcut option. Novice riders may just like to ride along the well surfaced (and flat) 'Test Way' path that runs between Horsebridge and West Down, where there is the very good Mayfly pub.

TECHNICAL RATING

This ride doesn't have lots of technical trails, but there are some fun, fast descents, some singletrack and some rooty trails to keep things entertaining.

TERRAIN

This route does pretty well in the wet weather, largely thanks to the 6 mile section along the 'Test Way' which is surfaced with gravel and tree lined.

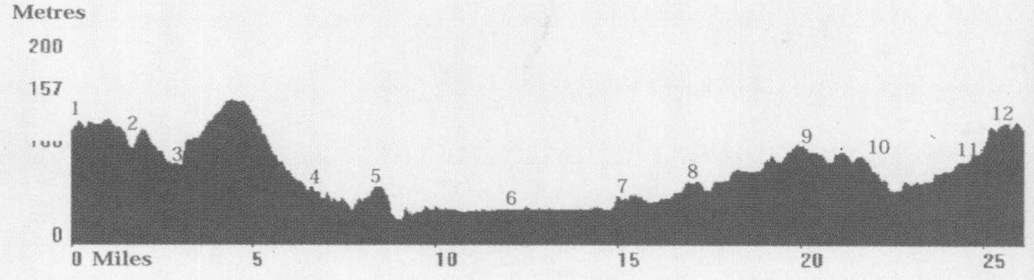

ROUTES

36

🚗 **GETTING THERE**

This ride starts from (one of the many) Farley Mount Country Park (FMCP) car parks, in the south east corner of West Wood. The car park is just west along a minor road of where Sarum road crosses Sparsholt road, then shortly on the right (433/292). There are also some toilets here and a BBQ and hut for hire.

🛏 **ACCOMMODATION**

B&B in Winchester (nr Sarum rd) on: 01962 861166
B&B in Comton (just south of Winchester) on: 01962 712162
YHA in Winchester on: 0870 7706092
Camping off the B3049 (between Crawley & Sparsholt): 01962 776486
Winchester T.I. on: 01962 840500

🚲 **BICYCLE SHOPS**

Peter Hargroves cycles in Winchester, (on Jewry Street) on: 01962 860005

🍽 **REFRESHMENTS**

There are pubs at Horse-bridge, Stockbridge, The (very good) Mayfly in West Down, Chilbolton and Crawley and a BBQ for hire at the FMCP (tel: 01962 846034).

26.2 miles & 475 metres of climbing

1 **START.** Go back to the entrance of the car park and turn R on a BW (horse-shoe sign) just before and parallel to the rd. This rejoins the rd after 0.6m and you keep SA/R on the rd. After 0.4m at a (rd) T-J (419/291) go SA on a BW (ROW), for 0.75m to a DT (410/284).

2 Turn R on the DT, UH, for 0.6m to a X-tracks (grassy DT SA and field on R), (401/282) and turn L on a grassy DT. Bear L, then R around a farm and barn, to a T-J with a rd and turn R on this for 0.25 to a fork (402/272) and bear R.

3 UH for 0.5m to an off-set X-rds (395/269) and turn R (Farley church, no through rd). Through a farm, UH, for 0.5m to a X-tracks (391/284) and go SA on the DT, into the woods (ST on L avoids the wet DT). Keep SA on this main track for 2.3m to a rd (368/301) and turn L on this or see the shortcut.

4 Turn L on the rd, for 0.4m then turn sharp L (363/304), for 0.15m then R on a BW (364/302). To another rd and go SA on the BW, bearing R (towards houses) for 0.3m and follow the BW as it turns L (360/307). After 0.65m (parallel to a rd) turn R over the rd, and go SA on the BW (351/301).

5 0.4m to a rd and turn R, down to a fork and bear L (Houghton), over a bridge and turn immediately R on the 'Test way' (345/305). Follow this nice track for 3m, joining a drive, to a round-about (358/350), with the White heart inn on the R, and go SA.

6 0.2m to another roundabout and go SA/L, for 0.4m then turn L at a lay-by, on the 'Test way'. Keep SA on this for 2.5m then turn R immediately after passing under a brick bridge, to a rd (382/389).

7 Turn L on the rd and keep L for 1.1m (on Coley lane, then L on Village street, past the post office and Abbots mitre pub) to a grass triangle (395/401). Turn R on Winchester street (Newton stacy), which bears L to some X-rds (405/403), and turn R (Winchester).

8 UH for 1.1m, then bear R on a BW as the rd bears L (415/390). After 0.25m keep SA/L on a grassy DT, and keep SA on this for 0.75m to a rd. Go SA for another 1.1m to a X-tracks (434/362) and take the 2nd R (SA/R), through a sil-ver gate (out of the woods).

9 Keep SA for 0.85m, through a gate and turn L (424/353), becoming a rd, to a T-J (425/348)by the church in Crawley. Turn R on the rd for 0.9m to a T-J with the B3049rd and go SA on the BW.

10 0.55m to a rd (411/331) and go SA on the BW, for 0.9m to a DT and turn L on this. After 0.4m, past a barn, turn R on a BW (417/313), and go through a wooden gate into the woods.

11 Keep SA on the DT in the woods, for 0.6m then keep SA out of the woods, past three wooden stumps. As you exit the woods bear L, UH, across the com-mon, to a rd at the top (419/291) and turn L on this (been here before).

12 After 0.3m take the ST (you used before) on the L (425/293), just after a BW (and a DT entrance to the woods), back to the car park (433/292).

1 R on the rd and keep SA between some buildings, becoming the Claren-don Way (C.W.) ByW. This bears R, DH, then L to a rd (390/296) and turn R on the C.W. BW just before the rd.

2 UH on this for 0.7m then turn L on the C.W. BW at the top (397/290) and follow this for 0.7m, DH, to a rd. Turn R on this for 0.7m to a fork in the rd (419/291) and turn L (been here before) and rejoin the main route at no12.

The well surfaced 'Test Way' track makes up a long section of this ride..

BRACKNELL

BRACKNELL FOREST

BRACKNELL FOREST

■ **MAIN ROUTE:** Various

■ **SHORTCUTS:** Various

■ **EXTENSIONS:** Various

THE RIDE

SUITABILITY
This route is not designed to guide you around a set course as there are so many good tracks in this 650 acre woodland you would spend the day looking at the map and trying to figure out where you are and where to go. Instead we show the markers present in the forest and suggest some areas to visit, and leave it to you to choose the distance and trails you want to ride.

TECHNICAL RATING
Non-technical fireroads, or technical twisty, rooty singletrack, jumps, drops, etc - it's your choice.

TERRAIN
Sandy, gravel and hard packed forest trails, with twisty woodland singletrack through the ferns and pine trees. There are not really any big hills, but definitely enough ups and downs to work your legs and lungs.

■ **NOTE:** You need to purchase a £1 permit to ride, which is available from the reception at the Look Out by the car park (which is free).

🚗 GETTING THERE

This ride starts from the (free) car park at the Look Out Discovery Centre car park (877/661). This is just off the B3430, west from the roundabout on the A322, just south of Bracknell itself, and is signposted (Lookout / Discovery outpost). There is a railway station in Bracknell, but use the Martins Heron station and follow the B3430 rd (south), all the way to the 'Look out'.

🛏 ACCOMMODATION

B&B's in Crowthorne on: 01344 773876, 750698, 775959 & 772645. **Camping** in Finchampstead (past Crowthorne) on: 0118 9733928. **YHA** in Windsor on: 0870 7706096 **Bracknell T.I.** on: 01344 354409

🚲 BICYCLE SHOPS

Wellington Trek at the Lookout do bike hire, on: 01344 772797 / 874611, Mountain Trax at the Wyevale Garden Centre, off the B3430 on: 01189 891999, and Berkshire Cycle Co in Crowthorne on: 01344 774529

🍽 REFRESHMENTS

There is a cafe and toilets at the Discovery centre (car park), which you will never be that far from, so you can pop back here for a cup of tea and some cake at any point.

■ MARKERS AND KEY AREAS

It is easy to lose your sense of direction in this Forest as you duck and dive around the trails. There are numbered marker around the forest which we have shown on the map to help you locate your position. There is also a mountain bike specific area (see right for more information) that we have drawn a blue border around, on the map, which has lots of good singletrack and no walkers.

①	876/660 The Look out
①	885/659
②	887/651
③	887/643
④	881/645
⑤	875/640 (Lower star post)
⑥	871/645
⑦	865/645 (Upper star post)
⑧	864/654
⑨	876/649
⑩	882/653

There are also names for some of the forest tracks, which are as follows:
Bracknell road between markers 1 & 2
Windsor ride between markers 1 (via marker 10) past marker 5 and on, into the danger area.
Pudding hill between markers 1 & 9
Ladies mile between markers 6 & 8
Lake Ride between marker 3 and Rapley lake.
Vicarage lane is the track on the north-east side of the MTB area
Mill ride runs parallel to Bracknell road (on the east side)
Devils highway goes west to Crowthorne from marker 4

MOUNTAIN BIKING AREA

The MTB specific area (inside the blue border, marked on the map), has some great singletrack and no walkers. The red posts and arrows around this area will guide you back to marker no.3. A popular singletrack starts by a sandy area, through a small gap into the woods at GR 889/636.

There are some man-made jumps if you head south-west from marker no.3, towards the 'Hydrant' and turn left at some X-tracks about 50 meters along here. The jumps are on the right after 0.15m (885/641), but are difficult to see from the track, as they are down in a dip.

OTHER INFORMATION

Cycling (and horse riding) in these woods requires a permit, which costs £1 for the day, and is available at the Look out reception, and Wellington bike hire. For more information contact the 'Look out' reception on tel: 01344 354400.

Berks on bikes (BOB) MTB club have regular rides around here, visit www.bobm-bc.com for more information.

■ **NOTE**: There are some areas that are out of bounds to cyclists, but these are well signposted, and are usually double-tracks, so who cares, just stay off them and ride the singletrack.

This is a very versatile ride, which will have something suitable for all abilities.

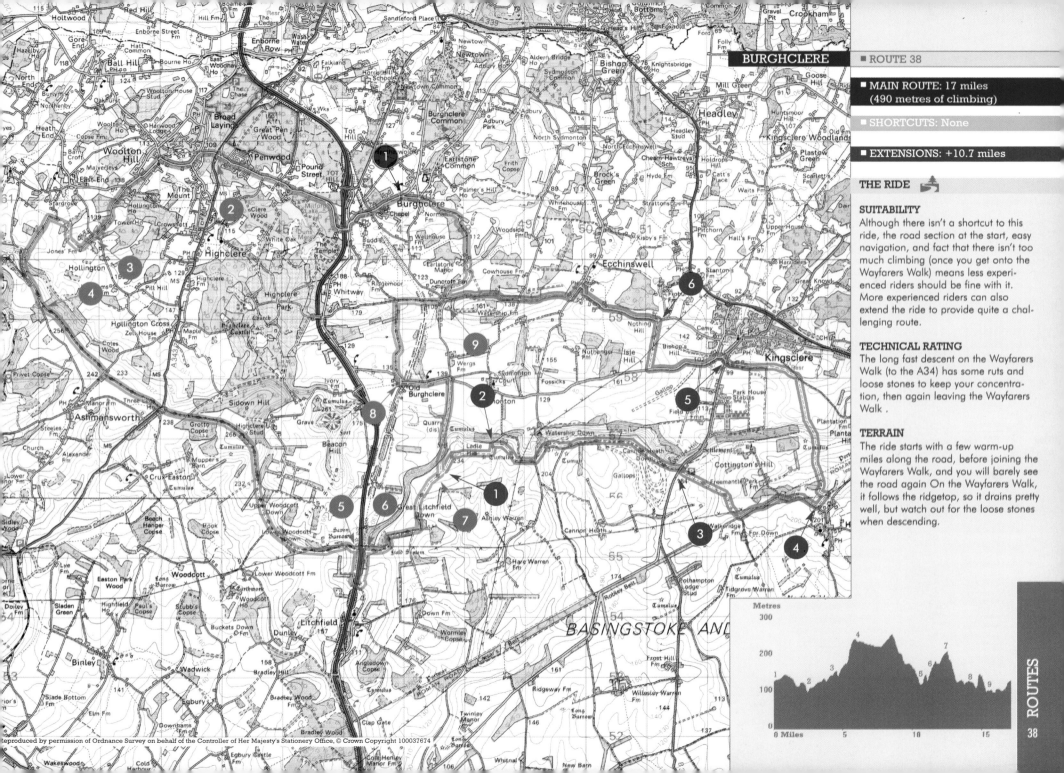

■ **MAIN ROUTE: 17 miles**
(490 metres of climbing)

■ **SHORTCUTS: None**

■ **EXTENSIONS: +10.7 miles**

THE RIDE

SUITABILITY
Although there isn't a shortcut to this ride, the road section at the start, easy navigation, and fact that there isn't too much climbing (once you get onto the Wayfarers Walk) means less experienced riders should be fine with it. More experienced riders can also extend the ride to provide quite a challenging route.

TECHNICAL RATING
The long fast descent on the Wayfarers Walk (to the A34) has some ruts and loose stones to keep your concentration, then again leaving the Wayfarers Walk .

TERRAIN
The ride starts with a few warm-up miles along the road, before joining the Wayfarers Walk, and you will barely see the road again On the Wayfarers Walk, it follows the ridgetop, so it drains pretty well, but watch out for the loose stones when descending.

■ MAIN ROUTE

17 miles & 490 metres of climbing

1 START. Go back to the main (Harts) rd and turn L on this for 0.7m, through Burghclere, bearing L, and take the 2nd R (bridge over the A34 road). **Follow this rd for 1.7m to a X-rds with the A343 and go SA** (Highclere).

2 0.15m to a T-J (436/618) **and turn L on this rd for 0.5m, then turn L on Church Rd** (by the church) (430/617). **0.45m to a fork in the rd, and bear L** (Hollington), **0.65m to a grass triangle and bear R, then SA/L on a BW** (rd) (419/603).

3 Becomes off-road, and bears R **to the corner of a track** (413/606) **and turn L on this. Keep L, UH to a rd** (407/599) **and turn L on this for 0.5m, then bear L on the Wayfarers Walk (WW), ByW** (410/592).

Quick guide: Stay on 'Wayfarers walk' for 4.7 miles to the A34 rd (463/551) and rejoin main route directions at no.5.

4 1.75m to the A343 rd (430/575), **bear L then R back on the WW. After 1.4m** (going DH), **bear R after the metal gates** as the DT bears L, to the top of the field. Through a field to some metal gates and bear L, into the woods, **to the A34 rd** (462/551).

5 Turn R just before the rd, which bears L under the bridge (A34) and immediately turn L into a field (not signposted) (462/545). Follow the LHS of the field (parallel to the rd) **for 0.5m** (old bridge on the L), **then turn R, up the valley** (463/551).

6 After 0.75m, turn L on another DT, following the white wooden arrow (472/555), near some woods. After 0.7m on this, bear L at a very feint fork (476/564), before the top of the hill, or see the extension.

7 DH, to the LHS of the hill top, going north, **along the BW track for 1m to a rd** (477/579). **Turn L**, into Old Burghclere, over a bridge, **bearing R, then keep SA on the ByW**, as the rd bears L, (468/580).

8 0.75m to a X-tracks (469/593) **and turn R**, for 0.5m, **to a rd and turn L, then immediately bear R at the rd fork, then turn immediately L on a BW** (477/593), before another rd T-J.

9 0.45m to a DT and turn L on this, then shortly R on the BW (if this is overgrown - follow the DT, past the manor, and rejoin the BW. **Follow this to a X-rds** at a grass triangle, (472/610) **and go SA** (Church lane) **back** to the car (470/610).

EXTENSION:

+10.7 miles & +320 metres of climbing

1 Bear R at the fork (staying on the WW), then shortly, keep SA through the gates, as track bears R. **To the top of the hill and bear R** on grassy a DT, to a T-J and turn (sharp) **L for 0.1m then turn R through the wooden gate**, by a green gate (484/568).

2 Through the field, and bear L at a metal gate, onto a good track (under the elec. cables), **UH to a rd** (491/566). Go SA on a ST BW, UH through some wooden gates, and join a DT, bearing L and follow this for 1.2m, **to a rd** (515/564).

3 Turn L on the rd, then immediately (sharp) R on the (WW) BW and follow this for 0.8m to a rd (525/556). Turn L on the rd (leaving the WW) **for 0.9m, then turn L on a BW** through some metal gates (538/558), just before entering Hannington village.

4 Bear sharp L at end of the field, and keep SA/L for 1.25m to a T-J (535/580) at the end of a path through the middle of a field **Turn L**, to a fork and bear L on the ST, and keep SA, becoming a drive, **to a rd**.

5 Turn R on the rd, then immediately L on Bear Hill rd (by some houses), over the stream, to a T-J (522/583). Turn L on this rd (Sydmonton) for 0.75m, then turn R on a BW (large stone in the middle) (510/581), **for 0.5m to a rd** (512/589).

6 Turn L on the rd for 0.95m to a T-J in Ecchinswell village, (Royal Oak pub here), **and turn L, for 0.15m then turn R on another rd** (497/593) (Burchclere). **After 1.4m bear R at the fork** (477/593), **and immediately turn R again on a BW** (before the blue HGV sign) **and rejoin the main route at no.9.**

🚗 **GETTING THERE**

The ride starts in village of Burghclere, which just off the A34 rd, south of Newbury. Follow the signs for Burghclere off the A34 and go through the village, past the Carpenters Arms pub, then turn R on Church lane (by the church) and park in the lay-by on the left just here (470/610).

🛏 **ACCOMMODATION**

B&B in Burchclere on: 01635 278305
B&B in Newtown on: 01635 43097
Camping at Oakley farm (off the A343), on: 01635 36581
Newbury T.I. on: 01635 30267

🚲 **BICYCLE SHOPS**

The Cycle shop in Newbury, on: 01635 582100

🍴 **REFRESHMENTS**

The Carpenters Arms in Burghclere or just off the route in Woolton hill and Ashmansworth. or in Hannington, Kingsclere and Ecchinswell on the extension.

ROUTES

38

HIGHLY RECOMMENDED

■ ROUTE 39

■ **NORTH LOOP: 21.6 miles**
(515 metres of climbing)

■ Shortcut: -8.3 miles

■ **SOUTH LOOP: 16.2 miles**
(430 metres of climbing)

THE RIDE 🌲

SUITABILITY

This will be 2 rides to most mere mortals, as both loops ridden together would be very difficult - be warned. Both are superb and you should find time to do both. The north loop is longer, has more climbing, and the ups and downs are long, but it does reward you with some great singletrack. The southern loop is a bit easier, but still has some great trails - especially the superb flowing singletrack alongside the river to point G.

TECHNICAL RATING

Lots of superb twisty singletrack that gets more technical the faster you go. There are also some steps, roots, ruts etc to keep you awake.

TERRAIN

Lots of twisty, flowing, woodland singletrack. Can get muddy in places in the wet which can make the going slow and tiring, and the wet roots need to be ridden carefully.

ROUTES

39

GETTING THERE

This ride starts from Woodcote village hall car park. Woodcote is north west of Reading, and just off the A4074. The (free) car park is in the centre of the village (645/820) by the playground and village green (and Red Lion pub). There is a railway station in Goring and Pangbourne.

ACCOMMODATION

B&B in Woodcote on: 01491 680461
Campsites in Crowmarsh / Wallingford on: 01491 836860 or ask at Wallingford TI for more information. YHA in Streatley/Goring on: 0870 770 6054
Wallingford T.I. on: 01491 826972

BICYCLE SHOPS

Mountain High in Pangbourne on: 0118 9841851 and Rides on Air in Wallingford on: 01491 836289

REFRESHMENTS

Shop and pubs in Woodcote. More pubs on the north loop in Hailey, Stoke Row, and nr Kingswood common. On the south loop in Goring Heath, Whitchurch, and Cray's pond.

21.6 miles & 515 metres of climbing

1 START. Exit the car park and turn L on the rd to some X-rds and turn R for 0.5m to the A4074 rd (643/827). Cross the rd onto the track opposite and keep L on this for 0.6m then turn L on a BW, as the rd bears R (650/831), **DH**, through the woods, **to a rd.**
■ NOTE: The RATZ club has a good (private) singletrack race course in these woods.

2 Turn L on the rd for 0.8m to a fork (633/840) and bear R (Ipsden), **keeping SA** for 1m to a X-rds (638/857). Turn R (Well Place zoo) on the rd for 0.8m, then keep SA on a BW, as the rd bears R (647/852) and follow this for 1.2m, UH, to a rd (667/854) **and turn L** for 0.3m to a X-rds (668/859) or see the shortcut.

3 Turn L (dead end) on the BW and keep SA, DH, on this for 1.9m to a fork by some woods and bear R on a DT, past a farm, to a rd (636/872). Turn R on rd for 0.2m then L on the Ridgeway BW (636/875).

4 SA over a minor rd after 0.4m, for another 0.9m to a gate (617/879) by the A4074 rd. Turn around and go back the way you came to the 2nd rd (636/875) and turn R on this for 0.4m. L at the rd T-J for 0.7m then L on the rd (637/858) (Hailey).

5 Past the King William **pub**, becoming a rough DT, UH, for 2.2m to a rd and turn R then shortly L on a BW (668/856).

6 Follow this BW for 1m, and join a drive and keep SA on this for another 0.35m to a T-J (681/841). Turn L on the rd (or R to a shop) for 0.55m, past a pub, **then turn R** on a BW opposite Clare house (689/840), UH.

7 0.45m to a fork and bear R (past some wooden posts), to a fork and bear R again, over a DT, to a T-J (694/831) and turn L, to a rd and turn R on this for 0.3 the turn R on a BW (697/828). Keep SA through the woods, to a drive and go SA on a BW, on the L of Holly Tree cottage (693/827).

8 DH, to a rd and keep SA on the (Hazel grove) BW (the pub is on the left), keeping to the LHS of some houses, for 2.25m, over a drive and 3 minor rds) to the A4074 rd. Go SA on the rd opposite (Goring) for 0.4m, then turn R on a BW (663/800).

9 SA for 1.2m, out of the woods, onto a drive and keep SA/L on this for 0.15m to a rd (645/812). Turn R on this, to a fork and bear L, DH, for 0.4m to a T-J by a shop and turn R. 0.1m to some X-rds and turn R, then shortly R again to the car park (645/820).

SHORTCUT:

-8.3 miles & -210 metres of climbing

1 Turn R off the rd after 0.01m on a BW (681/841), rejoin the main route at no.6.

16.2 miles & 430 metres of climbing

A START. Exit the car park and turn L on the rd to some X-rds, and turn L (past an pub), for 0.1m then L on Whitehouse rd (by the Post Office). UH, 0.4m to a T-J (645/814) and turn R for 0.1m then turn L on a BW/ drive (Green Lane) opposite a rd on on the R (646/812).

B After 0.15m keep SA/R into the woods, as the drive bears L, for 0.5m to a X-tracks (654/808). Keep SA, following the white arrows, for 0.8m to a rd. Go SA on the BW opposite for 0.8m (keep L at the stagnant water, becoming a DT, to a fork by a house (672/791) and turn R.

C After 0.15m turn R on a BW, bearing L around the stagnant water, to a rd (663/789) and turn R on this. 0.4m to some X-rds (658/792) by the old post office and turn L immediately L again on a BW, by the red phone box. 0.35m to a X-rds and turn R to a fork (658/786) and bear R on a BW.

D Go over a rd after 0.4m, for 0.2m to another rd (653/794) and turn L on this for 0.45m then and turn L on a BW (646/792). UH, along, then DH to a rd (649/784) and turn L on this, steep UH, for 0.25m then R on a drive, as the rd bears L (652/785).

E Keep SA on the DT, into the woods, follow this main track, R then L, DH, to a drive (658/778). Turn R on this for 0.45m, past some stables, to a X-rds and keep SA on the rd (although shortly after the farm, there is a ST in the trees on the R, parallel to the rd) for 1.1m to a T-J (634/775) in Whitchurch.

F Turn R, UH, for 0.05m then turn L on th Thames path BW (by a 40mph sign) for 0.75m and keep SA. **WARNING** there ar some steps down (and back up) here. Kee SA on this ST for 1.5m (be careful of other path users) to a X-tracks (610/798) by some houses, **and turn R** on the stoney DT.

G UH, to a rd and turn R on this for 0.3m then keep SA, on the ROW as the rd bears L. UH, for 0.5m to a fork (623/795) and bear L to and on the rd (this is a FP). After 0.3m turn R on a BW (by an old shack on L), on a thin ST, on the RHS of the fence.

H Into the woods and keep SA for 0.4m to a fork (625/799) and turn L, DH, and keep R after 0.25m through some gate posts (but no gate) to a T-J in the open (624/805). Turn R and keep SA for 0.85m UH, through gates, past a house, join a drive, to a rd (636/801).

I Turn L on the rd for 0.25m to an (off-se X-rds (637/806) (White Lion pub SA) and turn R on the B4526 rd (Reading). After 0.6m turn L on a BW (Exlade) just past the log yard on the R (645/801) and keep SA on this ST for 0.4m to a rd.

J Go SA on the BW for 0.3m to a X-track (654/808) (been here before) and turn L, joining the drive and keep SA/L on this the rd and turn R to a fork (645/813) and bear L. DH, for 0.4m to a T-J by the post office and turn R for 0.1m to the X-rds and turn R and shortly R back to the car park (645/820).

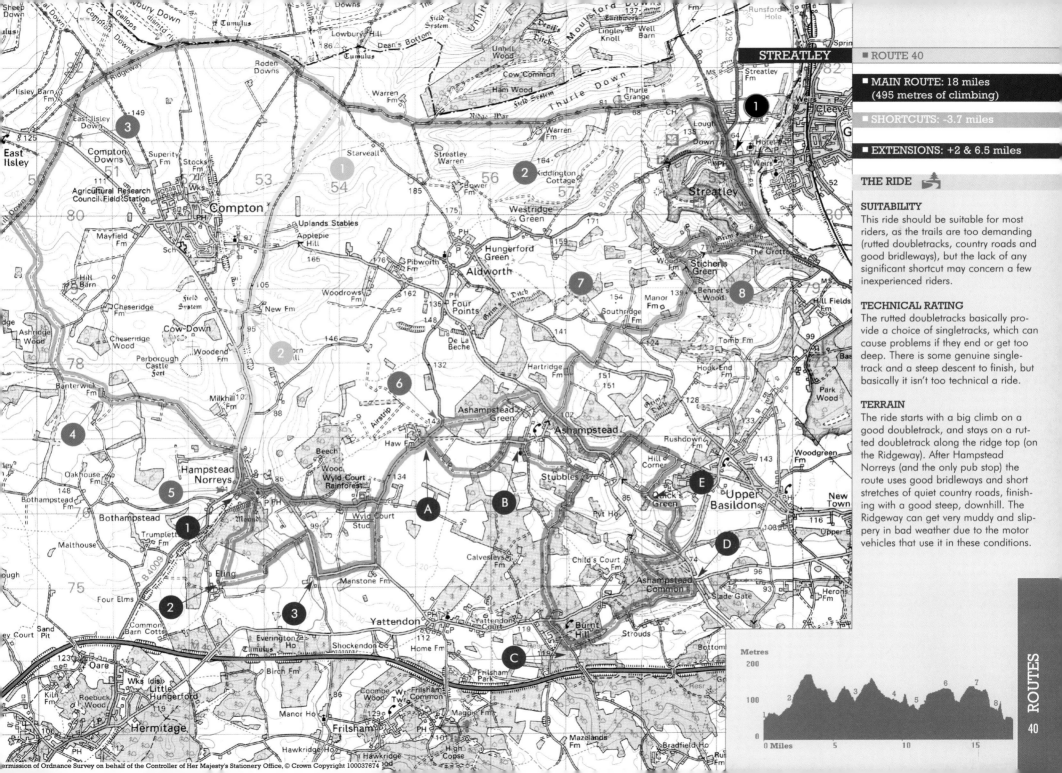

■ **MAIN ROUTE:** 18 miles
(495 metres of climbing)

■ **SHORTCUTS:** -3.7 miles

■ **EXTENSIONS:** +2 & 6.5 miles

THE RIDE

SUITABILITY
This ride should be suitable for most
riders, as the trails are too demanding
(rutted doubletracks, country roads and
good bridleways), but the lack of any
significant shortcut may concern a few
inexperienced riders.

TECHNICAL RATING
The rutted doubletracks basically provide a choice of singletracks, which can
cause problems if they end or get too
deep. There is some genuine singletrack and a steep descent to finish, but
basically it isn't too technical a ride.

TERRAIN
The ride starts with a big climb on a
good doubletrack, and stays on a rutted doubletrack along the ridge top (on
the Ridgeway). After Hampstead
Norreys (and the only pub stop) the
route uses good bridleways and short
stretches of quiet country roads, finishing with a good steep, downhill. The
Ridgeway can get very muddy and slippery in bad weather due to the motor
vehicles that use it in these conditions.

ROUTES

40

GETTING THERE

The ride starts in the village of Streatley (which is separated from the village of Goring by a bridge over the river Thames). There is a free car park in Goring (follow the signs), or on the side of Rectory road (off the A417) which is part of the route. There is a railway station in Goring.

ACCOMMODATION

B&B in Goring on: 01491 872829
B&B in Streatley on: 01491 872048
YHA in Streatley on: 0870 7706054
Camping in Crowmarsh / Wallingford on: 01491 836860
Wallingford T.I. on: 01491 826972

BICYCLE SHOPS

Mountain High in Pangbourne on: 0118 984 1851 and Rides on Air in Wallingford on: 01491 836289

REFRESHMENTS

There is a pub in Streatley, or pubs, restaurants and a shop in Goring. On the route the only pub is the White Heart in Hampstead Norreys (1/2 way around the route).

ROUTES

40

MAIN ROUTE

18 miles & 495 metres of climbing

1 START. From the X-rds (in Streatley, by the pub) **head north** (pub behind you) on the A329, for 0.2m then bear L on the A417 (Wantage). After 0.25m turn L on Rectory rd (Ridgeway) (589/814), and follow this **for 1.4m** to Warren farm.

2 Keep SA/R, UH on the Ridgeway, and stay on the Ridgeway (main DT) **for 4m** or see the shortcut. At some X-tacks (508/819) (0.7m after a bridge that goes over nothing), go SA (East Ilsley) as the Ridgeway goes R. After 0.2m at another X-tracks (506/817) **turn L, DH** to a rd (503/810).

3 Go SA on the BW for 0.8m, UH, to a blue height limit sign **and turn L on a** (grassy) rough and rutty BW (497/799), (you can probably hear the A34 rd, SA). After 1.1m bear R at a fork, for another 0.4m to a X-tracks (in some woods) (503/778).

4 Turn L, into a field, becoming a DT by a farm and keep SA on this **for 1.3m** to a rd and turn sharp R, to a T-J (526/763).

5 Turn L over a bridge, on the B4009 through the village, or see extension 1. As you exit the village, keep L at the fork on the B4009 (Wyld court rainforest) **for 1.5m** to a rd on the R (559/761). Stay on the B4009 or see extension 2, **for 0.15m** then turn R on a BW into the woods (553/771).

6 Keep SA for 0.85m, DH to a rd (565/776) and turn R on this for 0.25m to a X-tracks (568/772) and L on Hartridge lane. 6a - R at a T-J after 0.6m (Upper Basildon) for 0.1m then L on a BW at Blackwood house (574/780), SA to a rd (576/784).

7 Turn R on the rd, and keep L on this for 1m then bear L on a ByW as the rd goes DH and R, DH to a rd (583/795). Turn R on this, to a T-J (589/794) and turn L, UH on a drive (Ash Hill), between the brick posts.

8 After 0.2m go SA on a BW, as the drive bears L, steep DH on a ST to the A417 rd (595/798). Turn L on this for 1m back to the X-rds/lights in Streatley (591/808) (pub on L), and the end of the ride.

SHORTCUT:

-3.7 miles & -117 metres of climbing

1 After 1.8m (from Warren farm) turn L at a X-tracks (540/815) on a ByW (just after a ByW joins from the L). DH for 1.35m, joining Downs road, and keep SA to a X-tracks (530/795) and go SA on Coombe rd for 0.6m to New farm (527/787).

2 Go past the farm to a fork and and bear L, to another rd and bear L on this. After 0.85m bear R at a fork (526/768), to a T-J and rejoin the main route at no.5.

The Thames at Goring & Streatly.

EXTENSION 1:

+2 miles & +50 metres of climbing

1 Just over the bridge turn R towards the village hall, and into some woods and turn R on a BW as soon as you enter these woods (528/761). Keep SA to a fence (525/755) and turn R, across a field to the other side (524/751).

2 Turn L in front of the house (unmarked BW), along field edge for 0.35 to the far end **and turn L.** Through some woods and over a stream, then UH **to a rd** (535/757) and turn R on this for 0.3m then turn L on a nother rd (Yattendon 1m) (537/751).

3 After 0.45m turn L on a BW (opposite Manstone farm) (545/753) as rd bears R. Keep SA as this becomes a concrete track, to the B4009 rd (545/761) and turn R/SA on the rd. After 0.7m stay on the B4009 or see extension 2, for another 0.15m then turn R on a BW into the woods (553/771), and rejoin main route at no.6.

EXTENSION 2:

+6.5 miles & +160 metres of climbing

A Turn R on the BW before the rd on the R (opposite the white house), **through a green gate and turn L** on a concrete track, bearing L (555/765) to a rd. Turn R on this for 0.15m then turn R on Church lane as you enter the village (564/769).

B Turn L just past the church on a R.O.W. (565/767), through a field, **bearing R** parallel with a rd. To a thatched cottage (572/765) and turn R on the DT BW, and keep SA **for 1.25m** to a rd and go SA on a ST rd, for 0.25m then L after HGV sign (570/743) on a BW.

C Keep SA for 0.6m (SA at X-tracks and SA/L by a house), to a X-tracks (ByW on R & ROW on L) (578/746). Go SA then immediately bear R at the fork and ride along the bottom (RHS) of the wood for 0.7m, bearing L to a T-J (586/750), near a rd.

D Turn L for 0.2m to a fork and turn R, UH to a rd and go SA/R, to the edge of the wood (579/753) and turn R. After 0.35m at a rd (584/754), turn L on the BW, UH to a T-J and bear L, to a rd by some houses (580/762).

E Turn R on the rd for 0.4m, then turn L on a BW as the rd bears sharp R (584/767). Keep to the R of converted barns, and **bearing L,** DH to a rd (575/767). Turn R on this rd for 0.7m to a X-rds (568/773) and turn R on Hartridge lane, **and rejoin main route at no.6a.**

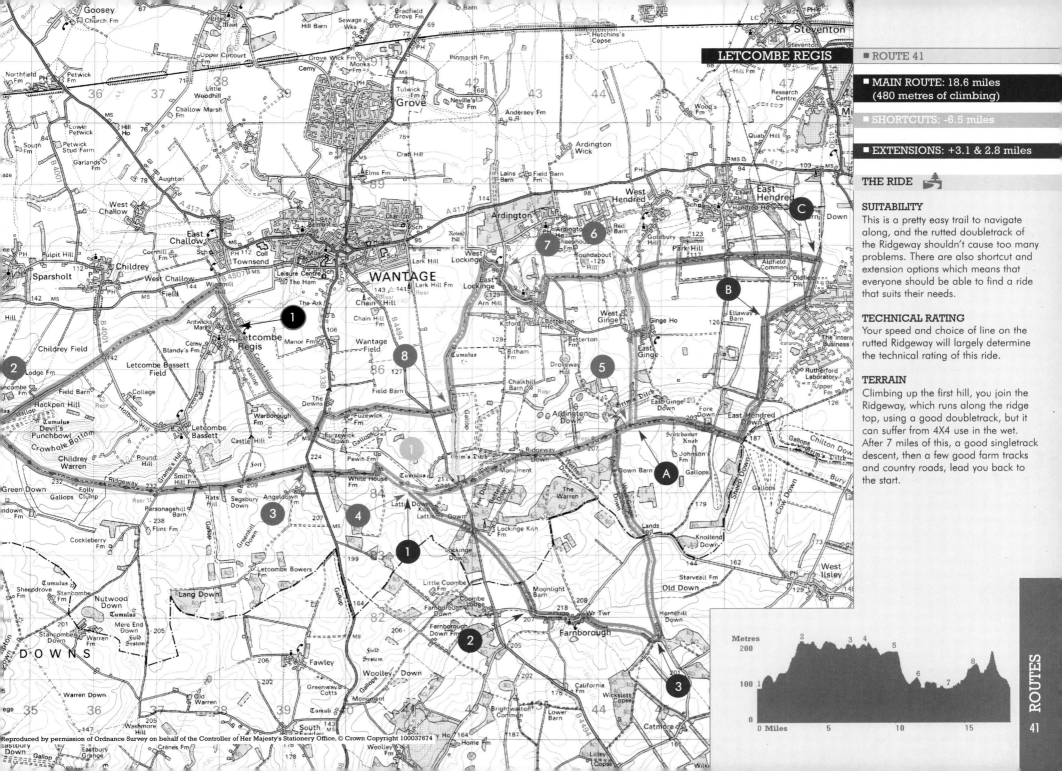

ROUTE 41

MAIN ROUTE: 18.6 miles
(480 metres of climbing)

SHORTCUTS: -6.5 miles

EXTENSIONS: +3.1 & 2.8 miles

THE RIDE

SUITABILITY

This is a pretty easy trail to navigate along, and the rutted doubletrack of the Ridgeway shouldn't cause too many problems. There are also shortcut and extension options which means that everyone should be able to find a ride that suits their needs.

TECHNICAL RATING

Your speed and choice of line on the rutted Ridgeway will largely determine the technical rating of this ride.

TERRAIN

Climbing up the first hill, you join the Ridgeway, which runs along the ridge top, using a good doubletrack, but it can suffer from 4X4 use in the wet. After 7 miles of this, a good singletrack descent, then a few good farm tracks and country roads, lead you back to the start.

GETTING THERE

The ride starts from the village of Letcombe Regis, which is just south west of Wantage. Go to Wantage (where the A338 and A417 cross) and exit here (west) on the B4507 (Ickleton rd) signposted 'Ashbury'. After 1 mile turn left to Letcombe Regis on Court hill rd, then right on Main street into the village (382/866) and park considerately. The nearest railway station is in Didcot (about 5 miles away - go through Harwell on the B449, then right on the A417 and join the route at extension 2 letter C).

ACCOMMODATION

B&B's in Letcombe Regis on: 01235 762860 and 765827.
YHA 2 miles south of Wantage, off the A338, on: 0870 7706064.
Wantage T.I. on: 01235 760176

BICYCLE SHOPS

Ridgeway cycles in Wantage on: 01235 764 445

REFRESHMENTS

There is a pub in Letcombe Regis, or shops, chippy, etc in Wantage, but nothing else on the main route. However, there is a pub just off the main route in Ardington.

ROUTES

41

MAIN ROUTE

18.6 miles & 480 metres of climbing

1 START. Go back to the main (Court Hill) rd and turn L (north) for 0.2m (over water) and keep SA/L on Windmill hill rd (East Challow). After 0.2m UH on this rd, turn L on a ByW (380/873). After 1.4m, at a rd going 3-ways, and go on the B4001 rd, UH for 1.25m then L on the Ridgeway (opposite a rd on the R) (344/851).

Quick directions: Keep SA on the Ridgeway for 7 miles, and the rejoin directions at no.5.

2 Keep SA on the Ridgeway for 3.5m to the A338 rd (394/844).

3 Turn R on the rd them immediately L back on the Ridgeway. After 0.75m turn R at a T-J (then keep L on the Ridgeway), for 0.35m to a fork (410/841), and bear L (staying on Ridgeway) or see extension 1.

4 Go to and over the B4494 rd (418/841) and go SA on the Ridgeway for another 1.9 miles or see the shortcut.

5 Shortly after some trees on the L, and a DT crossing the Ridgeway, turn L, DH, on a ST BW (445/851) or see extension 2.
5a - Go DH for 0.9m to a rd, and turn R on this, into East Ginge (448/866), staying sharp L on the rd, for 0.6m, turn L on the ByW which crosses the rd (446/875).

6 After 0.9m join a rd and keep SA/L, then very shortly turn L on a DT, bearing sharp R (432/875). 0.3m to a rd (429/870) and turn R/SA on this, for 0.6m past a church, and turn L on a rd (West Lockinge), just past a car park & telephone box (425/876).

7 After 0.15m, turn L through a farm (421/877), and follow this BW for 1.6m, then turn R on a DT (417/853) by the hedges, after a small climb and before the slight DH, to the B4494 rd ().

8 Go SA on the ByW for 1.1m to a A338 rd (396/852). Turn L on rd, steeply UH for 0.25m. Turn R on the (Court hill) rd (394/849), and do DH for 1.35m, then turn L, back in to Letcombe Regis and the start/end (382/866).

SHORTCUT:

-6.5 miles & -140 metres of climbing

1 Turn L on a BW (off the Ridgeway) immediately after crossing the rd, DH, keeping SA at the X-rds after 0.35m. After another 0.5m turn L on a DT, (417/853), by the hedges, and turn L to the B4494 rd, and rejoin the main route at no.8.

The Ridgeway.

EXTENSION 1:

+3.1 miles & +65 metres of climbing

1 Bear R at the fork (off the Ridgeway) for 0.85m to a rd (420/833) and cross this, through a gate. Go through the middle of a field, (farm on L), for 1m to a rd (430/821).

2 Turn L on the rd for 0.5m (through Farnborough) then R on a BW just past a red telephone box (437/820). After 0.75m at some X-tracks in the woods (449/816), turn L, which bears L, out of woods.

3 Keep SA for 1m, DH to a rd (448/833), and go SA (on the RHS of the house) on a BW, through a farm. 1.2m to a X-tracks with the Ridgeway (443/850) and turn R for 0.15m, then L on a ST, and rejoin the main route at no.5a or see extension 2.

EXTENSION 2:

+2.8 miles & +70 metres of climbing

A Keep SA on the Ridgeway for another 1.1m, (0.3m past a rough car park) and turn L on a rough DT BW (462/849) (don't worry the track improves). DH for 0.45m to a X-tracks and keep SA alongside the high (research laboratories) fence on the R, for 0.8m to a fork (466/867).

B Bear R at the fork (by the old tyres & tank), for 0.5m then bear L on the BW, into the trees (473/871). After 0.4m at a X-tracks (475/877), turn L on the DT ByW.

C Keep SA on this ByW for 1.75m to the 2nd rd crossing (446/875) and rejoin the main route at no.6.

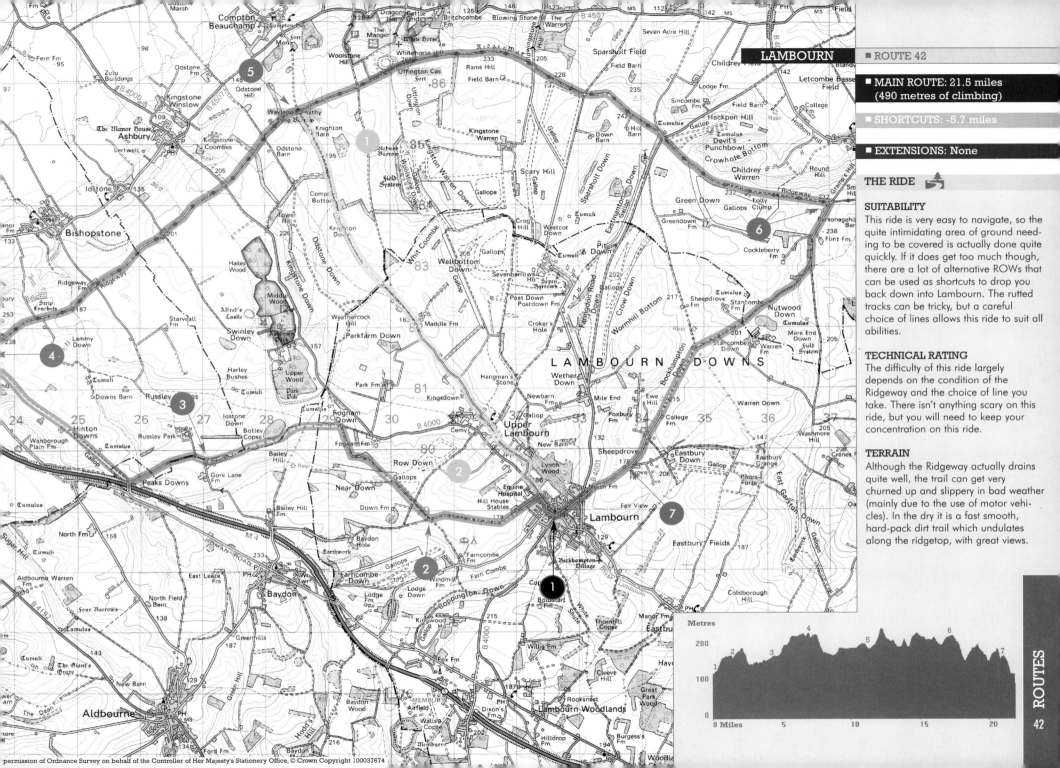

■ MAIN ROUTE: 21.5 miles
(490 metres of climbing)

■ SHORTCUTS: -5.7 miles

■ EXTENSIONS: None

THE RIDE

SUITABILITY

This ride is very easy to navigate, so the quite intimidating area of ground needing to be covered is actually done quite quickly. If it does get too much though, there are a lot of alternative ROWs that can be used as shortcuts to drop you back down into Lambourn. The rutted tracks can be tricky, but a careful choice of lines allows this ride to suit all abilities.

TECHNICAL RATING

The difficulty of this ride largely depends on the condition of the Ridgeway and the choice of line you take. There isn't anything scary on this ride, but you will need to keep your concentration on this ride.

TERRAIN

Although the Ridgeway actually drains quite well, the trail can get very churned up and slippery in bad weather (mainly due to the use of motor vehicles). In the dry it is a fast smooth, hard-pack dirt trail which undulates along the ridgetop, with great views.

ROUTES

42

■ MAIN ROUTE

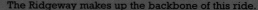

GETTING THERE

This ride starts from the village of Lambourn, which is just north of junction 14 of the M4, on the B4000 (and B4001). There is a car park near the library, as well as some spaces outside the church or down quiet roads.

ACCOMMODATION

B&B in Shefford Woodlands (by junction 14 of the M4): 01488 648466
B&B's in Letcombe Regis on: 01235 762860 and 01235 765827.
YHA (2 miles south of Wantage on the A338) on: 0870 7706064
Camping (nr Lambourn) at Farncombe farm on: 01488 71833
Wantage T.I. on: 01235 760176 or
Newbury T.I. on: 01635 30267

BICYCLE SHOPS

Ridgeway cycles in Wantage on: 01235 764 445

REFRESHMENTS

There is a pub and shop in Lambourn and a water tap at GR 264/835. There aren't any pubs on the route, but there are some just off the northern side of the Ridgeway.

21.5 miles & 490 metres of climbing

1 **START**. From the X-rds in the centre of the village (326/789) by the church, head north on Parsonage lane, for 0.3m, then turn L on Folly rd (323/792). Keep SA on this for 1.2m becoming a ByW, to a X-tracks (306/788) and turn R.

2 Keep SA after 0.2m at another X-tracks, for 0.3m and keep SA on a feint ByW **track**, as the DT bears L (300/794). 0.85m to a X-tracks (292/803) and turn L on the ByW, and keep SA on this for 1.45m to a rd, by a bungalow (270/798).

3 Basically, keep SA on the Ridgeway for 10 miles, to a minor rd (370/840) and rejoin the main route at no.6 or see below for more detailed information.

Go SA/R on the rd for 0.85m, then turn R on the BW (258/794) just before the bridge over the M4. Turn R immediately through a single gate, then turn L on a feint track (alongside the Gallop - horse bit). Keep SA for 1.95m, towards the satellite tower, **and turn R** behind the barn on the Ridgeway (235/815).

4 1.3m to a rd and go SA, (water tap on the L, after 0.85m by the barns), **for another 1.7m to the** B4000 rd (273/843). Go SA for 0.6m to a X-tracks and go SA for 0.45m past the neolithic Weyland Smithy burial mound, from around 2800BC at (280/853) **to a X-tracks (285/855) and keep SA for 2.5m to a rd** or see the shortcut.

5 Go SA at the rd (322/862), for 0.6m to a X-tracks and go SA, UH (track splits, but rejoins shortly) for 1m to a rd. Bear R on this minor **rd**, to the B4001 rd (343/851) **and go SA** on the Ridgeway, for another 1.9m to a minor **rd** (370/840).

6 Turn R on this rd, for 0.4m to a fork just past a farm, **and bear L on the ByW, for 0.3m to a X-tracks (367/829) and turn R.** 0.9m, and keep SA on the concrete track, UH, **for 0.5m to a barn** (348/816). **Keep SA** on the concrete track **for 1.4m where a rd joins from the L** (338/797).

7 **Turn R into the field** on the RHS of the rd, behind the hedge, **bearing L**, DH, parallel to the rd. This rejoins the rd, and keep you SA, DH, to the B4001 rd and bear L on this. 0.3m back to the X-rds in the centre of Lambourn (326/789), **and go SA, back to the car park.**

1 Turn R at the X-tracks, DH, **for 2m to a X-tracks, and go SA** on the DT. After 1.7m, past Maddle farm, **bear R with the rd to a T-J** (314/805) **and turn L.**

2 After 0.05m bear R to the B4000 rd (313/803) and turn L on this for 1.2m, to a X-rds in Lambourn (326/789), and turn R back to the car park.

The Ridgeway makes up the backbone of this ride.

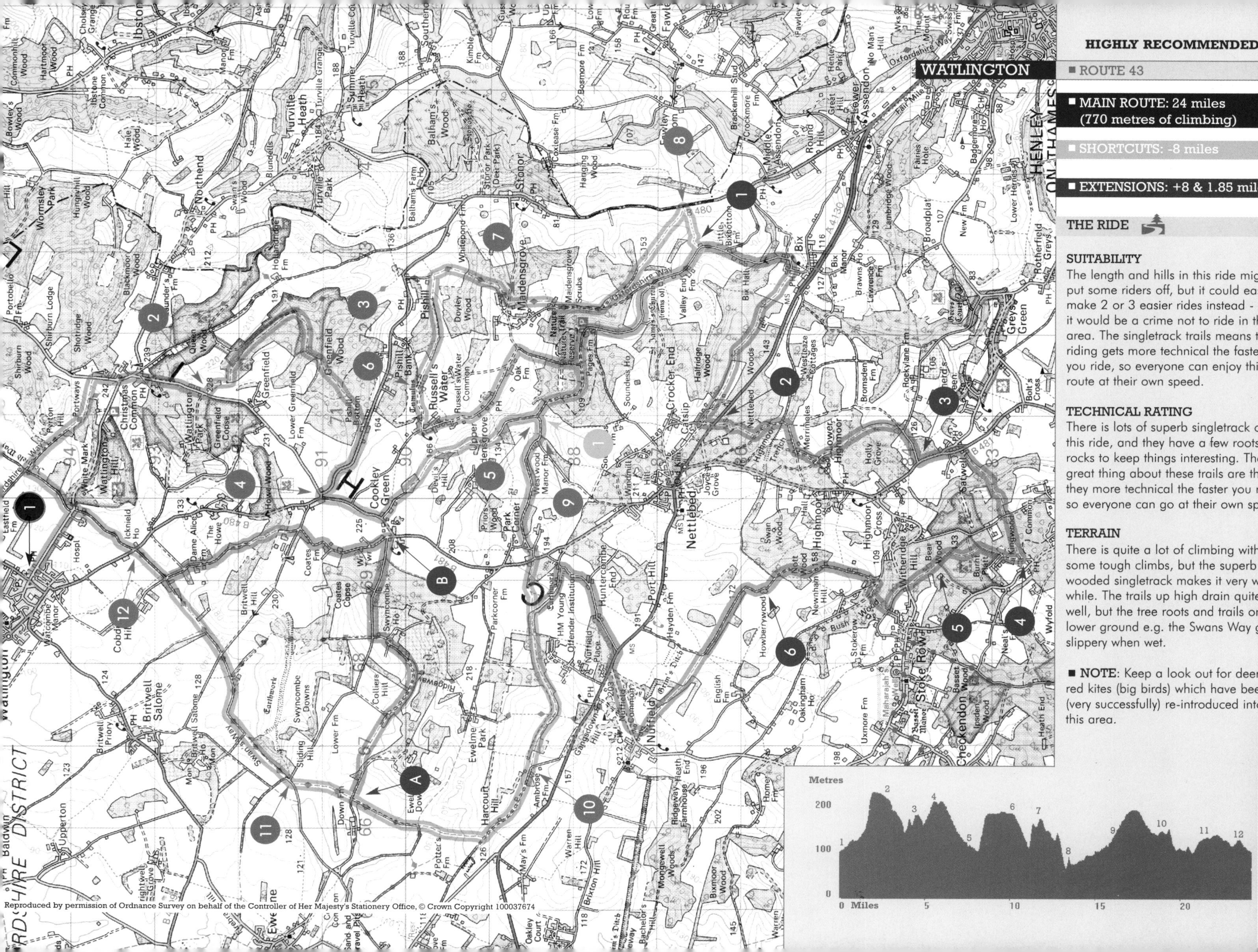

HIGHLY RECOMMENDED

■ ROUTE 43

■ MAIN ROUTE: 24 miles
(770 metres of climbing)

■ SHORTCUTS: -8 miles

■ EXTENSIONS: +8 & 1.85 miles

THE RIDE

SUITABILITY

The length and hills in this ride might put some riders off, but it could easily make 2 or 3 easier rides instead - and it would be a crime not to ride in this area. The singletrack trails means the riding gets more technical the faster you ride, so everyone can enjoy this route at their own speed.

TECHNICAL RATING

There is lots of superb singletrack on this ride, and they have a few roots and rocks to keep things interesting. The great thing about these trails are that they more technical the faster you ride, so everyone can go at their own speed.

TERRAIN

There is quite a lot of climbing with some tough climbs, but the superb wooded singletrack makes it very worthwhile. The trails up high drain quite well, but the tree roots and trails on the lower ground e.g. the Swans Way get slippery when wet.

■ NOTE: Keep a look out for deer and red kites (big birds) which have been (very successfully) re-introduced into this area.

GETTING THERE

The ride starts from the town of Watlington, which is on the B4009, just 3 miles south junction 6 of the M40. Follow the signs to the (free) car park, down Hill road (690/944) or there is another (free) car park at Christmas Common (708/936). The nearest railway station is at Henley-on-Thames (take the A4130 west towards Wallingford for 1 mile then turn right on the B480 for 1.5 miles and turn left on the BW and join the route at no.8.

ACCOMMODATION

B&B's in Pishill on: 01491 638601 or another on: 638351
Camping in Henley on: 01491 573419
YHA in Bradenham (nr High Wycombe) on: 0870 7705714
Wallingford T.I. on 01491 826972 or **Henley T.I.** on: 01491 578034

BICYCLE SHOPS

Rides on Air in Wallingford on: 01491 836289

REFRESHMENTS

Shops, pubs, etc in Watlington. Pubs on the route in Pishill (Crown), Maidensgrove (Five horseshoes), Christmas Common (Fox & Hounds), and Nuffield (Crown).

24 miles & 770 metres of climbing

1 START. Turn R out of the car park, to a T-J (pub on L) and go L/SA on the rd. After 0.55m turn L on a BW (698/ 940), for 0.5m to a ST rd (703/946) and turn R on this. Keep SA on the grass, as the rd bears R, UH, to a rd (715/937). Turn R and keep SA on this rd for 0.85m (0.5m past Fox & Hounds pub), & turn L on a BW (712/923).

2 DH for 1m to multiple X-tracks in a clearing (723/913). Turn R, and follow white 'CW' arrows, UH into woods. Follow the arrows, bearing L and DH to a X-tracks (716/910) at the bottom.

3 Go SA, UH to a X-tracks at the top and keep SA, DH then UH to a clearing, and keep R. Follow the white 'CW20' arrows through the woods, DH to Grove farm (708/905) and go through the gates to a rd (701/910). Turn R on the rd, UH, keep L to a T-J with the B481 rd (700/910).

4 Turn L on the rd for 0.5m, then L after the first house, on a gravel BW (697/902). Keep SA, becoming a ST between the trees, keeping R at fork after 0.7m, for 0.85m to a T-J (710/884) and turn L or see the shortcut

5 After 0.6m turn L at a X-tracks on a steep UH (716/879), for 0.6m to a rd (718/887). Turn L on the rd for 1m, to Russell's water then R on a gravel track just past a pond (708/898). Onto the common and keep SA on the garvel DT to a farm (713/898).

6 Go SA through the farm onto a ST for 1.25m to a T-J (at end of tunnel of trees) (727/897). Turn R, along the LHS of the field, DH to a X-tracks at bottom and go SA, steep UH, to the top and bear L, following

the white 'OW PS17' arrows to a rd (724/888).

7 Go SA, UH on the BW (Oxfordshire cycleway & white arrows), exiting the woods and across the field, between the houses to a farm and turn R, then immediately L at a grass triangle (on the cycle track). After 0.35m bear L at a fork (723/877), (SW33), and follow this for 1m, going DH to a DT T-J at the bottom (735/867).

8 Turn R on the DT, UH in the field, then back DH, bearing to the R of the house, to a rd (731/865) and turn R on the rd or see extension 1. After 1m, keep SA the Nature Reserve on the L (721/877) becoming off-road. Keep SA on this for 0.85m to a T-J (709/884) (you were here earlier) and bear L (haven't been up here before).

9 Bear to the R of the farm, UH to a minor rd and bear L to a T-J with another rd (693/885). Turn R on rd for 0.05m then L on BW (opposite house) and keep SA, DH on the ST for 1.7m.
9a - Exit the trees and bear R to a concrete track and turn R on this, past some houses.

10 Alongside the field for 0.8m to the top (near a clump of trees on the R) and turn R on a feint BW (easy to miss) (658/891). DH, and keep SA on the DT for 0.6m to a minor rd (663/906) and go SA or see extension 2. Through a field to a rd (665/914) and turn R on this, then immediately L/SA, as rd bears sharp R, on the (Swans Way) BW.

11 Keep SA on BW for 1.2m to a rd (681/922) and go SA, (the nice ST on RHS in the trees along here is a FP). 0.8m to some X-tracks with a concrete track (690/929) and keep SA to B480 rd.

12 Go SA (Icknield way) for another 0.6m to a rd (698/940) and turn L on this, DH (came up this at the start). After 0.55m keep SA, as rd bears L, by the pub, and shortly L back into the car park (691/944).

SHORTCUT:

-8 miles & -300 metres of climbing

1 Turn R at the T-J (710/884) and rejoin main route, which returns to this T-J on the track to the L, at no.13.

EXTENSION 1:

+8 miles & +160 metres of climbing

1 Turn L on the rd, then shortly R at a fork (Bix) to a T-J at the top (729/854) and turn R. Shortly along here keep SA on a BW, as rd bears L, across a field and into the woods, for 1.25m to a drive (709/864). Go SA, then shortly bear L on a DT by a house and tree, to a rd and turn L to the main rd (709/863) and go SA on the ST BW.

2 Shortly bear R at the (white arrow) fork, DH to a DT and turn L on this, to a T-J (709/855). Turn R. for 0.25m to X-tracks and L to another X-tracks and turn L again by buildings (704/851). Keep SA for 0.9m to a driveway (708/840) and turn R to a rd and bear R on this to the main rd.

3 Turn L on this for 0.35m, then R on a BW (706/833), keep R at a fork, DH (white arrows) to X-tracks at the bottom. Keep SA (UH) to a rd (698/828) and go SA on ST, forking R on the BW, and keep SA to a rd opposite Holly Tree cottage (693/827).

4 Turn R on the rd to the end and keep SA

on the ST BW (faded sign on silver gate, on LHS of a worksite). Keep L at the next two forks, over a DT for 0.25m to another fork (just after wooden posts) and turn L, following the blue arrow (693/836).

5 Follow this to a rd and go SA, keeping L (high) to the corner of a rd (686/843) and turn R (white arrows), DH, keeping R at a fork, on a ST to a rd. Go SA on the BW, UH to a X-tracks and go SA on this rd, (becomes off-road), for 0.8m to a fork (689/858) and bear L, past the houses.

6 After 0.75m, keep SA on a (hidden) BW as the DT bears R (681/864) and keep SA to a minor rd (670/872). Turn R on the rd, to a T-J with main A4130 rd, turn R on this for 0.15m then L on (Park corner) rd. After 0.9m (house SA and rd turns sharp R) turn L on Digberry lane (692/882). To a T-J with a BW (686/885) and turn L on this for 1.25m and rejoin the main route at no.9a.

EXTENSION 2:

+1.85 miles & +75 metres of climbing

A Turn R on the rd, UH for 0.2m then turn L on a BW (666/905) by the brick pillars, along the field edge, joining a DT and bear R on this. 0.7m to a church and bear R, then L, UH, to a rd T-J (683/903). Turn R on this rd for 0.75m to a (grass triangle) T-J (695/902) and turn L on the rd (FP).

B Follow this, keeping R by the farm, to a rd (696/913) and go SA (Woods farm - pig sign). After 0.1m turn R on a BW (into the trees), DH, keep SA on the main trail. Becomes a drive and keep SA, to a X-tracks (690/929) and turn R on a concrete track, and rejoin the main route at no.12.

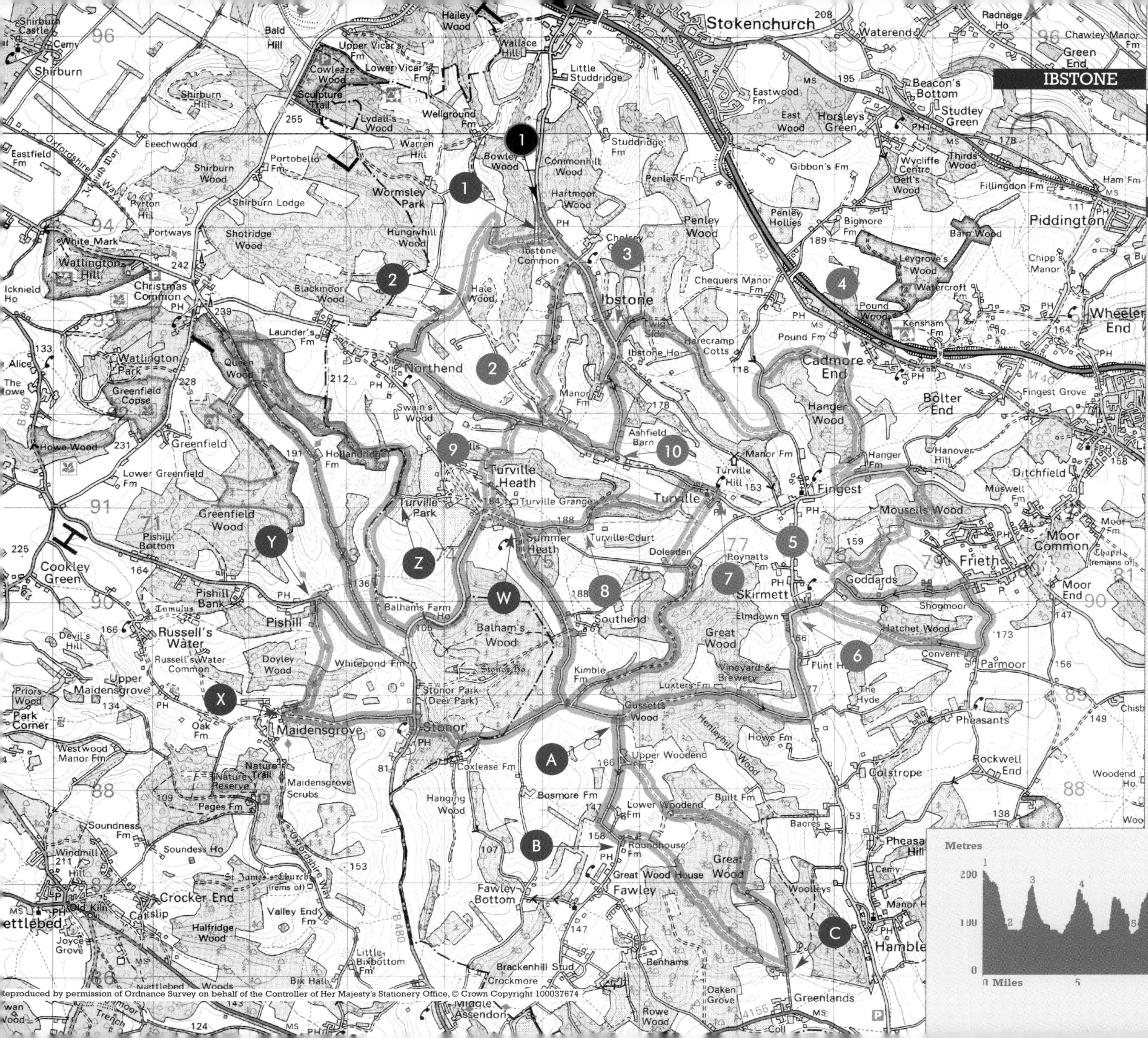

HIGHLY RECOMMENDED

■ ROUTE 44

- ■ **MAIN ROUTE: 20.5 miles** (800 metres of climbing)
- ■ **SHORTCUTS:** Various Possibilities
- ■ **EXTENSIONS:** +1.75, 4.7 & 10 miles

THE RIDE

SUITABILITY

This ride is nearly always going up or down one of the 7 big hills (more with the extensions), which makes it pretty tough. However, there are various shortcut opportunities, and it could actually make 2 or 3 good rides (rather than 1, with 36 miles and over 1,400 metres of climbing). This ride uses so many great trails you simply have to give it a go, regardless of all those hills.

TECHNICAL RATING

The superb, steep, tight singletrack with drops, rocks and other obstacles on this ride, mean it is a technical ride.

TERRAIN

This is a stunningly beautiful and unspoilt part of the country, with great trails and village pubs. It uses hilly, woodland or tree-lined tracks, with little or no rest between the ups and downs. The higher trails drain quite well, but some tracks can suffer after rain (and horses).

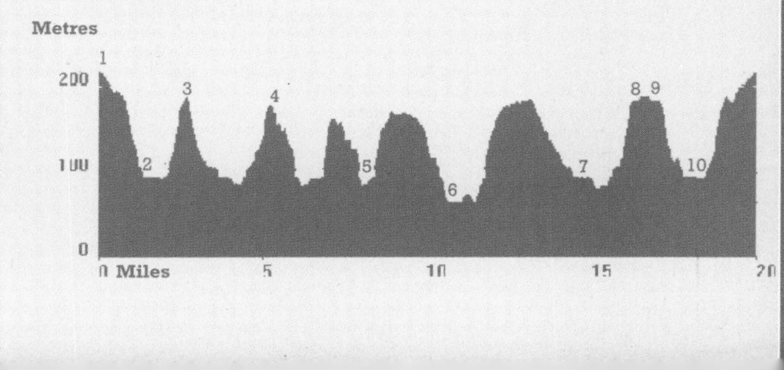

ROUTES

44

Reproduced by permission of Ordnance Survey on behalf of the Controller of Her Majesty's Stationery Office, © Crown Copyright 100037674

ROUTES

■ MAIN ROUTE

20.5 miles & 800 metres of climbing

1 START. Go south (past the Fox pub on your L) on the rd for (about) 0.4m to a X-rds (753/937), at the end of the common, or see extension 1. **Turn R on Grays lane, and keep SA to the end of the lane, then bear L into the woods on a BW, going DH, to the bottom** (751/919) **and bear L on the BW.**

2 0.5m to a rd (757/916) **and turn L on the rd, UH, to a T-J. Turn L on the rd for 0.1m, then turn R on a concrete track behind the school** (758/927).

3 Go DH on a concrete track **for 0.2m, then turn R on a ST BW,** through the woods (760/930), as the concrete track deteriorates. Exit the woods and **go over a DT, to a T-J and turn R on this, for 1.3m to a rd** (774/918). **Turn L on the rd for 0.45m then turn R on a BW** (773/924) **into woods, UH, to the top,** (781/925).

4 Bear R, DH to a T-J and keep R/SA on a good track, past a house and out of the woods, through a gate and **to the rd** (781/912). **Turn L on the rd for 0.45m to a fork and bear R** (Frieth). **After 0.15m turn L into the woods** (789/912), past a fence and steep UH on a BW. **After 0.3m turn R at the X-tracks** (signposted as a FP, but it is a BW) (791/908).

5 After 1m bear L onto the rd (780/902) **and turn L, UH on this for 0.9m to a T-J** (793/902) **and turn R on Parmoor lane.** Pub here in Frieth. Follow this rd **for 0.55 then bear R off the rd,** towards the convent (795/895) **and keep SA, on a fast ST DH to a rd. Turn L on the rd, DH to a T-J** (776/899) (or there is a pub to the right).

6 Go L/SA on the rd **for 1m to a X-rds** (777/888) **and turn R** (Vineyard) **on a steep, long UH. To the corner of a rd** (758/888) **and turn R/SA or see** extension 2.
6a - After 0.3m turn R on the BW at Kimble farm (753/889), and follow this, as it becomes a ST, DH. Follow the main track, keeping R, **for 1.5m to a rd** at the bottom (764/904).

7 Turn L on the rd **for 0.1m then R on a BW** (763/904) along the edge of a field, through a gate and **SA** through a tunnel of trees. Join a drive, past a school, **to a T-J in** Turville village (768/911). The Bull & Butcher pub is on the R. **Turn L on the rd, out of the village and immediately L on a BW** (765/912), **which bears R, then L after 0.5m, UH into the woods.**

8 Go UH to a T-J at the top (755/910) **and turn L on a DT, through a gate** (brick wall opposite) **and turn R on a drive.** To a T-J with a rd **and go SA/R for 0.3m and keep R at the fork** (by some houses) (748/908) or see extension 3. **After 0.25m at the X-rds** (744/910), **and go SA/R on the BW** (between the rd's going SA and R.

9 Through the trees, into clearing **bearing L across the common** area **going DH on the BW** just past Turville Heath farm. 0.55m to a rd (748/919) **and turn R on this for 0.15m** (by a track on the L), **then use the BW on the L,** running parallel to the rd (used this BW before).

10 0.5m to a rd (757/916) **and turn L on this, UH to a T-J and turn L,** through Ibstone, **back to the car** (751/941).

EXTENSION 1:

+1.75 miles & +100 metres of climbing

1 Shortly, turn R onto the common, along the edge of the woods (750/938) **to the far side and turn R on a BW** into the woods **then immediately L at a fork. Keep L,** DH, on this technical ST, **to a T-J** (745/941) **at the bottom** in the open (745/941), **and turn L, and follow this** BW to a (private) rd.

2 Go SA onto the BW, steep UH, to a surfaced **track and bear L, UH on this.** Follow this, through a gate and **to a rd** (735/926), **and turn L on the rd,** DH (the good ST alongside the road on the R is a FP). After 1m, by a track on the L, **use the BW on the L, parallel to the rd, and rejoin the main route at no.2** (751/919).

EXTENSION 2:

+4.7 miles & +190 metres of climbing

A Turn L on the rd for 0.85m, then turn L on a BW , by the Roundhouse, as the rd bears R (758/875).

B Follow the BW **for 1.5m** (watch for tree roots as you exit the woods), **and go DH on the grass, to a DT** (775/861).

C Turn L on the DT, UH, following the BW to Upper woodend farm (758/883). Bear L, to the rd and turn R on this (been on this rd earlier) to the T-J and turn L, and rejoin the main route at no.6a (758/888).

EXTENSION 3:

+10 miles & +380 metres of climbing

W Turn L on rd and follow this for 1.3m to a T-J (752/889) and turn R on the rd for 0.65m, then bear R/SA on a BW (Stoner 0.5m), as rd bears sharp L (743/885). After 0.1m, turn R on a (easy to miss) BW, DH to a rd (737/886). Turn R on this rd, for 0.1m then L on another rd (Maidensgrove), UH, for 0.9m and turn R on a BW (724/888).

X Into the woods, and keep L, then follow the track R, steeply DH (careful of the drop-off half-way down). Go SA at the X--tracks at bottom, UH and keep R to exit the field onto a driveway, and go DH (past a church) to a T-J with a rd (727/900).

Y Turn R on the rd for 0.75m then turn L on the Oxfordshire cycleway BW (just past an old barn) (733/895). UH for 2.25m and just before you exit the wood turn R on the Oxfordshire 'PS3' BW (718/928). 0.25m to a fork and bear R (OW18) to a DT and bear L, to a X-tracks and go SA on a BW, staying on track to a farm (735/911).

Z Keep SA, past the farm (735/911) on a grassy DT, along the field edge, to a rd (736/896). Turn L on the rd, UH, for 1.1m to a fork in the rd and bear R (Turville, Fingest), to a X-rds (744/910). Go SA then immediately L at the gravel area into the trees on a BW, and rejoin the main route at no.9.

🚌 GETTING THERE

The ride starts from the village of Ibstone (which is west of High Wycombe). Exit the M40 at junction 5 and head south for 2 miles to Ibstone and park in one of the lay-by's on the right, near the Fox pub (751/941).

🛏 ACCOMMODATION

B&B's in Pishill on: 01491 638351 and638601 (nr the Crown pub) **Camping** at Henley (on the A4155) on: 01491 573419 or visit www.swiss farmcamping.co.uk **YHA** is in Bradenham (nr High Wycombe) on: 0870 7705714 **High Wycombe T.I.** on: 01494 421892

🚲 BICYCLE SHOPS

Saddle safari in Marlow on: 01628 477020 or Bucks Cycle Centre in High Wycombe on: 01494 451972.

🍽 REFRESHMENTS

There is a pub in Ibstone at the start/end and more on the route in Fingest, Freith, Skirmitt, and Turville. There are also pubs in Stoner, Pishill and Christmas Common on extension 3.

HIGHLY RECOMMENDED

ROUTE 45

- **NORTH LOOP: 20 miles** (630 metres of climbing)
- **EXTENSION: +1 mile**
- **SHORTCUT: -4.6 miles**
- **SOUTH LOOP: 11.5 miles** (430 metres of climbing)

THE RIDE

SUITABILITY

This route is 2 rides really. The northern loop is the friendlier to less experienced riders, as the south loop has the more technical trails and bigger hills, which come straight after one another.

TECHNICAL RATING

These routes have some great sections of singletrack which get more technical the faster you ride them (which can be pretty fast on the long descents). There are also a couple of technical sections that need to be taken with care i.e. the descent at the start of the northern loop which has some very deep ruts, and the fast, narrow, stoney, descent at point C on the southern loop.

TERRAIN

Lots of good, hilly, woodland or tree-lined singletracks and the (easy to follow) lowland doubletrack of the Ridgeway. The Ridgeway can get very slippery, sticky and rutted in bad weather, but the rest of the trails fair pretty well, mainly because there are so few riders around here.

Metres
300

200

100

0

Miles 0   5   10   15

ROUTES

45

GETTING THERE

The ride starts from the (free) 'Cowleaze Wood Sculpture Trail' car park near Stokenchurch. Exit the M40 at junction 5 and head north west on the A40, after 0.6m turn L on another rd (Sculpture Trail) for 1.5m and the car park is on the left (725/955). There is a train station in Chinnor, close to the route.

ACCOMMODATION

B&B in Radnage on: 01494 484835.
B&B in Great Kimble (in the Bernard Arms) on: 01844 346172
YHA in Bradenham (nr High Wycombe) on: 0870 7705714
High Wycombe T.I. on: 01494 421892

BICYCLE SHOPS

Bucks cycle centre in High Wycombe on Oxford rd, on: 01494 451972

REFRESHMENTS

North loop: Pubs in Chinnor (& shops) Bledlow Ridge, Piddington, Beacon Bottom, The City, Stokenchurch (& shops).
South loop: There are pubs in Ibstone and Christmas Common.

■ NORTH LOOP

20 miles & 630 metres of climbing

1 **START**. Turn R out of the car park then R on the rd for 0.25m then L on a DT. DH, for 0.8m then R on the Ridgeway BW (720/968), just past a house. Under the M40 and keep SA on this BW, over 3 rds, for 4.2m to a fork (770/011), or see the extension.

2 Bear R, past a house, on the Ridgeway ByW for 0.9m to a rd (783/011). Turn R on this for 0.2m then keep SA through a gate, on a BW, at a lay-by. Keep SA for 0.95m to the end of the field (795/996) and bear R then L (effectively SA) alongside a hedge.

3 Joining a good track and keep SA, past a farm, to a rd (803/983). Turn R on rd, UH, into Bedlow, to a T-J and turn L them immediately R on a BW. DH, to a rd and turn L then immediately R on a BW and keep L, UH, to a rd (791/964).

4 Turn L, or see the shortcut, on the rd for 0.4m, then turn R on a BW, DH, into some woods for 0.25m to a T-J (794/957). Turn L and follow this for 1m, joining a good track, keep SA on this, to the A40 rd. Cross this rd onto Chipps Hill rd opposite, and keep R and immediately turn R on a BW (806/942).

5 UH, for 1.45m, past a farm, to a rd (785/945) and turn R on this rd, UH, for 0.5m to the A40 rd . Turn R on this rd for 0.15m then L on Water End rd (788/952). 0.8m to a T-J and turn R for 0.3m then L on a BW (Pophleys) (781/966).

6 Bear R, between houses, DH, to a rd and turn L on this, bearing R, UH. Keep SA on track (C14) when the rd ends (772/978). Follow the white (RA35) arrows along the edge of the wood, for 0.8m to a (BW) T-J (761/982) and turn L.

7 0.5m, UH then DH, to a T-J with a DT (760/975) and turn R on this. Keep L for 1m, heading towards a radar mast, to a rd and turn L on this, to a T-J with the A40 rd. Turn L on this then immediately R on another rd and follow this for 1.55m back to the car park (on the L) (726/958).

EXTENSION:

+1 mile & +80 metres of climbing

1 After 3.3m at the 3rd rd (760/002), turn R on this, UH, for 0.5m to a T-J and turn L (Chinnor hill), for 0.25m then bear L on Hill Top Lane (764/997).

2 Keep SA to a car park, and go SA on a BW to the L of the car park, (not L on a BW, DH). Go between 3 wooden posts, DH (the higher track on the L is rooty), to a T-J with the Ridgeway, at the bottom, and turn R to a fork and rejoin the main route at no.2.

SHORTCUT:

-4.6 miles & -130 metres of climbing

1 Turn R on the rd and follow this, keeping L, for 0.7m, then turn R, off the rd, onto a BW (Pophleys) (781/966) and rejoin the main route at no.6.

■ SOUTH LOOP

11.5 miles & 430 metres of climbing

A **START**. Exit the car park and turn R on the rd. After 1m cross the rd (R) on to a BW (737/963) by the start of a crash barrier, before going over the M40. Through a gate into Wormsley Estate, and keep SA on the main track following the white arrows, DH, for 1m, to a drive at the bottom (744/949).

B Go SA on a BW, steep UH, into the woods, bearing L to a rd (750/951). Turn R on the rd for 0.6m then cross the rd (R) onto a BW, into the woods. Keep SA on this for 0.15m then turn R at an off-set X-tracks (749/938), before you exit the woods.

C DH, following the main track (BW), in the trees, tricky in places, to a T-J at the bottom, in the open (745/940). Turn L for 0.6m to a (private) rd and go SA on the BW, steep UH, to a tarmac track and bear L, UH, on this.

D Becomes off-rd again, and bears R, then through a gate, to a rd (734/926). Turn R on the rd, for 0.45m then turn L on a BW (728/928), into the woods. Bears R, through a gate, and turn L, through another gate and go SA, DH, along the LHS of a field.

E 0.6m to a X-tracks (728/918) and turn R on a BW. UH, for 1m to a drive and turn R on this for 0.05m then turn L on a BW by a house (717/929). Keep SA, through the woods, to a rd (714/928) and turn R on this, for 0.35m to a fork.

F Keep R for another 0.2m then turn L on a BW (714/937). DH, for 0.9m, keeping SA as you join a tarmac track by a timber yard, to a X-tracks (703/945), and turn R on the Ridgeway (BW).

G Follow this for 1.85m to a rd (720/968) before going under the M40, and turn R on this, past a farm, becoming off-road and bearing R, UH. To a rd at the top and go SA, into the car park at the end/start (726/958).

The Ridgeway / Ickneild way at Watlington.

HIGHLY RECOMMENDED

- ■ ROUTE 46

- ■ MAIN ROUTE: 19 miles
  (640 metres of climbing)

- ■ SHORTCUTS: -11.5 & 2.7 miles

- ■ EXTENSIONS: +2.4 & 5.5 miles

THE RIDE

SUITABILITY

There are a few steep hills and some technical rooty sections of singletrack on this ride, so it probably isn't suitable for novice riders. However, extension 2 isn't actually very technical, and would make a good, short ride - don't mistake this for extension 1, which has a steep, technical descent though.

TECHNICAL RATING

The rooty singletrack and fast descents with a few obstacles to test your reflexes provide some quite challenging trails.

TERRAIN

This is a hilly ride with quite a few peaks to climb. A lot of the trails are woodland singletracks, which have plenty or twists and turns and littered with roots to make the going difficult in wet weather.

■ NOTE: Aston Hill, a MTB'ing specific area (with a 4 mile XC course, a duel slalom and some downhills), is near Wendover (see the 'Other places to ride' section for more information).

GETTING THERE

This ride starts from a (free) height restricted car park just outside the town of Princes Risborough. Exit the A4010 on Peters Lane (at the north edge of Princes Risborough / Monks Risborough) and follow this uphill for 0.8m and the car park is on your left (824/035). There is also a railway station in Princes Risborough.

ACCOMMODATION

B&B in Little Hampden (at the Rising Sun pub) on: 01494 488393/488360
B&B in Wendover on: 01296 696759
YHA in Bradenham (nr High Wycombe) on: 0870 7705714
Princes Risborough: 01844 274795

BICYCLE SHOPS

Bolton Bikes & Tandems (behind Lloyds), in Princes Risborough on: 01844 345949

REFRESHMENTS

There is a pub in Little Hampden, The Lee, Lee Gate, and pubs and shops in Wendover (Le Petit cafe is good) and Princes Risborough. There is also a pub in Great Hampden on extension 2.

ROUTES

46

19 miles & 640 metres of climbing

1 START. Exit the car park, back to the rd and turn L for 0.15m then L on a BW (drive) (826/034). Bear to R of the house to some X-tracks (after a hut with satellites on it) (828/034) and turn L into the woods. 1a - Keep L at the start, DH for 0.3m to an off-set X-tracks and bear R then L, to stay on the BW, to a rd (833/045).

2 Go over the rd and turn immediately sharp R on a BW running parallel with the rd for 0.25m then bearing L into woods. To some X-tracks and keep SA and follow the BW to a rd (843/046). Cross the rd and turn L on a BW (parallel to the rd), bearing R along the field edge, emerging by a farm.

3 Go SA (to the LHS of the farm), UH on the Ridgeway for 0.2m to a X-tracks (848/050) and turn R. To a rd after 0.45m and go SA (L at T-J, then R through green gates) on the BW , and turn R by a house, to the 'Rising sun' pub (857/040). Turn L on the (Chilterns way) BW, DH for 0.55m, to a DT at the edge of the woods (860/047) and turn R (not on the DT), or see shortcut 1.

4 UH, in the woods, to the top and turn R along the edge of the woods for 0.75m, to a rd (869/036). Go SA on a BW and SA again at the X-tracks. After 0.55m as you exit the woods, (878/030) bear L at a fork, DH, in a tunnel of trees, then under a tunnel, to a main rd (884/033).

5 Turn R on the rd for 0.2m, then L on Leather lane (The Lee) (888/029). 0.8m, UH to a T-J (898/033) and turn L (The Lee), for 0.5m and bear L at the grass triangle (897/038) and follow the blue cycle signs.

After 1.4m at a T-J in Kingsash (888/056) turn R or see shortcut 2.

6 After 0.3m bear L/SA on a BW, for 0.65m and join rd keeping SA/L on this. Keep L on this rd for 0.8m (ignoring 3 rd's on the R) then turn L on a BW (Ridgeway) (897/074) as rd drops DH. Follow the BW, DH, bearing R, for 1.4m to a T-J (882/064) and turn R on the DT for 0.7m to a X-rds (874/071) and go SA on church lane.

7 Follow this past a church to a T-J (869/072) and turn R on South street, to a roundabout (867/078) in Wendover and turn L (867/078), past the train station on Pound street. 0.3m over the railway bridge, turn L on a BW (864/074) as the rd bears R, and immediately L at the fork on the track for MTB's and horses.

8 Go UH for 0.9m then bear L on a BW (853/067) and keep SA on this for 1.2m to a rd (861/052) and turn R on the rd, steep DH (or go SA for 0.35m and turn R, DH, on a BW you came up earlier, then use the shortcut to rejoin the main route). After 0.15m turn L off the road, as it bears R (dead end) for 0.15m then turn R (between the stables) on a BW, UH, in to the woods.

9 0.3m to a 5-way X-tracks and take the 2nd R i.e. SA, on the (only) BW track, DH to a rd at the bottom (847/057). Turn sharp L back on yourself on a BW, for 0.5m to a X-rds (848/050) (been here before) and turn R, DH, to the rd (846/049).

10 Retrace your earlier wheel tracks, along the BW in the field on the LHS of the rd,

over the rd (843/046), in the woods, SA at the X-tracks. Parallel to, then over the rd (833/046), UH, for 0.65m to a fork and turn R (829/036) - haven't been here.

11 Keep SA/L for 0.6m to a T-J (822/038) with a good track and turn L back into the car park (823/035) or see extension 1 or 2.

SHORTCUT 1:

-11.5 miles & -350 metres of climbing

1 Turn L on the DT for 0.15m then turn L between the horse stables (859/050), and rejoin the main route at no. 9.

SHORTCUT 2:

-2.7 miles & -60 metres of climbing

A Turn L at the T-J, for 0.1m then R on a drive (Concord House) for 0.2m then bear L on a BW (885/059). DH, ST, and join a DT and the bottom and keep SA on this for 0.7m to a X-rds (874/071) and go SA on church lane and rejoin main route at no.6.

+2.4 miles & +135 meters of climbing

1 Exit the car park on the (good) DT in the rear left, shortly to and through a gate, to a clearing (822/039). Keep SA and through a single gate (Ridgeway), steeply DH, into the woods. Keep L at the fork, to a drive and bear L, DH on this to a rd (819/044).

2 Turn L on the rd to a T-J and go SA on the BW for 0.75m to a rd (812/031). Turn L on the rd for 0.15m, then L (Kop Hill) for 0.85m to a T-J at the top (824/035) and turn L then R, to the car park (824/035)

EXTENSION 2

+5.5 miles & +120 meters of climbing

A Exit the car park and turn L on the rd for 0.6m, then R on a BW (830/029) at the start of the woods. Keep SA on this BW for 0.6m, exit the wood to a track and turn L on this to a rd (827/019). Go SA/L on the rd for 0.35m then turn R on a BW (Redland End sign on the L) into woods (833/018).

B After 0.3m at a DT, as you exit the woods, turn L on this BW (830/014) past Lily farm, for 0.6m to a X-tracks and turn L (836/007) off the main track, between the hedges. 0.5m to a X-rds (843/011) and go SA/L on a rd (844/011). 0.25m to a T-J and turn R, then L at grass the triangle.

C After 0.6m turn L on a big posh drive (Hampden House and church) (851/022), and keep SA on the BW when the drive ends. Keep SA for 1.4m to a (BW) X-tracks (by a hut with satellites on it) and go SA, bearing L, to a rd and turn R on this, for 0.15m then R into the car park (824/035).

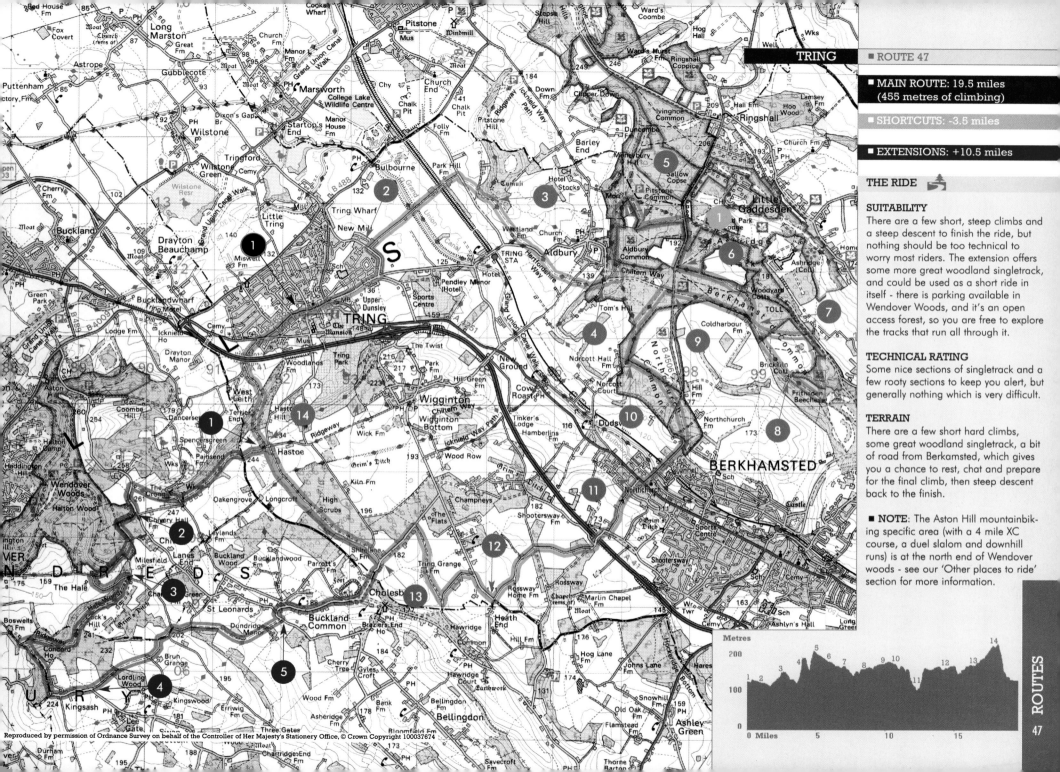

■ **MAIN ROUTE: 19.5 miles**
(455 metres of climbing)

■ **SHORTCUTS: -3.5 miles**

■ **EXTENSIONS: +10.5 miles**

THE RIDE

SUITABILITY

There are a few short, steep climbs and a steep descent to finish the ride, but nothing should be too technical to worry most riders. The extension offers some more great woodland singletrack, and could be used as a short ride in itself - there is parking available in Wendover Woods, and it's an open access forest, so you are free to explore the tracks that run all through it.

TECHNICAL RATING

Some nice sections of singletrack and a few rooty sections to keep you alert, but generally nothing which is very difficult.

TERRAIN

There are a few short hard climbs, some great woodland singletrack, a bit of road from Berkamsted, which gives you a chance to rest, chat and prepare for the final climb, then steep descent back to the finish.

■ **NOTE:** The Aston Hill mountainbiking specific area (with a 4 mile XC course, a duel slalom and downhill runs) is at the north end of Wendover woods - see our 'Other places to ride' section for more information.

ROUTES

47

GETTING THERE

This ride starts from the town of Tring, on the A41, between Hemel hempstead and Aylesbury. There is a car park in the centre or a choice of side streets. If you are going to do the extension, there is also a car park (with toilets) in Wendover woods (follow the brown signs off the A4011). There is also a railway station in Tring.

ACCOMMODATION

B&B's in Tring on: 01442 826638 and 828327
B&B in Wendover on: 01296 622351
YHA Ivinghoe (3 miles north of Tring) on: 0870 7705884
Camping in
Tring T.I. on: 01442 823347

BICYCLE SHOPS

Mountain Mania Cycles in Tring on: 01442 822458 or Dyson's in Dunstable, on: 01582 665 530

REFRESHMENTS

Lots of choice in Tring (try Tringfellows cafe) and Aldbury. A cafe at Pitstone common, a shop in Berkhamsted. Pubs in Cholesbury, and in Buckland common on the extension.

MAIN ROUTE

19.5 miles & 455 metres of climbing

1 START. Exit the car park and turn L (on the High st), to a roundabout (by the Robin hood pub) and go SA, then immediately bear L on Station rd. Keep SA for 0.5m to some X-rds (934/123) and turn L on Grove rd (934/119), for 0.3m then turn R on Marshcroft lane (932/123).

2 Keep SA for 1.1m over the canal and railway (look out for the dogs), to a rd (945/134). Turn R. on the rd then very shortly turn L on a BW, keeping SA at a DT, just inside the woods, to a X-tracks (951/129) and go SA on the Ridgeway.

3 0.4m to the X-tracks and keep SA (leaving the Ridgeway), to a rd and bear L on this. After 0.2m keep SA on a BW, as the rd bears L, to a rd (962/118), and go SA on a BW. Steep UH, to the top and bear L to a rd, and turn R on this, for 0.15m then turn L on a BW (969/119).

4 Keep SA over a DT (drive), bearing R to a (feint) X-tracks (968/121) and keep SA, UH, on a DT. After 0.35m go SA at the X-tracks, then shortly bear R at a fork (968/128). UH to the top by the monument, past the Visitor centre/cafe to the rd and turn R into the car park (970/131).

5 Exit the car park at the far left on a good track, for 0.5m to some X-tracks (972/126) and turn L on the BW. 0.45m to a rd (978/128), and turn R on the main rd, for 0.5m then L on the (Chiltern way) BW (977/120), or see the shortcut.

6 Keep SA for 0.65m to a drive (987/117), and bear R on this, for 0.25m, UH, to the top (988/112). Turn

L, through the trees, on a BW as the drive bears R, for 0.1m then bear L at a fork. Into the open, and bear L along the edge of the woods (twisty ST's in there).

7 0.3m to the DT on the other side near a rd (997/110), and turn R on the DT for 0.25m, then bear L on a BW, into the woods, as the DT bears R. Go SA at the 1st X-tracks to another X-tracks (999/101) and turn R, for 0.35m to a gravel DT.

8 Turn R on the DT, then shortly SA/L (to the RHS of the house), on a BW, into the trees, leaving the DT as it bears R. SA for 0.6m to a fork (been here earlier) and bear L. To a drive (988/112) and turn L on this and keep SA on the BW, to a rd (977/116), and go SA on the rd opposite

9 After 0.1m turn L on a BW (975/117), for 0.5m and bear L at a feint X-tracks (971/112), keeping along the LHS of the woods. 0.35m to another X-tracks (970/106), and turn L, out of the trees, and bear R, along the edge of the common (woods on the RHS).

10 After 0.4m (dips DH then UH) bear R, on grassy DT, BW (975/103), before the car park. Keep SA to a rd, and go SA on a BW, and keep SA at some X-tracks, over a drive to a rd (979/0945) and turn L/SA on this, DH, over a bridge, to a T-J.

11 Turn R then shortly L (972/088) on **Darrs lane** (by the One stop shop), steep UH for 0.6m, to the top. Turn R on the rd, bearing L over the A41 (966/080) and keep L at the fork, and follow this rd for 1.25m to some X-rds (951/071).

12 Turn R for 0.3m to a fork (948/074) and bear L (Cholesbury), for 0.45m, then R on a BW. Keep R at Tring Grange farm, to a rd (939/081) and turn L on this for 0.45m then turn R on Kiln lane (934/076).

13 After 0.1m keep SA/L on a ByW as rd bears R, and keep SA for 1.4m to a X-rds. Turn L then immediately R on a ByW at a grass triangle (917/093) or see the extension.

14 Keep to the RHS of the house, DH on the ByW (Hastoe Lane, becoming West lieth lane), to a rd T-J (914/105). Turn R under a bridge, to the main B4635 rd, and turn R on this, back into Tring (921/113), and the car park is on the L.

SHORTCUT:

-3.5 miles & -60 metres of climbing

1 Keep SA on the rd, for another 0.25m, then turn R on another rd (977/116) and rejoin the main route at no 9.

EXTENSION:

+10.5 miles & +300 metres of climbing

1 Keep SA on the rd for 0.25m, then go SA/R on the Ridgeway BW, as the rd bears sharp L. Follow this for 0.75m to a rd (905/085) and turn R then immediately L on the Riders route Ridgeway. To a rd (897/087) and turn L on this for 0.25m, then turn R on a tarmac drive (898/083) into Wendover woods.

■ **NOTE**: Wendover Woods is an open access FC wood, so you are welcome to explore the trails within it if you so wish.

2 After 0.2m turn L off the drive (as it bears R) (895/082), for another 0.2m to a X-tracks (897/079). Go SA (bearing R) on the Ridgeway, staying DH on the BW for 0.5m to a rd (892/074). Turn L on the rd, steeply UH, for 0.45m, then R, back on the Ridgeway (897/074).

3 Follow the Ridgeway for 1.4m, DH, to a T-J (881/063) and turn sharp L, UH on a ST BW. 0.4m to a drive and bear R on this, to a rd (886/056) and turn L on it. After 0.4m keep SA on a DT BW, leaving the rd as it bears R.

4 Keep SA for 0.6m to a rd (900/062) and turn L on this and keep L at a fork, to a T-J. Turn R for 0.15m then turn R onto a BW just after the house (906/066). Follow this for 0.9m, past a manor house, to a rd (919/067) and bear L on this.

5 Follow the rd as it bears R, for 0.9m and turn L on a rd to Wigginton (931/071). After 0.4m turn L on Kiln rd (934/076) and rejoin the main route at no.13.

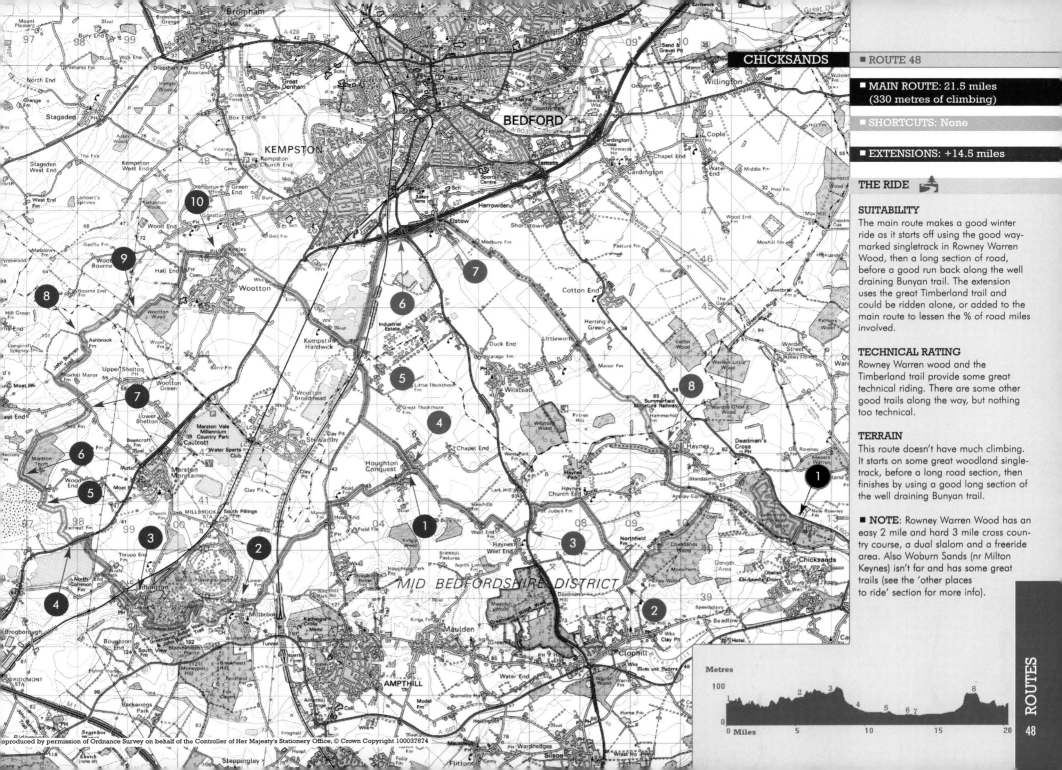

CHICKSANDS ■ ROUTE 48

- ■ **MAIN ROUTE:** 21.5 miles (330 metres of climbing)
- ■ **SHORTCUTS:** None
- ■ **EXTENSIONS:** +14.5 miles

THE RIDE

SUITABILITY

The main route makes a good winter ride as it starts off using the good way-marked singletrack in Rowney Warren Wood, then a long section of road, before a good run back along the well draining Bunyan trail. The extension uses the great Timberland trail and could be ridden alone, or added to the main route to lessen the % of road miles involved.

TECHNICAL RATING

Rowney Warren wood and the Timberland trail provide some great technical riding. There are some other good trails along the way, but nothing too technical.

TERRAIN

This route doesn't have much climbing. It starts on some great woodland single-track, before a long road section, then finishes by using a good long section of the well draining Bunyan trail.

■ **NOTE:** Rowney Warren Wood has an easy 2 mile and hard 3 mile cross coun-try course, a dual slalom and a freeride area. Also Woburn Sands (nr Milton Keynes) isn't far and has some great trails (see the 'other places to ride' section for more info).

ROUTES

48

reproduced by permission of Ordnance Survey on behalf of the Controller of Her Majesty's Stationery Office, © Crown Copyright 100037674

GETTING THERE 🚗

This ride starts from Sandy Lane car park (124/403) in Rowney Warren Woods, by Chicksands and Shefford. This is halfway between Hitchin and Bedford on the A600 road which goes between the two. There is a railway in Kempston Hardwick on the route.

ACCOMMODATION 🛏

B&B's in Wootton on: 01234 767210 and 84100
YHA in Bradwell Village (Milton Keynes) on: 0870 7705716
Camping in Houghton conquest (at the Chequers) on: 01525 404853
Bedford T.I. on: 01234 215226

BICYCLE SHOPS 🚲

Roy pinks in Newport Pagnel (nr Milton Keynes) on tel: 01908210688 and a Halfords Bike Hut in Bedford on: 01234 262212

REFRESHMENTS 🍽

Shops and pubs in Shefford near the start / end. Pubs in Houghton Conquest, Kempston Hardwick, and Haynes. Also on the extension in How End, Millbrook, Lidlington and Wootton.

ROUTES

48

21.5 miles & 330 metres of climbing

1 START. Follow the red (or easier blue) waymarked MTB route all the way around back to here, then retrace your along the Bunyan trail, to the rd (105/411). **Turn L on** the Greensand ridge walk **BW**, and follow this, over a small wooden bridge, UH, **to the end of the woods.**

2 Keep SA, as the GRW bears L through a hedge and across the stream, **for 0.3m to** rd (089/393). **Turn R on this rd for 1.3m to a T-J (080/410) and turn L**, on Church end rd **for 0.85m to the A6.**

3 Turn L on this for 0.05m then turn R on another rd (069/404), **for 0.2m to a junc-tion (067/403), and turn R on London lane.** 1.7m to a T-J in Houghton conquest, **and turn L on Chapel End rd, for 0.05m to a fork, and turn R on Bedford rd (046/416)** or see the extension.

4 Follow this rd for 0.95m to the B530 rd (036/426) **and turn R on this for 1m to Kempston Hardwick** (036/441).

5 Head north on the B530 rd (Bedford) **for 1.45m then turn R through metal gate** (041/463), before crossing the A421rd. Careful of broken glass under the bridge. **Onto the old track to the left of the line of** trees, going east, **to a BP petrol station and cross the road SA to a silver gate** (046/465).

6 Follow this track, past Pear tree fm, **to a rd** (051/467) (phone box opposite), **and turn L on the rd, then immediately R** (before going over the A421) **on Medbury lane** (John Bunyan trail).

7 Follow this JB Trail, which becomes off-road, **for 4.4m** (2.6m to a rd and turn R then immediately L on Elms Lane, UH, through the fields) becoming tarmac, **to a T-J with a rd in Haynes** (097/420).

8 Turn R on Plummers lane, DH, for 0.4m, to a T-J (097/414) **and turn L** (Ireland) **for 0.6m then keep SA on the John Bunyan trail**, as the rd bears L. **Follow this** (been here earlier) **for 1.25m to a rd** (122/401), **and turn L on this back to the car park** (124/403).

1 Keep SA/L on the High street, becoming the Grove, **for 1.3m to the B530 rd** (030/409). **Turn L on this for 0.25m, then turn R onto another rd** (030/405), and fol-low this **for 1.65m to a fork.**

2 Bear R (on Sandhill close) **for 0.1m then turn L on a BW** (011/389) (business park SA). **Follow the signposted** Marston Vale **Timberland trail for 2.6 m** (between the golf course and vehicle proving ground) **to a rd in Lidlington.**

3 Turn L on this rd for 0.05m then turn R (991/389) on Church street, **for 0.4m** (over the railway) **and go SA/R on Thrupp end rd** (986/393), as the rd bears L. **0.8m to the** (busy) **A507 rd** (982/402) **and turn L on this for 0.3m** (past two lay-bys) **then turn R through a wooden gate** (978/401).

4 Along a tree-lined, bumpy grass BW for 0.2m then bear R (north) (976/403), **for 0.35m**, over a stream and bumpy field, and through a hedge, and **turn L** (west) (977/408). **To some fencing, around the edge of a field, for 0.3m and join a good track going R** (973/409).

5 Turn R alongside the fence, towards a wooded area, **over a bridge and turn L into a car park** (973/412). **Go through a wood-en gate and follow the BW** through the woods. **Go through a gate after 0.3m** at the corner of the wood (969/415), **then R through another gate.**

6 Follow the Marston Vale forest trail signs (north) **for 0.8m then turn L out of the woods**, (974/424) leaving the MV trail, as it

bears R and DH. **Turn R and follow the BW** around the edge of the wood, past Hill farm, **to the rd** (982/429).

7 Turn L on the rd, for 0.15m to an off-set X-rds and go SA (R then L), UH, **to a big green barn** at Roxhill Manor farm. **Turn R** between the buildings **on a BW** (975/435), **for 0.8m to a fork** (980/444) by an old wooden building (980/444) **and bear R** on the JB trail.

8 Keep on the LHS of a line of trees, for 0.65m, until a dirt rd crosses you (988/452) **and turn R on this**, under the elec. pylons. 0.3m to the corner of a wood (991/448) **and turn L on the track**, alongside the edge of the wood.

9 After 0.55m, with a school SA, turn L (998/451), **diagonally across a field, for 0.2m**, to the bottom corner **and join a rd. Turn L on this** (Hall end) **rd, for 0.4m**, past the Checkers Inn pub, **to a T-J** (001/461). **Turn R** on Keeley lane, **for 0.45m then turn L** on Wooton rd.

10 After 0.15m turn R through the wood-en gates on a BW (009/462), by a 'Wooton' sign (009/462). **Go across the fields for 0.9m, to a the A421 rd** (021/454) **and go SA on Manor rd.** Follow this rd for 1.3m back to the B530 rd, (036/442) **and rejoin the main route at no.5.**

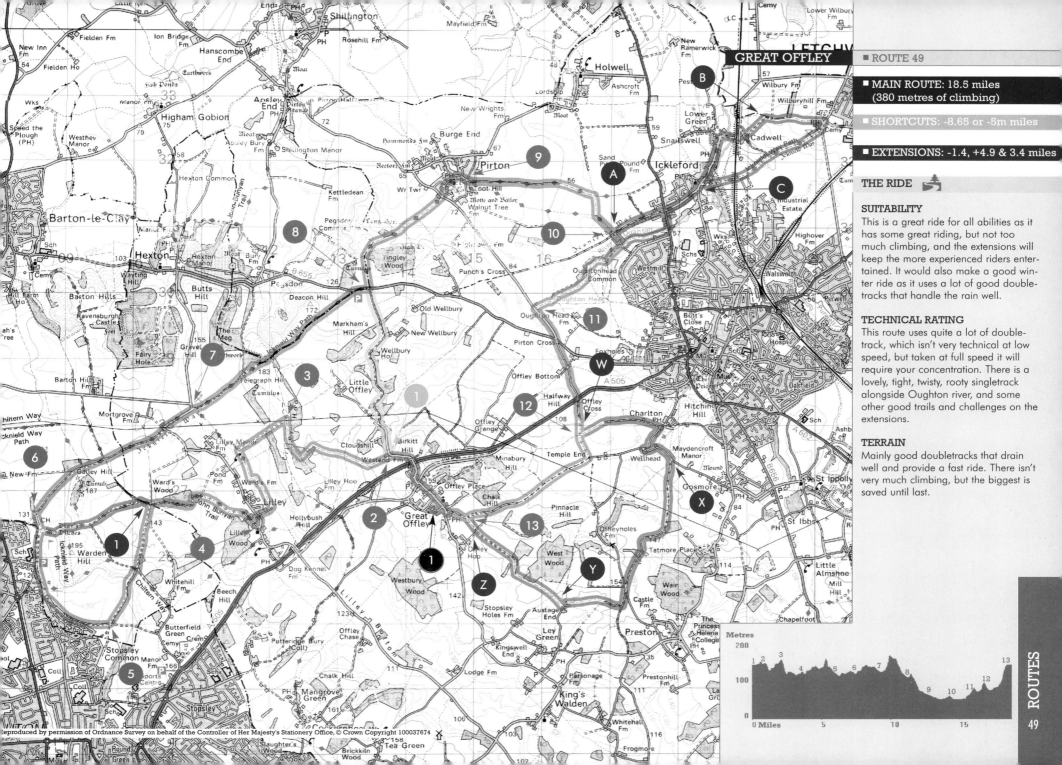

ROUTE 49

- **MAIN ROUTE:** 18.5 miles
  (380 metres of climbing)

- **SHORTCUTS:** -8.65 or -5m miles

- **EXTENSIONS:** -1.4, +4.9 & 3.4 miles

THE RIDE

SUITABILITY
This is a great ride for all abilities as it has some great riding, but not too much climbing, and the extensions will keep the more experienced riders entertained. It would also make a good winter ride as it uses a lot of good doubletracks that handle the rain well.

TECHNICAL RATING
This route uses quite a lot of doubletrack, which isn't very technical at low speed, but taken at full speed it will require your concentration. There is a lovely, tight, twisty, rooty singletrack alongside Oughton river, and some other good trails and challenges on the extensions.

TERRAIN
Mainly good doubletracks that drain well and provide a fast ride. There isn't very much climbing, but the biggest is saved until last.

ROUTES

49

Reproduced by permission of Ordnance Survey on behalf of the Controller of Her Majesty's Stationery Office, © Crown Copyright 100037674

GETTING THERE

This ride starts from the visitors car park in Great Offley (which is between Luton and Hitchin), on the A505 that runs between the A1 and M1. Turn onto the High Street (by the Green man pub) then right on Gosling rd, then left on Clarion Close, then left again into the car park (143/267). There is a railway station in Hitchin (2 miles from the route).

ACCOMMODATION

B&B in Lilley (at the Lilly Arms) on: 01462 768371
B&B in Charlton (at the Greyhound pub) on: 01462 440989
Hotel (at the Lord Lister) in Hitchin on: 01462 432712
Luton T.I. on: 01582 401579

BICYCLE SHOPS

C J Frost and Sons in Hitchin on: 01462 434433.

REFRESHMENTS

There are 4 pubs and a post office shop in Great Offley. On the route there are pubs in Lilley and Pirton, Ickleford and Letchworth on extension 2 and in Charlton on extension 3.

■ MAIN ROUTE

18.5 miles & 380 metres of climbing

1 START. Go back to the X-rds by the Greene Man pub (141/271) and go SA on School lane. 0.2m after crossing the A505, keep SA/L on a BW as the rd bears R or see the shortcut.

2 After 0.2m bear R at the fork (134/273), keep SA at the X-tracks after 0.25m, through a field, then bearing L around the back of some trees. UH, in the woods to a T-J (124/275) and turn R, for 0.4m to junction under the electricity pylons (122/280).

3 Turn L on the DT, DH for 0.5m then turn L on a BW as the DT turns sharp R (115/276). Keep SA for 0.65m through the gates to a X-tracks (in a clearing and FP only SA) and turn R (120/267). To a rd and turn L for 0.1m then turn R on West Street (118/264), which becomes a ByW.

4 Follow this (John Bunyan trail) for 1.2m (bearing to the LHS of the woods), DH to some X-tracks (102/268) and turn L, or see extension 1. Go UH for 0.6m to some X-tracks and keep SA, back DH towards the houses (Luton).

5 0.6m to the X-tracks at the end of field (097/250), turn R on a track going on the RHS of houses. 1.5m to some X-tracks just past the golf clubhouse (086/266) and turn R (after Tee no.10), on the Icknield way.

6 Keep SA on the main track (note: signposts may still be incorrect) for 1.6m to a rd and go SA/L on the rd. After 0.3m keep SA, back onto the Icknield way path, as the rd bears sharp L (109/282).

7 Keep SA on the Icknield way for 2m (L at a fork after 0.5m, by the Telegraph hill sign) to a rd (132/300). Turn R on the rd for 0.15m then L on a BW (134/301).

8 Keep SA on this for 1.25m to Pirton village (145/314) and go SA on the (Crab tree lane) rd opposite. Past the Motte & Bailey pub to a T-J (with the High street) opposite the Fox pub and turn R (147/317).

9 0.1m to a T-J and go SA through a gate on the good, wide Icknield way BW. After 1.15m bear R (167/314), staying on the good track (Hitchin 1m), to a grass triangle, and bear R then L through a white gate., or see extension 2.

10 Keep SA, over the river then immediately R on a BW along the river (171/307). 10a - After (about) 1m, by the end of the woods bear R then L (SA) to a rd (158/297).

11 Turn L on the rd for 0.35m to a X-rds and go SA on Wibbly Wobbly lane. 0.6m to a dual carriageway (165/284) and (carefully) cross this onto a ByW opposite. 0.3m to a X-tracks and keep SA or see extension 3.

12 After another 0.25m at some X-tracks, turn R on a R.O.W. (166/275), under the electricity pylons and keep SA for 1m (become a good track). To a fork and bear R, emerging by the Red Lion pub (146/266).

13 Turn R (on the High street), then shortly L on Salisbury lane then R on Clarion Close, back to the car park (143/267).

SHORTCUT:

-8.65 miles & -200 metres of climbing

1 Keep R on the rd for another 0.35m and bear R at the fork (136/280) by the houses (New Wellbury). Follow this for 1.45m to a rd (134/300) and go SA on the (Icknield way path) BW, and rejoin the main route at no.8.

■ **NOTE:** This shortcut can also be used the other way, to reduce the ride by 5 miles and 100 meters of climbing.

EXTENSION 1:

-1.4 miles, but uses a steep DH

1 Keep SA for 0.1m then bear L at the fork (100/268), and keep SA for 1m (down a steep hill) to some X-tracks (086/264). Turn R, past the golf club house and then turn R again past Tee no.10, and rejoin the main route at no.6.

EXTENSION 2:

+4.9 miles & +65 metres of climbing

A Turn L on a lane (Icknield way) for 0.5m to the A600 rd and go SA on Turnpike lane. Keep SA at the roundabout, on Arlesey rd, under the railway bridge. 0.1m under the bridge turn R on a BW (188/324), for 0.1m then turn L through Cadwell farm (189/323)

B After 0.3m turn R at a fork (192/326), UH, for 0.5m, into a wood by the picnic area, bearing R, for 0.1m then R on a ByW (200/324), DH, past the railway, back to Arlesey rd in Ickleford (183/316).

EXTENSION 3:

+3.4 miles & +40 metres of climbing

C Turn L, to the roundabout then SA/R on Turnpike lane for 0.3m to the main (A600) rd (177/312). Turn L on this rd for 0.2m then turn R on a BW (178/309) just over a bridge. After 0.5m alongside the river rejoin the main route at no10a (171/307).

W Turn L, DH into Charlton (good pub here) to a T-J with a rd (177/279) and turn R. UH for 0.25m to a barn (174/276). Turn R on Maydencroft lane (unsuitable for HGV's), for 0.3m then turn R on a DT (ROW) (178/274) (unsuitable for motors).

X Keep SA (ignore BW on R at start) on this for 1.4m to a rd (172/255), and go SA/L on this (not on the BW opposite). Very shortly bear off the rd, to the RHS of a house, on a ByW. After 0.2m on this bear R at the fork (171/252) for 0.15m then bear R on a BW.

Y 0.35m to a T-J and turn L towards the houses, then shortly R through a metal gate on a PRUP (162/252). Follow this BW for 1.15m, and keep SA on the grassy BW as the DT bears sharp R (150/264).

Z Rejoin the DT and keep SA/L, back into Great Offley, emerging by the Red lion pub (146/267), and rejoin the main route at no.13.

GETTING THERE

The most common direction to ride the Ridgeway is from west to east (although you finish at almost exactly the same altitude). The start is in an inconspicuous dirt car park (118/680), just off the A4 near Avebury (4 miles west from Marlborough, and finishes at Ivinghoe Beacon (nr Ivinghoe). If you can't get a lift to the start, you could leave your car in Marlborough, although we can recommend using the train (see below).

By Train: Get the train to Swindon and follow our map and instructions to get to the Ridgeway (which is 7 miles away, but it also joins the Ridgeway 7 miles from the start). There is also a train station in Cheddington near the end of the ride and more on or near the Ridgeway at: Didcot (6m), Goring (on it), Saunderton (2m), Princes Risborough (on it), Wendover (on it), and Tring (on it).

ACCOMMODATION

Distance (in miles) from the start/Avebury:

0 - B&B in Avebury, tel: 01672 539294
29 - Ridgeway YHA, near Wantage, tel: 0870 7706064, GR 393/851.
43 - Streatley YHA, (on the route), tel: 0870 7706054, GR 591/806.
49 - B&B in Wallingford, tel: 01491 837834
66 - B&B in Princes Risborough: 01844344508
66 - Bradenham YHA, 4 miles off the route, tel: 0870 7705714, (GR 828/972).
89 - Ivinghoe YHA (1.5m from the end) tel: 0870 770 5884, GR 945/161.

Phone the tourist information for more choices:
Marlborough on: 01672 513989
Wantage T.I. on: 01235 760176
Wallingford on: 01491 826972
Princes Risborough on: 01844 274795
Wendover on: 01296 696759
Tring on: 01442 823347

REFRESHMENTS

There aren't many refuelling places actually on the route, but there are plenty of pubs and village shops just off the route. There are some water taps on the route however, these can be found at grid references: 263/835, 338/855, and 506/823 (19, 25 and 37 miles from the start respectively).

BICYCLE SHOPS

Bertie Maffoons bicycle co in Marlborough, on: 01672 519119, Ridgeway cycles in Wantage on: 01235 764 445, Halfords Bike hut in Didcot: 01235 511643, Rides on air in Wallingford on: 01491 836289, and Bolton bikes & tandems in Princes Risborough on: 01844 345949.

■ **MAIN ROUTE: 89 miles**
(2,125 metres of climbing)

THE RIDE

SUITABILITY
At almost 90 miles long, this ride should not be taken lightly. However, ridden sensibly over 2 or 3 days, most people should be fine to ride it.

TECHNICAL RATING
The technical challenge in the first half of the ride comes from the rutted doubletrack, while the second half has twisty, rooty, woodland singletrack. It will require your attention and test your skills, especially when (not if) you start getting tired and complacent.

TERRAIN
The Ridgeway dates back over 5,000 years to when it was a busy drove road for transporting livestock. Nowadays it makes a superb epic MTB ride, which takes in the typical terrain of the south east i.e. chalk escarpments, beech woods and amazing views over rolling farmland and fields. The first half is well signposted and uses well draining doubletracks, although these can become very muddy and slippy in the wet (as motor vehicles use the trail). The second half uses twisty woodland singletrack, and has to detours off the official trail a few times where it becomes a footpath.

So what are you waiting for? Phone some friends and start planning it now...

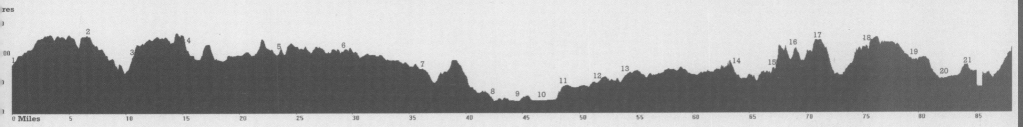

Start from Swindon station:

1 Exit the train station and turn L on Station rd, to some X-rds/lights (bridge on L) and go SA for 0.3m to a (big) roundabout (156/854). Turn R (County road) for 0.45m to a multiple round-about and turn R on Drove rd (by the Fire station) (159/858). After 0.6m keep L at the fork (by a cathedral), keeping SA at a mini roundabout, to big roundabout (159/830) and go SA at this, on Pipers Way rd.

2 After 0.5m turn L on a BW (159/822) as the rd starts bearing R. Over the M4, UH, to a rd (161/803) and go SA/L on this (Brimble hill), for 0.25m then keep SA on another rd as the rd bears L. Keep SA on this for 2.7m, past a car park on the R, and a farm and cafe on the L, and turn L onto the Ridgeway (158/758) and rejoin the main route at no.2.

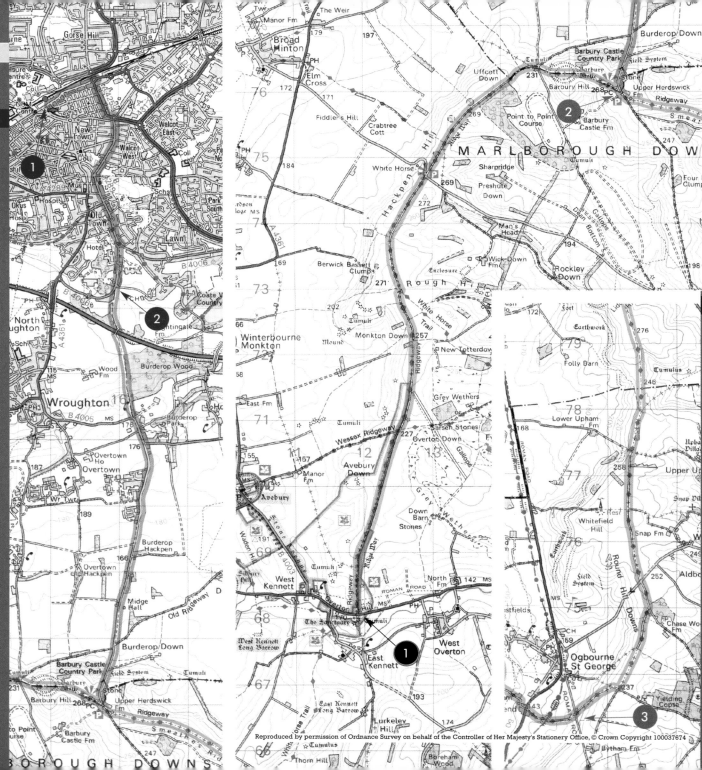

Start from Avebury

1 **START**. Head north, following the main DT, over a rd after 4.4m (129/747), for another 1.5m to a rd (145/763). Turn R on this rd, (not SA on the BYW/old RW) then shortly turn L through a gate, UH. Keep SA at the top, through a car park, to a min rd and bear R on this, past the farm and cafe, then shortly turning L, back off-road on a DT (RW) (158/758).

2 Follow this for 2.35m to a rd (192/746) and turn R on this, then shortly keep SA off-road, as the rd bears L. 0.55m to a fork and bear L, DH, to the A346 rd (197/734), and go SA, past an old (broken) bridge, to a fork and bear L, to a rd and go SA, UH, on the RW.

3 Bearing R to a X-tracks (211/731) at the top and turn L, DH, to a rd, and turn L on this, for 0.25m to a r T-J (214/753) and go SA. 1.25m to an off-set X-tracks. Go SA (R then L) for 0.4m

to a 3-way split (214/779), and go SA on a ST (RW), as the DT bears R, for 1.75m to a rd and turn L on this.

4 After 0.15m turn R on another rd (217/806), for 1m, to a X-rds (by the Shepherds rest pub), and go SA for 0.15m then turn R, off-road, on the RW (232/814). Keep SA, off-rd, on the RW (water on the L after 0.9m, by some barns), for 3.2m to the B4000 rd (273/843) and keep SA for another 3.6m (past Wayland Smithy's) to a rd (322/862).

5 Keep SA (water tap after 1.15m, nr Hill barn) to a minor rd and go SA/R on this, to the main B4001 rd (343/851), and go and keep SA, off-rd, for 3.4m to the A338 rd (394/844) the YHA is L 0.3m on this rd. Turn R on the rd, then immediately L back off-rd on the RW, which bears L after 0.6m, to a good track and turn R on this, then immediately keep SA/L at a fork, as the good DT bears R.

6 Go 1m to a rd (418/841) and keep SA, for 1m to a fork and bear L. Past a car park after 1.6m (458/850), and keep SA, over a rd after 1.5m, for 0.8m going under a bridge/A34 rd (490/834). Bear R then L, following the main track, and keep L at 2 forks after 0.95m, (Note: There is a water tap by the farm entrance on the R) for another 0.4m to a X-tracks and go SA for 0.15m to another X-tracks (508/819).

7 Turn L (on the RW). Keep SA for 1.2m to a fork (526/823) and bear R, for 0.5m to a fork and bear R, keeping SA over 2 X-tracks. 0.5m to a X-tracks and go SA to a fork (540/814) and bear L, for 0.6m to a fork and bear L. Keep SA for 2.6m, DH, becoming a rd, to a T-J (589/815) with the A417 rd, and turn R on this. 0.3m to a T-J with the A329 rd and turn R on this, into Streatley, to a X-rds (with traffic lights) (591/807). The YHA is SA, just past the Bull pub, on the R.

8 Turn L at the X-rds, DH, over the river Thames, for 0.4m and turn L just after the 2nd bridge, on Thames rd (598/808). Follow this rd bearing R (leaving the RW, which goes SA and becomes a FP), to a T-J and turn L on Cleeve rd (RW rejoins you). After 0.3m keep SA on the RW, as rd bears R (becoming Mill rd), 1.1m to a rd .

9 Keep SA/L on the rd, through the village, for 0.3m and bear R on the rd (RW on L, becomes a FP). Go under a bridge, to the B4009 rd (602/837) and turn L on this. After 0.7m turn L on a rd (to Little Stoke village), bearing R by Little Stock Manor (601/850), for 0.75m, then keep SA on a DT (off-road), as the rd bears R.

10 0.5m to a rd and keep SA/L on this, rejoining the RW, and keep SA for 1m to a fork in Carmel college (611/877). Turn R, UH, to the A4074 rd, then turn L on this rd, for 0.1m then R, on the RW, just before the roundabout (617/879).

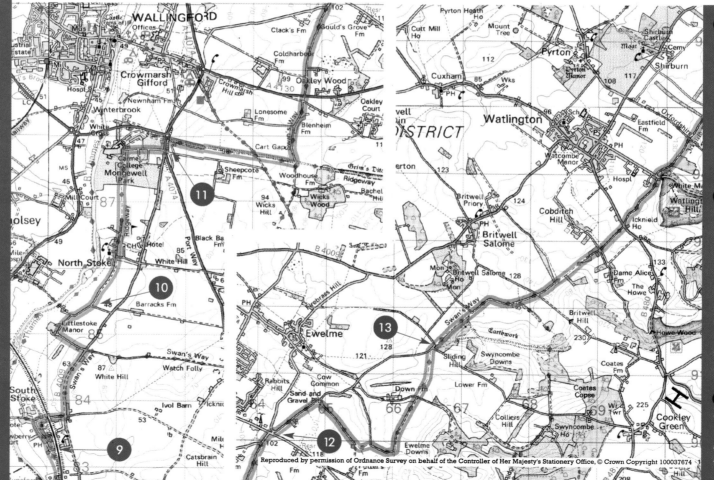

11 0.85m to a rd and go SA, for 0.4m to a rd (636/875) and turn L on this (leaving the RW) joining the Swan's way (636/875), for 0.6m to a X-rds and go SA, to a X-rds with the A4130 rd. Go SA (past the refuse site), for 0.9m to a T-J, and turn R/SA, to an off-set X-rds (641/901) and go SA (R then L).

12 Keep R at the fork, for 0.5m then turn R on the BW (648/905), for 0.55m then bear L (Swan's way) to a fork and keep L, to a T-J with a DT. Turn R, for 0.25m to a X-tracks (660/898), and turn L (on a good DT), over a minor rd after 0.55m, for another 0.45m to a rd (665/913). Turn R on the rd, then shortly keep SA/L off-road as the rd bears R, on Swans way.

13 Keep SA (RW rejoins you just along here) on the RW for 9.3m (SA over 2 rd's, L then immediately R at the 3rd, under the M40 rd, across the A40 rd,

ROUTES

over another rd, for 0.8m after another rd) and keep R on the ByW (RW) by a house, and keep SA (leaving the RW, which becomes a FP and bears R) on this for 0.95m to a rd (783/011).

14 Go SA at the grass triangle, on the Upper Icknield way (UIW), and keep SA for 1.65m to the A4010 rd (806/018). Turn L on the rd, for 0.4m, then turn R on the UIW (805/025), over a rd after 0.6m, for another 0.7m (leaving the RW), to a (Peters lane) rd. Go SA on for 0.2m (past the Red lion pub) then turn R on the UIW (819/043), going steeply UH.

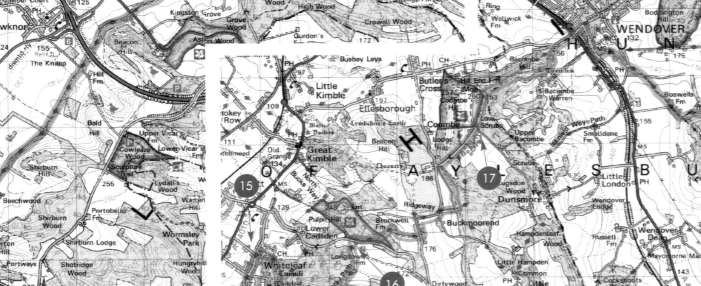

15 Shortly (by the houses) turn R on the Riders Icknield way, through a gate and keep SA/R on the BW RW (not the RW FP on the L) to the top. Go through a (open?) gate, for 0.1m and turn L on a BW (easy to miss), before you get to a car park, and follow this to a T-J (829/036). Turn L, DH, keeping R at a fork (easy to miss), to a rd and go SA on the BW, which immediately bears R, alongside the rd.

16 Follow the Icknield way (IW) signs, to a rd and cross this and turn L on a BW, alongside the rd. This bears R, to the corner of a rd, and go SA (off-rd) back on the RW, UH, for 0.15m, to a X-tracks (848/050), and turn L (leaving the Ridgeway again). DH, to a rd and turn R on this UH, for 0.45m to the top, and bear L on a BW through the car park (851/062).

17 Follow the main track, keeping R, for 1.3m, DH, to a rd and turn R on this, over a bridge, into Wendover. Turn R at the roundabout (867/077) on South street, then turn L after 0.3m on Church lane (St Mary's church), for 0.35m to X-rds (rd bears sharp L), and go SA, back on the RW. Keep SA for 0.7m to a fork (881/063) in the woods and bear L, then shortly R at another fork (signposted FP, but is a BW), 1.4m through the woods to a rd. Turn L, DH, for 0.4m then turn R on a BW.

ROUTES

50

18 Follow the BW, UH, to a rd (900/080) and turn L (leaving RW) for 0.55m then turn R on the IW (riders route) BW, (898/087). 0.5m to a rd (905/085) and cross this, back onto the RW, for 0.75m to a rd and turn L on this. 0.3m to a X-rds (918/093) and turn R on a ByW (leaving the RW), for 1.35m to a rd and go SA/R on this, to a T-J (934/076).

19 Turn L on the rd, for 0.8m to a T-J and turn L (Wigginton), for 0.35m then turn R (Crawleys lane), for 1m, under the A41/bridge, to a fork and bear R. 0.35m to a T-J with the A4251 and turn R then immediately L, over a bridge, and immediately turn L on the other side (959/103) on a BW, alongside the canal.

20 After 1.45m just past/under the 2nd bridge, turn R up the steps to a rd (948/121). Turn L on the rd, then bear L on the RW (concrete track) after 0.35m, and keep SA on the grass as the track bears L to a farm, through a gate to some X-tracks (954/125). Turn L (on the RW), for 0.4m to a X-tracks and keep SA on the BW just inside the wood, (leaving the RW, which is now a FP to the end).

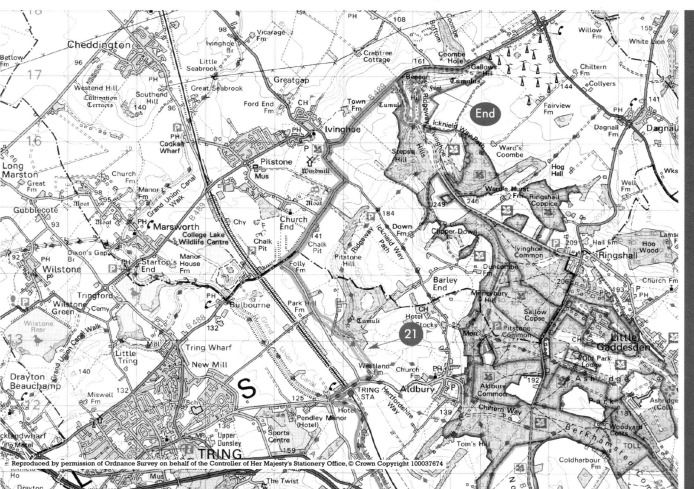

21 Keep SA, over a DT, to a rd and turn R on this, for 0.65m to a roundabout (940/141), and turn R (Ivinghoe). After 1.45m bear R at the fork (Dunstable) (947/159), for another 0.9m then turn R (957/169) on a minor rd, over a cattle grid. UH, for 0.5m, then turn L (960/163) (Note: This track is a footpath, but it is the only way to the end of the Ridgeway), for 0.35m to the viewpoint which marks the end of the Ridgeway (960/168).

■ **NOTE:** The nearest train station is Cheddington station (922/184). Go back down the B489 road and turn right through Ivinghoe village, heading north west on the B488 rd and the station is 2 miles down this road.

■ ROUTE 51

GETTING THERE

The most common direction to cycle this epic route is from West to East i.e. from Winchester to Eastbourne. The ride starts from Winchester train station, and although you could leave your car in Winchester, we would advise using the train (see below).

By Train: The ride starts from Winchester station and there are more railway stations in Petersfield, Houghton (Amberley), Brighton, Hassocks, and nr Rodmell (on the route), and in Eastbourne at the end.

REFRESHMENTS

There are a few pubs and shops on (or close to) the route e.g. in Warnford, QECP, Pyecombe, Cocking, Amberley, Alfriston.

There are water taps at Hill barn in Cocking (878/166), Parkfield farm near A24, Anchor Bottom near the A283, Saddlescombe and Itford farm (433/056) near the A26.

BICYCLE SHOPS

Peter Hargroves cycles in Winchester on tel: 01962 860 005, The Sensible bicycle co. in Petersfield on: 01730 266 554, Phoenix Cycles in Eastbourne on: 01323 729 060 (more in Brighton), Bike & Hike in Alfriston.

ACCOMMODATION

Distance (in miles) from the start / Winchester:

0 - Winchester YHA on tel: 0870 7706092, at GR 486/293.

35 - B&B in Cocking tel: 01730 814370

43 - Camping / hut at Gumber Bothy farm, tel: 01243 814484, GR 961/118.

44 - Arundel / Warning Camp YHA, (4.5 miles off the route, south on the A284), tel: 0870 7705676, GR 032/074.

45 - B&B in Bury, tel: 01798 831843

47 - B&B in Amberley tel: 01798 831787

61 - Truleigh Hill on the route (near Upper Beeding, tel: 0870 7706078, GR 220/105.

65 - Brighton YHA (3 miles off the SDW, GR 300/088), use the Sussex Border Path by Pyecombe) tel: 0870 7705724.

66 - B&B in Pyecombe tel: 01273 843766

80 - Telscombe YHA, 1.5m off the route, on:0870 7706062, (GR 405/033).

88 - Alfriston YHA, tel: 0870 7705666, GR 518/019.

97 - Eastbourne YHA, tel: 0870 7705806, GR 588/990.

For more info see www.vic.org.uk or phone: Winchester TI on: 01962 840500
Petersfield TI on: 01730 268829
Brighton TI on: 0906 7112255
Lewes TI on: 01273 483448
Eastbourne TI on: 01323 414400

SOUTH DOWNS WAY

■ MAIN ROUTE: 97 miles (3,850 metres of climbing)

THE RIDE

SUITABILITY
At almost 100 miles long and 4,000 metres of climbing this ride will challenge all abilities of rider. However, as it is easy to follow, isn't too technical and can be ridden over a few days, most riders can give it a go. Some (very fit) people can ride it 1 day, but 2 or 3 days is more common (and sensible).

TECHNICAL RATING
The trails never get too technical, but there are lots of long, fast rutted descents that require your concentration, and it gets very slippery when wet.

TERRAIN
This ride is virtually all off-road and very hilly. The west part of the ride is mainly rolling farmland, the central part steeper and wooded, and the east is along good doubletracks on open grassland, with views of the sea.

■ **NOTE**: The waymarking from Winchester to Queen Elizabeth Country Park isn't very good. There are some diversions for cyclists as well, these are: between the M3 and Chilcomb at the start, between Beacon Hill and Old Winchester Hill, between Alfriston and Eastbourne (leaving the coastal footpath), and the last mile to Beachy Head at the end (where cyclists have to use the road).

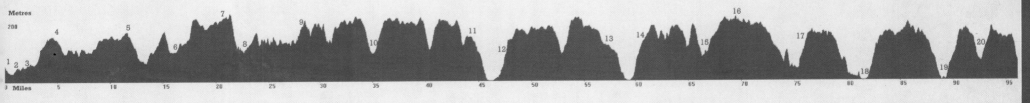

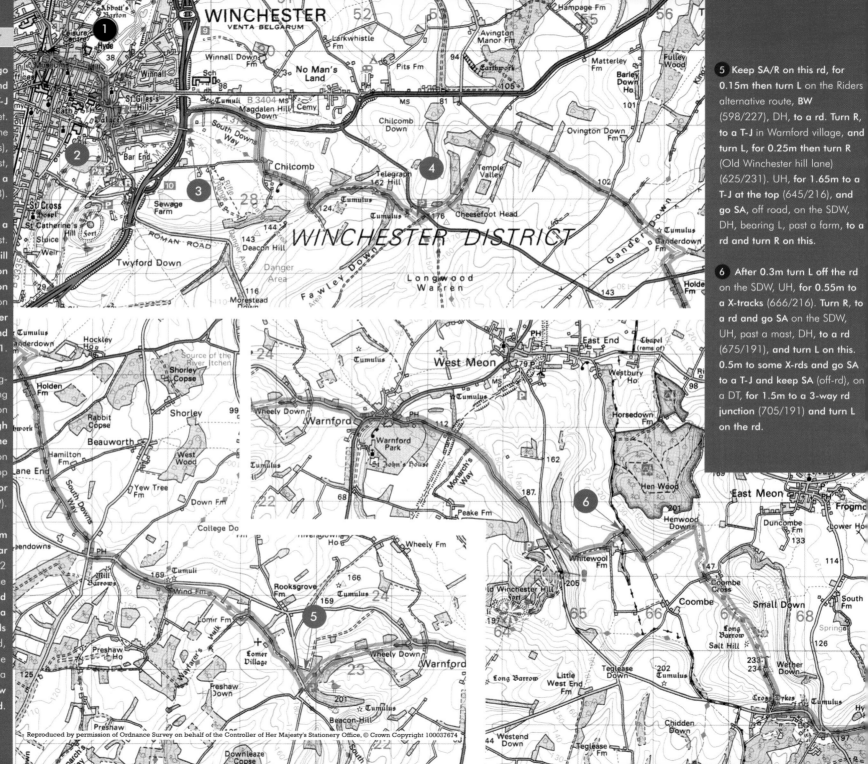

1 START. From Winchester train, go south on Station rd, to a junction and turn L on Gladstone st, to another T-J (478/298) and turn L on Sussex street. To a X-rds (479/299) and turn R on the B3404 (City rd, becoming North Walls), for 0.4m then bear R on Union st, becoming Eastgate st, for 0.2m to a roundabout (485/293).

2 Turn L on High st, over a bridge, to a fork and bear R (south) on Chesil st. After 0.2m turn L on East hill (486/289), for 0.1m then bear R on Petersfield rd, for 0.2m then bear R on Fivefields rd (492/290) and keep SA on this rd (SDW). This becomes a FP, over the M3 and A31 rd's (478/299), and turn L (north) alongside the A31.

3 To a roundabout and turn R, alongside the A31(can get overgrown along here), for 0.45m then turn R on Chilcomb rd, and keep L, through Chilcombe. Go to the end of the the dead end rd (513/278) and turn L on the SDW, UH, to a X-tracks at the top and turn L, to and over a rd. DH, for 1m to a X-tracks (537/289).

4 Turn R, and keep SA for 1.95m (under elec. cables) to a fork and bear R, then shortly L, to the A272 rd (560/269). Go SA on the SDW, for 0.9m to a rd, and keep SA/R on this for 0.6, to a T-J and turn R, to a X-rds (569/245). Turn L on the rd, for 0.7m then bear R off the rd, on the SDW, through a farm (579/241), and follow this for 1.45m to a rd.

5 Keep SA/R on this rd, for 0.15m then turn L on the Riders alternative route, BW (598/227), DH, to a rd. Turn R, to a T-J in Warnford village, and turn L, for 0.25m then turn R (Old Winchester hill lane) (625/231). UH, for 1.65m to a T-J at the top (645/216), and go SA, off road, on the SDW, DH, bearing L, past a farm, to a rd and turn R on this.

6 After 0.3m turn L off the rd on the SDW, UH, for 0.55m to a X-tracks (666/216). Turn R, to a rd and go SA on the SDW, UH, past a mast, DH, to a rd (675/191), and turn L on this. 0.5m to some X-rds and go SA to a T-J and keep SA (off-rd), on a DT, for 1.5m to a 3-way rd junction (705/191) and turn L on the rd.

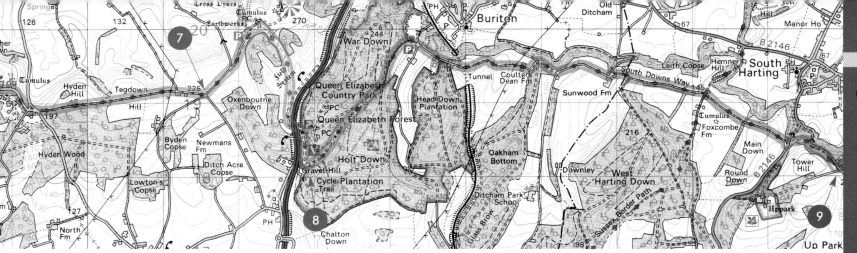

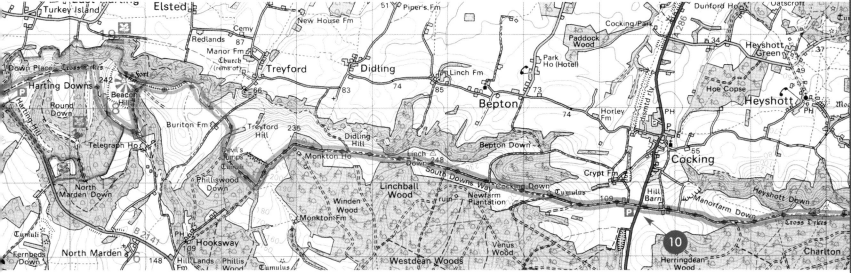

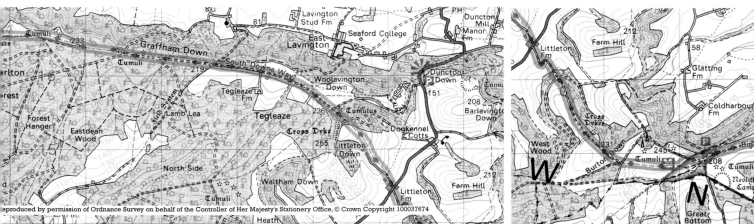

7 Bear R at the fork after 0.3m, for 0.4m to the car park and toilet, **and turn R** (712/200), DH, **going under the A3 rd**, to the Queen Elizabeth country park **visitors centre** (nice cafe here). **Use the path to the LHS of the visitors centre** (orange markers), **for 0.2m to a forest track** (718/181), just before the gravel hill car park, **and turn L, UH.**

8 Keep SA on this track for 1.6m, DH, through a car park, to a 3-way rd junction (733/197) and go SA. Keep SA for 1.9m (varying surface) then turn R off the rd, just past Sunwood farm, just after the rd bears sharp L (759/193). Follllow the SDW over the B2146 rd, then alongside and over the B2141 rd, onto Harting Downs.

9 Follow the grassy track SA across Harting downs, for 0.9m to a X-tracks (803/185) at the base of a steep hill (Beacon hill), and turn R, UH, for 0.75m to a DT (809/176). Turn L. on this, for 0.5m to a X-tracks (809/183) and turn R, UH, and follow the SDW signposts for 5 miles, to the A286 rd (875/166) nr Cocking.

10 Go SA over the rd, past a farm, UH, for 5.3 miles across Graffham Down, DH, to the A285 rd (950/144), and go SA, UH. Follow the SDW signs for 2m, bearing L to a car park (973/129), then to the RHS of a minor rd, for 2.5m up then down Bignor hill and Westburton hill, to the A29 rd (004/119).

11 Turn R on this, then immediately L, back off-rd, on the SDW and follow the signs, for 2m, DH, over a rd, then over the river, then a railway line, to the B2139 rd (027/124). Turn R with the B2139 rd, for 0.1m, then cross it, onto a minor rd (027/122), UH, for 0.4m then keep SA/R, leaving the rd as it bears sharp L, off-rd on the SDW.

12 Follow the SDW signs for 5.5m (L at a fork after 4m, slight UH), dropping DH, to and under the A24 rd (119/118), then bearing R, off-road, UH. Follow the SDW signs for 3.7m (past Chanctonbury ring) down to a minor rd, and keep SA on this for 0.55m then turn L (165/089), off-rd and DH, keeping SA on the feint track.

13 Join a DT and bear L to a rd (186/095) and turn R on this, for 0.25m then bear L onto a DT. To a X-tracks, and keep SA, over the river, to the A283 rd (197/093). Turn L alongside this rd for 0.1m then turn R over the rd, onto a BW (SDW), UH, to a rd and car park at the top (208/096) and turn L along the rd.

14 Keep SA on the SDW, for 3.6m to a minor rd (258/107) and go SA over this. Keep to the RHS of the valley, DH, to a rd and cross this, bearing R around the buildings, and bear R at the 1st fork, then L at the 2nd, up West hill. Keep SA/L at the top, DH, to a fork and bear L, to the A23 rd, and bear L then R over this.

15 Go into Pyecombe (291/126) (pub and tea shop here), and exit on School lane, to the A273 rd. Turn L alongside this rd for 0.15m then turn R on a DT, UH, through golf course, to a X-tracks and turn L. 0.2m to a T-J (305/132) nr the windmills and turn R, and follow this track for 1.9m, through Ditchling Beacon car park, to a

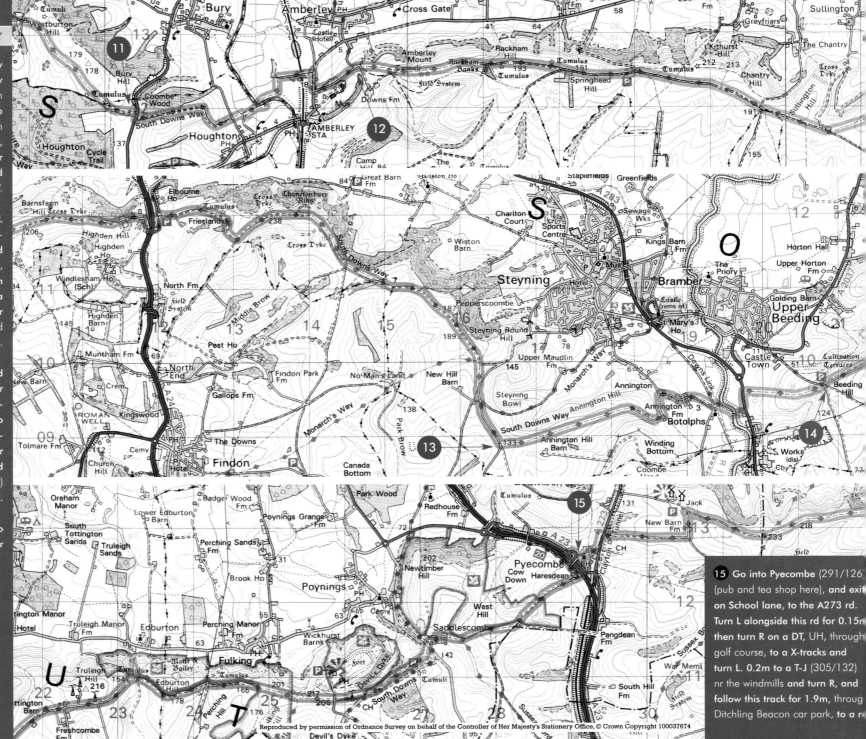

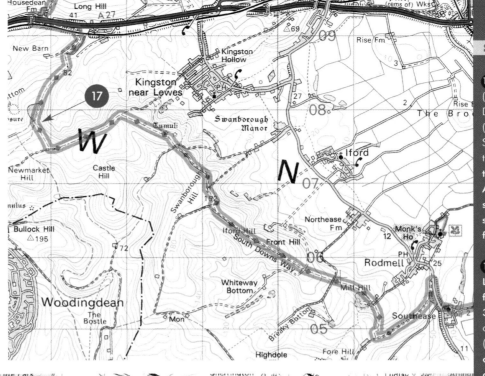

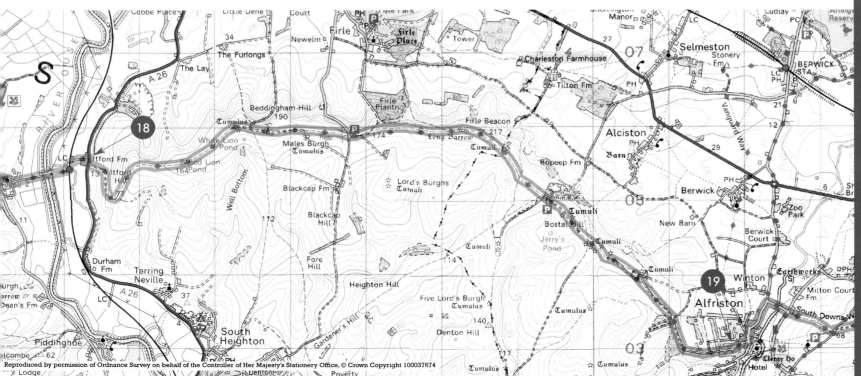

16 Go SA, for 2.3m to a X-tracks (369/125), and turn R, through a gate, DH, for 0.65m to a fork and bear L (364/116). DH, for 1.1m to a fork (FP SA/L) and bear R, DH, to some woods, then UH, then back DH, to a farm and turn R after this, then shortly L over the A27 rd (367/092). Turn L on the other side, between the rd and railway, then shortly turn R, under the railway, UH, for 0.9m to a 3-way junction.

17 Bear L, to a T-J (369/074) and turn L on this, for 0.65m and bear R at the fork, on the SDW, and keep SA for 3.1m, along the top, becoming DH, over some DT's, to a T-J at the bottom (412/048). Turn L, to a rd and turn R on this for 0.25m then turn L onto another rd (421/053) and keep L, over the river (Ouse), to the A26 (433/056)

18 Turn R on the rd, then shortly L back off it, UH, bearing L after 0.45m, UH, for 2.25m, past a radar mast, to a car park/rd (467/058). Go SA, for 1.9m, DH, to a car park (493/050) and keep SA, UH, then DH, for 2.3m, joining King's rd, then Star lane, to the High street in Alfriston.

■ NOTE: Alfriston is where the walkers and riders go their separate ways, to the end of the SDW.

19 Turn L then immediately R on River lane, over Cuckmere river (523/031) and turn L for 0.3m then turn R (opposite a bridge on the L), off-rd, UH, for 0.45m to a rd and go SA, on the SDW, up Windover hill. Follow the SDW for 2.9m, along the hill top, then DH, through some trees, keeping SA, onto Church lane, to the main rd in Jevington. Turn R on this rd, then immediately L (562/013) off the main rd, on a DT (SDW), UH.

20 1m to a X-tracks at the top and keep SA, DH, for 1.6m, along the edge of some woods, to the A259 rd and go SA. 0.25m to a 3-way (SDW) junction (587/982) and bear L or see the extension. DH, for 0.7m, between the trees, to a (Paradise) rd, by Compton place, and the end of the SDW (597/981).

■ **NOTE:** To get to Eastbourne train station, turn R on Paradise drive, becoming Carlisle rd, to Meads rd (603/982) and turn L. After 0.4m keep SA/L on Grove rd for 0.2m to a roundabout and turn R (Terminus rd) to the station (609/991).

EXTENSION:

1 Bear R, and keep SA at an off-set X-tracks, to and over a rd (589/975). Keep SA for 0.4m then turn R, (593/969) back to the rd and turn L on this for 0.65m to the view-point (seaside end point for the SDW) on the R (588/955).

OTHER PLACES TO RIDE

other places to ride in the UK...

This section of the book brings you information on the mountain bike specific trails and areas in the UK, as well as some long distance / epic rides you may want to attempt.

Man-made mountain bike trails may not provide the sense of adventure and achievement that you get from natural trails, but there is no denying the fact that you get an easy-to-follow route, which flows fantastically, and provides some superb technical challenges. The man-made courses in Wales and Scotland are world famous, suitable in all weather conditions, and free, so are well worth a visit at some point - you'd be crazy not to.

Other places to ride in the UK

Over the next few pages, we have compiled a list of mountain biking areas that offer riding such as waymarked cross country and downhill courses and areas to ride in any direction. Finally, we have also listed some long distance rides that would make excellent adventures over a bank holiday weekend.

■ NOTES:

The long distance rides are shown as lines (in their country's colour) on the map.

The broken white lines show the country borders.

Many Forestry Commission forests are open to the public and some have waymarked (family) cycle routes, see www.forestry.gov.uk for more information.

Before heading off, it is always best to check that the cycle trails are open (see the contact details).

Please check that the route you have chosen to ride is suitable to your abilities - some of these man-made courses are very technical.

ENGLAND

01 - Aston Hill
02 - Bewl water & Bedgebury Forest
03 - Blandford
04 - Bracknell / Swinley / Crowthorne forest
05 - Bringewood
06 - Cannock Chase
07 - Chicksands
08 - Combe Sydenham
09 - Dalby Forest
10 - Deers Leap MTB park
11 - Delamere Forest
12 - Dunster Woods / Croydon Hill
13 - Eastridge Wood
14 - Forest of Dean (FoDCA)
15 - Friston Forest
16 - Grizedale
17 - Guisborough Forest
18 - Hamsterley Forest
19 - High Action Ltd
20 - Hopton Woods
21 - Kielder Forest
22 - Penshurst Off-Road Centre (PORC)
23 - Queen Elizabeth Country Park (QECP)
24 - Redlands Trails
25 - Sherwood Pines
26 - Stainburn forest
27 - Thetford Forest
28 - Timberland Trail
29 - Wharncliffe Woods
30 - Whinlatter Forest Park
31 - Woburn Sands

LONG DISTANCE RIDES
32 - Cheshire Cycleway
33 - Coast to Coast
34 - Downs Link
35 - Pedders Way
36 - Pennine Bridleway
37 - Ridgeway
38 - South Downs Way
39 - Devon Coast to Coast

WALES

01 - Afan Argoed
02 - Brechfa Forest
03 - Coed Trallwn
04 - Coed Y Brenin
05 - Cwm Carn
06 - Gwyder Forest (Betws y Coed)
07 - Llanwrtyd wells
08 - Machynlleth (Mach trails)
09 - Nant yr Arian
10 - Nant Mawr Quarry
11 - Penmachno
12 - Snowdon
13 - Y Tri Chwn (Three valleys)

LONG DISTANCE RIDES
14 - Glyndwrs Way

SCOTLAND

01 - Achray & Loch Ard Forest
02 - Ae
03 - Argyll Forest
04 - Craik Forest
05 - Dalbeattie
06 - Fort William (Aonach Mor downhill)
07 - Glentress
08 - Glentrool Forest
09 - Innerleithen
10 - Kirroughtree Forest
11 - Laggan
12 - Mabie
13 - Newcastleton Forest
14 - Pitfichie Forest

LONG DISTANCE RIDES
15 - Great Glen Cycle Route
16 - Speyside Way
17 - West Highland Way

● ENGLAND

● WALES

● SCOTLAND

ENGLAND

If you mention purpose built mountain bike routes to most riders, they will think of Wales and Scotland. However, there are a lot of purpose built trails in England if you know where to look.OK, so there aren't the hills and vast forests of Wales and Scotland, but there is plenty of the superb twisty woodland single track that makes English MTB'ing great.

Pine forests also exist in England - and they are home to some superb single track.

01 - Aston Hill

Trails: A 4 mile XC course, a duel slalom, a BSX course, 4 downhill courses (Red, Black, DH3 and Ultimate pursuits DH), bomb holes and 100 acres of FC woodland set aside for MTB'ers.

Getting there: In Buckinghamshire, near Aylesbury. Take the B4009 from Wendover, towards Tring, past RAF Halton, to the top of the hill and turn right, (signposted Wendover Woods). Keep straight ahead, past Wendover Woods on the right and Chiltern Hills golf club on the left, to the top of the hill, and the car park is on the left.

Other information: It is meant for members, but for £4 a day, visitors are welcome at weekends and in holidays. There is a shop on site with basic parts, spares, bike hire and refreshments and there are regular events and training courses available from the pro's.

Contacts: See: www.astonhill.com e-mail; info@firecrestmtb.com, or tel: 01296 489729. Wendover TI on 01296 696759.

02 - Bewl Water & Bedgebury Forest

Trails: A 12 mile waymarked circuit of Bewl water, and a short and easy green waymarked trail in Bedgebury forest.

Getting there: Bewl water is south east of Royal Tunbridge wells, on the A21 (and Bedgebury forest is on the other side of the A21). Follow the signs for the Bewl water visitor centre to the car park.

Other information: The Bewl water trail is open from May to October for cyclists (and horse riders). The Bewl water visitor centre has refreshments, etc (open everyday except X-mas), and there are also hot and cold snacks available at the Pinetum in Bedgebury forest.

Contacts: Tunbridge wells T.I. 01892 515675 or the recreation officer on 01420 520212. Bike hire is available during the summer months, at Bewl water on 07801 670 999.

03 - Blandford

Trails: Several freeride courses, a downhill, a duel course, Area 51 (various), north shore, and some jumps.

Getting there: In Dorset, on Oakford hill, which is near Okeford Fitzpaine. Take the A357 to Shillingstone (north-west from Blandford forum) and turn left to Okeford Fitzpaine. In Oakford Fitzpaine turn left, then shortly left again, uphill for about 1 mile and the car park is on the right and the mountain bike area is at the end on the track on the left.

Other information: A dedicated Freeride park designed for all skill levels. It is meant for members, but day passes are available. There are also lots of great R.O.W.'s in the surrounding area.

Contact: www.mountainbikefreeride.com.

04 - Bracknell Forest (a.k.a. Crowthorne or Swinley Forest)

Trails: No waymarked trails, but 650 acres of woodland with lots of superb singletrack, and a MTB specific area.

Getting there: On the southern edge of Bracknell town (not far from Reading). Follow the signs for the Lookout / Discovery centre, on the B3430 and use this free car park.

Other information: You need to buy a cycle permit (£1) for the day from the Lookout centre by the car park. They also have a map of the forest, toilets, and a cafe. There are more good trails just over the M3 in Bagshot heath and around Lightwater.

Contacts: Wellington Trek bike hire on tel: 01344 874611, Berkshire cycles in Crowthorne on 01344 774529, or the Berks on bikes club website on www.bobmbc.com.

05 - Bringewood & Haye Park

Trails: A DH course in Bringewood and great (unmarked) trails in Haye Park.

Getting there: On the south-west edge of Ludlow, off the the A49, in Shropshire.

Other information: The DH is used for races, and there are plans to expand the trails into Haye Park (which is an open access FC forest).

Contacts: Pearce cycles on 01584 876016 or visit www.pearcecycles.co.uk in Ludlow, or ludlow T.I. 01584 875053.

06 - Cannock Chase:

Trails: Various loops to make a XC ride of up to 30 miles, and a downhill area.

Getting there: In Staffordshire, by Cannock (north of Birmingham), off the M6 at junction 12. Follow signs for the Forest office / Birches valley visitor centre on the B5012 (Penkridge bank road).

Other information: There is lots of cycling in these woods - although not all of them are legal. The Birches valley visitor centre has a cafe, free car park, bike shop, bike wash and servicing. Bike hire is available at Swinnerton cycles bike shop. Other places to ride around in Birmingham include Sandwell Valley Country Park (mid west), the Lickey hills (south west) and Sutton Park (north).

Contacts: Swinnerton cycles bike shop or 01889 575170, www.chasetrails.co.uk, website www.cannockchasedc.gov.uk or Litchfield TI on 01543 308209.

07 - Chicksands

Trails: An easy 2 mile (blue), and a hard (red) 3 mile waymarked XC courses, a dual slalom, and a freeride area in the bomb holes.

Getting there: South-East of Bedford, off the A600, just north of Chicksands (nr Shefford) - park in Sandy lane car park.

Other information: Basic and small, but great fun. The course is managed and maintained by the Beds Fat Trax MTB bike club. The freeride area is in the north-east corner of the woods, and is accessed from the XC course.

Contacts: Ranger on 01780 444394 or www.bedsfattrax.supanet.com.

08 - Combe Sydenham

Trails: A DH course, with more planned.

Getting there: Just south of Monksilver, off the B3188, south of Watchet, off the A39 rd, near the Quantock hills.

Other information: Open Feb-Oct and request you put £5 in the honesty box. Lifts back up are sometimes available, see www.sightdirect.co.uk/racing.

Contacts: See above, or tel Bridgewater tourist info. on tel: 01278 427652.

Crowthorne Forest - see Bracknel

09 - Dalby Forest

Trails: A black 6 mile route, a red 15 mile route, a blue 8 mile route, and 2 easier green routes 6 and 2.5 miles fire road route, and a downhill being built.

Getting there: Inland on the A170 from Scarborough, in north Yorkshire. Head north at Thornton Le Dale, following the brown signs, to the visitor centre, on the Dalby forest drive toll road. You can also gain access from the north of Scarborough via minor roads through Hackness and Langdale end.

Other information: There is a shop, toilets, refreshments and bike hire available. The toll road is around £5 (£2 out of season) per car - cyclists and walkers go free.

Contacts: e-mail: north.york.moors.fdo@forestry.gsi.gov.uk or telephone the recreation manager on 01751 472771.

10 - Deers Leap Mountain bike Park

Trails: A MTB specific trail and 230 acres to explore.

Getting there: South of East Grinstead, by Weir Wood reservoir. Exit the A22 and following the brown signs, onto the B2110 (Turners hill road) in East Grinstead. Turn left after 1.2 miles onto Saint Hill road and it's on the left about 1 mile down here.

Other information: Mostly easy riding, but some more technical tracks there if you want. There is a shop with spare parts, bike hire, and maps to borrow. Parking costs £3.50, which also pays for the days cycling.

Contacts: Tel: 01342 325858 or see www.deersleappark.co.uk.

11 - Delamere Forest

Trails: A freeride area, duel slalom, BSX course, jumps, downhills, and some singletrack. There is also the 7 mile Whitemoor and 4 mile Hunger hill trails, family XC trails.

Getting there: At the end of the river Mersey, between Chester and Northwich. The car park is by Delamere train station, just off the B5152.

Other information: Great place for all types of riding, but especially freeriding.

Contacts: The area Forester) on tel: 01606 882167.

12 - Dunster Woods / Croydon Hill

Trails: 1 mile family trail (green), 6 mile intermediate (orange), and 9 mile advanced (brown) trail.

Getting there: Near Minehead, on the the north coast of Devon. Turn off the A39 on the A396, past Dunster castle and about 0.5 miles after Dunster turn left on a minor rd to the car park and trails.

Contacts: Minehead T.I. 01643 702624

13 - Eastridge Wood

Trails: Open access F.C. woodland, with some technical XC and downhill trails.

Getting there: Eastridge woods is near a place called Snailbeach, but the car park for the woods is near Habberly. Head south-west on the A488 from Shrewsbury, to Pontesbury and turn left to Habberly. In Habberly, take the (small) Minsterly road, up the hill to some parking places on the left hand side, and you should see the cycle tracks sign.

Other information: The woods themselves are small, but steep, and home to some nice singletrack. The NPS races come here, and walkers and horse riders tend to stay away.

Contact: Shrewsbury T.I. on 01743 281200

14 - Forest of Dean (FoDCA)

Trails: Over 100 miles of forest fire roads, a range of different length 'easy' routes, a (pink) family route, and the technical 9.5 mile FoDCA trail, plus a skills area just behind the cycle centre.

Getting there: The Forest of Dean is on the border of Wales, south of Ross-on-Wye, where the M50 ends. Follow the B4234 south (towards Cannop valley), cross the A4136 for 1.4 miles then turn right (west) into the car park (by Pedalabikeaway).

Other information: The Sallow Vallets enclosure (where the FoDCA trail is) behind Pedalabikeaway is the only off-road cycling area you are free to roam, otherwise keep to the main forest tracks. Pedalabikeaway has spares and bikes for hire (see pedalabikeaway.com or phone 01594 860065 or 01989 770357).

Contacts: See www.fodca.org.uk, or phone Ross-on-Wye T.I. on tel: 01989 562768. Church farm does self catering accommodation on 01594 541211.

15 - Friston Forest

Trails: A 7 mile technical (purple) XC route, and an easy 4.5 mile (green) route. There are also a few downhill tracks and jumps (parallel to the A259 nr Friston, ending at the Exceat car park), and lots of other trails in the forest.

Getting there: The trails start at the Cuckmere cycle co bike shop and visitor centre just off the A259 (east of Seaford) in the Seven sisters county park car park.

Other information: Cuckmere cycle shop has cycle parts, accessories and bikes for hire (see contacts below). There are more good tracks to explore in this open access FC forest.

Contacts: Cuckmere cycles on 01323 870310 or: www.cuckmerecycle.co.uk. Eastbourne TI on 01323 411400.

16 - Grizedale

Trails: The 14 mile Silurian way, 7 mile Moor top trail, and the 10.5 mile Hawkshead Moor trail, none of which are very technical. There is also the easy Grizedale tarn and Goosey Foot tarn.

Getting there: In Cumbria, near Coniston, west of lake Windemere, off the B5285.

Other information: The visitor centre has cycle hire and a cafe, etc. The cycle trails aren't very technical, but there are plenty more unmarked trails to explore.

Contacts: mountain bike visitor centre on tel:01229 860369

17 - Guisborough Forest

Trails: A technical 7.5 mile black route, and a 4.5 mile blue family route.

Getting there: Take the A171 from Middlesbrough (north Yorkshire), towards Guisborough and turn right at the roundabout (just before Guisborough) on the A173 for 300 meters and there it is.

Other information: A visitors centre with refreshments, toilets and maps.

Contact: The recreation manager on tel: 01751 472771.

18 - Hamsterley Forest

Trails: 4 XC routes: the technical 7 mile (black) Bedborn bash, the challenging 10 mile (red) Neighbour moor tour, the easy-moderate 9 mile (blue) Spurls Wood Valley ride and the easy 3 mile (green) Windy Bank trail. A great DH suitable for most riders, by use of chicken runs to avoid 25ft table top jumps and the like. There are also plans for a freeride and a quad descend course.

Getting there: West of Bishop Auckland in county Durham, north Pennines. Follow the brown tourist signs for Hamsterley forest from the A68 near Hamsterley.

Other information: The car park is £2 for the day, and the riding is free. There is a visitor centre with toilets, a cafe, shop, and mini-bus / trailor back up the downhill.

Wonderful dappled, woodland single track trails in England.

Typical English forest single track.

Contacts: Visitor centre on 013884 88312 Hamsterley cycle hire on 01388 488188 and Avanteee bike shop (Bishop Auckland) 01388 608397. The Hamsterley outdoor centre sleeps around 30 tel: 01388 488080 or Gore house B&B in the woods on 01388 488203 or the YHA on 01833 622228.

19 - High Action Ltd
Trails: A north shore obstacle trail course with varying difficulty levels.

Getting there: Near Churchill (where the A368 and A38 cross), south of Bristol. Aim for High Action ltd / Avon ski centre at Lyncombe lodge.

Other information: Open 11-5 on Sundays and costs £5 for 2 hours or £7 for the whole day and has a minimum age of 12). There is also general cycling on the 230 acres, which is suitable for family riding.

Contacts: Tel 01934 853314 or 852335 or visit www.highaction.co.uk.

20 - Hopton Woods
Trails: 4 XC courses: a hard red route, challenging amber, moderate green, and a blue family route. There are also 3 (national championship standard) downhill courses (marked in black).

Getting there: Hopton Titterhill wood is 12 miles west of Ludlow. Head along the A4113, then on to the B4385, and head for Hopton Castle, and the trails are (just south of) here.

Other information: There is a picnic area, free car park, and maps for the area are £1 from Pearce Cycles in Ludlow, who give lifts back up (book in advance).

Contacts: Ludlow T.I. on 01584 875053, Pearce Cycles on: 01584 876016 or www.pearcecycles.co.uk.

21 - Kielder Forest:
Trails: 15 waymarked routes, and miles and miles of unmarked trails to explore.
01 - Bull crag - easy 6 miles.
02 - Cranecleugh - easy 5 miles.
03 - Cross crags - easy 6 miles.
04 - Humble loop - easy 10 miles.
05 - Swinburne selection - moderate to demanding 6, 8 or 10 miles.
06 - Kielder water circuit - a moderate to demanding 16 miles.
07 - Border railway - easy 7 miles.
08 - Scaup - easy 8 miles.

09 - Castle hill - easy 7.5 miles.
10 - Sidewood - demanding 17 miles
11 - Kershope - easy 7 miles
12 - Cross border trail - moderate 13 miles
13 - Cross Border - demanding 11 or 17miles
14 - Archercleugh - Trail quest cyclo-orienteering course area.
15 - Leaplish crags off-road area - hard 13 hectares to explore (very good).

■ NOTE: Graded by the F.C.

Getting there: By the Scottish border. Exit the A68 on the B6320 and follow signs to Kielder on the minor roads. There are two main centres; the Leaplish waterside park (south-west side of the lake) and the Kielder castle forest park (northern end of the lake).

Other information: Over 600 square kilometres, makes this the biggest forest in Britain. There is a bike wash, hire, shops, toilets, and lots of places to park, stay, eat and drink, as well as lots of other activities for all to do.

Contacts: Kielder partnership on 01434 220643 for accommodation information or the YHA on 01434 250392. Bike shop / hire available at Leaplish cycling hire centre: 01434 250312 or Kielder bikes: 01434 250392.

Mary Towneley Loop - see the Pennine bridleway (in the Long distant rides section).

22 - Penshurst Off-Road Centre (PORC).
Trails: Over 40 acres of woodland for XC, lots of DH's, BSX / Slalom course, jump area and a (national standard) 4-cross course.

Getting there: Penshurst in Kent, South East England. Drive south out of Penshurst on the B2188 for about 1/2 mile and turn right on Grove road, and the centre is less than 1 mile on the right.

Other information: A charge of £4 (or £2.50 in under 18) and free parking for the day. There is hot food and refreshments and coaching, etc available.

Contacts: Coaching enquiries (PORC) on 01892 870136 or www.pork-online.co.uk.

23 - Queen Elizabeth Country Park (QECP).
Trails: A technical 3 mile (orange) route, and an easy 3.7 mile (purple) route. Also, 2 further trails starting in the park and leading out into the surrounding countryside: the 10 mile Queen Elizabeth and the 10 mile Meon Valley.

Getting there: 3.5 miles south of Petersfield, off the A3. Follow the brown tourist signs to the QECP car park.

Other information: The car parks is £1 mon-sat and £1.50 sun. There is 1,400 acres of open access woodland and downland with an additional 500 acres for specific events and club use. A visitors centre with a shop, cafe, toilets, adventure play trail, orienteering, wayfaring, BBQ sites to hire.

Contact: Telephone 023 92 595040

24 - Redlands Trails
Trails: 2 mile Summer lightening trail and lots of good unmarked trails.

Getting there: Exit the M25 at leatherhead and follow signs to Dorking. Go round the one way system and exit to Leith hill, (the exit after Horsham). About 3 miles to to the Plough pub in Coldharbour and use the FC car park. The trail is up Wolvens lane (byway), (GR 150/445).

Other information: Redlands are a small team who are building these trails for the local riders, to provide some alternatives to the superb, but very busy trails around Leith hill, Holmbury hill and Pitch hill.

Contacts: See www.justriding along.com

Rowney Warren Woods - see Chicksands.

25 - Sherwood Pines
Trails: A 1.5 mile training circuit, a duel descender, the 'Jungle' where locals can build some trails, and a black off-road area with some great variable length singletrack XC. There are also two easier routes, a 6 mile blue (easy), and a 3 mile green (family) route.

Getting there: Head east from Mansfield (off the M1), in Nottinghamshire, on the B6030, and follow the brown tourist signs for Sherwood Pines Forest Park.

Other information: Cycling for all abilities, and often races are held here. Bike hire is available at the cycle centre 01623 822855.

Contacts: Visitor centre on 01623 822447 or the T.I. on 01623 824545.

26 - Stainburn forest
Trails: Very technical 2.5m Stainburn forest boulder trail.

Getting there: 10 miles north of Leeds, near Otley, off the B6451.

...ther information: A very technical trail
...h more riding available.

...ontacts: www.singletraction.org.uk

...winley Forest - see Bracknell

...7 - Thetford Forest
...ails: 3 XC courses; a technical black 8
...le trail, a 6.5 mile easy / moderate
...ue trail, and a 6.4 mile green trail for
...ginners.

...etting there: The rides start from the
...itors centre (signposted) between
...etford and Brandon, off the B1107, or
...ve parking at Brandon Country Park.
...e nearest railway is in Brandon, just a
...w miles away.

...ther information: A large forest with
...ads of undulating singletrack and forest
...acks. There is a restaurant, toilets, shop
...d bike hire (see Bike Art below) and a
...sitor centre where the trails all start
...om. There are also more developments
...anned for the area.

...ontacts: The 'Bike Art' bike shop on
... 842 8100090 or visit www.bike-
...t.com, or Thetford 01362 656235 for
...ccommodation information.

...8 - Timberland Trail
...ails: A 7 mile, waymarked woodland
...ngletrack XC trail, and plenty more trails
...ound this area.

...etting there: The ride starts in Ashton
...ourt by the gate house, near Clifton
...spension bridge (west Bristol). There
...e 2 car parks in Ashton court, one SA
...nd on the left, and another on the right,
... the golf club and cafe.

...ther information: There are many many
...ore (unmarked) twisty woodland
...ngletracks around this area e.g. Leigh
...oods, Ashton hill, 50 acre wood (near
...len farm) which is mostly open to
...clists. The pitch & putt cafe in the

middle of Ashton court has a cafe, and
there is usually an ice cream van (in the
summer) at the car park. 3 good bike
shops nearby in Bristol: Bike (UK), Dave
Baters, and Mud Dock (with restaurant).

Contacts: www.timberlandtrail.com or
Mud Dock on 0117 9292151 or see
www.visitbristol.co.uk/acc for
accomodatioon information.

29 - Wharncliffe Woods:
Trails: A technical 10 mile black XC
route and an easy green, family route.
Lots of great downhills (legal and
otherwise), and lots of unmarked trails for
all abilities i.e. wide firetrack and
technical singletrack.

Getting there: 5 miles north of Sheffield
near the village of Grenoside. Exit the
M1 at junction 35 and head West on the
A629 for 2.5m (though Chapeltown), to
a T-J with the A61 and turn left (towards
Sheffield). After 1.5m turn right on
Norfolk hill (in Grenoside) and right at
the X-roads, for 0.4m on to Main Street
(Wortley) for about 0.7m to a car park.

Other information: Superb area for
freeriding, with lots of technical trails,
and home to Steve Peat - nuff said! For
the DH's, bear right from the car park
and keep right at next 3 forest roads,
now take your pick of any DH's on the
left (GR306/949). Also, on the black
route look out for a DH course on the left
(in to the woods) on a stoney doubletrack
shortly after the sign for Wharncliffe
moor). Follow the black markers (keeping
left) to get back to the car park. There is
also a northshore style course around
grid reference 312/942.

Contacts: T.I. on 0114 2211900

30 - Whinlatter Forest Park
Trails: Various waymarked trails,
including 2 junior trails, 2 orienteering
courses, an all ability trail, a 7.5 mile
purple route, and a 6 mile orange route.

Getting there: Off the B5292, north west
of Keswick, in Cumbria.

Other information: Around 1,200
hectares, a visitor centre, shop, tearoom,
riding for all abilities, toilets, picnic sites
and more.

Contacts: Recreation ranger on 01768
778469, or visit www.forestry.gov.uk.

31 - Woburn Sands
Trails: There are loads of trails in the 800
acres of woodland, including a play area
with jumps, downhills, etc.

Getting there: The riding is in Aspley
Heath, on the south east edge of Milton
Keynes. There are 3 car parks around the
wood, or a big grass verge on Woodland
way, off Hardwick rd from the High Street
(A5130) where you can enter the woods
through the gate in the fence.

Other information: You will need to get a
permit, costing £2 for the day, or £10 for
the year (see the ranger contact for more
details) to ride around here. Salcey forest
(just up the M1) is an open access FC
forest with parking and toilets. It is more
family style riding, but there are a few
good (unmarked) singletrack trails.

Contacts: See www.woburntrails.co.uk or
speak to the Stockgrove Country park
ranger on tel: 01525 237760.

LONG DISTANCE ROUTES

32 - Cheshire Cycleway
Trail: A non-technical, signposted 176
mile route alongside canals and byways.

Getting there: Starts in Chester, (south of
Liverpool), at the end of the M53 & M56.

Other information: Starts in Chester and
goes along the Shropshire union canal,
through Acton bridge, Bollington,
Marton, Malpas, and back to Chester. It
is signposted from both directions, but is
still probably worth using Ordnance
Survey Landranger maps no.117 & 118.

Contacts: Chester T.I. on 01244 402111
or order the Cycling explorer pack on tel:
01244 603107 or visit www.visit-
cheshire.com/form.htm.

33 - Downs Link
Trail: A 34 mile, signposted, one-way
trail, linking the North Downs Way to the
South Downs Way.

Getting there: From St Martha's hill (just
east of Guildford), on the NDW, to the
SDW, just south of Bramber.

Other information: Uses mainly off-road
trails, and joins the south downs way, just
south of Upper Beeding (nr Brighton).

34 - Coast 2 Coast (C2C):
Trail: Over 200 miles (mostly off-road)
across the Lake district, Pennines, Dales
and the Moors, taking around 3-5 days.

Other information: There is no single,
authentic route from one coast to the
other. Sustrans have opened their route
(from Whitehaven to Sunderland), which
mainly uses cycle paths and quiet lanes.
Off-road routes often start from around
Whitehaven / St Bees / Ravenglass and
finish around Whitby pier or Robin Hoods
bay. You will need 6 OS Landranger
maps (93, 94 and 96-9).

Contacts: See www.c2c-guide.co.uk.

England has it's fair share of man-
made trails as well.

LONG DISTANCE ROUTES continued...

Be well prepared when tackling a long distance ride.

Mary Towneley loop- see no.5 'The Pennine Bridleway' (below).

North Downs Way - forget it there are too many diversions for MTB'ers.

35 - Peddars Way (& Norfolk Coast Path)

Trails: 93 miles from Knettishall in Suffolk, to Cromer in Norfolk, along unsurafced country roads and well draining chalk tracks.

Getting there: Continuing on from the Icknield way path, in Knettishall Heath country park, just south of the A1066, east of Thetford.

Other information: The first 43 miles from Knettishall Heath Country Park to Old Hunstanton on the north coast is open to bicycles. The last section (along the coast) to Cromer i.e. the Norfolk coast path, is not open to bicycles, however Sustrans have created the Norfolk coast cycleway, which is slightly inland, using quite roads. The map is available from north Norfolk District council tel: 01263 513811.

Contact: Peddars Way & Norfolk Coast Path National trail on 01328 711533.

36 - Pennine Bridleway

Trails: 347 miles from Middleton Top in Derbyshire, north, across two national parks, to Byrness in Northumberland.

Getting there: Middleton is in Derbyshire (Peak District), south-west off the A6, from Cromford (south of Matlock).

Other information: Due for completion in 2005/6 - see the contacts for latest info. This long distance (national) route has been designed especially for cyclists and horseriders as an alternative to the actual Pennine way, which we are asked not to ride our bikes on. It will take a good few days to complete, but there are YHA's on the way. There is also the Mary Towneley

loop, starting at Hebden bridge (west of Halifax). This loop is 47 miles long, and you can get (free) maps from the Blazing saddles bike shop in Hebden.

Contact: The Pennine bridleway project team on 0161 2371061 or visit the website: www.nationaltrail.co.uk. Blazing saddles bike shop in Hebden bridge on 01422 844435 or see the website www.blazingsaddles.co.uk.

37 - Ridgeway

Trail: 89miles & 2,125 metres of climbing

Getting there: The ride starts from an inconspicuous dirt car park, just off the A4 near Avebury (4 miles west of Marlborough. The nearest train station is in Swindon (7 miles away).

Other information: Although you finish at almost exactly the same altitude, it is usually ridden from west to east. The first 43 miles are easy to follow, rutted doubletracks, and is all open to cyclists, but the 2nd half has a few diversions. There are some well placed YHA's to stay at along the way, and a few water taps.

Contacts: For maps and further info see our South East book (www.roughride guide.co.uk or www.nationaltrail.co.uk).

38 - South Downs Way

Trail: 100 miles of well signposted, (nearly all) off-road riding from Winchester to Eastbourne with around 4,000 metres of climbing.

Getting there: Get the train to Winchester (north of Southampton) and the train back from Eastbourne at the other end.

Other information: Usually attempted over 2-3 days. There are places close to the route to spend the night. The shortened route of 76 miles, starts from the Queen Elizabeth Country Park (south of Petersfield, off the A3). There are a few small diversions for

MTB'ers, including the very start and end, but should be signposted.

Contacts: South downs way national trail officer on: 023 9259 7618 or visit: www.nationaltrails.gov.uk.

39 - Southern C2C:

Trail: Over 100 miles from Plymouth to Ilfracombe.

Getting there: Start from Plymouth or Ilfracombe.

Other information: A non technical trail, using the Plym valley, Granite way, Tarka trail cycleways, and quite roads. Requires OS maps no.180, 190, 191 and 201.

Contacts: Sustrans (www.sustrans.gov.uk).

South West Coast Path - It's a footpath so stay off.

Thames Path - It's a footpath so stay off.

●ENGLAND

●WALES

●SCOTLAND

WALES

The country that pioneered the purpose built mountain bike courses in the UK is still holding a very strong position, and has been voted as having the best riding in the world in 2003. It's not surprising when the country looked like it was built for MTB'ing before the 'trail pixies' picked up their magic shovels to make it even better.

Most of the mounatin bike centres have more than one route, and seeing as it can take a while to get there it is well worth making a weekend of it by staying over - that's the whole idea of the trails being built and receiving the funding. If you like a challenge, take a week off work and try to complete all the rides in ; Gwydyr, Coed-y-Brenin, Nant-y-Arian, Afan, and Cwm carn for a truly superb and memorable few days of riding.

Being Wales it's used to the rain, and the mountain bike trails have been cleverly designed and built so that they are not really affected by the rain - making it a very good place to head to when all your local trails are a muddy mess.

Visit the www.mbwales.com website for more information.

01 - Afan Argoed

Trails: The 14 mile Wall, 13.5 mile Penhydd. 5 miles further up the valley at Glyncorrwg ponds is the 10 mile Whites level, and 28 mile Skyline. Less technical trails include the 24 mile (one-way) Celtic high level scenic trail from Neath to Pontprydd and a 7 mile family route.

Getting there: In south Wales near Port Talbot. Exit the M40 at junction 40 and go north on A4107 to Afan forest park.

Other information: A cafe, toilets and (very basic) campsite at the Afan car park. At Glyncorrwg ponds there is a better campsite, MTB centre with a cafe, bike wash, and Skyline cycles bike shop.

Contacts: Skyline cycles on 01639 850011, or Afan visitor centre on 01639 850564, www.mbwales.com. Afan Valley Bike hire (www.afan-valley-bike-hire.co.uk) on 07952 577316 or Argoed cycle hire on 01639 850564.

Betws Y Coed - see Gwydyr Forest

02 - Brechfa Forest

Trails: 9 mile (red) route, and loads of unmarked trails in the surrounding forest.

Getting there: The trails starts at the car park in Aber Gorlech (GR 586/337), on the B4310 - 10 miles north of Llandeilo on the B4302.

Other information: Free car park, with a picnic site and miles and miles of unmarked trails to explore.

Contacts: Carmarthen TI on 01267 231557 or Llandovery TI on 01550 720693 or www.forestry.gov.uk.

03 - Coed Trallwn

Trails: 3 loops: an easy (blue) 2 mile, moderate (red) 2.5 mile and a difficult (black) 3 mile. These can all be linked to make one ride.

Getting there: Take the A483 west from Builth wells for 8 miles to Beulah, then take a minor rd for 3.5 miles and Trallwn will be on the right.

Other information: Run on a private farm near Builth wells, there is no charge for the ride or the car park though. The routes use natural trails, with forest roads for the climbs and singletrack for the descents. Set in a great position with holiday cottages available.

Contacts: George Johnson on 01591 610229 or visit www.forestcottages.co.uk

04 - Coed y Brenin

Trails: The technical trails are the 6.8 mile 'Red Bull', 23.6 mile Karrimor, and the 13.7 mile MBR. There is also an intermediate 9.3 mile Sport route and a 6.8 mile Fun route for beginners.

Getting there: Near Dolgellau, in Snowdonia. Take the A470 north from Dolgellau, and the visitor centre is on the left after about 7 miles.

Other information: A shop with some bike parts, good cafe, toilets and bike wash on site. Dolgellau has lots of places to stay, eat and drink, shop and a couple of bike shops. There is also the easy, hard-packed Mawddach trail of 9 miles, along a discussed railway track, between Bramouth and Dolgellau.

Contacts: CyB visitor centre on 01341 440666, Dolgellau T.I. on 01341 422888 or the Forestry enterprise on 01341 422289. Plas Isa self catering accomodation in Dolgellau on 01766 540569, or in the log cabins just north of Coed-Y-Brenin on tel: 01766540219 or see www.logcabins-skiwales.co.uk.

05 - Cwmcarn

Trails: Technical 10 mile Twrch trail and a superb downhill course (with an uplift).

Getting there: North west of Newport. Exit the M4 at juntion 28 on the A467, past Risca, and turn R at the roundabout (staying on the A467), and follow the signs to Cwn Carn forest car park.

Other Information: These is a visitor centre with a cafe, bike wash, and camping. There are also things to do for the whole family i.e. forest drive, walking, sculpture trail, an adventure playground. Martyn Ashfield bike shop in Risca has parts and hire tel:01633 601040.

Contacts: Visitor centre on 01495 272001 or Graham on 07789 927395. Newport TI 01633 842962.

06 - Gwydyr Forest / Betws y Coed

Trails: 16 mile 'Marin' trail, with great singletrack and hundreds of miles of unmarked trails in the surrounding area.

Getting there: Near Betws-Y-Coed, in North Wales. Take the A470 towards Llanrwst (before Betws Y Coed), and the trail is (west) in the village of Trefriw. Follow the green forestry parking signs with a bike. There is also a railway station in Llanrwst, not far from the trail.

Other informations: Betws-y-coed has lots of cafes, restaurants, pubs, outdoor shops, etc. There is also another 20 mile route being built in Penmachno, close to Betws-y-Coed, which should be finished in 2005. For bike parts and hire, go to Beics Betws bike shop tel: 01690 710766 or 01690 710829 or visit: www.bikewales.com.

Contacts: Betws-y-coed TI on 01690 710426. YHA in Betws-Y-Coed on 01690 710796 or www.betws-y-coed.co.uk.

07 - LLanwrtyd Wells

Trails: 6 routes from an easy 8 miles to some longer and more technical rides.

Getting there: Take the A483 from Builth Wells, until you get to Llanwrtyd wells.

Other information: It used to be the home of the famous Man v Horse v Bike race, which has now been replaced by other riding and beer festivals. The routes use bridleways, forest tracks and quiet roads. Route maps are available from the T.I. and Ifron cycles on tel: 01591 610710 or www.cyclesirfon.co.uk. There are also miles of unmarked trails in the surrounding mountains and forests.

Contacts: Llanwrtyd T.I. on: 01591 610666, and Stonecroft lodge on 01591 610332 / 329 or www.stonec-roft.co.uk.

Wales - Home to some of the best MTB riding in the world.

08 - Machynlleth / Mach trails

Trails: 10 mile Mach 1, 14 mile Mach 2, and 19 mile Mach 3, and the more technical 12.5 mile Cli-machx trail. Also planned is the 25 mile Mach Epic.

Getting there: Starting from the town of Machynlleth at the bottom of Snowdonia. The town is south of dolgellau on the A487, and just off the A470 on the A489 and a a railway station in town.

Other information: Suitable for most abilities, while the Cli-machx offers more singletrack. There are also acres and acres of the Dyfi forest to explore.

Contacts: T.I. on 01654 702401, Greenstiles cycles on 01654 703543 have spares, and guided rides by arrangement, and Red bike hire on 01654-703622 or see the website: www.redbikehire.co.uk.

09 - Nant yr Arian

Trails: The 10 mile Summit Trail, 5.6 mile Pendam trail, and the 22 mile Syfydrin trail (which uses all of the Summit and Pendam trails, and a bit more).

Getting there: Nant-Y-Arian is about 8 miles inland, along the A44 from Aberystwyth (mid Wales on the coast), where there is also a railway station. Park in the Forestry Commission car park, where the trails start from.

Other information: There are plenty of places to eat, drink and stay, close to Nant-yr-Arian, with hot food and drinks at the centre Red Kite café (famous amongst roadies and motor bikers). There is also lots of unmarked riding just north, in the Cambrian mountains.

Contacts: Visitor centre on 01970 890694, Aberystwyth T.I. on 01970 612125, or Summit Cycles bike shop in Aberystwyth on 01970 626061 (www.summitcycles.co.uk).

10 - Nant mawr Quarry

Trails: A 3.5 mile XC circuit (for all abilities by using chicken routes), a downhill course and a quad slalom course (although it's usually only for competitions), and over 200 acres for freeriding, jumping, etc.

Getting there: Leave the Oswestry by-pass (A5/A438) at the Little Chef roundabout, on to the A483 towards Welshpool. After 4 miles turn right at the White Lion pub, Llynclys, onto the A495 for 3 miles, then turn right opposite a quarry entrance. Uphill to a T-junction and turn left for 0.5 miles and the entrance is on the right.

Other information: There is a bike wash, hot showers, club room, accommodation, and coffee bar on summer weekends and during events. £4 a day (£3 for under 16's) cash-in-the-box payment, so take the correct change. Some areas may be limited on event days, and you must wear a helmet, and not be on your own.

Contacts: Tel: 01691 659358

11 - Penmachno (planned):

Just south of the Gwydyr forest (Marin trail), is another 20 mile technical XC course being built for 2005/6.

12 - Snowdon

Trails: The Llanberis track up Snowdon involves a 4 mile climb of about 1,000 metres, then back down again the same track again.

Getting there: In Snowdonia (of course), which is in north-west Wales. Park in Llanberis, which is on the A4086 and is well signposted.

Other information: There are other tracks e.g. Ranger path & Rhyd-du, but they are more dangerous. There is a voluntary ban of bicycles on the mountain between 1st May to 30th September, between 10am and 5pm (confirm these dates & times). Please abide by these or it could become an outright ban. Bikes are not allowed on the train and it will take 2-4 hours to get up and back down for most riders, so you will have to set off around 7.00am if you go in the morning. There is a café / restaurant at the top and bottom and plenty of B&B's around.

Contacts: Tourist info. on 01286 870765

13 - Tilhill (Llandegla forest)

Trails: A 7.5 mile family trail and a 9.5 intermediate trail.

Getting there: Llandegla forest lies between Wrexham and Ruthin. Leave the A483 at Wrexham and follow the A525 towards Ruthin for 6.5 miles and the forest is on the left (south).

Other information: Due to open in the spring of 2005, there will be a bike shop with parts, clothing, bike hire and a cafe.

Contacts: www.forestry.gov.uk

14 - Y Tri Chwm (three valleys)

Trails: A waymarked 30 or 50 mile ride on natural trails, with shortcuts available, to provide a moderate to hard ride.

Getting there: Tredegar is about 20 miles north of Cardiff. Exit the M4 at junction 28 and follow signs to Risca, then pick up the A4048 past Blackwood for 10 miles, and turn left at the 2nd roundabout to a (free) car park. The trail starts by the Hobo backpackers hostel.

Other information: Ranch cafe (and others) in Tradegar, the Motor world shop has some bike parts, or there is a Halfords in Merthyr, and a good bike shop in Blackwood.

Contacts: Hobo backpackers is behind the design of the trail, and also the best place to stay, tel: 01495 718422 or see www.hobo-backpackers.co.uk.

LONG DISTANCE ROUTES

1 - Glyndwrs Way

Trails: Around 130 miles, from Knighton to Welshpool / Y Trallwng, through the Welsh mountains, on some technical trails.

Getting there: Knighton is west of Shrewsbury, where the A4113 meets the A488 running north to south. There is also a train station here and at the other end in Welshpool.

Other information: Listed as a Welsh walk, but there are only a few places where it is footpath only, and alternative routes are fairly easy to find. It is well signposted (although the part between Macynlleth to Llanbrimair is not very clear) and shown on OS maps. It will probably take 3-4 days, but there are plenty of places on the route to stay.

Contacts: T.I. no's: Knighton 01547 528753, Llanidloes 01686 412605, Macynlleth 01654 702401, Llanwdyn 01691 870346, and Welshpool 01938 552043. Bike shops: Les's bike shop in Llanidloes, Greenstiles bike shop in Macynlleth on 01654 703543, and Brook cycles in Welshpool on 01938 553582.

Offa's Dyke - This is a footpath, so don't ride it.

Pembrokeshire Coast Path - This is a footpath, so don't ride it.

Glorious weather(!), superb trails, what more could you ask for?

●ENGLAND

●WALES

●SCOTLAND

SCOTLAND

Scotland has always had numerous waymarked cycle trails in their forests, but they have mostly been family orientated. Recently though, the "Seven Stanes" project is aiming to build 23 purpose built trails, with around 200 miles of trails, in 7 locations (Tweed Valley, Dalbeattie, Mabie, Kirroughtree, Newcastleton, Ae, and Glentrool).

The countryside in Scotland is amazing and the thought that has gone into building these trails has created some absolutely amazing rides that are strongly challenging Wales for their title of best MTB trails in the world. The routes generally involve quite technical riding, but less experienced riders haven't been forgotten about. Each of the trails will have a marked password or historical theme on each "stane" (stone) which the rider will find on their bike ride. Once the rider has collected all the passwords from each trail they can apply for a certificate to prove they have ridden the 'Seven Stanes'.

For accommodation and other information on Scotland tel: 0845 225 5121 or see www.visitscotland.com or www.7stanes.gov.uk.

01 - Achray & Loch Ard Forests

Trails: The 5 mile Achray Forest Single track (with plans for a black and a red route), the 7 mile (red) Leanach West Achray Forest loop, the 9 mile (purple) Lochan Ghleannain (starting in Milton). There is also the 15.5 mile (red) Bonity Burn loop (starting in Crinigart) which includes the High Corrie loop), and the 9 mile Balleich trail. There are also 2 non-technical rides in Loch Ard Forest; the 20 mile Orbital route (green with red stencils) and the 8 mile South Loch Ard route (yellow). There is also an 11.5 mile trail between Braeval and Loch Achray.

Getting there: Go to Aberfoyle (where the A821, A81, and A873 all meet), east of Loch Lomond, in the Queen Elizabeth Forest Park. There is a car park at the west end of the village, off the main street (south), at the crossroads.

Other information: As most of the trails are not mountain bike specific, they are generally non-technical. Maps are available at the David Marshall Lodge Visitor Centre, in Aberfoyle. The Glasgow MTB club have an annual race at Braeval near the lodge, and hope to have trail markers put up. Cycle hire is available at Cobleland camp site on 01877 376284, and Liz MacGregor's tea room is good.

Contacts: The recreation team on 01877 382383 or Aberfoyle T.I. on 382352.

02 - Ae

Trail: There is a (black) DH course, a freeride area and a technical (red)12 mile XC course. For less experienced riders there is the (blue) 15 mile Upper Ae cycle, 7.5 mile Gubhill & Whaup Knowe, and 10 mile Windy Hill routes. Also, see right column for Drumlanrig.

Getting there: 6 miles north of Dumfries on the A701. In the village Ae, turn right, down past the forestry offices, then left at the sharp bend onto a forest road, and the car park is 100 metres on the right, (just after a road junction on the right).

Other information: Access to the downhill course is by permission from Riks bike shed, tel: 01848 330080 - please check in advance. Also see the note right.

Contacts: The ranger on 01387 860247 or e-mail: feae@forestry.gsi.gov.uk. Dumfries TI on 01387 253862.

Aonach Mor - see Leanachan forest

03 - Argyll Forest

Trails: The (easy) 5 mile Cat Craig loop (with the blue 6 mile Shoe extension), (moderate) 20 mile Ardgartan peninsula circuit, both at Ardgartan. There are also 3 more routes at Glenbranter (top of Loch Eck): hard 5.6 mile Glenbranter splash, easy 7.5 mile Glenshellish loop, and the south-bound one-way Shore trail, along the loch.

Getting there: The A82 north from Glasgow leads into the Argyll forest, then the A83 goes to Ardgartan (Glenbranter is off the A815).

Other information: Not very technical trails. This is a working F.C. forest, so please take heed of their cycle code.

Contact: Cowal forest: 01369 84666.

04 - Craik forest

Trails: An easy, blue route of 4 miles, a moderate purple route of 11 miles, a strenuous green route of 9 miles, and a difficult red route of 10 miles.

Getting there: Craik Forest is 12 miles south-west of Hawick in central southern Scotland. Take the A7 out of Hawick towards Langholm and Carlisle, then the B711 on the right after 2 miles, then just follow the signposts.

Other information: You can mix and match the different routes as you go e.g. start and finish with the Blue route, but also do the western section of the Purple.

Contacts: Visit www.forestry.gov.uk or tel the T.I. on 0870 6080404.

05 - Dalbeattie

Trails: Easy 11 mile Ironhash hill on fire roads, the easy-moderate 7 mile Moyle hill route, and the infamous 18 mile Hardrock trail graded red (intermediate) with very difficult (black) sections.

Getting there: From Dumfries in west Scotland, go south on the A711, past Dalbeattie on the A710 for 1 mile and the car park is off the road on the right.

Other information: The Hardrock trail has been created using some huge natural granite rock formations inc. Moby dick and the Slab. There is no visitor centre, but there are a choice of bike shops in Dumfries.

Contacts: Ranger on: 01387 860247, Dumfries TI on 01387 253862 and www.dumfriesandgalloway.co.uk for accommodation information.

06- Fort William
(Aonach Mor downhill)

Trails: The 1.9 mile world cup Aonach Mor downhill course, as well as other downhills, a 4-Cross course (by the finish to the DH), and the 5 mile XC world cup 'Witches trail' in the Leanachan Forest. There is also over 30 miles of alternative way-marked XC routes to explore in the forest (graded from easy to expert) and a permanent trailquest route for families to solve riddles along their journey.

Getting there: In Torlundy, 3 miles north of Fort William, (over 100 miles north of Glasgow) on the A82. Follow the signs for the Nevis ranges / Aonach Mor ski centre and the free car park. There is a railway station in Fort William.

Other information: The Nevis Range ski resort transforms into a downhill MTB mecca in the summer. The Aonach Mor downhill starts from 2150ft and finishes at just 200ft. It is the longest and only DH in the UK with a cable car back up. It is open daily between mid-May and mid-September and there are toilets, café, bike hire (www.offbeatbikes.co.uk or tel: 01397 704008).

Contacts: Fort William TI on tel: 01796 472215, or www.nevis-range.co.uk. For accommodation information see www.scotland-inverness.co.uk/fortwill.htm

A MTB'ers heaven.

■NOTE: There are some good way-marked MTB trails at Jedburgh (forest), on the A68, south east of Galashiels in the Scottish Borders. Here you will find the 25 mile Justice Trail and 3 shorter family routes. For more info see www.jedforesttrails.org.

■NOTE: The superb Drumlanrig country park is just 3 miles up the A76 from Thornhill, which is home to some great natural trails, suitable for all abilities. Contact Rik's bike shed on 01848 330080 for more information.

Scotland has some of the best man-made and natural trails in the world.

07 - Glentress (Tweed Valley)

Trails: Starting by the hub cafe is an 8 mile (blue) beginners route, 10.6 mile moderate (red) route, and a difficult (black) 19 mile route known as the Helly-Hanson V-trail. Further up the track, at Buzzards nest car park, is an easy (blue), a moderate (red) freeride area, and a skills loop for beginners. There is also the 'Heritage' trailquest, the 1.5 mile 'Janet's Brae' or the 4 mile Green hill routes for less experienced riders.

Getting there: Glentress is about 20 miles south of Edinburgh, on the A72, inbetween Innerleithan and Peebles. Turn (north) off the A72 in to the Gletress forest on a forest road and take the 2nd left off this, to the Hub car park.

Other information: There is suitable riding for all abilities, and Innerleithen with more trails is just down the road. The Hub cafe (run by pro bikers Emma Guy and Tracy Brunger), also have bike hire, bike wash, weather information, maps, spare parts, accessories and organised night rides (inc light hire and food).

Contacts: The Hub cafe on 01721 721736 or www.thehubintheforest.co.uk or Peebles TI on: 0870 6080404.

08 - Glentrool Forest

Trails: Plans for a natural 35 mile XC course, as part of the 7 Staines project. There are also lots of singletrack and forest trails to explore.

Getting there: West of Dumfries, and north on the A714 from Newton Stewart. The start of the trails are to be confirmed, but should be near the visitor centre.

Other information: Based around the visitor centre, the trail is planned to be technical and tiring, using part of the southern upland way.

Contacts: Visit the www.forestry.gov.uk or www.7stanes.gov.uk.

09 - Innerleithen

Trails: The famous 1.5 mile Red Bull world class downhill, another 3 downhills, and the 12.5 mile technical (red) Traquair XC.

Getting there: In the Elibank & Traquair forest on the south side of the A72, by Innerleithen. Turn off the A72 at Innerleithen, and take the B709, over the bridge and turn left, and this is where all the DH's finish.

Other information: You will need a day pass, which includes lifts back up (cheaper for members - see www.redbullprojectdownhill.co.uk). There are also plans for the Cardrona forest towards Peebles on the left. There are toilets, bike wash, and a chill out cabin with refreshments. Bike sport (tel: 01896 830880) in Innerleithen have spare parts, bike hire, etc. Progravity do Safari tours and bike hire (info@progravity.com).

Contacts: To book lifts or join the Innerleithen riders mountain bike club, contact Neil Stoddart, the site manager on info@innerleithenriders.com or call 0775 3691484 or Progravity on www.redbullprojectdownhill.co.uk or 0708922478. ProBike sport self-catering accommodation on tel: 01896 830880 or www.probikesport.com/bunkhouse.htm or Peebles TI on: 0870 6080404.

10 - Kirroughtree Forest

Trails: An 8.7 mile Red (Twister) trail which forms part of the 18 mile Black (Craigs) trail. Also a 3.7 mile Green (Bargaly wood) trail and a 5 mile (Laghill) with a 2.5 mile (Doon hill) extension.

Getting there: On the west side of Scotland, just north of Newton Stewart. From here take the A75 (Dumfries), for 3 miles then turn left at Palnure, which is signposted 'Kirroughtree Visitor Centre.'

Other information: This is home to big slab of rock known as McMoab. There is also miles and miles of great unmarked singletrack to explore in the forest.

Contacts: www.forestry.gov.uk, www.7stanes.gov.uk, or Newton Stewart TI on: 01671 402431.

11 - Laggan (Achduchil Forest)

Trails: There are 3 Laggan Wolftrax trails: a very technical (double black) 4 mile route, a moderate 3.9 mile (red) route and a (blue) 0.9 mile 'fun park' trail.

Getting there: The trails are in Achduchil Forest (part of Strathmashie Forest) in Strathspey & Bedenochwork, near Loch Laggan, on the A86, south of Aviemore.

Other information: There is a cafe, toilets, bike hire and repair services at the Laggan base camp. Please note that the black double diamond route is very difficult in places and body armour is recommended.

Contacts: www.basecampmtb.com or tel: 07891 169817.

Leanachan Forest - see Fort William.

Loch Ard - see Achray & Loch Ard forests.

12 - Mabie

Trails: The technical 10.6 mile Phoenix trail (red) route and the 1.5 mile Dark Side northshore style raised boardwalk trail. There are also some easier forest road rides; the 3 mile Big Views loop, 7 mile Woodhead loop and the 12 mile Lochbank loop.

Getting there: Mabie forest is 4 miles south of Dumfries, on the A710 (Solway Coast) road. Go through Islesteps village and the entrance to the forest is shortly on the right. The car park is to the right, 500 metres up a narrow tree lined drive.

Other information: Well signposted, singletrack trail with a natural feel to it. Rik's bike shed (shop) has demo and hir bikes, and offers skills courses (tel: 01387 270275).

Contacts: Recreation ranger on 01387 860247 or Dumfries TI on tel: 01387 253862. Marthown of Mabie bunkhouse on tel: 01387 247900 or www.dumfriesand galloway.co.uk for more accommodation info.

13 - Newcastleton Forest

Trails: Plans for a technical 4 mile loop, a long XC course and a family trail, as part of the 7 staines project.

Getting there: The town of Newcastleton is on the B6357, on the Scottish border. From the southern end of the village, take the unclassified road and follow the signs for Dykecrofts.

Other information: Trails are planned to link up to the villages of both Newcastleton and Kielder, for use of their facilities. Dykecroft visitors centre has bike hire, food & refreshments.

Contacts: Forestry on: 01750 721120.

14 - Pitfichie Forest

Trails: 17 mile red, route, a blue family route and plenty of other trails (including an informal DH built by locals).

Getting there: Near Monymusk, west of Aberdeen, on the B993, north of the A944 rd.

Other information: Aberdeen TI on 01224 632727.

(The) Trossachs - see Achray fores

Tweed Valley - see Glentress and Innerleithen.

LONG DISTANCE ROUTES

1 - Great Glen Cycle Route

Trail: 80 miles from Fort William along Loch Lochy, and Loch Ness, to Inverness.

Getting there: Start from either Fort William or Inverness, both of which are on the A82 road, and have train stations.

Other information: Don't get this confused with the Great Glen way (a walking route), although some parts are the same. It mainly uses forest roads, but also has some bits of canal tow paths, purpose-built tracks and road. The section between Fort William and Laggan is the easiest part, then it gets very hilly north-east of Laggan, and the final section to Inverness involves a stretch on the road. This ride will take you several days and require Ordnance survey landranger maps numbers 41, 34, and 26. This long distance ride could also be linked with West Highland way long distance ride to form a really, really long distance ride.

Contacts: The route manager 01320 366633 or www.greatglenway.com, or the recreation ranger on 01320 366322 or e-mail: fort@forestry.gsi.gov.uk.

2 - Speyside way

Trail: 84 miles linking Buckie (on the the Moray coast), to Aviemore.

Getting there: Start from either Aviemore (on the A9) or Tomintoul (on the A939), and finish in Spey bay or Buckie on the coast.

Other information: The trail generally follows the valley of the River Spey, but it does also fork half-way (nr Ballindalloch castle), to Tomintoul. Bicycles are required to make a few detours, so see the website below. Be aware that although it states there is no cycling between Tomintoul and Ballindalloch, the Glenlivest estate offices actually have some of these 'no cycling' tracks, signed as cycle routes through the estate!

Contacts: Check out the website www.speysideway.org for more info on cycling, accommodation, etc.

3 - West Highland Way

trail: 95 miles from Milngavie (north Glasgow) to Fort William.

Getting there: Start from Glasgow or Fort William, both of which have train stations.

Other information: Start at either Glasgow or Fort William. Parts of the trail are not accessible by bicycles, and the 30 miles just north of Glasgow gets used a lot by walkers, with the best riding being up from Loch Lomond. This long distance ride could also be linked with Great Glen way long distance ride to form a really hard challenge.

Contacts: See www.west-highland-way.co.uk, or speak to the ranger on tel: 01360 870502 for more information. Also, Off Beat bikes in Fort William on tel: 01397 704008, or the Fort William T.I. on tel: 01397 703781.

Take some time out and enjoy the views.

brought to you by rough ride guide ltd

rough ride guide ltd   publishing

keep things running smoothly   MAINTENANCE

Due to the punishment you put your mountain bike through it is always useful (as well as safer, cheaper and reassuring) that you know how to look after and repair it.

You might not have the first clue of what all the bits are on a bike, or you might be a budding new mechanic, but whatever your level, this section is aimed to make you aware of mechanical problems, then take you through maintaining, repairing, and upgrading your components, from the simple puncture to changing a bottom bracket.

MAINTENANCE: ESSENTIALS

Essential MAINTENANCE
SECTION

This section covers the essential information you should know
about your mountain bike before you venture into taking it apart to
work on. It shows what is what on the bike, explains about nuts and
bolts, the tools you need, how to clean your bike, and a trouble
shooter to determine what is wrong with it in the first place.

TOP TIP: Hob nobs (chocolate), doughnuts, or similar are a good way to sweeten up the mechanic working on your bike.

■ **NOTE:** Warranty issues are with the (bike) shop you made the purchase from - your contract is with them and not the manufacturers or distributors.

THE KNOWLEDGE: One of the most important factors of bicycle maintenance is establishing a state of awareness. No, this isn't a load of hippy nonsense, what we mean is to become aware of how well the bike is set up and how to nip a problem in the bud before it causes any long term damage. Having some mechanical knowledge will intensify your enjoyment of the sport as you will be able to stop those annoying chain skips, poor gear shifting, squealing brakes, etc. You will gain confidence and understanding of the bike and it's parts and feel more involved with the sport, as well as saving you money and time in waiting for a window in a shops busy schedule.

REASONS FOR LEARNING HOW TO FIX YOUR BIKE

* Firstly, a well working bike is not only more fun to ride, it is safer.

* If something does break while out on a ride, you might be able to fix it, rather than having to walk miles back home.

* A clean and well-maintained bike will work better and last longer than a dirty, shoddily set up machine, and you won't have to pay someone else to do it.

* There is also the wholesome feeling of having done a worthwhile job.

Bikes may seem like complicated machines, but once you understand how the parts work, and get over the fear of taking things apart and getting dirty, you will soon start enjoying yourself. Basically all you need to remember is to keep the parts clean & correctly lubricated and if something doesn't work, take it apart, clean & re-grease it, then put it back on again, or if it's worn out, replace it.
    However, you must also realise when the job is beyond you skills, or tools and go to a bike shop before you wreck something. Repairing your bike is not always simple or clear what exactly needs to be done, so consider why you are performing the job yourself, the time taken to learn and perform the repairs, the investment in tools, and how often you will be doing the job. It could be a false economy (especially if you are in a reasonably well-paid job), and you risk damaging your expensive parts.

WORKING ON YOUR BIKE

Not everyone has access to a bike workshop, but it can really help to try and recreate one when working on your machine. A bike stand is particularly useful, however pro quality models cost hundreds and take up lots of space. Folding stands or devices that hold up the back wheel to let you spin the cranks and tune the gears work very well, or failing that, turn the bike upside down, or suspend it by the saddle from the ceiling.

It's important to work somewhere well lit and with decent ventilation if you're using solvent-based cleaning products. Bear in mind you can make a bit of a greasy mess, but also small parts may go flying and get lost in heavily patterned carpets or down the floorboards. A work mat made from spare lino can be ideal, and can be rolled up and tucked away if space is limited.

It always pays to be organised with your tools, losing that all important 5mm hex key can be extremely frustrating. If you've got space, attach them to the wall workshop style; otherwise keep a well-ordered toolbox.

Before you start taking bits apart, ensure that they and the bike are all clean first, and as you remove the parts, place them in the order they have come off the bike, to make replacing them simple and not a memory recall test.

TOP TIP: Try to recreate a workshop in your available space - a bright clean space, with a bike stand and an organised tool lay-out will make working on your bike a whole lot easier and more enjoyable.

DEVELOPMENTS

We have done our best to cover most components on the bikes people are actually riding the UK trails on right now. The speed at which new componentry develops, new designs pop up, etc is another reason for us using this folder design (the extractable maps being the other advantage). This means that you will also be able to add new maintenance instructions etc (from RRG or MTB magazines as they come about), to the book, to keep it up-to-date, without having to buy a whole new book.

Older components such as cantilever and U-brakes, and cup-and-cone bottom brackets are not included as they are becoming less and less common, while many components are very specific to make and model, prime examples being suspension forks and cartridge bearing hubs. For these components, please refer to the manufacturers service instructions, which are often to be found on the internet. We have provided the web-site addresses where necessary.

To try and cover all the suspension forks on the market would take up lots of pages and is already covered very well by the manufacturers and available on their websites (provided in the suspension maintenance section). You can then off the relevant maintenance instructions for your suspension fork and add it to the folder.

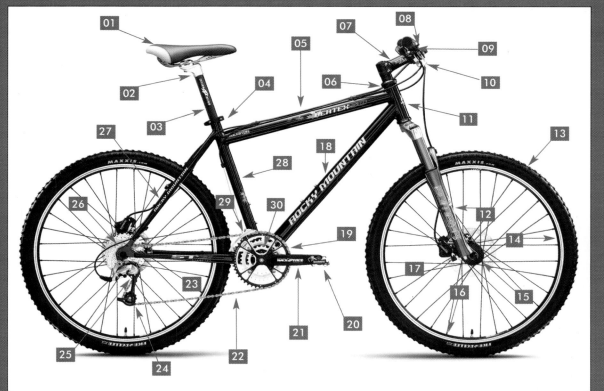

THE DIAGRAM (LEFT) SHOWS THE PARTS COMMON TO MOST MOUNTAIN BIKES.

First things first. **LEARN where** and **what** all the bits are on the bike. This will make following the instructions later on in this maintenance section, make a whole lot more sense, and be easier to understand.

The diagram shows a **'hardtail'** bike (old motorcycle term) meaning that it has front, but no rear suspension.
This remains the basic design for most bikes, although suspension designs, can make them look pretty different.

■ NOTE: A bike with no suspension is called a **'rigid'** bike, and a bike with front and rear suspension is a 'full suspension' bike.

KNOW YOUR BACK TO YOUR FRONT

OK, so now you are starting to get to grips of what's what on a bike, lets confuse matters some more. Because bikes are not symmetrical, you will need to know which side we are referring to when following the instructions.

The directions 'Right', 'Left', 'Front' and 'Rear' are always used from the perspective of a rider sitting on the bike.

The terms 'Drive side' (Right) and 'Non-drive side' (Left) are frequently used, referring to the position of the chainrings and derailleur i.e. drivetrain.

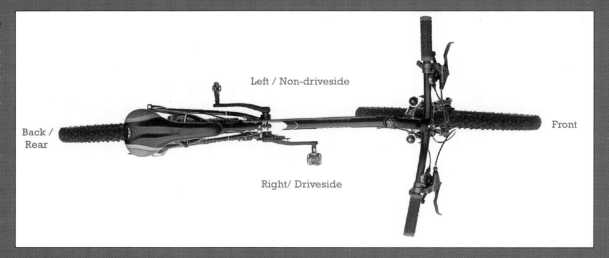

Left / Non-driveside

Back / Rear

Front

Right/ Driveside

Before diving in the deep end with your new tool box, take a minute to read through this introduction to gain an understanding of things like bolt and threads sizes, different types of bearings, torque strengths, tightening multi bolt components, etc so that you don't do any harm anything before you even start.

METRIC AND IMPERIAL

Irritatingly, both systems are commonly used on bikes.

A rear wheel for example may take a 26" tyre, have a 135mm axle, use a 25mm wide rim and spin on 1/8" bearings. Throughout the book, we use whatever measurement is commonly used in the bike industry.

■ **NOTE:** Just because a larger hex key is used to do up a bolt it doesn't necessarily imply it should be done up with more force.

■ **NOTE:** Stainless steel bolts can be tightened more, and are less likely to get seized, threaded or rounded off than softer alloy ones.

01: NUTS, BOLTS AND THREADS

Most parts on MTB's are secured with 'Hex' (a.k.a. Allen keys) type bolts, although Torx head bolts e.g. T25, are becoming more popular as they have a low profile and don't round off as easily as small aluminium alloy hex bolt heads.

Many bike parts use threaded parts so that they can be tightened and adjusted. Most things we encounter in day-to-day life have 'normal' threads, tightening clockwise and loosening anticlockwise - this is called a 'Right hand Thread'.
    Several bike parts however, e.g. non-drive side pedal, and drive side bottom bracket cups have 'Left hand threads' that work in the opposite way, often to stop them becoming loose by your pedalling.

Threads are described by their diameter and 'pitch' (distance between threads / ridges). Both are usually measured in millimetres with a M in front of the diameter - so a M6 x 1 bolt has a 6mm diameter thread with a pitch of 1mm.

02: MULTIPLE BOLTS

Whenever you encounter a component with more than one bolt to do up, it is important that you tighten or loosen each one little by little. This stops a single bolt becoming unduly stressed and allows the components seat into position correctly. Common examples are chain-ring bolts and removable front-plates of many handlebar stems (see pic below on how not to do up a stem). Always ensure that bolts are tightened equally and that the look symmetrical.

02

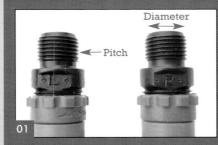

01

Left-hand thread   Right-hand thread

■ **NOTE:** You can recognise a left hand thread as it goes up to the left, and a right hand thread goes up to the right.

03: BEARINGS

Wherever a bike moves it needs bearings - e.g. at the hubs in the middle of the wheels, or bottom bracket on which the cranks spin.

The simplest types of bearings are 'bushings' where two tight-fitting pieces of metal slide over one another- these are frequently used at the pivots of full-suspension bikes. Most moving parts use ball bearings- the bearings move on bearing surfaces or 'races'.

The most common set-up is to have 'loose' ball bearings spinning directly on the component (see pic 03). The place where the bearings touch will be specially polished and shaped. This is an efficient and low friction method of creating a bearing, however if dirt and grit contaminate the bearing and scratch the surfaces, the whole component will need replacing. Many high quality mountain bike parts use 'cartridge bearings' (see pic 03A). These bearings tend to look like a metal Polo and comprise of the two surfaces the bearings run on (the races) and the ball bearings all held in place by plastic seals. The big advantage of these bearings is that when they wear out, the cartridge can be replaced and the part can run as good as new.

03

03A

■ **NOTE:** There's often confusion about 'sealed' bearings. Pretty much any bearing on a bicycle has to be sealed from the elements in some way e.g. the ball bearings in a simple headset use plastic lip seals, while Shimano hubs use a 'labyrinth' of rubber covers to keep water and dirt out.

04: TORQUE SETTINGS

It's fairly obvious that you don't need to tighten the small bolts that hold your brake levers as much as the large bolt that holds your crank in place. Each bolt on every part will have a correct recommended force with which it should be tightened or 'torque' specified by the manufacturer. These can be really important e.g. when screwing a steel bolt into the soft magnesium alloy of fork lower legs, and failing to observe these recommendations can damage parts and invalidate the warranty.

The correct tightening force can be measured with a 'torque wrench'. We have mentioned some of the forces recommended, but parts and materials vary, so always refer to the recommendations that came with that product. The forces are commonly measured in Newton meters (Nm), 43inches per pound (in-lbs), or pounds per foot (ft-lbs).

TOP TIP: Think of what torque forces actually mean (especially if you don't have a torque wrench) i.e. a torque of 1Nm = 0.7376lbs on the end of a 1 foot long spanner, or 8.851lbs on the end of a 1inch long spanner / hex key.

04

■ **NOTE:** 1Nm = 8.851 in-lbs = 0.738 ft-lbs

The Norbar SLO torque wrench has a torque range of 1-20Nm (10-180lbs) and will do most jobs on a bicycle and what it doesn't do e.g. bottom bracket, it's big brother will.

HOME MAINTENANCE TOOLS ▶

01 BOTTOM BRACKET (BB) TOOL - Slots in to the splines of the BB shell (there are various types available)

02 CABLE CUTTERS - Bike specific

03 CASSETTE LOCKRING - To remove the cassette (all MTB's use the same lockring)

04 CHAINRING (TL-FC20) TOOL - For tightening chainring bolts (used with a 5mm hex key)

05 CHAIN CLEANER - An easy, non-messy way to clean the chain

06 CHAINWHIP - Holds the cassette still (used with a cassette lockring tool)

07 CONE SPANNERS - Thin headed spanners for loose ball and cup hubs which range between 13-20mm.

08 CRANK PULLER/EXTRACTOR - Screws into the crank and pushes the crank arms off (2 sizes: one fits the older square taper BB and other size fits the ISIS and Octalink BB's)

09 FILE - For smoothing rough edges

10 FREEWHEEL TOOLS - Removes a freewheel (found on some old bikes)

11 GREASE GUN - For tidy greasing, and the lube ports found on some forks and headsets

12 HAMMERS - Hard and soft headed

13 HEADSET WRENCHES - For threaded headsets (usually 36mm)

14 PEDAL SPANNER (15mm) - For easy & secure, pedal removal and re-fit

15 PIN SPANNERS - To hold the BB cup while you adjust the lockring (with a ring spanner)

16 RING SPANNER - For threaded rings e.g. a lockring on an old BB

17 SOCKET SET (metric)

18 SPOKE KEY - For truing your wheels (they are different sizes)

19 STANLEY KNIFE

20 STAR-FANGLED NUT TOOL - For setting the star-fangled nut in the fork steerer tube

21 - TAPE MEASURE

22 TORQUE WRENCH - For tightening bolts accurately

■ **NOTE:** A vice also makes a useful 3rd (strong) hand

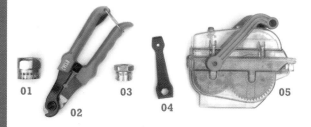
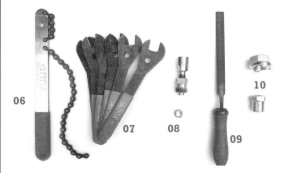
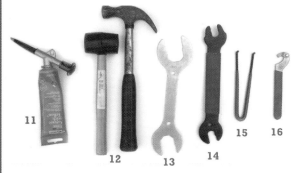
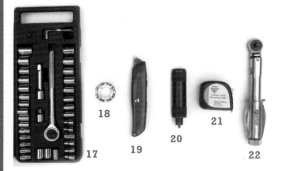
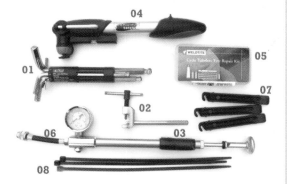
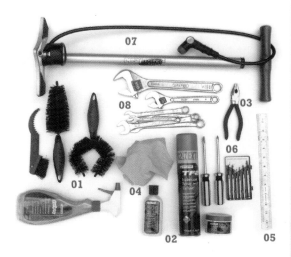

TOOLS THAT ARE EXPENSIVE AND / OR NOT USED ENOUGH TO JUSTIFY BUYING:

ALIGNMENT GAUGES - To find any bends in the frame or forks, that the eye would probably not see.

HEADSET CUP REMOVAL TOOL - For removing the headset cups from the frame.

HEADTUBE FACING TOOL - Cuts a thread and faces the headtube.

HEADSET PRESS - To fit headsets cups accurately.

BB TAP - Cuts a thread and faces the BB shell.

WHEEL JIG - For truing your wheels professionally (there are some cheapish ones around).

◀ ESSENTIAL RIDING TOOLS:

01 HEX KEYS - (a.k.a. as Allen keys) sizes 1.5-10mm.
NOTE: Some non-bike specific sets may omit the 2.5 and 8mm

02 CHAIN TOOL

03 GAFFA TAPE - wrap it around a pump to save space

04 MINI PUMP

05 PUNCTURE REPAIR KIT

06 SHOCK PUMP (if you have air suspension shocks)

07 TYRE LEVERS

08 ZIP-TIES

◀ RECOMMENDED MINIMUM HOME TOOLS:

01 BRUSH CLEANING SET

02 LUBE - Grease, chain oils, water displacement, etc

03 PLIERS

04 RAGS - You can never have too many

05 RULER

06 SCREWDRIVERS - Flat and posi-drive, and the tiny jewellers ones

07 TRACK PUMP - Faster, easier tyre pumping

08 WRENCHES or AN ADJUSTABLE SPANNER - Various sizes

TOP TIPS:

If you don't have any tools, a toolbox set can be a cheaper way to obtain a collection of the most useful tools.

It is also worth stocking up on spare tubes, brake pads, cables, chain, and some nuts and bolts.

Different parts on the bike require different lubricants, of the correct thickness or viscosity, so make sure you choose the right lube for the right job. It will make a marked difference in performance, and reduce wear, making your expensive parts last longer, therefore it is worth getting the good quality lubricants.

GREASE (LITHIUM)

SUSPENSION FORK OIL

CHAIN LUBES

WATER DISPLACERS

LOOSE & SEIZING BOLTS

TOP TIP: Car mechanics use barrier cream to stop grease and oil sticking to their skin, then a citrus hand cleaner to get really clean afterwards.

■ NOTE: Never pour any products away that aren't completely bio-degradable - visit your local skip or Halfords for a safe disposal.

■ NOTE: Aerosol cans are quick to use and can get in to hard to reach places, but bottles will allow a more controlled application.

GREASE (LITHIUM)

Thick waterproof grease should be used in bearings (e.g. hubs and headsets) and whenever metal parts are tightened together (e.g. the threads of bolts and the seat-post) to prevent seizing and corrosion and to get a snug fit.

Look for a high performance grease that will not attack plastic or rubber seals. White lithium grease is the classic stuff to use but cannot be used in suspension forks as it wrecks the bushings and seals.

■ NOTE: A motorbike shop can be a top place to pick up a decent sized pot at a bargain price such as the red, glittery 'Silkolene RG2 Racing grease'.

SUSPENSION FORK OIL

Oil is used in many suspension forks to lubricate the internals and as the medium in the damping systems.

There are different weights of oil, and each fork has a recommended weight (and volume). You can also alter the affects of the suspension damping on the forks by using different weight oils.

If you service the forks yourself, buying oil from a motorbike shop can make savings. Don't be scared of the beards and tattoos, the guys in motorbike shops are fellow bikers and can be really helpful.

TOP TIP: If you service your suspension forks yourself, buying the oil from motorbike shops can be much cheaper - don't be scared off by the beards and tattoos, they are fellow bikers.

CHAIN LUBES

These come in a few varieties. Dry conditions lubes work well in good weather and don't pick up too much dirt, but are washed off by rain and mud. Thicker winter 'wet' lubes are stickier, so pick up more dirt, but don't wash off so easily on wet rides. There are also, wax lubes, which can be for dry or wet conditions, and are very effective, as long as the chain is clean to start with.

Added protection - PTFE (Polytetrafluoroethylene), or it's trade name of Teflon, has non-stick properties. Also Kyrtox (trademark of Du Pont) is a substance that keeps metals apart, even under high pressures, but needs to be put on a clean chain.

■ NOTE: Don't use anything as heavy as 3 in 1 oil - this is too thick and will quickly become filthy and difficult to clean off - leave it for the lawn mower.

WATER DISPLACERS

Spray lubes such as TF2, WD40 and GT85 are used for expelling water ('WD' stands for 'Water Dispersant').

These generally, don't actually have long lasting lubrication properties, but are useful for expelling water and lifting greasy dirt. However, added PTFE / Teflon, makes it slippery and has some protective qualities, making it a bit more versatile, so it can be used on the likes of cables, shifters, etc.

■ NOTE: The solvents in these products can remove grease - so don't spray them into greased bearings e.g. hubs and headsets.

LOOSE & SEIZING BOLTS

Where bolts may be in danger of coming loose, a thread locking solution can be very useful. The threadlock will stop bolts vibrating loose, and will simply crumble away when you come to undo it. It can be quite hard to get hold of though - try phoning around iron mongors, or car spares shops (Halfords have their own brand).

Where there is a danger of metal parts seizing in place (e.g. anything screwed into the frame e.g. BB, or cleats on the bottom of shoes) a copper-based anti-seize compound can be useful. Titanium is particularly prone to this, so apply 'Ti prep' to any titanium threads, and avoid screwing one Ti part in to another.

If you are already too late and the parts have seized, use some GPO (graphite penetrating oil) to aid the separation process.

PROBLEM	POSSIBLE CAUSES	REMEDY	SEE PAGE
Bearings squeak or creak	Bearings dry or loose	Service	
Creaking or clicking by feet	Worn, loose bad fitting or cracked shoe cleat	Replace cleats	
	Cracked shoe sole	Replace shoes	
	Dry or loose BB	Grease/Tighten BB	G9
	Dirty, dry or loose crank arm or pedal	Service and tighten crank arm and/or pedal	G7 & M7-8
	Play in pedal bearings	Service or repair pedal	M7-8
	Loose or dry chainring bolt(s)	Remove, grease and tighten the chainring bolt(s)	G7
Other Creaking	Dry / rusty seat post or seat post clamp	Clean and grease seat post	M9
	Loose seat post	Check post size	M9
	Dry handlebars / stem	Grease inside stem clamp	M4
	Cracked frame	Check frame - repair or replace frame if cracked	
	Steel bolts in alloy threads or vice versa	Apply anti-seize	E6
	Rear suspension pivots dry or too tight	Service	M11
Rubbing / scraping	Front derailleur rubbing when pedalling	Adjust derailleur, get stiffer frame, or loose weight	G11
	Bent chainring	Straighten or replace chainring	G8
	Chainring rubs frame	Move BB over or replace with longer BB	G9
	Tyre rubs frame / fork when not pedalling	Straighten wheel or fit narrower tyres	W9 or W3
	Brake rubbing rim	Adjust brakes, true the wheel, or replace the bent rim	B3-7 or W9
	Dry hub dust covers	Clean and lube	W10
	Chain on big chainring and small cog or visa versa	Stop using this combination	
Squeaking	Dry V-brake springs	Lube the springs with candle wax	
	Dry hub or bottom bracket bearings	Service hubs or bottom bracket	W10 or G9
	Brake rubbing rim	Service pedals	M7-8
	Squeaky saddle	Replace saddle	M9
	Dry suspension	Service suspension	M11
	Rusty or dry chain	Clean and lube or replace	G3-4
Rattles	Usually indicate something is loose, worn, or wrong fit.	Check all nuts and bolts	
Forks clunk	Something is loose inside	Get them serviced	M11
	Headset loose or worn	Adjust headset or service	M5-6
	Forks are topping out	Upgrade the forks	M10
	Forks bottom out	Add air/fit a stronger spring	
Pedals move laterally or clunk	Pedal not in properly, bearings loose or axle bent	Secure pedal, tighten bearings or replace	M7-8
	Loose or bent crank arm	Tighten or replace the crankarm	G7
	Loose BB or bent axle	Tighten or replace the BB	G9
SPD pedal entry is difficult	Tension too high	Lower tension via screw on the pedal	M7
	Shoe soles are thick	Trim soles with a knife	
	Cleats or pedals are dirty or have mud etc stuck in them	Clean and lube the pedal and cleats	
Pedal entry/release is easy	Release tension is too low	Increase tension via the screw on the pedal	M7
	Cleats are worn	Replace	
Pedal exit is difficult	Tension is too high	Reduce the tension via the screw	M7
	Loose or incorrect cleats	Tighten the cleat bolts or replace the cleats	

PEDALS

	PROBLEM	POSSIBLE CAUSES	REMEDY	SEE PAGE
CHAIN & GEARS	**Chain falls off the rear cogs** **Chain jams (falls off between the rear cogs and the frame)**	Stop screws are not set properly The rear mech is mis-adjusted The chain is too wide (for the cogs) Poor frame clearance Rear wheel is not in the frame correctly Rear mech/hanger is bent	Adjust the rear derailleur stop screws Adjust / index the gears correctly Replace the chain with a wider one Return to dealer Reposition the wheel Straighten or replace the mech/hanger	G10 G10 G4 W5 M2 or G10
	Chain falls off the front chainrings	Chainring is loose, worn or bent Chainline incorrect Chain too long Front mech is not set up correctly	Tighten, bend back or replace - see Check (adjust) chainline Check chain length Adjust	G8 G9 G3 G11
	Chainsuck i.e. chain gets jammed between the chainring and the frame chainstay.	Dirty or worn chain The chainring teeth are bent Chain is too narrow (for the chainring teeth) The chainline is incorrect The chain links are stiff	Clean or replace the chain Straighten or replace the teeth Replace the chain with a wider one Adjust it as required Loosen and lube the links	G3-4 G8 G2-4 G9 G4
	The chain skips	Worn chainrings / Cogs Chain links are stiff (or bent) Mis-adjusted mech Bent rear derailleur / hanger	Replace chainrings / cogs and the chain Loosen and lube the chain links (or replace chain) Adjust Straighten or replace	G7-9/4-6 G4 G10-11 M2 or G10
	Chain slaps chainstay	Chain too long Weak rear mech spring Bumpy terrain	Remove some links from the chain Replace spring Ignore or use large front chainring or fit a chain device for DH riding	G4
GEARS	**Front mech rattles / scrapes**	Loose mech pivots BB loose, or not adjusted Chainrings bent	Replace mech Tighten or adjust or replace Bend back or replace	G11 G9 G8
	Poor rear shifting	Damaged, stiff, or poorly lubed chain Indexing not set correctly Sticky or damaged cable Loose (or worn) rear cogs	Fix, replace or clean and lube chain Adjust rear mech Replace cable Seat and tighten (or replace) the cogs	G3-4 G10 G14 G5
	Chain won't shift to the smallest screw	Stop screw in too far	Make (small) adjustments to the high screw	G10
	Derailleur hits the spokes	Poorly adjusted rear derailleur Broken spoke Bent rear derailleur / hanger	Adjust low gear limit screw Replace spoke Straighten or replace derailleur / hanger	G10 W9 M2 or G10
	Chain skips and doesn't engage on rear sprockets (ghost shifting) - common when on the larger cogs and riding a bumpy uphill, or pedalling hard out of the saddle.	The gear cable outer is compressed (by rear suspension movement), pinching the cable inside. A flexible rear end, on some rear suspension designs, can affect the chainline/mech.	Use smooth, gradual cable routing. Pedal smoothly or change your frame.	G14
	Chain doesn't 'freewheel' and can't pedal backwards	Freehub body is stuck Rear mech jockey wheels seized or full of debris.	Service or replace Service, clean or replace the jockey wheels.	W11 G10

PROBLEM	POSSIBLE CAUSES	REMEDY	SEE PAGE
Rolling resistance	Tyre rubs frame	Check wheel is in straight	W5
	Brakes dragging on wheel rim	Adjust brakes, true the wheel	B3 & W9
	Low tyre pressure	Pump up tyres	W3
	Hub bearings worn, dirty or too tight	Service or adjust the hubs	W10
	Brakes are rubbing	Service and set-up the brakes	B3 or B5-7
Resistance while pedalling	BB tight	Adjust BB	G9
	BB dirty or worn	Service or replace	G9
	Chain dirty, dry or rusty	Clean, lube or replace	G3-4
	Pedal bearings too tight	Adjust bearings	M7-8
	Pedal bearings dirty/worn	Service pedals	M7-8
Poor braking	Poorly adjusted brakes or worn pads	Adjust brakes or replace pads	B3 or B5-7
	Greasy / dirty wheel rims	Clean	E11
	Sticky brake cable	Lube or replace	B2
	Steel rims in wet weather	Use aluminium rims	
	Bent or sticky lever	Replace or lube (disc brakes only)	B3
	Contaminated disc rotor/pads	Clean rotor with alcohol & replace pads	B6
Spongy brake levers	Air in the hydraulic brake system	Bleed the brakes	B8 or 9
	Too much/poor quality cable outer	Shorten or replace cables and outers	B2
	Flexible frame	Fit horseshoes style brake stiffner	
Chattering and vibrating	Greasy or bent / dented wheel rim	Clean the rim or replace if bent	E11
	Wheel not round	True wheel	W9
	Loose headset	Tighten	M5
	Loose or worn brake pivots	Tighten bolts or replace brakes	B3
	Flexible seat stays on the frame	Fit brake booster plate	
	Anything else loose e.g. wheel reflectors, etc	Identify and tighten correctly	
Brakes rub rim	Pads not aligned	Set brake pads correctly	B3 or B5-7
	Wheel out of true	True wheel via spoke tension	W9
	Flexible fork	Fit stiffer hub or replace fork	M10
	Loose hub bearings	Service hub	W10
Seatpost loose	Post incorrect size	Measure the frame & get correct post	M9
Bent wheel:	Loose or broken spoke	Tighten spokes or replace spoke	W9
	Bent rim	Replace rim	
Steering is stiff	Tight, dirty or pitted headset	Loosen, clean or replace	M5-6
Bike wobbles at high speeds or pulls to one side	Cracked or bent frame or fork	Replace frame or fork - steel frames can be welded	M10
	Wheels out of true	True wheels	W9
	Loose hub bearings	Adjust hubs	W10
	Headset too loose or tight	Adjust	M5
	Flexible frame	Loose weight or change frame	

RESISTANCE

BRAKES

MISCELLANEOUS

■ NOTE: See M53 for the suspension troubleshooter.

YOUR PRIDE AND JOY

OK some of you may take pride and care in maintaining your bike and stare at it for hours on end each night, but many will give it a half-arsed wipe after a ride and hide it out of sight and so out of mind, until the next ride. For these (latter) people, the pre-ride check is important and not to be skimmed over or left out all-together. You may be lucky and get away with only minor inconvenience, but if you are out riding you could end up miles from civilisation, breaking something on your bike, or even worse injuring yourself.

PRE-RIDE CHECKS:

TOP TIP: Don't leave the pre-ride check until two minutes before you're meant to leave on a Sunday when the shops are shut. Doing it the day before will avoid missing things or carrying out frenzied emergency repairs with any old bits you have lying around, because the shop is shut.

FRAME REPAIR & RE-SPRAY

Argos Racing (Bristol) on 01179724730 or see www.argoscycles.com
Arthur Caygill Cycles (Yorkshire) on 01748825469 or see www.arthurcaygill.co.uk
Bob Jackson Cycles (Leeds) on 01132551144 or see www.bobjacksoncycles.co.uk
Chas Roberts Cycles (Croydon, Surrey) on 02086843370 or see www.robertscycles.com
M Steel Cycles (Newcastle-upon-Tyne) on 01912344275 or see www.msteelcycles.co.uk
Psychlo Sport (N. Yorkshire) on 01423545413 or see www.psychlosport.co.uk

* Check tyres for wear, splits and correct air pressure - especially with tubeless tyres as these can tend to lose air after a few days. Around 40p.s.i. will suit the average rider - to make tyre checks quicker, get used to the squeeze feel at this pressure.

* Check the chain is clean, moving freely and lubricated (turn the pedals backwards and look for any stiff links as they roll over the rear sprockets).

* Check the stem lines up with front wheel and is done up securely.

* Check the saddle is at the correct height, straight, and secure.

* Check the quick release levers are done up tightly - this is especially important on the front wheel as it could fall out. Check the wheels are in straight by picking the bike up and spinning them - they should spin without wobbling and not rub the brakes.

* Check the brakes work. Pull the front brake and try to push the bike forwards, next pull the rear brakes and try to push the bike backwards - the wheels should lock both times.

* Check the brakes are centred, don't rub the rims, and that the pads have at least 2mm rubber remaining (or 1mm of the pad, for disc brakes). If they don't, replace them. If you wear the pads down completely, the metal will scratch and ruin your rims or rotors.

* The levers should move easily and pull tight halfway to the handlebar. If they are hard or sticky to move, remove the cable from the lever and clean or replace the cables. If the lever reaches the handlebars, the cable needs tightening (at the anchor bolt by the brakes), or hydraulic brakes need bleeding or adjusting.

* Finally, take the bike for a quick spin and ensure the gears are easy to operate and click in to position correctly. If the shift levers are hard to move, try cleaning or even replacing the cables if they are very bad. If they skip and jump may need to twiddle some screws and knobs to set them up properly (see the front or rear mech sections).

■ NOTE: See right for how to check the headset, hubs, crank and bottom bracket for any play before you go out riding.

CHECK THE HEADSET, HUBS, CRANKS & BOTTOM BRACKET FOR PLAY:

Play in the Headset ▶

Turn the handlebars (wheel) sideways to the front of the bike. Pull the front brake on and place your other hand around the headset to feel for movement as you rock the bike back and forth - be sure it's not the movement n the fork bushings, that you are feeling.

If feels loose you will need to tighten it or you will have a shaky n' rattly ride - see section M40.

Play in the Wheel Hubs ▶

Hold onto the frame with one hand and the top of the wheel with the other. Now try pushing the wheel from side to side and see if it moves - check that the axle skewers are tight, and it's not these allowing the wheel to move.

Movement with a small knocking sound means you will need to service the hubs - see section M35 and M36 for further details on how to do this.

Play in the Crank & BB ▶

Hold the frame steady with one hand and grip the crank (near the pedal) with the other hand. Now pull and push the crank arm back and forth and feel for any movement i.e. an obvious clunking noise - if this happens see section M19.

■ NOTE: Riding with loose cranks can cause permanent (and costly) damage.

TYRE PRESSURE

For the average rider i.e. 11 to 12 stone, have the pressure around 40p.s.i.

Add more for: Heavier riders, hard non-technical trails, better efficiency, and to stop pinch punctures. You will have less grip and a harsher ride though.

Less air for: Light riders, more grip, and a softer and more comfortable ride. You may have less control though, as the tyres can 'squirm', have more rolling resistance, and you have a higher chance of getting a pinch puncture, and hitting and denting the wheel rims.

THE COST OF NOT CLEANING

Mountain bikes are designed for use on rough trails and can be used in equally rough weather. There is a tendency, therefore, to assume that they'll happily cope with being neglected and dirty. While it is possible for a bike to just about keep going provided you oil the chain sometimes and fix punctures when you have them, the bike really won't thank you for it.

A bike must be kept clean and properly lubricated to stay happy. If it isn't lubricated, it will cause friction and corrosion, but on the other hand, oil and grease that is full of gritty dirt will wear out metal parts alarmingly quickly.

DIRT AND WATER WILL CAUSE:

: Cables to stop moving smoothly, causing most brake and gear problems.

: Chain to wear out which in turn wrecks chain-rings and sprockets.

: Wear of bearings (e.g. headset, bottom bracket and hubs).

: Prematurely worn brake pads and wheel rims.

: Contamination of suspension systems- wearing out bearings, bushings and corroding internals.

: Your bike to look old quickly - not just bad from an aesthetic point of view but in terms of the resale value.

CLEANING YOUR BIKE

Just like doing the washing up, start with the least greasy bits (glasses and mugs become frame, saddle, bars, etc), then move to the dirtier bits (pans i.e. chain).

Use a bike cleaning product such as 'dirt wash' or a car shampoo, but avoid washing up liquid (it's bad for seals). Also avoid using power hoses as these force water in to bearings and pivots, causing them to corrode. With the cleaner, a hose or bucket of water, and a sponge or soft-bristled brush that won't scratch the bikes finish, clean everything except the chain, gears and disc brakes.

■ NOTE: Leave cleaning the disc brake rotors to the end (in case you accidentally get grease etc on the discs while cleaning the other parts of the bike) and use a specific disc brake cleaner (see pic 01).

With rim brakes unhook them and carefully clean the wheel rims and pads - this removes grit, which could otherwise wear them down quickly. Remove the cable outers from their frame guides/slots and slide the cable outers back to expose the inner cable - to get the cable slack enough to do this, unhook the brakes at the wheel/brake arm, or with the gears, shift the chain to the biggest cog and largest chainring, then (without pedalling) click both shifters the other way. Now spray the inner cable with a light lube e.g. TF2, wipe with a rag then put everything back in place.

SUSPENSION:

If you have suspension boot covers, lift them to let the water out and get to the stanchions (inner legs). With a clean rag, wipe the stanchions clean and drip a little bit of oil containing teflon on the stanchions and seals, then compress them a few of times, and wipe off any excess oil. Replace the boots (with air holes facing out).

THE CHAIN AND REAR COGS:

These are the greasy roasting tins in our washing up analogy, and should be cleaned last to avoid smearing dirty chain oil over the rest of the bike.

Rear cogs will get mud, grass, etc stuck down in between them; this can build up and make the gears skip and jump on the rear, so it needs to be cleaned out every so often - the easiest way is with a specially thin brush tool (see pic 02).

A simple way to clean the chain is to pinch the lower length with a rag and spin the cranks backwards, scraping off the dirty oil. Similarly, loosely pinch a rag on the jockey wheel teeth and turn the cranks, to remove any build up of dirt (see pic 03). Penetrating spray e.g. TF2 will help shift stubborn gunk which is fine when the chain isn't too dirty, but doesn't clean inside the rollers.

A more rigorous method is to remove the chain and shake it in a plastic container filled with petrol or diesel, and then allow the chain to drip dry (don't try to burn the remaining fuel off to save time!). This does a really good job of stripping dirty oil from the chain, but splitting the chain will weaken it (unless you use a special link - see chains for further info) and disposing of the fuel is a pain and must be done responsibly i.e. at the local tip. A chain-cleaning device cleans the chain very effectively without you having to remove the chain - use a biodegradable cleaning product in it first, then water to wash off the fluid (see pic 04).

Once the chain has been cleaned, and dried, use a water displacement spray and wipe down. Next, use an appropriate lubricant - trying to get just one drop of lube on each chain roller (see pic 05). The links do not need to be covered in oil, so spin the cranks a few times to get the lube moving around, then wipe the excess oil off with a rag.

01

02

03

04

05

TOP TIPS:

A special bike cleaner will help lift oil and muck, while a specialist brush set will get to those hard to reach areas (see pic below).

Keep solvents away from the tyres as it can damage them.

To make your bike look good and be easier to clean, spray some car trim on the frame only, to stop dirt sticking easily.

Pump sprayers (available from garden centres for about £20) make great portable hoses - perfect for flat dwellers.

Leaving the cleaner on for a short while will help dissolve the grim.

MAINTENANCE: WHEELS

Wheels MAINTENANCE
SECTION

This section takes you through the basic tasks of removing and replacing the wheels and fixing inner tubes, to the more technical jobs of truing wheels and servicing freehubs.

THE WORD 'BICYCLE' MEANS 'TWO WHEELS'!

The wheel is all the metal bits - rim, spokes and hub. When you accelerate a bike, the wheels & tyres count as 'rotating weight', which is harder to get moving than the non rotating bits (almost everything else). For this reason, the wheels and tyres are the number one place to shed weight if you want the bike to be livelier, but remember they still need to be strong enough to take whatever punishment you plan on giving your poor bike.

Well-built wheels have evenly tensioned spokes and are the result of painstaking attention to detail. Hand built wheels are almost always better than the machine made ones that come on most production bikes. While outside the scope of this section, wheel building can be learnt with the help of a decent instruction (human or book), the right equipment (a wheel truing stand and dishing tool) and plenty of practice.

THE WHEEL

- Rim
- Spoke
- Nipple
- Hub

WHEEL WEBSITES:

www.bontrager.com
www.chrisking.com
www.dtswiss.com
www.hopetech.com
www.mavic.fr
www.ritcheylogic.com
www.rolfwheels.com
www.royceuk.freeserve.co.uk
www.sapim.be
www.sheldonbrown.com
www.wheelpro.co.uk

■ NOTE: If you like the idea of building your own wheels read 'The Art of Wheelbuilding' book by Gerd Schraner (ISBN no. 0-9649835-3-2)

RIMS

Rims are where much of the wheels strength comes from, and range from narrow, lightweight models for cross-country use, to wide, burly constructions for big impacts and big tyres. Good quality rim features include: box-section alloy construction, a smooth join where the rim is held together, and reinforcing eyelets around the spoke holes.

When rim-brakes (V-brakes) are used, the rim doubles as the braking surface. This can eventually wear out (quickly if worn down pads are used) so it is worth cleaning (with emery paper or similar) and checking the rims for dents, cracks, and wear.

■ NOTE: A ceramic coating on the rim tends to double the price of rim, but also probably extends it's life by about twice, as well as improving the braking quality.

SPOKE LACING PATTERNS

The rotational force coming from the hub (the pedalling force on a rear hub or disc brake) causes the spokes to twist or 'wind up'. To resist this, spokes are put at angles, causing them to cross another 1, 2, 3 or 4 spokes depending on lacing pattern.

The most common spoke lacing design is the '3 cross' (see pic below), which offers an excellent compromise between strength and resistance to the rotation of the hub. Wheels built in the most direct path from hub to rim (i.e. a straight line) are called 'radially spoked' (see below right). These are stiff, strong, aerodynamic and lightweight, and used on many performance wheels - but can't be used with disc brakes.

BEARINGS

Broadly speaking, there are two types of hub, depending on what sort of bearing is used: cup-and-cone, or cartridge bearings.

A: Cup-and-Cone Bearing Hub
Used on Shimano hubs and on much original bike equipment. This system features loose bearings that spin on a polished surface inside the hub body and a nut with a second bearing surface called a cone. The cones screw onto the threaded axle and are held in place by being tightened against a locknut.

The advantage of these hubs is that tightening up the cones can eliminate any small amount of bearing play. With regular maintenance, these hubs can last a long time, and replacement bearings and cones are both cheap and easy to get hold of. However, if the bearing surface is damaged by incorrect adjustment and dirt, they cannot be repaired and the hub will need replacing, which means the expense of re-building the whole wheel.

B: Cartridge Bearing Hubs
Favoured in the U.K. and featured on many high-quality hubs such as those from Hope and Mavic, these tend to last a long time (partly due to the seals provided by the hub, and partly due to the quality of the cartridge). A good cartridge has smooth running bearings and surfaces, good seals and a high 'grease fill'.

The hubs run on bearings in a sealed cartridge (containing the bearing surfaces) which sits inside the hub body on a plain or threaded axle, usually covered by a spacer doubling as an extra seal. The advantage of this system is that, on the whole, only the cartridge bearings themselves wear out and can be replaced (usually) making the hub spin like new again. Replacing cartridge bearings is usually just a matter of knocking the old bearings out using a soft hammer on the axle, and carefully pressing new ones in.

■ NOTE: Due to the diversity of cartridge bearing hub designs, and that special tools are often required, we refer you to the manufacturers instructions for the correct procedure.

TYRES

Choosing tyres that suit your specific riding requirements can really aid your riding. There are lots of different designs around though; some designed for both front and rear in any conditions,(mud, dry, downhill), and others may be designed to be used specifically for the front or back. Front tyres are designed to corner and decelerate, so tend to be round with forward pointing knobs, while the rear tyre has the additional role of acceleration, so will probably be squarer with lateral paddle knobs to lay down maximum traction.

TYRE DESIGNS

Generally, narrower tyres are lighter and faster, while wider tyres are more comfortable, and provide better traction and more impact protection for the wheel rims. Pump up to around 35psi to provide you with good grip and a low rolling resistance. Pump them up higher for less rolling resistance, and lower for more comfort and traction.

A: GENERAL USE TYRES
General purpose off-road tyres are usually 1.9-2.1" wide, with smallish knobbles. This gives them a reasonable volume of air for comfort, while still offering speed in the dry and traction on loose ground.

B: MUD TYRES
Mud tyres have long knobs (to dig into the mud for traction) which are widely spaced (so the mud falls off the tyre). Some are narrow e.g. 1.8" and should be pumped up hard, to cut through the mud and give good frame clearance, while others are wide e.g. 2.1" and use a low pressure to 'float' over the mud.

C: SEMI-SLICK TYRES
These tyres have a low centre tread to minimise rolling resistance, and knobbles on the sides to grip around corners. These should be pumped up hard, and are good for racing on dry, hard terrain.

D: SLICK TYRES
These tyres are for road use as they don't have any knobbles to minimise rolling resistance, although they usually have groves to channel water away. They vary between 1" (for speed) to 2" (for comfort) and should be pumped up hard.

E: DOWNHILL TYRES
These tyres are 2.3" + width with tough carcasses so they can be ridden when flat (if in a race). The bigger size gives more cushioning (comfier), and the big tread is designed for maximum traction.

OTHER INFORMATION

FOLDING BEADS: Rather than being made from steel, the bead holding the tyre on the rim is made of Aramid (called Kevlar if made by DuPont), which saves weight, allows the tyre to be folded up, and makes it easier to fit and remove.

SOFTER RUBBER: Stickier rubber compounds can offer more grip on hard surfaces - although they may not be as durable as their cheaper counterparts.

BETTER CASING: The 'casing' or body of the tyre can be made of more tightly woven material (greater number of threads per inch - TPI). This improves puncture resistance and allows the tyre to be more supple, grip the terrain better and improves comfort.

WRITING ON THE WALL
The tyre sidewall is will usually tell you the diameter (usually 26"), the width (something like 1.5 to 3"), recommended air pressure to use, and often whether the tyre is for front or rear use and which way it goes on (the rotation direction).

TUBELESS TYRES

Most tyres are used with inner tubes, however the UST (Universal System for Tubeless) system does away with tubes, by having special airtight rims and tyres (these UST rims can also use normal tyres if needed). The advantage of these systems is that they roll better, are not likely to pinch puncture, and can be run at low pressures for more grip and comfort.

So why doesn't everyone use them then? They are still fairly expensive and heavy, and it is difficult to find the puncture when it does happen. They also require specialist parts.

An alternative to special rims and tyres is NoTubes. Remove the inner tubes (weighing between 100 to 200 grams) and replace them with 'No Tubes' latex (weighs about 60 grams) by Stan. This lightweight system seals or stops most punctures. However it is relatively expensive, and the tyres can fall off the rim and lose air, which is why not everyone uses them.

■ **NOTE:** Follow the recommended tyre pressure written on the side of the tyre. Use a higher pressure for faster rolling on smooth surfaces and better puncture protection, and a lower pressure for better traction and shock absorption.

■ **NOTE:** Replace tyres when the tread is worn and the tyre no longer offers sufficient grip. Many new tyres have wear indicators to comply with E.U. regulations, but be aware that both time and UV light can age tyres, making the rubber brittle and crack - making punctures more likely.

TOP TIP: When installing tyres position the label on the tyre over the valve to make the valve easier to find when you have a puncture - and it shows everyone that you're a real hard-core pro rider or wannabee.

 A

 B

 C

 D

 E

■ **NOTE:** Tyres are a rotational weight, which greatly affects the acceleration of the bike. Therefore saving weight here can be very beneficial - especially good mud tyres that shed that heavy mud.

WHEEL REMOVAL

Often the first thing you have to do often when buying a new bike is to take off the wheels to fit it in the car. The wheels also need to be removed to change an inner tube in the case of a puncture, so this can be a pretty frequent job. It is also one that people assume they know how to do because it looks easy and usually needs no tools. All to frequently however, wheels are replaced incorrectly and insecurely, which could lead to a horrific accident if one slipped or came off. As with many jobs on a bike, this is straightforward, but not immediately obvious how to do correctly.

REMOVING THE FRONT WHEEL

■ NOTE: Sometimes quick release skewers are replaced with hex key skewers. These require you to undo a bolt at one end rather than flip the QR lever. On older bikes (and some cheaper ones) the wheel will be held in place by axle nuts, which need to be undone with a spanner (usually 14mm front wheel, 15mm rear wheel) on both sides of the wheel.

■ NOTE: If you have disc brakes, make sure no-one / thing squeezes the brake levers, on some systems (e.g Hayes, Hope Mini's) the brake pads will stay closed together and be difficult to separate (and you won't be able to fit the wheel).

Start with the front wheel, as this does not have the gears in the way of things. The first step is to undo the brake if you have rim-brakes (brakes where a pad hits the side of the wheel near the tyre). If you have disc brakes, this stage can be skipped. You want to move the brake pads away from the wheel rim so you can remove the wheel - the method varies depending on what type of brakes you have:

■ NOTE: Magura Hydraulic brakes have a lever on the right side of the brake which is pulled down to release the entire right side of the brake, including the horseshoe shaped bridge. Lift this away from the frame being careful not to loose the washer that sits under the brake.

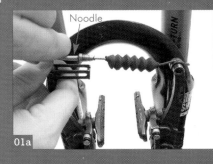
Noodle
01a

01b

02

01a Vee Type Brake ▲
First slide the rubber boot to the right. Next, push the brake arm on the left towards the tyre and pull the metal 'noodle' towards you. This should allow you to unhook the cable and open the brake.

01b Cantilever Brake ▲
Push the straddle wire towards the brake arm, and unhook the metal circle on the end of the cable away from the brake arm.

02 Undo the Quick Release Lever ▲
Pull the quick release lever away from the bike. The wheel will rattle around but shouldn't come out, as it will be held in place by metal tabs on the end of the fork (safety dropouts), designed to retain the wheel in case of accidental loosening. Undo the nut on the opposite end of the axle a few turns and lift the wheel out.

REMOVING THE REAR WHEEL

The rear wheel has the added complication of the chain getting in the way, but is still not a difficult job by any means.

TOP TIP: It is probably easiest to do this job with the bike upside down.

01

02

01 Change Gear ▲
Change gear, so the chain is sitting on the smallest sprocket at the rear. Now undo the brake and QR or wheel nuts - there won't be any safety tabs, so the skewer doesn't need to be unwound as far as at the front wheel.

02 Move the Mech ▲
Lift the rear wheel (or have the bike turned over) off the ground and move the derailleur backwards to get the chain out of the way. Push downwards on the QR skewer or gently push / punch downward on the tyre to remove the wheel.

01a

This is a simple job, but mistakes can still be made - but don't be scared as this is by no means difficult, it just needs to be done carefully. If the wheels are not put in properly, they could come loose, and even if done slightly wrong the gears and brakes won't work correctly.

01

01b

02

NOTE: When the wheels are off the bike, ensure that nothing heavy rests across the empty frame and forks - as these can be bent surprisingly easily.

01 PUT THE WHEEL IN PLACE ▲

First ensure that the wheel is facing the right way - there are often arrows on tyres showing you the direction they should go, and the QR lever should usually go on the left of the bike. Even if you have a work stand, it is best to replace the wheels on the ground, as this will make it easier to get the wheel sitting correctly in the dropouts.

■**NOTE:** Check (using the arrows on tyres) that they are going in the right direction.

Make sure the wheel is sat all the way in to the fork or frame dropouts on both sides; check by looking at the top of the tyre to see if it is centrally aligned.

01c

REPLACING THE REAR WHEEL ▲

01a Change into the highest gear (smallest sprocket at the back) and lift the chain out of the way.

01b Now manoeuvre the wheel and bike so that the upper part of the chain sits on the smallest sprocket, then pull the derailleur back and the wheel towards the dropouts - if you have disc brakes, ensure that the rotor is headed between the brake pads.

01c Finally make sure that the wheel axle is sitting all the way in the dropouts.

02 SECURE THE WHEEL ▲

Do up the nut on the skewer most of the way (so the lever starts to bite halfway) then move the lever to the 'Closed' position, tight enough to leave a white mark on your hand. Do not make the mistake of twirling the QR lever clockwise until it feels tight.

Ensure that the QR lever is closed completely, not resting on the fork or frame and the lever points up or backwards, to minimise the risk of it catching on something and becoming undone.

If your wheel doesn't use QR levers, simply tighten up the wheel nuts or Hex-key skewer.

03 RE-ATTACH THE BRAKES ▲

Re-attach the vee-brakes (or cantilevers) by squeezing the arms together, and hooking the cables back in to position. For vee-brakes, slide the rubber boot back on to the noodle.

To re-attach Magura hydraulic rim brakes, slide the brake over the brake post and locate the brake stiffener (arch). Now line up the pad with the rim and close the release lever.

With disc brakes, after you have fitted the wheel (with the rotor back in between the brake pads) and fastened up the QR (or similar), you should be ready to go. Sometimes you need to squeeze the lever a couple of times to re-align the brake pads

MAINTENANCE

A puncture is probably the most common single mechanical mishap a mountain biker will have to put up with. Unless you have a one legged fork e.g. Cannondale 'Lefty' or USE SUB fork, the first thing to do is to remove the wheel (see W4).

The next challenge is to remove the tyre. The difficulty of this depends largely on the tightness of the tyre on the wheel rim. Some manufacturers can sometimes make their wheel rims slightly larger, and some tyres are slightly smaller than others, both going towards creating a tight fit. Fortunately, as tyres age they do tend to get a bit slacker and easier to pull on and off.

■NOTE: Tyres may lose air over a few days/weeks (especially light weight inner tubes).

01: Remove the valve cap and deflate the tyre. With a Schrader valve (pic 01a), push the stem in the middle of it (use a fingernail or twig). With a Presta valve (pic 01b), undo the tiny nut a bit and press it down (this needs to be re-tightened after inflating the tube again or it may leak slowly). You may need to squash the tyre to remove all the air from it.

01a   01b

Schrader valves are tough, and can be tightened with a special tool (useful if you use air shocks), but they are heavier than presta valves.

Presta valves are easier to pump up and can achieve a higher pressure, but the inner part can bend and leak - it is replaceable, but is hardly worth it.

02: The next step (big bike shop secret here) is to make sure that the tyre is unattached from the rim all around the wheel.

Do this by pushing in on the tyre with your thumbs as shown in the photo and make sure to do this on both sides and all around the tyre or you will find it difficult to get off.

02

Ideally, the tyre should be removed and replaced without tyre levers, to minimises the risk of damaging the tube or tyre. This is easiest with a tyre that is a loose fit on a rim, but with practice and strong thumbs can be done on most tyres.

You want to create a 'high spot' opposite the valve by pulling the tyre away from the rim with one hand (call this the 12 O'clock position). With the valve in the 6 O'clock position, use the other hand, moving from 4 O'clock round to 12 O'clock, try and shove the tyre upwards, then do the same from the 8 O'clock through to 12 O'clock.

Now try and pull the tyre from the wheel rim. Grab the tyre at your 'high spot/12 O'clock position and try and pull it up and over the wheel rim.

03: Insert a tyre lever between the wheel rim and tyre sidewall, hooking under the tyre bead (careful not to pinch the inner tube). If the lever has a hook, attach it to the nearest spoke.

Now add another lever a few inches away, then a third lever and slide this sideways to move the tyre off the rest of the rim.

03

Find out what caused the puncture or it may happen again straight away! If you hit something quite hard just as you got the puncture, and the tyre went down very quickly, you've probably got a 'pinch flat' - where the tyre folds under the impact and pinches the tube against the rim. If this is the case, put in a new or fixed tube and pump the tyres up to a higher pressure.

Otherwise, look for what may have made a hole in the tube by carefully running your fingers around the inside of the tyre - you should find a thorn etc. Remove this (poke it back through with something hard), and don't assume it's the only one - check the whole tyre - our best was 12 thorns. A less common cause is a hole in the tyre wall, which will need to be repaired - see bodge repairs on page M2.

04: Next pull out the damaged inner tube.

* If you want to fix the hole now, go to the 'tube repair' section on the next page.

* If out on the trail or racing, it is quicker just to pop in a spare tube - you did remember to bring one didn't you?

04

05: Inflate the new or repaired tube slightly, to give it some shape, then place the valve through the corresponding hole in the wheel rim.

Now push the inner tube in to the tyre, evenly - making sure there are no overly stretched bits or folded over sections, as these will cause problems later on.

05

Using your thumbs, pop the tyre back on to the rim. Start at the valve and work around in both directions. If you can't get the last bit of tyre back on, prise it on with tyre levers, but be careful no to pinch the inner tube against the rim.

Before you pump it all the way up, make sure the tube is not pinched underneath the tyre and the rim. Do this by pushing the tyre wall inwards (see pic above).

01: FIND THE HOLE.

A hole or slit up to 6mm diameter should be repairable, anything bigger and the tubes' life is over, likewise, if the tube has split by the valve (see 01b).

Inflate the tube then look and listen for the escape off air. If the position of the hole is not obvious, run the tube under your ears, or if in a noisy place under your (wet) lips, which are surprisingly good at detecting the rush of air out of a tube.

02: APPLY RUBBER SOLUTION.

Clean (using a buffer / cleaning solution is ideal, but spit may have to do), then dry the area around the hole, then rough it up with sandpaper Next apply a thin layer of solution, a bit bigger than the patch you're going to use.

■ NOTE: Glueless patches save time waiting for solvent to dry, but their effectiveness varies.

03: PUT A PATCH ON

Give the area 5 minutes to dry, or until there are no more wet looking areas.

Remove the backing from the patch and press it on as hard as possible, (push from the middle out towards the edges) making sure all the edges are stuck down securely.

04: PEEL OFF BACKING

Now peel the other sheet from the patch (some makes have a slit down the middle to avoid pulling the edges of the patch off the inner tube) - if it looks like removing the backing will take the patch with it, just leave the backing in place.

Grate some chalk on the back of the repair kit and dust the patch. This will aid the drying up of any excess solution.

05: TALC THE INNER TUBE

Inflate the tube some more to check that there are no other holes you missed. Leave it for 24 hours to 'cure' if you can, otherwise dust the inner tube in talcom powder and replace it in the tyre. Talc stops the tube sticking to the tyre and keeps it supple, which helps avoid punctures

TOOLS: Puncture repair kit. Tyre levers and talcom powder are optional.

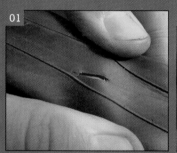

01

02

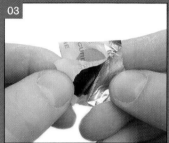

03

04

05

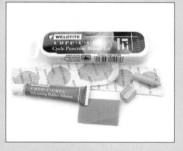

TOP TIP: If you get a puncture on a ride and are all out of repair patches, and your spare inner tube has a hole, you could still get home without walking - see M53.

01b

PREVENTION IS BETTER THAN CURE

MORE AIR

Heavier or big hitting riders who frequently get 'pinch flats' can benefit from using slightly higher air pressure, and/or bigger volume tyres.

TOUGH INNER TUBES

You could also try heavy duty tubes e.g. Michelin C6 or Hutchinson greenlight.

ANTI-PUNCTURE TYRES OR RIM STRIPS

Strips made from Aramid (generic name for Kevlar) around the inside of the tyre (see pic right) will protect the inner tube from thorns etc. Some 'armoured' tyres have puncture proof casing or kevlar belt under the tread to stop thorns etc getting through. They may also have thicker sidewalls to avoid pinch flats.

TYRE SEALANT

A 'slime' (see pic right) can be used to fill and prevent air leaks from small holes in a tube, or used in tubeless tyres. You can buy tubes with the sealant already in them tubes or you can inject it into the tube through a schrader valve.

An alternative to conventional inner tubes is 'liquid latex'. Stan's sealant is the original, but Art latex is cheaper (see www.justridingalong.com). It involves converting your wheel rims, with tape, fitting a sealed valve, then pouring in the liquid and inflating the tyre very quickly, then spinning the wheel - it will probably dry up in about a year, so top it up. This system will let you ride at a lower p.s.i. without getting pinch flats. The results are variable, some love it, while others still get punctures and their tyres fall off.

Puncture protection products will add weight to your wheels - but it is a price many riders are happy to pay.

01c: If you can't find the hole, immerse the inflated tube in water and look for the bubbles of air.

TUBELESS TYRES

NOTE: The most widely used system is 'UST' (Universal System for Tubeless) pioneered by leading rim and tyre manufacturers.

NOTE: You will need to use 'tubeless' rims to use 'tubeless' tyres, however you can usually run a regular tyre on your tubeless rims.

NOTE: DO NOT use tyre levers when fitting or removing tubeless tyres as they can dent the rim or damage the tyre, wrecking the seal.

Tubeless tyres do not need inner tubes because they create an air tight seal by using specially designed wheel rims and tyres. The advantages of this is that they can be run at a lower pressure, giving greater traction and comfort without suffering from a pinch flat. However, when you do puncture they can be harder to repair than normal inner tubes (especially when out on the trail), as the hole is difficult to find, the tyres are difficult to get on and off, and they need to be pumped up very quickly to get the (tyre rim) seal to pop into place. Therefore it may be worthwhile carrying a spare inner tube out on a ride, taking a CO2 inflation device, or even using a tyre sealant slime or latex solution.

TOOLS: Tubeless puncture repair kit, track pump or CO2 canister, wet sponge.

NOTE: CO2 canisters are perfect for inflating tubeless tyres quickly (to pop the seals in place) when out on the trail.

TOP TIP: A quick and easy trailside puncture repair is just to use some super glue in the hole / puncture.

01a

02

03

04

EXTERNAL REPAIR

This method of hole repair is very useful for when out on the trail as you don't have to remove and replace the tyre which can be difficult.

01a: First find the hole - this can be trickier than on a regular tube. Try to listen for the rush of air escaping. If this proves fruitless, inflate the tyre then immerse it in water and look for the bubbles escaping.

Once you have identified the hole, remove the foreign object if applicable and mark it's position.

01: Apply the rubber solution to the rasp tool and work it into the hole - to lube and clean the hole.

02: Now insert the strip of sticky material into the eye of the needle tool so there are equal lengths either side of the eye.. Now apply some rubber solution to this strip of material.

03: Insert the tool/strip into the hole until around 1/2 of the strip is inside / outside the tyre.

04: Now SLOWLY pull the needle out of the hole leaving the strip in the tyre / hole. Without stretching the strip of material cut it off about 3mm from the tyre surface. Now inflate the tyre to the desired riding pressure.

INTERNAL REPAIR

01a: As external repair step 01a.

01: Deflate the tyre by depressing the valve. Next 'unseat' the bead of the tyre from the rim on one side by pushing one side of the tyre (starting near the valve) into the centre of the rim, and continue all around the tyre.

Now roll the tyre off the rim by shoving it in the opposite direction - this may be difficult, but resist the temptation to use tyre levers. Go all around the tyre until one bead is completely off then un-seat the other side of the tyre, again starting near the valve, then remove the tyre.

02: Clean, roughen and apply some glue to the area. Allow to dry then press a patch over the hole.

03: Wet the tyre rim beads or use a tyre rim wax to help pop the tyres on and create a seal·between the tyre and rim.

04: Place one side of the tyre into the centre of the rim (starting at the valve) and work around to pop the rest of the tyre into position. Now push the second tyre bead into position, finishing at the valve. Now inflate the tyre to 50psi as quickly as possible using a track pump or CO2 to force the beads into position - you may need to manipulate the tyre so it holds the air, then let out the air to your desired pressure for riding.

01

02

03

04

WHEEL MAINTENANCE

Dish out too much punishment to your wheels and they will go out of 'true', wobbling left and right and if you're unlucky up and down as well. Check for loose spokes by gripping and squeezing two spokes together (rim side of where they cross), and if they feel loose or make a grating noise, they are loose. The movement, to a certain extent, can be removed by adjusting the spoke tension to 'true' the wheel (see steps 1-4); if the spoke is broken however, it will require replacing.

A: Nipple
B: Threads
C: Bend / Neck
D: Spoke head

TOOLS: Spoke key, zip-tie (or a truing stand if possible).

UPPERS AND DOWNERS

'High spots' & 'low spots' can be corrected by adjusting spoke tension, but it is tricky so may be best left to an experienced wheel builder with an accurate wheel stand.

Adjust the markers so that they just touch the top of the rim. Working in groups of 3 spokes at a time, tighten ones on the 'high' side of the wheel and loosen the spokes opposite, and the opposite for 'low spots'.

Now check the dish (centre) of the wheel by having the hub central in the drop-outs and have both markers touch the edge of the rim (as for side to side truing). Now take the wheel out, turn it around and replace it in the drop-outs. If the markers don't still touch the rim tighten every spoke 1/4 turn on the side that doesn't touch the marker, centre the marker, flip the wheel, check, and keep repeating until centred.

REMEMBER: A wobble to the left can be corrected by tightening 'right' spokes & loosening 'left' spokes.

REPLACING SPOKES

Spokes vary in materials, thickness or gauge, butting, and length. The nipples (where the spokes tighten - usually at the rim) can be made of alloy or brass. Alloy nipples can save some rotating weight and they're often available in a range of colours - but will seize in time.

'Butted' spokes (get thinner in the middle where there is less stress) save weight, while thicker 'plain gauge' spokes will stretch less and are better for bigger riders, heavy duty wheels and use with disc brakes.

The most important factor is spoke length, which will depend on the rim, hub and lacing combinations. Most good bike shops should be able to work out the correct spoke length from your combination of rim, hub and lacing pattern. Otherwise, look at the neighbouring spoke, and measure the distance from the head to where it goes in to the nipple, and add 4mm, or check out the www.wheelpro.co.uk website.

■ NOTE: Be aware that spoke lengths tend to differ on the left and right of a rear hub or disc hub to compensate for the space taken up by the sprocket or disc (this is called the 'dish').

Study the lacing pattern (way the spokes cross one another) of the spokes on your wheel and copy this pattern to put your new spoke in place. Thread the spoke through the flange hole in the hub - the spoke may need to be flexed slightly.

If replacing the spokes on the same side of the wheel as a disc rotor or rear sprockets, these items will usually need removing (see G5 for sprocket removal and B5 for disc rotor removal).

First insert the spoke head of the new spoke through the hub flange. Apply a dab of grease to the spoke thread and attach the nipple in to the old nipple head if it's not damaged - otherwise, you will need to remove the tyre and rim-tape to inset a new nipple from the rim-side with a spoke wrench or home-made one using an old spoke (see pic below).

Now check you have laced the spoke correctly, tighten the spoke to the same tension as its neighbours, and assess how true it is (see 'Truing a wheel' - right).

■ NOTE: Spoke nipples can seize in place with time; your efforts with the spoke key will just twist the spokes if this happens, so remove the rim-tape and apply a penetrating lube to the tops of the spokes to get them moving.

TRUING A WHEEL

01: INSPECTION
Take the tyre off the wheel and inspect the rim for cracks and dents. If you find a crack (usually at the join) the rim will need to be replaced. You can try to straighten any dents in the rim with pliers or an adjustable spanner, but be careful not to chew up the metal.

02: LOCATION, LOCATION, LOCATION
Place the wheel in a wheel-truing stand or put it back on the bike and turn the bike upside down. Adjust the feelers of the stand / brake pads or if you have disc brakes, you can use a zip-tie or tape some card to the frame/fork so that they almost touch the rim and spin the wheel to locate the wobble(s) - it's off to the left in the pic.

03: TRUTH
Where the rim touches the pad / feeler / card you will need to loosen spokes coming from the same side of the hub, and tighten spokes coming from the opposite side.

■ NOTE: Always tighten and loosen spokes in pairs to maintain even tension through the wheel. With the spokes at the bottom of the wheel, tighten anticlockwise and loosen clockwise.

04: EASY DOES IT
Turn the spokes 1/4 a turn at a time, making your adjustments more subtle as you get further from the highest point of the movement and as it decreases. Re-adjust the feelers / pads as the wheel begins to straighten-up, and continue until the wheel is as straight as you can (a couple of millimetres is fine) if the rim is damaged you are unlikely to get it perfect.

01

02

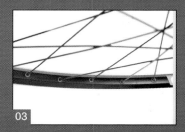
03

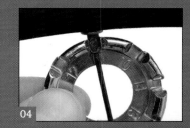
04

THE HUB sits in the middle of the wheel, providing the main bearing and the attachment point for the spokes. The rear hub also contains the freewheel mechanism (the 'freehub body') on most MTBs and transmits the power from the drivetrain to the wheel rim and tyres. If the bike has disc brakes, the hub additionally provides the point of attachment for the disc rotor and transfers breaking forces to the rest of the wheel.

SAWN UP CUP & CONE HUB

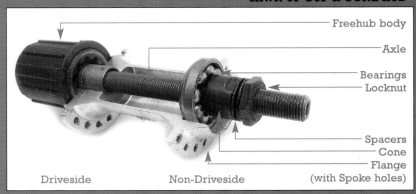

- Freehub body
- Axle
- Bearings
- Locknut
- Spacers
- Cone
- Flange (with Spoke holes)

Driveside   Non-Driveside

CUP AND CONE HUB SERVICE

Except for clicky noises made when freewheeling, hubs should move noiselessly. Any unhappy rumbling sounds indicate the hub is in bad need of servicing.

The hub should also be free of lateral movement or 'play' around the axle. Check this by holding the bike by the frame and tyre and trying to move the wheel left and right. Any movement or noise is bad and indicates that the bearings need to be tightened.

■ **NOTE:** If you are reasonably sure the hub needs tightening but not a full service, simply loosen the locknut as in step 01, then adjust the cones and tighten as in step 06.

01: Take the wheel off the bike and remove the quick release skewer, axle nuts and any large plastic seals (usually on Shimano hubs). If working on a rear hub, remove the cassette or freewheel (G5/6) and start work on the non-driveside. Attach the cone spanner to the cone (you can usually see two little flats) then a regular spanner to the locknut and undo this anticlockwise.

02: Spin off the locknut, spacer and cone, line them up to make sure you remember the order they came off in. Pull the axle out of the opposite side of the hub (leave the cone and locknut in place) and poke the bearings out with something pokey.

03: Clean up everything to the best of your abilities. Run a rag through the hub body and polish the inside bearing surfaces, using a cleaner if necessary. Inspect the condition of the cones and bearings - if pitted or dull they can be replaced - take the parts to a bike shop to make sure you get the correct replacements.

■ **NOTE:** You can now remove, clean and grease the freehub body - see W11.

04: Smear waterproof grease over both bearing surfaces inside the hub a few mm deep. Place the bearings in the side you pulled the axle from.

The bearings should be spaced evenly with perhaps a small gap left over. Put more grease over them, then gently lower the axle back into position, making sure it doesn't knock any bearings inside the hub. Hold the axle in place and gently flip the wheel over.

05: Pull the axle down just far enough to give you room to pop the second set of bearings in to position.

Use a small screwdriver or similar to prod the bearings into place. Wipe some more grease over them and pull the axle up.

06: Screw the second cone, spacer and locknut gently onto the bearings. With the cone spanner, adjust the cone so it turns smoothly with very little play then tighten down the locknut. It's OK for there to be a small amount of bearing play at this stage, as clamping down the skewer will tighten everything up.

■ **NOTE:** This will probably take a few attempts to get right - just be very careful not to over-tighten the cone, or it can ruin the inside of the hub.

Now, put the wheel back in the frame, tighten up the quick release skewer / axle nuts. Test the wheel for play and spin it to see how free-rolling it is. If your adjustment isn't quite spot on, hold the hub by both locknuts and tighten to remove play, or hold it by both cones and loosen to free it up.

Once the wheel is spinning sweetly, replace any external seals and rear sprockets and you're done!

TOOLS: 2 Cone spanners, pointy thing, rag, grease, container for catching and holding the bearings.

TOP TIP: When you take the hub apart, the bearings like flying everywhere, especially under things or down between floorboards, so count them and perform this service over a container to catch them.

01
02
03
04
05
06

The freehub is the cylindrical part which is attached to the rear hub, and uses a splined cylinder to hold the cassette cogs. It is found on most modern derailleur bike hubs, and allows the wheel to spin while coasting and engage when force is applied to the pedals.

The common freehub has bearings, pawls and springs inside it and we advise that you don't bother trying to take it apart. The only replaceable parts will be the bearings and if these are worn it's likely the whole lot needs replacing.

The freehub will wear out over time becoming rough, slipping or seizing. The freehub body can usually be removed, then cleaned, and re-lubed (some even have a grease port to make this easier), but if this doesn't solve the problem you will need to replace it with a new one. Make sure you get the correct model i.e. 7 or 8/9 speed to ensure all the seals fit correctly.

BROKEN OR BENT AXLE

If you notice that the axle is bent or broken, take the opportunity to service your hubs. Buy a replacement axle of the same width and pitch (i.e. make sure your old cones will screw on).

When you pull the old axle, out measure the distance between the end of the axle and the locknut (see the picture right). Take the locknut, spacer and cone from the damaged axle and put them in place on the new one with exactly the same spacing and continue with the hub service.

TOOLS: 2 cone spanners, 10mm hex key, vice (optional), spanner, and grease.

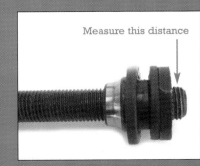

Measure this distance

01

02

To service the freehub, first remove the cassette (see G5 or G6), then follow the cup and cone hub service instructions (see W10) until you have removed the axle and bearings.

01: With the cassette and axle hub removed you can now insert a 10mm hex key and unscrew the freewheel (anticlockwise) - this can require quite a bit of force.

02: Lift off the old freehub body, taking note any spacers behind freehub.

03

04

03: You can clean the old freehub by flushing a cleaning solvent through the body and cleaning under the dust cap - but do not remove the righthand side dust cap, as you could cause some damage. Once this has dried out completely, add some (liquid) lubricant in the back, side and front, and spin the freehub to work lube around inside.

04: Grease the cleaned (or new) freehub mounting-bolt, and install the freehub back onto the hub body, adding any spacers as required. Tighten to about 360 inch-pounds. Now continue with the hub service.

■ NOTE: It is possible to squeeze a little more performance out of a Shimano freehub body, but it is fiddly and requires the Shimano TL-FH40 tool which is hard to get hold of. The tool fits into two slots in the 'body fixing race' and will enable you to:

1: Put thicker grease into the freehub - making it more weather proof.
2: Replace or add more pawl springs to give more positive engagement (and cope with thicker grease).
3: Remove play from the freehub body - reducing wear and sharpening shifting.

MAINTENANCE: GEARS

Gears MAINTENANCE
SECTION

This section tackles the transmission of the mountain bike,
and should result in smooth gear changes and longer
wearing parts. It may seem complicated now, but this
section will make the words 'splines, top pull, and spider'
make a whole lot more sense. If it's all still too much there is
also a page on how to get ride of all but one of the gears.

LOVE & HATE

The part of a bike that is the most complex and responsible for the most common source of worries are the gears, also known as the drivetrain or transmission (see pic below).

■ **NOTE**: Bikes are usually fitted with front chainring sizes of 42-32-22 (big-middle-small), although older bikes and pre-2002 XTR have 48-36-24 (for racing).

■ **NOTE**: Use the right chain lubricant for the weather conditions i.e. dry or wet weather lubes and wipe off excess lube as it just attract dirt.

It comprises of shift levers, cables, front & rear derailleur, chain-set, bottom bracket and sprockets. Many people are a little bit scared of gears, as explorative attempts to sort out problems often end up badly, and what is assumed to be a worn out chain often ends up being a load of worn out parts and a big bill at the bike shop.

HOW MANY GEARS?

The number of gears has steadily increased over the years, with top quality mountain bikes now having nine rear sprockets (Mega 9 or nine speed), while older or lower-end bikes may have 8, 7, 6 or even 5 rear sprockets.

Most mountain bikes will also have 3 chainrings at the front (downhill bikes will usually just use one large chainring at the front and a device to keep the chain in place), so combined with the choice of rear sprockets you get 27, 24, 21 etc geared bikes. There are even some people who ride a 'Singlespeed' mountain bike - yes, just one gear. Having just one gear is growing in popularity, and has the advantage of the chain not slipping or sucking, and enables you to concentrate on riding - but are may not be good for the weaker knee amongst you.

Having more gears enables either a greater range of gear ratios to be used (e.g. faster high gears and lower low gears for climbing) or the ratios to be closer together for more consistent cadence (revolutions of the pedals per minute). 8-speed cassettes typically have 11-30, and 9-speed 11-32 or 12-34.

Despite all this, the most important thing is that they work correctly - 27 gears will do you no good at all if the chain slips when you stomp on the pedals.

UPGRADING - MIX 'N' MATCH

While there is nothing wrong with older systems such as the 7 or 8 speed, it is getting getting harder and harder to get quality replacement parts. This is an issue because of the compatibility between different 'speed' components.

Each bit of the drive train (except the cables) is specifically 6, 7, 8 or 9 speed. Ask the component manufacturers and they will tell you that you must only use complete systems of one type, and to get the best results it is usually worth following this advice.

If you thinking of upgrading your old 8 (or even 7) speed drivetrain to a 9-speed, you will need to consider the following points:

Cassette: You will need a new 9-speed cassette (sprockets), which will fit in the place of the old 8-speed one.

Chain: 7 and 8 speed chains are the same, and 9 speed chains can work on a 8 speed set-up, but a 9-speed cassette uses thinner sprockets, so thinner 9-speed chains are required (8 speed won't work on a 9-speed set-up) - remember to get the thinner joining pins as well.

Chainrings: Again, 9-speed chainrings are narrower than 8-speed and have a different ramp design (for better shifting). You should be able to replace the old 8-speed chainrings with 9-speed ones without having to replace the crank arm.

Hubs: The freewheel (bit of the rear hub where the rear cogs fit on) is either 7 speed or 8/9 speed. The wider 8/9 speed size will fit 7 speed, but if you are upgrading from 7 to 8 or 9 speed you will need a new hub.

■ **NOTE**: Some XT hubs prior to the 9-speed, are not compatible with new 9-speed cassettes.

Rear Mech: On the whole, rear mechs are fairly interchangable. 9 speed mech work well on 7 and 8 speed systems and although not designed to take the big 32 or 34T cogs, 7 and 8 speed mechs can often work fine on a 9 speed system.

■ **NOTE**: It is getting very hard to find high quality 7 and 8 speed rear mechs.

Front Mech: The 9-speed is thinner which seems to stop it working with 7 & 8 speed components.

Shift Levers: These don't mix 'n' match at all. The rear shifters each have a different number of 'clicks', and pull a different amount of cable. Shimano also says that the amount of cable pull is different on left-hand shifters as well, so you will need two new shifters.

OTHER CONSIDERATIONS

SRAM & SHIMANO

Most mountain bikes come fitted with Shimano derailleur and gear shifters - and most other makes work to their specifications. The exception is the SRAM ESP system. An ESP shift lever pulls about twice as much cable as a Shimano unit. This system was designed to overcome cable friction and give lighter action gear shifting, but it means ESP shifters and derailleur must be used together and not mixed with standard Shimano parts.

HG, IG, & SRAM

Most Shimano chainrings, cassettes & chains will be either 'Hyperglide' HG or 'Interglide' IG. Each uses a slightly different system of profiled teeth and shaped chain, and is meant to be used as an all 'HG' or all 'IG' system, so avoid mixing the two.

Components by other manufacturers e.g. SRAM chains and Truativ chainrings tend to work irrespective of if they are HG or IG - just make sure that you are using all 7,8 or 9 speed bits.

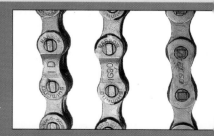

CHAIN WEAR

Dirt and grit in the chain causes wear, making the chain fit together sloppily and elongate or 'stretch'. When this happens, the chain cannot sit correctly on the chainrings and sprockets - only the top few teeth engage. This means that the load on the chainrings and sprockets isn't being spread evenly, and this makes them wear out quickly.

A complete set of chain, chainrings and rear sprockets typically costs around £100, and usually the price of individual chainrings means that you might as well get a complete chainset (cranks + chainrings) while you're at it - making the bill even higher. The way to avoid this (for as long as possible) is to replace the chain BEFORE it becomes worn out and damages everything else.

MEASURING CHAIN WEAR

1: The quickest (and laziest) way to check for chain wear is to try and lift the chain up off the largest cog. If the chain comes away from the teeth of the cog, it may well need replacing, so either replace it, or measure it more accurately.

01

2: You could invest in a check checker, or simply take your bike to a bike shop and ask them to use their tool to check your chain for wear. This is an easy and accurate way of measuring for chain wear, and there are a choice of tools whose prices tend to range from around £5 to £25.

02

3: A cheaper method is just to measure with a ruler. Each link of a new chain measures exactly one inch. To take an accurate measurement, look at 12 links at once. Place a ruler next to the upper part of the chain, and straighten the chain by pushing on the crank.

03

4: A new chain should be 12inches. If you are using alloy sprockets, replace the chain if 12 links measure 12 1/16th inches, whereas if you are using steel ones you have until it is 12 1/8th inches.

■ NOTE: These are alloy sprockets - so it looks like we need a new chain.

04

SPECIAL CHAIN JOINING METHODS

Whenever you join the chain by pushing a pin in, it widens the hole in the outer plate slightly, making the chain more likely to break at that point. To reduce the risk of this, some chains use special joining methods.

SHIMANO CHAINS MUST be joined with a 'special pin' and never split again with this joining pin. This looks like a regular chain pin with a thinner bullet tipped extra section.

When joining the chain, the special pin fits easily in to the chain, then is driven in to position by the chain tool. The bullet-shaped tip must then be snapped off with pliers.

■ **NOTE:** A 9-speed Shimano chain uses a silver (6.5mm) pin and the 7 & 8-speed a black (7.1mm) pin.

SRAM & TAYA CHAINS have tool-free links that join up two inner links.

The Sachs/Sram Powerlink is made of two identical pieces that join up '69' style, the Taya Master link has one piece with both pins and a second which snaps over the top. This is used for both connecting and disconnecting again and again.

Both join easily and make a great emergency fix but can be hard to undo when the chain is rusty or oily and your hands are cold and numb. If you can't get the link to work, use a chain tool elsewhere on the chain.

■ **NOTE:** A 9-speed chain uses a gold SRAM powerlink, and an 8-speed uses a silver SRAM powerlink.

TOP TIP: A SRAM powerlink is a great quick fix to a broken chain when out on the trail. It even works on a Shimano chain (although you should fix it properly with a pin when you get back). Simply get two identical ends of the chain and snap the powerlink in place.

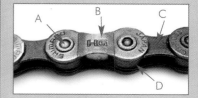

A: JOINING PIN - connects the inner and outer links.
B: OUTER LINK - shaped to aid the shifter.
C: INNER LINK - rotates around the barrel.
D: ROLLER - goes between the teeth on the cogs & chainrings.

■ **NOTE:** Chains are 7, 8 or 9 speed.

Sachs, Shimano and Taya all make a variety of chains. Sachs chains are labelled PC then 2 no.'s. The first number (4-9) shows the quality; 4 being low and 9 being high. The second number shows what speed chain it is; 8 is an 7/8 speed chain, and 9 is a 9 speed chain. Therefore a PC48 is a cheap 7/8 speed chain, and a PC99 is a quality 9 speed chain. Shimano will be either HG or IG. HG can be 7, 8 or 9 speed, and IG is 7 speed.

CHAINSUCK is when the chain gets jammed between the chainring and the frame chainstay because the chain isn't releasing from the chainring teeth properly. This can be caused by a dirty or worn chain, bent chainring teeth, stiff links, incorrect chainline, or a narrow chain.

MAINTENANCE

G3

REMOVING AND REPLACING THE CHAIN:

You will need to remove the chain when replacing it or doing some serious cleaning, and to do this will need a chain tool.

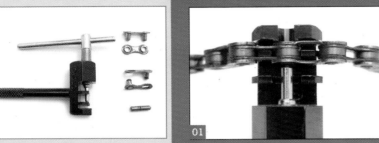

NOTE: It only takes a very small misalignment of a pin i.e. it protrudes too much on one side, to cause failure.

TOOLS: Chaintool & Shimano pin or SRAM link.

TOP TIP: Protect the frames chainstay from being chipped by the chain (which slaps around) by wrapping an old inner tube (road tubes work best) or specially made neoprene covers around the chainstay.

01: REMOVING THE CHAIN

Place a chain tool so that the chain is slotted in to the last channel of the tool as in the picture. Now drive the chain link out by turning the handle of the tool clockwise (remove pins on Shimano chains which have 2 parallel lines on the ends).

NOTE: Chaintools have a driving pin which is used to push the pin / rivet out, and a cradle that holds the chain. Some chaintools have 2 cradles; the one furthest from the driving pin pushes the rivet / pin in and out, and the closer cradle is used for loosening tight links.

You may need to wriggle the chain about to get it to disconnect, and then remove it from the derailleur. If you are going to use the chain again, don't push the pin all the way out, leave it poking through the outer link plate to make rejoining the chain easier.

NOTE: If it's a Shimano chain then drive the pin all the way out, as you will need to fix it with a 'special pin' (mentioned earlier).

02: CUT TO LENGTH

If you are fitting a new chain, compare it in length to the old one (bear in mind links may have been removed from previous breakages).

Alternately, wrap the chain around the big chainring and biggest sprocket, but NOT through the derailleur. Pull the chain together, and then add one link (an inner link + an outer link) to get the correct chain length. Remove additional links by using the chain tool in the same way as you did to remove the chain. For most chains ensure that you are left with an 'outer' end and an 'inner' end.

NOTE: On a full suspension bike the suspension action may affect the chain length. Therefore it is advisable to move the suspension around (this may require you to disconnect the spring from the shock or let the air out) to find the point where the sprockets are furthest from the chainrings, then work out chain length.

03: ROUTING

Next, shift gear to select the smallest chainring and smallest sprocket.

Feed the chain through the derailleur as shown in the diagram. Pay special attention to the rear, making sure the chain isn't touching any part of the cage that holds the jockey wheels in place.

04: JOINING THE CHAIN

Put the chain in the furthest channel in the chain tool and drive the pin back in to the chain, so it is flush with the outer link.

NOTE: To get the two ends of chain closer for joining, lift the chain off the front chainring, put the bike on its side / and hold the links in place with a chain hook - you can make one from a wire coat hanger, but it needs to be exactly the right length or it won't help much.

Then flex the join / link with your hands to loosen it up until it feels free. Now spin the pedals backwards and watch the rear derailleur - the jockey wheels will move forwards slightly as the stiff link tries to resist being fed through.

05: GOT A STIFFEE?

If the link is still stiff, flex it in with your hands again, or put the stiff link in the near channel of the chain tool and push the pin SLIGHTLY to open up the link.

THE REAR SPROCKETS / COGS

The rear sprockets provide a range of fasirly closely spaced gear ratios. The majority of shifting is done over the rear sprockets in response to gradual changes in the terrain. The sprockets engage and transfer power when pedalling and disengage when you coast - this is called 'freewheeling'.

Almost all MTBs use the cassette system where the rear hub includes a cylindrical section that performs the freewheeling action and that the rear cogs mount on to. These are recognised by the 12-notch lockring on top of the smallest sprocket - see right. Older bikes may use a 'freewheel' design, which is a simple hub with a threaded section, which the sprockets and ratchet mechanism (which is one piece) screws onto - recognised by not having a lockring - see below for a picture and M20 for maintenance instructions.

CASSETTE HUB
This has a lockring on the outside of the sprockets, and is the most common design on most new MTB's.

FREEWHEEL
Recognisable as it doesn't have a lockring - see page G6 for more information on servicing freewheels.

CASSETTES

Most sprockets have profiled teeth (chunks missing from certain ones) to help the chain shift between them. To ensure that the teeth on the sprockets are lined up correctly, freehub bodies have a system of different shaped splines (slots and teeth), which correspond with the inside of the sprockets - this only allows the cassette to go on one way. It is also worth remembering that cassette tooth wear is caused by a stretched chain. Keep your chain clean to extend it's life, and try to replace it before the cassette is too worn to accept a new chain or you will need to replace everything.

■NOTE: The width of the freehub body can vary depending on the number of sprockets it is designed for. A seven-speed freehub body is only wide enough to take cassettes with seven sprockets. Eight / nine speed freehub bodies are slightly wider to take the wider eight or nine speed cassettes, and seven-speed cassettes can be fitted to these by using a washer to take up the additional space.

MAINTENANCE

The only real maintenance that needs doing to cassettes is cleaning and replacement when worn.

When the cassette is at the end of it's life the chain will jump around or 'skip' when you pedal. Replacing the chain will only make this worse as a new chain doesn't interface correctly with worn sprockets

■ NOTE: If you are replacing the cassette, it is usually best to replace the chain as well, for maximum life of both.

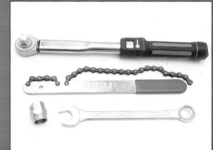

TOOLS: Chain whip, lockring tool, large spanner, (torque wrench).

TOP TIP: You can bodge a chainwhip with some old chain and a piece of wood, or use a car oil filter removal tool.

01: REMOVAL

Take off the rear wheel and skewer and fit a lock-ring-remover tool in to the cassette (you can hold it in place with the skewer to stop it slipping).

Brace the cassette with a chain-whip on middle or larger cog, and turn the lock-ring tool anticlockwise with a large adjustable spanner. Remove the skewer and undo the lock-ring and pull the old cassette off the hub.

TOP TIP: It will release a bit suddenly, so make sure you don't skin your knuckles.

02: FIT NEW CASSETTE

Cassettes come in several pieces, some of which are rivetted together or held on an alloy carrier. The new cassette should come with an assembly diagram.

Basically put them on in descending order of size, usually with spacers between individual pieces, making sure the sprockets are evenly spaced. Each piece will only go on one way - line up the largest tooth on the inside of each with the large slot on the freehub body.

03: TIGHTEN UP

Now grease the lock-ring and tighten it on with an adjustable spanner - the recommended torque may be written on the lock-ring e.g. 40Nm.

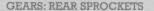

01

02

03

■ **NOTE:** A 'Freewheel' can be recognised by the lack of lockring retaining the smallest cog.

■ **NOTE:** Freewheel removal and replacement requires a tool that fits in to the body of the freewheel - there are several different shapes of tool. Take your bike to a shop where you get one and check that it fits.

TOP TIP: You can beef up a Shimano freewheel by adding extra springs (if you can find any).

This will enable you to use thicker grease in the hub to protect it, and the freehub will still lock up and perform effectively.

MAINTENANCE

On some older bikes the sprockets and ratchet mechanism is one piece (called a 'freewheel'), which screws on to a thread on the hub. It is a mechanism of bearings, pawls and ratchets. When freewheeling (rolling without pedalling) the pawls slide over the ratchet (giving a clicking sound) and when pedalling, the pawls engage the ratchets, to drive the wheel.

This system is rare on quality geared mountain bikes, as 8 or 9 speed freewheels are very hard / impossible to find and the design does not support the rear axle as well. It is however, used on most BMXs and other single speed bikes (see right) and old or cheap bikes. It is relatively easy to replace, oil & grease the bearings, but the whole thing will need replacing when either the sprockets are worn or the freewheel mechanism is broken i.e. spins both ways or becomes loose or hard to turn.

REMOVING & FITTING A FREEWHEEL

01: REMOVAL
Take off the rear wheel and remove the skewer or axle nuts. Fit the freewheel removal tool in place and hold it down with the skewer or an axle nut. Fit a large spanner to the flats of the tool and undo anticlockwise - loosening the skewer / nut as the freewheel comes off.

TOP TIP: For more leverage, clamp the tool in a vice and spin the wheel anticlockwise.

02: LUBRICATING THE FREEWHEEL
Multiple speed freewheels have fiddly internals and are not always possible to disassemble. If you have a continual high pitch squeal, try oiling between the spokes and cogs to fix it.

■ **NOTE:** Ison Distribution (ID) do a 'freewheel buddy' tool, which (although expensive and hard to find) can be used to pump grease into the freewheel.

03: REPLACEMENT
Make sure your replacement has the same number of sprockets and the largest sprockets aren't too big for your rear derailleur to cope with.
Grease the threads on the hub and screw on the new freewheel by hand. Tighten it up with a chain-whip or the freewheel tool. Alternately, put the wheel back on the bike and a few (careful!) pedal strokes will finish the job.

SINGLE-SPEED FREEWHEEL SERVICE

The BMX type freewheel (often used by single-speed riders) don't have great seals, so often need servicing to keep them running smoothly.

This service can be done with the freewheel on the bike, or you can remove it with the freewheel removal tool. If you are not taking the freewheel off the bike, all you will need is a pin spanner.

01: REMOVE THE COVER
Remove the QR skewer or axle nuts and clean up the teeth. Use a pin spanner to unscrew the cover (see pic 01a) of the freewheel (left-hand thread - unscrews clockwise). Pull the silver toothed section of the freewheel up and off the central body - make sure you know which which way up it goes! You should also find between 1 and 4 thin spacing washers sitting on top of the main body - remove these for later.

02: CLEAN
Clean everything and inspect the ball bearings and surfaces for wear. Examine and clean the pawls (the sprung catches that allow a freewheel to move one way and lock the other). Shimano use 2 pawls and 1 circular spring, ACS use 4 pawls with individual leaf springs. Other makes are usually copies or rearrangements of ACS and Shimano.

— Spring

— Pawl

03: GREASE
Line the bearing surfaces inside the toothed section with grease (marine grease for outboard motors is a winner). If the old bearings clean up OK, re-use them, otherwise purchase some new ones and install them in both sides of the toothed section. Carefully lower this into position on to the main freehub body (you may have to use something to retract the pawls).

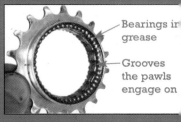

— Bearings in grease

— Grooves the pawls engage on

04: PUT BACK TOGETHER
Finally, drop the spacing washers in place and screw down the top cover section (anti-clockwise). Spin the freewheel and check for smooth running and play - if the freewheel wobbles a little, re-assemble and leave out one of the spacing washers - this should eliminate unwanted play and noises.

— Cover

— Pin spanner

CRANK MAINTENANCE

When the rider stands out of the saddle, the chainset and bottom bracket bear nearly all their weight and when going over obstacles the chainrings are a prime target for getting bashed. The chainset must therefore be strong and stiff to prevent breakage and deliver power efficiently - any looseness can quickly wreck it, so it is important that everything is adjusted correctly.

THE CHAINSET

A: Outer chainring
B: Chainring bolt
C: Spider
D: Driveside crank arm
E: Bottom bracket
F: Non-driveside crank arm

TOP TIP: Put the chain on the outer chainring, so that when you are undoing the cranks, as they suddenly undo, the chain will protect your knuckles from the chainring teeth.

■ NOTE: Some cranks e.g. Truvativ and Bontrager have washers to go in between the hard steel pedal and the soft alloy cranks to stop over tightening and reduce creaking.

REMOVING & REPLACING CRANKS

You will need to remove the cranks to change them, adjust the bottom bracket, change chainrings, or if the chain gets horribly stuck behind the chainrings.

SELF-EXTRACTORS

Some cranks (including most splined cranks) come fitted with 'self extracting' or 'captured' bolts, recognisable by having a crank bolt surrounded by a circular metal disc with two circular holes opposite one another (pic 01). Simply turn the hex bolt anti-clockwise to pull the cranks off.

■ NOTE: These bolts are available to be fitted to older cranks.

CRANK PULLER

If you don't have self extracting bolts (or Hollwtech cranks - see right), you will need a crank extracting tool (crank puller). This has two parts - an outer that screws in to the crank and an inner piece that pushes against the bottom bracket and shoves the crank off.

Remove the crank bolt (pic 02) by un-screwing anticlockwise (usually an 8mm hex key - older bikes may need a 14 or 15mm socket). Make sure that the inner part of the crank puller is not protruding from the outer, then with your fingers, screw the outer part of the tool, into the crank thread. If your cranks use a splined system insert the Shimano TL-FC16 (metal cap shown in the tools pic) or a 5p piece over the end of the BB axle to give the crank puller something to push against. Now turn the inner part of the crank tool with a spanner (pic 03) or if the tool has a handle attached use that. Tighten the inner part of the crank puller (usually with

TOOLS: Crank puller, spanners, and hex keys.

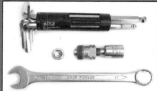

■ NOTE: Shimano Hollowtech II cranks and Race Face X-type cranks require the BB shell faced (a job for a good bike shop) and the Shimano TL-FC 32 and TL FC 16 tools.

a 17mm spanner) to pull the crank off. Make sure it is screwed in as far as it can go - otherwise attempting to remove the crank may simply rip its' threads out. If this happens, ride the bike gently with the crank bolts removed. This will loosen the crank's hold on the BB.

To replace the cranks, ensure that tapered bottom brackets are clean and un-greased, splined systems can be lightly greased. Push the crank on by hand making sure the left and right cranks are at 180° to one another (easy to get slightly wrong with splined systems). Grease the crank bolt, and do it up very tight (usually between 20-23ft/lbs, or see the recommended torque for your specific design).

HOLLOWTECH CRANKS

Loosen the hex bolts (pic 04) on the left crank, then using the specialist tool remove the cap from the crank arm (pic 05). Now slide the left arm off, then pull the right arm (and connected spindle) out the other side.

To replace them, push the spindle (attached to the crank) through the driveside of the BB shell. Grease the spindle splines and pop the left crank onto the spindle (the splines ensure it goes on at 180° to the right crank arm). Now tighten (hand-tight) the cap on the LH crank using the specialist tool and tighten the hex bolts 10-15Nm.

01

02

03

04

05

CRANK PROBLEMS

LOOSE

Check by holding the bike by the frame and try to push and pull the crank. If a single crank moves, it is loose, and if both cranks move it indicates that the BB is loose or worn out - see E10. Riding with a loose crank will quickly wreck the inside of the crank where it joins on to the BB. This will cause the cranks to continually come loose and so will need replacing. If you notice in time, simply tighten the crank bolt.

If the crank comes loose again, try cleaning where the crank and BB join, and apply Loctite to the crank bolt threads to stop it coming loose.

CREAKY

Remove the cranks, clean thoroughly and replace, ensuring the crank bolt and splines are greased. Note that the noise could also be due to creaky pedals or bottom bracket.

CRACKED OR BENT

Replace bent or cracked cranks with stronger ones designed for your riding style. If you have damaged the threads inside the crank, it will be difficult to remove. Some bike shops might have a tool that can remove the crank. If you are willing to replace the crank, you could simply remove the crank bolt then ride (somewhere non technical and with no traffic) until the crank falls off. Bear in mind doing this may ruin the crank.

MAINTENANCE

CHAINRING SIZES

■NOTES:

There are many chainring sizes, so take your old stuff to a bike shop when buying replacements, or take careful measurements to ensure you get the right size.

You may need to remove the cranks (see page G7) to replace the outer & middle chainrings, and definitely for the small one.

Steel bolts can be tightened tighter and are less likely to thread or seize than the (softer) alloy bolts.

Chainring bolts can be the cause of creaking - if this is the case, undo them, grease and retighten.

TOP TIP: If weight isn't a major issue with you, but replacement costs are, use steel chainrings as they are more hard wearing than aluminium chainrings.

Chainrings fit on to the cranks and turn the chain. They come in different sizes (number of teeth) and numbers of bolt-holes. Generally they bolt on to the crank with chainring bolts, either straight on to 'tabs' on the crank, or a removable 'spider' (that can be replaced if bent).

The 'bolt circle diameter' (BCD) of chainrings can vary, so make sure any replacements are the correct size. There are two measurements, the outer BCD (for middle and outer chainrings) and the inner BCD for the inner chainring. Most new four arm cranks have a outer BCD of 104mm and 64mm inner BCD. Five arm 'compact drive' cranks have an outer BCD of 94mm and 58mm for the inner ring, while XTR and older 'standard drive' five arm cranks have an outer BCD of 110mm and inner BCD of 74mm.

TOOLS: TL-FC20 or a flat screwdriver, 5 & 8mm hex keys.

02

03

01

02A

Line-up

04

01 CHAIN SUCK

Chain suck is a strange phenomenon whereby the chain doesn't release from the front small or middle chainring. Instead it wraps around it, where it can get jammed in the frame; when riding this means you will suddenly be unable to turn the pedals.

We don't need to tell you this can be a bit of a surprise, taking a bite out of the frame, or just getting wedged in between the chainring and chainstay. If the chain is stuck tight (especially if you carried on trying to pedal) use a screwdriver or similar to flex the chainring out and free the chain.

Inspect the chainrings and sort out any defects or replace if too far gone. Clean and lube the chain, and inspect it for any stiff links, or even try using a wider chain or thinner (steel) chainrings.

02 WORN CHAINRINGS

To assist shifting, chainrings usually have an assortment of shaped teeth, pins and ramps. To the untrained eye, this looks as if they are twisted or worn but they're really designed like that, honest!
When chainrings wear, they develop burrs and scratches, or even missing and hooked teeth (see pic 02). This is caused by being unevenly loaded by a stretched chain and will encourage the chain to skip or wrap around causing chainsuck. Replacing the chain at this stage is too late, as a new chain will still not sit happily on the worn chainrings. Chains should therefore be periodically checked for wear, and replaced when necessary.

02A SORTING OUT DEFECTS

Burrs can be carefully removed with a file, and bent teeth straightened with pliers. Pay special attention to the smaller sprockets as these tend to wear out quicker as they have less teeth across which to spread weight. If you do a lot of technical riding where the chainrings are in danger of being bent by hitting obstacles, the outer chainring can be replaced with a solid 'bash guard'.

03 REMOVING A CHAINRING

The outer and middle chain rings can often be replaced without removing the crank. Undo the outer chainring bolts with a 5mm hex key. The rear nuts may spin around, so hold them in place with a chainring bolt tool e.g. the Shimano TL-FC20 (see pic 03) or a screwdriver.

■NOTE: If you can't get the rings off, or need to take the granny ring off, remove the cranks (G7).

04 REPLACING A CHAINRING

When replacing the chainrings, look for a feature on the outer ring such as an extended pin, designed to stop the chain falling behind the crank or an inward facing tooth that lines up with the crank arm (see pic 04). Ensure all shifting ramps are on the 'inside', and try and make any writing stamped in to the rings lines up. Grease or threadlock the bolts and screw gently back into position.

■NOTE: Tighten one bolt a bit, then the one opposite, then the opposite but one, and continue round, to prevent the chainrings from bending.

THE BOTTOM BRACKET (abbreviated to BB).

This component is the big axle and bearings on which the cranks spin. It supports most of your weight when you're standing and it's in the firing line of plenty of mud. Older style cup and cone BBs had an axle, two cups and two sets of bearings. These often went out of adjustment and have pretty much been replaced by sealed BBs that you will use 'till they go wobbly or grindy' and then just replace the whole thing.

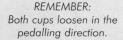

01 HOLLOWTECH II   SQUARE TAPER   ISIS DRIVE (10 SPLINES)   SHIMANO OCTALINK (8 SPLINES)   1996-2002 SHIMANO XTR (8 SPLINES)

REMEMBER:
Both cups loosen in the pedalling direction.

A   B   C

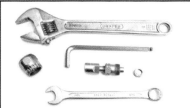

02   03   04   05

CARTRIDGE BOTTOM BRACKET

A: Non-driveside / free-cup
B: Axle - usually steel, but also available in light-weight titanium
C: Driveside / fixed cup.
The BB usually comes in two parts: the bearing unit and axle attached to the fixed cup (on the driveside) and the removable cup (on the non driveside). The cups screw into the threads in the BB shell of the frame, and require a special tool to fit the splines inside the cup.

CREAKING

Check it's not coming from the pedals, loose chainring bolts, etc. On a new BB it may be paint in between the driveside cup and the shell, or the shells outside edge isn't parallel to the BB threads - take to a bike shop for facing. If it's an old BB, remove it, clean, and grease the threads (and inside the cups).

CHAINLINE

For the gears to operate perfectly & noiselessly, the middle (or only) chainring should be in line with the middle rear sprocket, which should in theory be parallel with the vertical plane of the bike. On production bikes with their original kit the chainline is usually fine and nothing to worry about.

TOOLS: 8mm hex key, crank puller, BB tool, large adjustable spanner, grease.

Clean and re-grease the threads every 6 months to prolong the life of your BB and stop it getting stuck in.

01: REPLACEMENT INSTRUCTIONS

First remove the cranks (see G7) and look at 01 above to work out which sort of BB system you need to use. The (various) splined designs are popular as they are stiffer, stronger and give better contact than the old square taper design.

02: MEASURE UP

Measure the 'BB shell' of the frame to get the 'shell width' (68 or 73mm). Also measure the axle width (ISIS and Octalink are 113mm, but square taper designs vary e.g. 110 or 113mm). You will need to quote these numbers when you buy the replacement.

03: OUT WITH THE OLD

Attach a BB tool to the teeth inside the left / non-driveside cup. It can help to hold the tool in place with a washer and the crank bolt to prevent slippage. Attach a large adjustable spanner to the tool and undo anti-clockwise to remove the BB - if it is very stiff use some pipe over the spanner for more leverage.

■ **NOTE:** If you have trouble removing the BB, spray a penetrating lube e.g. GPO around the cups and down the seat-tube and leave overnight. If it still doesn't move, put the BB tool (splines up) in a vice, remove the bikes wheels and place the cup onto the tool and turn the whole frame.

Next, remove the right / driveside cup with the BB tool (clockwise), and remove the main BB unit.

04: CLEAN OUT

Clean out the threads in the BB shell with a rag and check they are in good condition (no crossed threads, or slivers of metal). Next apply some clean grease to the threads.

■ **NOTE:** A shop can 'chase' the threads if they've become corroded or damaged.- this may also be needed on a new frame to remove any paint.

05: IN WITH THE NEW

Grease the threads and inside the BB cup then work out which side of the BB is left and right (usually printed L + R), and screw the non drive-side (L) cup clockwise 2 turns by hand (this should be easy to do, any resistance indicates that the threads are damaged). Now screw in the

driveside (R) and main body of the BB (anti-clockwise). Tighten up the driveside (R) cup really hard (around 50-70NM) until the 'lip' is flush with the frame, then tighten the left side (there is no lip here) and put the cranks back on.

■ NOTE: Race Face X-Type cranks are very similar to Shimano Hollowtech cranks, but the spindle is attached to the non-driveside crankarm.

INSTALLING HOLLOWTECH (II) BOTTOM BRACKETS & CRANKS

■ **NOTE:** Before installing Hollowtech cranks and BBs, it is very important to have the threads tapped and BB shell 'faced' (by a good bike shop), as the bearings run on the outside of the frame.

01: Grease the BB shell face and threads then fit the internal plastic sleeve to the right (R) cup and insert this into the driveside of the BB shell (anti-clockwise) - fit 1 spacer on a 73mm BB shell or 2 on a 68mm (less one spacer if using an E-type mech).

02: Install the left (L) cup (add one spacer on 68mm shells) on the non-driveside (and the rubber compression seals on XTR), and tighten both cups (clockwise) to 35-50 Nm, using the specialist tool.

03: Now put the spindle (attached to the crank) through the driveside - if it catches the shell requires machining. Now attach the LH crank - see G7 for more info.

01   Spacers

02

03

MAINTENANCE

G9

The rear mech moves the chain over the rear sprockets and takes up any slack in the chain. Keep it clean and lubed to help prolong it's life.

Although it looks fiddly, setting up a rear mech is pretty straight forward, and by following these instructions, sweet, smooth shifting will be yours.

QUICK FIX GUIDE:

Constant clicking in low gears - the jockey wheel may be hitting the cassette - adjust the B-screw.

Won't shift into smaller sprockets - check cables are clean and lubed, if so - turn the barrel adjuster clockwise.

Won't shift into smallest sprocket - check high screw limit

Won't shift into larger sprockets - turn barrel adjuster anticlockwise

Won't shift into biggest sprocket - check low screw limit

Mech isn't working - check the cable is fastened securely at the cable fixing bolt, and check the mech and jockey wheels for wear.

B-SCREW: Alters the distance between the jockey wheel and cogs. For optimum shifting get them as close as possible, but not touching. With the chain on the small chainring and largest cog, turn the cranks backwards while turning the B-screw anticlockwise, then do the same with the chain on the smallest cog.

MAINTENANCE

A: FIXING HEX BOLT
B: HIGH & LOW LIMIT SCREWS
C: BARREL ADJUSTER
D: CABLE STOP BOLT.
E: LOWER (tension) JOCKEY WHEEL
F: TOP (guide) JOCKEY WHEEL
G: (REPLACEABLE) GEAR HANGER
H: B-SCREW

REMOVING / INSTALLING THE MECH

To remove the rear mech without breaking the chain, have the chain on the small ring at the front and back. Unscrew the tension screw, loosen the cable bolt and remove the cable from the mech. Undo (with a hex key) and remove the lower jockey wheel. Slide the 2 halves of the cage apart to remove the chain, then undo the fixing bolt with a 6mm hex key.

Follow these steps in reverse to fit a new mech. Check the top jockey is still tight at the end (as it can come loose) and grease the mounting bolt.

01

02

03

04

TOP TIP: If the gears become noisy use the barrel adjuster on the rear mech (see pic 04) to adjust the cable tension.

■ **NOTE:** Jockey wheels can be removed and cleaned or replaced if they become hard to turn or the teeth are sharp. They are not identical though - the upper one usually has a small amount of 'play' to allow it to centre easily over a sprocket, while the lower wheel is relatively rigid.

ADJUSTING THE REAR MECH

For this job you will need to get the back wheel off the ground, so you can spin the cranks to check your adjustments.

Start with the limit screws - these decide how far your derailleur can move in and out, and so stop the chain falling over the biggest sprockets into the spokes or off the smallest sprockets in to the frame; they are usually as follows:

Top (H) screw controls the limit for high gears (high gear = small sprockets)

Low (L) screw, controls the limit for low gears (low gears = big sprockets)

TOP TIP: Start with the rear gear cable disconnected (as it's easier when their is no tension in the rear gear cable).

01: HIGH-GEAR LIMIT SCREW

First, align the top jockey wheel with the small sprocket. Screw the barrel adjuster in and shift the chain to the large chainring at the front. Tightening the screw with a small screwdriver (clockwise) moves the derailleur towards the sprockets, and loosening it moves it towards the frame.

Check your adjustments by spinning the cranks clockwise and with your hand push the derailleur towards the bigger cogs then releasing. The chain should fall quickly onto the smallest sprocket, but not over-shift into the frame or be noisy.

02: LOW-GEAR LIMIT SCREW

Align the jockey wheels with the largest sprocket. Shift the chain to the smallest chainring. Tightening the screw moves the derailleur nearer the sprockets, and loosening it moves it towards the wheel.

Check your adjustments by spinning the cranks clockwise and very carefully pushing the rear derailleur toward the wheel. The chain should be able to reach the largest sprocket, but not fall in to the spokes of the wheel.

03: CABLE SLACK

Shift the chain into the largest chainring at the front and click the rear shifter into the high gear position i.e. smallest cog (keep clicking until it won't let out any more cable). Tighten any barrel adjusters on the rear derailleur and rear shift-lever (clockwise), then back off 1 turn to give you some adjustment. Pull the cable tight with some pliers, be sure it is sitting in the grove and tighten down the cable fixing bolt.

04: INDEXING GEARS

Shift up one gear from the smallest sprocket while turning the pedals. The chain should quickly shift on to the next sprocket. If it doesn't shift or is slow, tighten the cable by turning a barrel adjuster 1/4 turn anticlockwise. The barrel adjustor on the rear mech is the easiest to use, but some e.g. SRAM twist Shift don't have one, so use the one at the lever. Shift back to the highest gear - the chain should go back - if it doesn't loosen the cable slightly. Keep going back and fourth between the two smallest sprockets until the chain shifts sweetly.

FINALLY make sure it works in all gears. Shift into the middle chain-ring at the front. Shift up and down through the complete range of gears, making subtle adjustments by tightening the cable (anticlockwise) if the chain is reluctant to shift to a bigger sprocket or loosening it (clockwise) if the chain shifts slowly to smaller sprockets.

Test out every front chainring and rear sprocket combination - it should shift sweetly in all but the most crossed over gears i.e. big chainring and big sprockets or small chainring and small sprockets.

STILL NO JOY? Check the cables aren't dirty, the chain and cassette aren't worn, the chain is clean, lubed & free of stiff links, the derailleur hanger isn't bent OR the rear mech isn't bent or worn and wobbly around it's pivots.

THE FRONT MECH

This moves the chain between the front chainrings. Keep it clean and lubed to help prolong it's life. To check the mech, hold the cage and try moving it gently - if it wobbles it is probably best to start looking for a replacement. Some models are (allegedly) serviceable, but it's usually better just to get a new one - what a wasteful society we inhabit.

DIFFERENT DESIGNS

Although it looks simple enough, you need to know the clamp size, if it's a top or bottom pull, and the number of gears it's designed for e.g. 7, 8 or 9.

Band size: Most designs attach to the frames seat tube with a band, and as seat tube diameters vary, so do the front mech clamp sizes - the three common sizes are; 28.6, 31.8, and 34.9mm.

Other designs: Some Shimano derailleurs attach to the bottom bracket, and either rest against the frame or have a special attachment point on the frame. Rotational and height adjustments are limited, and they only work with chainrings of specific sizes. Limit screw and cable tension adjustments can be performed as for regular, band clamp derailleurs.

Top or bottom pull: Where does the cable enter the derailleur? If the cable runs along the top tube and enters the mech from above you need a top pull mech, and if the cable runs along the downtube, and enters the mech from below, you require a bottom pull mech. However, some designs of derailleurs e.g. the new Shimano XT, are 'dual pull' enable the cable to be routed through the top or bottom.

■ **NOTE:** The 'top pull' mech are meant to have a lighter action and provide better clearance on some full suspension designs, while the conventional 'bottom pull' fits more frames and is slightly less affected by dirt.

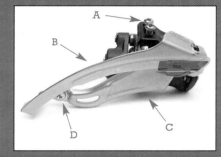

CONVENTIONAL FRONT MECH

A: HIGH & LOW LIMIT SCREWS
B: OUTER CAGE
C: INNER CAGE
D: CAGE TAIL SCREW
E: CABLE CLAMP BOLT (out of view on conventional mech above)

TOP PULL FRONT MECH (below)

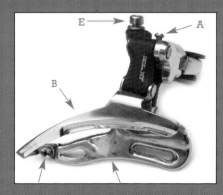

INSTALLING AND ADJUSTING (BAND TYPE) FRONT DERAILLEURS

01: ATTACH AND POSITION
Clamp the band of the front derailleur around the seat tube and do up the bolt loosely. Route the chain through the derailleur either by undoing the cage tail screw or if there isn't one, by breaking the chain and feeding it through.

Next adjust the height of the derailleur so that the outer cage passes between 1 and 2 mm of the large chainring with the chain on it (you'll have to push the derailleur into position by hand).

■ **NOTE:** New mechs will usually come with stickers on, showing where the chainrings should go.

Now move the derailleur so that, when viewed from above, the inward sides of the cage are parallel to the chainrings. Move the shift lever to the lowest gear then attach the gear cable.

■ **NOTE:** Shimano recommends that the chain rubs the front mechs inner plate lightly, when in the middle ring and largest sprocket, or is 1/2mm away when on the smallest chainring and largest cog.

02: 'L' (LOW-GEAR) LIMIT SCREW
Leave or let the cable out. Shift between the middle & inner chainrings while in the large cog and spin the cranks clockwise.

- If the chain drops off the inner ring on to the frame, tighten the limit screw (clockwise) using subtle adjustments (half or quarter turn) at a time.
- If the chain does not easily shift on to the inner ring, loosen the screw (anticlockwise).

03: 'H' (HIGH-GEAR) LIMIT SCREW
Again make subtle adjustments, this time shift between the middle and outer chainrings, while in the smallest sprocket.

- If the chain over-shifts i.e. the chain falls off the outer chainring - tighten the limit screw (clockwise).
- If the chain cannot shift to the outer chain-ring, (or is reluctant to do so), loosen the limit screw (anticlockwise).

04: CABLE TENSION
Shift to the lowest chainring and take up any slack in the cable and clamp it down. Use the shifter barrel adjuster to ensure the cable is tight enough so the mech moves as soon as the shifter is pushed, but still shifts easily to the inner ring.

QUICK FIX GUIDE:

CHAIN FALLS OFF:
The outer ring - turn high screw clockwise 1/4 turn
The frame side - turn the low screw clockwise 1/2 turn

POOR SHIFTING:
Between mid to large - turn high screw anti-clockwise 1/8 turn
Between mid to small - turn low screw anti-clockwise 1/4 turn or turn barrel adjuster clockwise
Between big to middle - turn barrel adjuster clockwise
Won't shift from small to middle - turn barrel adjuster anticlockwise
Chain misses mid ring when coming from largest - turn the cable barrel adjuster (by the gear shifters) anti-clockwise 1 or 2 turns
Won't go into big ring - turn barrel adjuster and/or high limit screw anti-clockwise
Won't go into big ring - the cable needs to be taught when in the small chainring - so tighten it
General bad and erratic shifting - clean, lube or replace cable - check for play in the mech

CHAIN TOUCHES / RUBS:
Inner mech plate on largest ring - turn top screw clockwise 1/8 turn
Outer mech plate on largest ring - turn top screw anti-clockwise 1/8 turn and check the cage alignment
Inner plate when on mid ring and largest sprocket - turn cable barrel adjuster clockwise 1 turn
Mech rubs small ring - turn low limit screw anticlockwise

MAINTENANCE

G11

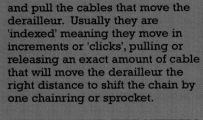

01

02

03

04

01	RAPIDFIRE
02	GRIPSHIFT
03	THUMBSHIFTERS
04	DUAL CONTROL

Shift levers attach to the handlebars and pull the cables that move the derailleur. Usually they are 'indexed' meaning they move in increments or 'clicks', pulling or releasing an exact amount of cable that will move the derailleur the right distance to shift the chain by one chainring or sprocket.

SHIMANO RAPID-FIRE SHIFTERS

A: Barrel Adjustor
B: Gear Indicator
C: Bar clamp
D: Gear shift levers

Most recent bikes have Shimano 'Rapid Fire Plus' shifters where a large paddle operated by the thumb pulls cable and a smaller trigger operated by the first finger releases it. If the gear lever is joined to the brake lever, this is a 'STI' unit (Shimano Total Integration).

Many older bikes feature the near-indestructible thumb-shifters made by Shimano and Suntour, or the original **"Rapid Fire Minus"** units, where both up and down shifts are performed with buttons operated by the thumb.

Shimano also produce dual control shifters (see picture 04, left), where the brake levers are moved to change gears (much like road bikes often use).

INNER CABLE REPLACEMENT (for Rapid-Fire, Thumb-Shifters and many older, mystery shifters) - see the next page for Twist Grip cable replacement.

Fitting most shift-levers is simply a matter of removing the grips and old shifters, (see the bars and grips on page M4) sliding on the new shifters and brake levers (remembering most shifters mount inboard of the brake levers, while twist grip shifters go outboard). Next you will have to plumb in the cables (see below).

MAINTENANCE

TOOLS: 5mm hex key, Cable cutters, Screwdriver.

Shimano Rapid Fire shifters are both amazingly durable and very fiddly inside (so don't take them apart!). When shifting becomes problematic it is often down to dirty, kinked or frayed cables. Therefore keep the cables clean and lubed, and replace the cable when it becomes frayed or rusty.

Thumb-Shifters should be taken off their clamps and cleaned occasionally.

01: DETACH THE OLD CABLES

First shift gear so that the maximum amount of cable is released (highest gear on rear shifter, lowest at the front). Detach the cable from the derailleur and snip off the end cap.

02A: PULL OUT THE CABLE

If there is a plastic screw covering the cable-entry hole on the shifter remove it with a screwdriver - you will now be able to push the cable out.

02B: Some XT and XTR Rapid-fire shifters made after 1996 have a little hatch covering the cable entry port.
To get in to it, undo the two tiny crosshead screws with a small screwdriver - it can help to loosen the clamp bolt on the shifter and turn it around the bar so that the cover is facing upward.

03: POP IN NEW CABLE

Look through the cable entry hole to see where the cable head sits. Push the new cable through until the cable head is seated. (XT & XTR - slot the new cable into position).

Pull on the cable and operate the shifter to check that it is pulling and releasing cable OK.

04: ROUTE THE INNER CABLE

Feed the inner section through the outer sections adding cable donuts (rubber washers) where the inner cable is exposed, and attach it to the rear derailleur. Ensure the outer cables are seated in the cable stops, and then tune in the gears. Now crimp a cable cap on the end of the cable to stop it fraying

01

02A

02B

03

04

GRIPSHIFT SHIFTERS:

Grip shifters mount to the handlebars between the grips and brake levers. The rider grips the shifter body and rotates it to shift between gears - towards them to lower gear and away for a higher gear. The advantages of these over other types of shifters is that they allow constant grip on the handlebars even when changing gear and are lighter.

■ **NOTE:** There have been a few different versions over time so the cable installation may vary. The modern lever has an access hole under a plastic or rubber cover. Some may have a small hex head screw over the cable end, or a small clip which needs to be pried back with a small screwdriver

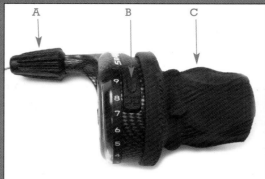

A: Barrel adjuster
B: Cable cover
C: Shifter body

CABLE REPLACEMENT

SRAM (Grip shift) and SACHS Twist shifters from 1998 and on have a cable hole cover, making changing the cables very easy. Pre 1998 Grip shifters require taking apart to change the cable.

01: Disconnect the cable at the derailleur and cut off the end cap. Then twist the shifters to let out the cable i.e. '8 or 9' on the rear and '1' on the front.

02: Models will vary on how you expose the cable head, so either:

lift the cable hole cover and use a small screwdriver to lift the tab that stops the cable end coming out (see pic 02).

OR

slide the cover aside to view the cable on from shifters or remove the 2.5mm hex screw to reveal the cable head on rear shifters.

OR

peel back the corner of the rubber grip to expose the cable head.

03: Push / pull the old cable out then grease and thread the new cable in (through the cable outers and guides).

04: Replace the hex screw if applicable and pop the cable cover back down.

Pull the new cable tight and (after making sure you are still in the highest gear i.e. smallest sprocket or smallest chainring) clamp the cable to the derailleur and cut off the excess cable. Finally, adjust the gears - see page G10 / G11 for more information.

■ **NOTE:** With Pre 1998 Grip shifters you will probably have to remove the grips and undo the screw holding the triangular cover to slide the shifter apart. While it is all apart clean everything up with a special gripshift solvent or soapy water and a toothbrush or similar) then apply some silicon grease to touching surfaces.

TOOLS: Pliers, cable cutters, hex keys.

■ **NOTE:** Make sure you use the 1.1mm cable (not the more commonly available 1.2mm).

TOP TIP: Grip shift gearshifters can be a good idea for female riders, as they are more accommodating for smaller hands.

■**NOTE:** If you use twist-grip shifters, it is important that the brake lever is designed to reach over the shifter, so that your fingers can reach the lever.

01

03

02

04

CABLES

■ **NOTE:** Don't use brake cable outers in place of gear cable outers, as they can compress and change length when bent.

TOP TIP: Protect the frames paintwork from the outer cable rubbing it, by using frame protection stickers (or electrical insulation tape) - clean the frame with meths first.

Although they may seem like a very lowly item, neither expensive nor very exciting, cables are of prime importance when it comes to getting your gears to shift smoothly.

Cables consist of the 'inner wire' and an 'outer', which is designed to compress as little as possible. Gear 'outer' cables can be recognised by the lengthways steel strands running down them (brake cables have coiled steel strands).

A: Cable splayed open - notice the straight outer wire and low friction inner in which the gear cable lies.
B: Outer and inner cable
C: New cable outer with a 'ferrule'

For indexed gear systems to operate correctly, quality cables must be used (not brake outers). It is also more or less essential to use proper bike cable cutters - anything else will cause the inner cables to fray and make it hard to cut the outer cables straight.

At each end of a piece of outer a ferrule (a cap for the end of the cable housing) should be used; these contain seals that keep dirt out of the system. Inners should be tidied up with an end cap. Where the inner cable is exposed, small rubber donuts should be placed over the cable to stop it slapping the frame and damaging the paint.

TOOLS: Cable cutters (bike specific), 5mm hex key, small screwdriver, and pliers.

CABLE MAINTENANCE

The majority of poor gear shifting is caused by dirty, rusty, or frayed cables. As cables age and get dirty, it gets harder for the shifter to pull the cable, (felt by more thumb force being required) and harder for the springs in the derailleur to take up the slack (shifts to smaller sprockets are sluggish).

■ **NOTE:** Often a new set of cables is the cheapest performance hop up you can make to your bike.

Ideally you should clean cables before they get to this state - by shifting the chain to the biggest cog and largest chainring, then (without pedalling) operate both shifters to create slack in the cable. Now pop the outer cables out of their stops and slide back to reveal the inner cable, spray with a light lube e.g. TF2, wipe with a rag, spray some lube down the outer then reposition the outer cables.

If you have let things get too bad you will probably need to replace the cables.

POSH STUFF!!

BETTER SEALED CABLES
If you're fed up with cables becoming dirty on mucky rides, try using sealed cables with additional liners such as Ride-On 'Gore-Tex' or Avid 'Flak Jackets'. They are more expensive and require careful installation, but can reward you with sweeter shifting for longer.

AIR ASSISTED SHIFTING
For a number of years, Shimano has been experimenting with pneumatic shifting - powered by a can of air attached to the bike.

The shifting is lightning fast but unfortunately Shimano has not declared the system ready for general use. A few pro riders have sets, and a few were sold (for $1,400), but the rest of us will have to wait.

01: Cut the outer cable to length
If you're replacing the old cable, cut identical length segments to the one you're replacing.

If you don't have this as a guide, link the cable stops with a smooth curves of the outer, ensuring that they are not kinked or stretch when the bars are turned, or affected by the suspension moving.

01

02: Open Up
When you cut the outer cable the liner inside gets squashed shut. Use something pointy to poke inside the inner lining to open it up. Next, fit a ferrule (cap for the end of the cable outer).

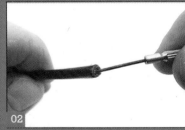

02

03: Route Down
Fit the inner cable in to the shifter (see previous page), then thread it through the outer and fit donuts to exposed sections of cable.

Take up the slack in the cable with some pliers, then tighten the cable clamp bolt on the derailleur. Pull the cable to eliminate stretch, then tune in the derailleur (see G10/11).

03

MAINTENANCE

WHY GO SINGLESPEED?

Taking all but one of the gears off your bike, or even specially going out and buying a 1-speed machine may seem like an odd thing to do, but it has it's advantages: low weight, less clutter, fewer mechanical problems, quieter, less affected by mud, cheaper way to build a hack bike, looks cool, no noisy chain slap, and your brain is less occupied with changing gears, and more focused on the actual riding.

For some people, nothing can beat the super-responsive & reliable feel of a single-speed, and while the one gear may lead to some frenzied pedal spinning when trying to keep up on flat tarmac, the inevitably aggressive climbing style required may make you first to the top of every hill.

IS IT FOR ME?

Admittedly the strain of getting up those hills may not be suitable for people with problematic knees or backs, so think twice if you've had a problem here. However, if you think the pros outweigh the cons and would like to give single-speeding a go, but don't want to spend a lot of money, follow our D.I.Y. guide to going singlespeed.

CONVERTING TO SINGLESPEED

First, think about how you're going to un-gear your bike. Read through all the steps, decide on your chain-tensioning method, and work out what gear to run - most riders go for a 2:1 ratio, e.g. 32 teeth chain-ring and 16 teeth rear sprocket. Remove those subversive shifters, derailleur, cables, cassette and other superfluous gear from your bike. Now follow the next 3 steps - either doing it properly, or if finances are tight (or you are) and you might want to change back to gears when your knees give out, use the bodge it (B) guide.

01: CHAINRING (PROPER)

A popular add on is a bash-guard to protect the chainring. It allows the use of regular chainring bolts and also attempts more ambitious log-crossings without tooth-loss misery.

■ **NOTE:** Many singlespeeds are set up with longer-than-normal crank arms (e.g. 180mm instead of usual 175mm) for improved leverage for climbing.

Male   Female

01B: CHAINRING (BODGE)

Remove the front chainrings, and replace with a single ring. Profiled teeth and shifting ramps aren't really any good, so go for a chainring with plain teeth.

■ **NOTE:** You'll usually need shorter (BMX) chainring bolts or you could file down the 'female' side of a set of regular bolts (see above).

02: HUB / FREEWHEEL (PROPER)

Use a screw-on hub that will accept a singlespeed BMX style freewheel. There are many hubs designed for singlespeed MTBs available.

Alternatively, use an old BMX or road hub, rebuilding it with a MTB axle and spacing it to be compatible with the 135mm dropout spacing of a MTB. Some manufacturers offer singlespeed cassette hubs, which have superior seals and freewheel mechanisms (but at a price).

02B: HUB / FREEWHEEL (BODGE)

The most popular option for hubs (usually involving the least investment) is to use a Shimano style cassette hub and a single sprocket with spacers. This can be obtained in a kit from single-speed friendly manufacturers - use a cassette lockring to hold it in place.

Alternatively use the spacers from old cassettes, file the heads off the rivets on the back and pull apart, or try using some plastic piping e.g. a drain pipe of the right diameter. Now line up the rear sprocket with the front chainring - this gives a good chainline to keep things running smoothly and quietly.

03: CHAIN TENSIONING (PROPER)

Horizontal BMX-style track ends / drop-outs allow the wheel to be slid back to tighten the chain, and so do some old frames with forward-facing dropouts. If wheel slippage is a problem, try using chain tugs or tapping a thread into the axle and using bolts instead of a quick release.

■ **NOTE:** Elliptical bottom brackets do away with the 'faff' of moving the wheel in the drop-outs.

03B: CHAIN TENSIONING (BODGE)

If you have a regular bike with vertical drop-outs you cannot tension the chain by moving the wheel forwards of backwards. If you're lucky, you may be able to get the chain to the right length without further palaver. Otherwise, use a chain tensioner or bodge one out of an old rear mech - use the 'H' screw or put a small bit of cable in the mech and adjust with the barrel adjuster to adjust the jockey wheels.

TOP TIP: You may also want to get a **different chain e.g. a BMX change as they are tougher and stretches less.**

DISC BRAKES ON SINGLESPEEDS

Fitting a disc brake to a regular frame using a chain tensioner is easy, but with specific singlespeed bikes it can be a fiddle.

If the rear wheel moves to tension the chain, the disc calliper must also move. Designs that enable this include a slotted disc tab (pic A), a moving tension arm, or an elliptic BB shell (pic B), where the BB can be moved to tension the chain, thus allowing the use of regular drop-outs and disc brakes.

MAINTENANCE: BRAKES

Brakes MAINTENANCE
SECTION

This section will bring your riding to a halt. Your brakes need to perform well for obvious reasons, but they will also allow you to ride faster, because to ride faster you need to be able to stop faster. This section explains how to set-up and service V-brakes and the ever more popular disc brakes (hydraulic and cable operated) to get the optimum performance from them.

BRAKE LEVERS & CABLES

A: **Shimano LX** - slide the leverage screw between H & L.
B: **Shimano XT** - add or remove the 'half moon' washers.
C: **Shimano XTR** - wind the small screw in or out.
D: **Avid** - often a thumbscrew protruding from front of the lever, or move a plastic spacer.

In the UK, bikes are set up so the right lever controls the front brake and the left lever for the rear, while Americans and mainland Europeans tend to go right / rear, left / front - we just love to be different.

Brake cables consist of an inner wire with a round nipple soldered on the end, and an outer of coiled steel with plastic casing and liner. The cable outers should be sealed with a ferrule at each end, and inners should be tidied up with lead end caps.

THE PERSONAL TOUCH

There are a couple of adjustments that you can make to your brake levers so that they suit your hands and preferences:

POWER: The leverage (mechanical advantage) of the lever can be adjusted. Moving the cable pivot nearer the bar gives more 'feel' and power, while moving it away gives more cable travel, but less power - the exact way this is done varies between designs (see A-D left).

LEVER REACH: You can usually adjust the distance between the brake lever and bars to fit your hand size better. This is usually done with a small grub-screw in the lever body (see pic 02), turned with a hex key to move the lever toward (anticlockwise) or away (clockwise) from the bar (you may need to change cable tension after doing this), or hydraulic brake levers usually have a small bolt behind the brake lever.

TOP TIP: Grip shift gearshifters (see G13) are more accommodating for smaller hands. However, as they go between the brake lever and the grip the lever needs to be designed to reach over the shifter, so that your fingers can reach the lever.

■NOTE: If you are upgrading from cantilever brakes to the modern 'V-brakes' you must use V-brake compatible levers, which pull around twice as much cable as cantilever levers. There are things called V-adaptors available which alter the amount of cable pulled io enable compatibility.

MAINTENANCE

Cables need to be kept clean and lubed or they will get sticky / stiff, and if you leave them for too long, they will need to be replaced. Most cables are Teflon lined although smoother (but more expensive) Gore-Tex cables are available. The end caps have small rubber seals inside them to keep the grime out, but (more expensive) sealed cables use a sheath to seal the inner cable from the brake lever to the brake, protecting it from grime to give you longer lasting, smooth braking.

TOP TIP: You can make your own sealed cables, by using outers all the way along the inner cable, and you will probably have to zip-tie the cable or file out the cable stops on the frame to secure it.

01 CLEANING CABLES

Unhook the noodle to release the brakes (see pic 01). Now remove the cable from the frame stops and slide the outer cable back to reveal the inner cable. Clean this inner cable with a rag and lightly lube it (with chain lube). Now replace everything and check they (how) work. If this has failed to improve things enough, you need to replace the cables.

02 REMOVING THE CABLE

Unhook the brakes, squeeze the cable cap end with pliers and remove it, undo the allen bolt (see pic02). Slide the rubber boot and noodle off the inner cable, now line up the slots in the barrel adjuster (see pic 02a) and unhook the nipple and pull the cable out. It is usually work replacing the cable outers as well as the inner cable, so remove these as well.

01
02

■NOTE: MTB brake cables have a barrel nipple (01) and a coiled steel outer (02).

03 ROUTING NEW CABLES

Cut the new cable outer (using bicycle specific cable cutters) to the desired length - use the old ones as a guide if they fitted well, i.e. didn't restrict the handlebar movement. Open-up the squashed ends of the outers, file down any burrs and squirt some grease into the cable outer and brake noodle. Next, fit the ferrules / outer caps onto the cable outer, except where they enter the noodles and crimp them down. Attach the inner cable nipple to the brake lever, feed the cable through the outers (but never pull a frayed inner cable through an outer, as it will destroy the lining). Pop the outer into the frame guides (see pic 03), and add cable donuts to the exposed sections of cable (see G12 pic 04). Feed the inner cable through the noodles, add the rubber boots and clamp in place. Snip off the cable leaving 3-5cm and tidy with a crimped-on end-cap.

TOP TIP: Standard cable cutters won't usually cut the cable or the outer housing cleanly. However, by heating up the cable with a lighter you may be able to get a good enough cut.

04 REMOVING SLACK IN THE CABLE

Cables stretch and brake pads wear, causing some slack in the cable. To tighten the cable, back the barrel adjuster (pic 04) away from the lever body (anticlockwise) then screw the locking washer against this to hold its position; if more than 4 turns are required, screw the barrel in and pull the cable taught at the brake end and re-clamp it.

01

02

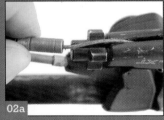
02a

03

04a

MAINTENANCE

Introduced in the mid 90's, V-brakes were the original name for Shimano's linear pull brakes; now, most straight arm pull cantilevers are referred to as V-brakes. When set-up correctly and in dry conditions, they provide good stopping power and are lightweight and simple.

V-brakes work by pulling the two parallel arms on either side of the wheel rim together and pinching the wheel rim. Springs push the arms back when the lever is released. The condition of your cables is critical to the performance of V-brakes - keep them and the noodles as clean as possible and replace when they get slow and full of friction.

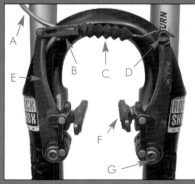

V-BRAKE
A: NOODLE
B: CRADLE
C: GAITER/BOOT
D: CABLE-CLAMP BOLT
E: BRAKE ARM
F: BRAKE PAD
G: BRAKE BOSS BOLT

01: REMOVE & FIT BRAKE ARMS
Remove old brakes by undoing the hex bolt into the brake bosses (pic 01), and clean and grease the brake bosses on the frame.

Slide each brake arm over the boss, ensuring the spring-pins fit into the middle or only hole (pic 01a). Grease the bolts and screw them in to the bosses.

02: FITTING & REMOVING PADS
The brake pads are changed by undoing the nut (with a 5mm hex key), on the brake arm. You can re-arrange the thin and thick concave washers to alter the spacing between the brake arms and wheel rim.

03: SETTING UP
Adjust the washers so that the brake arms are vertical when the pads engage - they should hit the rim straight and at the same height on both sides.

TOOLS: Hex keys, small cross-head screwdriver, long nose pliers.

05: CENTRING PADS
Most V-brakes have a spring tension adjustor at the base of the brake arm that may take a X-head screwdriver or small hex key. Adjust these screws so that the pads are the same distance from either rim and engage at the same time.

These use a metal brake shoe, which replacement rubber pads slide into. They come on high-end brakes or can be purchased separately and provide sharper braking, as well as cheaper pad replacements. Be careful not to wear down to the metal holders or they will erode the wheel rims.

To change the pads, remove the split pin (see pic 07) and slide out the old pad (thin nose pliers can help). Insert a new pad and line up the channel in it with the hole in the cartridge, and replace the pin. The 'closed' end of the pad must be oriented to the front of the bike, to stop the rubber insert slipping out when braking.

■**NOTE:** The deafening squealing noise that accompanies some riders down hills is often due to dirty or greasy wheel rims, pads or maybe an unlucky pad / rim combination. If you are sure all is clean of contamination it may be worth using a different brand of pads.

■**NOTE:** Disengage the brake springs and hold the brake arms in place with a rubber band to help your adjustments.

04: CLAMP THE CABLE
When the pad spacing and position is correct, tighten the nut with a 5mm hex key. Re-attach the springs, then attach cables, noodles (90° rear or 120° front) and rubber boots. Clamp the cable onto the brake arm, leaving 1-2mm clearance between brake pads and wheel rim.

■**NOTE:** Having the leading edge of the pad 2mm closer to the rim (toe-ing in) can help stop squealing brakes.

■**NOTE:** If there are no spring tension screws or they don't provide enough adjustment, un-hook the spring and bend it outwards - this will pull that arm further away from the wheel rim.

06: CHECK THEY WORK
Squeeze the brake levers a few times as hard as you can to eliminate cable stretch. Now (if necessary) undo the cable clamp bolt, pull the cable tight again and re-tighten the clamp bolt.

■**NOTE:** As brakes age the pivots can wear causing vibration and noise - either put up with it or replace them.

TOP TIP: Make sure the split pin in cartridge brakes don't stick out or it could wear/rip the tyre sidewall.

■**NOTE:** Brake pads can wear out very quickly e.g. after just one ride if the conditions are hilly, wet and gritty, so keep an eye on them.

DISC BRAKES

Disc brakes use a rotor attached to the wheel hub. When the rider pulls the brake lever the hydraulic fluid (or cable) pushes the pistons in the calliper, which in turn pushes the brake pads against the rotor, which slows the bike down.

Good disc brakes offer superior stopping power compared to conventional rim brakes. They have become very popular in the UK as they are suited to our wet and muddy climate as well as consistent braking in the wet or dry, no mud clogging between the tyres, frame and brakes, no dirty cables (for hydraulic discs), and no premature rim wear.

■ **NOTE:** A good set of brakes can actually make you ride faster - as you will have more confidence, and be able to brake later.

A: **LEVER**
B: **LEVER REACH ADJUST SCREW**
C: **RESERVOIR**
D: **BAR CLAMP**
E: **CALLIPER FIXING BOLT HOLES**
F: **BRAKE PADS**
G: **HYDRAULIC HOSE**
H: **BANJO**
I: **BLEED SCREW/NIPPLE**
J: **PAD RETENTION SCREW**

MECHANICAL or HYDRAULIC

Many budget systems are mechanical - using a regular brake cables and levers to activate the brake calliper. This system is simple and can work superbly, although the cables need to be kept clean, can stretch, and as the brake pads wear down, you will also need to manually adjust the pads closer to the rotor.

Most quality disc brakes are Hydraulic - meaning the brake lever pushes fluid down a hose to activate the brake calliper. The hose lines are sealed from dirt and water and are generally more efficient, powerful and provide a better 'feel' than mechanical systems, but they are also more expensive and fiddly to fit.

■ **NOTE:** While most systems on the market are 'open' systems, there are also some 'closed' systems available.

OPEN - have an expansion chamber which means they self adjust for pad wear and fluid expansion (caused by extensive use i.e. long downhills, which heats the fluid). The 'biting' point is decided by the volume of fluid.

CLOSED - these use springs inside the calliper to pull the pistons (and pads) apart. This design lets you fine tune the modulation and lever feel (usually by a thumbwheel on the brake lever), but it doesn't automatically adjust for pad wear or fluid expansion - so you have to adjust the pad-rotor distance manually, and they can 'pump up' if they get too hot.

BRAKE PADS

The brake pads are usually held apart by a spring, and held in the calliper with a clip and/or retaining pin (usually has a clip at one end to stop it undoing itself) - see page B6 for info on changing disc brake pads.

Disc brake pads tend to last considerably longer than rim brake pads, but must be changed when there is approximately 0.5mm of pad material remaining. If you wait too long and get down to the metal you will lose braking power, damage the rotors, and could heat up the fluid resulting in the system locking up.

Resin pads (fitted on many bikes) help to increase stopping power and reduce brakes heating up in hot, dry conditions. However, UK conditions are usually wet, muddy, and gritty, causing them to wear down incredibly quickly. Therefore it is best to switch to sintered pads (which contain copper to harden the pad) for longevity and increased power. However, these can be noisier, heat up causing pump up (especially on smaller volume systems), and may not be compatible with your brakes. Soft organic pads have great stopping power, but don't last and are usually best left for downhillers.

■ **NOTE:** Brake pads need to be bedded / burnt in to create a hard braking surface or they will quickly wear down. Do this by riding along then braking, spraying the rotor with water and repeat about 20-30 times before riding off-road.

OTHER 'BITS'

THE FLUID in hydraulic brakes will either use automotive brake fluid (usually given a number such as DOT 5.1) or mineral oil (which is more biodegradable). You MUST use the correct type for your brakes! The wrong stuff can damage the seals and cause the brakes to leak and fail (most likely when you most need them).

■ **NOTE:** Be very careful when using DOT fluid as it's nasty stuff: don't let it get on your skin or in your eyes and keep it away from painted surfaces and the brake pads and rotors.

PISTONS: Most systems use 2 pistons (aka pots) which push the pads to the rotor, although some brakes (usually on downhill bikes) use 4 or even 6 pistons to provide more power and a better 'feel'.

ROTOR SIZE is usually around 160mm for XC use, 200mm for downhill or heavy riders who require more stopping power. The holes / writing / patterns and wavy edges in the rotor makes them lighter, and cool down quicker, cope with mud etc better, as well as looking better.

■ **NOTE:** Use a specialist disc brake cleaner, isopropyl alcohol, or meths, but NOT white spirit, to clean the disc brake rotors.

■ **NOTE:** If you like to stand out from the crowd, Hope disc brake manufacturers will laser cut any text you may want, into your disc rotors - see www.hopetech.com for more details.

DISC BRAKES

The actual fitting of disc brakes onto the bike is fairly straight forward, but the wheel hubs and frame mounts must be disc brake compatible. You will also need to ensure that the disc brakes you buy will fit the style of the frame mounts on your frame and fork.

ARE YOU READY FOR DISC BRAKES?

our frame and forks will need **disc mounts** - most use the international standard (IS) attachment, but many (e.g. Manitou forks, some Trek, Gary Fisher, and Klein frames) use the Hayes post mount style, and some older exceptions may also exist. The IS mount uses two bolt holes on a plate aligned parallel to the brake rotor, making the alignment rely on the frame mounting alignment and using washers to get the spacing right. Hayes use a pair of bolt mounts perpendicular to the rotor face with a slotted mount on the calliper to enable sideways movement.

International standard   Hayes, post mount

our wheels must be **disc compatible**. They must be made with the spokes laced in the 3 or 4 crossed pattern (not radial!) and most disc rotors bolt on to the hub via the 6-bolt standard (44mm BCD). Some hubs (older Hope, King, XTR) use a spider to attach the disc while others use 4 (Coda) or 5 (Hope) bolts.

■ **NOTE**: It's rarely economical to have old rims built up with new hubs and spokes - so in most cases get a new set.

you are using **hydraulic discs** you will need separate gear shifters (unless you have the integrated XTR or XT gear / brake levers); mechanical discs simply need a standard V-brake lever and cable.

FITTING DISC BRAKES

01: ATTACH THE ROTOR
Look on the rotor to check the rotating direction (not super important - but Hope have the spokes curving with the direction of the wheel rotation, while Hayes, Magura & Shimano run them the opposite way) and put in place. Make sure the bolts (hex-heads or a TORX 25 bolt head) are clean and apply a drop of thread-lock to each. Tighten each bolt a bit at a time to avoid stripping bolts or warping the disc.

■ **NOTE**: Shimano use a system of flat 2-bolt washers and triangular bolts (see pic 01) - bend the washers over the bolts (if you can) to stop them loosening.

If using a 'spider' system - bolt the adaptor and disc in place with the appropriate tool - with Hope hubs it's a pin-spanner, while with 2003 XTR and some SRAM hubs, it's a cassette lockring remover tool.

02: ATTACH THE BRAKE LEVERS
Remove grips and old equipment and fit the new levers (see M4 for more info).

03: ATTACH THE CALLIPER
Make sure the pistons are fully retracted, using a hard flat object to push them back e.g. a plastic tyre lever (pic 03), then bolt the brake calliper onto the frame or forks (pic 03a) and centre the calliper over the rotor: If using international standard mounts, it's a matter of trial and error, using a combinations of different thicknesses of washers in between the frame / fork mounts and the calliper (see pic 03b) - a dab of grease holds them together, making them easier to handle. For post mounts, squeeze the lever to centre the disc, then tighten the calliper bolts.

■ **NOTE**: Paint built up on the mount surfaces can stop the calliper and disc lining up. Good bike shops can 'face' the mount with a special tool to enable perfect set-up.

04: ROUTING THE CABLE / HOSE
If your frame has no disc cable guides, use zip-ties or add-on hose guides (pic 04) that screw into the now obsolete cantilever brake bosses. The main thing is to make sure that the cable doesn't foul the wheels, get in your way, or rub on the frame (as it will damage the hose and the paint on the bikes frame.

Mechanical Brakes
Use continuous runs of cable outer and inner between the lever and calliper for both front and rear brakes. Wind in the calliper and brake barrel adjusters, then route the cable and clamp in place and cut off the excess cable to prevent it fouling the calliper - see page B7.

Hydraulic Brakes
Cut the hose / cable to a length that allows a smooth run from lever to calliper, through any guides on the frame and ensuring that the line cannot be fouled when the suspension compresses.

■ **NOTE**: The Hydraulic systems will use either automotive brake fluid (given a number such as DOT 5.1) or mineral oil. You MUST always use the correct fluid for your system, as the wrong one could damage the system leaving you with no brakes.

01

02

03

03a

Washers
03b

04

TOP TIP: Most brake levers will have a small screw to adjust the reach (the distance of the lever to the bar), to suit the size of your hands - see the picture of the lever page B4 or B2 for more information.

WHAT! NO DISC MOUNTS?
There are devices that bolt into the drop-outs and provide a disc mount are available (www.a2zcomponents.com). The torsion bar is a sensible but inelegant design that attaches at both the drop-out and cantilever brake stud, distributing the braking force and putting less stress on the drop-out area.

You could also get a welder (see page E10) to weld a mount on to the frame for you (see pic above). Check with your frame manufacturer to see if any of these devices affects the warranty.

Disc brakes are great! - they offer powerful braking even in our wet and muddy British conditions. However, this fantastic stopping power may become a thing of the past, the pads continually (and irritatingly) rub on disc rotor, and when you touch the brake levers the brakes start squealing loudly, making everyone's heads turn and dogs come running from miles around - but how do you keep your disc brakes working quietly and effectively?

FOR FURTHER INFO TRY THE MANUFACTURER'S WEBSITE:

www.avidbike.com
www.cannondale.com (Coda)
www.Clarks.co.uk
www.Diatech.co.uk
www.formula-brake.it
www.grimeca.com
www.hayesdiscbrake.com
www.hopetech.com
www.magura.com
www.promax-usa.com
www.shimano.com
www.suntour.com

■ **NOTE:** If the lever feels spongy / soft, air or water may have got into the hydraulic system. To rectify this you will need to 'bleed' the brakes - see page B8 for Hope disc brakes or B9 for Shimano disc brakes.

Formula and Hayes disc brakes both require a bleed kit (which should come with instructions. Formula uses a syringe to draw the fluid out through the lever bleed hole, while Hayes forces fluid from the calliper bleed nipple through the system and out at the lever.

MAINTENANCE

Cable disc brakes will need the same maintenance care as regular cable brakes i.e. regular cleaning and lubing - see page B2. Hydraulic brakes on the other hand, require very little maintenance as the system is sealed, so just keep the rotor clean and remove the pads now and again and rub them with an abrasive pad to remove any glaze. It is also recommended that you change the hydraulic fluid about every 4 years.

The performance of disc brakes is greatly reduced by contamination of the disc rotors or brake pads. Therefore it's very important that you are careful when using oil, spray lubes, brake fluid, and cleaning products, etc anywhere near them - even oil from your hands can effect them.

If your disc brake rotors are dirty, clean them with a specific disc brake cleaner, or isopropyl alcohol (try the chemists), or meths, but NOT white spirit. If the brake pads have been contaminated you can try rubbing them down, or using a cleaner on them also - for very badly contaminated pads, try soaking them in a cleaner, if this doesn't work, you'll have to bin them and be more careful next time. Also, don't touch the rotors, as the oil from your hands could affect braking performance, and the rotors also get very hot when used.

■ **NOTE:** A notchy feeling at the brake lever is often due to dirt becoming trapped around the pistons. Remove the brake lever and clean the pistons, then apply a tiny amount of brake fluid where they go in to the calliper.

REPLACING PADS

Disc brake pads usually last very well (see M32 for more info), but will need changing when the pad material is down to about 0.5mm - don't leave it until it gets to the metal backing or you will damage the rotors.

The pads are held in the calliper with a clip and/or retaining pin. Remove the clip if applicable and slide the retaining pin out (see pic 01) - this may use an hex key screw. Now remove the pads.

If using an 'Open' system, push back the brake pistons with a plastic tyre lever or similar (see pic 02) to make room for the new pad material. If the piston is stiff (with pads removed) pour some brake fluid on it and squeeze the lever gently to free it up. With a 'Closed' or mechanical system, back off the pad adjustor or cable tension withe the relevant adjuster.

Put the new pads in, making sure you get the correct type for your brakes as there are no 'standard' pads for disc brakes.

Assemble the pads and spring by facing the pads inwards, the spring between them, with the prongs either side of the pad material and resting on the material backing plate. Put it back into the calliper - the holes in the pads and spring should line up, and insert the retaining pin.

If using an 'Open' system, squeeze the brake lever a few times to return the pads to their correct position.

SQUEALING LIKE A PIG

* Disc brakes can refuse to reach full power, pads can rub irritatingly on the disc or squeal when you brake for a number of reasons:

* The pads may be vibrating against the piston head - put a small amount of high temperature grease e.g. copper slip on the back of the pad or chamfer the back edge of the pad at an angle (see pic 03).

* Dirt/brake dust build up on the calliper, pads, or fixing bolts - clean them.

* 'Lazy' piston (not moving freely) - put a small amount of (the correct type for your system) brake fluid on it to lube and free it up (see pic 04).

* Poorly aligned disc mounts /callipers, due to imprecise manufacture or thick / uneven paint - have the disc mounts of the frame / fork 'faced' by a bike shop.

* Contaminated rotors or pads - clean the rotor and/or clean or replace the pads (see pic 05).

* The calliper is not centred - re-centre the callipers - see B5 or B7.

* A flexible or loose disc mount or rotor - tighten all the mount and rotor bolts.

* Bent rotor - very carefully bend the disc back in to shape using a special tool (by Stan at www.no-tubes.com) or you could try bending it by hand or with pliers.

* File off the leading edge of the pad - effectively toeing the pads in (see pic 06).

CABLE DISC BRAKES

These are some very good cable (aka mechanical) disc brakes, which as well as being cheaper and easier to fit than hydraulic designs, you can also use your old V-brake levers and are pretty straight forward to fit, and adjust (once you know how).

SETTING UP CABLE DISC BRAKES

01: First, attach the disc rotor to the hub / wheel (see B5 for more info). Run the brake cable and outer all the way from the brake lever to the calliper, in a smooth line. Make sure the cable doesn't touch the front wheel when the fork compresses - you can buy special hose guides, but zip-ties are cheap and work.

■ **NOTE:** The front brake always has a continuous run of cable outer from the lever to calliper, but also doing it on the rear brake keeps it clean and gives a firmer feel.

02: Make any adjustments to the lever reach adjuster (see pic) before you attach the inner brake cable - doing it afterwards may affect the calliper set-up. Attach the brake cable to the brake lever and screw down the barrel adjuster on the brake lever (and on the calliper if it has one) - this will give you maximum adjustment to tighten the cable slack (as the pads wear).

03: Cable disc brakes usually have a fixed pad (inboard i.e. closest to the wheel) and one which moves (activated by the cable). Sometimes the fixed pad can be adjusted via a dial or hex key, to enable you to set the space between the pad and calliper (you will need to do this when the pads wear down as well). Wind the adjuster all the way out (usually anti-clockwise) to move the inboard brake pad away from the rotor, then turn back 1/2 a turn. If there is also a dial for the outer pad, do this one as well.

03a: If the pads don't offer any adjustment you'll need to use washers to position the calliper (centrally) over the rotor.

04: Lightly grease the cable and thread it through the cable outer / housing. Pull the cable tight and fasten the calliper cable bolt down. Pull the brake lever and check the pads engage the disc rotor - if they don't, loosen the cable clamp bolt and move the calliper arm further up the cable (this moves the outer pad closer to the rotor) and tighten the cable bolt back down, and re-check.

■ **NOTE:** For maximum power, the calliper arm should be at a right angle to the cable stop at the point the pads contact the disc.

05: Next pull the lever and hold it in and tighten the calliper mounting bolts (see pic 05) - the calliper should be centred over the disc rotor. Now turn the pad adjusters to create a small and equal amount of clearance between the pads and rotor, so the wheel spins without rubbing.

If the rotor is rubbing the brake pads or the gaps between the pads and rotor are uneven, loosen the calliper mounting bolts, reposition the calliper over the rotor and re-tighten the calliper mounting bolts.

Finally, cut off the excess cable so that it can't get caught in the rotor, and attach a cable cap end.

■ **NOTE:** As the brake pads wear down you will need to move the pads closer to the disc rotor. To move the outer pad closer, turn the brake lever barrel adjuster, and to move the inboard pad, turn the adjuster / dial at the brake calliper.

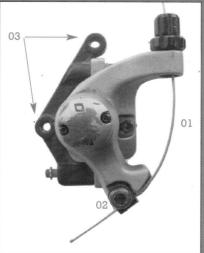

CABLE DISC BRAKES

01: Cable
02: Cable clamp bolt
03: Calliper mounting bolts

TOOLS: Cable cutters, hex keys, zip ties or cable guides.

01

03

04

02

Washers
03a

05

■ **NOTE:** Cable disc brakes have the same maintenance requirements as cable V-brakes i.e. keep them clean and lubed, and adjusted when the cable becomes stretched, or replaced when they become too worn, dirty, kinked, or frayed.

Hope make some very good disc brakes, which makes them a popular upgrade.

WARNING!
Hope disc brakes use DOT hydraulic fluid which is nasty stuff, so don't get it on your skin, paintwork or anything else you value. Wear hand and eye protection and avoid leaving the fluid exposed to the air, as it quickly absorbs water vapour.

■ NOTE: Hope's 'My little bleeder kit' bleed kit, helps bleed the brakes quickly, easily, with less messily and accurately (tel: 01282 851200).

This bleed kit works by attaching a hose to a bottle with DOT 5.1 and to a car tyre (at 20psi) valve, another hose from the bottle to the lever reservoir and another hose to the bleed nipple and another bottle which collects the fluid which is forced through the system from the reservoir.

DISCONNECTING THE HOSE

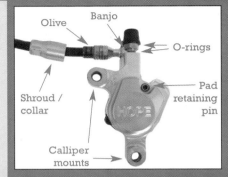

Olive · Banjo · O-rings · Shroud / collar · Pad retaining pin · Calliper mounts

If you need to shorten the length of the brake hose, or want to disconnect it in order to run it through hose guides, you will need to disconnect it at one end.

At the brake calliper end, unscrew the silver metal collar, and slide it down the hose. Prise the brass olive open with a thin, flat screwdriver, then ease the hose off the connector.

■ NOTE: If you need to replace the hose (e.g. because it is damaged or too short), it detaches at the brake lever end in an identical fashion.

CUT, ROUTE & CONNECT

Be careful with the open hose - don't let it swing about or it can spill fluid. To shorten the hose, make a clean cut using a sharp blade on a flat surface or use a guillotine-style hose cutter. You can now carefully route the hose through any guides on the frame. Next, push the hose back on to the connector, slide the brass olive back in to position and tighten the silver connector.

■ NOTE: If you have disconnected the hose you will need to bleed the system, as it will most likely have air inside it now - see above.

BLEEDING HOPE DISC BRAKES

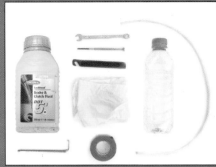

TOOLS: Small screwdriver, 2mm hex key, tape, hydraulic fluid, hose, tyre lever or similar, tissue, bottle, 8mm ring spanner.

01: REMOVE THE BRAKE PADS
Remove the brake pads and push the pistons back into the brake calliper with a tyre lever. Make sure they go in straight - they may become stuck if at an angle! Now put a spacer between the pistons to keep them apart until the end.

02: REMOVE RESERVOIR CAP
Position the brake lever so that the master cylinder is horizontal. Unscrew the tiny bolts on the master cylinder with a 2mm hex key, then remove the cylinder cap and rubber diaphragm.

03: ATTACH HOSES
Tape a small plastic bottle to the the frame or fork leg near the calliper.

Pull the plastic cap off the bleed nipple, then put an 8mm ring-spanner over it. Run a length of clear plastic hose from the nipple to the bottle to collect the waste brake fluid. The hose has to be a good fit on the nipple to prevent leakage - we bought a hose meant for fish tanks from a pet shop.

■ NOTE: Hope make a bleeding kit to make things easier (see the note in the left column for more information).

01

02

03

04

05

06

04: ADD HYDRAULIC FLUID
Fill the master cylinder with DOT 5.1 fluid. Open the bleed nipple a quarter turn (anti-clockwise) then gently squeeze the brake lever and hold it against the handlebar. Close the bleed nipple then release the brake lever. Repeat this until you only see fluid and no air bubbles coming out of the bleed nipple (remember to top up the master cylinder as it empties).

■ NOTE: To change all the fluid, fill the master cylinder 4 times.

05: REPLACE RESERVOIR CAP
Check that the pistons haven't pushed out - if necessary retract them again.

Surround the underside of the master cylinder with tissue paper or rag, and fill the reservoir to the brim with DOT 5.1 fluid. Replace the diaphragm and

cylinder cap then replace the screws - and be ready to mop up the fluid as it overflows when you tighten the screws / cap down.

06: REPLACE BRAKE PADS & TEST
Remove the spanner, hose, bottle and pad spacer. Make sure your hands are clean, then replace the brake pads and wheel.

Squeeze the lever 1/2cm repeatedly to allow the brake to move the pads closer to the rotor. Check the brake for any signs of leakage and ensure they work correctly before using the bike off road or in traffic.

BLEEDING SHIMANO HYDRAULIC DISC BRAKES

The popular hydraulic disc brakes from Shimano all use an 'open' system and can be maintained in the same way. When they were first introduced, only pre-cut lengths of hose were available, so you would have to determine the size you needed before purchase. Fortunately, Shimano have now produced cutable hose - much more convenient for installing for the first time.

Although mineral oil is not as nasty as DOT hydraulic fluid we still recommend wearing eye and hand protection and working in a well ventilated area. Also, remove the wheel and brake pads (and place a spacer between the pistons to stop them from closing together).

01: CUTTING THE HOSE
With the brake lever, calliper and rotor installed, determine the correct length of hose required. Either buy the correct pre-cut length or chop it down to size.

02: ATTACH THE HOSE
Position the olive about 5mms from the end of the hose, then insert the hose into the lever or calliper and screw down the sleeve with a 6mm spanner. This makes the olive expand and hold the hose in place, but don't over-tighten it or you will permanently deform the olive.

■ NOTE: Some designs may use a connection similar to Hope (see previous page) where the hose fits into a Banjo (as above). The Banjo then attaches to the lever or calliper. Check the O-ring seals are in their grooves either side of the Banjo hole and put the banjo bolt through and tighten it up to around 5-7NM torque.

03: POSITION THE BRAKE LEVERS
Adjust the brake lever so that it is parallel with the ground, then remove the screws from the reservoir and take the top off and rubber filler out.

04: BLEED HOSE AND CONTAINER
Put the bike in a stand, otherwise prop up securely. Attach a 6mm (box) spanner to the bleed nipple on the calliper, then attach a piece of hose leading into a plastic container to catch waste oil - tape this bottle / container to the bike to prevent spillage.

05: NIPPLE TWEAKING
Open the calliper bleed nipple 1/8 of a turn (anticlockwise). Fill the reservoir with Shimano mineral oil then gently squeeze the brake lever to push the fluid down the hose, and top up the reservoir as it empties - always have some fluid in the reservoir or air will also be sucked down into the hose.

Continue topping up the reservoir and squeezing the lever until you see oil coming out of the hose at the calliper end, then close the bleed valve.

06: SQUEEZE UNTIL STIFF
Gently squeeze the brake lever - any air in the system should bubble up to the reservoir. Shake the hose and tap the calliper to dislodge air.

Squeeze the lever again - it should be 'stiff'- i.e. doesn't move close to the bar.

07: FINAL NIPPLE SQUEEZE
Next, squeeze the brake lever and quickly open and shut the bleed nipple to remove any remaining air from the calliper. Repeat a couple of times, then close the nipple (3-5Nm Torque).

08: MOP UP LEAKAGES
Surround the reservoir with tissue paper then fill it to overflowing then replace the reservoir top back on and tighten down - catching any fluid over flow with the tissue / rag. Remove the pad spacers and replace the brake pads and wheel - and test they work.

Calliper mounts — Banjo — Pad retention screw — Bleed nipple (SHIMANO Deore)

TOOLS: 5mm hex key, knife, tape, bottle, mineral oil, 6mm spanner, and tissue.

01

Olive — Sleeve — Lever connection
02

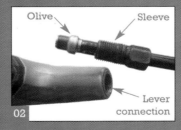
03

04

05

06

07

08

■ NOTE: The basic Shimano bleed kit (50ml of fluid, short piece of hose, and a small plastic bag is very expensive for what it is - you can easily get the bits yourself for much less.

TOP TIP: 'Back bleeding' is an effective method of bleeding, but it is messy and can contaminate parts if not done sensibly.

It involves attaching a hose to the calliper bleed nipple and forcing hydraulic fluid through the system (using a squeezy bottle or syringe with mineral oil in). The hydraulic fluid is then forced out at the reservoir on the lever which needs to be collected. This can be tricky, so it is advisable to remove or cover up rotors, brake pads and anything else you don't want covered in hydraulic fluid.

MAINTENANCE: MISC

Miscellaneous MAINTENANCE
SECTION

This section covers all the other bike parts that didn't fall into the other categories. It will enable you to service, adjust and replace handlebars, stems and headsets, keep your pedals turning, change your forks, service your suspension and try and get you home with trailside repairs.

WHEN YOU ARE OUT AND ABOUT

It's all well and good fixing your bike back at home in the warm and dry, with the correct tools, parts, etc, but the likelihood is that you will break something when out on a ride. If you can hobble back home or to the car, that's fine, but sometimes you might be miles from anywhere, without (m)any tools, and any which way to get you rolling is a blessing.

■ **NOTE:** These are just "get you home" bodges, which will require fixing properly once you get back from the ride.

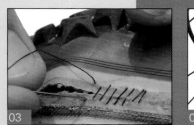

01: PUNCTURE:

If you have a puncture but no tubes or patches left, you could tie a knot or zip tie the tube, either side of the hole. Then replace the tube, inflate to around just 20psi and hobble home.

01A: If you don't have any puncture repair patches left but do have an old inner tube you don't mind cutting a section out of, you can use this as a puncture repair patch. Roughen this and the inner tube with the hole it, up and apply some vulcanising solution (aka glue) to them and stick them together.

02: SNAPPED MECH CABLES:

Front - You can continue in the small ring or tighten the inner adjustment screw to get it into the middle ring.

Alternatively, have the chain bypass the mech altogether (preferably by undoing the mech cage, rather than breaking and reconnecting the chain) and change between the chainrings manually.

02A: Rear - You can continue on the smallest cog, or move the chain to a larger cog and line up the mech by pushing it inwards with your hand and tightening the high adjustment screw - make any adjustments to the stop screw to stop it skipping if necessary.

■ **NOTE:** If you don't have a screwdriver to make the adjustments, push the mech inwards while turning the cranks (with the wheel off the ground), then jam a stick between the mech cage plates to stop it moving back down to the small cog.

03: RIPPED TYRE WALL:

If you remembered the sewing kit (as suggested in the general section), you can repair it. Sew the tear up, and put an (energy bar) wrapper, business card or similar inside the tyre - this will stop the inner tube bulging out when the tyre is inflated.

■ **NOTE:** Check to see what caused the tyre wall to tear. It is usually the v-brakes touching the tyre or the pin used to hold the replacement cartridge pads in.

04: BROKEN SPOKE:

Remove the spoke from the nipple and hub, or wrap / tape a broken rear driveside spoke to another spoke. If you need to adjust the spokes but don't have a spoke key tighten a zip-tie around two parallel spokes to effectively tighten them.

05: BENT WHEEL:

For small buckles, adjust the spoke tension - gradually tighten spokes near the bend to pull the rim inwards, or slacken them to move it away.
For a big dents, remove the wheel and hold either side of it with the high point of the buckle at the bottom and furthest away from you. Now hit the tyre firmly against the ground and repeat until the wheel becomes rideable again.

06: BROKEN FREEWHEEL:

If the sprockets just spin when you pedal, the pawls have probably died.
Zip-tie the largest sprocket to the spokes, but note that you won't be able apply much pressure, and will have a fixed wheel i.e. you can't freewheel / coast.

07: MANGLED MECH:

This is often caused by the rear mech going into the wheel, so check the low limit screw is set correctly - see G10.

First check to see what has been bent: th rear mech hanger, or the mech itself. Many frames use (screw / bolt on) replaceable gear hangers that are designed to bend before the frame does. Others (usually steel) may have the mech hanger as part of the frame, and if this bends you can bend it back - get it straightened properly by a bike shop with the right tool when you can though.

07: GEAR HANGER - You may be able to bend the gear hanger back into or near it's correct position by securely holding the mech, and pulling firmly, but smoothly.

07A: MECH - If the mech cage plate is bent, try bending it back with your hands or levering it with any suitable tool.

■ **NOTE:** If you can't straighten the mech or hanger, you can singlespeed your bike - you can't do this on rear suspension designs unless you have a lockout optio though (as the chain tension changes as the suspension moves, which the mech usually allows for).

Place the chain on the middle sprocket and middle chainring (as you need to have a straight chainline) and get the chain as tight as possible - if the top jockey wheel is working, screw the high and low mech screws, otherwise take some links out of the chain.

INTRODUCTION TO STEMS

Since the mid 1990s, most MTBs come fitted with the 'Aheadset' system, where the handlebar stem clamps onto the steerer tube of the fork and the stem is pushed down by a top cap which screws into the star fangled nut inside the steerer tube. This system is lightweight, easy to adjust, strong and stiff, but only allows minor adjustments to handlebar height without replacing the stem.

Older MTBs and some modern comfort-oriented models have the threaded headset system that uses a 'quill stem'. Here the steerer tube of the fork is threaded and the headset screws on (the flat surfaces on the headset allow for adjustments with a spanner). The quill stem slides in to the fork and tightens with an expander wedge. The advantage of this system is that handlebar height can be adjusted easily.

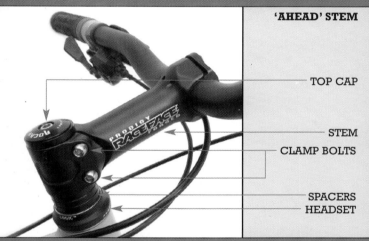

'AHEAD' STEM

- TOP CAP
- STEM
- CLAMP BOLTS
- SPACERS
- HEADSET

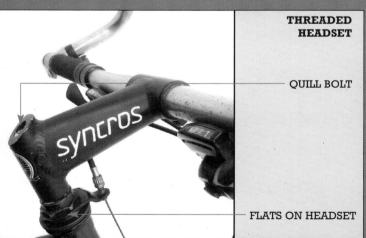

THREADED HEADSET

- QUILL BOLT
- FLATS ON HEADSET

CHANGING AN 'AHEAD' STEM.

01: MEASURE UP
First, make sure that the 'clamp height' of the new stem is no greater than that of the old stem plus any spacers.

If the new stem is taller than the old stem and the spacers don't buy it! If the new stem is smaller than the old stem alone, you will need spacers to take up the difference.

02: REMOVE OLD STEM
If the existing stem has a removable front plate, undo the bolts and take it off. If not, you'll have to remove the grips and controls from one side of the handlebar and slide it off (see M4). Undo the top cap bolt, loosen the clamp bolts and remove the old stem and spacers.

03: FIT NEW STEM
Check the inside of the new stem for sharp edges and gently file off anything that feels sharp. Slide the new stem in to position, adding or removing spacers so that there is 3mm between the top of the steerer tube and stem (see pic 03). This is for adjustment purposes and to enable you to compress the headset bearings.

04: ADJUST
Grease the top cap bolt and replace but don't tighten. Replace the handlebar and line up the stem with the front wheel (see pic 04), then tighten up the top cap bolt to eliminate play from the headset (see M5). Finally, evenly tighten the stem clamp bolts (usually around 5-7Nm), not too tight or you could damage the bars.

01

02

3mm

03

04

HOW TO ADJUST OR REPLACE A QUILL STEM

01: ADJUSTING (QUILL) STEM
First loosen the quill (top) bolt a couple of turns. Give the bolt a sharp tap with a plastic hammer to get the stem moving. You can then move the stem up or down (don't go above the minimum insertion mark though) and tighten the quill bolt again to hold position.

02: REPLACING A QUILL STEM
First detach the handlebars (see M4), then loosen as described in the last step. You should then be able to pull the stem free and replace with a new model. Grease the quill and expander wedge well to prevent corrosion, then replace handlebars and tighten in place.

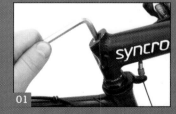
01

02

HANDLEBARS

■ **NOTE:** Bars need little maintenance, but you should regularly inspect them for damage i.e. cracks, white stress marks, as it can be dangerous if they fail. Be aware that over-tightening the stem can cause damage to the bars.

Most MTB handlebars are made of aluminium, which is light and durable. Some old / lower end bikes may come with steel bars, but these can be bone shakingly stiff and heavy (an ideal item to upgrade!). Fancier handlebars may be made of carbon-fibre or titanium, to provide a low weight bar with good shock-absorbing properties, but are quite expensive. Riser bars (kinked up at the ends) provide better handling (greater leverage) and a comfier riding position, while narrow, straight bars put you into a faster riding position.

REMOVING AND FITTING HANDLEBARS

HANDLEBAR SHAPES & SIZES:

Handlebars come in a variety of shapes and sizes, to help get your hands in a comfortable position. You will have choice of widths, rise (between flat and around 3"), and sweep (usually 3-5°). Wide bars offer good leverage for cornering, however if too wide they may be uncomfortable and hard to squeeze through the trees (use the width of your shoulders + hands as a guide). Most aluminium bars can be sawn down with a hacksaw or pipe-cutter if required (check with the bar manufacturer if you're not sure), but always remember to fit bar plugs (compulsory in racing) for safety.

If you buy a replacement bar be aware that the clamp area of most MTB handlebars is 28.6mm and most stem are made to fit this standard. However, some heavy duty bars may use a wider diameter, so will need a stem to match.

01: REMOVE THE GRIPS
Squirt some light lube e.g. GT85 or water under the grips from both sides, and wriggle them off.

If you're binning the old grips you could cut them off but be really careful not to scratch the bar (or mechanic).

02: REMOVE THE CONTROLS
Loosen the clamp bolts on the gear and brake levers, and then slide them off the bar. You may have to turn the bars to get some controls off because of restrictive gear / brake cables.

03: REMOVE THE HANDLEBAR
Loosen the bolt(s) at the front of the stem and slide out the bar. If the clamp is 'closed' it may help to put a penny in the gap, reverse the bolt and gently tighten to open up the clamp. Make sure you don't damage the stem doing this!

04: FIT NEW BARS
Check the inside of the stem clamp for sharp bits and gently file away any you find. Clean and grease the stem bolt(s), place the new bar in position (look for markings on the bar to help you get it central) and loosely tighten the bolts.

05: POSITION THE BARS
As a guide, try pointing riser bars straight up, and have the sweep going up and back. Experiment to find out what puts your hands at the most natural angle. Do up the stem bolts a little at a time, ensuring they are evenly tightened.

06: REPLACE THE CONTROLS
Slide the gear & brake levers back onto the bar, then replace the grips (sprays such as GT85 can help the grips slide on, then stick when dry - see 08 below for more info). Position the levers so they are easy to reach. Tighten the bolts enough so that they stay in position when used, but move rather than break in a crash.

07: FITTING BAR-ENDS
Handlebar extensions, or 'bar-ends', can be fitted to flat bars to give a greater variety of hand and riding positions. Check that your bars are OK for use with bar ends, as some light weight models e.g. carbon fibre, may require reinforcement plugs. Now, slide the controls and grips inboard and clamp them on at your preferred angle (usually between flat and 20°).

■ **NOTE:** Putting bar-ends on riser bars is a serious faux pas and is punishable with severe scathing looks.

08: SLIPPY GRIPS
The grips (especially in wet conditions) may slip around on the bars, which is both annoying and dangerous. Check they are not worn out or eroded - if they are, replace them. It's possible to glue grips down with hair spray, touch-up paint or an adhesive, but it will also make them harder to remove when you need to. Bolt-on grips, held in place with narrow aluminium collars are more expensive than normal grips, but they don't slip and are easy to fit and remove.

THE HEADSET

s the large set of bearings on which he fork turns. Most are licensed ersions of Dia Compe's 'Aheadset' ystem, which uses a thread-less, ush-fit system of a smooth steerer ith bearings and spacers that slide nto place. The Aheadset stem then lamps around the steerer tube and he whole lot is held in place by a op cap: this presses down onto the op of the stem by tightening a bolt hat goes into a starfangled nut SFN) inside the headtube (although here are alternatives to the SFN). The most common headtube iameter is 1 1/8". There are older " threaded headset / steerers /hich use a stem that plugs inside, ut these are heavier and not as nechanically efficient, although ney do offer easy height djustment. Some freeride bikes and Cannondales) use 1.5" eadtubes for added strength so ong travel single crown forks can e used - but you can fit reducer ups into the frame to enable you to t conventional forks i.e. 1 1/8".

ALTERNATIVE HEADSET DESIGNS
NTEGRATED HEADSETS

ome frame manufacturers produce MTB rames with the bearing cups actually in he headset. This design does away with he need for separate cups to be pressed nto the headset thus saving fitting time, veight, keeps the muck away from the earings. It also looks good as the frame, eadset and stem all blend together. The nanufacture of these integrated / internal eadsets needs to be very precise so will e found on top end bikes.

ERO STACK HEADSETS

hese headsets are somewhere between headsets and Integrated headsets as ney use separate cups pressed into an ver-sized headtube, but the cups are idden from sight and muck. This design as evolved because it is much easier nd therefore cheaper) to manufacture.

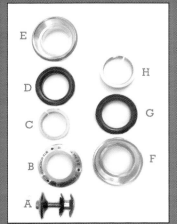

THE 'AHEADSET'

(above the frames headtube)
A: Top cap & starfangled nut
B: Top cover
C: Centring sleeve
D: Bearings (sealed)
E: Upper headtube cup

(below the frames headtube)
F: Lower headtube cup
G: Bearings (sealed)
H: Fork crown race

■ NOTE: The headset parts will vary between designs.

CHECKING THE HEADSET

The headset needs to be kept adjusted so that it is neither too tight, nor too loose. Too tight and the steering will be stiff, too loose and the forks will rattle about and the headset will wear quickly. It is important therefore, that you keep an eye on it.

Basic headsets contain ball bearings (often held in a clip). Higher quality units have better seals and / or cartridge bearings to keep out dirt, and you can simply replace the cartridges (bearing races and balls combined), without needing to get the cups in & out of the frame. There are also integrated headsets which use cartridges inside the frames headtube (see info left).

01: CHECK HEADSET
Turn the bars 90° and put your fingers over the upper part of the headset. Now rock the bike back and fourth and feel (and listen) for any movement by your fingers, which would indicate that the headset needs tightening.

■NOTE: Make sure that any movement is not coming from worn out suspension forks e.g. worn bushings.

02: REMOVE PLAY
First loosen the clamp bolts (on the side of the stem) which hold the stem in place. Next carefully tighten the top cap bolt 1/4 turn (see pic above) and check the headset as before, and continue to tighten until there is no play.

Finally, align the stem with the wheel and tighten the clamp bolts on the stem. Lift the wheel and turn the bars to ensure it's not too tight and binding.

HEADSET MAINTENANCE

The headset will benefit from periodically being taken apart and cleaned. Do this regularly or whenever turning the bars starts to feel gritty, indicating that dirt has found it's way in. Bearings cost very little, so are worth replacing if you've taken the headset apart anyway.

01: REMOVING THE STEM
This is best done in a work stand with the front wheel removed and front brake disconnected. Loosen the stem clamp bolts, then undo the top cap bolt all the way and remove the top cap.
Pull the stem and any spacers off the forks steerer tube.

02: PULL OUT THE FORK
While holding the lower part of the fork, either bop the top of the fork with a plastic faced mallet (or hammer and protecting piece of wood), or open the split in the compression ring of the headset. Gently lower the fork out of the frame, keeping a look out for loose bearings.

03: CLEAN OUT
Paying close attention to the order the bits are in, you should now be able to pull everything apart with your fingers.

Clean everything thoroughly with rags and cleaner. Replace dull or pitted bearings - get new ones in a 'race' or use loose balls. Also replace worn / gritty cartridge bearings where necessary.

04: RE-GREASE
When everything is clean, put fresh grease in the headset cups and stick the bearings in place. Put extra grease over the bearings, then slide the fork (and any seals) in place. Replace the upper parts in the order you removed them, then replace spacers, stem and top cap.

Tighten the top cap bolt until there is no play, align the stem and wheel and then tighten the stem side bolts and check it all works - see left 'checking the headset'

01

02

03

04

■ NOTE: See page M6 for maintenance of Cannondale headsets.

MAINTENANCE

M5

REPLACING HEADSETS

If servicing cannot remedy headset looseness or tightness, then it will need to be replaced.

Replacing headsets is best done by a shop mechanic (especially Cannondale designs) with the correct tools as it is very easy to damage the headset and frame, and some high quality headsets will not tolerate any misalignment. You can bodge it (see the alternative 'A' guide), but don't blame us if you damage anything,

■NOTE: It is recommended that new frames have the headtube reamed (rounded) and faced (makes the top and bottom of the headtube parallel). These are both jobs for a good bike shop to do - NOT YOU.

REMOVING THE OLD HEADSET
Remove the stem (see page M3) and if you have a cup-less internal headset (bearings seated on steps inside the frames headtube), remove the bearings and go to step 02.

REMOVE THE UPPER & LOWER CUPS
01: Use a headset cup remover tool. Push the non-splayed end of the tool through the headset, until the splayed ends spread. Now tap the sealed end of the tool to pop the cups out.
01A: If you don't have this tool and don't mind damaging the headset you are removing, use a long, blunt screwdriver - be VERY careful not to damage anything.

REMOVE THE CROWN RACE
02: Next, turn the fork upside-down and place a fork crown remover tool against the crown and tap that off.
02A: If you don't have this tool, use a screwdriver and gently tap one side then the other of the crown - there is usually a small notch front and back.

FITTING THE NEW HEADSET
Frames with internal headsets just require the bearings dropped in place, then go to step 04.

FIT THE UPPER & LOWER CUPS
Grease the cups and frame and make sure the outer flanges (NOT the inner bearings) are being pushed, and that they go in dead straight.

03: Press the new cups in place with a proper headset press (recommended).
03A: If you don't have this tool, use a threaded rod with 2 flat screw plates on it - or the RRG (non-patented) gate hinge available at hardware stores for under £5

FIT THE CROWN RACE
04: Use a crown race slide punch to fit the crown race tight onto the forks crown.
04A: If you don't have this tool, use some plastic drain pipe or similar. Finally, assemble the headset - see M5.

01

01A

02

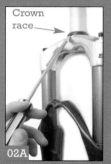
Crown race
02A

03

03A

04

04A

Cannondale often use their own design of front suspension i.e. 'headshoks' where the suspension is on the steerer tube and the 'lefty' which has just one telescopic leg on the left-hand side. These forks use contact bearings (rather than bushings as on conventional forks) which are very smooth if looked after - so check and service them regularly.

HEADSET BEARING MAINTENANCE
01: Undo the hex key bolt on top of the damping dial and remove the dial, then loosen the stem bolts & remove the stem.

02: Lift the bearing seal to expose the headset bearings and clean and lube them with a light lube e.g. TF2 then put everything back in place and tighten.

FORK BEARING MAINTENANCE
03: Undo (on Lefty forks) or cut (on Headshok forks) the top zip-tie that holds the protective boot. Check boot isn't torn (or it could affect the warranty). Pull the boot down to expose the bearing races and clean then grease them.

04: On Headshok designs lift the o-ring up and clean and grease this and where the steerer meets the fork crown.

05: On Lefty forks, check the lower collar is tight (with a green pin spanner). Now remove the brake calliper and unscrew the axle bolt and clean the axle.
Cut the zip-tie off the bottom of the air filter boot and pull the air filter out from under the boot. If it needs cleaning, pull it over the boot and axle and gently clean it in soapy water, rinse, dry, then spray with a light lube e.g. TF2, refit it and use a new zip-tie to secure the boot.

05a: Grease the bearing seats, axle, and axle bolt threads, then replace the wheel. Screw the bolt on until it engages the axle and tighten it down, then replace the brake calliper. Pull the boot back up and secure it with the new zip-tie.

Damping dial →
01

02

03

04

05

05a

PEDALS

Pedals put up with loads of abuse, being dipped in puddles and clonked on rocks, but often don't actually need much looking after. After a ride the pedal body only requires a clean, spray with a water displacer, then a dab of grease on the spring (and cleats if they need it). However, it is worth especially if they have developed some 'play') dismantling, cleaning, re-greasing and re-adjusting them now and again, to keep them turning nicely and living longer. The pedals can also be damaged if put under a lot of stress i.e. taking your weight after landing a jump. Remove the pedal and rotate the axle, feeling for any stiffness - if they are stiff you may have bent the axle, so take it out and have a look. Don't remove the springs from SPD pedals though, as there is no need and they are very difficult to get back in.

There are two broad categories of pedals: loose ball bearings (this page) and cartridge bearings (next page).

■ NOTE: Pedals screw into the cranks so that they don't loosen through pedalling. The right pedal (usually marked with an R on the axle) has a normal (right hand) thread (tightens clockwise), while the left (marked L) has a left handed thread (tightens anticlockwise).

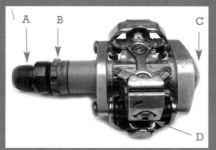

SPD PEDAL

A: Axle
B: Knurled collar (Shimano)
C: End cap
D: Release tension screw

■ NOTE: To adjust the SPD cleat release tension (looking from the back of the pedal) turn the tension adjustment screw clockwise to increase the tension, and anti-clockwise to reduce the tension of the cleat on the top side of the pedal.

CUP AND CONE PEDAL MAINTENANCE

Most flat and clip-and-strap pedals, together with some clipless pedals use loose ball bearings and can be serviced as follows:

01: Remove the pedal from the crank, then remove the dust cap. You may need a screwdriver to prise this out, or unscrew with either a large screwdriver or a hex key.

You should see the end of a nut. On the left pedal this undoes anticlockwise, on the right it undoes clockwise. Undo this with the appropriate socket.

02: Remove the washer that sits under the locknut. Position the pedal over a container, as bearings will soon start flying.

Insert a flat screwdriver on to one side of the cone underneath, then slowly unscrew. Carefully pull the axle out of the pedal and catch and count all the bearings.

03: Make sure you remove all the bearings from the pedal body. Inspect the bearings, and if they're worn (dull and pitted), buy replacements.

Clean everything with rags and cleaner then grease the pedal bearing surfaces and put half the bearings evenly on to the 'inside' bearing surface.

04: Carefully replace the axle, then replace the remaining bearings in place on the 'outer' side, using a small screwdriver or similar to poke them in place. Put fresh grease over the top then carefully screw down the cone. Put the washer back then tighten down the locknut. This may take a few attempts and re-adjustments of the cone until the pedal can spin freely without play. Then pop the dust-cap back on and you are finished.

TOOLS: 15mm spanner, socket set, degreaser, grease, and a screwdriver.

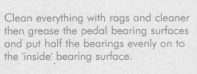

01

02

03

04

REMOVING PEDALS

Most pedals can be taken off with a 15mm pedal spanner and/or a 6mm hex key on the frame side of the crank.

The right pedal undoes anti-clockwise and the left pedal undoes clockwise. An easy way to remember which way to undo the pedals, is to put the crank facing forward and attach a spanner / key so that it's horizontal and facing back. Now push downwards to undo the pedal - this can be stiff, if so use a pole attached to the spanner for extra leverage.

REPLACING PEDALS

Clean then grease the pedal threads and threads in the cranks arms. Screw the pedal into the cranks - do the first few threads by hand to check it's going in correctly then hold the pedal axle with a spanner and turn the cranks backwards until snug.

QUICK PEDAL MAINTENANCE

To get fresh grease into the pedal bearings quickly, unscrew / ping off the dust cap from the end of the pedal (if it has one).

A: Fill the end of the axle and the cap with some grease.

B: Now put the cap back in place and screw it down, forcing the clean grease into the pedal body and the dirty grease out on the other side of the pedal - *keep repeating this procedure until the grease coming out the other side is clean grease.*

CARTRIDGE BEARING PEDALS

High quality XC mountain bikes come with a set of SPD style clipless pedals - usually of pretty good quality and (if they're not Shimano) tending to use either loose bearings (see M7) or a combination of cartridge bearings and a bushing.

If you haven't got a manual for them, the only way to find out what's inside is to open 'em up! The cartridge type are fairly easy to service as there are no flying bearings, but getting parts can be difficult to get hold of.

01: Remove the pedals from the crank arms (see M7) then prise or unscrew the end cap off, with a hex key or whatever else fits in the end.

02: Hold the axle steady with a 15mm spanner then undo the lock-nut with the correct sized socket (usually 7-8mm). The nuts are conventionally threaded on the left pedal, and have a left-hand thread on the right pedal.

Remove any other washers or nuts you find underneath.

03: Pull the pedal body off the axle - you may need to tap the end of the axle with a mallet to get it to move.

You may find that the bearing and the bushing stay in the pedal body - if so tap them out with a screwdriver from the reverse side.

04: Clean all the parts inside, re-grease and re-assemble.

If the pedal still has some play, you will need replacement bearings and / or bushings - the best way to find these is to ask your local bike shop to phone the company that distributes the pedals.

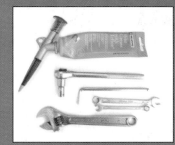

TOOLS: 15mm pedal spanner, hex key, socket set, and grease.

01

02

03

04

SHIMANO CARTRIDGE BEARING PEDALS

Shimano have a system where the pedal is only open at the crank end - keeping it sealed from dirt and water. They have also managed to retain loose ball bearings so that they don't fly about when you service them. These pedals are recognisable by the knobbly collar on the crank side (which requires the TL-PD-40 tool) and the absence of a dust cap. Some older pedals may use loose bearings.

■ **NOTE:** Some pedals have a recessed locknut so require the TL-PD-73 tool (this has two sockets, one to hold the cone and the other to turn the locknut see pic

01: Remove the pedals from the crank arms (see M7). Put the TL-PD-40 tool facing up in a vice or large spanner, and slot the pedal onto the tool and turn clockwise to undo a right pedal or anti-clockwise to undo a left pedal.

02: Pull the axle out of the pedal to reveal the bearing assembly inside. If not very dirty, the bearings can be cleaned with some cleaner and a rag. The sleeve should rotate freely and without play. Loosen the locknut (7mm socket) then adjust the cone (10mm spanner) and re-tighten the locknut to remove play.

03: Hold the axle still with a 15mm pedal spanner at the crank end and remove the locknut with a 7mm spanner. Remove the cone with a 10mm spanner / socket then pull off the sleeve over a container to catch the bearings. Clean everything up and inspect the bearing surfaces.

04: Grease the races and stick the clean / new bearings in, then re-insert the axle and replace the cone and locknut. Adjust the cone and tighten the locknut on top of it so that the sleeve turns smoothly with no play - this may take a few attempts to get this right. Finally, screw the axle back into the pedal body.

TOOLS: TL-PD-40 tool, vice / large spanner, 15mm pedal spanner, 7 & 10mm spanners or TL-PD-73 tool

01

Locknut →
Cone →
02

03

04

SADDLE & SEATPOSTS

The saddle is a 'sore point' for many people. They are generally made of a plastic shell with padding on them, and have 'rails' that fit into a clamp that is attached to the top of the seatpost. There are lots and lots of designs of saddles as peoples bums are different, so take your time choosing and trying out different designs.

Saddles and seatposts need little maintenance, but over time you may want to change / replace them for performance or cosmetic reasons, but there are a few things to consider before you do so.

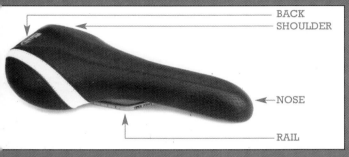

BACK
SHOULDER
NOSE
RAIL

CHOOSING A SADDLE

A comfy saddle for one person is not necessarily comfy for someone else, so try before you buy (good shops should let you do this). The most important factor in finding a comfy saddle is that it fits the rider correctly. Soft padding (foam or gel) may feel comfortable, but it is the way that it supports the pelvic bones that is most important, and unnecessary material may cause uncomfortable chaffing.

Saddles come in all shapes, sizes and designs (see right). Designs with soft or missing central sections aim to relieve and alleviate numbness in sensitive 'downstairs' areas. Women should also try designs designed specifically for their wider pelvic bones.

The rails are usually made of cromo alloy. Titanium rails are lighter, provide more of a spring and take some trail 'buzz' out of the ride, but of course cost more. Some saddles have removable rails, that can be replaced if damaged.

When you have decided on your favoured perch, start off with it positioned level to the ground; if this is uncomfortable, experiment by tilting the nose up or down slightly. Try to position the clamp in the centre of the rails, because if it is near the front or back the rails may bend (use a seatpost with some lay-back to get the correct riding position if necessary - see seat clamp designs).

Saddles require very little maintenance. Give them a wash with soap and water, don't let leather covers become dried out (by continuous soakings or exposure to solvents), and grease the rails to stop any annoying creaks (see the picture below).

SADDLE DESIGNS
A: Normal
B: Gel section
C: Hole / 'Love' channel
D: Ladies

A

B

C

D

THE SEAT-POST

These are made of two parts, the main shaft and the clamp that holds the saddle in position. It is vitally important that the post is the correct diameter for your bike frame. Sizes vary by as little as 0.2mm and even a slightly undersized seatpost will not tighten securely. Not only will this cause the seatpost to slip down, but it could damage your frame. If you're not sure what diameter seatpost to use, most shops have a set of drop-in frame measuring device or contact the frame manufacturer and ask.

To avoid producing lots of sizes of seatposts, manufacturers sometimes use 'shims'. These are collars of metal or plastic which allow a smaller diameter seatpost to fit a wider seat tube. Some seatposts MUST be used with a shim to protect the post from any imperfections in the seat tube; if you have an unusual frame size, a shim may be the only way to replace a broken seatpost.

■ NOTE: Make sure the 'minimum height' mark on the seatpost is inside the frame.

TOP TIP: 2-piece telescopic seatposts available, which allow you to drop the saddle height, without the seatpost getting in the way of some full suspension frame designs.

SEAT POST CLAMP DESIGNS

A variety of clamp designs exist on the market (see right). Some are extremely minimal and designed to save as much weight as possible, others put adjustability and strength at a premium. The more the amount of seatpost held by the clamp the less likely it is to break or bend.

TOP TIP: Some riders may benefit from a seatpost with layback i.e. the seat-clamp is positoned behind the top of the seat post) as it increases the distance between the seat and handlebars.

SEATPOST CLAMP DESIGNS
A: Twin jacking syncros style
B: One bolt
C: Layback
D: Cheap & weak

MAINTENANCE

FITTING FORKS

Fork upgrades are common; we recommend you get a bike shop to fit them. If you want to have a go anyway, be aware of the tricky bits i.e. fitting the crown race straight, cutting the steerer tube to the right length and straight. Also, ensure the new forks are compatible with your brakes i.e. have the correct mounts, steerer tube diameter, and consider the affect that longer forks will have on your steering (i.e. approximately every 20mm of travel exceeding the original forks travel will reduce the headtube angle by 1 degree - making the steering slower).

01: Firstly, remove the front wheel, then the stem top cap, the stem itself, and the spacers (see M3). Take the cables out of the guides and hang the bars out of the way and slide the forks out - you may need to prise the cir-clip type part of the headset open (see pic) and / or tap the top of the steerer tube with a rubber mallet to persuade it.

02: Check the condition of your headset: if it's good, remove the lower crown race from your old forks, and fit them to your new forks (see M6). Measure the old steerer tube length (from the base of the crown to the top of the steerer) and cut the new steerer the same length, file off any rough edges and go to step 04.

03A: Another method to get the correct steerer length is to put the lower bearings on the crown race and the upper bearings in the top cup, and slide the new fork into the frame. Fit any spacers you require (above or below the stem) to get the correct height, and put the stem on. Mark the steerer at the top of the stem, and now remove the stem, spacers, fork and bearings.

03B: The top of the steerer tube needs to be cut 3-4mm below the top of the stem, to enable you to preload the headset bearings (because when the top cap is tightened it pulls the steerer tube up). Cut the steerer tube with a hack-saw or pipe cutter 3mm below the mark you made on the steerer tube. File the rough edges (use a round file for the inside, and a flat one on the outside and top) and clean any swarf away.

04: If you are using a starfangled nut (SFN) to tighten the steerer to the aheadset, it must go into the steerer tube straight. A threadless nut setter tool will help you achieve this, otherwise use an old 5mm bolt.

Screw the star nut onto the setting tool or 5mm bolt and tap the tool/bolt gently until the star-nut is about 1cm down the steerer tube and in straight.

04A: There are alternatives to the star fangled nut. The 'Ring-go-star' uses two spacers that go under the stem, which tightens the headset against the stem by expanding the top spacer, by tightening the lower spacer. Another design is a head-lock device, which runs through the steerer tube.

■**NOTE:** These alternative designs will come with detailed fitting instructions.

05: Grease the headset cups and bearings and re-fit the fork into the frame.

06: Slide the spacers and stem on top - making sure the cables are in the correct place. Now tighten the top cap bolt until there is no play (see M5), check the stem is straight, then tighten the stem side bolts. Lift the wheel and turn the bars to make sure it turns easily.

Do a final check that all the other bolts are tight before riding off into the sunset on your new bouncy forks.

A: STEERER TUBE
B: CROWN
C: INNER LEGS / STANCHIONS
D: FORK BRACE
E: V-BRAKE BOSSES
F: LOWER LEGS
G: DISC BRAKE MOUNTS
H: DROP-OUTS

ARE YOUR FORKS BENT?

Spin the wheel - if it leans one way, remove it and turn it around and spin it again. If it leans to the same side the forks are probably misaligned, but if it leans the other way, it's a bent wheel.

TOOLS: File, small flat bladed screwdriver, hammer, 5 & 6mm hex keys, grease, rubber mallet, hack-saw or pipe cutter.

■**NOTE:** A crown race seating tool, star fangled nut fitting tool, and a workstand will all come in handy.

01

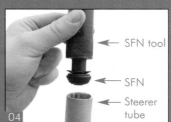

04

← SFN tool
← SFN
← Steerer tube

02

04A

03A

05

03B

06

CARING FOR YOUR SUSPENSION

The amount of attention your suspension requires will depend on the conditions you ride in, style of riding, the design, etc. Most manufacturers have a recommended time schedule that you should try and stick to.

The seals and oil in the suspension will gradually deteriorate (faster the more you ride and the worse the weather), requiring them to be serviced. Servicing suspension is a specialist job / skill that may require specialist tools and mechanical knowledge, and there are so many different designs, makes, and models of forks, covering them it is outside the scope of this book, so we would recommend you let the professionals do it - see right.

If you are a confident and competent mechanic, fancy a challenge, or are just a cheapskate with a basic idea, you can visit the manufacturer's web-site (see right) where you can usually obtain their very comprehensive servicing instructions for your specific forks. Print this information off and add it to the RRG folder.

Don't let us scare you off totally from doing anything to your suspension however, as correct set-up, basic checks, cleaning, and lubing are essential to maximise performance and prolong the life of the components.

SUSPENSION SPECIALISTS:

CVI: Tel: 01405 760030 or see www.cvi.co.uk.
Headshock Doc: Cannondale specialist at www.headshockdoc.com.
Mojo suspension: Tel: 01633 615815, or see www.mojo.co.uk.
TF Tuned Shox: Tel: 01373 834 455 or see www.tftunedshox.com

FRONT SUSPENSION

* After every ride it is advisable to wipe the stanchions down carefully with a dry, soft cloth and check for scratches. If the suspension has a protection cover / boot clean under this.

TOP TIP: Dripping a bit of teflon - containing lube on the stanchions and seals will help keep them sliding smoothly for longer (especially if being left un-used for a while), and keep grit and water out of the internals.

* If you have an air fork, check the air pressure regularly.

* Inspect the fork regularly for loose bolts, bends, cracks, and stresses (paint ripples can indicate hidden problems).

* Change the fork oil (if applicable) every year or two. The volume and weight of oil used varies between manufacturers and forks, so use the manufacturer's recommendations.

* Hold the front brake and gently rock the bike back and forth to check for any play / movement between the fork legs and stanchions (make sure it's not a loose headset you are feeling). If there is some play, the bushings may require replacing. New bushings almost always mean a professional job needs doing.

REAR SUSPENSION

* Suspension seatposts are pretty low maintenance, but stripping, cleaning and re-greasing the internal parts is fairly easy (follow the specific manufacturers instructions) and will keep them running smoothly. Pivot bushings will also wear over time, but are fairly easy to get to and replace. If the seat rotates on telescopic seatposts, it is probably due to worn 'keys' i.e. small nylon strips.

* Most rear suspension systems use solid bushings or replaceable cartridge bearings so they can be ridden until they fall apart- this doesn't mean you should forget about them though!

* Look out for rear suspension bearing stiffness or looseness, clean grit and grim away, avoid jet washes, and keep the bushings greased (not the white lithium grease though), to prolong their life. If the bushings pressed into the eyes on either end of the shock are red or black don't grease them, but you can grease the grey ones.

* **DO NOT** attempt to service a rear shock as they can contain pressurised nitrogen (up to 300psi) and will blow apart if taken apart incorrectly.

* A squishing noise, may indicate 'cavitation' i.e. the damping oil mixes with the nitrogen or air in the rear shock, and reduce the viscosity of the oil, leading to less damping and a springy shock.

FITTING A REAR SHOCK

* Rear shocks are all different shapes and sizes, so you will need to know the length (distance between the 2 eyes / mounting points), eye width, stroke length. Not all frames will accommodate the piggy-back reservoir so check yours will.

* Coil springs are tough and reliable, so should last a good few years - although the more preload it has dialled in, the shorter it's life will be. Make sure you get the same length spring, and take note of the numbers written on the spring e.g. 500X3 will mean 500lbs is required to compress the spring by 1 inch, and it has 3 inches of movement (so 1,500lbs is required to fully compress the spring).

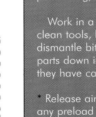

AIR   COIL

A: EYE
B: PIGGY BACK RESERVOIR
C: SPRING
D: SHAFT
E: SHOCK BODY
F: EYE

TIPS & ADVICE

* Suspension performance will probably deteriorate gradually, making you unaware of it's slow demise - don't be fooled into thinking it's performance still feels fine even after 4 years, as it probably isn't.

* If the suspension springs back and forth like a pogo stick, you may have a damaged seal in the damping system - look for signs of oil on the outside of the fork to confirm your fears.

* The (nitrogen) bubbles in elastomer / MCUs will slowly escape the 'stack' leaving you with duff suspension.

* Silkolene (motorcycle fork oil) or Redline (car suspension fluid) are good performing, cheap fork oil alternatives.

* Work in a well lite, clean area, with clean tools, bike, etc. Also when you dismantle bits, clean, inspect and lay the parts down in the order and orientation they have came off.

* Release air on air shocks, and remove any preload on coil or elastomer springs, before taking them apart.

* Never use flammable or corrosive solvents to clean the parts, as these could damage the seals. Use detergents that are not corrosive, non flammable and preferably biodegradable.

MANUFACTURERS WEBSITES:

Fox: www.foxracingshox.com
Magura: www.magura.com
Manitou: www.answerproducts.com
Marzocchi: www.marzocchi.com
Maverick: www.maverickamerican.com
Pace: www.pace-racing.co.uk
RockShox: www.rockshox.com
Romic: www.romicmfg.com
Rond: www.rond.nl
RST: www.rst.com.tw
Stratos: www.stratashock.com
Sun tour: www.srsuntour-cycling.com
White brothers: www.whitebrotherscycling.com

■ **NOTE:** Open bath forks are self lubricating, and generally require less maintenance than sealed cartridge systems.

MAINTENANCE

	PROBLEM	POSSIBLE CAUSES	REMEDY
STEERING	Twangy or poor steering at high speed	Flexy fork or too heavy (or fast) rider	Get stronger / stiffer fork or beef up fork with a stiffer hub.
	Understeers i.e. feels like it doesn't steer responsively enough.	Too little rebound damping Too much compression damping Spring too hard (not enough sag)	Increase rebound damping Decrease compression damping Decrease spring rate/preload
	Oversteers i.e. feels twitchy, like it is steering too quickly or front wheel tucks under	Spring too soft (too much sag) Too little compression damping Too much rebound damping	Increase spring rate/preload Increase compression damping Decrease rebound damping
	Steering feels slow	New longer fork has slackened head tube angle	Fit a shorter stem
	Forks judder when braking	Loose headset Fork bushings worn	Adjust headset correctly Replace bushings (fork service)
MECHANICAL	Oil leaking onto stanchions or legs	Oil seals or stanchions worn / internals broken	Replace oil seals (fork service)
	Dirt and oil ring on stanchions	Fork internals contaminated/seals leaking	Service and replace seals
	Oil leak from bottom of fork legs	Loose bottom nut, seal / nut o-ring around the bolt at the bottom of the fork leg worn / blown fork cartridge	Service and replace worn parts
	Air fork gets soft quickly	Air leaking- from air seals Air leaking from valve	Lubricate or replacing the seals. Lubricate valve with spray and push valve stem in and out.
	Back wheel feels 'loose' and sloppy or bike is noisy / knocking coming from (near) the rear shock	Rear shock bushings worn	Replace bushings
	Suspension compresses (bobs) under pedalling forces.	Active suspension design or not enough rebound damping	Increase the rebound, or get a new frame!
	Shock makes a squishing noise and has gone springy.	Damping oil is mixing with the air/nitrogen, reducing the viscosity of the oil.	Get it serviced professionally
SUSPENSION SEATPOST	Seat rotates (telescopic post)	The 'keys' (small nylon strips) are worn Pivot bushings are worn	Get the appropriate service kit and replace the 'keys' Replace
	Stiff or sticky compression and extension	In need of servicing	Unscrew (by hand) the collar, connecting the two parts of the seatpost, clean, and re-grease.